$$h \to 0 \qquad \frac{5h^2 + 6h}{2h^3 + 3h}$$

$$\lim x \to 2 \quad \frac{3x^2 - 2x + 7}{x^3 + 5x}$$

$$x \to -2 \quad \frac{(x+2)(x^2 - x + 3)}{x^2 + 3x + 2}$$

$$x \to -1 \quad \frac{x^2 - 1}{x^2 - 2x - 3}$$

The Brookhaven particle accelerator for developing proton energies in excess of 2 billion electron-volts. This so-called synchrotron is partly surrounded by a shield of concrete blocks for protecting personnel against atomic rays and particles emanating from the machine. The three units between the synchrotron and shield are pumps for evacuating the chamber that is embedded in the giant ring magnet and in which the particles are accelerated.

CONSULTANTS FOR THE FOURTH EDITION

DEAN J. WILLIAM BUCHTA
University of Minnesota

DR. REGINALD G. LACOUNT
Professor of Physics
Northeastern University

PHYSICS

by

ERICH HAUSMANN

Dean Emeritus and
formerly Thomas Potts Professor of Physics
Polytechnic Institute of Brooklyn

AND

EDGAR P. SLACK

Adjunct Professor of Physics and
formerly Chairman, Undergraduate Physics
Polytechnic Institute of Brooklyn

FOURTH EDITION

D. VAN NOSTRAND COMPANY, INC.

PRINCETON, NEW JERSEY

TORONTO   LONDON

NEW YORK

D. VAN NOSTRAND COMPANY, INC.
120 Alexander St., Princeton, New Jersey (*Principal office*)
257 Fourth Avenue, New York 10, New York

D. VAN NOSTRAND COMPANY, LTD.
358, Kensington High Street, London, W.14, England

D. VAN NOSTRAND COMPANY (Canada), LTD.
25 Hollinger Road, Toronto 16, Canada

First Published September 1935

Seven Reprintings

Second Edition, August 1939

Twenty-seven Reprintings

Third Edition, August 1948

Twelve Reprintings

Fourth Edition, June 1957

Reprinted January 1958, September 1959

PREFACE

The purpose of this textbook is to present the principles and methods of Physics to college students, particularly those who major in Science and Engineering. During the past few years much attention has been directed to what should be taught in an introductory course in Physics and how it should be taught. In the extensive revision for this new edition, the authors have availed themselves of the guidance afforded by a report on the Role of Physics in Engineering Education, prepared in 1955 by a committee of the American Institute of Physics.

As in previous editions of this textbook, the presentation is designed to give a gradual and logical approach to the subject, to develop and illustrate the fundamental concepts clearly, and to help the diligent student master the basic principles of this stimulating branch of physical science. To those who study Physics for its cultural value, the text should aid in developing a power of analysis that will be of service in any career. The place of Physics in our affairs today is discussed informally in an Introductory Statement to the Student.

Emphasis in this edition is placed on principles and methods. Descriptions of devices, such as measuring instruments, heat engines, and electrical machines, have been omitted or curtailed, and engineering applications have been restricted to those believed necessary for student motivation. More stress has been put on the contributions of the great scientists to the thinking of their time and to the development of the scientific method of today.

Certain rearrangements of subject matter have been made for more effective teaching. In the Mechanics section, uniform and accelerated linear motion have been presented in a single chapter; the discussion of force has been expanded into two chapters to enlarge the treatment of momentum and center of mass; and material has been added on the gravitational field and earth satellites. In the Electricity and Magnetism section, the subjects of electrical machinery and communications have been rewritten to meet the new objectives and are now more appropriately placed under new chapter headings: Magnetic Circuits and Electrical Radiation, respectively. A new chapter, Solid State Electronics, has been added to serve as an introduction to a field of growing importance. The divisions on Heat, Wave Motion, and Light have also been thoroughly revised, and the chapter on Radiation and Atomic Structure has been rewritten in the light of recent developments.

Many of the illustrations have been changed, some added, and all are redrawn. The problems at the ends of chapters are new and have been increased in number, but more importantly, they have been prepared to be more thought-provoking. The answers to the odd-numbered problems are given in the Appendix.

In the matter of units, it should be remarked that when the first edition of this textbook was published two decades ago, physicists and engineers expressed but little preference between unit systems. Today, they seem to favor the cgs and British gravitational units in Mechanics, mks units in Electricity and Magnetism, and cgs units in Modern Physics. These are the units used in the present edition. However, the esu system is explained at appropriate places to enable the student to refer intelligently to books in which the older system is used.

The opening chapters of the book lead the student by the hand, so to speak, explaining every step fully, cancelling units, and solving numerous illustrative problems, so that the material should be well understood even by a student who has had no previous training in Physics. Later parts of the book are treated more and more concisely, consistent with the student's mastery of the subject and confidence in his ability. The illustrative problems have distinctive side heads by which they can be located easily. In most problems, the data are given to one or two digits only, so that the mathematical work may not obscure the physical concepts, but are to be regarded as correct to three or four significant figures, as explained in the text. The solutions are carried out to the precision obtainable with the 10-in. slide rule.

The book should be found suitable for a one-year course in Physics, or for individual courses based on its main divisions. Calculus is not considered a prerequisite, but is used to a limited extent in the later divisions of the book in the thought that many students will then be able to avail themselves of the simplicity which it affords. Class work should be supplemented by demonstration lectures and laboratory experiments.

The authors wish to express their thanks to Professor J. W. Buchta of the University of Minnesota and Professor Reginald G. Lacount of Northeastern University, who served as consultants, for their review of the entire manuscript and for their searching criticisms; to many teachers, particularly our associates at the Polytechnic Institute of Brooklyn, for helpful suggestions and generous assistance; to several industrial organizations for technical data and illustrations; and to a host of students who, intentionally or otherwise, have pointed out difficulties that they encountered in earlier editions of the book. Thanks are also expressed to Dr. Walter H. Brattain of the Bell Telephone Laboratories for reviewing the chapter on Solid State Electronics. Largely because of help from these sources, we feel that this revised textbook should be a more useful and teachable book.

Erich Hausmann
Edgar P. Slack

INTRODUCTORY STATEMENT
TO THE STUDENT

Physics plays a dual role in our affairs today. It is both a foundation science for engineering and a basic field of endeavor in itself. The future of both will be profoundly affected by our increasing knowledge of the atom.

The engineer turns hopefully to the atom as an abundant source of energy to offset our diminishing supply of natural fuels. The physicist sees opportunities for utilizing the properties of the atom in his own research projects and in such related fields as chemistry, botany, metallurgy, and medicine. Not only the engineer and the scientist, but every well-informed business man and executive, must become familiar with the atom and its possibilities. Little wonder that nowadays many choose to pioneer in this exciting field.

The study of the atom is a part of Physics. It is called atomic or "modern" physics to distinguish it from the older Newtonian or "classical" physics, which deals with sizable objects and not the tiny particles within the atom. As a student who looks forward to taking part in the world's activities, very likely in engineering or science, you will need to study atomic physics. But in order to prepare yourself, you must first lay a firm foundation in classical physics. In this discipline, you will learn certain facts. What is more important, you will absorb certain ideas and methods of approach. Most important of all, you will get a proper grasp of a few broad, basic principles and understand where they apply and where they do not. Through this study, you will acquire a point of view and attitude of mind that will enable you later to master the more abstract and complex problems of atomic physics and present-day engineering. And you will no doubt find classical physics fascinating in itself. It will certainly be useful. Employers of technical graduates are on the alert for recruits who have a thorough basic knowledge of physics and mathematics.

Never were the opportunities so great as they are now. Much about the atom is known, but much more still is to be learned. Great discoveries lie ahead. It is not too much to say that the world looks to you to complete the task—just begun—of harnessing the atom for the peaceful service of mankind.

In your college course, it will not matter too much whether a particular topic has any practical application at the time. Many physical concepts thought of as abstract a few years ago are used in practical engineering today. Who can say what engineering practice will include ten years hence?

Just one more thought. Since the turn of the century, the science of Physics probably has advanced more than it did up to that time throughout the entire history of the world. The same can hardly be said of many other fields of human endeavor. To match the progress made in Physics, much more attention must be given to our social, economic, and spiritual well-being.

In this book, the authors have tried to place before you the ideas, methods, and principles of classical physics—with a suitable introduction to atomic physics—in a manner that they believe best suited to your needs. Your teacher can only guide you; the hard work, the joy of learning, and the satisfaction of achievement, will be all your own.

E. H.

E. P. S.

CONTENTS

MECHANICS

1

FUNDAMENTAL QUANTITIES

1. Matter.   Physics takes its place among the physical sciences with astronomy, chemistry, and geology, in applying the laws of nature to inanimate objects, and some of its principles apply to living things as well. The fields of knowledge of these sciences overlap considerably and give rise to such areas as astrophysics, physical chemistry, geophysics, and biophysics.   The ideas and principles of Physics are concerned broadly with matter, energy, and radiation, together with such related topics as force and motion.   These are fundamental to all parts of the subject, comprising mechanics of solids and fluids, heat, electricity and magnetism, sound, and light.   The scope of Physics is continually widening as new knowledge is gained, particularly in the divisions of this science that deal with the structure of matter.

Matter is the name given to anything that makes up a physical object. It cannot be defined in terms of anything more fundamental.   Matter can be recognized in three phases, as a solid, liquid, or gas.   Water, for example, can exist as ice, liquid, and vapor at appropriate temperatures, and these phases can exist in contact with each other at specific temperatures and pressures.   But whatever phase water assumes, its chemical composition remains the same.

The various known substances can be classified broadly into *elements* and *compounds*, elements being basic substances and compounds being formed by the chemical union of two or more elements in definite proportions. Each element is composed of *atoms;* the atom is regarded as the smallest particle into which matter can be divided by purely chemical means. Combinations of atoms are called *molecules;* for example, two atoms of hydrogen form a molecule of hydrogen gas.   The molecules of any one compound differ from those of another; thus, two atoms of hydrogen combined with one of oxygen form a molecule of water, and an atom of hydrogen combined with one of chlorine forms a molecule of hydrochloric acid. All told, approximately a hundred elements have been discovered, but the number of compounds that can be formed from them is almost without limit.

The following table gives a few examples of elements and compounds and shows whether they are solids, liquids, or gases at ordinary temperatures.

ELEMENTS AND COMPOUNDS

Solids		Liquids		Gases	
Elements	Compounds	Elements	Compounds	Elements	Compounds
Aluminum	Copper sulfate	Bromine	Alcohol	Argon	Acetylene
Carbon	Lead dioxide	Gallium	Fuel oil	Helium	Carbon dioxide
Copper	Quartz	(melts in	Gasoline	Hydrogen	Hydrogen sulfide
Iron	Sodium chloride	the palm	Glycerine	Neon	Methane
Tin		of hand)	Sulfuric acid	Nitrogen	
Zinc		Mercury	Water	Oxygen	

A solid usually consists of an aggregation of *crystals*. Investigation with x-rays shows that the atoms in these solids, instead of being associated with particular molecules, are arranged within the crystal in an orderly three-dimensional pattern. The arrangement of the atoms in the crystal is characteristic of the substance. Sodium chloride (NaCl), for example, consists of alternate rows of sodium atoms and chlorine atoms, spaced in such a way as to build up a series of cubes, repeated again and again, with the atoms at the corners. Other substances, such as glass and plastics, although commonly called solids, do not exhibit a crystalline structure and differ in this respect from "true" solids.

Some combinations of matter that are not brought about by chemical action are recognized as *mixtures* and others as *alloys*. For example, the atmosphere is a mixture of a number of gases, mostly oxygen and nitrogen in the proportion of about one to four by volume, and contains, among other elements, small quantities of argon, helium, and neon. An alloy is usually a union of metals, produced by melting them together. Thus, brass is formed by the fusion of copper and zinc, and bronze by the fusion of copper and tin. Steel is essentially an alloy of iron and carbon, the carbon ranging from a few hundredths of 1% to about 1.6%, depending on the type of steel.

Two general properties of matter, of whatever kind, are of outstanding importance. (1) Every object exerts a force of attraction on all others. Thus, a stone is pulled to the earth, giving weight to the stone; the water of the sea is attracted by the sun and moon, causing tides; and the planets are attracted by the sun, maintaining them in their orbits. Such a force exists between any two objects, large or small; this universal force is called *gravitation* and will be discussed in Chap. 4. (2) Every object tends to maintain its condition of rest or uniform motion. This is evidenced in many everyday occurrences, as, for example, in the sudden starting or stopping of a train. When it starts abruptly the passengers are pressed back against their seats, and when it comes to a sudden stop they pitch forward. Because bodies behave in this manner, they are said to have *inertia*. These general properties of matter, together with its elastic, thermal, electric, magnetic, optical, and other specific properties, form a large part of the material with which the science of Physics deals.

2. Structure of the Atom. Extensive research over many years has shown that atoms, although extremely small, are made up of still smaller particles of three kinds, two of which have electric charges, § 191. The *electron* is the tiniest of these particles; it has a definite charge that is designated as negative. The *proton* is 1836 times as heavy as the electron; its charge is exactly the same as that of the electron in amount but produces opposite effects and is therefore termed positive. The neutron is about as heavy as the proton and has no charge. Electrons, protons, and neutrons are now recognized as the fundamental particles of which all atoms of matter are built.

The atom can be pictured as consisting of a central core or *nucleus*, with one or more electrons whirling around it. The motions of these electrons are often complex, but for simplicity the paths are regarded as circular or elliptical orbits similar to those of the planets about the sun. The nucleus is very minute and very dense, and it contains all the protons and neutrons of the atom, collectively called *nucleons*. These are held together somehow in a compact cluster that requires a tremendous force to break apart. When the atom is in an electrically uncharged or "neutral" condition, the number of orbital electrons equals the number of protons in the nucleus, so that the negative and positive charges just balance each other. The number of orbital electrons in an atom for the natural elements varies from 1 in hydrogen to 92 in uranium; for the so-called transuranic elements produced by physicists since 1940 this number extends to 101.

The simplest atom is that of hydrogen; it is pictured as having a single proton for its nucleus and one electron whirling around it. The dimensions of the hydrogen atom, with its components assumed to be spherical, are of the following order of magnitude: radius of nucleus and radius of the electron, each about 2×10^{-13} cm, § 3; least radius of electronic orbit, about 5×10^{-9} cm. A better appreciation of the relative proportions of these quantities can be obtained by imagining the atom to be magnified until the electronic orbit is a mile in diameter. The electron would then be represented by a sphere a little smaller than a baseball and would revolve around a nucleus of about equal size.

Two numbers are used in describing atoms. The number of protons in the nucleus (equal to the number of orbital electrons in a neutral atom) is called the *atomic number*; it determines the electrical charge of the atom and its chemical properties. The total number of protons and neutrons in the nucleus, that is, the number of nucleons, is called the *mass number* of the atom. Chemical reactions have no effect on the nucleus of the atom. When two or more atoms unite to form a molecule, each atom retains its own individuality, but their outer electronic orbits become interlinked.

Every natural element, with rare exceptions, is a mixture of atoms that have the same nuclear charge or atomic number but different masses. These are called *isotopes* of the element. The isotopes of an element differ in the structure of the atomic nucleus; they have different numbers of neutrons and so have different weights, but they have the same number of protons and so are essentially alike in their chemical properties. Hydrogen, for example, has three isotopes, and in this case they are given separate names: the most abundant one has no neutron in the atomic nucleus, the next with one neutron is called deuterium (a part of "heavy water"), and the third, with two neutrons, is called tritium.

The *average* weight of the atoms in any one element is called its *atomic weight.* The atomic weight of oxygen is taken as the base and given the value of exactly 16, and the atomic weights of all the other elements are expressed relative to this value. Thus, chlorine consists of two isotopes, one of atomic weight 35 and the other 37; in natural chlorine three-quarters of the atoms are of the first kind, and hence the atomic weight of chlorine is $(\frac{3}{4} \times 35) + (\frac{1}{4} \times 37) = 35.5$.

Figure 1 illustrates the foregoing terms for a few elements: hydrogen, helium, and oxygen. For chemical reactions these elements are symbolized

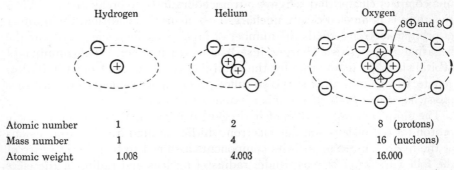

	Hydrogen	Helium	Oxygen
Atomic number	1	2	8 (protons)
Mass number	1	4	16 (nucleons)
Atomic weight	1.008	4.003	16.000

FIG. 1. Constituents of a few simple atoms in the neutral state. Protons are marked $+$ and electrons $-$; neutrons are unmarked

as H, He, and O, respectively. For nuclear reactions they are frequently symbolized as $_1H^1$, $_2He^4$, and $_8O^{16}$, respectively, wherein the subscript indicates the atomic number and the superscript the mass number. Isotopes of the elements can thus be designated definitely; for example, $_1H^2$, $_2He^3$, and $_8O^{17}$, each of which has one neutron more or less in its nucleus than in the most abundant form of the element.

Natural processes by which certain elements change into others have been known since the beginning of this century, and some twenty years later the same result was produced artificially by bombarding nuclei with atomic particles. In recent years particles of atomic nuclei have been split in two, a process called fission, and also some nuclei have been merged with others, a process called fusion. Atomic energy is made available through such processes.

3. Measurement. A definite knowledge of natural phenomena, and of the precise relations among them, is based upon information determined by experiment. If this information were indefinite or ambiguous it would be subject to different interpretations, and the conclusions drawn therefrom would be open to speculation. To have definite meaning, the evidence obtained must be quantitative. Evidence of this type is obtained by *measurement*, one of the most important operations in all scientific work.

The usual way to measure a quantity is to compare it with some other quantity of the same kind used as a basis of comparison. Everyone is familiar with the process of measuring the length of an object by laying a foot-rule alongside and expressing the result in feet and inches. A statement that a pole is 15 feet in length enables anyone having a foot-rule to form a correct conception of that length by laying off a distance equal to 15 one-foot distances. The length of the pole can also be expressed as 180 inches. This illustration shows that *the measurement of a quantity involves two things*: *a number and a unit.* To say that the pole measures 15 or 180 is an incomplete statement; it is necessary to say 15 feet or 180 inches. The unit shows how large a quantity is used as the basis of comparison, and the number shows how many of these units are contained in the quantity being measured.

Some statements based on physical measurements are given below to indicate the necessity for both number and unit: The rating of a certain automobile engine is 115 horsepower. The speed of a large steamship was found to be 30 knots. Comfortable room temperature is 68 degrees fahrenheit. Atmospheric pressure is about 14.7 pounds per square inch. The angular speed of a particular motor is 1800 revolutions per minute. The speed of light in a vacuum is 30,000,000,000 centimeters per second. The wavelength of yellow sodium light is 0.0000589 centimeter.

Numbers expressed in thousands or larger and those expressed in thousandths or smaller are usually written with 10 raised to the appropriate power, either positive or negative. Thus, the last two numbers of the preceding paragraph are customarily written 3.00×10^{10} and 5.89×10^{-5}. This notation is specially useful where such numbers are to be multiplied or divided.

Among the quantities with which Physics deals, three are generally regarded as fundamental, namely, *length*, *mass*, and *time*. These fundamental quantities and their measurement are considered in this chapter, together with some computations involving their use.

4. Standards and Units of Length. The units of length commonly employed belong to two groups, British and metric, and these are based upon definite distances on bars that are preserved as standards. The *yard* is the standard of length in British units. The Imperial yard is the distance at 62 degrees Fahrenheit (°F) between two fine lines engraved on gold plugs in a bronze bar kept at the Standards Office in Westminster, London. The *meter* is the standard of length in metric units and is the distance at 0 degrees centigrade (°C) between the centers of two lines traced on a platinum-iridium bar kept in a subterranean vault of the International Bureau of Weights and Measures at Sèvres, France.

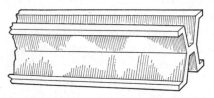

FIG. 2. Part of a standard meter bar. The defining lines are engraved on the center rib

Several standards of length are kept at the National Bureau of Standards in Washington, D. C. Because of difficulty in marking and because of shrinkage and expansion since construction, the distance between marks on any one meter bar is not precisely 1 meter; for example, the length of Meter Bar No. 27 is 1.5 ± 0.1 micron short as certified by the most recent comparison with the standard meter bar at Sèvres. Fig. 2 shows a portion of a standard bar.

The multiples and submultiples of the yard and of the meter in common use, together with their equivalents, are given below:

UNITS OF LENGTH

British	Metric
1 mile (mi) = 1760 yards	1 kilometer (km) = 1000 meters
1 yard (yd) = 3 feet	1 meter (m) = 100 centimeters
1 mile (mi) = 5280 feet	1 centimeter (cm) = 10 millimeters
1 foot (ft) = 12 inches	1 meter (m) = 1000 millimeters
1 inch (in.) = 1000 mils	1 millimeter (mm) = 1000 microns

It is often necessary to convert expressions of length in one group to corresponding ones in the other group. The fundamental relationship between the U. S. yard and the meter, as fixed by an Act of Congress in 1866, is: 1 yard = $\frac{3600}{3937}$ meter. In consequence, the following relations hold with sufficient exactness for most purposes; the last two relationships are frequently used and should be remembered.

CONVERSION FACTORS FOR LENGTHS

1 mile	=	1.6093 kilometers
1 kilometer	=	0.6214 mile
1 foot	=	30.48 centimeters
1 meter	=	3.281 feet
1 meter	=	39.37 inches
1 inch	=	2.540 centimeters

In carrying out computations involving lengths or other physical quantities, *the units should be included throughout;* they can be cancelled, multiplied, or divided as though they were numbers.

For example, it may be desired to convert a length of $\frac{5}{16}$ in. to centimeters. Since 1 in. = 2.54 cm, it follows that $\frac{2.54 \text{ cm}}{1 \text{ in.}}$ equals unity, the numerator and denominator being equal. Hence, the given length can be multiplied by the *unit factor* $\frac{2.54 \text{ cm}}{1 \text{ in.}}$ without changing its value, and the inch units cancelled, as follows:

$$\frac{5}{16} \text{ in.} = \left(\frac{5}{16} \text{ in.}\right)\left(\frac{2.54 \text{ cm}}{1 \text{ in.}}\right) = \frac{12.70 \text{ cm}}{16} = 0.794 \text{ cm}$$

Illustrative Problem

Find the number of kilometers in a mile, by using the relation 1 m = 39.37 in.

In this problem, use several unit factors, converting 1 mi first to feet, next to inches, then to meters, and finally to kilometers, thus:

$$1 \text{ mi} = (1 \text{ mi})\left(\frac{5280 \text{ ft}}{1 \text{ mi}}\right)\left(\frac{12 \text{ in.}}{1 \text{ ft}}\right)\left(\frac{1 \text{ m}}{39.37 \text{ in.}}\right)\left(\frac{1 \text{ km}}{1000 \text{ m}}\right)$$

$$= \frac{5280 \times 12}{39.37 \times 1000} \text{ km} = 1.609 \text{ km}$$

This procedure may seem laborious for such a simple computation, but in more involved calculations there is a distinct advantage in carrying all units through to avoid ambiguity and error.

5. Area and Bulk. The areas and volumes of regular geometric figures are often found by calculation from measurements of their linear dimensions. A few formulas frequently used for this purpose in physical calculations are given herewith:

AREAS AND VOLUMES

Figure	Area	Figure	Volume
Triangle of altitude h and base b	$\frac{1}{2}hb$	Right cylinder of altitude h and base of area B	hB
Triangle of sides, a, b, and c, and semi-perimeter s, that is $s = \frac{1}{2}(a + b + c)$	$\sqrt{s(s-a)(s-b)(s-c)}$	Pyramid or cone of altitude h and base of area B	$\frac{1}{3}hB$
Trapezium of altitude h and bases b and b'	$\frac{h}{2}(b + b')$	Sphere of radius r	$\frac{4}{3}\pi r^3$
Circle of radius r	πr^2		
Sphere of radius r, surface area	$4\pi r^2$		

The units in which areas and volumes are expressed are usually the squares and cubes respectively of the regular length units: for example, square feet (sq ft or ft^2); square centimeters (sq cm or cm^2); and cubic meters (cu m or m^3). Other units met with and their equivalents appear in the following table:

SOME UNITS OF AREA AND VOLUME

Circular mil = area of circle 1 mil in diameter
(cir mil)
Acre   = 43,560 ft^2 = $\frac{1}{640}$ square mile
Gallon (gal) = 4 quarts (liquid measure) = 231 in.^{3} = 3.785 liters
Liter   = 1000 cm^3 = 61.02 in.^{3} = 1.057 quarts (liquid measure)
Bushel   = 32 quarts (dry measure) = 2150.4 in.^{3}

1 ft^3 = 1728 in^3 7.48 gal/ft^3

6. The Concept of Mass. A fundamental property of matter known as inertia was described in § 1. The concept of mass is based upon this property; thus, the mass of an individual object is a measure of its inertia.

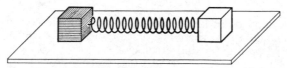

FIG. 3. Spring experiment to illustrate the concept of mass

This concept can be illustrated with two blocks of the same size, one of lead and one of wood, connected by a coiled spring, as in Fig. 3. The blocks are pulled apart, stretching the spring, and then placed on a smooth level surface and released. The spring pulls the blocks toward each other, but it is observed that the lead block does not travel as far as the wood block; it has more inertia and therefore a larger mass than the wood block. Thus, mass and inertia are essentially synonymous; a body with a large inertia is said to have a correspondingly large mass.

The metric standard of mass is the *kilogram*. The kilogram is defined as the mass of a certain block of platinum preserved at the International Bureau of Weights and Measures and known as the standard kilogram.

Fɪɢ. 4. An equal-arm balance. (*Courtesy of Central Scientific Company*)

One kilogram (kg) equals 1000 grams (gm), and one gram equals 1000 milligrams (mg). The British unit of mass is the pound and can be defined in a manner similar to the kilogram, but it will suffice to state that the U. S. pound is defined legally, to five significant figures, as 0.45359 kilogram.

The measurement of mass is usually accomplished with an equal-arm balance such as shown in Fig. 4. A mass to be measured is placed on one of its scale-pans; known masses are placed on the other; and the latter are varied until a balance is obtained. The operating principle is in reality the balancing of two forces, the earth's attraction for the mass on one pan being just counteracted by the earth's attraction for the known masses on the other.

The mass of a substance per unit volume is known as the *density* of that substance. For example, the mass of 1 cm³ of water is 1 gm, and therefore the density of water is 1 gm per cm³, or often written as 1 gm/cm³.

7. Measurement of Time. The regularity of the earth's motion around the sun serves as the basis for measurements of time. The earth revolves in its orbit once a year (about 365¼ days) and also rotates uniformly on its axis once a day. If the instants when the sun is directly overhead are recorded on two successive days, the elapsed time interval is a solar day. Since the earth's orbit is slightly elliptical, the earth travels faster in some parts of its orbit than at others, and consequently the solar day varies somewhat in length. The average throughout the year is known as the mean solar day. This period is divided into 24 hours (hr), each hour is subdivided into 60 minutes (min), and each minute into 60 seconds (sec), giving 86,400 sec in a day or about 3.156×10^7 sec in a year.

The basic standard of time is the *second*, defined until recently as 1/86,400 of a mean solar day. For greater accuracy the second is now officially defined as 1/31,556,925.975 of the tropical year for 1900.0, the zero after the decimal point indicating the beginning of that particular year. The reason for specifying a date is that the tropical year (which corresponds to the seasons) is decreasing by about 0.5 sec per century. The difference between the new definition and the old is slight, but is of interest in astronomy.

In scientific and engineering work, there is frequent need for measuring *intervals of time*, usually with the familiar stop watch. In laboratory experiments, clocks are used in which each sweep of the pendulum operates an electrical contact in a sounder circuit, the audible clicks of the sounder making the intervals easy to count.

8. Numerical Computations. The solution of numerical problems is an essential part of any serviceable course in Physics, and the observance of a few rules will make the work easier and more meaningful. Computations should be carried out far enough to be consistent with the data provided and the nature of the problem. Results should usually be stated to three or four significant figures, which can be obtained directly from a standard slide rule. In stating problems in this book, numerical values are usually given to only a few digits, for example, 7 ft or 0.12 mm. This is done in order that the mathematical work may not obscure the physical concepts; such values should be regarded as precise to three or four figures.

Where data are supplied to many figures, as in dealing with the wavelength of light, or where the effect under observation is very small, as in the expansion caused by heat, the number of figures to be kept in the computations and the result should be correspondingly increased. Care should be taken, however, not to state a result to more figures than are justified by the data. An example would be to compute the area of a rectangle from its base and height, with these lengths measured as 2.34 in. and 1.77 in., respectively. Here the data are precise to about 1 part in 200, or ½ of 1%, and since the area cannot be more precise than the lengths themselves, the result should be expressed as $(2.34 \text{ in.})(1.77 \text{ in.}) = 4.14 \text{ in.}^2$ It is needless and incorrect to express it with more figures, as *these would imply a precision not obtainable from the data provided.*

PROBLEMS

1. The uncharged atom of carbon (C) is formed of 6 protons, 6 neutrons, and 6 orbital electrons. The corresponding numbers of particles for copper (Cu) are 29, 34, and 29, respectively. Write the symbol for each of these elements with subscript and superscript.

2. (*a*) The symbol for deuterium is often given as $_1D^2$; express it in terms of an isotope of hydrogen. (*b*) What is the composition of the isotope of oxygen $_8O^{17}$ in the neutral state?

3. One of the transuranic elements produced in the development of the atomic bomb is called plutonium, and its symbol is $_{94}Pu^{239}$. How many neutrons does the nucleus contain? How many particles does each neutral atom have?

4. The air distance between Paris and Rome is approximately 1110 km. Express this distance in miles.

5. The height of the earth's highest mountain, Mt. Everest, has been recomputed, and the measurement now officially accepted by the Government of India is 29,028 ft. Convert this elevation to meters.

6. The Mackinac bridge designed by David B. Steinman and connecting the upper and lower peninsulas of Michigan is the longest suspension bridge in the world, the distance between cable anchorages being 8614 ft. It has two cables 24.25 in. in diameter, each composed of 12,876 wires that are 0.196 in. in diameter. Express these dimensions in the metric system.

7. Compute the radius of the earth in miles on the assumption that the distance from the equator to the pole along the earth's surface is exactly 10^7 m, as originally intended.

8. From the relation that 1 m $=$ 39.37 in., show that 1 km $=$ 0.6214 mi. Carry all the units through the computation.

9. The range of television broadcasting is at present limited largely to the "line of sight" from an elevated antenna to the horizon. The tallest television tower to date is at Oklahoma City and it rises to a height of 157? ft. Compute the broadcasting range in miles from the antenna at the top of this tower on the assumption that the earth is a smooth sphere 3960 mi in radius.

10. A piece of wire 10 m long is wound into a coil of 12 turns. Compute the diameter and area of the coil.

11. A certain tank holds 30 gal; find its volume in cubic feet.

12. A cylindrical quart measure for liquids is $3\frac{1}{2}$ in. in diameter; compute its height.

13. The liter is defined as the volume of 1 kg of pure water at the temperature of maximum density and under normal atmospheric pressure. The density of water under these conditions is 0.999973 gm/cm^3. From these data compute the number of cubic centimeters in a liter, and show by what percentage this number differs from 1000.

14. The usual fuel-oil tank is cylindrical and is installed with its axis horizontal. The depth of oil in the tank can be determined by inserting a stick

vertically through an opening in the top and measuring the length that has been wetted. (*a*) If such a tank holds 550 gal and if its internal diameter is 4 ft, what is its length? (*b*) If the oil is found to be 1 ft deep, how many gallons can be added to fill the tank?

15. An elevated storage tank has the form of a sphere and measures 20 ft in diameter. How many gallons of water does it hold?

16. In forming a spray, if each drop of water is broken up into 1000 droplets all of equal size, in what proportion is the liquid surface area increased?

17. The diagram shows an elevated water tank; the bottom is a hemisphere of 5-ft radius, the sides form a cylinder 10 ft high, and the top is a flat disk. Compute the total surface of the tank in square feet and its volume in gallons.

18. Take the density of steel to be 7.8 times that of water, and compute the mass of a solid steel rod 6 cm in diameter and 1 m long.

Problem 17

19. The dimensions of the molecules of certain substances can be determined by floating a known volume of the substance on water and measuring the area over which it spreads in forming a film one molecule deep. In myristic acid, the atoms in a molecule are held in chain fashion, and in forming a thin continuous film the individual molecules align themselves pointing upward from the water surface and stack together snugly. In a particular test, 0.03 mg of myristic acid, of density 0.862 gm/cm^3, formed a continuous film covering an area of 222 cm^2. (*a*) From these data find the lengths of the molecules, that is, the height of the upstanding atomic chains. (*b*) Take the mass of one molecule of myristic acid to be 4.20 × 10^{-22} gm, and from the number of molecules present, find the cross-sectional area per molecule, as viewed from directly above.

20. The wheels shown in Fig. 55 are solid disks of uniform thickness; they have the same dimensions, and are so proportioned that the mass of the combination remains unchanged when the metal and wood are interchanged as shown. If the density of the metal is 10 times that of the wood and if the outside diameter is 20 cm, what is the diameter of the central disk?

21. One of the pumping stations supplying a city with water can pump at the rate of 100 million gal per day (mgd). Express this rate in cubic feet per second.

22. The division of the United States into four time zones—Eastern, Central, Mountain, and Pacific—became effective in 1883. These zones correspond to the sun time at the 75th, 90th, 105th, and 120th meridians of longitude west of Greenwich, England. Given the longitude bearings of New York, N. Y. as 74.0° west; Chicago, Ill. as 87.6° west; and San Francisco, Cal. as 122.4° west; determine the actual sun-time difference between (*a*) New York and Chicago, (*b*) Chicago and San Francisco, and (*c*) New York and San Francisco.

2

VECTOR AND SCALAR QUANTITIES

9. Angular Measure. A large part of this chapter will be devoted to quantities that have definite directions. In calculations dealing with these quantities, the angles between their direction lines have to be taken into account. The total angle about a point is composed of 360 *degrees* (°), and a right angle has 90°. A degree has 60 *minutes* (′) of arc, and a minute has 60 *seconds* (″) of arc.

Another unit for measuring angles is based on the relative dimensions of a sector of a circle. In Fig. 5, the ratio of the arc s_1 to its radius r_1 is the same as that of any other arc s_2 to its radius r_2. This ratio of arc length to radius is not affected by the size of the circle but depends only upon the central angle θ (theta).

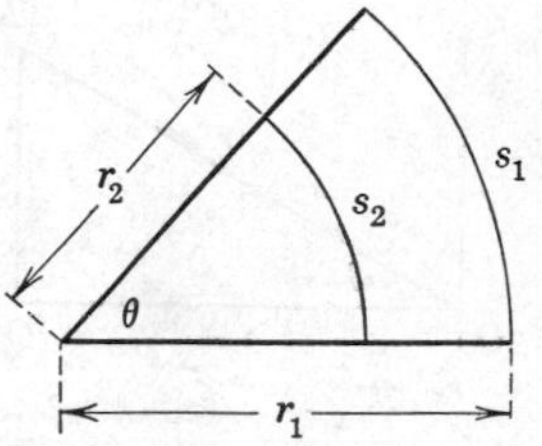

Fig. 5. Relation between arc and radius in radian measure

The angle subtended at the center of a circle by an arc equal in length to the radius is called a radian. Since the circumference of a circle is 2π (2 pi) times its radius r (that is, $2 \times 3.1416r$), the total angle around the central point is 2π radians. A right angle is one-fourth as large, or $\pi/2$ radians. In general,

$$\text{Angle in radians} = \frac{\text{arc length}}{\text{radius}}$$

or in symbols

$$\theta = \frac{s}{r} \tag{1}$$

The angle θ is a ratio of one length to another; the arc length s must be be expressed in the same unit as the radius r, and consequently the angle in radians is simply a number.

Conversion from degrees to radians, or vice versa, must often be made.

CONVERSION FACTORS FOR ANGLES

1 radian	— 57.3	degrees
1 degree	= 0.0175	radian
1 revolution	= 6.283	radians

$1^\circ = \frac{\pi}{180}$ 13

Since 2π radians about a point equal 360°, 1 radian $= 360°/2\pi = 57°\ 17'\ 45''$ or 57.3° approximately.

Angles can be measured and laid off with a *protractor*. In a simple form, this instrument consists of a semicircular plate with angles marked from 0 to 180° on lines radiating from the center.

10. Some Trigonometric Relations. In handling physical quantities that have specific directions, it is convenient to represent them by lines drawn at the appropriate angles. Often these lines form the sides of a triangle, some of the sides and angles being known and others unknown. The unknown quantities are generally determined by trigonometry.

The trigonometric functions most often used are the sine, cosine, and tangent (abbreviated sin, cos, and tan); they are defined below in connection with Fig. 6. This figure shows the X and Y rectangular coordinate axes, intersecting at the origin O, from which the radius r extends to the point P. The rectangular coordinates of this point are the abscissa x and the ordinate y; together with the radius they form the right-angled triangle OPQ. For the angle θ, the sine is the ratio of the length of the ordinate y to the radius r; the cosine is the ratio of the abscissa x to the radius r; and the tangent is the ratio of the ordinate y to the abscissa x. These statements are symbolized as follows:

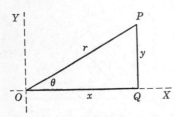

Fig. 6. Triangle for defining the trigonometric functions

$$\sin \theta = \frac{\text{ordinate}}{\text{radius}} = \frac{y}{r}; \quad \cos \theta = \frac{\text{abscissa}}{\text{radius}} = \frac{x}{r}; \quad \tan \theta = \frac{\text{ordinate}}{\text{abscissa}} = \frac{y}{x} \quad (2)$$

Numerical values of these functions for angles between 0 and 90° are tabulated in the Appendix. The values for angles larger than 90° may be obtained by applying the rules at the end of the table or by referring to Fig. 6 and following the usual convention as to signs, x being taken as plus when measured to the right of the origin O and minus when measured to the left, and y being taken as plus when measured upward from O and minus when measured downward.

For small angles, an approximation is often used to simplify computations, to the effect that

$$\sin \theta = \theta \text{ (in radians)} = \tan \theta \quad (3)$$

The accompanying table shows that these quantities are almost identical to the third decimal place for angles up to 10°, and hence they may be used interchangeably for such angles. Facility in handling these functions will be helpful in dealing with vector quantities.

FUNCTIONS OF SOME SMALL ANGLES

Degrees	Radians	Sine	Tangent
0	0	0	0
5	0.087	0.087	0.088
10	0.175	0.174	0.176
15	0.262	0.259	0.268

The *Law of Sines* expresses the relation between the sides of any triangle and the sines of the angles opposite them. For the triangles of Fig. 7, this law states that

$$\frac{a}{\sin A} = \frac{b}{\sin B} = \frac{c}{\sin C} \tag{4}$$

which shows that in any triangle, whether right-angled or oblique, the ratio of any side to the sine of the opposite angle is a constant.

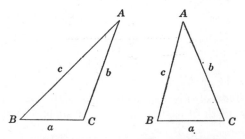

FIG. 7. Triangles for establishing the laws of sines and cosines

The *Law of Cosines* is used to solve an oblique triangle when two sides and the included angle are known and the length of the other side is required. This law states that in any triangle the square of any side is equal to the sum of the squares of the other two sides minus twice the product of these two sides and the cosine of the angle included between them. For example, in Fig. 7,

$$c^2 = a^2 + b^2 - 2ab \cos C \tag{5}$$

where C is the angle between sides a and b, and c is the side opposite this angle. When $C = 90°$, the last term disappears and the expression reduces to the form $c^2 = a^2 + b^2$, which is the familiar Theorem of Pythagoras for a right triangle.

11. Addition of Directed Quantities. Many quantities that are used in physical measurements or calculations can be added the way dollars are added: by simple arithmetic. Thus, a 600-watt percolator connected to an electric circuit in addition to a 60-watt lamp already connected makes a total load of 660 watts. Addition can be carried out in this manner when the quantities do not involve the idea of direction. Physical quantities that have directions can also be added; the process is more involved, but not difficult, and forms one of the important methods of Physics. It will now be applied to the addition of displacements.

When a body moves from one position to another it is said to undergo a displacement. *Displacement is change of position;* it is taken to be a directed quantity, with its direction away from the initial position of the body toward its final position. Fig. 8 shows a small subdivided area upon which distances are scaled off with respect to a fixed reference point O. The position of point A is 2 mi east and 1 mi north of O, and that of point B is 6 mi east and 4 mi north of O. When an object moves from A to B its displacement is represented by the straight arrow AB; this is true whatever path the body actually follows, either straight or curved, in moving from A to B. Thus, if the body moves in two straight lines via point C, the *length of path* traversed is $AC + CB$, but the *displacement* is still AB. The numerical value, or *magnitude*, of this displacement is $\sqrt{(6-2)^2 + (4-1)^2} = 5$ mi and its *direction* is north of east by an angle θ such that $\tan \theta = \frac{3}{4}$; that is, $\theta = 36.9°$.

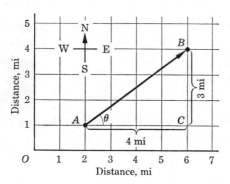

FIG. 8.   Illustrating position and displacement

Displacements can be added even though they are not in the same direction. Such an addition is necessary, for example, when a man walks a certain distance in one direction, another distance in a different direction, and so on, and desires to know his position with respect to the starting point. His entire journey can be mapped out as a series of displacements, one after another, each represented by an arrow of appropriate length and direction. An arrow from the beginning to the end of such a diagram represents the "sum" of the separate displacements with their directions taken into account; this sum is also called the *resultant* displacement. In arriving at the result *graphically*, the diagram is made carefully to scale, and the resultant is measured with rule and protractor to determine its length and direction. To obtain the result *analytically*, a rough diagram will suffice as a guide, and the length and direction of the resultant are calculated by mathematics. The contrast between the two procedures can be shown by a numerical example dealing with the addition of two displacements.

Illustrative Problem

Consider a pedestrian to walk 3 mi due east and then 2 mi in a direction 60° north of east. How far is he from the starting point and in what direction is he from that point?

Graphical solution. Lay off the arrows representing the displacements accurately to suitable scale and at the exact inclinations, with the tail-end of the second arrow placed at the head-end of the first, thereby forming two sides of a triangle, as in the plan view of Fig. 9. Draw the closing side of the triangle, and measure its length carefully to the same scale. This gives the numerical value of the resultant R as 4.4 mi. Measure the direction that this closing side of the triangle makes with the east direction by means of a protractor; this angle is marked θ in the diagram. This gives the direction of the resultant as north of east by an angle $\theta = 23°$.

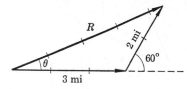

FIG. 9. Addition of two displacements

The accuracy of a graphical result depends not only upon care in using the correct lengths and directions, but also upon making the drawing of adequate size. If a directed quantity is represented as an arrow 6 in. long, an error of $\frac{1}{32}$ in. in its length means an inaccuracy of one part in $6 \times 32 = 192$, that is, an error of $\frac{1}{2}\%$. Graphical solutions like the foregoing can be depended upon for an accuracy of 1% if care is exercised. Much greater accuracy can be attained by analytical solutions since these do not require the making of drawings to scale.

Analytical solution. Make a rough sketch to resemble Fig. 9, and figure out the unknown parts of the triangle by trigonometry. First, use the Law of Cosines to determine the magnitude of the resultant R, the angle between the two known sides of the triangle being 120°. Thus

$$R^2 = 3^2 + 2^2 - 2(3)(2) \cos 120°$$

$$= 9 + 4 - 12(-\sin 30°) = 13 + 12(0.500) = 19.00$$

whence $R = 4.36$ mi. Next, apply the Law of Sines to find the direction of the resultant:

$$\frac{2 \text{ mi}}{\sin \theta} = \frac{4.36 \text{ mi}}{\sin 120°}$$

whence $\sin \theta = (2/4.36) \sin 120° = 0.459(0.866) = 0.397$. From trigonometric tables, the angle having this value for its sine is $\theta = 23.4°$.

An analytical solution is inherently more precise than a graphical one since it does not depend upon the accuracy of a drawing, but only upon the precision of the data given and the number of places to which the computation is carried out.

12. Parallelogram Method of Combining Displacements. In adding displacements or other directed quantities, several methods may be used. These are described in this and the following sections.

In the first method, two displacements a and b are laid off graphically to scale in the proper directions *from a common starting point S*, so as to form

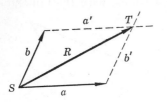

FIG. 10. Two displacements added by the Parallelogram Method; vectorially, $R = a + b$

two adjacent sides of a parallelogram, as shown in Fig. 10. The parallelogram is then completed by drawing the sides a' and b' parallel to a and b respectively and intersecting at T. The diagonal R drawn from the starting point, called the *concurrent diagonal*, gives the resultant both in length and direction. This method of finding the distance and direction from the starting point S to the terminal point T is called the Parallelogram Method of adding displacements. Since lengths b and b' are equal, the

resultant R is the same as though distance b' were added to distance a by the method described in the preceding section. Consequently the same mathematical steps used in the solution of the oblique triangle can be used to obtain an analytical solution by the Parallelogram Method.

The Parallelogram Method can be used for the addition of any number of displacements, by first finding the resultant of two of them, then adding another displacement to this resultant in the same way, and continuing this process until all are included.

The process of addition just described applies also to the reverse operation of *subtraction* with but a slight modification. Thus, one displacement, or other directed quantity, can be subtracted from another by *reversing its direction and proceeding as in addition.* For example, to subtract displacement b from displacement a in Fig. 10, b is first reversed by shifting it through 180° to the position $-b$ as in Fig. 11, and then a and $-b$ are added by the Parallelogram Method to get the difference D, as shown.

13. Polygon Method. In adding three or more displacements, the Parallelogram Method is somewhat unwieldy, and it is more convenient to follow a procedure called the Polygon Method. From a chosen starting point, one of the displacements is laid off to appropriate scale and in proper direction;

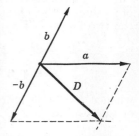

FIG. 11. One displacement subtracted from another; vectorially, $D = a - b$

from its terminal or head-end another of the displacements is laid off similarly; from the terminal of the latter the third is laid off; and so on until all are included. Lastly, the line is drawn that will close the figure and form a polygon; this is the resultant. The procedure is an extension of that used in the problem of § 11 in which only two displacements were added; in that case the polygon had the simpler form of a triangle. The Polygon Method is illustrated in Fig. 12, wherein the four displacements *a*, *b*, *c*, and *d* shown at the left are to be added. At the center of the figure the order of addition, starting at *S*, is *a*, *b*, *c*, *d*, and at the right is *c*, *a*, *b*, *d*;

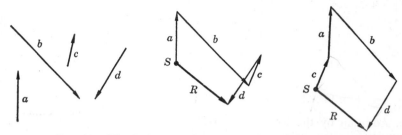

FIG. 12.   The Polygon Method of adding displacements

the resultant *R* is, of course, the same in magnitude and direction whatever the order followed in the additive process. It is to be noted that the resultant is directed away from the starting point.

14. Resolution of Directed Quantities. In the preceding sections, attention was focused upon methods by which displacements can be added to form a resultant. From the reverse point of view, the resultant displacement can be regarded as formed of *components*. Thus, in either diagram of Fig. 13, *R* is the resultant of *a* and *b*, and therefore *a* and *b* can be considered the components of *R*. The diagram at the left illustrates the most usual case, in which the components are at right angles to each other and hence are termed *rectangular components*. The process of breaking up a directed quantity into components is called *resolution*.

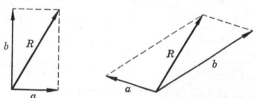

FIG. 13.   Resolution of a displacement; *R* is resolved into components *a* and *b*

To resolve a displacement into two components, it is desirable to follow the procedure illustrated in Fig. 14. At I is shown the displacement *L* to be resolved and the direction lines 1 and 2 along which the desired components shall lie. First, the displacement *L* and the two direction lines are drawn from a common point *S* as in II. Next, from the head-end of *L*, lines are constructed parallel to the direction lines 1 and 2, meeting those lines at points 3 and 4, as in III. Finally, the intercepts of these direction lines are replaced by the desired components *J* and *K*, with their head-ends located at the intersection points 3 and 4, as illustrated in IV. Naturally

J and *K* must be measured to the same scale that is used for *L*. This procedure is the same whatever the directions of the displacement to be resolved or the direction lines may be.

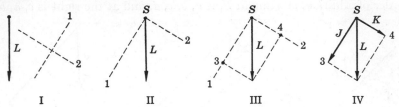

FIG. 14.   The process of resolving a vector into components

15. Addition by the Resolution Method. The process of resolution just described is extremely useful when applied to the addition of displacements analytically, particularly where there are more than two such quantities to be added. Under these circumstances, each of the displacements concerned is resolved into rectangular components, usually in the horizontal and vertical directions, then the horizontal and vertical components of all displacements are added separately, and finally these values are combined to form the resultant. The diagrams need not be drawn to scale, since the lengths are determined accurately by trigonometric methods.

Illustrative Problem

Use the Resolution Method to find the resultant of the displacements *a*, *b*, *c*, *d*, and *e* in Fig. 15.

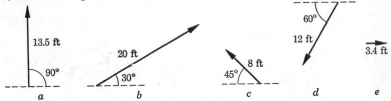

FIG. 15.   Displacements to be added by the Resolution Method

Displacement *a* is 13.5 ft vertically up and has no horizontal component. Displacement *e* is 3.4 ft horizontally to the right and has no vertical component. The other three displacements must be resolved into their horizontal and vertical components. This resolution is shown in Fig. 16, where

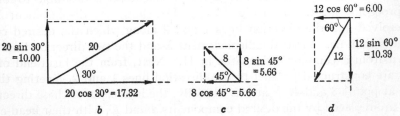

FIG. 16.   Resolution into rectangular components

the perpendiculars dropped from the head-ends of the displacements upon the horizontal and vertical direction lines fix the terminals of the components. Thus, the displacement *b* of 20 ft at an angle 30° up from the horizontal is replaced in the addition by a component 20 cos 30°, or 17.32 ft, horizontally to the right and another component 20 sin 30°, or 10.00 ft, vertically up. The addition of the components is tabulated below:

Displace- ment	Components			
	Up	Down	Right	Left
a	13.50	0	0	0
b	10.00	0	17.32	0
c	5.66	0	0	5.66
d	0	10.39	0	6.00
e	0	0	3.40	0
Totals	29.16	10.39	20.72	11.66
	10.39		11.66	
	18.77		9.06	

Consequently, the result of the addition is a displacement 18.77 ft vertically up and 9.06 ft horizontally to the right. The resultant *R* of these components is obtained in Fig. 17; its magnitude is $\sqrt{18.77^2 + 9.06^2} = 20.84$ ft, and its direction is upward from the horizontal datum by an angle θ of which the tangent is $18.77/9.06 = 2.072$, namely, 64.2°.

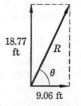

16. Vector Versus Scalar Quantities. This chapter deals principally with displacements and the methods by which they can be added. Many other physical quantities are like displacements in that they have direction as well as magnitude and are added by the same methods. *The term* vector *is applied to quantities that have both direction and magnitude, and that can be added the way displacements are added.*

Fig. 17. Combining components to form resultant

The last clause is needed in the definition because of situations like the following: Stream *A* flows south and the volume of flow is 500 ft³/sec. Stream *B* flows southwest and the volume flowing in that direction is 100 ft³/sec. These quantities might be thought of as having direction and magnitude; nevertheless they are not vector quantities since when added—that is, when *B* flows into *A*—the result is 600 ft³/sec, and not as given by vector addition.

Any vector quantity can be represented by an arrow drawn in the appropriate direction and having a length which represents, to some convenient scale, the numerical value of the quantity that it represents. The *displacement* of a box along a chute, the *velocity* of an airplane, and the *force* used in stretching a spring, all are examples of vector quantities.

Other physical quantities are expressed completely by magnitude alone. *The term* scalar *refers to quantities that have magnitude only.* As illustration of scalar quantities, the *volume* of a tank, the *length of path* traversed by a moving body, or the *horsepower* of a motor may be mentioned.

17. Vector Addition in More Than One Plane. The methods used in the preceding sections for determining the resultant of vector quantities can be extended to three dimensions.

In the diagram of Fig. 18, the axes OX, OY, and OZ represent the inter-

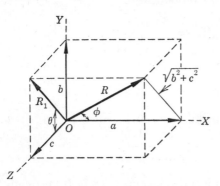

FIG. 18. Addition of forces in three mutually perpendicular directions; R is the resultant, shown in perspective

sections of three planes at right angles to one another, with the XZ plane horizontal; and a, b, and c represent forces acting along the directions of these axes. The resultant of any two of them is found exactly as before; for example, the resultant of b and c is R_1 and lies in the YZ plane at an angle $\theta = \tan^{-1} (b/c)$ with the horizontal XZ plane. This intermediate resultant R_1 is next combined with the third force a; the final resultant of the three forces a, b, and c is $R = \sqrt{a^2 + b^2 + c^2}$; its plane is inclined at the angle θ with the horizontal, and in this plane it makes an angle ϕ (phi) $= \tan^{-1} (\sqrt{b^2 + c^2}/a)$ with the axis OX.

In more involved problems, where the quantities to be added do not lie along mutually perpendicular axes, they can be resolved into components that do have these directions and the solution then carried forward in the same manner.

PROBLEMS

1. Determine approximately the percentage difference in length between the chord c and the arc s in the accompanying diagram, considering θ to be an angle of (a) 10°; (b) 30°.

2. City B is 200 mi east of city A, and city C is 150 mi northeast of city B. What is the air distance from city A to city C?

3. A uniform beam 10 ft long is suspended from a single point by two ropes a and b extending to its ends.

Problem 1

Rope a is 6 ft long and rope b is 8 ft long. The beam swings, and comes to rest with its midpoint directly below the point of support. What angles do the ropes make with the vertical?

4. To determine the width of a stream, a datum line 80 ft long is laid off along one bank, and from its ends a near-by point on the opposite bank is sighted. The angles that these lines of sight make with the datum line are 70° and 60°. Calculate the width of the stream.

5. To determine the height of a distant mountain, its peak is sighted at a point on level ground and found to be 30° above the horizontal; another sight of the peak at a point 1000 ft nearer the mountain gives the

angle of elevation as 35°. From these data, compute the height of the mountain.

6. Two bowling pins, centered 1 ft apart, stand crosswise of the alley. A bowler 62 ft away from the pins attempts to hit both by rolling a ball between them. The diameter of the ball is 8.60 in. and that of each pin is 4.76 in. What variation may be allowed in the direction of the ball if it is to hit both pins?

7. A boat in still water sails 12 mi due east and then 5 mi due north. How far is the boat from its starting point, and in what direction is it from that point?

8. An airplane in still air flies 100 km due north and then 125 km along a course 60° west of north. How far is the airplane from its starting point and in what direction from that point? Solve both graphically and analytically.

9. An object undergoes two displacements: $a = 30$ cm horizontal and toward the right, and $b = 20$ cm toward the left, in a direction 60° downward from the horizontal. Add a and b graphically by the Parallelogram Method.

10. In the preceding problem, subtract displacement b from displacement a; also, subtract displacement a from displacement b. Obtain the result for each part graphically.

11. A body undergoes three displacements as follows: (*a*) 3 mi south, (*b*) 1 mi east, and (*c*) 2 mi 30° north of east. Represent these displacements by a polygon, and find their resultant analytically.

12. A displacement of 10 m is directed vertically upward. Resolve this displacement into two components: one horizontal and toward the right; the other at an angle of 53.1° with the horizontal.

13. (*a*) A displacement of 4 ft is directed upward and toward the right, at an angle of 60° with the horizontal. Resolve this displacement into horizontal and vertical components. (*b*) A displacement of 20 ft is directed vertically downward. Resolve it into rectangular components which make angles of 30° and 60° with the horizontal.

14. A displacement of 10 cm directed horizontally toward the left has one component that has a magnitude of 20 cm and is directed vertically downward; find the magnitude and direction of the other component.

15. Find the resultant of the following displacements by the Resolution Method: (*a*) 80 ft north, (*b*) 100 ft northeast, (*c*) 60 ft directed 30° south of west, and (*d*) 110 ft west.

16. A body is acted upon by two forces: its weight W directed vertically downward, and a force N directed upward and toward the right at an angle of 60° with the horizontal. Their resultant R is known to be directed downward and toward the right at an angle of 30° with the horizontal. Find the magnitudes of both N and R.

17. A body undergoes three displacements in mutually perpendicular directions: 3 cm along the X axis, 4 cm along the Y axis, and 5 cm along the Z axis. How far is the body from its starting position?

3

LINEAR MOTION

18. Uniform Linear Motion. The concept of motion has wide application to machinery of all sorts, to locomotion on land and water and in the air, to astronomical bodies, and to tiny particles within the atoms of matter. Motion can be described as to the path followed, the uniformity of travel, and the changes in travel rate.

Linear motion is sometimes taken to mean motion along any kind of line, but often it is defined as motion along a straight line, and in this book it is used with that meaning. Thus, motion along a straight line is called *rectilinear* or simply *linear;* along a curve it is described as *curvilinear.* Rate deals with the rapidity of motion, whereas change in rate has to do with speeding up or slowing down. This entire chapter deals with motion along a straight line, and the first few sections (up to § 21) with straight-line motion at a steady rate—that is, *uniform linear motion.*

Many instances can be cited in which a body moves from one place to another along a straight line: for example, a crate hoisted by a rope, a train running on a straight track, or a car driven along a straight stretch of highway. In each of these cases the body moves along a straight line, and therefore its motion is *linear.*

The motion of such a body can be studied by observing the body carefully for a period of time and measuring the displacement that it undergoes every second. If the motion is *uniform*, these displacements are found to be equal. For example, if a car in uniform linear motion crosses a starting line and passes a point 50 ft away at the end of one second, it will pass another point 50 ft farther along at the end of the next second, and so on, undergoing the same displacement (namely, 50 ft in the direction of travel) during each second. If shorter time intervals are chosen, the same equality of displacement is observed. To generalize, a body has uniform linear motion if it undergoes equal displacements along the same straight line during equal intervals of time, however brief these intervals may be.

Often motion that is linear is not uniform; for example, a falling body is observed to travel faster as it approaches the earth. Also, the above-mentioned car acquires the uniform motion referred to after starting from rest and later loses that uniform motion when the brakes are applied. Many other examples will suggest themselves in which uniform motion is preceded or followed by periods of changing motion. In dealing with uniform

24

motion, it is assumed that the body has already started from rest and reached a state of uniform motion before any consideration of its motion is begun.

The *velocity* of a body in uniform linear motion is defined as *the displacement that the body undergoes divided by the time in which this displacement occurs.* In equation form,

$$\text{Velocity} = \frac{\text{displacement}}{\text{time interval}}$$

or, in symbols,

$$v = \frac{s}{t} \tag{6}$$

where v is the velocity of the body, s its displacement, and t the time during which the displacement occurs, all symbols that are commonly used for these quantities. From the fact that equal displacements occur in equal intervals of time, it is seen that the ratio of s to t in this equation remains constant; hence, if a body has uniform linear motion it has constant velocity. Velocity is a vector quantity, like displacement, and is directed along the line of motion.

All kinds of motion can be represented on a graph by plotting velocity as ordinates and time as abscissas. On such a graph, steady or uniform motion would be shown as a straight horizontal line through the appropriate value on the ordinate scale, as in the heavy line of Fig. 19. Nonuniform motion is represented by inclined or curved lines; the straight dotted line in the figure represents a uniformly increasing velocity and the curved one a gradually decreasing velocity.

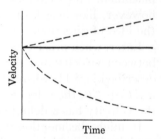

Fig. 19. Comparison of uniform and nonuniform motion; the horizontal line represents uniform motion

The unit in which velocity is expressed depends upon the units used in designating displacement and time. If the displacement is stated in miles and the time in hours, the velocity, from Eq. 6, is given in miles per hour; if, instead, the displacement is stated in meters and the time in minutes, the velocity is given in meters per minute. Any given velocity may thus be stated in many different ways, depending on the units selected for displacement and time. Although all of these may be correct, there are three particular units for velocity that are used quite generally in scientific and technological work, namely, *feet per second* in British units, and *centimeters per second* or *meters per second* in metric units. In expressing the velocity of ships the term *knot* is commonly used; the knot is 1 nautical mile per hour, which is equivalent to 1.152 (land) miles per hour.

A velocity expressed in miles per hour can be converted to feet per second by multiplying it by suitable unit factors, as in § 4. Thus,

$$30 \frac{\text{mi}}{\text{hr}} = \left(\frac{30 \text{ mi}}{\text{hr}}\right)\left(\frac{5280 \text{ ft}}{1 \text{ mi}}\right)\left(\frac{1 \text{ hr}}{60 \text{ min}}\right)\left(\frac{1 \text{ min}}{60 \text{ sec}}\right) = \frac{(30)(5280) \text{ ft}}{3600 \text{ sec}} = 44 \frac{\text{ft}}{\text{sec}}$$

It will be convenient to remember that 30 mi/hr is exactly equal to 44 ft/sec in converting from one of these units to the other.

19. Distinction Between Velocity and Speed. In describing the rate at which a body moves, a distinction is made between velocity and speed, just as a distinction was made between displacement and length of path in § 11. For a body in uniform linear motion, speed is defined as the length of path traversed divided by the elapsed time, or

$$\text{Speed} = \frac{\text{length of path}}{\text{time interval}}$$

Speed has the same units as velocity and is expressed by the same equation, Eq. 6, with *s* interpreted as the length of path traversed. In fact, for uniform linear motion the length of path traversed is identical with the displacement and therefore speed and velocity have the same value. Speed, however, like length of path, is a scalar quantity and does not involve the idea of direction.

Later, when other types of motion are studied, the need for the distinction between velocity and speed will be more apparent. Even in the example described in § 11, where the displacement is *AB* whereas the length of path is *AC + CB*, the velocity and speed clearly have different values; moreover, the velocity has a definite direction, namely, from *A* to *B*.

It might be mentioned again that length of path is not restricted to a straight line, and hence the foregoing definition for speed applies equally well to curvilinear motion. A body that moves along a curved path at constant speed nevertheless experiences a change in velocity at each instant because of the continual change in its direction of motion. To be sure, the numerical value of its velocity remains unchanged, but the fact that its direction keeps changing from instant to instant means that its velocity is also changing continuously.

Illustrative Problem

An example is afforded by atomic particles that are given high speeds for the purpose of breaking up atomic nuclei. In a test with a cyclotron protons move with a constant speed of 2.5×10^9 cm/sec around a semicircular path in a time of 5×10^{-8} sec; determine the radius of the semicircle.

From Eq. 6, the length of the semicircle is

$$s = vt = \left(2.5 \times 10^9 \frac{\text{cm}}{\text{sec}}\right)(5 \times 10^{-8} \text{ sec}) = 125 \text{ cm,}$$

and therefore the radius of the semicircle is $\dfrac{125}{\pi} = 39.8$ cm.

20. Relative Motion. It is difficult to conceive of absolute motion or of absolute rest, for actually only relative motion can be observed, that is, the motion of bodies with respect to one another. A person seated in a train at a railroad station and looking out of the window at another train near by is often unable to tell whether the train in which he is seated or the other train is in motion when one of them starts; he can observe only that one of them is moving relative to the other. Again, a house is commonly referred to as stationary, a statement which means, of course, that the house does not move with respect to the earth; nevertheless the house is in rapid motion relative to the sun, for it is carried along with the earth as the earth rotates on its axis and also as it moves in its orbit. In ordinary usage the term "velocity of a body" means its velocity with respect to the earth, and the expression "condition of rest" refers to a state of rest with respect to the earth. The concept of relative motion can be illustrated by some common examples.

Illustrative Problems

I. A man walks through a railroad train at 5 mi/hr while the train is moving eastward at 40 mi/hr; what is his velocity relative to the earth (*a*) if he walks forward in the train? (*b*) if he walks toward the rear of the train?

(*a*) The man is moving relative to the train at 5 mi/hr eastward, whether the train moves or not, and the train is moving relative to the earth at 40 mi/hr, also eastward. These velocities have the same direction and therefore can be added arithmetically, giving the velocity of the man relative to the earth as 45 mi/hr eastward. (*b*) Here the two velocities have opposite directions, and the velocity of the man relative to the earth is 35 mi/hr eastward.

II. An automobile 18 ft long driven at 50 mi/hr overtakes and passes a 28-ft truck moving along a straight road at 30 mi/hr. Compute the time occupied in passing and the distance traveled by each vehicle during this time. Assume that one car is passing the other so long as any point on it is opposite any point on the other. (Actually, the time of overtaking a vehicle and returning to the same traffic lane is much greater than the time of "passing" as here described.)

The velocity of the automobile relative to the ground is 50 mi/hr, or 73.3 ft/sec, and that of the truck is 30 mi/hr, or 44.0 ft/sec, both in the direction of travel. The velocity of the automobile relative to the truck is $50 - 30 = 20$ mi/hr, or 29.3 ft/sec in the same direction. The distance that the automobile travels relative to the truck while passing it is $18 + 28 = 46.0$ ft, whether the truck is moving or not. From these relative values, the time occupied in passing is found to be $t = s/v = 46.0$ ft/(29.3 ft/sec) $= 1.570$ sec. During this time the automobile travels a distance $s = vt = (73.3 \text{ ft/sec})(1.570 \text{ sec}) = 115.1$ ft, and the truck travels $(44.0)(1.570) = 69.1$ ft.

_____

In the more general situation, where a body has two motions at the same time with the paths of motion not parallel, the resultant velocity is found by applying the methods of vector addition described in Chap. 2. For definiteness, it may be supposed that an object *A* is moving relative to a second object (or medium) B with a velocity v_{AB}, while the second object is moving relative to a third object C with a velocity v_{BC}. Then the velocity of object A relative to object C, namely, v_{AC}, is the vector sum of v_{AB} and v_{BC}, or symbolically,

$$\overrightarrow{v_{AC}} = \overrightarrow{v_{AB}} + \overrightarrow{v_{BC}} \tag{7}$$

in which the arrows are used as a reminder that the expression represents a vectorial addition. This practice is not followed throughout this textbook, but only where deemed essential. Incidentally, there is but one vector equation connecting these velocities, and it does not matter which term is placed first. Thus, the foregoing equation might equally well be written $\overrightarrow{v_{AB}} = \overrightarrow{v_{AC}} + \overrightarrow{v_{CB}}$, as will be evident upon replacing v_{CB} by $-v_{BC}$ and transposing this term.

A traveling crane such as used in power plants and factories for moving heavy machinery from place to place within a building will serve as an illustration. The crane extends across the width of the building and rolls on tracks supported along the side walls near the eaves, as shown in Fig. 20.

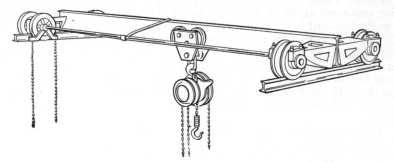

FIG. 20. A traveling crane for hand operation

A machine can be moved along the crane, crosswise of the building, at the same time that the crane is moving lengthwise of the building. The velocity of the machine with respect to the floor is then the resultant or vector sum of two separate velocities, that of the machine with respect to the crane and that of the crane with respect to the floor. In subscript notation, v_{MF} represents the velocity of the machine with respect to the floor, v_{MC} the velocity of the machine with respect to the crane, and v_{CF} the velocity of the crane with respect to the floor; then as a *vector addition*,

$$\overrightarrow{v_{MF}} = \overrightarrow{v_{MC}} + \overrightarrow{v_{CF}}$$

The principles of relative velocity are applied wherever an object travels through a medium which is itself in motion, for example, a projectile moving in a strong wind, an airplane flying in moving air currents, or a ship traveling through moving water.

Illustrative Problems

Suppose the machine just mentioned to be moved along the crane with a velocity $v_{MC} = 3$ ft/sec, while at the same time the crane is moving at right angles to this direction, its velocity with respect to the floor being $v_{CF} = 5$ ft/sec; find the resultant velocity of the machine with respect to the floor.

The resultant velocity v_{MF} is found by the Parallelogram Method as in Fig. 21. From the vector diagram, not necessarily drawn to scale, it is evident that

$$v_{MF} = \sqrt{v_{MC}^2 + v_{CF}^2} = \sqrt{3^2 + 5^2} = \sqrt{34} = 5.83 \text{ ft/sec}$$

and

$$\theta = \tan^{-1} \tfrac{3}{5} = \tan^{-1} 0.600 = 31.0°$$

This gives the velocity of the machine with respect to the floor as 5.83 ft/sec, in the direction shown, making an angle of 31.0° with the side walls.

Fig. 21. Determining resultant velocity in relative motion

In what direction should a ship be steered in order to reach a destination 80° east of north from the ship's position if it steams through the water at 20 mi/hr while the water is flowing due south at 8 mi/hr? The term "steered" denotes the direction in which the ship moves with respect to the water.

The velocity of the ship with respect to the land, v_{SL}, is along the direction 80° east of north; that of the ship with respect to the water, v_{SW}, is 20 mi/hr in an unknown direction, shown as east of north by an angle θ; and that of the water with respect to the land, v_{WL}, is 8 mi/hr south. The vector equation connecting these velocities, following the pattern of Eq. 7, can be written as

$$\vec{v}_{SL} = \vec{v}_{SW} + \vec{v}_{WL}$$

or $\vec{v}_{SW} = \vec{v}_{SL} - \vec{v}_{WL}$. To solve by the Polygon Method, draw v_{SL} and $-v_{WL}$ as in Fig. 22, and show v_{SW} as their resultant, forming the closing side of the triangle. The angle opposite the resultant is 100°, and it follows from the Law of Sines that

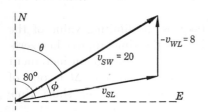

Fig. 22. Addition of relative velocities in ship problem

$$\frac{v_{SW}}{\sin 100°} = \frac{-v_{WL}}{\sin \phi}$$

Therefore $\sin \phi = (8 \sin 100°)/20 = 0.4(0.985) = 0.394$, from which $\phi = 23.1°$. Then $\theta = 80.0 - 23.1 = 56.9°$, showing that the ship should be steered in the direction 56.9° east of north.

21. Speed and Velocity in Nonuniform Motion. The speeds of moving bodies often change from moment to moment. Thus, a passenger bus is repeatedly started from rest, speeded up, slowed down, and stopped; its speed along a highway may be 30 mi/hr at one moment and 50 mi/hr at another. Such instantaneous speeds are indicated by the speedometer and are often controlled by driving conditions. An essential aspect of motion is the average speed maintained over a given period; in the operation of the bus, for example, the average speed is of importance in establishing and maintaining schedules.

The *average speed* of a body is the total length of path covered divided by the time taken to traverse it, or

$$\text{Average speed} = \frac{\text{total length of path}}{\text{total time}}$$

Nonuniform motion deals more often with velocity than with speed. The *average velocity* of a body is the total displacement divided by the elapsed time, or

$$\text{Average velocity} = \frac{\text{total displacement}}{\text{total time}}$$

Symbolically

$$v_{av} = \frac{s}{t} \tag{8}$$

where v_{av} represents the average velocity of a body that undergoes a displacement s during a time interval t. As the displacement under consideration is taken shorter and shorter, the elapsed time becomes progressively less also, and the velocity obtained by Eq. 8 is restricted to a correspondingly short portion of the entire displacement. If a body is displaced by 0.1 ft in 0.005 sec, its average velocity for that time interval is the displacement divided by the time, or $0.1 \div 0.005 = 20$ ft/sec. When the displacement and the time interval are taken as infinitesimals, then the velocity of the body is that for the particular instant selected, or its instantaneous velocity.

Strictly, the *instantaneous velocity* of a body is the limiting value of the ratio of the displacement to the elapsed time as the time approaches zero. The symbol Δ (delta) is commonly used as a prefix to denote an increment of a quantity; thus, Δs is an increment of displacement and Δt is one of time. If the body undergoes the short displacment Δs in the short time Δt, then the instantaneous velocity is the limit of the ratio $\dfrac{\Delta s}{\Delta t}$ as Δt approaches zero. In the limit, the ratio is represented by $\dfrac{ds}{dt}$, so that

$$\frac{ds}{dt} = \underset{\Delta t = 0}{\text{Limit}} \frac{\Delta s}{\Delta t}$$

Hence the limiting ratio of displacement to time becomes

$$\text{Instantaneous velocity} = \frac{\text{infinitesimal displacement}}{\text{infinitesimal time}}$$

for the particular instant under consideration.   If the instantaneous velocity is symbolized as v (without subscript) then

$$v = \frac{ds}{dt} \tag{9}$$

In the special case where a body has uniform linear motion, it has the same instantaneous velocity at every instant, and its average velocity is the same as its constant velocity.

22. Linear Acceleration.   Every car owner speaks of "getaway" as one of the requisites of a good automobile.   By this he means the rapidity with which the car gains velocity, a characteristic that is technically called acceleration.   If the car starting from rest and moving forward along a straight highway acquires a velocity of 4 ft/sec by the end of one second, gains an additional velocity of 4 ft/sec during the next second, and so on, the car is said to have an *acceleration* of 4 ft/sec in each second.   By the end of 5 sec, the velocity is 20 ft/sec, and continues to increase at a steady rate as long as the car can maintain the same acceleration.

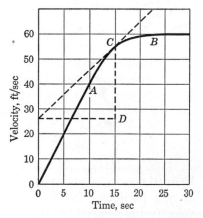

The instantaneous velocity values of an accelerating automobile when plotted against elapsed time yield a curve like that in Fig. 23.   The curve is straight from O to A, showing that during the first 10 sec the car gains velocity at a uniform rate; that is, the acceleration is constant.   The

Fig. 23.   Determining acceleration of an automobile from its velocity-time curve

curve slopes off beyond A, showing that the acceleration is reduced, and becomes horizontal at B, showing that the acceleration is zero.

The acceleration of a body is defined as the change of its velocity during any interval of time divided by the duration of that interval.   This definition can be stated in the form of an equation by referring to the motion of the body over some stated time interval.   If v_o is its initial velocity at the beginning of this period and v_f its final velocity at the end of the period, then the change in velocity is $v_f - v_o$, and if this change occurs in a time interval t, the average acceleration of the body over that interval is

$$\text{Average acceleration} = \frac{\text{final velocity} - \text{initial velocity}}{\text{time interval}}$$

or

$$a_{av} = \frac{v_f - v_o}{t} \tag{10}$$

The performance represented in Fig. 23 will now be analyzed in greater detail. The velocity of the car under consideration increases uniformly from 0 to 40 ft/sec in the first 10 sec of motion; then it increases from 40 to 60 ft/sec during the next 15 sec, but during this period the velocity does not increase uniformly, and therefore the acceleration varies from instant to instant. The *average acceleration* over this time interval can be found as above, by dividing the change of velocity during that interval by the duration of the interval. Thus, the average acceleration over the time interval from the tenth to the twenty-fifth second is

$$\frac{(60 - 40)\ \frac{\text{ft}}{\text{sec}}}{(25 - 10)\ \text{sec}} = 1.333\ \frac{\text{ft}}{\text{sec}^2}$$

As the time interval is taken shorter and shorter, the average acceleration approaches nearer and nearer to the *instantaneous acceleration*. In the limit, for an infinitesimal change of velocity dv occurring in an infinitesimal time interval dt, the instantaneous acceleration a is expressed as

$$a = \frac{dv}{dt} \tag{11}$$

Defined concisely, *acceleration is the time rate of change of velocity*. Its value at any particular instant is represented graphically by the slope of the velocity-time curve at the corresponding point. Thus, in Fig. 23, the instantaneous acceleration 15 sec after starting the car is found by drawing a tangent to the curve at point C where it crosses the 15-sec ordinate and determining the slope of the tangent. Since $CD = 55 - 26 = 29$ ft/sec, the slope is $29\ \frac{\text{ft}}{\text{sec}} \div 15\ \text{sec} = 1.930\ \frac{\text{ft}}{\text{sec}^2}$, and this is the value of the instantaneous acceleration at that particular moment.

When the acceleration is constant, its successive instantaneous values are all alike and the same as the average acceleration. In the remainder of this chapter attention is directed only to motion in which the acceleration is constant.

From the form in which acceleration is expressed, it is clear that any velocity unit divided by any time unit is an acceleration unit. The most usual acceleration units are feet per second per second, centimeters per second per second, and meters per second per second. These units are written respectively $\dfrac{ft}{sec^2}$, $\dfrac{cm}{sec^2}$, and $\dfrac{m}{sec^2}$. An acceleration of 10 cm per sec per sec means that during each second the velocity of the body concerned increases by 10 cm per sec. Other acceleration units are sometimes used in scientific and engineering work. Thus, an acceleration of one mile per hour per second $\left(\text{written } 1 \dfrac{mi}{hr \cdot sec}\right)$ means that during every second the velocity increases by 1 mi/hr.

The definitions of acceleration, although applied here to motion in a straight line, are valid for motion along any line, straight or curved. Acceleration is a vector quantity; in straight-line motion it has the same direction as the velocity when the velocity is increasing, and opposite when the velocity is decreasing.

23. Linear Motion with Constant Acceleration. The manner in which the initial velocity, final velocity, displacement, acceleration, and elapsed time are related in *linear motion with constant acceleration* can be expressed mathematically by four equations, wherein

v_o = initial velocity, that is, the velocity of the body at the moment the consideration of its motion begins,

v_f = final velocity, that is, the velocity of the body at the moment the consideration of its motion ends,

t = time interval between the two moments mentioned,

v_{av} = average velocity of the body during this interval,

s = displacement of the body, that is, the straight-line distance from its initial to its final position, and

a = acceleration, assumed constant.

I. The first equation of linear motion with constant acceleration follows directly from the definition of acceleration, as given in the preceding section. The acceleration of the moving body is the time rate of change of its velocity, or $a = (v_f - v_o)/t$, whence, by rearrangement,

$$v_f = v_o + at \tag{12}$$

II. The second equation is an expression for the displacement of the moving body in terms of its initial velocity, final velocity, and the elapsed time. Since the change in velocity during the time interval t is uniform, the average velocity is the mean of the velocities at the beginning and end of the interval, namely, v_o and v_f respectively; therefore the average velocity is $v_{av} = (v_o + v_f)/2$, *but only where the acceleration is constant*. Then the displacement during the interval is the product of the average velocity and the duration of the interval, as stated in § 21, namely, $s = v_{av}t$, or

$$s = \frac{v_o + v_f}{2}t \qquad\qquad S = \frac{V_F{}^2 - V_o{}^2}{2a} \tag{13}$$

III. The third equation also gives the displacement of the moving body, but expresses it in terms of the initial velocity, acceleration, and time. To obtain this expression, the value of v_f from Eq. 12 is substituted in Eq. 13, giving the displacement as

$$s = \frac{v_o + (v_o + at)}{2}t$$

or

$$s = v_ot + \tfrac{1}{2}at^2 \tag{14}$$

The inclined line in Fig. 24 represents graphically the motion of a body in which the velocity increases uniformly with time—that is, motion with

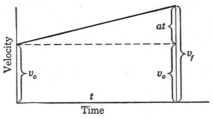

Fig. 24. Displacement is given by the area under velocity-time curve

constant acceleration. If the figure is compared with Eq. 14 it becomes evident that the area below the line represents the displacement of the body.

IV. The fourth equation is obtained from the first and second by eliminating the time interval t. This is accomplished by multiplying a from Eq. 12 and s from Eq. 13, as follows:

$$as = \left(\frac{v_f - v_o}{t}\right)\left(\frac{v_o + v_f}{2}t\right) = \tfrac{1}{2}(v_f - v_o)(v_f + v_o)$$

from which

$$a = \frac{V_F{}^2 - V_o{}^2}{2s} \qquad\qquad v_f{}^2 = v_o{}^2 + 2as \tag{15}$$

For the special case of a body that starts from rest, these equations become simplified, because $v_o = 0$. Thus, the third equation applied to a body starting from rest and moving with constant acceleration reduces to the form $s = \tfrac{1}{2}at^2$, showing that the displacement of the body is proportional to the square of the elapsed time. If the acceleration is 2 ft/sec^2, the dis-

placements in feet are given by $s = \dfrac{1}{2}\left(2\,\dfrac{ft}{sec^2}\right)(t\ sec)^2 = t^2$; these displacements for $t = 1$ sec, $\cdots$ 5 sec are marked off to scale in Fig. 25, which shows graphically how much farther the object moves each following second.

The four equations just derived are valid *only* for motion along a *straight line* with *constant acceleration*. These equations and their limitations should be thoroughly understood. It may be noted that displacement is

FIG. 25.   Displacements of an object moving with constant acceleration

missing from Eq. 12, acceleration from Eq. 13, final velocity from Eq. 14, and time from Eq. 15. These facts should help to indicate which equation to use in a particular example.

Illustrative Problems

I. While an automobile is being driven along a straight highway, the speedometer is observed to read 25 mi/hr at a certain instant and 49 mi/hr at an instant 8 sec later. Find the acceleration (assumed constant) of the car during this interval.

The acceleration is directed along the line of travel, and its magnitude, by Eq. 12, is

$$a = \frac{v_f - v_o}{t} = \frac{(49 - 25)\ \dfrac{\text{mi}}{\text{hr}}}{8\ \text{sec}} = \frac{24\ \dfrac{\text{mi}}{\text{hr}}}{8\ \text{sec}} = 3.00\ \frac{\text{mi}}{\text{hr}\cdot\text{sec}}$$

II. One of the devices used to accelerate atomic particles for nuclear bombardment is the linear accelerator, in which a charged particle has its velocity increased in steps as it moves along a straight line. In one such step a proton initially moving at 2.8×10^9 cm/sec is given a constant acceleration of 3.33×10^{17} cm/sec^2 for 1.2×10^{-9} sec. Compute the displacement of the proton, and its velocity at the end of this time interval.

The displacement, from Eq. 14, is

$$s = v_o t + \frac{1}{2}\, at^2 = \left(2.80 \times 10^9\ \frac{\text{cm}}{\text{sec}}\right)(1.200 \times 10^{-9}\ \text{sec})$$

$$+ \frac{1}{2}\left(3.33 \times 10^{17}\ \frac{\text{cm}}{\text{sec}^2}\right)(1.200 \times 10^{-9}\ \text{sec})^2 = 3.60\ \text{cm}$$

The final velocity is given by Eq. 12 as

$$v_f = 2.80 \times 10^9\ \frac{\text{cm}}{\text{sec}} + \left(3.33 \times 10^{17}\ \frac{\text{cm}}{\text{sec}^2}\right)(1.200 \times 10^{-9}\ \text{sec})$$

$$= 3.20 \times 10^9\ \frac{\text{cm}}{\text{sec}}$$

Both displacement and final velocity are in the direction of travel.

III. An object has a constant acceleration of 2 ft/sec². Compute its displacement during the fourth second after starting from rest.

The problem is solved by determining the displacements in 4 sec and in 3 sec, starting from rest. Eq. 14 with $v_o = 0$ gives these values respectively as

$$s = \frac{1}{2}\left(2 \frac{ft}{sec^2}\right)(4 \text{ sec})^2 = 16 \text{ ft}$$

and

$$s = \frac{1}{2}\left(2 \frac{ft}{sec^2}\right)(3 \text{ sec})^2 = 9 \text{ ft}$$

Consequently, the displacement during the fourth second is $16 - 9 = 7.00$ ft, in the direction of motion, as shown in Fig. 25.

IV. The velocity of a car moving along a straight highway is observed to be 20 mi/hr as the car passes a given point, and 50 mi/hr as it passes a second point 200 ft farther along. Assume the acceleration of the car to be constant, and compute its value.

The velocities in miles per hour are first reduced to feet per second; 20 mi/hr = 29.3 ft/sec = v_o, and 50 mi/hr = 73.3 ft/sec = v_f. Then from Eq. 15, the acceleration is

$$a = \frac{v_f{}^2 - v_o{}^2}{2s} = \frac{(73.3 \text{ ft/sec})^2 - (29.3 \text{ ft/sec})^2}{2(200 \text{ ft})} = 11.29 \frac{ft}{sec^2}$$

along the direction of motion.

24. Acceleration Due to Gravity. Everybody has observed that objects fall to the ground when not supported. They fall because the earth exerts a pull upon them. This pull, called the force of gravity, causes the object to accelerate while falling. Moreover, all objects fall with the same acceleration, whether they are light or heavy, provided the resistance of the air is neglected. This result was first established by the Italian philosopher and astronomer, Galileo Galilei (1564–1642). While professor of mathematics at the University of Pisa, he conducted actual tests, reportedly at the famous Leaning Tower, to refute the teaching of the Greek philosopher Aristotle (384–322 B.C.) that heavy bodies fall faster than light ones. But the influence of Aristotle persisted so strongly that Galileo encountered bitter opposition and was forced to resign his professorship. Galileo's contribution to present scientific thinking was threefold: (1) he was the first to appreciate the value of experiment and might well be called the father of experimental physics; (2) he was able to imagine an ideal situation, such as a frictionless medium, and thereby to explain discrepancies between actual and theoretical results; and (3) he recognized the value of mathematical analysis in the study of physical principles.

The force of gravity exerted upon a body, and consequently the acceleration due to the earth's attraction, depends upon the distance of the body from the center of the earth, being less at greater distances. The acceleration of a falling body if measured at points above the earth's surface is found to be less at greater elevations. But on the surface of the earth, this acceleration is nearly the same at all points. It is slightly greater at the poles than at the equator because the earth is flatter at the poles, its polar radius being 13 miles shorter than its equatorial radius. The rotation of the earth also makes the acceleration of a falling body less at the equator than at the poles, § 46. Actual values of the acceleration due to gravity at a few places are given below:

ACCELERATION DUE TO GRAVITY

Location	$\dfrac{\text{ft}}{\text{sec}^2}$	$\dfrac{\text{cm}}{\text{sec}^2}$	Location	$\dfrac{\text{ft}}{\text{sec}^2}$	$\dfrac{\text{cm}}{\text{sec}^2}$
Equator at sea level.	32.09	978.1	New York, N. Y....	32.16	980.2
New Orleans, La....	32.13	979.3	Paris, France......	32.18	980.8
San Francisco, Cal..	32.15	979.9	London, England...	32.19	981.2
Madison, Wis......	32.16	980.2	North Pole........	32.26	983.3

The symbol generally used for the acceleration imparted by the earth is *g*, and its numerical value is approximately

$$g = 32 \text{ ft/sec}^2 \quad \text{or} \quad g = 980 \text{ cm/sec}^2$$
$$= 9.8 \text{ m/sec}^2$$

These values may be used in problems unless other values or particular places are specified.

25. Falling Bodies. The laws of falling bodies are expressed by the same equations used for linear motion with constant acceleration, Eqs. 12–15, except that the acceleration due to gravity *g* is used instead of any acceleration *a*. To emphasize the fact that these equations apply to vertical motion, it may be useful to use *h* for height, instead of *s*, as the symbol for displacement. The equations as modified are:

$$v_f = v_o + gt \tag{16}$$

$$h = \frac{v_o + v_f}{2} t \tag{17}$$

$$h = v_o t + \tfrac{1}{2} g t^2 \tag{18}$$

$$v_f^2 = v_o^2 + 2gh \tag{19}$$

In applying these equations, some direction is arbitrarily taken as positive and the opposite direction as negative, and $+$ and $-$ signs are given accordingly to displacement, velocity, and acceleration.

A few problems will illustrate the laws of falling bodies. In these, air friction is neglected and the downward direction is regarded as positive.

Illustrative Problems

I. A ball is dropped and allowed to fall freely; compute the distances it travels in 1 sec, $\cdots$ 5 sec.

The ball has no initial velocity, making $v_o = 0$, and its displacements are given by Eq. 18 as

$$h_1 = \frac{1}{2}\left(32\ \frac{ft}{sec^2}\right)(1\ sec)^2 = 16\ ft \qquad h_2 = \frac{1}{2}\left(32\ \frac{ft}{sec^2}\right)(2\ sec)^2 = 64\ ft$$

and so on. The results are shown to scale in Fig. 26.

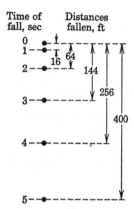

FIG. 26. Distances traveled by freely falling object

II. Suppose a ball to be thrown vertically downward with a velocity of 10 m/sec from a cliff 100 m high. With what velocity does it strike? and how long does it take to reach the ground?

In this problem, the initial velocity is $v_o = 10$ m/sec and the displacement is $h = 100$ m downward. The velocity at impact is found from Eq. 19 as follows:

$$v_f{}^2 = \left(10\ \frac{m}{sec}\right)^2 + 2\left(9.8\ \frac{m}{sec^2}\right)(100\ m) = (100 + 1960)\ \frac{m^2}{sec^2}$$

whence $v_f = 45.4$ m/sec. Then, from Eq. 16, the time of flight is

$$t = \frac{v_f - v_o}{g} = \frac{(45.4 - 10.0)\ \dfrac{m}{sec}}{9.8\ \dfrac{m}{sec^2}} = 3.61\ sec$$

Consequently the ball strikes the ground in 3.61 sec, with a velocity of 45.4 m/sec, downward.

III. Imagine a ball to be projected vertically upward with a velocity of 96 ft/sec from the top of a tower of the George Washington Bridge at New

York City, a level 600 ft above the water, as indicated in Fig. 27. (*a*) How high does the ball travel? (*b*) With what velocity does the ball pass the roadway of the bridge in its downward motion, if the roadway at that part of the bridge is 240 ft above the water? (*c*) What is the velocity of the ball on reaching the water?

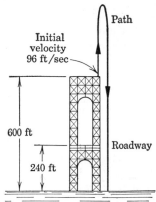

FIG. 27. Illustrating problem on ball projected upward

(*a*) In order to find how far up the ball travels, place the final velocity $v_f = 0$ and the initial velocity $v_o = -96$ ft/sec in Eq. 19, and solve for h. Thus

$$h = \frac{v_f{}^2 - v_o{}^2}{2g} = \frac{0 - \left(-96\ \frac{\text{ft}}{\text{sec}}\right)^2}{2\left(32\ \frac{\text{ft}}{\text{sec}^2}\right)} = -144 \text{ ft}$$

Hence the ball rises 144 ft beyond the top of the tower and reaches an elevation of 744 ft above the water.

(*b*) In descending, the ball is displaced by $744 - 240 = 504$ ft to reach the level of the roadway, and its velocity at that place is obtained from Eq. 19 by placing the initial velocity $v_o = 0$ and solving for v_f. Thus

$$v_f{}^2 = 0 + 2\left(32\ \frac{\text{ft}}{\text{sec}^2}\right)(504 \text{ ft}) = 32{,}300\ \frac{\text{ft}^2}{\text{sec}^2}$$

from which the velocity of the ball as it passes the roadway is $v_f = 180$ ft/sec.

(*c*) The same equation is used to obtain the velocity with which the ball strikes the water, but this time $h = 744$ ft. Thus

$$v_f{}^2 = 0 + 2\left(32\ \frac{\text{ft}}{\text{sec}^2}\right)(744 \text{ ft})$$

from which $v_f = 218$ ft/sec. As an alternate solution, consider the initial position of the ball to be at the top of the tower, its initial velocity to be

−96 ft/sec, and its displacement to be 600 ft. Then from the same equation,

$$v_f^2 = \left(-96\,\frac{\text{ft}}{\text{sec}}\right)^2 + 2\left(32\,\frac{\text{ft}}{\text{sec}^2}\right)(600\text{ ft})$$

from which $v_f = 218$ ft/sec, as before.

26. Combination of Uniform and Accelerated Motions. An experiment commonly used in the lecture room makes use of two metal balls supported at the same level near the ceiling, one having a compressed spring behind it, and the other having a trap door beneath it. By closing an electric circuit controlling both spring and door, both are released simultaneously; the spring strikes one ball horizontally and the door opens to allow the other ball to fall vertically. The experiment shows that the two balls strike the floor at the same instant, demonstrating that the horizontal motion imparted to the one ball by the spring does not affect its motion in the vertical direction.

The ball that is projected horizontally follows a curved path, moving both horizontally and vertically at the same time. The *horizontal motion* of the ball is *uniform*, there being nothing either to speed it up or slow it down along this direction, and is entirely unaffected by the fact that the ball is falling at the same time. The *vertical* motion is *accelerated*, like that of any falling body, and is neither helped nor hindered by the fact that the ball is moving horizontally while falling. Consequently, the motion of such an object can be studied by regarding it as made up of two parts, one horizontal and the other vertical, and by recognizing the fact that these motions occur *independently* of each other.

Illustrative Problem

Suppose that a ball is thrown horizontally from the top of a high building with a velocity of 50 ft/sec, and that a plot of its path is desired.

The horizontal motion is uniform and is determined by Eq. 6, namely, $s = vt$; that is, the displacement is equal to the product of the constant velocity and the time of flight. The vertical motion is accelerated and is determined by Eqs. 16–19. During the first second of its flight, the ball moves forward horizontally $(50)(1) = 50$ ft and falls $\frac{1}{2}g(1)^2 = 16$ ft. During the first 2 sec, it travels 100 ft horizontally and falls a total of $\frac{1}{2}g(2)^2 = 64$ ft. The horizontal motion with constant velocity and the vertical motion with constant acceleration result in the following displacements of the ball during the first few seconds:

Total time, sec	1	2	3	4	5
Horizontal travel, ft	50	100	150	200	250
Vertical drop, ft	16	64	144	256	400

These values are coordinated in Fig. 28, and the resulting parabola shows the trajectory of the ball. If the building were just 400 ft tall, the ball would strike the ground at a point 250 ft from the building. In this illustration, air friction is neglected, as heretofore. The actual distance traversed by the ball, that is, the length of the curve in the figure, has not been determined and is of little interest.

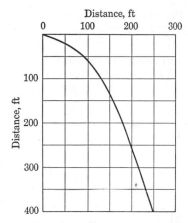

27. Projectile Motion. The composition of two motions, one uniform and the other accelerated, is of frequent occurrence in the study of ballistics to determine the range of projectiles and to trace their paths.

When a projectile is fired from a gun at a velocity v and at an angle θ upward from the horizontal, the initial velocity has a horizontal component $v \cos \theta$ and a vertical component $v \sin \theta$, as shown in Fig. 29. As long as the projectile is in flight, its *horizontal* motion is exactly the same as if it were moving forward horizontally with a *constant velocity* $v \cos \theta$ and without moving vertically; this horizontal motion is *uniform*

Fig. 28. Combining uniform horizontal motion and accelerated vertical motion

and is determined by Eq. 6. Meanwhile, the *vertical* motion of the projectile is exactly the same as if it were fired straight upward with an initial velocity $v \sin \theta$ and without moving horizontally; this vertical motion has a *constant acceleration g* and is determined by Eqs. 16–19. From these facts, any desired information regarding the motion of the projectile can be

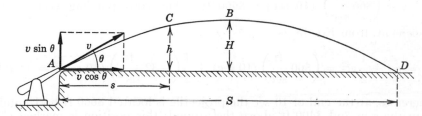

Fig. 29. Resolving the velocity of a projectile and determining its range

obtained. Two illustrations will explain the procedure; in each the upward direction is taken as positive and air friction is neglected.

Illustrative Problems

I. A projectile is fired from ground level over a horizontal terrain at 1000 ft/sec in a direction 30° upward from the horizontal, as in Fig. 29; determine (*a*) the maximum height H reached by the projectile (vertical range), and the time taken to reach this elevation; (*b*) the position of the projectile at an instant 10 sec after it is fired, and its velocity at that instant; and (*c*) the total time of flight, and the distance S from the gun at which the projectile strikes the ground (horizontal range).

For the horizontal motion, the velocity is constant at

$$v \cos \theta = (1000 \text{ ft/sec})(0.866) = 866 \text{ ft/sec}$$

For the vertical motion, the initial velocity is

$$v_0 = v \sin \theta = (1000 \text{ ft/sec})(0.500) = 500 \text{ ft/sec}$$

and the acceleration is $a = g = -32 \text{ ft/sec}^2$.

(a) Consider the vertical motion only, while the projectile moves from A to B in the figure. The vertical displacement H is found from Eq. 19,

$$h = \frac{v_f{}^2 - v_0{}^2}{2g}, \text{ with } v_f = 0 \text{ at the top point, whence}$$

$$H = \frac{0 - \left(500 \dfrac{\text{ft}}{\text{sec}}\right)^2}{2\left(-32 \dfrac{\text{ft}}{\text{sec}^2}\right)} = 3910 \text{ ft}$$

The corresponding time, from Eq. 17, is

$$t = \frac{2H}{v_0 + v_f} = \frac{2(3910 \text{ ft})}{(500 + 0) \dfrac{\text{ft}}{\text{sec}}} = 15.64 \text{ sec}$$

Therefore the projectile rises to a maximum height H of 3910 ft in 15.64 sec.

(b) The projectile is displaced both horizontally and vertically during the first 10 sec of its flight. The horizontal displacement, from Eq. 6, is $s = vt = \left(866 \dfrac{\text{ft}}{\text{sec}}\right) (10 \text{ sec}) = 8660 \text{ ft}$. The corresponding vertical displacement, from Eq. 18, is

$$h = v_0 t + \frac{1}{2} g t^2 = \left(500 \frac{\text{ft}}{\text{sec}}\right) (10 \text{ sec}) + \frac{1}{2}\left(-32 \frac{\text{ft}}{\text{sec}^2}\right) (10 \text{ sec})^2 = 3400 \text{ ft}$$

Therefore, at the end of 10 sec the projectile is located 8660 ft horizontally from the gun and 3400 ft above the ground; this position is marked C in the figure.

The velocity of the projectile at point C has a horizontal and a vertical component. The horizontal component is constant at $866 \dfrac{\text{ft}}{\text{sec}}$. The vertical component is found by considering the vertical motion only; from Eq. 16,

$$v_f = v_0 + gt = 500 \frac{\text{ft}}{\text{sec}} + \left(-32 \frac{\text{ft}}{\text{sec}^2}\right) (10 \text{ sec}) = +180 \frac{\text{ft}}{\text{sec}}. \quad \text{From these}$$

components, the actual velocity at the end of 10 sec of flight is

$$\sqrt{866^2 + 180^2} = 885 \frac{\text{ft}}{\text{sec}}$$

directed upward from the horizontal by an angle $\theta' = \tan^{-1}\frac{180}{866} = 11.7°$, as shown in Fig. 30.

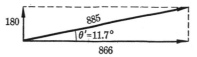

FIG. 30. Velocity at point C in projectile problem

(c) The total time of flight is found by considering the vertical motion only, while the projectile moves from A to D. Eq. 18, $h = v_o t + \frac{1}{2}gt^2$, with $v_o = 500 \frac{\text{ft}}{\text{sec}}$ and $h = 0$, becomes $0 = \left(500 \frac{\text{ft}}{\text{sec}}\right) t + \frac{1}{2}\left(-32 \frac{\text{ft}}{\text{sec}^2}\right) t^2$, whence the total time of flight is $t = 31.3$ sec.

The horizontal range is found by considering the horizontal motion only, while the projectile moves from A to D, as above. From Eq. 6, the horizontal range $S = vt = \left(866 \frac{\text{ft}}{\text{sec}}\right)(31.3 \text{ sec}) = 27,100$ ft.

II. A bomber flying with a constant velocity of 225 mi/hr at an elevation $h = 10,000$ ft is moving horizontally toward a point directly above its objective shown at O in Fig. 31. At what angle of sight ϕ with respect to the vertical should a bomb be released to strike the objective?

At the instant of release, the bomb has the same forward velocity as the bomber, and its path is exactly analogous to that of a ball thrown horizontally from the top of a building, as shown in Fig. 28. Its horizontal motion is uniform at 225 mi/hr or 330 ft/sec. Its vertical motion is like that of any falling body with an initial velocity $v_o = 0$ and an acceleration of 32 ft/sec^2 downward. From a consideration of the vertical motion only, Eq. 18 gives the time of fall as

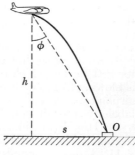

$$t = \sqrt{\frac{2h}{g}} = \sqrt{\frac{2(-10,000 \text{ ft})}{-32 \frac{\text{ft}}{\text{sec}^2}}} = 25.0 \text{ sec}$$

FIG. 31. Path of a bomb dropped from an airplane

From the horizontal motion of the bomb, the distance that it travels horizontally in this time is given by Eq. 6 as $s = vt = \left(330 \frac{\text{ft}}{\text{sec}}\right)(25.0 \text{ sec}) = 8250$ ft. Therefore, the desired angle of sight is $\phi = \tan^{-1}\frac{8250}{10,000} = 39.5°$.

The concept of acceleration is so fundamental that it is used as the means of defining motion of different types. Thus, in uniform motion the acceleration is zero, and in uniformly accelerated motion the acceleration is constant.

PROBLEMS

(Air friction may be neglected in these problems.)

1. The first speed law, passed in Connecticut in 1901, stated that no driver should drive faster than 12 mi/hr in the cities or faster than 15 mi/hr in the country. Express these speeds in feet per second.

2. To gain an idea of snail-pace, a snail was timed to travel 1 in. on a level surface in an average of 55 sec. At this pace, how long would it take the snail to travel 1 mi?

3. (*a*) Compute the speed of a point on the surface of the earth at the equator, due to the rotation of the earth around its axis, and state the result in kilometers per minute. The average radius of the earth is 6370 km. (*b*) At what latitude would the surface speed of the earth have half the value found in (*a*)?

4. Compute the average speed of the earth in its orbit around the sun; take the orbit to be a circle of 9.29×10^7 mi radius, and the year to consist of $365\frac{1}{4}$ days.

5. If an airplane can travel 300 mi due east and then return to its starting point in exactly 4 hr when there is no wind, what time would this round trip take if there were a wind blowing from east to west at 25 mi/hr?

6. A small motor-boat travels to a point 5 mi upstream and back again in a total time of 1 hr, 20 min. If the boat goes at 8 mi/hr in still water, what was the velocity of the stream?

7. Car *A* is moving due south on a highway at 30 mi/hr. Car *B* is moving due west on an intersecting highway at 40 mi/hr. Determine the velocity of car *A* with respect to car *B*.

8. A river 1 mi wide flows due south at 4 mi/hr. A boat that moves through the water at 10 mi/hr leaves a point on the west bank to reach a point 0.7 mi farther north on the opposite bank. (*a*) In what direction should the boat be headed? (*b*) How long does the trip take?

9. An airplane that travels at 200 mi/hr in still air leaves New York City for Pittsburgh, which may be taken as 300 mi away, due west. If the wind is blowing from north to south at 40 mi/hr, (*a*) in what direction should the airplane be headed, and (*b*) how long does the trip take? Use a clearly labeled vector diagram of velocities in solving.

10. How little time would be saved by driving a distance of 5 mi at an average speed of 60 mi/hr instead of 45 mi/hr?

11. A record non-stop round-the-world flight of 24,325 mi was made in 1957 by three Air Force B-52 Stratofortresses, refueling several times from aerial tankers enroute. The 8-engine jet bombers, with nine men each, took off from Castle Base near Merced, Cal., at 1:00 P.M. on Jan. 16, traveled eastward, and arrived at March Base at Riverside, Cal., at 10:19 A.M. on Jan. 18, both Pacific Standard Time. (*a*) What was the duration of the flight? (*b*) What was the average speed? (*c*) How many nights were the fliers underway?

12. An 8-mi stretch of highway passes through a town, and this fact cuts automobile speed to an average of 25 mi/hr over that distance during business hours. To relieve congestion, a 9-mi by-pass has been built which permits an average speed of 45 mi/hr. How much time is gained by traveling over the by-pass instead of the main road at the speeds stated?

13. John Landy, 24-year-old Australian, won two world records in one race in Finland on June 21, 1954, covering 1500 m in 3 min, 41.8 sec, and

1 mi in 3 min, 58 sec. Express his average speed in feet per second (*a*) during the first 1500 m, and (*b*) during the remainder of the race.

14. In a recent pigeon race, the winning bird, "Mr. Remington," was liberated at Remington, Va., at 9:45:00 A.M. and arrived at his home coop in Newark, N. J., 246.3 mi distant, the same day at 2:48:30 P.M. Compute his average speed in miles per hour, and express it also in the official Homing Pigeon Fancier's unit, yards per minute.

Problem 15

15. A wheel 40 cm in diameter rolls toward the right on level ground at the rate of 3 rev/sec as shown in the accompanying diagram. Compute (*a*) the velocity of the axle relative to the ground, and (*b*) the instantaneous velocity of a point on the rim of the wheel relative to the ground as the point sweeps through the position marked *P* in the diagram, 20 cm above the ground.

16. Strapped in a rocket-powered sled moving along horizontal steel rails at the Holloman Air Force Base in New Mexico, Col. John P. Stapp in December, 1954, reached a speed of 632 mi/hr—a record speed for travel on land—in sliding 2800 ft from a standing start. At that distance mark his sled was separated from the power unit and after coasting for $\frac{1}{2}$ sec was brought to a dead stop in 1.5 sec. Assume a speed loss of 10% while coasting, and determine the average acceleration to which the officer was subjected (*a*) while accelerating to top speed and (*b*) while stopping.

17. In a 15-sec interval the velocity of an automobile moving along a straight road increased from 20 to 50 mi/hr. Assume that the increase was at a uniform rate and compute for this time interval (*a*) the average velocity of the car and (*b*) its displacement.

18. A train starts from rest and accelerates at the constant rate of 2 mi per hr per sec while it travels a straight distance of 330 ft. (*a*) What is its velocity at the end of the stated distance? (*b*) In what time was the distance traveled?

19. A train going at 75 km/hr comes to a stop in 200 m. Assume that the acceleration (negative) is constant and compute its value.

20. Two cars 60 ft apart are traveling at 45 mi/hr along a straight highway. Both drivers observe an obstruction ahead and apply the brakes at the same instant. If the forward car decelerates at 25 ft/sec² and the other at 15 ft/sec², how far apart are the cars when they have stopped?

21. A ball is dropped from a point 10 m above the ground. In what time does the ball reach the ground, and with what velocity does it strike?

22. A ball is thrown vertically upward with an initial velocity of 96 ft/sec. (*a*) What is the displacement of the ball at the end of the fourth second of its flight? During the first 4 sec of flight, what is (*b*) the length of path traversed, (*c*) the average velocity of the ball, and (*d*) its average speed?

23. A ball thrown vertically from the roof of a building 100 ft high strikes the ground in exactly 5 sec. (*a*) Was the ball thrown upward or downward, and what was the initial speed? (*b*) With what velocity does it strike the ground?

24. An object that has been thrown horizontally from the top of a building may be regarded as moving horizontally and falling vertically at the same time. (*a*) If such an object has a velocity of 30 ft/sec horizontally and at a given instant also has a velocity of 45 ft/sec vertically downward, what is its actual velocity at that instant? (*b*) How far is the object vertically and horizontally from the starting point at the instant considered?

25. A block weighing 3 lb is projected horizontally with a velocity of 10 ft/sec toward the right from the edge of a table top 4 ft above the floor. What is its velocity just before it strikes the floor?

26. (*a*) A ball is thrown horizontally from an elevated point at a speed of 40 ft/sec. In a time of $\frac{1}{2}$ sec how far does the ball travel horizontally and how far vertically? (*b*) A rifle bullet is fired horizontally from an elevated point at a speed of 2000 ft/sec. In a time of $\frac{1}{2}$ sec, how far does the bullet travel horizontally and how far vertically?

27. In a cathode-ray tube, a beam of electrons is projected horizontally with a velocity of 10^9 cm/sec into the region between a pair of horizontal plates 2 cm long. Electric charges have been given to the plates, and as a result the electrons receive a constant acceleration downward while they are between the plates, but their horizontal motion is unaffected. Assume that the acceleration is 10^{17} cm/sec^2, and determine (*a*) the vertical displacement of the beam while it is between the plates and (*b*) the velocity of the beam as it emerges from the plates, both in magnitude and direction.

28. If a BB shot is fired horizontally at a vertical wall distant 25 m from the muzzle of an air rifle and strikes the wall at a point 10 cm lower than the rifle barrel, what is the muzzle speed of the shot?

29. A youthful hunter aims his air rifle 30° upward from the horizontal, directly at a monkey in a tree 70 ft away, and the shot leaves the rifle at a speed of 300 ft/sec. The monkey (having studied his Physics) decides to sit tight. How far below him does the shot pass?

30. With what speed is a golf ball driven if it leaves the tee at an angle of 10° above the horizontal and strikes the ground at the same level 200 yd away?

31. If a golf ball on a level fairway strikes the ground 2.5 sec after it was hit, how high did the ball rise in its flight?

32. A stream of water issues from the nozzle of a hose at 40 ft/sec; the nozzle is held 3 ft above level ground and is directed upward at 30° with the horizontal. If no wind is blowing, (*a*) how long does each particle of water continue to rise? (*b*) how long does each particle take to drop from its maximum height to the ground? and (*c*) how far from the nozzle, measured horizontally, does the stream strike the ground?

$$V = gT$$
$$S = \tfrac{1}{2}gT^2$$
$$V = \sqrt{2gS}$$
$$S = \tfrac{1}{2}g(2T-1)$$

$$S = V_0 T + \tfrac{1}{2}at^2$$
$$V_f^2 - V_0^2 = 2aS$$
$$V_f - V_0 = aT$$

4

FORCE AND MOTION; NEWTON'S LAWS

28. Effect of Force on Motion. In the preceding treatment of accelerated motion, little attention was paid to the means by which acceleration is brought about; the present chapter deals with the agency that produces it. Acceleration is always produced by force. Whenever a body is accelerating, a force is acting upon it to cause the acceleration. Thus, a force is applied to a body to set it in motion. Again, a force is applied to a body already in motion in order to speed it up, slow it down, or change its direction. Any change in velocity implies an acceleration, and this acceleration can be produced only by a force.

A force can be described as a push or a pull acting upon a body. A man pushing a lawn mower exerts a force on the lawn mower, a locomotive pulling a train exerts a force on the train, and a book resting on a table exerts a force on the table. In each of these illustrations it is necessary that the two bodies be in contact. Thus, in moving the lawn mower, the man must move along also and stay in contact with it if he is to continue to exert a force on it. Again, when a boy throws a ball, he exerts a force on it only so long as it stays in contact with his hand.

The principle that one body cannot exert a force on another unless the two are in contact is subject, however, to an exception that is continually met with in Mechanics. This exception is gravitation, by means of which a body—say, the earth—exerts a force of attraction on other bodies whether they are in contact with it or not. This gravitational action was mentioned in § 1, and will be considered more fully in § 31.

Although a force must act upon a body when it accelerates, it does not necessarily follow that a body will accelerate when a force acts upon it. For example, a man may exert a force on a crate while at the same time friction or some other agent exerts an equal force on it in the opposite direction; under these circumstances the two forces balance each other and the crate does not accelerate. But when all of the forces acting upon a body are taken into account and these do not balance, then the unbalanced force is the resultant force acting on the body; this resultant always causes acceleration.

29. Newton's Laws of Motion. The relation of force to motion was set forth by the English philosopher Sir Isaac Newton (1642–1727), one of the most profound scientists of all time. He interpreted and correlated many diverse observations in Mechanics and combined the results into three fundamental laws, known as Newton's Laws of Motion. In the following paragraphs, each of these generalizations is stated in terms of quantities already defined and is supplemented by a brief discussion.

FIRST LAW OF MOTION. *A body at rest remains at rest, and a body in motion continues to move at constant speed along a straight line, unless there is a resultant force acting upon the body.*

The first part of this law is evident from everyday experience; for instance, a book placed on a table remains at rest. In explanation, one might be inclined to say that the book stays at rest simply because no force is being exerted upon it. Further thought shows that this reasoning is not true, since it is known that the force of gravity pulls it downward and it can be inferred that the table pushes it upward. The fact is that these two forces *on* the book are equal and opposite, one balancing the other. Thus, the resultant force acting on the book is zero, and so the book stays at rest.

The second part of the law is more difficult to visualize; it states virtually that if a body is set into motion and left to itself, it keeps on moving without the action of any further force. This statement is correct; the body would continue to move without any reduction of velocity if no force acted upon it. However, experience shows that a retarding force is always present in the nature of friction. Thus, a block of wood thrown along a rough road comes to rest after sliding only a short distance, because the friction is large; along a floor it would slide farther, the friction being smaller; and along a sheet of ice it would slide much farther, since the friction is very small. From examples like these, it is reasoned that if friction could be eliminated entirely, a body once set into motion on a level surface would continue to move indefinitely with undiminshed velocity. Therefore, uniform motion is a natural condition and maintains itself without the action of a resultant force.

An example of the first law is an airplane traveling horizontally at constant speed. The forces acting on the airplane are indicated in Fig. 32: wherein

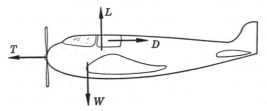

FIG. 32. Forces on an airplane moving with constant velocity

T is the propeller thrust acting forward along the propeller axis; D the backward drag of air friction; W the weight acting vertically downward; and L the "lift" acting upward at right angles to the the thrust of the propeller.

When the thrust equals the drag and the lift equals the weight, then the resultant force on the airplane is zero, and the velocity it has attained continues without change as long as the propeller thrust can be maintained.

It is interesting to note that whether a body is at rest or moving with constant speed along a straight line, its acceleration is zero. Hence the first law of motion means that a body accelerates only while some resultant force acts upon it.

SECOND LAW OF MOTION. *The acceleration of a body takes place in the direction of the resultant force acting upon it; the acceleration is directly proportional to the resultant force and inversely proportional to the mass of the body.*

Expressed mathematically, the law states that when a mass m is acted upon by a resultant force F, the acceleration of the mass is

$$a \propto \frac{F}{m}$$

A constant of proportionality k may be introduced to form an equation; thus,

$$ka = \frac{F}{m}$$

The meaning of the second law can be illustrated by two identical boxes being moved across a floor; if more force is applied to one than to the other, the box subjected to the larger force is found to have the greater acceleration. Or if a full box and an empty one are drawn across the floor with exactly equal forces, the empty box has the greater acceleration. In general, the greater the resultant force and the smaller the mass, the greater is the acceleration. Later, the applied force is reduced to a value just equal to the backward force of friction which the floor exerts on the box. Then one force pulls the box forward and an equal force drags it backward, and therefore the resultant force acting upon the box is zero. Hence, the acceleration of the box is also zero; the box neither speeds up nor slows down, and so continues to slide with constant speed, as expressed in the first law.

THIRD LAW OF MOTION. *For every action, there is an equal and opposite reaction, and the two are directed along the same straight line.*

In this statement, the term "action" means the force that one body exerts on a second body, and "reaction" means the force that the second body exerts on the first. A useful way to express this law is as follows: If body A exerts a force on body B, then B must exert an equal and opposite force on A.

Some illustrations will clarify the meaning of the third law. If a book presses downward on a table with a certain force, then the table presses upward on the book with the same amount of force. Evidently the ability to exert a force depends not only on the agent that is exerting the force, but also on the object that is supplying the reaction. A truck striking a tree can exert only as much force on the tree as the tree is able to exert against the truck.

Two objects are involved in each of these illustrations, and it should be noted that the action and reaction are never exerted on the same object. Thus, *action and reaction, although equal and opposite, can never balance each other*, since in order for two equal and opposite forces to balance each other, they must be exerted on the same object.

Newton's Third Law is not restricted to the forces that bodies exert on each other when in contact; it also applies to the gravitational forces, § 1, exerted by bodies that may be far apart. The earth and the moon, for example, exert forces of attraction on each other, which, in accordance with this law, are equal and opposite, and each is given an acceleration such that

$$m_1 \vec{a_1} = m_2 \vec{a_2}$$

In this vector equation, subscript 1 refers to one of the bodies and subscript 2 to the other.

The first and second laws deal with forces on a single body; the third law deals with the mutual forces between two bodies.

30. Absolute Units of Force. Of the three laws of motion discussed in the preceding section, only the second law deals quantitatively with the relation between force, mass, and acceleration. The mathematical statement of the law can be written

$$F = kma$$

in which a is the acceleration produced in a mass m by the resultant force F, and k is a proportionality constant depending in value upon the units used in the expression. Several systems of units are in common use, in which k is chosen as unity, for simplicity, and the units of mass and acceleration determine the unit of force. Thus,

$$F = ma \tag{20}$$

and the force F becomes unity when m is unit mass and a is unit acceleration. This equation is one of the most widely used expressions in Physics.

In metric units, there are two so-called absolute systems. One of these is known as the *cgs* system because the centimeter, gram, and second are respectively the units chosen for the fundamental quantities: length, mass, and time. In this system, since the unit mass is 1 gm and the unit acceleration $1 \dfrac{\text{cm}}{\text{sec}^2}$, the unit of force becomes

$$F = ma = (1 \text{ gm}) \left(1 \frac{\text{cm}}{\text{sec}^2}\right) = 1 \frac{\text{gm} \cdot \text{cm}}{\text{sec}^2}$$

which is read "gram centimeter per second per second." This awkward name is replaced by a simpler one, the *dyne*. *The dyne is the force needed to give a mass of 1 gm an acceleration of 1 cm per sec*^{2}. The term "dyne" can always be replaced by its equivalent, $\dfrac{\text{gm} \cdot \text{cm}}{\text{sec}^2}$.

The other absolute metric system is the *mks* system, in which the meter, kilogram, and second are selected as the units of length, mass, and time. In this system, the unit of force becomes the $\dfrac{\text{m} \cdot \text{kg}}{\text{sec}^2}$ and is called the *newton*. *The newton is the force needed to give a mass of 1 kg an acceleration of 1 m per sec*^{2}. The term "newton" can always be replaced by its equivalent, $\dfrac{\text{kg} \cdot \text{m}}{\text{sec}^2}$. It is easy to show that 1 newton $= 10^5$ dynes. The *mks* system is much used in electrical calculations.

In British units, the absolute system is called the *fps* system, because the foot, pound, and second are respectively the units of length, mass, and time. The pound (lb) of mass is defined in § 6. In the *fps* system, unit force becomes $F = ma = (1\ \text{lb})\left(1\ \dfrac{\text{ft}}{\text{sec}^2}\right) = 1\ \dfrac{\text{lb} \cdot \text{ft}}{\text{sec}^2}$ and is called the *poundal*. The poundal is the force needed to give a mass of 1 lb an acceleration of 1 ft per sec^2.

The systems just described are referred to as "absolute" systems because the mass units involved in their definitions are independent of the acceleration due to gravity; these are in contrast to the gravitational units to be discussed in § 34. To give practice in the handling of absolute units, some basic illustrations will be considered in which objects are caused to slide along surfaces designated as "smooth," that is, surfaces on which friction may be neglected. All illustrations make use of Eq. 20, $F = ma$.

Illustrative Problems

I. Suppose that a body of 100-gm mass, initially at rest on a smooth, level surface, is acted upon by a horizontal force of 5000 dynes, and that the resulting acceleration of the body is to be found.

Since there is no backward force of friction, the applied force of 5000 dynes is the resultant force on the body, and the acceleration is

$$a = \frac{F}{m} = \frac{5000\ \text{dynes}}{100\ \text{gm}} = \frac{5000\ \dfrac{\text{gm} \cdot \text{cm}}{\text{sec}^2}}{100\ \text{gm}} = 50.0\ \frac{\text{cm}}{\text{sec}^2}$$

in which the term "dyne" is replaced by its equivalent, $\dfrac{\text{gm} \cdot \text{cm}}{\text{sec}^2}$.

II. An object having a mass of 5 kg is placed on a smooth horizontal plane; what horizontal force must be applied to the object to give it an acceleration of 3 m/sec^2?

By the same method,

$$F = ma = (5 \text{ kg})\left(3\,\frac{\text{m}}{\text{sec}^2}\right) = 15\,\frac{\text{kg}\cdot\text{m}}{\text{sec}^2} = 15.00 \text{ newtons}$$

III. A mass of 20 lb is placed on a smooth, level plane and acted on by a horizontal force of 160 poundals; calculate the acceleration of this mass. As before,

$$a = \frac{F}{m} = \frac{160 \text{ poundals}}{20 \text{ lb}} = \frac{160\,\frac{\text{lb}\cdot\text{ft}}{\text{sec}^2}}{20\,\text{lb}} = 8.00\,\frac{\text{ft}}{\text{sec}^2}$$

The fps system of units, applied in illustration III above, is used less than formerly and will not be considered further in the present book except for reference purposes, § 35.

31. Law of Universal Gravitation. Newton's investigations in Mechanics were not limited to the principles now incorporated in his three laws of motion, but extended to the general subject of gravitation. He showed that every particle in the universe attracts every other particle, and explained how this attraction is affected by the masses of the particles and the distance separating them.

LAW OF UNIVERSAL GRAVITATION. *Each particle of matter attracts every other particle with a force that is directly proportional to the product of their masses and inversely proportional to the square of the distance between them.* Expressed mathematically, the law states that the attractive force between two particles is

$$F = G\,\frac{m_1 m_2}{r^2} \tag{21}$$

where m_1 and m_2 are the masses of the particles, r is the distance between them, F the force with which either particle attracts the other, and G a quantity known as the *gravitational constant*. The constant G should not be confused with the acceleration due to gravity, symbolized by g. When F is expressed in dynes, m_1 and m_2 in grams, and r in centimeters, G has the value $6.67 \times 10^{-8}\,\frac{\text{dyne}\cdot\text{cm}^2}{\text{gm}^2}$; thus, two particles each having a mass of 1 gm and located 1 cm apart attract each other with a force of 6.67×10^{-8} dyne. The law can be extended to give the gravitational attraction between symmetrical spheres by considering their masses concentrated at the centers.

The gravitational constant was originally measured long after Newton's time by the English physicist and chemist Henry Cavendish (1731–1810), with a torsion balance such as represented schematically in Fig. 33. Two small spheres *mm* are mounted at the ends of a slender rod which is suspended

in a horizontal position by a quartz fiber.   The spheres of this moving
system are placed close to a pair of massive lead globes MM, mounted in
the same horizontal plane.   When the globes are moved to another position,
the spheres of the moving system follow them by attraction and give the
suspension fiber a slight twist.   A narrow beam of light is directed upon a
mirror carried by the moving system and the reflected beam falls upon a
scale, thus allowing the twist to be measured.   From a separate test to

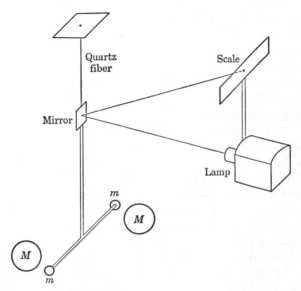

FIG. 33.   The Cavendish experiment

determine the stiffness of the quartz fiber, the force of attraction can be
computed; and then, from a knowledge of the masses and their separation,
the gravitational constant can be determined.

   32. Pull of Gravity; Weight.   The most familiar illustration of universal
gravitation is the force of attraction which the earth exerts upon objects
near it, causing the objects to accelerate downward when they fall.   If an
object is restrained so that it cannot fall when released, the earth exerts
the same force on it, but the pull of the earth is balanced by some equal and
opposite force exerted by the restraining agent.   Thus, a box resting on a
table is pulled downward by the earth, but is pushed upward by the table,
so that with the forces balanced it stays at rest.   If the table were in-
capable of pushing upward on the box as much as the earth pulls it downward (that is, not strong enough to support the box), there would then be
a resultant force acting upon the box which would make it accelerate
downward, and the table, being in the way of its motion, would collapse; a
result that might be expected with a very heavy box on a frail table.   The

force of attraction that the earth exerts on a body, that is, the pull of gravity on it, is called the *weight* of the body. The weight of a body is a force and can be treated in exactly the same way as any other force. Its direction is, however, always toward the center of the earth.

It was shown in § 24 that the acceleration due to gravity varies slightly from point to point on or near the earth's surface; hence a body dropped at the pole would have a slightly greater acceleration than when dropped at the equator. The increased acceleration at the pole shows that there is an increased force of gravity acting on a body there; in other words, the body weighs slightly more at the pole than at the equator. The correctness of this statement can be reasoned from the Law of Universal Gravitation, for the earth, although slightly flattened at the poles, can still be regarded as a sphere; the body at the pole is thus nearer the center of the earth than if located at the equator, and the force of attraction is greater at the pole.

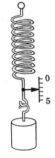

It is a matter of everyday experience that objects having different masses also have different weights. A full barrel not only has a larger mass than an empty one, but it also has the larger weight. This result also is to be expected from the Law of Universal Gravitation. If m_1 represents the mass of the earth and $m_2 = m$ the mass of another object, then F becomes the weight W of this object, and for any particular separation r, it follows that $W \propto m$. Hence, at a given location, the weights of objects are directly proportional to their masses.

Fig. 34. Elements of a spring balance

Weight or force is often measured with a spring balance, the essential parts of which are shown in Fig. 34. The body to be weighed is suspended by a spring; as it settles downward the spring stretches and exerts an increasing upward force upon it, and a balance is reached when the restoring force due to the spring equals the downward pull of gravity on the body. Such a device is calibrated by hanging bodies of known weight on the spring and marking its corresponding extensions on a scale. The spring balance can then be used to measure any weight or force within its range.

33. The Gravitational Field. A concept which in itself does not explain why objects attract one another but which may help sometime in solving this puzzle is that of the gravitational field. The *gravitational field* of an object is the surrounding region within which it would exert a gravitational force upon another object. A similar concept is used with electric charges and magnetism, §§ 197 and 207.

It is supposed that every object sets up, or establishes, a gravitational field throughout the surrounding region, and that this field exerts a force upon any particle located within it. The greater the force acting upon a given particle, the stronger the field. Indeed, the strength, or intensity, of the field at any point is defined as the force F that it exerts upon a particle there divided by the mass m of the particle.   In symbols,

$$\text{Gravitational field intensity} = \frac{F}{m}$$

Field strength is a vector quantity, and its direction at any point is the same
as that of the gravitational force F.   The field produced
by a spherical body is directed radially toward its center
as in Fig. 35.

The gravitational field of the earth is of special interest, and its study is simplified by the fact that the field
around a spherical body is the same as if the mass of the
body were concentrated at its center.   From Newton's
Law of Universal Gravitation, the pull of the earth on a
particle within its field is $F = \dfrac{GMm}{r^2}$, where M represents
the mass of the earth, m the mass of the particle, and r
the distance from the center of the earth to the point
where the particle is located.   Hence, the field strength
at that point is $\dfrac{F}{m} = \dfrac{GM}{r^2}$, which shows that the field strength (at points
outside the earth's surface) varies inversely as the square of the distance
from the center.

Fig. 35.   Vectors
showing intensity
of gravitational
field at some points

It is also interesting to note that the force F is the weight W of the particle,
and that the ratio $\dfrac{W}{m}$ is the acceleration due to gravity, namely, g.   Thus,
the intensity of the earth's field at any point in the surrounding region is
identical with the acceleration due to gravity at that point; hence

$$g = \frac{GM}{r^2}$$

The mass of the earth can be determined by applying the foregoing considerations to a particle located near the earth's surface, where the acceleration due to gravity is known to be $g = 980 \text{ cm/sec}^2$, and where the separation r may be taken as the radius of the earth, namely, 6.37×10^8 cm.   With
the gravitational constant G taken as 6.67×10^{-8} dyne·cm²/gm², the result
gives the mass of the earth as $M = 5.98 \times 10^{27}$ gm.

34. Gravitational Units.   In gravitational systems of units, force is taken
as a fundamental quantity instead of mass.   In the British gravitational
system, the unit of force is the *pound of force* (lb), and is defined as *the force
exerted by the earth on a 1-pound mass;* that is, it is the weight of a pound of
mass, § 6.   For exactness, the definition specifies that this weight shall be
as measured at 45° latitude and at sea level, but for ordinary purposes this

limitation is neglected. The ton and the ounce are other force units related to the pound as follows: 1 ton = 2000 lb; 1 lb = 16 ounces (oz).

The British unit for acceleration, whether in the gravitational or absolute systems, is 1 ft/sec². With the units for force F and acceleration a given, and these quantities related by the equation $F = ma$, the unit for mass is determined. This unit is called the slug; thus, *the slug is defined as a mass that is given an acceleration of 1 ft/sec² by a resultant force of 1 lb.* When the foregoing units are used in the equation $F = ma$, it is seen that

$$1 \text{ lb} = (1 \text{ slug}) \left(1 \frac{\text{ft}}{\text{sec}^2} \right)$$

hence the term "pound of force" can be replaced by its equivalent, $\dfrac{\text{slug} \cdot \text{ft}}{\text{sec}^2}$.

Further Analysis of Newton's Second Law. The underlying principles by which force and motion are related are not affected by the units used in applying such relations. Nevertheless, it will be of value in studying gravitational units to restate these principles with particular reference to the subject of weight.

Newton's Second Law of Motion states that the acceleration of a body is directly proportional to the resultant force that produces it. Thus, if a force F acting upon a body gives it an acceleration a, some other force F_1 acting upon the same body would impart a different acceleration a_1 such that

$$\frac{F}{F_1} = \frac{a}{a_1}$$

If the body were released so as to fall freely, the resultant force acting upon it would be its weight W, and the acceleration would be that due to gravity, or g; thus, F_1 may be replaced by W and a_1 by g, giving

$$\frac{F}{W} = \frac{a}{g} \tag{22}$$

In this expression, a is the acceleration produced by a resultant force F acting upon a body of weight W, and g is the acceleration due to gravity.

The form of this equation shows that if the accelerations a and g are expressed in the same units of acceleration, then the forces F and W are in the same units of force. In British gravitational units, the accelerations are commonly stated in feet per second squared and the forces in pounds.

The analysis leading to Eq. 22 gives a useful relation between the weight of a body and its mass, since the equation $F = ma$ applied to a freely falling body becomes

$$W = mg \tag{23}$$

Thus, the weight of a slug of mass is

$$mg = (1 \text{ slug})\left(32 \frac{\text{ft}}{\text{sec}^2}\right) = 32 \frac{\text{slug} \cdot \text{ft}}{\text{sec}^2} = 32 \text{ lb}$$

Therefore,

1 slug of mass weighs 32 lb

Similarly,

1 gm of mass weighs 980 dynes

and

1 kg of mass weighs 9.80 newtons

Illustrative Problem

To illustrate the use of gravitational units, calculate the acceleration of a body weighing 64 lb, when placed on a smooth, level plane and acted upon by a horizontal force of 10 lb.

The problem can be solved by using either Eq. 20 or 22. Since the body weighs 64 lb, its mass is $\frac{64}{32}$ or 2 slugs, whence, by Eq. 20,

$$a = \frac{F}{m} = \frac{10 \text{ lb}}{2 \text{ slugs}} = \frac{10 \frac{\text{slug} \cdot \text{ft}}{\text{sec}^2}}{2 \text{ slugs}} = 5.00 \frac{\text{ft}}{\text{sec}^2}$$

Or, by Eq. 22,

$$a = \frac{Fg}{W} = \frac{(10 \text{ lb})\left(32 \frac{\text{ft}}{\text{sec}^2}\right)}{64 \text{ lb}} = 5.00 \frac{\text{ft}}{\text{sec}^2}$$

35. Application of Principles. In applying Newton's Laws of Motion to the solution of problems dealing with force and acceleration, much difficulty can be avoided by following a definite procedure, at least until a thorough familiarity with the subject is attained. The following steps are suggested:

1. Select some one body for consideration. Usually this is the body that is in motion, but it may be a single member of a structure or a single portion of a moving system, isolated for study. Such an isolated part is called a "free body."

2. Construct a force diagram, entirely apart from any "space" diagram or picture that may be used to show the conditions of the problem. On this force diagram, let a point represent the body selected, and indicate *all* of the forces acting *on* this body by suitable vectors. Be careful that no forces are omitted, and that only forces acting on the body are used (not forces that the body may be exerting on other things). If any forces are unknown, represent them also by vectors, but mark them as unknown quantities.

3. From the force diagram, find the resultant force acting on the body. When some forces are unknown, the expression for the resultant force will involve these unknown quantities.

4. Choose a consistent set of units. The systems most frequently used in practice and the ones presented in this textbook are listed in the table below: the *cgs* and *mks* absolute systems and the British gravitational system. The *fps* system, § 30, is included for reference purposes only. Use the units in the column appropriate to the data given.

BASIC MECHANICAL UNITS

Quantity	Absolute Units			British Gravi-tational Units
	cgs	mks	fps	
Length............	cm	m	ft	ft
Mass..............	gm	kg	lb	slug
Time..............	sec	sec	sec	sec
Velocity...........	cm/sec	m/sec	ft/sec	ft/sec
Acceleration........	cm/sec^2	m/sec^2	ft/sec^2	ft/sec^2
Force..............	dyne	newton	poundal	lb

5. Next, find the acceleration or force, whichever is unknown, by using either Eq. 20 or 22.

6. Finally, should the problem ask for the distance traversed or the velocity acquired, then use the equations of accelerated motion, Eqs. 12–15, to find the quantity required.

Illustrative Problems

I. Find the acceleration produced by a force of 25 lb applied horizontally to a body weighing 30 lb, placed on a rough horizontal plane; assume the plane to exert a backward force of 10 lb on the body because of friction.

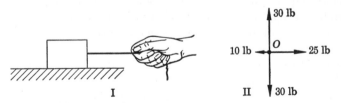

FIG. 36. Analysis of forces acting on a block; the first step in computing its acceleration

In Fig. 36, the body pictured in part I is indicated by a point at O in part II, and all the forces that act upon the body are represented by vectors drawn roughly to scale from this point in the appropriate directions. Of the 25-lb force applied to the body, 10 are balanced by friction, and so the resultant or unbalanced force acting on the body is 15 lb. Eq. 22, with terms rearranged, gives the acceleration as

$$a = \frac{Fg}{W} = \frac{(15\ \text{lb}) \left(32\ \dfrac{\text{ft}}{\text{sec}^2}\right)}{30\ \text{lb}} = 16.00\ \frac{\text{ft}}{\text{sec}^2}$$

II. A block weighing 10 lb is released at the top of a smooth plane 5 ft long, inclined 30° with the horizontal. In what time does it slide to the bottom of the incline?

The block shown on the plane in part I of Fig. 37 is chosen as the body for consideration and is indicated at O in the force diagram shown as part II. Only two forces act upon the block: the downward pull W due to gravity, and the outward push P of the plane. Since the plane is smooth, it can

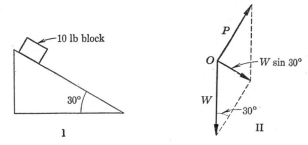

FIG. 37.   Forces on a block sliding down frictionless plane

exert no frictional drag on the block parallel to the plane; the force P is therefore at right angles to the plane, but its magnitude is unknown. The resultant of these forces is directed downward along the incline, because this is the direction in which the block accelerates. Hence, starting at the head end of vector W, construct a parallelogram having W and P for its adjacent sides. The angle indicated in part II of the figure is 30°, its sides being mutually perpendicular to the incline and the base in part I; and the resultant, represented by the concurrent diagonal of the parallelogram, is consequently $W \sin 30°$. This is the resultant force F acting on the block, and its value is $F = 10 \sin 30° = 5$ lb. The mass of the block is $m = \frac{10}{32}$ slug, and it follows from Eq. 20 that the acceleration is

$$a = \frac{F}{m} = \frac{5\ \text{lb}}{\frac{10}{32}\ \text{slug}} = \frac{5\ \dfrac{\text{slug} \cdot \text{ft}}{\text{sec}^2}}{\frac{10}{32}\ \text{slug}} = 16\ \frac{\text{ft}}{\text{sec}^2}$$

The time of descent of the block is obtained from Eq. 14, $s = v_o t + \frac{1}{2}at^2$, with $v_o = 0$, as

$$t = \sqrt{\frac{2s}{a}} = \sqrt{\frac{2(5\ \text{ft})}{16\ \dfrac{\text{ft}}{\text{sec}^2}}} = 0.791\ \text{sec}$$

III. What upward force must be applied to the cable of an elevator weighing 5 tons in order that the car may have an upward acceleration of 3 ft/sec², if friction is neglected?

The elevator, shown in part I of Fig. 38, is acted upon by two forces: the downward pull W due to gravity and the unknown upward pull P of the cable. In part II, these forces are represented by vectors at O, pointing in the appropriate directions. The elevator is to accelerate upward; hence the upward force is greater than the downward force, and the difference between them, $P - W$, is the resultant force acting upward on the elevator. Since $W = (5)(2000) = 10,000$ lb, it follows from Eq. 22, $F = \dfrac{W}{g}\,a$, that

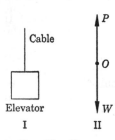

$$P - 10,000 \text{ lb} = \left(\frac{10,000 \text{ lb}}{32 \text{ ft/sec}^2}\right)\left(3 \frac{\text{ft}}{\text{sec}^2}\right) = 940 \text{ lb}$$

Fig. 38. Forces on elevator

hence the upward force on the elevator is

$$P = 10,000 + 940 = 10,940 \text{ lb}.$$

IV. In Atwood's machine, used in the study of accelerated motion, a cord with masses at the ends is hung over a pulley, as represented in part I of Fig. 39. When one of the masses is 400 gm and the other 300 gm, what is the tension in the cord? and what is the acceleration of the moving system? Assume friction to be absent, and neglect the mass of the cord and that of the pulley.

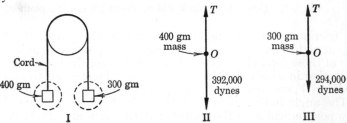

Fig. 39. Elementary Atwood's machine

In solving the problem, each mass is considered as a free body in turn, and in each case the direction in which the free body accelerates is taken as positive. The 400-gm mass is shown at O in part II of the figure; it is acted on by two forces: the downward pull of gravity, which equals $(400)(980) = 392,000$ dynes, and the unknown tension T in the cord pulling upward. Since this mass accelerates downward, the downward force is greater than the upward force, and the difference between them, namely, 392,000 dynes $- T$, is the resultant force acting on the 400-gm mass. The expression $F = ma$ is set up for this body alone, thus:

$$392,000 \text{ dynes} - T = (400 \text{ gm})a$$

This equation cannot be solved by itself since it contains two unknown quantities, T and a.

Next, consider the 300-gm body; it is acted on by a downward force of $(300)(980) = 294,000$ dynes, and by the upward force T, as indicated in part III. The resultant force acting on this body is $T - 294,000$ dynes, and therefore, from the same equation,

$$T - 294,000 \text{ dynes} = (300 \text{ gm})a$$

This provides another equation relating the magnitudes of T and a. The two equations can be solved simultaneously; the results give the tension T in the cord as 336,000 dynes, and the acceleration a of the moving system as 140.0 cm/sec².

PROBLEMS

1. A block of 500-gm mass is pushed along a smooth level surface by a constant horizontal force of 20,000 dynes. Compute the acceleration of the block.

2. State the reaction to each of the following forces: (a) downward push of a book on a table, (b) downward pull exerted by a man on a rope, (c) downward attraction of the earth on a book, (d) push of the hand against a wall, (e) force exerted by a boxing glove on chin, (f) force with which car A strikes car B, and (g) force with which rear tires push back against roadbed.

3. What force in newtons will give an object of 2-kg mass an acceleration of 1.25 m/sec² along a smooth horizontal surface?

4. A constant horizontal force applied to a block of 2000-gm mass moves it 150 cm along a smooth level surface in 5 sec, starting from rest. Compute the value of the applied force.

5. A constant horizontal force of 2.5×10^6 dynes is exerted upon a body of 5000-gm mass, initially at rest on a level surface. What velocity does the body acquire in 2 sec, if friction exerts a steady backward force of 10^6 dynes upon it?

6. What horizontal force should be applied to a mass of 50 gm to increase its velocity from 100 to 250 cm/sec in sliding 200 cm along a level plane, if friction meanwhile exerts an opposing force of 5000 dynes upon it?

7. An object of 2000-gm mass is moving at 60 cm/sec. If it is desired to bring the object to rest in 1.25 sec, what retarding force should be exerted upon it?

8. A block of 400-gm mass is sliding along a horizontal plane. Beginning at an instant when the velocity of the block is 50 cm/sec, a constant force of 140,000 dynes is applied to the block in the direction of its motion. What is the velocity of the block 2 sec later, if its motion is retarded by a constant force of 100,000 dynes due to friction?

9. An electron is projected horizontally from an electron gun at 1.5×10^9 cm/sec through an electric field that exerts a constant sidewise force of 5×10^{-10} dynes upon it. Take the mass of the electron as 9.11×10^{-28} gm, and compute (a) the time in which the electron moves forward a distance of 3 cm in the field and (b) the distance it moves sidewise in this time.

10. (a) Assume the earth's gravitational field to have an intensity of 32 lb/slug at the surface of the earth, and compute its intensity at an elevation of 300 mi. The earth's radius may be taken as 3960 mi. (b) If an artificial earth satellite weighs 20 lb at the surface of the earth, what does it weigh at the stated elevation?

11. If a man weighs 200 lb at the surface of the earth, what would he weigh at the surface of the moon? The mass of the moon is 7.34×10^{25} gm and its radius is 1.75×10^8 cm.

12. The distance from the earth to the moon (center to center) varies from 225,000 to 252,000 mi, and its average value may be taken as 240,000 mi. If a "space ship" were located between the earth and moon at a point such that the gravitational pulls of these bodies upon it were equal, how far would the ship be from the center of the earth? Additional data appear in the preceding problem.

13. Some gold is placed on a spring balance in the far north, at a place where the intensity of the gravitational field is 32.25 lb/slug, and is found to weigh $16\frac{1}{8}$ oz. How much would this gold weigh on a spring balance near the equator at a place where the gravitational intensity is 32.10 lb/slug?

14. An airplane climbing at an angle of 20° upward from the horizontal is acted upon by four forces: its weight $W = 12,000$ lb; the propeller thrust $T = 4800$ lb in the direction of motion; the lift L, perpendicular to the propeller thrust; and the drag D of air friction, opposite to the direction of motion. Assume that the airplane is moving with constant velocity, and calculate the values of the lift and the drag.

15. What upward pull should be applied to the cable of an elevator weighing 4000 lb to raise the elevator 30 ft in 4 sec, starting from rest? Assume that friction is negligible.

16. An automobile that weighs 2400 lb is being pushed by a constant force of 420 lb and acquires a velocity of 15 mi/hr in moving a distance of 50 ft, starting from rest. Calculate the backward force of friction acting on the automobile.

17. A man who weighs 180 lb stands in an elevator that is accelerating upward at 4 ft/sec². With what force does he press against the floor of the elevator?

18. A constant horizontal force of 15 lb is applied for 3 sec to a box and causes it to accelerate from rest along a level surface. The box weighs 40 lb and its motion is opposed by a constant frictional force of 12 lb. (*a*) How far does the box move during the 3-sec period while the force is applied? (*b*) At the end of the 3-sec period the force is discontinued, but the force of friction remains unchanged. How much farther does the box move before it stops?

19. A block of mass m starts from rest and slides down a frictionless plane inclined at an angle θ with the horizontal. Derive an expression for the distance that the block slides down the plane in a time interval t.

20. An airplane catapulted from a carrier leaves a 60-ft runway at a speed of 90 mi/hr. (*a*) Assume the acceleration of the airplane to be constant and compute its value. (*b*) If the pilot weighs 160 lb, with what force does he press against the back of his seat during the acceleration period?

21. A box that weighs 20 lb slides from rest down a plank 12 ft long inclined at 36.9° with the horizontal. How long does it take the box to slide down, if friction exerts an opposing force of 4 lb upon it?

22. An object of 2000-gm mass is pulled up a smooth plane inclined at an angle of 30° with the horizontal, by a constant pull applied for 5 sec parallel to the plane. If the object, starting from rest, moves a distance of 200 cm along the plane in this time interval, (*a*) what is the value of the applied pull? and (*b*) what is the velocity of the object at the end of the 5-sec interval?

23. A block of 1000-gm mass is drawn along a smooth, level table top by a cord that passes horizontally over a frictionless pulley, extends downward,

and supports a second block, of 50-gm mass, at its lower end, as shown in the diagram. Find the acceleration of the system and the tension in the cord.

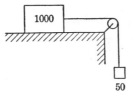

Problem 23

24. A block of 1000-gm mass is initially at rest on a smooth plane inclined at 45° with the horizontal. A cord attached to the block extends upward parallel to the plane, passes over a small frictionless pulley, and extends downward to another block attached to its lower end, as shown in the diagram. The latter block has a mass of 100 gm. When the system is released,

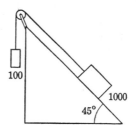

Problem 24

(a) does the large block move up or down the plane? (b) what is its acceleration? and (c) how far does it move during the first second?

25. Two weights, one of 2.0 lb and the other of 2.4 lb, are fastened to opposite ends of a cord, and the cord is placed over a frictionless pulley. Compute the acceleration of the moving system.

26. A sled that weighs 50 lb is drawn along smooth level snow by a pull of 10 lb applied in a direction 30° above the horizontal. Determine (a) the acceleration of the sled and the distance it moves in 3 sec, starting from rest, and (b) the upward push of the snow upon the sled.

5

PRINCIPLES FURTHER
RELATING TO FORCE

MOMENTUM

36. The Concept of Momentum. Among the concepts of Physics that have to do with force and motion, one of the most fundamental is momentum. *The momentum of a body is defined as the product of its mass and its velocity.* This concept prompts a further consideration of Newton's Second Law of Motion.

In accordance with Eq. 20, this law states that a body of mass m acted upon by some resultant force F receives an acceleration a such that

$$F = ma$$

where the acceleration can be expressed as $a = (v_f - v_o)/t$, in terms of the velocity v_o at the beginning of the time interval t during which the force acts and the velocity v_f at the end of that interval. The second law can thus be stated more fundamentally as

$$F = \frac{mv_f - mv_o}{t} \tag{24}$$

where the terms in the numerator represent the final and initial values of the momentum and F is the average force exerted during the time t. This equation gives a basic definition of force as the time rate of change of momentum.

The foregoing expression can also be transformed to read

$$Ft = mv_f - mv_o \tag{25}$$

wherein the product of a force and the time during which it acts is called *impulse*. Hence the second law in this form states that *a body acted upon by some resultant force undergoes a change of momentum which is equal to the impulse of that force*; this is basically the form in which the law was stated by Newton. Both impulse and momentum are vector quantities; the impulse Ft has the same direction as the force, and the momentums mv_f and mv_o have the same directions as the velocities.

37. Conservation of Momentum. The foregoing principles will now be applied to a system of two or more bodies, and to the special case where the resultant force acting upon the system is zero; such a system is said to be isolated. Then in Eq. 25, the resultant force $F = 0$, and consequently $mv_f = mv_o$, which means that the momentum of the system remains constant. More generally, this equation can be expressed as

$$m_f v_f = m_o v_o \qquad (26)$$

to anticipate possible change of mass with velocity, § 444. This equation expresses the law of Conservation of Momentum, a principle which states that *the total momentum of an isolated system stays constant regardless of any interactions that may take place among its parts.*

Two blocks sliding toward each other on a smooth level surface and colliding will serve as an illustration. Here the system comprises the two blocks, and since the resultant force acting on the system as a whole is zero, its momentum is not affected by the collision. The same conclusion would be reached by considering the blocks individually. When they collide, they exert equal and opposite forces on each other, in accordance with Newton's Third Law, and obviously the time intervals over which these forces act are identical. Therefore the colliding blocks are subjected to equal and opposite impulses and so undergo equal and opposite changes in momentum; the amount of momentum lost by one block is gained by the other. The forces just referred to are internal forces that the different parts of the system exert upon each other, and not forces acting on the system as a whole.

Additional illustrations of the Conservation of Momentum are afforded by the operation of a jet engine, the firing of a bullet from a gun, or the bursting of a shell into several fragments; others will doubtless suggest themselves. This law is applicable to atomic processes, including nuclear reactions and radiation, and to interactions of all kinds. The principle of Conservation of Momentum is one of the great generalizations of Physics.

This law is frequently applied in specific situations by expressing the momentums along rectangular axes. The collision between two objects provides a simple illustration. If the objects have masses m_1 and m_2, and if their respective velocities along the X axis are v_{1x} and v_{2x} before impact and v_{1x}' and v_{2x}' after impact, then, by the Law of Conservation of Momentum,

$$m_1 \vec{v}_{1x} + m_2 \vec{v}_{2x} = m_1 \vec{v}_{1x}' + m_2 \vec{v}_{2x}'$$

and similarly along the Y and Z axes. Expressed more simply,

$$\Sigma mv = \Sigma mv' \qquad \text{along any direction} \qquad (27)$$

where Σmv represents the momentum of the system before collision, and $\Sigma mv'$ the momentum after collision, in the direction considered. The letter Σ (sigma) is used to represent "sum"; consequently Σmv means the sum of a number of terms each of which is a mass multiplied by a velocity.

Illustrative Problem

Suppose a block of wood having a mass of 5000 gm to be sliding along a smooth, level plane at 120 cm/sec and that a bullet having a mass of 10 gm, known to be moving at 42,000 cm/sec, is fired horizontally into the block in a direction at right angles to its motion. If the bullet remains embedded within the block, through what angle is the block deflected?

Suppose the block to move along the X axis and the bullet along the Y axis. Then, from Eq. 27, with masses in grams and velocities in centimeters per second,

<table>
<tr><td></td><td>Before
Impact</td><td>After
Impact</td></tr>
</table>

Along X axis: $(5000)(120) + (10)(0)$ $= 5010v_x'$

Along Y axis: $(5000)(0) + (10)(42,000) = 5010v_y'$

In Fig. 40, part I represents the conditions at the moment of contact, and

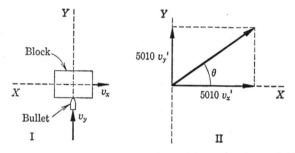

FIG. 40.   Momentums involved in collision of bullet and block

part II shows the momentum of the system after collision in terms of its components. From the vector diagram,

$$\tan \theta = \frac{5010v_y'}{5010v_x'} = \frac{(10)(42,000)}{(5000)(120)} = 0.700$$

and therefore $\theta = 35.0°$ is the angle through which the block is deflected.

FRICTION

38. Force of Friction. The surface of any solid if magnified sufficiently is found to be rugged and uneven, with minute hills at some places and valleys at others. If two surfaces are pressed together, these irregularities intermesh somewhat; contact is established chiefly at the peaks, and these become flattened by pressure until the area of actual contact is sufficient to withstand the applied force. Because of these surface irregularities, opposition is encountered to the sliding of one surface over another. This opposition, called *sliding friction*, increases as the contacting surfaces are pressed more firmly together. Recent experiments with metal surfaces in sliding contact indicate that increased pressure may result in high local temperatures at the contacting areas, followed by seizure, in which portions of the two surfaces become welded together, with the subsequent tearing away of relatively large particles. A frictionless or so-called smooth surface represents an ideal that is never attained in practice. Notwithstanding its disadvantages, friction has certain useful aspects; indeed, a person could not walk on the ground without friction.

The information available on the subject of friction relies more on experiment than on theory. From the experimental results, the following statements can be made, but they should be regarded as true only approximately, even for dry surfaces. It is found that the amount of friction depends upon the materials in contact, the condition of the surfaces, and the force with which these surfaces are pressed together. Friction is virtually independent of the speed of sliding over a wide range. Actually, the amount of friction is somewhat greater when a body is starting from rest than when sliding, but this effect will be neglected. Friction depends little, if any, on the apparent area of the sliding surfaces; some recent evidence, however, indicates that it is proportional to the area of actual contact between them.

When a body slides over another body, a force acts upon it called the *force of friction*. Much can be learned about the force of friction by merely sliding a book around on a table top. It soon becomes apparent that the force of friction always opposes the motion of the book along the plane of sliding. No matter which way the book is moved, the force of friction acts on it in the opposite direction.

When one exerts a horizontal force of $\frac{1}{4}$ lb on the book toward the right and the book does not move, then the resultant force acting on it is zero, and therefore the surface of the table is exerting a force of friction on it of $\frac{1}{4}$ lb toward the left. In this test, the force of friction cannot be greater than $\frac{1}{4}$ lb, for if it could be greater than the applied force the force of friction would move the book backward!

Next, if the force applied to the book is increased to $\frac{1}{2}$ lb and still the book does not move, the force of friction has also increased to $\frac{1}{2}$ lb. Finally, if the force is increased little by little until the book is set into motion, and if a horizontal force of 1 lb is found just sufficient to keep it moving with constant speed, the resultant force again is zero, and hence friction is now exerting a force of 1 lb on the book. It is evident that in this case the force of sliding friction is as great as possible for these particular bodies, but is insufficient to hold the book at rest.

39. Coefficient of Friction. The maximum force of friction that one object can exert upon another is directly proportional to the normal force *pressing their surfaces together*. Thus, if f is the maximum force of friction between two objects and N is the force with which either object presses against the other perpendicular to their contacting surfaces, then $f \propto N$, or

$$f = \mu N$$

where the proportionality factor μ (mu) is the *coefficient of friction* between the surfaces. This expression can be transposed to read

$$\mu = \frac{f}{N} \qquad (28)$$

from which the coefficient of friction is defined as *the ratio of the maximum force of friction between two bodies to the normal force pressing the surfaces together.* It is evident from Eq. 28 that, since f and N are both forces, they may be expressed in any desired force unit so long as the same unit is used for both, and that μ is simply a number.

Since the frictional force f is always in the plane of sliding, and the normal force N pressing the two surfaces into contact is perpendicular to this plane, it follows that f and N are always at right angles to each other. Fig. 41 shows the forces acting upon a block which has been set in motion toward the right and is now sliding to rest along a rough, level plane. In this example, the supporting surface is horizontal, and so the normal reaction N of the plane is equal and opposite to the weight W of the block. The force of friction f is at right angles to N and opposite to the direction of motion and is the resultant force acting on the block.

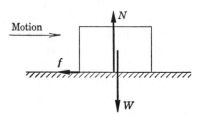

FIG. 41.   Forces acting upon block sliding to rest

The coefficient of sliding friction is found by experiment to be fairly constant for any two surfaces; it depends only on the materials involved and the condition of the surfaces in contact. Some representative values for dry surfaces appear in the accompanying table.

COEFFICIENTS OF SLIDING FRICTION

Wood on wood.........	0.25 to 0.5
Metals on wood........	0.2 to 0.6
Metals on metals.......	0.15 to 0.2
Leather on wood........	0.27 to 0.38
Leather on metals.......	0.56

For surfaces that are carefully machined and thoroughly lubricated, the coefficient of sliding friction is much smaller and depends upon the area of contact.

Illustrative Problem

As a typical example involving sliding friction, consider a sled being pushed along level snow by a constant force of 6 lb applied at an angle $30°$

downward from the horizontal. If the sled with its load weighs 60 lb and if the coefficient of friction between the sled and the snow is 0.05, in what time does the sled travel 100 ft, starting from rest?

In accordance with the procedure of § 35, the sled, shown in part I of Fig. 42, is indicated at O in part II, and all the forces acting on it are represented by vectors drawn from this point, as follows: the downward pull of gravity, W (60 lb); the push P (6 lb) applied in the direction shown; the upward reaction of the snow, R (unknown); and the backward force of friction, f (also unknown). The push P is resolved into a horizontal component

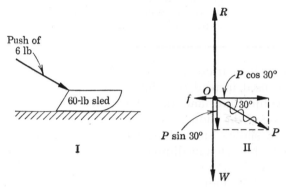

FIG. 42. Forces on sled that is pushed along horizontal surface

$P \cos 30° = 6 \times 0.866 = 5.20$ lb that shows how much of the push is effective in moving the sled horizontally, and a vertical component $P \sin 30° = 6 \times 0.500 = 3.00$ lb that shows how much the sled is being pushed down, increasing its force against the snow. The push P may now be disregarded and is crossed out, since it is replaced by its components.

The total force that the sled exerts downward on the snow is $60 + 3.00 = 63.0$ lb, and hence the upward thrust R of the snow on the sled is also 63.0 lb, this being the normal force between the sliding surfaces. The frictional force is obtained from Eq. 28 as $f = \mu N = 0.05 \times 63.0 = 3.15$ lb. Since the vertical forces are balanced, the resultant force acting on the sled is toward the right and amounts to $5.20 - 3.15 = 2.05$ lb. Consequently the acceleration of the sled, from Eq. 22, is

$$a = \frac{Fg}{W} = \frac{2.05 \, \text{lb} \times 32 \, \dfrac{\text{ft}}{\text{sec}^2}}{60 \, \text{lb}} = 1.093 \, \frac{\text{ft}}{\text{sec}^2}$$

Finally, this acceleration value is substituted in Eq. 14, namely,

$$s = v_0 t + \tfrac{1}{2}at^2 = 0 + \tfrac{1}{2}at^2$$

in order to find the time taken for the sled to travel 100 ft. The result is

$$t = \sqrt{\frac{2s}{a}} = \sqrt{\frac{2 \times 100 \, \text{ft}}{1.093 \, \dfrac{\text{ft}}{\text{sec}^2}}} = \sqrt{183.0 \, \text{sec}^2} = 13.53 \text{ sec}$$

Rolling friction is the opposition that occurs when one body rolls upon another and is probably due to slight deformations of the bodies at the points of contact. In problems, rolling friction and sliding friction are treated in the same way. Some typical values of the coefficients of rolling friction follow.

COEFFICIENTS OF ROLLING FRICTION

Cast-iron wheels on rails............	0.004
Ball bearings in rolling contact........	0.001 to 0.003
Roller bearings in rolling contact.....	0.002 to 0.007

It is because rolling friction is so small compared with sliding friction that wheels are used instead of runners on wagons, that casters are provided on heavy furniture, and that, for many purposes, ball bearings are preferred to those of the sliding, or sleeve, type.

In addition to sliding and rolling friction, opposition is offered to the motion of objects through a medium such as air or water. This skin friction, as it is called, depends in amount on the size and shape of the moving object and the velocity of its motion; as the velocity rises, the friction increases more than proportionately.

Skin friction has an important effect on the motion of an object falling through the air. When first released, the object begins to fall freely, but as it gains speed it encounters more and more air resistance and finally reaches a constant "terminal" velocity at which the upward drag of friction equals the weight of the falling object. For example, a man falling with unopened parachute could reach a terminal velocity of 100 to 150 mi/hr.

TORQUE

40. Rotational Effect of Force. Under appropriate circumstances, a force applied to a body may cause it to rotate about some axis. The rotational effect depends upon the direction of the force and also upon the position of its line of action with respect to the axis of rotation. This statement can be verified readily in opening a heavy door, by exerting a force upon the door knob in the various directions shown from 1 to 4 in part I of Fig. 43. The force needed in direction 2 to open the door is smaller than in direction 3, and a force along direction 4, parallel to the door, produces no rotational effect, however large the force may be. The most favorable direction is that along direction 1, perpendicular to the door, for the least force is required along this line.

Again, if the door is pushed at various places along its width in a direction at right angles to the door, as in part II, the least force is needed at position 8, along the edge farthest from the hinges, to open it; more and more force must be exerted in approaching the hinges, positions 7 and 6; and a force applied at the hinges, position 5, will not produce rotation, however great it may be.

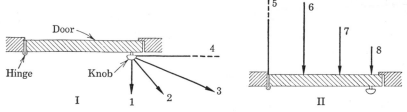

FIG. 43.   Various forces needed to open a door

41. Moment of Force: Torque.   A variety of experiences with forces acting on movable bodies, such as turning the door in the previous section, shows the need of expressing definitely the effectiveness of a force in setting a body into rotation.   The rotational effect is known as the *moment of force*, or *torque*, and is measured by *the product of the force and the perpendicular distance from the axis of rotation to the line of action of the force.*   This perpendicular distance is called the *lever arm;* consequently,

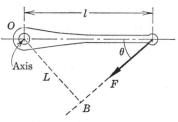

FIG. 44.   The torque *FL* tends to turn the crank about the axis *O*

Torque = force × lever arm

In symbols, the force is represented by F and the lever arm by L, and the torque becomes

$$T = FL \tag{29}$$

For example, with the crank shown in Fig. 44, the moment of force F tending to turn the crank clockwise about an axis O, is equal to $F \times OB$ for the position shown, where OB is the lever arm.   The lever arm L is not the length l of the crank, but is the perpendicular distance from the axis at O to the line of action of the force at point B.   The lever arm can, of course, be expressed in terms of the crank length l by replacing L by its equal, $l \sin \theta$; hence the torque $T = Fl \sin \theta$.   Another way to obtain this result is to resolve the force F into two components, namely: $F \cos \theta$ along the crank, and $F \sin \theta$ at right angles to the crank.   The latter component multiplied by the length l of the crank yields the correct value of the torque.

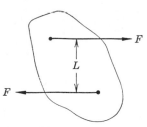

FIG. 45.   A pair of equal and opposite forces not in the same line constitute a couple

Another example illustrating torque is shown in Fig. 45, which represents a pair of forces acting upon a body to set it into rotation. Two equal and opposite forces that do not act along the same line constitute a *couple*. The torque exerted by a couple is equal to the product of one of the forces, F, and the perpendicular distance, L, between their lines of action; Eq. 29 applies to this example also.

The units of torque depend on the units selected for the force and for the lever arm; the units commonly used are dyne·cm and lb·ft.

CENTER OF MASS

42. Motion of a Rigid Body; Center of Mass. Until the subject of torque was introduced in the preceding sections, it was assumed that forces applied to a body would cause the body as a whole to accelerate in the direction of the resultant force. Such motion, in which every particle of the body has the same velocity and the same acceleration, is called *translation*. But a torque acting upon a body may produce an entirely different kind of motion, in which the particles of the body describe concentric circles about a fixed line as an axis, a motion known as *rotation*. In general, a body may undergo translation or rotation, or a combination of these motions, depending on how the forces are applied with respect to a particular point called the *center of mass* of the body.

Before considering the location of this point, some of its properties will be described. This description will be limited to *rigid bodies*, in which the particles maintain their relative positions, so that the bodies remain unchanged in size and shape regardless of the forces acting. Most solid objects closely approximate rigid bodies unless abnormally large forces act upon them. The properties of the center of mass are:

1. When a force is applied to the center of mass of a body, the resulting acceleration of the body is one of pure translation. Such a situation exists with many forces acting on a body if the line of action of their resultant passes through the center of mass of the body; a force through this point results in no rotational effect whatever.

2. When one or more forces act upon a body, whether at the center of mass or not, the motion of the center of mass is the same as if all the mass of the body were concentrated at that point and all the forces were applied there. Thus, if a long stick is picked up and thrown, its center of mass moves in a parabolic path, as though the resultant force acted upon a concentrated mass at that center, § 26.

3. A body set into rotation rotates about an axis through its center of mass if free to do so. Thus, the stick just mentioned rotates about its center of mass while that point moves along the parabolic path.

The term "center of mass" is also applied to a combination of two or more bodies. It is interesting to consider the behavior of such a system upon which the resultant force is zero. A man afloat in a canoe serves as an illustration of such a system. If the man crouches down and dives out of the canoe, say at one end, then the man and the canoe exert forces upon each other, but these are merely internal forces that one part of the system exerts upon another part, and no external force is applied to the system as a whole, if friction of the water is negligible. Under these circumstances, if the center of mass of the system is initially at rest it remains at rest; thus, while the man moves through the air one way, the canoe moves through the water the other way, and the location of the center of mass of the combination does not change. The same conclusion would be reached from the law of conservation of momentum, § 37, for the momentum acquired by the man is equal and opposite to that acquired by the canoe.

43. Location of Center of Mass. From the properties of the center of mass described in the preceding section, it is possible to determine the location of this point for a given body or system. The method will be illustrated by a system composed of two particles having masses m_1 and m_2 and joined by a rod of negligible mass, as indicated in Fig. 46. If the center of mass of the combination is at C, a force F applied at this point produces a linear acceleration a which is the same for both masses, since the system moves with translation only. The force F can be regarded as the resultant of two parallel forces F_1 and F_2, acting respectively on m_1 and m_2, where F_1 = $m_1 a$ and F_2 = $m_2 a$. Since there is no rotation, the clockwise moment

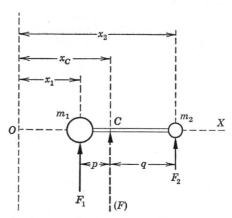

FIG. 46. Location of the center of mass of a system of particles

of F_1 tending to produce rotation about C must equal the counterclockwise moment of F_2 about the same point; that is, $F_1 p = F_2 q$, an equation that can be restated as $(m_1 a)p = (m_2 a)q$, or simply

$$m_1 p = m_2 q$$

The distances p and q and the location of the center of mass can be expressed in terms of coordinates along the X axis, namely, x_1, x_2, and x_C as shown, and therefore the foregoing result can be written as $m_1(x_C - x_1) = m_2(x_2 - x_C)$, whence

$$x_C = \frac{m_1 x_1 + m_2 x_2}{m_1 + m}$$

By extending this method to apply to more than two mass particles and to more than one of the coordinate axes, the following general equations result for the coordinates of the center of mass:

$$x_C = \frac{\Sigma m x}{\Sigma m} \qquad y_C = \frac{\Sigma m y}{\Sigma m} \qquad z_C = \frac{\Sigma m z}{\Sigma m} \qquad (30)$$

where each numerator represents the sum of the products of the masses and their distances from the axis, and each denominator the sum of the masses.

In symmetrical objects of uniform density, the center of mass is at the geometrical center; thus for a sphere it is at the center, and for a rectangular sheet it is at the intersection of the diagonals. Nonsymmetrical objects can often be divided into parts that are symmetrical, making it possible to determine the center of mass by the method just described. Practically, the center of mass coincides with the center of gravity, and its location can be found experimentally as described in § 79.

Illustrative Problem

Consider the three concentrated masses shown in Fig. 47, located in one plane at the positions indicated; determine the location of the center of mass of the combination with respect to the 40-gm mass.

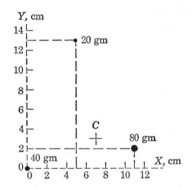

Fig. 47. System of three particles and its center of mass C

From Eq. 30, with masses in grams and distances in centimeters:

$$x_C = \frac{\Sigma mx}{\Sigma m} = \frac{(40)(0) + (20)(5) + (80)(11)}{40 + 20 + 80} = 7.00$$

$$y_C = \frac{\Sigma my}{\Sigma m} = \frac{(40)(0) + (20)(13) + (80)(2)}{40 + 20 + 80} = 3.00$$

hence, the coordinates of the center of mass of the system considered are $x_C = 7.00$ cm and $y_C = 3.00$ cm. This location is marked C in the figure.

44. Translation and Center of Mass. A further deduction can be made from the properties of the center of mass stated in § 42, and dealing with the behavior of a body that accelerates while moving with pure translation. With such motion, the resultant force acting on the body passes through the center of mass. Naturally, this force produces no torque about this axis. The resultant may be made up of several forces, and an important principle follows: *Where a body moves with translation only, the sum of the moments of all the forces acting upon it, taken about an axis through the center of mass of the body, equals zero.* In symbols,

$$\Sigma T_C = 0 \text{ for translation only} \tag{31}$$

Illustrative Problem

Fig. 48 represents a box 4 ft high and 3 ft wide, with its center of mass C at its center. The box has a weight $W = 80$ lb and is caused to slide along a level floor by a horizontal force P applied at its top edge. For simplicity, assume that the box touches the floor only at the front and rear edges, and that the normal forces exerted by the floor at these places are N_1 and N_2, as indicated. Take the coefficient of friction between box and floor to be 0.25, and compute: (*a*) the values of N_1 and N_2 when the box is caused to accelerate at 2 ft/sec^2, and (*b*) the maximum value of the force P that can be applied without causing the box to tip over.

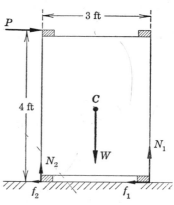

(*a*) The mass of the box is $m = \frac{80}{32} = 2.5$ slugs, and the force of friction is $f = \mu N = 0.25 \times 80 = 20$ lb, divided between f_1 and f_2. The resultant force on the box is $P - f$, and the equation of motion, $F = ma$, becomes $P - 20$ lb $= (2.5 \text{ slugs})(2 \text{ ft/sec}^2) = 5$ lb, whence $P = 25$ lb.

FIG. 48. Forces on a box being pushed along level surface

Next, take moments about C, in accordance with Eq. 31, with forces in pounds and lever arms in feet; then

$$P(2) + N_2(1.5) + f_1(2) + f_2(2) - N_1(1.5) = 0$$

whence $(25)(2) + (f_1 + f_2)(2) = (N_1 - N_2)(1.5)$. But $f_1 + f_2 = f = 20$ lb, and therefore $N_1 - N_2 = 60$ lb. Also, the sum of N_1 and N_2 must equal the weight W of the box, or $N_1 + N_2 = 80$ lb. These two equations when solved simultaneously give the reactions of the floor as $N_1 = 70.0$ lb and $N_2 = 10.00$ lb.

(*b*) When the box is about to tip over, N_2 and f_2 become zero, and under this condition $N_1 = W = 80$ lb, and $f_1 = \mu W = 20$ lb. The equation of moments about C becomes: $P(2) + f_1(2) - N_1(1.5) = 0$, or $2P = (80)(1.5) - (20)(2)$, whence $P = 40.0$ lb. This is the maximum force that can be applied along the top edge of the box without causing it to tip over.

CENTRIPETAL FORCE

45. Acceleration in Circular Motion. A body that moves in a curved path is accelerated because its velocity is changing continually, even though the body travels at constant speed. This change is one of direction and not magnitude. Since acceleration is defined as the rate of change of velocity, § 22, a change in either magnitude or direction of velocity implies acceleration. Thus, if the velocity is continually changing in direction, additions are continually being made to it even though the magnitude of the velocity remains the same.

When a body moves at constant speed v around a circle of radius r, as shown centered at C in part I of Fig. 49, its velocities at A and B can be represented by vectors v_1 and v_2, each equal numerically to v and tangent to the circle at the respective points. Since these velocities differ in direction, some additional velocity must be given to the body as it moves from A to B in order to change its velocity from v_1 to v_2. To find this additional velocity, v_1 and v_2 are drawn from a common point in part II of the figure;

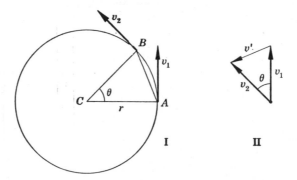

FIG. 49.   Diagram for deriving the expression for centripetal force

the closing side v' of the velocity diagram is clearly the vector added to v_1 to obtain v_2. If t is the time in which the body moves from A to B, then the added velocity v' divided by this time interval is the average acceleration of the body. But the isosceles triangles in the two parts of the figure are similar, whence $\dfrac{v'}{v_1} = \dfrac{AB}{r}$, and therefore the magnitude of this acceleration is

$$\frac{v'}{t} = \frac{v(AB)}{rt}$$

where v replaces v_1, the subscript being omitted since the velocity has the same magnitude at all points in the circular path.

To find the instantaneous acceleration, the time interval t is regarded as having the small value Δt, and the added velocity is designated Δv. As Δt becomes smaller and smaller, the chord AB approaches the arc $AB = v \cdot \Delta t$; also the ratio $\Delta v / \Delta t$ approaches the instantaneous acceleration; its magnitude is derived from the centered equation above as $a = \dfrac{\Delta v}{\Delta t} = \dfrac{v(v \cdot \Delta t)}{r \cdot \Delta t}$, or

$$a = \frac{v^2}{r} \tag{32}$$

where v is the speed of the body in its circular path and r the radius of the circle.

The direction of the acceleration is that of the added velocity v'; the shorter the time interval taken, the more nearly v' becomes perpendicular to v_1 and v_2; in the limit it is perpendicular to both these vectors and points directly toward the center of the circle. This acceleration toward the center is called *centripetal* acceleration.

Therefore, when a body revolves at constant speed in a circular path, (*a*) it does have an acceleration, (*b*) the magnitude of this acceleration is $\dfrac{v^2}{r}$ at every instant, and (*c*) the direction of the acceleration is toward the center of the circle.

46. Force in Circular Motion. It was shown in the preceding section that a body moving in a circular path at constant speed is constantly accelerating toward the center of the circle. This statement implies that a force is acting upon the body; this force is also directed toward the center of the circle and is called the *centripetal force*. Since the acceleration is known to be v^2/r, the force can be found at once either by Eq. 20, $F = ma$, or by Eq. 22, $\dfrac{F}{W} = \dfrac{a}{g}$, with units as tabulated in § 35. Thus, the centripetal force in dynes acting upon a body of mass m gm that is moving with a speed v cm/sec around a curve of radius r cm is

$$F = m\,\frac{v^2}{r} \qquad \text{Centripital} \tag{33}$$

Again, the centripetal force in pounds acting upon a body of weight W lb that is moving with a speed of v ft/sec around a curve of radius r ft is

$$F = \frac{Wv^2}{gr} \tag{34}$$

Many examples show the existence of this centripetal force needed for motion along a curve. When a stone is whirled around at the end of a cord, the cord becomes taut and pulls inwardly on the stone. When a locomotive encounters a curve, the outer rail presses against the flanges of the wheels and provides the centripetal force that enables the locomotive to follow the curved track. The earth in moving along its orbit is always drawn toward the center by the gravitational attraction of the sun. In contrast, an automobile may be unable to make a sharp turn on a slippery street. All these examples illustrate the same principle: an object cannot move around a curve unless it is constrained to do so by a centrally acting force.

Since for any action there is an equal and opposite reaction, the moving object exerts an equal force radially outward upon the constraining agent.

This reaction is called the *centrifugal force;* in the foregoing illustrations the force that the stone exerts on the cord, or that the locomotive exerts on the rail, or that the earth exerts on the sun, are examples of centrifugal force. The centripetal and centrifugal forces are equal and opposite, as is always true for action and reaction, but can never balance each other, because they never act upon the same body. In the study of circular motion, the centrifugal force is of little interest because it does not act on the body moving in the circle; *the centripetal force is important as the only force acting on the moving body.*

In problems dealing with motion in a circle at constant speed, the forces acting on the moving object are analyzed and represented by vectors as usual. Since the object is known to be accelerating toward the center of the circle, the resultant of all the forces acting upon it must lie in the plane of the circle and be directed along the radius toward the center. *This resultant is the centripetal force*, and its magnitude is given by either Eq. 33 or Eq. 34. With this knowledge, the force diagram can be completed and the desired information obtained. If the speed of the object along the curve is not constant, then the object has a tangential acceleration in addition to its centripetal acceleration, and the force necessary to produce this tangential acceleration is treated separately.

Illustrative Problems

I. A charged particle moving horizontally in a vertical magnetic field experiences a constant horizontal force that is always perpendicular to the direction of its motion. Describe the path of an electron moving in the manner described if its speed is 5×10^9 cm/sec and if the field exerts a force of 15×10^{-9} dynes upon it.

The electron moves in a circle, the centripetal force for this motion being provided by the field. The radius of the circle is found from Eq. 33, $F = m\dfrac{v^2}{r}$, where m is the mass of the electron, which may be taken as 9.11×10^{-28} gm. Therefore, the radius of the circle is

$$r = \frac{mv^2}{F} = \frac{(9.11 \times 10^{-28} \text{ gm})(5 \times 10^9 \text{ cm/sec})^2}{15 \times 10^{-9} \text{ dyne}} = 1.518 \text{ cm}$$

II. A highway on flat, level country has a curve of 800-ft radius. At what angle from the horizontal should this curve be banked in order that a car moving at 60 mi/hr (88 ft/sec) can round the curve without depending upon friction?

The car in part I of Fig. 50 is indicated at O in part II. Two forces only act upon it: the downward pull W of the earth and the outward push P of the road, and this push P is at right

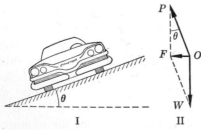

FIG. 50. Forces on a car rounding a banked highway curve

$$a = \frac{v^2}{R}$$

angles to the road if friction is assumed absent. The car moves around a horizontal circle, and therefore the resultant force F acting upon it is the centripetal force, directed horizontally toward the center of this circle. Hence the forces W and P are so proportioned that their resultant F is horizontal. Since the two angles marked θ are equal, it follows that

$$\tan \theta = \frac{F}{W} = \frac{\dfrac{Wv^2}{gr}}{W} = \frac{v^2}{gr} = \frac{\left(88 \dfrac{\text{ft}}{\text{sec}}\right)^2}{\left(32 \dfrac{\text{ft}}{\text{sec}^2}\right)(800 \text{ ft})} = 0.303$$

whence the correct banking angle is $\theta = \tan^{-1} 0.313 = 16.8°$.

III. A ball weighing $\frac{1}{4}$ lb is whirled in a vertical circle at the end of a cord 2 ft long. Compute the tension in the cord (*a*) as the ball passes through the lowest point of the circle with a speed of 20 ft/sec, and (*b*) as it passes through the highest point of the circle with a speed of 12 ft/sec.

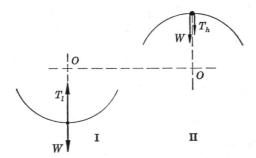

Fig. 51. Forces on a ball moving in vertical circle

At either of these points, two forces only act upon the ball: the downward pull W of the earth and the tension T in the cord. At the lowest point, these forces are opposite in direction, as shown in part I of Fig. 51, and T is larger than W, since the ball is accelerating toward the center of the circle at O. Hence the centripetal force at this point is $T_l - W = \dfrac{Wv_l^2}{gr}$, where $v_l = 20$ ft/sec. From this equation, the tension is $T_l = 1.813$ lb.

When the ball is at the highest point, T and W both act downward, as shown in part II of the figure, and the centripetal force is $T_h + W = \dfrac{Wv_h^2}{gr}$, where $v_h = 12$ ft/sec. The resulting tension in the cord is $T_h = 0.313$ lb.

The rotation of the earth about its axis causes the apparent weight of an object to be less than its actual weight. A body resting on a platform scale at the equator, at the point marked 1 in Fig. 52, is acted upon by two forces, the attractive force W of the earth, which is the true weight, and the outward push P of the scale, which shows the apparent weight.

The resultant force, $W - P$, acts toward the center of the earth and is the centripetal force $\dfrac{Wv^2}{gr}$, where v is the speed of the earth's surface at this point about the axis, and r is the radius of the earth. At places away from the equator, as at point 2 in the figure, the forces W and P are not directly opposed, since their resultant F must act in the plane of the circular motion

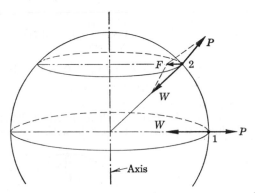

FIG. 52.   Effect of earth's rotation on apparent weight

as shown; at such places the true weight of the object acts toward the center of the earth, but its apparent weight does not.

47. Earth Satellites.   One of the most spectacular scientific projects of our time is the launching of several artificial earth satellites during the International Geophysical Year 1957–58, for the purpose of learning more about the earth and its atmosphere.   Such satellites will be filled with a variety of instruments and the information gathered by them will be automatically transmitted by radio to stations on the ground.   Some of the basic principles involved in satellite motion follow:

A satellite moving at constant speed in a circular orbit around the earth is acted upon by only one force, namely, its weight.   This force is directed toward the center of the earth and is the centripetal force that is necessary for circular motion.   Thus the basic expression for the motion of the satellite is

$$mg = m\,\frac{v^2}{r}$$

where m is the mass of the satellite, r the radius of its orbit from the center of the earth, g the acceleration due to gravity at the orbit, and v the speed of the satellite.   Hence,

$$v = \sqrt{rg}$$

showing that the radius of the orbit determines the speed of the satellite in its path.

Scientists have figured that a height of 300 mi above the surface of the earth is desirable, because at that elevation the satellite could be observed in clear weather and the atmosphere there would be of such low density that friction would not impede its motion too much, and the satellite could stay aloft for months. At low elevations, where the atmosphere is dense, the energy expended in friction would heat the satellite to incandescence and cause it to vaporize.

At an assumed elevation of 300 mi, taken as constant, this value added to 3960 mi, the earth's radius, would give the orbital radius r of the satellite as 4260 mi, which is equivalent to 2.25×10^7 ft, or 6.85×10^8 cm. Reference to § 33 shows that the acceleration g due to gravity at this distance from the center of the earth is GM/r^2, where G is the gravitational constant, namely, $6.67 \times 10^{-8} \dfrac{\text{dyne} \cdot \text{cm}^2}{\text{gm}^2}$, and M is the mass of the earth, which is 5.98×10^{27} gm. From these values, g is found to be 850 cm/sec^2, or 27.9 ft/sec^2. Hence the speed of the satellite in its orbit would be

$$v = \sqrt{rg} = \sqrt{(2.25 \times 10^7 \text{ ft})(27.9 \text{ ft/sec}^2)} = 25{,}100 \text{ ft/sec}$$

or about 17,000 mi/hr. The corresponding time for one traversal of the orbit is 1.563 hr, or about 94 min.

In launching, the satellite is projected, raised to the desired height, and given the necessary speed by using a three-stage rocket, the first to push the satellite through the stratosphere, the second to carry it up into the ionosphere, and the third to accelerate it in its orbit, each rocket falling away when its function is completed. The amount of energy available for launching puts a limit to the mass that the satellite may have. Once the orbit is established, its plane remains fixed, but, while the satellite goes around its orbit once, the earth beneath it makes approximately $\frac{1}{16}$ of a rotation about its axis. Thus the satellite travels over a different area of the earth in each transit.

Actually the orbit is not the ideal circle as described, but instead forms an ellipse, chiefly due to variations from the correct speed and direction of launching. Such an orbit shortens the life of a satellite, because in each transit it encounters a stretch of denser air near the earth and loses some energy through friction.

The earliest satellites were launched in the Soviet Union during the latter months of 1957, their reported masses are 184 lb for the first and 1120 lb for the second. One of the satellites built in the United States is a sphere of 20-in. diameter with a mass of 20 lb; its kinetic energy when traveling at 17,000 mi/hr is comparable with that of a 200-ton locomotive traveling at 120 mi/hr.

The satellites will be instrumented to give continuous data on cosmic rays, solar ultraviolet and x-rays, magnetic field strength, and meteoric dust. From the earth, the density of the upper atmosphere can be determined by plotting the decay of the satellite's orbit. The satellites will be visible with binoculars and, under favorable conditions, with the naked eye. The best time for observation should be at dawn and twilight, when the sun is below the horizon and illuminates the satellite against a dark background.

PROBLEMS

1. The standard baseball weighs 5 oz. Compute the momentum of the ball when thrown horizontally with a velocity of 100 ft/sec.

2. A bullet that weighs 0.4 oz is fired straight through a board 1 in. thick. It enters the board at 2000 ft/sec and emerges at 1200 ft/sec. Assume the deceleration constant, and compute (*a*) the time in which the bullet passes through the board and (*b*) the force exerted by the bullet on the board.

3. A sphere of 400-gm mass and one of 500-gm mass hang side by side in contact, each supported by a long cord. The smaller sphere is moved away in the plane of the cords; it is then released and strikes the larger sphere with a velocity of 135 cm/sec. If provision is made to keep the spheres together after impact, what is their joint velocity?

4. From a multiple-exposure photograph of Bobby Jones driving a golf ball, measurements show that the velocity of the club before impact was 166 ft/sec and after impact 114 ft/sec. Take the head of the club to weigh 7.4 oz and the ball 1.62 oz; neglect the effect of the shaft of the club. What velocity was given to the ball?

5. In a test to determine the velocity of a bullet, a wood block of 10-kg mass is projected along a level surface with a velocity of 100 cm/sec and the bullet is fired horizontally into it at right angles to its motion. The bullet has a mass of 15 gm and remains embedded within the block. Suppose the block to be deflected through an angle of 40° and determine the initial velocity of the bullet.

6. Sphere *A* of 200-gm mass moving at 1000 cm/sec on a level surface strikes sphere *B* of equal mass that is initially at rest. After the collision, sphere *A* is deflected toward the left of its original direction by an angle of 36.9° and its speed is reduced to 700 cm/sec. Determine the velocity of sphere *B* just after impact, in both magnitude and direction.

7. Modern theory shows that the mass of a moving body is not the same at all speeds but varies in accordance with the expression $m = m_o \div \sqrt{1 - v^2/c^2}$, where m_o is its mass at rest, m its mass at speed v, and c is the speed of light, 186,000 mi/sec. To show that this effect is unimportant except at very high speeds, determine the speed at which the mass of a body would increase by 1%.

8. A block is projected with an initial velocity of 300 cm/sec down a plane inclined at 20° with the horizontal. If the coefficient of friction between the sliding surfaces is 0.5, how far does the block slide before it stops?

9. A box thrown along a level surface slides a distance of 16 ft in 2 sec in coming to rest. (*a*) With what velocity was the box thrown? (*b*) Show a diagram of the forces acting upon the box while it is sliding to rest. (*c*) Compute the coefficient of friction between the box and the surface.

$N = W = mg$

10. A box weighing 40 lb is dragged up a plane inclined at 30° with the horizontal, by a constant pull of 30 lb parallel to the plane. The coefficient of friction between the box and the plane is 0.25. (*a*) What is the acceleration of the box? (*b*) If the box starts from rest, what is its velocity after it has been moved 10 ft? (*c*) If the pull is then discontinued and the box allowed to come to a stop, will it remain at rest or slide back? Why?

11. It is found that a block of 5000-gm mass slides at constant speed down a plane inclined at 25° with the horizontal. What force parallel to the plane is needed to push the block at constant speed up the plane?

12. A block weighing 24 lb is drawn along a level table top by means of a horizontal cord which passes over a frictionless pulley and thence hangs downward, as shown in the diagram. The coefficient of friction between the block and table top is 0.25. What is the acceleration of the block (*a*) if a body weighing 8 lb is attached to the end of the cord? (*b*) if, instead, a downward force of 8 lb is applied to the end of the cord?

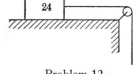

Problem 12

13. A thin stick of negligible weight is pivoted at one end so that it can move in a vertical plane. A mass of 900 gm is attached to the stick at a point 60 cm from the pivot, and the weighted stick is held horizontal by a force applied at a point 100 cm from the pivot. What is the magnitude of this force (*a*) if it is directed vertically upward? (*b*) if it is directed at an angle of 30° with the vertical?

14. The "wheel and axle" shown in the diagram consists of two pulleys clamped together and mounted on a fixed horizontal shaft at the center. One pulley has a radius of 4 in. and the other has a radius of 9 in. A rope attached to the small pulley supports a 60-lb load at its lower end. What force should be applied to the rope attached to the large pulley in order to raise the load at constant velocity? Friction may be neglected.

Problem 14

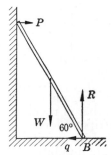

Problem 15

15. The diagram represents a uniform ladder 20 ft long, resting against a smooth wall and making an angle of 60° with the ground. Four forces act upon the ladder. Two of these are vertical: the weight W of the ladder acting at the midpoint and the reaction R of the ground at the base; the other two are horizontal: the force of friction f at the ground and the outward push P of the wall. Take W and R as 40 lb each, and f and P as 11.55 lb each. Give the moment of each of the forces W, R, f, and P, about an axis through B, the base of the ladder, and perpendicular to the plane of the paper.

16. Determine the location of the center of mass of the earth-moon system. Pertinent data appear in § 33 and in Probs. 11 and 12 of Chap. 4.

17. An automobile has a wheel base of 10 ft and weighs 3200 lb; its center of mass is midway between the wheels and 2 ft above the ground. The

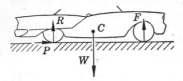

diagram shows the forces acting upon the automobile while it is accelerating along a straight level road, friction being neglected. W represents the weight of the car, acting downward at its center of gravity, F is the combined upward reaction of the ground at the two front tires, R is similarly the reaction at the rear tires, and P is the forward push

Problem 17

of the roadbed. When the acceleration is 4 ft/sec², what are the values of P, F, and R?

18. The bookcase in the diagram has dimensions as shown; it weighs 160 lb and has four short legs, and its center of mass C is at its geometric center. The bookcase is being moved along a level floor by a constant horizontal push $P = 70$ lb applied at a point 1 ft above the floor. Assume the coefficient of friction between the bookcase and floor to be 0.4, and compute (*a*) the acceleration of the bookcase and (*b*) the force with which each of the front legs F and each of the rear legs R presses against the floor.

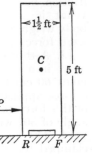

Problem 18

19. In the diagram, AB represents a uniform platform 12 ft long, which weighs 140 lb and carries a 500-lb load centered 3 ft from A; the platform is supported by two vertical ropes, one at each end. Suppose the two ropes to be paid out with equal speeds by a windlass, lowering the loaded platform for a short distance with an acceleration of 2 ft/sec², and compute the tension in each rope.

Problem 19

20. In a hydrogen atom, the electron may be regarded as revolving at constant speed about the nucleus in a circular orbit having a radius of 5 × 10⁻⁹ cm, the centripetal force being provided by a constant attraction of 9.2 × 10⁻³ dynes exerted by the nucleus. Take the mass of the electron as 9.11 × 10⁻²⁸ gm, and determine (*a*) the speed of the electron in its orbit and (*b*) the number of revolutions it makes per second.

21. The centripetal force acting upon the moon as it revolves about the earth is provided by gravitational attraction. Assume the moon's orbit to be a circle having a radius of 240,000 mi, and compute (*a*) the speed of the moon in its orbit and (*b*) the time in days during which it moves once around its orbit. For numerical constants, see § 33.

22. One of Kepler's laws of planetary motion states that the squares of the periodic times of the planets are proportional to the cubes of their mean distances from the sun. Derive this law on the assumption that the planets move in circular orbits around the sun and on the fact that the centripetal force acting on a planet is the gravitational attraction of the sun, Eq. 21.

23. A ball fastened to the end of a cord 30 cm long is whirled around in a horizontal circle, the cord describing the surface of a cone. If the ball completes a revolution every second, what angle does the cord make with the vertical?

24. A 3.8-mi test track of the General Motors Corporation at its proving ground in Michigan is five lanes wide; the upper lane at the sharpest turns has a radius of 661 ft and a slope of 77% (that is, a vertical rise of 0.77 ft for each foot of horizontal width). At what speed in miles per hour can an automobile round such a curve with its wheels pressing perpendicularly against the roadbed?

25. A ball that weighs 1 lb is whirled around in a vertical circle at the end of a cord 2 ft long. What is the tension in the cord as the ball passes through the lowest point of its circular path if its speed is 20 ft/sec at that point?

6

ROTATIONAL MOTION

48. Uniform Angular Motion. In previous chapters mention has been made of rotation as a type of motion distinct from translation; such rotational motion takes place about an axis, usually the axis of symmetry. Motion of this type is easily recognized and takes place in such objects as a turning wheel or pulley, a spinning chuck in a lathe, or a train of rotating gears. Details of rotational motion will now be developed.

The motion of a rotating body is often studied by referring to a radius extending from the axis to any point on the body. As the body rotates, this radius turns through an angle; thus in 1 rev the displacement is 360° or 2π radians. For this reason, rotation is also called *angular motion*. Many properties of angular motion can be visualized by analogy with linear motion.

If the body is rotating uniformly, it is displaced by equal angles during each unit of time. For example, if a flywheel in uniform angular motion revolves 40 times in one minute, it revolves 40 times in the next minute, and so on. Uniform angular motion is defined as motion about a fixed axis in which the rotating body undergoes equal angular displacements in equal intervals of time, however short. The rotation of the earth and of the hands of an electric clock are familiar examples of uniform angular motion.

The *angular velocity* of a body in uniform angular motion is defined as *the angle by which the body is displaced divided by the time in which this displacement occurs*, that is

$$\text{Angular velocity} = \frac{\text{angular displacement}}{\text{time interval}}$$

or

$$\omega = \frac{\theta}{t} \tag{35}$$

where ω (omega) is the angular velocity, θ the angular displacement, and t the time in which the displacement occurs. For uniform angular motion, the ratio of θ to t is constant and the rotating body has a constant angular velocity.

Angular velocity is commonly expressed in revolutions per minute (rev/min), a unit often used by engineers, and radians per second (radians /sec), which is simpler for scientific work. Since 1 rev = 2π radians, it follows that 1 rev/min = 2π /60 radians/sec.

The distinction between velocity and speed, which was pointed out for linear motion in § 19, applies also to angular motion. The *angular speed* of a body that is rotating at a steady rate about a given axis is defined as the *angle swept through divided by the elapsed time*, that is,

$$\text{Angular speed} = \frac{\text{angle swept through}}{\text{time interval}}$$

Angular speed is expressed in equation form by Eq. 35, with θ interpreted as the angle swept through, and has the same units as angular velocity. For a body in uniform angular motion, the angle swept through is identical with the angular displacement, and the angular speed and angular velocity have the same numerical value.

Illustrative Problem

Find the number of revolutions a wheel makes in 3 min if it is turning at a constant speed of 50 radians/sec.

From Eq. 35, the angle swept through is

$$\theta = \omega t = \left(\frac{50 \text{ radians}}{\text{sec}}\right)(3 \text{ min})\left(\frac{60 \text{ sec}}{1 \text{ min}}\right)\left(\frac{1 \text{ rev}}{2\pi \text{ radians}}\right) = 1432 \text{ rev}$$

Angular speed is a scalar quantity and is not affected by a change in the direction of the axis. Angular velocity is a vector quantity and undergoes a change if there is a change in the direction of the axis of rotation. The distinction between the two is of importance in gyroscopic action, which will be discussed in § 59.

49. Angular and Tangential Velocities Compared. As a body rotates about a fixed axis, the different points on the body describe concentric circles about that axis. Hence, while the body as a whole has angular motion, the individual points on it have curvilinear motion. These motions will be compared by reference to a wheel such as shown in Fig. 53. If the wheel, in uniform rotation, is displaced about its axis by an angle θ radians in t sec, its angular velocity, clockwise in this instance, is $\omega = \theta/t$ radians/sec. In the same time interval, a point P at a distance r cm from the axis moves over an arc of length $s = \theta r$ cm. Consequently, the speed of this point in its circular path is $v = s/t$ or $\theta r/t$ cm/sec; its velocity has the same magnitude, $v = \theta r/t$, and is directed along a tangent to the circle, as shown. A comparison of the angular velocity of the wheel, $\omega = \theta/t$, and the tangential velocity of the point considered, $v = \theta r/t$, shows that

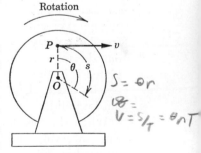

FIG. 53. Comparing angular and tangential velocities

$$v = r\omega \tag{36}$$

$v = R$ *in* ω

which states that *the tangential velocity of any point on a rotating body is equal to the product of the radius extending to that point and the angular velocity of the body in radian measure.*

In this equation, the angular velocity ω is expressed in *radians per unit time*, and the length unit used in expressing the tangential velocity v is the same as that used for r. With ω in radians per second, if r is expressed in centimeters, then v is given in centimeters per second; if r is expressed in feet, then v is given in feet per second. An angle in radians is a ratio of one length to another and can always be replaced by "cm/cm" or "ft/ft" in balancing units.

Where direction is not important, Eq. 36 may be applied to speeds, by taking ω as the angular speed of the rotating body and v as the curvilinear speed of some point on it.

Illustrative Problem

As an example, determine the maximum allowable speed of a cast-iron flywheel having a radius of 10 ft, assuming that the speed of the rim is not to exceed 6000 ft/min.

From Eq. 36,

$$\omega = \frac{v}{r} = \left(\frac{6000 \frac{ft}{min}}{10 \; ft} \right) \left(\frac{1 \; rev}{2\pi \; radians} \right) = 95.5 \; rev/min$$

50. Accelerated Angular Motion. The principles of acceleration, as developed in Chap. 3 for linear motion, apply also to rotational, or angular, motion. Thus, angular acceleration is always associated with a change in angular velocity. Such a change may be due either to a change in the speed of rotation of a body or a change in the direction of its axis. Throughout the present chapter, except in §§ 59 and 60, the only change contemplated is in the speed of rotation, and the direction of the axis is assumed to remain fixed. Unless this condition is satisfied, the conclusions drawn may not be valid.

When the angular velocity of a rotating body changes from ω_o to ω_f in a time interval t, then its average angular acceleration α (alpha) over this interval is

$$\alpha_{av} = \frac{\omega_f - \omega_o}{t} \tag{37}$$

and if the change of angular velocity takes place at a uniform rate, then the angular acceleration is constant at this value. By analogy with Eq. 11, the instantaneous angular acceleration is expressed as

$$\alpha = \frac{d\omega}{dt}$$

where $d\omega$ is the infinitesimal change of angular velocity occurring in the infinitesimal time interval dt. Hence *the angular acceleration of a body is defined as the time rate of change of its angular velocity.*

From the similarity between angular and linear motion, the equations for angular motion *with constant acceleration* are analogous to those of § 23 and can be written as follows:

$$\omega_f = \omega_o + \alpha t \tag{38}$$

$$\theta = \frac{\omega_o + \omega_f}{2} t \tag{39}$$

$$\theta = \omega_o t + \tfrac{1}{2}\alpha t^2 \tag{40}$$

$$\omega_f{}^2 = \omega_o{}^2 + 2\alpha\theta \tag{41}$$

Herein θ is the angular displacement in the time t, α is the angular acceleration, ω_o the initial angular velocity, and ω_f the final angular velocity.

Illustrative Problem

Suppose that a pulley is accelerated from a state of rest to a speed of 1200 rev/min in 20 sec. Compute the angular acceleration of the pulley (assumed constant) and the number of revolutions that it turns through during this interval.

The angular acceleration is obtained from Eq. 38, $\alpha = \dfrac{\omega_f - \omega_o}{t}$, where $\omega_f = 1200 \dfrac{\text{rev}}{\text{min}}$, $\omega_o = 0$, and $t = 20$ sec. Hence, the angular acceleration is

$$\alpha = \frac{(1200 - 0)\,\dfrac{\text{rev}}{\text{min}}}{20 \text{ sec}} = \frac{60\,\dfrac{\text{rev}}{\text{min}}}{\text{sec}} = 1\,\frac{\text{rev}}{\text{sec}^2}$$

The angular displacement is then found from Eq. 40 with $\omega_o = 0$; thus,

$$0 = \frac{1}{2}\,\alpha t^2 = \frac{1}{2}\left(1\,\frac{\text{rev}}{\text{sec}^2}\right)(20 \text{ sec})^2 = 200 \text{ rev}$$

When a body has angular acceleration, any point upon it has a corresponding acceleration along a tangent to its circular path. The angular acceleration of the body can be expressed as $\alpha = \dfrac{\omega_f - \omega_o}{t}$, and the tangential acceleration of the point as $a = \dfrac{v_f - v_o}{t}$, in accordance with Eqs. 38 and 12. The relation between these quantities can be found by applying the expression $v = r\omega$ as given in Eq. 36, in which r is the distance from the axis of rotation to the point in question. It follows that

$$a = \frac{\omega_f r - \omega_o r}{t} = r \left(\frac{\omega_f - \omega_o}{t} \right)$$

or

$$a = r\alpha \tag{42}$$

which states that the *tangential acceleration of any point on a rotating body is equal to the product of the radius extending to that point and the angular acceleration of the body in radian measure.*

When motion along a line is compared with motion about an axis, an interesting generalization appears from an examination of Eq. 1, $s = r\theta$; Eq. 36, $v = r\omega$; and Eq. 42, $a = r\alpha$. In all three, the quantity measured along a line, whether distance, velocity, or acceleration, is equal to the radius multiplied by the corresponding angular quantity.

51. Relation of Torque to Angular Acceleration. Consideration will now be given to what is called the dynamics of rotation: the means by which angular acceleration is brought about, and the factors that determine its amount. It will be shown that the angular acceleration imparted to a body depends upon the torque acting, and upon the distribution of the mass of the body about its axis of rotation. Here, again, the analogy between angular and linear motion will become apparent as the study proceeds. Attention is first directed to a single particle constrained to move in a circular path.

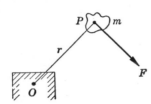

FIG. 54. Torque producing angular acceleration about axis O

In Fig. 54, a particle of mass m is attached to the end P of a crank that is pivoted on a fixed axis at O, and a steady force F is applied to the mass in a direction always at right angles to the crank OP, itself assumed as weightless. Then as the particle moves, the crank pulls it toward the center and makes it travel in a circular path, and at the same time the tangential force F causes it to move along the circle with increasing speed, giving it a tangential acceleration a such that

$$F = ma$$

In the meantime the crank has an increasing angular velocity, and if the crank has a length r, its angular acceleration can be expressed as

$$\alpha = \frac{a}{r}$$

in accordance with Eq. 42. The force F acting on the particle produces a torque about the axis O which amounts to

$$T = Fr$$

by Eq. 29. From the three foregoing equations, the torque can be expressed as

$$T = Fr = ma \times r = mr^2\alpha$$

where the product mr^2 is a constant for the particular combination of mass m and crank length r. The single letter I is used to designate this constant, whence the torque becomes

$$T = I\alpha \tag{43}$$

where T, I, and α are all measured or computed about the same fixed axis. This expression is similar to that expressing Newton's Second Law but applies to rotation instead of linear motion. The expression $T = I\alpha$ is the basic equation for rotation just as $F = ma$ is for linear motion; and the quantities T, I, and α play respectively the same roles in rotational motion as do F, m, and a in linear motion.

The constant I is called the *moment of inertia* of the particle; this "rotational" inertia depends both upon the mass moving and its distance from the center of rotation.

52. Moments of Inertia of Rigid Bodies. For a rigid body consisting of many particles, the moment of inertia depends not only upon the entire mass of that body but also upon the distribution of the many tiny masses of which it is composed. For example, the two wheels in Fig. 55 are solid disks composed in part of metal and in part of wood. Both wheels have the same radius and are so designed as to have the same mass. The wheel with the heavy rim is found to require a larger torque than the other to start it spinning, and hence it has the

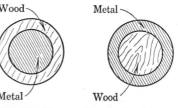

Fig. 55. Composite wheels of same size but having different moments of inertia

larger moment of inertia. The constant I for a rigid body is independent of the speed of the body and of the forces acting upon it.

In order to show how the distribution of mass about the axis of a body affects its moment of inertia, a rigid body will be considered as divided into a number of particles and subjected to a torque. This torque is transmitted from one particle to another through cohesion and thus is equivalent to a number of individual torques acting severally on the particles. First the torque on each particle and the acceleration that it produces will be investigated, and then the results will be collected for the entire body.

A body is shown in Fig. 56 pivoted at O, and several of its particles are indicated by

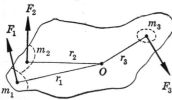

Fig. 56. Diagram used in determining the moment of inertia of a body

dotted lines. The masses of these particles are designated as m_1, m_2, m_3, $\cdots$, their radial distances from the axis as r_1, r_2, r_3, $\cdots$ respectively, and the forces acting perpendicularly to these distances as F_1, F_2, F_3, $\cdots$ respectively. The torque produced by F_1 acting on particle m_1 is given as in § 41 as

$$T_1 = F_1 r_1 = m_1 a_1 r_1 = m_1 r_1^2 \alpha$$

where α, the angular acceleration of the body, is the same for all of its particles and so does not need a subscript. Similarly, for the other particles, the torques are

$$T_2 = m_2 r_2^2 \alpha \qquad T_3 = m_3 r_3^2 \alpha$$

and therefore the resultant torque on the body is

$$T = m_1 r_1^2 \alpha + m_2 r_2^2 \alpha + m_3 r_3^2 \alpha + \cdots$$
$$= (m_1 r_1^2 + m_2 r_2^2 + m_3 r_3^2 + \cdots)\alpha = (\Sigma m r^2)\alpha$$

where the expression in parentheses contains a number of terms of the same type and is replaced by the symbolic form $\Sigma m r^2$. Here Σ represents a summation; consequently $\Sigma m r^2$ means the sum of a number of terms, each of which is a mass multiplied by the square of its distance from the axis of rotation. This result when compared to Eq. 43, $T = I\alpha$, shows that $\Sigma m r^2$ is the moment of inertia of the body. Consequently,

$$I = \Sigma m r^2 \qquad\qquad (44)$$

or in words, *the moment of inertia of a body about a given axis is the sum of a number of terms, each representing the mass of a particle multiplied by the square of its distance from the axis, the summation including all the particles of the body.*

The moment of inertia of a single particle of mass m located a distance r from the axis of rotation is simply $m r^2$, since there is but one particle and no need for summation as called for in Eq. 44. In a thin ring the mass is distributed all around the axis, but the various particles are equally distant from the axis; thus r is constant and the moment of inertia becomes $r^2 \Sigma m = M r^2$, where M represents the total mass of the ring. These values follow directly from the definition of moment of inertia, but for most geometric shapes the application of the expression $I = \Sigma m r^2$ requires the methods of calculus, because the correct result is obtained only where the body is considered to be made up of a vast number of particles.

The units for moment of inertia follow from its definition, Eq. 44. Moment of inertia is always the product of a mass and the square of a distance; in metric (cgs) units it is expressed in gram·centimeters², and in British gravitational units it is expressed in slug·feet².

53. Computing the Moment of Inertia of a Stick. The moment of inertia of an object can often be approximated without calculus by considering the object divided into relatively few particles, determining the moment of inertia of each, and adding the results. The procedure will be applied to a uniform slim stick with a transverse axis through one end.

The stick, of mass M and length l, is divided into two equal particles as a first approximation; these are centered at C_1 and C_2, as shown in part I of Fig. 57. Here $m_1 = m_2 = \dfrac{M}{2}$, $r_1 = \dfrac{l}{4}$, and $r_2 = \dfrac{3l}{4}$. Hence the moment of inertia of the stick becomes

$$I = m_1 r_1{}^2 + m_2 r_2{}^2 = \frac{M}{2}\left(\frac{l}{4}\right)^2 + \frac{M}{2}\left(\frac{3l}{4}\right)^2 = \frac{10}{32}Ml^2 = 0.313 Ml^2$$

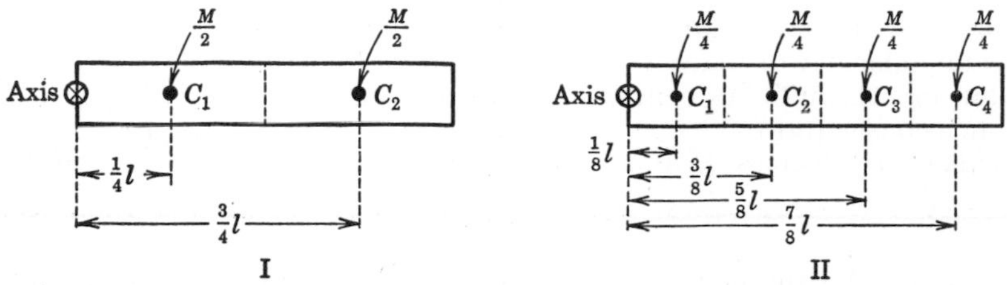

FIG. 57. How moments of inertia are approximated

As a second approximation, the stick is divided into four equal particles located at C_1 to C_4 in part II of the figure. Here

$$m_1 = m_2 = m_3 = m_4 = \frac{M}{4} \qquad r_1 = \frac{l}{8} \cdots \qquad r_4 = \frac{7l}{8}$$

and the moment of inertia becomes

$$I = \frac{M}{4}\left(\frac{l}{8}\right)^2 + \frac{M}{4}\left(\frac{3l}{8}\right)^2 + \frac{M}{4}\left(\frac{5l}{8}\right)^2 + \frac{M}{4}\left(\frac{7l}{8}\right)^2 = \frac{21}{64}Ml^2 = 0.328 Ml^2$$

If this process of subdivision is continued until the stick is divided into an infinitely large number of particles, a summation by calculus gives the moment of inertia of the stick correctly as

$$I = \tfrac{1}{3}Ml^2 \quad OF \quad STICK$$

Incidentally, the second approximation, in which the stick is divided into quarters, gives the result to within 2% of the correct value.

54. Moments of Inertia of Some Shapes. The values of the moments of inertia for objects of various geometric shapes are not derived in this textbook, but several are given in the accompanying table. These will be helpful in applying the principles of rotational motion to objects having the shapes indicated.

MOMENTS OF INERTIA

Shape	I
Slim rod of mass M and length l, about a transverse axis through one end..................................	$\frac{1}{3}Ml^2$
Same, but transverse axis is through center...........	$\frac{1}{12}Ml^2$
Hollow cylinder (thin wall) of mass M, radius r, and of any axial length, about its geometric axis............	Mr^2
Solid cylinder or disk of mass M, radius r, and of any axial length, about its geometric axis...............	$\frac{1}{2}Mr^2$
Solid disk of mass M and radius r about any diameter..	$\frac{1}{4}Mr^2$
Rectangular bar of mass M, length l, and width b, about an axis through its center and at right angles to dimensions b and l...................................	$\frac{M}{12}(b^2 + l^2)$
Solid sphere of mass M and radius r about any diameter	$\frac{2}{5}Mr^2$

Sometimes the moment of inertia of a body about a particular axis is known and it is desired to find its moment of inertia about another axis parallel to the first. This can be done in a simple manner when one of the axes passes through the center of mass of the body. Analysis shows that if the moment of inertia of a body of mass M about an axis *through its center of mass* is I_C, then the moment of inertia about a parallel axis distant h from the first is

$$I = I_C + Mh^2 \qquad (45)$$

Illustrative Problems

I. A solid cylinder rolls on a flat surface; find the moment of inertia of the cylinder about its line of contact with the surface.

The moment of inertia of the cylinder about its geometric axis is $I_C = \frac{1}{2}Mr^2$ from the foregoing table, and the distance between the axes is $h = r$. Therefore the moment of inertia of the cylinder about the contacting line on its cylindrical surface is $I = I_C + Mh^2 = \frac{1}{2}Mr^2 + Mr^2 = \frac{3}{2}Mr^2$.

II. Find the moment of inertia of a slim rod of mass M and length l about a transverse axis midway between one end of the rod and the center. Assume that the only value known for the moment of inertia of a slim rod is that about a transverse axis through one end, that is, $I = \frac{1}{3}Ml^2$.

First find the moment of inertia about the center of mass, namely, I_C, by using Eq. 45 with $h = \frac{1}{2}l$, thus: $\frac{1}{3}Ml^2 = I_C + \frac{1}{4}Ml^2$, whence $I_C = \frac{1}{12}Ml^2$.

Then, with I_C known, the value of I for the rod about an axis midway between one end and the center is given by the same equation, taking $h = \frac{1}{4}l$, thus: $I = I_C + Mh^2 = \frac{1}{12}Ml^2 + \frac{1}{16}Ml^2 = \frac{7}{48}Ml^2$.

55. Radius of Gyration. The moment of inertia of a body embodies the masses of the particles that make up the body and the squares of the individual radii that extend from these particles to the axis. Moment of inertia is often expressed quite differently, however, in terms of the total mass of the object and a single length called the radius of gyration.

The *radius of gyration* of a body is defined as the *distance from the axis of rotation to a point at which the entire mass of the body could be considered as concentrated without altering the moment of inertia.* A rotating object of any shape can be imagined to have its entire mass concentrated into a single particle that is so located with reference to the axis of rotation that the particle has the same moment of inertia as the object itself. If K is the radius extending from the axis to the particle, then K is also the radius of gyration of the body about the same axis; hence, the moment of inertia of the body of mass M is

$$I = MK^2 \qquad \text{Rof Gyration} \qquad (46)$$

Illustrative Problem

Find the radius of gyration of a meter stick about an axis through one end perpendicular to the stick.

The moment of inertia of the stick about an axis through one end is given in the table of the preceding section as $I = \frac{1}{3}Ml^2$. From Eq. 46 it follows that

$$\tfrac{1}{3}Ml^2 = MK^2$$

whence the radius of gyration of the stick of length 100 cm about a transverse axis through one end is

$$K = \frac{l}{\sqrt{3}} = \frac{100 \text{ cm}}{1.732} = 57.7 \text{ cm}$$

Radius of gyration should be thought of as a convenient means of computing moment of inertia. Manufacturers of rotating machinery, such as engines, turbines, and generators, indicate the radii of gyration of the rotating parts so that the users can readily compute the moment of inertia of these odd-shaped elements.

56. Application of Principles. The relationship between angular motion, torque, moment of inertia, and radius of gyration will be best understood by considering several numerical examples.

Illustrative Problems

I. A cylindrical grindstone 24 in. in diameter weighs 96 lb; it is turned by a handle fastened to a crank at a distance of 10 in. from the center of the grindstone, as shown in Fig. 58. What steady force applied perpendicularly to the end of the crank will bring the stone from rest to a speed of 90 rev/min in 10 sec, if friction is neglected?

FIG. 58. Action of torque on a grindstone

The grindstone has a mass $M = \frac{96}{32} = 3$ slugs and a radius $r = 1$ ft. Since it is a solid cylinder rotating about its geometric axis, its moment of inertia is $I = \frac{1}{2}Mr^2 = \frac{1}{2}(3 \text{ slugs})(1 \text{ ft})^2 = \frac{3}{2} \text{ slug} \cdot \text{ft}^2$. Its final angular speed is $\omega_f =$

$$90 \; \frac{\text{rev}}{\text{min}} = \frac{90 \text{ rev}}{60 \text{ sec}} = 3\pi \; \frac{\text{radians}}{\text{sec}} \; , \text{ and is to be attained in a time } t = 10 \text{ sec,}$$

starting from rest. Therefore its angular acceleration, from Eq. 38, is

$$\alpha = \frac{\omega_f - \omega_o}{t} = \frac{3\pi \; \dfrac{\text{radians}}{\text{sec}}}{10 \text{ sec}} = \frac{3\pi}{10} \text{ radians/sec}^2$$

The torque needed to produce this angular acceleration, from Eq. 43, is

$$T = I\alpha = \left(\frac{3}{2} \text{ slug} \cdot \text{ft}^2 \right) \left(\frac{3\pi}{10} \frac{\text{radians}}{\text{sec}^2} \right) = \frac{9\pi}{20} \text{ lb} \cdot \text{ft}$$

Consequently the force needed at the end of the crank of length $l = \frac{10}{12}$ ft, as given by Eq. 29, is

$$F = \frac{T}{l} = \frac{\dfrac{9\pi}{20} \text{ lb} \cdot \text{ft}}{\frac{10}{12} \text{ ft}} = 1.697 \text{ lb}$$

II. A wheel of mass 2×10^4 gm and radius 15 cm, which is turning at 150 rev/min in stationary bearings, is brought to rest by pressing a brake shoe radially against its rim with a force of 10^6 dynes. If the radius of gyration of the wheel is 10 cm, and if the coefficient of friction between the shoe and the rim is constant at 0.2, how many revolutions does the wheel make in coming to rest?

The normal force applied to the brake shoe does not of itself produce any torque upon the wheel, but it causes a force of friction to act tangentially upon the rim of the wheel, and this force sets up the retarding torque that stops the wheel. If the direction of rotation is taken as positive, the retarding force of friction, from Eq. 28, is $f = \mu N = -0.2 \times 10^6$ dynes, and the torque due to this force, from Eq. 29, is $T = Fr$, where r is the radius of the wheel. Thus, the torque is $T = (-0.2 \times 10^6 \text{ dynes})(15 \text{ cm}) = -3 \times 10^6$ dyne·cm.

Next, the moment of inertia of the wheel is computed from the mass M and the radius of gyration K by Eq. 46; its value is

$$I = MK^2 = (2 \times 10^4 \text{ gm})(10 \text{ cm})^2 = 2 \times 10^6 \text{ gm} \cdot \text{cm}^2$$

With the torque T and the moment of inertia I known, Eq. 43 gives the angular acceleration of the wheel as

$$\alpha = \frac{T}{I} = \frac{-3 \times 10^6 \text{ dyne} \cdot \text{cm}}{2 \times 10^6 \text{ gm} \cdot \text{cm}^2} = -1.5 \; \frac{\text{radians}}{\text{sec}^2}$$

To find the angle that the wheel turns through in stopping, use Eq. 41, $\omega_f{}^2 = \omega_o{}^2 + 2\alpha\theta$, in which $\omega_f = 0$, $\omega_o = 150 \; \dfrac{\text{rev}}{\text{min}} = \dfrac{150 \text{ rev}}{60 \text{ sec}} = 5\pi \; \dfrac{\text{radians}}{\text{sec}}$, and $\alpha = -1.5 \; \dfrac{\text{radians}}{\text{sec}^2}$. Thus,

$$\theta = \frac{\omega_f{}^2 - \omega_o{}^2}{2\alpha} = \frac{0 - \left(5\pi\,\dfrac{\text{radians}}{\text{sec}}\right)^2}{2\left(-1.5\,\dfrac{\text{radians}}{\text{sec}}\right)} = \frac{25\pi^2}{3}\,\text{radians}$$

this is equivalent to

$$\frac{25\pi^2}{3}\,\text{radians} \times \frac{1\ \text{rev}}{2\pi\ \text{radians}} = \frac{25\pi}{6}\,\text{rev} = 13.09\ \text{rev}$$

III. A pulley 16 cm in diameter is mounted on a horizontal shaft in frictionless bearings and, around its rim, is wound a light cord to which a 100-gm mass is attached. When released, the mass is observed to descend 40 cm in the first second, without slippage of the cord. Compute the moment of inertia of the pulley.

Before the torque acting upon the pulley can be determined, the tension in the cord must be computed. To find this tension, isolate the 100-gm mass and treat it as a free body. In part I of Fig. 59, this mass is indicated

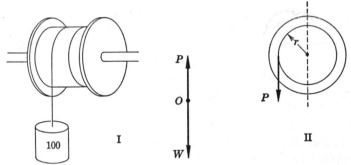

FIG. 59. Measuring moment of inertia. Part I shows forces on descending mass and Part II force that exerts torque on pulley

at O; the forces acting on it are its weight $W = 100 \times 980 = 98,000$ dynes downward and the upward pull P of the cord, as yet unknown. Since the mass accelerates downward, W is larger than P, and the difference between them, $W - P$, is the resultant force acting on the 100-gm mass. To find the acceleration of this mass, substitute the test data in Eq. 14, $s = v_o t + \frac{1}{2}at^2$, with $v_o = 0$; the acceleration is

$$a = \frac{2s}{t^2} = \frac{2 \times 40\ \text{cm}}{(1\ \text{sec})^2} = 80\,\frac{\text{cm}}{\text{sec}^2}$$

These values substituted in Eq. 20, $F = ma$, give: $98,000$ dynes $- P =$ $(100\ \text{gm})\left(80\,\dfrac{\text{cm}}{\text{sec}^2}\right) = 8000$ dynes; whence the tension in the cord is $P =$ $90,000$ dynes.

Next, find the torque on the pulley. If the pulley is isolated, as in part II of the figure, the torque acting on it, by Eq. 29, is clearly $T = Pr$, where P is the tension in the cord and r the radius of the pulley. Thus, $T = 90,000$ dynes $\times$ 8 cm $= 720,000$ dyne·cm. This torque gives the pulley an angular acceleration

$$\alpha = \frac{a}{r} = \frac{80 \dfrac{\text{cm}}{\text{sec}^2}}{8 \text{ cm}} = 10 \frac{\text{radians}}{\text{sec}^2}$$

Finally, Eq. 43 gives the moment of inertia of the pulley as

$$I = \frac{T}{\alpha} = \frac{720,000 \text{ dyne·cm}}{10 \dfrac{\text{radians}}{\text{sec}^2}} = 7.2 \times 10^4 \text{ gm·cm}^2$$

57. Vector Representation of Angular Quantities.

Angular quantities have direction as well as magnitude; also most of them can be added the way linear displacements are added and hence are vector quantities, § 16.

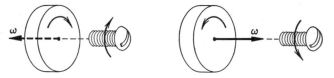

FIG. 60.　Vector representation of angular velocity

Thus, angular velocity, angular acceleration, and torque are all vector quantities. Angular displacement is an exception because vector methods cannot be applied to the addition of angular displacements unless these are infinitesimal, and so angular displacement does not conform to the definition of a vector quantity.

The manner in which an angular vector quantity is represented is illustrated for angular velocity in Fig. 60. The angular velocity of a wheel or other rotating body is represented by an arrow *directed along the axis* of rotation; the length of the arrow indicates to some suitable scale the numerical value or magnitude of that velocity, and the direction of the arrow is chosen as that in which the usual right-handed screw advances when turned in the same direction that the body rotates. This method is also used to represent angular acceleration and torque, as well as other angular quantities to be considered later, but not angular displacement.

It will now be clear why it was necessary in describing *uniform* angular motion, § 48, to specify that the direction of the axis should remain fixed, for a change in the direction of the axis would shift the position of the velocity vector, and this would mean a change in the angular velocity of the rotating body. In this instance, the change would be one of direction only, but any change in velocity is inconsistent with uniform motion.

58. Angular Momentum.   The close analogy between linear and angular quantities, already pointed out, applies also to momentum.   The *angular momentum* of a body is defined as the product of the moment of inertia of the body and its angular velocity.   Hence, if I represents the moment of inertia and ω the angular velocity of a rotating body, both about the same axis, then

<u>Angular momentum $= I\omega$</u>

an expression similar to that for linear momentum, § 36.

Just as the resultant force acting upon a body for a certain time causes a change in its linear momentum, so a resultant torque T acting for a time t upon a body causes a corresponding change in its angular momentum, thus,

$$Tt = I_f\omega_f - I_o\omega_o \qquad T = I\alpha \qquad (47)$$

where the different subscripts for the moment of inertia allow for a possible change in the shape of the body itself while its speed changes.   The product Tt is called an *angular impulse*, just as in Eq. 25 the product Ft is called a linear impulse.   The principle underlying Eq. 47 states that *the resultant angular impulse about any axis* causes a *change in the angular momentum of a body about the same axis* and, moreover, that *these two quantities are numerically equal.*

Both angular impulse and angular momentum are vector quantities; angular impulse Tt has the same direction as the torque T, and angular momentum $I\omega$ has the same direction as the angular velocity ω.

Actually, the foregoing equation is identical with Eq. 43, $T = I\alpha$; however, the present form is useful in that it leads to a generalization regarding angular momentum.   When $T = 0$ in the equation, then

$$I_f\omega_f = I_o\omega_o \qquad (48)$$

which means that the product $I\omega$ is constant.   Stated in words: *If the resultant torque acting upon a body or system of bodies is zero, the angular momentum of the body or system about any fixed axis remains unchanged.*   This generalization is known as the principle of *Conservation of Angular Momentum.*

Examples of this principle are numerous.   A wheel or other rigid object turning without any friction would continue to rotate with undiminished speed.   The earth closely approximates a rigid body; it rotates at a uniform rate and its axis stays nearly fixed in direction.   A skater whirling around on his toes keeps turning at the same speed as long as his moment of inertia remains the same, since the ice offers little frictional resistance.   If he extends his arms, thus increasing his moment of inertia, his speed diminishes so as to keep the product $I\omega$ constant; but if he draws the arms in to his sides, his speed of rotation increases.

59. Motion of Precession. When a rotating body is given an additional angular velocity about the same axis, the two angular velocity vectors have the same direction, and the resultant is their algebraic sum. Thus, if a body rotating at 20 radians/sec in a clockwise direction receives an additional angular velocity of 3 radians/sec in a counter-clockwise direction, then its resulting velocity is 17 radians/sec clockwise about the same axis. However, when the added velocity is about a different axis from that of the original rotation the resultant velocity can be obtained only by vector addition.

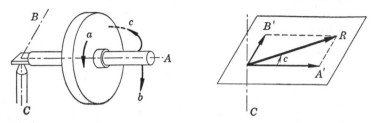

FIG. 61. Precession of rotating wheel about pivot at one end of axle

The addition of two angular velocities about separate axes gives rise to an angular motion about a third axis; this motion is called *precession*. To explain this type of motion, reference will be made to a wheel mounted loosely between collars on an axle A, as shown in perspective in Fig. 61, and set in rotation by some agency not illustrated. The shaft does not rotate with the wheel and one end of it is set horizontally upon a pivot on the vertical support C, the other end of the shaft being free. If the wheel were not rotating, the free end of the shaft would drop and the whole system would fall off the vertical support. But with the wheel rotating, the tendency for the free end of the shaft to drop causes the wheel and shaft to describe horizontal circles about the pivot; that is, the wheel precesses in the horizontal plane. A simplified description of the process follows.

The angular velocity of the wheel spinning in the direction a about axis A is represented by the vector A' in the vector diagram at the right. This diagram is also in perspective, and A' is drawn parallel to shaft A. The pull of the earth upon the wheel produces a torque that tends to turn the entire moving system about the axis B in the direction shown by arrow b. This torque sets up an angular acceleration and gives the body an additional angular velocity about axis B which is represented in the vector diagram as B'. If this velocity B' is added to the spin velocity A' in the same horizontal plane, the resultant is R. Accordingly the shaft shifts its position to point in the direction R, turning about the vertical axis C as shown by arrow c. This motion of precession occurs, therefore, about an axis that is perpendicular to both the other axes, A and B. This motion continues, for as soon as the wheel reaches the position R, it is subject to another torque due to the tendency of the free end of the shaft to drop, the corresponding change in angular velocity is at right angles to R, and a new resultant is formed, to which position the shaft progresses, and so on. As described, it would appear that the shaft progresses in discrete steps, but the process is actually one of infinitesimally small angular shifts, thus producing a constant velocity of precession.

It can be shown that the angular velocity of precession Ω (omega) of a wheel is given by the expression

$$\Omega = \frac{T}{I\omega} \tag{49}$$

in which T is the torque that tends to change the direction of the axis, and the product $I\omega$ is the angular momentum of the wheel.

60. The Gyroscope. A gyroscope is a wheel and axle supported in gimbal rings so that it can be set in rotation with its axis in any desired direction. When rotating, the wheel maintains its axis in the given direction, even though the gyroscope as a whole is moved from one position to another, because with negligible friction the force exerted on the gyroscope is not transmitted through the gimbal rings to produce a torque on the wheel.

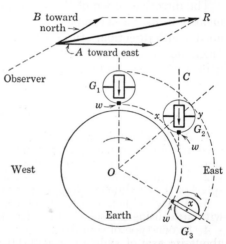

The action of the gyroscope as a compass is an application of the vector addition of angular velocities. In Fig. 62, the earth is viewed from a point in space beyond the south pole; as seen from that point the earth rotates in a clockwise direction. The gyroscope is shown at the equator in various positions; that at G_3 is the ultimate one and

FIG. 62. The use of a gyroscope as a compass. The observer is imagined in space looking northward toward the earth

the other two are disturbed positions used in explaining the action. The arrows on the wheel in positions G_1 and G_2 indicate the direction in which the rim of the wheel nearest the reader is moving. A weight w, placed on the inner gimbal ring, always seeks the position nearest the center of the earth wherever the gyroscope may be situated.

If the gyroscope is placed at position G_1 with its axis directed arbitrarily from east to west, the vector representing the angular velocity of the rotating wheel is directed axially toward the east, as shown at A in the vector diagram. As the earth rotates and carries the gyroscope to position G_2, its axis continues to point eastward, thereby bringing the weight w out of line with the earth's radius. The earth's attraction for this weight sets up a torque which tends to produce clockwise rotation of the gyroscope about an axis perpendicular to the page. The additional angular velocity produced by this torque is represented by a vector directed into the paper; it is shown in perpective as B in the vector diagram. The addition of A and B yields the resultant R as the direction toward which the axis of the wheel turns. Consequently the shaft-end y moves northward (into the paper) and the shaft-end x moves southward (out of the paper); this precessional motion occurs about the axis C. As the gyroscope is carried farther by the earth the precession continues until the shaft of the wheel becomes parallel to the axis O of the earth, with the shaft-end x pointing toward the reader as at G_3. When the gyroscope reaches this position the earth's pull on weight w exerts no further torque action and the gimbal ring remains in a plane with the earth's axis. The gyroscope wheel thus assumes a position such that its axis points north and south.

The directive action of the earth upon the gyroscope permits this instrument to be used as a compass which indicates on its scale the true geographic north-south direction. In contrast, the magnetic compass points along the magnetic meridian, and furthermore, its indications are influenced by magnetic variations and by the presence of magnetic materials near by.

PROBLEMS

1. A wheel in uniform rotation completes 100 rev in 5 sec. (a) How many revolutions does it make in 15 min? What is its angular speed (b) in revolutions per minute? and (c) in radians per second?

2. The earth rotates around its axis once a day. Compute the angular speed of the earth (a) in degrees per minute and (b) in radians per second.

3. A flywheel is to rotate at 800 rev/min. How large may its diameter be without causing the speed of the rim to exceed 6000 ft/min?

4. In one type of spin drier, a perforated drum 20 in. in diameter rotates about its axis of symmetry at 1100 rev/min. (a) Compute the tangential speed of the cylindrical wall of the drum. (b) If 1 lb of wet clothing in the drum is in contact with the cylindrical wall, what radial force does it exert upon the wall?

5. A wheel of 20-cm radius is mounted in stationary bearings, and a cord is fastened to the rim and wound around it. If the cord is pulled perpendicularly to the axis at a speed of 10 cm/sec, what angular speed is imparted to the wheel?

6. The front sprocket of a bicycle has 24 teeth and drives the rear sprocket by means of a chain. The rear sprocket has 8 teeth and is attached to the rear wheel. With wheels of 13-in. radius, at what rate should the front sprocket be driven in order to travel along at a speed of 10 mi/hr?

7. One pulley 12 in. in diameter and turning at 400 rev/min drives another, 18 in. in diameter, by means of a belt. Assume that the belt does not slip and compute (a) the speed of the belt in feet per minute and (b) the angular speed of the driven pulley in revolutions per minute.

8. The armature of a large motor starting from rest reaches its rated speed of 1200 rev/min in 30 sec. Assume the angular acceleration to be constant,

and compute (*a*) the value of the angular acceleration and (*b*) the number of revolutions the armature makes during the starting period.

9. The flywheel of a metal punchpress slows down from 75 to 50 rev/min in turning $\frac{3}{4}$ of a revolution during the punching operation. Assume that the angular acceleration (negative) of the flywheel is constant and determine its value. Also find the time occupied by the punching operation.

10. A wheel having a radius of 12 cm is mounted in frictionless bearings; a cord attached to its rim and wound around it extends downward and carries a weight at its lower end. If this weight descends with a linear acceleration of 20 cm/sec^2, what is the angular acceleration of the wheel?

11. Suppose that the pulley system referred to in Prob. 7 comes to rest from the speed given in 15 sec, and compute the angular acceleration of each pulley and the acceleration of the belt while stopping.

12. What torque should be applied to a wheel which has a moment of inertia of 20 slug·ft^2 in order to bring it from rest to a speed of 360 rev/min in 45 sec?

13. A constant torque of 8×10^6 dyne·cm is applied to a motor armature; assume that 5% of this torque is used in opposing friction and the remainder brings the armature from rest to a speed of 1200 rev/min in 10 sec. At that time the applied torque is discontinued. Compute (*a*) the moment of inertia of the armature and (*b*) the time in which friction stops the armature upon removal of the applied torque.

14. (*a*) Suppose that a slender rod 30 cm long is marked off in three equal parts and that a 100-gm sphere is clamped to the midpoint of each part. If the spheres are considered as particles and the mass of the rod as negligible, what is the moment of inertia of the combination about a transverse axis through one end of the rod? (*b*) For comparison, compute the moment of inertia of a thin rod 30 cm long and of 300-gm mass about a transverse axis through one end.

15. A washer is a disk of uniform thickness with a central hole. Assume the disk to have inner and outer radii of R_1 and R_2 respectively, and to have a mass M. Show that the moment of inertia of the washer about its geometric axis is $\frac{1}{2}M(R_1{}^2 + R_2{}^2)$.

16. Compute the moment of inertia of a slender rod 100 cm long and having a mass of 1000 gm, about a transverse axis 20 cm from one end.

17. Three slender sticks, each of mass M and length L, are fastened together to form a letter H, with the cross member at right angles to the other two and joining their midpoints. Find the moment of inertia of the combination about an axis perpendicular to the plane of the H and passing through the base of one of the vertical members.

18. Compute the moment of inertia of a solid disk having a mass of 10 gm and a radius of 2 cm, about an axis at its rim, the direction of the axis being (*a*) perpendicular to the plane of the disk and (*b*) in the plane of the disk.

19. (*a*) What is the moment of inertia of a meter stick of 150-gm mass about a transverse axis at one end? (*b*) If the meter stick could be squeezed into a concentrated mass, where should this mass be located with respect to the axis mentioned, in order to have the same moment of inertia as the original stick?

20. Find the radius of gyration of a solid sphere having a radius of 6 in. and a weight of 16 lb (*a*) about an axis through the center and (*b*) about an axis tangent to the surface.

21. A sphere having a radius of 10 cm and a mass of 3 kg rolls without sliding down a plane 7 m long inclined at 30° with the horizontal. If the

sphere starts from rest at the top of the incline, in what time does it reach the bottom?

22. To measure the moment of inertia of a pulley, of 5-cm radius, the pulley is mounted in horizontal frictionless bearings and a cord with weights at the ends is placed on its cylindrical rim (not smooth), as in Atwood's machine, § 35. One weight has a mass of 500 gm and the other has a mass of 440 gm. When the moving system is released, the 500-gm mass is observed to descend 90 cm in 3 sec, starting from rest. As a preliminary step, find the tension in each part of the cord, and finally compute the moment of inertia of the pulley.

23. A cord wound around a thin-walled tube is fastened to a support and the tube is released with its axis horizontal, unwinding the cord as it descends. Suppose the cord to be under a tension P, and the cylinder to have a mass M and a radius r, and write expressions for the resultant force acting upon the tube and for the torque acting upon it about an axis parallel to the tube through its center of mass. From these expressions, determine the acceleration of the tube.

24. A constant torque of 20 lb·ft is applied to a wheel mounted in stationary bearings; part of this torque opposes friction and the remainder sets the wheel into rotation, increasing its speed from standstill to 1200 rev/min in 1.5 min. Upon removal of the torque at this speed, the wheel comes to rest in 10 min. Determine the moment of inertia of the wheel.

25. A small 20-gm mass is fastened to the lower end of a cord 10 cm long, the upper end of which is attached to a vertical shaft of negligible mass that rotates in frictionless bearings. (*a*) At what speed does the shaft rotate when the cord is inclined at 30° with the vertical? (*b*) What is then the angular momentum of the system? (*c*) What torque applied to the shaft for 3 sec will cause the cord to take up a position at 45° with the vertical?

26. The apparatus shown in the diagram is designed to illustrate the conservation of angular momentum. The small block attached to the cord is set revolving in a circle of 6-in. radius on a frictionless table top, and is observed

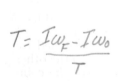

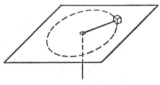

Problem 26

to make 5 rev in 4 sec. If the block is then pulled toward the center by means of the cord, at what rate does the block revolve when the radius is 2 in.?

27. A board upon which an electric motor is mounted is held in a horizontal position by two men, A and B, one at each end. The pulley of the motor faces A and rotates in a clockwise direction as viewed by A. If A lifts his end of the board vertically upward, in what direction does that end of the board precess?

28. The flywheel of an automobile engine rotates clockwise as viewed from the front. If the car is moving forward on a level road and the driver turns it to the right, in what direction does the front end of the car precess?

7

MECHANICAL ENERGY

61. Work. In popular language, the term "work" is applied to any form of labor, physical or mental, for producing any kind of result. In science and engineering, on the other hand, "work" has a definite technical meaning, which the following illustration will make clear.

When a man moves a box along the floor by a steady push or raises it from the floor to the top of a table, two things should be noted: first, that the man exerts a *force* on the box, and second, that the box undergoes a *displacement* in the direction of the force. Under these conditions the man or the force that he exerts is said to do *work* on the box. Many such illustrations show that *whenever a force is exerted on an object and the object is displaced in the direction of the force, the force or the agent applying it does work on the object.*

The amount of work done is the product of the force and the displacement of the object while the force is being applied. In symbols, when a constant force F is exerted on an object while the object undergoes a displacement s in the direction of the force, the amount of work done on the object is

$$E = Fs \qquad (50)$$

The symbol E is used instead of W to represent work in order that W may continue to represent weight, as previously, without confusion.

In § 41, the product of force and length was considered, but there the force and length vectors are at right angles to each other, and their product, torque, is a vector quantity. Here, the force and length vectors have the same direction, and their product is a scalar. Work is a scalar quantity, and hence amounts of work can be added arithmetically.

Since work is the product of a force and a length, the unit for work is the product of a force unit and a length unit. The cgs unit of work is the erg. One *erg* of work is done on a body when a force of 1 dyne is exerted upon it while the body is displaced 1 cm in the direction of the force. The mks unit of work is the joule. One *joule* of work is done on a body when a force of 1 newton is exerted upon it while the body is displaced 1 m in the direction of the force. This work unit is named after the British experimenter, James P. Joule (1818–1889). Since 1 newton = 10^5 dynes and 1 m = 10^2 cm, it follows that 1 joule = 10^7 ergs. The British gravitational unit of work is the foot·pound. One *foot·pound* (ft·lb) of work is done on a body when a force of 1 lb is exerted upon it while the body is displaced 1 ft in the direction of the force.

A unit of work much used in atomic physics is the electron·volt, § 258. Although derived from electrical principles, this unit is not restricted to electrical calculations. One electron·volt = 1.602 × 10⁻¹⁹ joule, or 1.602 × 10⁻¹² erg. A million electron·volts is often used as an energy unit and is abbreviated by the initials Mev; 1 Mev = 1.602 × 10⁻⁶ erg.

It frequently happens that the force exerted on the body is not in the same direction as the displacement of the body. In such cases, the term F in Eq. 50 should be interpreted as that component of the force which is

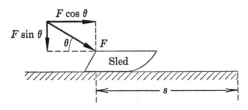

FIG. 63. Work being done in sliding an object

along the direction of s. For example, a boy may push a sled with a force F that makes an angle θ with the horizontal, while the sled is displaced a distance s along a level surface, as shown in Fig. 63. Here F can be resolved into two components, $F \cos \theta$ along the direction of the displacement and $F \sin \theta$ at right angles to this direction. Only the first of these components is effective in doing work on the sled, while the other component increases the pressure of the sled against the snow and thereby causes the backward drag of friction to increase. The amount of work done is therefore

$$E = Fs \cos \theta \tag{51}$$

This is a general expression for the work E done on a body by a force F exerted on it while the body is displaced an amount s, the directions of F and s making an angle θ with each other. It should be noted that F is the force *applied* to the body and is not, in general, the resultant force acting upon it.

Illustrative Problem

As an example, calculate the work done by a porter in dragging a trunk along a level floor by applying a constant force of 40 lb to it at an angle of 30° upward from the horizontal while the trunk moves 3 yd along the floor. From Eq. 51, the work done is $E = Fs \cos \theta = (40 \text{ lb}) (3 \text{ yd})(\cos 30°) = (40 \text{ lb})(9 \text{ ft})(0.866) = 312 \text{ ft·lb}$.

Sometimes a body moves in opposition to the force exerted upon it; for instance, a heavy weight may slide down an incline in spite of attempts to to pull it upward. In such cases, *the body does work instead of having work done on it;* Eq. 51 may be used as before, but since θ is larger than 90° its cosine is negative; a negative value for E indicates that the work computed is done *by* the body instead of *upon* it.

62. Work Done in Rotation. The amount of work done upon a rotating body can also be calculated from the foregoing equations, but usually is obtained more directly in terms of the angular quantities, torque and angle.

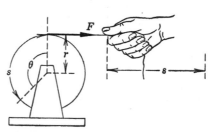

FIG. 64. Work being done in rotating an object

The desired expression can be found by supposing that a drum of radius r has a cord fastened to its rim, as represented in Fig. 64, and that the cord is pulled with a force F for a distance s along its length. The amount of work done upon the drum is $E = Fs$, where F and s are to be replaced by angular quantities. The torque T resulting from the force F is $T = Fr$, whence $F = T \div r$. As the cord is pulled, every point on the rim of the drum travels over an arc of length s, and therefore the drum rotates through an angle θ such that $s = r\theta$. When these values are substituted for F and s, the expression for work becomes

$E = Fs = \left(\dfrac{T}{r}\right)(r\theta)$, whence

$$E = T\theta \tag{52}$$

In general, the work done upon a rotating body by a torque T exerted upon it while the body undergoes an angular displacement of θ radians is equal to the product $T\theta$.

If the body rotates in opposition to the torque applied to it, as when a rotating wheel continues to turn in a certain direction even after a brake is applied which exerts a torque in the opposite direction, then T and θ have opposite signs, and their product E is negative. In such cases Eq. 52 represents the amount of work done *by* the rotating body instead of the amount of work done *on* it.

63. Energy. A body is said to possess energy if it is able to do work. For example, a man or a horse can do work and so possesses energy; the steam within the cylinder of a steam engine possesses energy since it is able to move the piston; the mainspring of a watch possesses energy when wound, since it is able to drive the hands of the timepiece. Moreover, *when a body does work, its energy is reduced by an amount exactly equal to the work done.* Work and energy are expressed in the same units.

There are many different forms of energy; thus, the spring just mentioned has mechanical energy, coal has chemical energy, a hot substance has internal energy, a charged capacitor has electrical energy, and so on. In the study of Mechanics, mechanical energy is naturally the type that is of interest.

A body or a system of bodies may possess mechanical energy from either or both of two causes. First, whenever a body is in motion it is able to exert a force and do work in coming to rest; a moving body always possesses energy by virtue of its motion; this is called *kinetic* energy. A moving hammer has kinetic energy, and this enables it to do work in driving a nail. Second, a body that has been moved to a new position is sometimes able to do work because of this fact; for example, a raised weight can do work in falling and is commonly said to possess energy by virtue of its position; this is called *potential* energy. Strictly, it is not correct to regard potential energy as possessed by a particular object, but rather as possessed by a system which includes that object. Thus, while a weight is being raised it is being separated from the earth against their mutual attraction; in the process work is done and the potential energy of the system, made up of the weight and the earth, is increased. Nevertheless, the potential energy is customarily ascribed to the weight since it is the tangible part of the system which makes that energy available.

A body is not necessarily given potential energy by displacing it, but only when it can do more work in its new position than it could originally. A weight that has been raised is thereby given potential energy, but if it is merely moved along a level floor from one position to another its potential energy is not changed.

64. Conservation and Transformation of Energy. Whenever a body does work, its capability of doing further work is lessened, and this means that it possesses less energy than before. This reduction must not be regarded as a loss of energy, for in doing work the body has imparted an equal amount of energy to some other body, which, together with the first, constitute a system. The energy given up by a body is imparted to others without loss, and thus within the system the total amount of energy remains unchanged. This illustrates a basic principle known as the *Conservation of Energy*, which states that *energy can neither be created nor destroyed.* Expressed differently, *the total amount of energy in the universe remains constant.*

This principle will be illustrated by considering a body which is raised to the top of an inclined plane and then allowed to slide down. A certain amount of work is done on the body in raising it, thereby increasing its potential energy. As the body slides down the incline, it gives up potential energy and gains kinetic energy; and if no work is done against friction, the increase of kinetic energy equals the reduction of potential energy. If, however, part of the potential energy possessed by the body is expended in doing work against friction on the way down, then the kinetic energy of the body at the bottom will be less than before by this amount. This example shows that, although energy can be transformed from one kind to another, it is not destroyed in the process. When energy is expended in work against friction, it is said to be wasted, that is, rendered unavailable for useful purposes; but it is not destroyed, for it is converted into heat, which is recognized as a form of energy.

When the work done on a body is expended mechanically, it can be accounted for entirely by one or more of the following effects: (1) *increase in the kinetic energy of the body*, (2) *increase in its potential energy*, or (3) *production of heat due to friction*. Hence the Law of Conservation of Energy can be expressed by the equation

$$E = \Delta E_k + \Delta E_p + E_f \tag{53}$$

where E is the work done on the body, ΔE_k the increase in its kinetic energy, ΔE_p the increase in its potential energy, and E_f the energy used in opposing friction. This equation expresses in symbols one of the most important principles in the whole subject of Physics.

65. Kinetic Energy. *Kinetic energy is the kind of energy that a body has by virtue of its motion.* As applied to motion of translation, an expression for kinetic energy can be derived by applying the law of Conservation of Energy to a body that is caused to slide along a surface without change of potential energy and without waste of energy by friction, for then the work done on the body appears entirely as an increase in its kinetic energy.

If a block of mass m is initially at rest on a smooth level plane, and a constant horizontal force F is exerted on the block while it is displaced by a distance s, then the amount of work done on the block is $E = Fs$. Since there is no friction, the force F is the resultant force acting on the block, and hence the block moves with a constant acceleration a such that $F = ma$. From the laws of accelerated motion, § 23, the displacement of a body starting from rest with a constant acceleration a and acquiring a velocity v is found to be $s = v^2/2a$. The change in kinetic energy ΔE_k of the block equals the work done upon it, and is obtained by substituting for F and s the values found; it becomes $\Delta E_k = Fs = (ma)(v^2/2a) = mv^2/2$. Hence, with respect to zero motion, the kinetic energy of the block is

$$E_k = \frac{mv^2}{2} \tag{54}$$

A more general treatment would show that the work done upon a body by *all* forces acting on it (or by their resultant) equals the change in kinetic energy of the body.

The foregoing expression is adapted to any of the systems of units listed in § 35. Thus, with the mass in grams and the velocity in centimeters per second, it is easily shown that the kinetic energy is in centimeter·dynes, or ergs. With the mass in slugs and the velocity in feet per second, the kinetic energy is in foot·pounds.

It is important to note that the kinetic energy of a body is determined entirely by its mass and its present state of motion and is completely independent of the manner in which the forces acted upon it while its kinetic energy was being acquired.

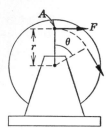

To find an expression for kinetic energy due to rotation, reference is made to Fig. 65, which represents a body, initially at rest, and free to turn in frictionless bearings. A force F is applied to a pin A at the end of a radius r, with F always at right angles to the radius. This force produces a torque $T = Fr$, causing the body to accelerate in accordance with Eq. 43, $T = I\alpha$; in sweeping through an angle θ it reaches a velocity ω such that $\theta = \omega^2/2\alpha$. But the change in kinetic energy of the body equals the work performed upon it, which, from Eq. 52, is $T\theta$. Hence, with respect to zero motion, the kinetic energy of rotation is $E_k = T\theta = (I\alpha)(\omega^2/2\alpha)$, or

FIG. 65. Diagram used in calculating kinetic energy due to rotation

$$E_k = \frac{I\omega^2}{2} \qquad (55)$$

where I is the moment of inertia of the body and ω its angular velocity. The student should have no difficulty in showing that with I expressed in slug·feet^2 and ω in radians per second, E_k is in foot·pounds, and similarly for the other systems of units.

A body like a rolling wheel possesses energy due to both translation and rotation. If the mass of the body is m and the velocity of its center of mass is v, the kinetic energy of the body due to translation is $mv^2/2$. If the moment of inertia of the body is I and its angular velocity is ω, both taken about an axis through the center of mass, the kinetic energy of the body due to rotation is $I\omega^2/2$. The total kinetic energy of the body is therefore

$$E_k = \frac{mv^2}{2} + \frac{I\omega^2}{2}$$

66. Potential Energy. *Potential energy is the kind of energy that a body has by virtue of its position or configuration.* When a body is raised to a higher level, it is able to do a certain amount of work in falling back again, and hence it has acquired this amount of potential energy. Although elevating a body is not the only way to give it potential energy, it is perhaps the most usual way. If the body is raised without increasing its kinetic energy and without waste of energy on account of friction, the work done in raising it is all expended in increasing the potential energy of the body.

Fig. 66 shows a body of mass m being raised from one level to another at constant speed (no change in E_k) along a smooth plane (no friction), the second level being a vertical distance h above the datum level. The plane has a length l and makes an angle θ with the horizontal. The force F necessary to move the body along the plane with constant speed is $mg \sin \theta$. Since this force is exerted through a distance l, the work done on the body, and hence the change in its potential energy, is $\Delta E_p = (mg \sin \theta)(l) = \left(mg\dfrac{h}{l}\right)(l)$. Consequently, the potential energy of the body with respect to the given datum level is

$$E_p = mgh \qquad (56)$$

which shows that the increase in potential energy of a body in raising it from one level to another depends only on the weight mg of the body and the vertical distance h between the two levels. Since the result is independent of the value of θ, the path of the body may be inclined at any angle, it may have different inclinations at different points, or it may be curved. The change in potential energy of a body is not affected by the path over which it is moved in reaching a fixed elevation.

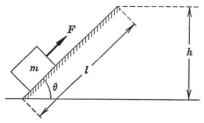

FIG. 66. Diagram used in calculating potential energy due to elevation

Potential energy due to configuration is illustrated by a stretched spring. Work must be done to stretch (or compress) a spring, and an equal amount of potential energy is stored in the spring because it can do that amount of work in returning to its original length. An experiment described in § 96 shows that the force F required to stretch a spring is directly proportional to the amount of elongation x; that is, $F \propto x$, or $F = kx$, where k is called the "spring constant." For a total elongation x, the stretching force varies from $F = 0$ at the start to $F = kx$ at the end, and the average force is $\frac{1}{2}kx$. This average force exerted on the spring through a distance x represents an amount of work $\frac{1}{2}kx^2$ done on it, and hence the potential energy of a spring when stretched by an amount x is

$$E_p = \frac{kx^2}{2} \qquad (57)$$

Potential energy and kinetic energy are expressed in the same units; these were discussed in the preceding section.

67. Alternate Form of Energy Expressions. The expressions just developed for the kinetic and potential energy of a body can be stated in terms of its weight W rather than its mass m. Since $W = mg$, from Eq. 23, kinetic energy of translation $E_k = \dfrac{mv^2}{2}$ becomes

$$E_k = \frac{Wv^2}{2g} \qquad (58)$$

Also, potential energy due to elevation $E_p = mgh$ becomes

$$E_p = Wh \qquad (59)$$

Thus, in the British gravitational system, with the weight W in pounds and the other quantities in their appropriate units for this system, § 35, the energy E_k or E_p is in foot·pounds. Kinetic energy due to rotation is found in foot·pounds most simply by using the expression $E_k = \dfrac{I\omega^2}{2}$ with I in slug·feet^2, as stated in § 52.

68. Energy Expended in Friction. *Whenever one body moves upon another, some work is done because of friction that exists between them.* The amount of energy expended in this manner can be found by supposing work to be done upon a body under such conditions that neither the kinetic nor the potential energy is increased, since all the work done is then expended against friction. These conditions apply when a body, having been started from rest, is moved at constant velocity along a rough horizontal surface. To give the body this motion, the force exerted upon it is equal and opposite to the maximum force of friction f. The work done in exerting this force while the body undergoes a displacement s is equal to the product fs, and hence the energy wasted through friction is

$$E_f = fs \qquad (60)$$

The method of calculating f was discussed in § 39.

The work done against friction is converted into heat and is usually wasted. Frequently the heating is so slight as to escape notice, but sometimes it is quite evident, such as the heating produced in an automobile brake, in an overheated bearing, or in striking a match.

69. Application of Energy Principles. The principles of work and energy provide a method by which many problems can be solved independently of the dynamical method described in Chaps. 4 and 6 and often with less difficulty.

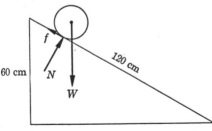

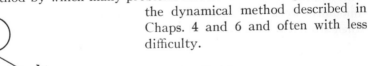

FIG. 67. Forces on cylinder rolling down inclined plane

Illustrative Problems

I. A solid cylinder and a thin-wall hollow cylinder start from rest at the top of an inclined plane and roll without sliding to the bottom. Find the time taken by each cylinder if the plane is 120 cm long and has one end 60 cm higher than the other. The conditions of the problem are represented in Fig. 67.

The method of solution is the same for either cylinder. As the cylinder rolls down the incline, the reduction of potential energy equals the gain of kinetic energy, friction being neglected. Thus,

$$-\Delta E_p = \Delta E_k$$

From this relation, the final velocity of the cylinder (upon reaching the bottom of the plane) can be found, and the desired time then obtained from the laws of accelerated motion. Hence, for either cylinder,

$$mgh = \frac{mv^2}{2} + \frac{I\omega^2}{2}$$

where m is the mass of the cylinder and v the final velocity of its center of mass; I is the moment of inertia of the cylinder and ω its final angular velocity, both taken about an axis through the center of mass; h is the elevation of the upper end of the plane, and g the acceleration due to gravity.

For the solid cylinder, the moment of inertia about its central axis is $I = \frac{1}{2}mr^2$, from the table in § 54, and its angular velocity at the bottom of the incline is $\omega = \dfrac{v}{r}$; therefore the last term of the equation can be replaced

by $\left(\dfrac{1}{2}mr^2\right)\left(\dfrac{v^2}{2r^2}\right) = \dfrac{mv^2}{4}$. Hence $mgh = \dfrac{mv^2}{2} + \dfrac{mv^2}{4} = \dfrac{3mv^2}{4}$. Therefore,

the linear velocity of the cylinder as it reaches the bottom is

$$v = \sqrt{\frac{4gh}{3}} = \sqrt{\frac{4\left(980\ \dfrac{\text{cm}}{\text{sec}^2}\right)(60\ \text{cm})}{3}} = 280\ \frac{\text{cm}}{\text{sec}}$$

The time of descent, from Eq. 13, is

$$t = \frac{2s}{v} = \frac{240\ \text{cm}}{280\ \dfrac{\text{cm}}{\text{sec}}} = 0.857\ \text{sec}$$

Evidently, any solid cylinder, whatever its mass or dimensions, would roll down this plane in the same time.

Similarly, for the hollow cylinder $I = mr^2$ and again $\omega = \dfrac{v}{r}$; therefore $\dfrac{I\omega^2}{2} = (mr^2)\left(\dfrac{v^2}{2r^2}\right) = \dfrac{mv^2}{2}$. In this case, $mgh = \dfrac{mv^2}{2} + \dfrac{mv^2}{2} = mv^2$, whence the velocity at the bottom is $v = \sqrt{gh} = \sqrt{(980)(60)} = 242$ cm/sec, and the time of descent is $240/242 = 0.992$ sec. Thus a hollow cylinder takes longer to roll down the plane than a solid cylinder.

The foregoing results can be verified by applying the dynamical method of Chap. 6 and using the forces represented by the vectors W, N, and f in the figure.

II. Prob. II of § 23 deals with a linear accelerator in which a proton initially moving at 2.8×10^9 cm/sec is accelerated to a velocity of 3.2×10^9 cm/sec. Compute (*a*) the initial kinetic energy of the proton and (*b*) the increase in its kinetic energy due to the acceleration. Express the results in terms of electron·volts. The mass of the proton may be taken as constant at 1.672×10^{-24} gm.

(*a*) The initial kinetic energy

$$\frac{mv_o^2}{2} = \frac{1}{2}(1.672 \times 10^{-24} \text{ gm})\left(2.8 \times 10^9 \frac{\text{cm}}{\text{sec}}\right)^2$$

$$= 6.56 \times 10^{-6} \text{ erg} \times \frac{1 \text{ Mev}}{1.602 \times 10^{-6} \text{ erg}} = 4.10 \text{ Mev}$$

(*b*) The increase in kinetic energy is

$$\frac{m}{2}(v_f^2 - v_o^2) = \frac{1.672 \times 10^{-24}}{2}[(3.2 \times 10^9)^2 - (2.8 \times 10^9)^2]$$

$$= 2.009 \times 10^{-6} \text{ erg, or } 1.254 \text{ Mev}$$

III. A level surface AB, 8 ft long, is smoothly joined at B to a plane inclined at 36.9° upward from the horizontal, as shown in Fig. 68. A block weighing 12 lb is initially at rest at point A. A horizontal force of 9 lb is applied to the block while it moves from A to B, but not beyond. Take the

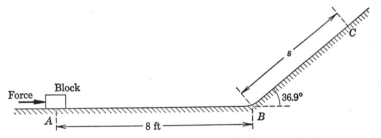

FIG. 68. Block sliding on level surface and up incline

coefficient of sliding friction between the block and each surface that it slides upon as 0.25, and compute the distance $BC = s$ that the block slides along the incline before it comes to rest.

In this example, work is done upon the block by the applied force. Part of this work is done against friction from A to B and from B to C; the remainder appears as potential energy of the block at C. Stated in terms of Eq. 53,

$$E - (E_f)_{AB} - (E_f)_{BC} = (E_p)_C$$

The work done on the block is $E = (9 \text{ lb})(8 \text{ ft}) = 72 \text{ ft·lb}$; the work done against friction from A to B is $(E_f)_{AB} = (0.25)(12 \text{ lb})(8 \text{ ft}) = 24 \text{ ft·lb}$, and from B to C is $(E_f)_{BC} = (0.25)(0.8 \times 12 \text{ lb})(s)$; and the potential energy of the block at C is $(E_p)_C = (12 \text{ lb})(s \sin 36.9°) = (7.2 \text{ lb})(s)$. With these numerical values, the energy equation becomes

$$72 \text{ ft·lb} - 24 \text{ ft·lb} - (2.4 \text{ lb})(s) = (7.2 \text{ lb})(s)$$

from which $s = 5.00$ ft is the distance that the block slides along the incline before it comes to rest.

70. Rate of Doing Work: Power. In practice, where work is done upon a body, both the amount of work and also the time during which that work is done are important. For example, if a motor-driven hoist has to raise its load quickly, a more powerful hoist and a larger driving motor are needed than if more time were allowed. Usually the size of machinery is determined, not by the total amount of work to be done, but by the rate at which it is to be done; that is, the amount of work required per unit of time. *The time rate of doing work is called power.*

In general terms, the average power P delivered by any agent that performs an amount of work E in a time interval t is given by the relation

$$P = \frac{E}{t} \tag{61}$$

If a machine operates steadily, performing the same amount of work every second, the power that it provides is constant. But if a machine works irregularly, doing more work during some intervals than in others, the power fluctuates from moment to moment. Under these circumstances, Eq. 61 gives the *average* value of the power throughout the time interval considered.

The power provided to a body can be expressed in terms of its velocity as follows: In motion of translation, $E = Fs$, from Eq. 50, and $s = vt$, from Eq. 6. But power is $P = E/t$, whence

$$P = Fv \tag{62}$$

where F is the force applied to the body and v its linear velocity. Similarly, in motion of rotation, $E = T\theta$, from Eq. 52, and $\theta = \omega t$, from Eq. 35, therefore

$$P = T\omega \tag{63}$$

where T is the torque applied to the body and ω its angular velocity, both with respect to the axis of rotation.

Since power is the time rate of doing work, the unit for power in any system of units is found by dividing the work unit in that system by the time unit. Thus, in the cgs system, power is expressed in ergs per second, and in the British gravitational system it is expressed in foot·pounds per second. If a machine working steadily performs 150,000 ft·lb of work in 10 min, it does work at the rate of 15,000 ft·lb every minute, and its power output is therefore 15,000 (ft·lb)/min or 250 (ft·lb)/sec. In addition to the units of the standard systems, other practical units of power are in general use. *The horsepower* (hp) *is the power provided by an agent while doing work at the rate of 33,000 (ft·lb)/min, or 550 (ft·lb)/sec.* The *watt* is a rate of doing work equal to 1 joule/sec and is named after the Scottish engineer, James Watt (1736–1819). The kilowatt (kw) is a power unit used in rating electrical machines.   The relations between some power units are given below:

UNITS OF POWER

$$1 \text{ watt} = 10^7 \frac{\text{ergs}}{\text{sec}} = 1 \frac{\text{joule}}{\text{sec}}$$

$$1 \text{ hp} = 550 \frac{\text{ft} \cdot \text{lb}}{\text{sec}} = 33,000 \frac{\text{ft} \cdot \text{lb}}{\text{min}}$$

$$1 \text{ hp} = 746 \text{ watts}$$
$$1 \text{ kw} = 1000 \text{ watts} = 1.34 \text{ hp}$$
$$1 \text{ ft} \cdot \text{lb per sec} = 1.356 \text{ watts}$$

Illustrative Problems

I. A horse pulls a wagon $\frac{1}{2}$ mi in 10 min along a level road; what force would he exert on it in developing exactly 1 hp?

The horse in walking $\frac{1}{2}$ mi in 10 min covers an average of 264 ft in 1 min, and since he is to do 33,000 ft·lb of work each minute, the force he must exert, from Eq. 50, is

$$F = \frac{E}{s} = \frac{33,000 \frac{\text{ft} \cdot \text{lb}}{\text{min}}}{264 \frac{\text{ft}}{\text{min}}} = 125.0 \text{ lb}$$

II. What power is represented by the friction in a sleeve bearing that supports a 2-in. shaft turning at 500 rev/min, if the shaft presses against the bearing with a force of 1200 lb, and the coefficient of friction between the sliding surfaces is 0.005?

The force of friction, from Eq. 28, is $0.005 \times 1200 = 6$ lb.   This force is tangent to the shaft at its rim, 1 in. from the axis through the center.   The torque due to friction is therefore $T = 6 \text{ lb} \times \frac{1}{12} \text{ ft} = \frac{1}{2} \text{ lb} \cdot \text{ft}$.   The shaft is turning at 500 rev/min or 52.4 radians/sec, and hence the power represented by friction, from Eq. 63, is $T\omega = (0.5 \text{ lb} \cdot \text{ft})(52.4 \text{ radians/sec}) = 26.2 \text{ ft} \cdot \text{lb/sec}$, which is equivalent to 0.0476 hp.

The relation between work and power is emphasized by transposing Eq. 61 to read

$$E = Pt$$

In this form, the expression shows that, if an agent provides an amount of power P continuously for a period of time t, the agent does an amount of work E which equals the product of P and t.   This conception of work as the product of power and time leads to some energy units that are widely used in engineering practice.   The *horsepower·hour* (hp·hr) is thus a unit of work, being the amount of work performed when the rate is one horsepower over a period of one hour. Similarly, the kilowatt·hour (kw·hr), the unit upon which the cost of electrical energy is based, is the amount of work performed when the rate is one kilowatt over a period of one hour. Thus, if an engine delivers 80 hp steadily for 5 hr, it does $80 \times 5 = 400$ hp·hr of work; if a motor takes 15 kw steadily for 4 hr, it receives $15 \times 4 = 60$ kw·hr of electrical energy.

71. Simple Machines. It is a matter of common experience that a stone firmly embedded in the ground can be dislodged with a crowbar, and that a heavy automobile can be raised by means of a jack. The crowbar or jack serves as an intermediate device upon which work can be done and which in turn does work upon some other object. A device that accomplishes this result is technically called a *machine*. The complex machines used in industry are found upon analysis to be made up largely of certain elements that may be considered simple machines in themselves. These simple machines are generally taken to comprise the lever, the wheel and axle, the pulley, the inclined plane, the screw, and the wedge.

Usually a machine is employed in order to lessen the force required in doing a certain piece of work. Thus, if a 500-lb weight is to be lifted, a machine can be used to exert this amount of upward force upon it while the person operating the machine exerts perhaps only 50 lb. It is thus possible, and indeed usual, to obtain a larger force from a machine than that which is exerted upon it. Of course, *this statement applies to force and not to energy;* according to the law of Conservation of Energy, *more work cannot be obtained from a machine than the energy supplied to it.* Since work = force × distance, when the operator exerts a smaller force than does the machine, he exerts the smaller force through a correspondingly greater distance. The ratio of the force W exerted by a machine on a load to the force F exerted by an operator on the machine is called the *mechanical advantage* of the machine.

If it is assumed that the machine operates without friction, the ratio of W to F becomes the *ideal mechanical advantage* of that machine. Hence, if friction is neglected, the ideal mechanical advantage is

$$A = \frac{W}{F} \tag{64}$$

Under this assumption the energy output would equal the energy input, an ideal condition that cannot actually be attained. Thus, the machine may exert the force W through a distance h while the operator exerts a force F through a distance s. Then the energy output is Wh and the energy input is Fs; if these quantities are equated, $Wh = Fs$; whence, $\dfrac{W}{F} = \dfrac{s}{h}$. Therefore the ideal mechanical advantage can also be expressed in terms of these distances, as follows:

$$A = \frac{s}{h} \tag{65}$$

If, on the other hand, friction is considered in calculating the mechanical advantage of a machine, or if the mechanical advantage is found by actual test, in which case friction is present and affects the result, the actual force ratio W/F becomes the *actual mechanical advantage* of the machine.

72. Mechanical Advantage of Basic Machines. It is often useful to predict the mechanical advantage of a machine from its dimensions. The *actual* mechanical advantage cannot be determined in this manner with great exactness, for such a calculation involves a knowledge of the frictional forces, and these are uncertain because the coefficient of friction is not very definite, § 39. The *ideal* mechanical advantage, on the other hand, can be calculated without difficulty, since friction is assumed to be absent. Eq. 65 will be applied in determining the ideal mechanical advantage of several of the simple machines mentioned. The procedure in each case will be to assume that the machine exerts a force W through a distance h while the operator exerts a force F through a

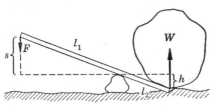

FIG. 69.   Crowbar used as a lever

distance s; the ratio $\dfrac{s}{h}$ is then expressed in terms of the dimensions of the machine, and gives the ideal mechanical advantage A.

I. In the *lever*, one class of which is shown in Fig. 69, a bar rests on a fulcrum, dividing its length into two parts l_1 and l_2. In order for the machine to raise a load W through a height h, the operator exerts a force F downward through the distance s. From the properties of similar triangles, $\dfrac{s}{h} = \dfrac{l_1}{l_2}$, and the ideal mechanical advantage of the lever shown is

$$A = \frac{l_1}{l_2}$$

II. The *pulley* is used in a variety of ways. In a typical pulley system, shown in Fig. 70, each block consists of two pulleys or sheaves encased in a frame or shell. The upper block is fixed and the lower one moves with the

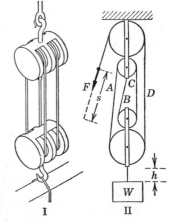

FIG. 70.   Block and tackle

load. A rope passing around the several pulleys is fastened at one end and extends to the operator at the other. Part I of the figure represents a common type of construction, and part II shows the pulleys separated for clearness. Evidently, in order to raise a load W through a height h, each of the four ropes A, B, C, and D must be shortened by this amount, and hence the operator must exert a force F through the distance $s = 4h$. Thus, $\dfrac{s}{h} = 4$, and the ideal mechanical advantage of the arrangement shown is 4, corresponding to the four ropes used to support the load.

III. An inclined plane is also used to reduce the force needed to raise

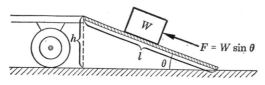

FIG. 71.   The inclined plane

an object. To push an object of weight W up a smooth plane inclined at an angle θ with the horizontal, as shown in Fig. 71, requires a force $F = W \sin \theta$ along the plane, and in order to raise the object through a vertical height h, this force must be exerted through a distance $s = l$. The ratio of W to F or the ratio of s to h equals $\dfrac{1}{\sin \theta}$ or $\dfrac{l}{h}$. Therefore, the ideal mechanical advantage of an inclined plane, where the force is exerted along the direction of the incline, is

$$A = \frac{l}{h}$$

IV. The *screw* may be looked upon as an inclined plane wrapped around a cylinder. In a common form of screw jack, an upright screw threads into a stationary base and supports a load at the top, the screw being turned by means of a horizontal bar, as shown in Fig. 72. In order to raise the load W a distance h equal to the pitch p of the screw, the operator exerts a force F at the end of the bar through a circle of length $s = 2\pi l$, where l is the

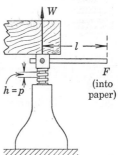

FIG. 72.   A screw jack

length of the bar. Hence $\dfrac{s}{h} = \dfrac{2\pi l}{p}$, and the ideal mechanical advantage of the screw jack is

$$A = \frac{2\pi l}{p}$$

73. Efficiency of a Machine. Friction is present in all moving machinery, however well designed; consequently, the energy delivered by a machine is less than that supplied to it. More definitely, the principle of conservation of energy shows that

Energy input = energy output + energy wasted

if no energy is stored up in the machine. This statement is true over any period of time and hence applies to unit time; and since energy used per unit time is power, it can also be said that

Power input = power output + power wasted

The efficiency of a machine is defined as the ratio of its output to its input, both output and input being expressed in the same units of energy or power. Thus,

$$\left.\begin{aligned}\text{Efficiency} &= \frac{\text{energy output}}{\text{energy input}} \\[2mm] \text{Efficiency} &= \frac{\text{power output}}{\text{power input}}\end{aligned}\right\} \tag{66}$$

The ratio of output to input is always less than unity; in practice it is usually multiplied by 100 and expressed in per cent. High efficiency in a machine implies that in a given time a large part of the energy supplied to it is delivered by the machine to its load and only a small part wasted. The efficiency of a large electrical generator may be as high as 98%. In some of the simple machines—a screw jack, for example—considerable friction is necessary to prevent the load from running down after it has been raised; because of the energy wasted in friction the efficiency of a screw jack is less than 50%.

Machines are rated in terms of their *output;* thus, a 5-hp motor is one that can *deliver* 5 hp without exceeding its design limitations; if its efficiency is 80%, the power input to the machine is 5 hp/0.80 = 6.25 hp.

Illustrative Problem

Suppose an operator to exert a force of 16 lb in raising a load weighing 2 tons with a screw jack that has a bar 1.5 ft long and a screw with 6 threads to the inch. Compute (*a*) the actual and ideal mechanical advantage of this machine and (*b*) its efficiency.

The actual mechanical advantage of the machine is $\dfrac{W}{F} = \dfrac{4000 \text{ lb}}{16 \text{ lb}} = 250$

and the ideal advantage is $\dfrac{2\pi l}{p} = \dfrac{2\pi \times 1.5 \text{ ft}}{\frac{1}{6} \times \frac{1}{12} \text{ ft}} = 679$. In one turn of the screw, the load is raised $\frac{1}{6}$ in. or 0.01389 ft, and the distance through which the operator exerts his force is $2\pi \times 1.5 = 9.43$ ft. Hence for each turn the energy output is (4000 lb)(0.01389 ft) = 55.56 ft·lb, and the energy input is (16 lb)(9.43 ft) = 150.9 ft·lb. The efficiency is therefore $\dfrac{55.56 \text{ ft·lb}}{150.9 \text{ ft·lb}}$ × 100 = 36.8%. Note that this result is the same as the ratio of 250 to 679 given above.

It may be stated that the efficiency of a machine always equals the ratio of the actual mechanical advantage to the ideal mechanical advantage.

PROBLEMS

1. A crate weighing 2500 lb is hoisted vertically upward from the hold of a vessel a distance of 30 ft at constant velocity. Compute the amount of work done on the crate.

2. A block having a mass of 10 kg, initially at rest, is pushed along a smooth, level surface by a constant force of 50,000 dynes applied for 3 sec. How much work is done on the block?

3. A box that weighs 50 lb is moved 15 ft in 5 sec at constant speed along a rough horizontal surface by a horizontal pull. If the coefficient of friction between the sliding surfaces is 0.25, how much work is done on the box?

4. How much work would be done on an elevator that weighs 2 tons in accelerating it upward from rest at the rate of 3 ft/sec² for 4 sec?

5. A freight car rolls slowly along a track. A man walking beside the track exerts a steady forward push of 5 lb on the car while the car moves forward 50 ft. Did the man do work on the car, and if so how much?

6. How can the work done in Probs. 1, 2, 3, and 4 above be accounted for?

7. Refer to Prob. 25 of Chap. 3 and determine (a) the kinetic energy of the block at the instant it leaves the table top, (b) the amount of kinetic energy it gains by falling to the floor, and (c) its kinetic energy just before it strikes the floor.

8. A big-league baseball weighs 5 oz. If a pitcher exerts a constant forward force on the ball for 0.05 sec and throws it with a speed of 100 ft/sec, (a) what force does he exert on the ball? (b) how much work does he do on the ball? and (c) how far does the ball move while the forward force acts upon it?

9. In § 23, Prob. II deals with an accelerating proton. Take the mass of the proton to be constant at 1.672×10^{-24} gm and compute (a) the initial kinetic energy of the proton and (b) the increase in its kinetic energy due to acceleration. Express the results in electron·volts.

10. A wheel that weighs 40 lb has a radius of 15 in. and a radius of gyration of 10 in. What is the kinetic energy of the wheel when rolling along the ground at 60 mi/hr?

11. A pendulum bob of 50-gm mass hangs at the end of a thread 50 cm long. The pendulum sweeps through an angle of 30° on each side of its midposition as it vibrates to and fro. What is the kinetic energy of the bob as it moves through the midpoint of its path, and what is its velocity at that point?

12. Compute the amount of work done on each of the following objects in raising it from a position flat on the ground to one in which it stands upright: (a) a slender rod 16 ft long, of negligible weight, and carrying a weight of 50 lb at its midpoint; (b) the same rod but carrying five 10-lb weights, one

at each end and the others equally spaced between them; and (c) a uniform ladder 16 ft long and weighing 50 lb.

13. A wheel that has a mass of 3 slugs and a radius of gyration of 6 in. is turning at 480 rev/min in stationary bearings, and is brought to rest by pressing a brake shoe against its rim. (a) How much energy is converted into heat? (b) If the wheel has an outside radius of 9 in. and makes 40 rev while stopping, what is the force of friction acting at its rim?

14. Refer to Prob. 3 and suppose that the applied force is discontinued when the box has moved 15 ft. How much farther will the box slide?

15. A block of 1500-gm mass, initially at rest, is caused to slide along a level surface by a constant horizontal push of 6×10^5 dynes. When the block has moved 100 cm the push is discontinued, but the block slides 20 cm farther before it stops. Compute the coefficient of sliding friction between the block and the surface.

16. In Prob. 25 of Chap. 5, what is the speed of the ball as it passes through the highest point of its circular path?

17. A dumb-waiter that weighs 100 lb starts from rest and is given an upward acceleration of 4 ft/sec², its motion being opposed by a frictional force of 20 lb. (a) From the laws of accelerated motion find the velocity of the dumb-waiter at an instant when it is 10 ft above its starting point, and compute its kinetic energy at that instant. (b) Compute the work done on the dumb-waiter by the applied force during this 10-ft displacement, and apportion this work between that expended in opposing friction and in increasing its kinetic and potential energy. (c) Show that the work done by the resultant force equals the increase in kinetic energy.

18. A box weighing 50 lb is pushed a distance of 8 ft up a plane inclined at 36.9° with the horizontal, by a constant *horizontal* force of 100 lb. The box starts from rest, and the coefficient of friction between the box and the plane is 0.20. Compute (a) the amount of work done upon the box, (b) the energy used in opposing friction, (c) the kinetic energy imparted to the box, and (d) the final velocity of the box.

19. A spring that requires a force of 50 lb to compress it 1 in. is compressed a total amount of 3 in. and is placed behind a block weighing 10 lb at the bottom of a smooth plane inclined at 30° with the horizontal. The spring is released and projects the block up the incline. (a) How far does the block slide up the plane before it comes to rest? (b) What is the maximum compression produced in the spring by the block upon returning?

20. Solve the preceding problem on the assumption that the plane is not smooth; take the coefficient of friction between the block and the plane to be 0.25.

21. A solid sphere starts from rest and rolls without slipping down a plane 300 cm long inclined at 30° with the horizontal. Assume that no energy is wasted through friction and compute the speed of the sphere when it reaches the bottom of the incline.

22. A pump rated at 10 hp is used to pump water into an elevated tank. How many gallons can it pump per minute to an average height of 20 ft without exceeding its rating?

23. A train that weighs 200 tons is to be moved along a level track. Assume that the backward force of friction amounts to 8 lb per ton of weight, and compute (a) the power required to bring the train from standstill to a velocity of 50 mi/hr in 30 sec and (b) the power required to pull it at a constant velocity of 50 mi/hr.

24. An inclined plane is 10 ft long, and one end is 4 ft higher than the other. A force of 125 lb parallel to the plane is found necessary to push a 200-lb box up the plane at constant velocity. Consider this inclined plane as a simple machine and compute (*a*) its ideal mechanical advantage, (*b*) its actual mechanical advantage, and (*c*) its efficiency.

25. A motor drives a hoist that raises a 1-ton elevator 120 ft in 10 sec at constant speed. If the efficiency of the motor is 80% and that of the hoist is 50%, what power is supplied (*a*) to the elevator, (*b*) to the hoist, and (*c*) to the motor?

$$E = \frac{mv^2}{2}$$

$$E = FS$$

$$E = \frac{I\omega^2}{2}$$

$$E = T\theta$$

$$E = Wh \uparrow$$

$$E = mgh \downarrow$$

$$mgh = \frac{I\omega^2}{2} + \frac{mv^2}{2}$$

$$R\omega = v$$

$$v = at$$

$$F = \frac{mv}{T}$$

$$25000$$

$$A = \frac{W}{F} = \frac{S}{h} = \frac{l_1}{l_2} = \frac{2\pi l}{p} = \frac{l}{h}$$

8

STATICS

74. Equilibrium. In this chapter a study will be made of bodies that are in equilibrium and of the requirements that must be fulfilled in order to maintain them in this condition. *A body is said to be in equilibrium if its acceleration is zero.* The term "equilibrium" thus applies to an object that remains at rest and also to an object that moves uniformly in a straight line. Under both circumstances, the object has no acceleration, and the principles of statics apply equally to each. But the body at rest must *remain* at rest in order to be in equilibrium. Although a ball thrown upward comes to rest *momentarily* before it starts to fall, it has a downward acceleration due to gravity even at that instant. Hence it is not in equilibrium.

A body accelerates if it is acted upon by either a resultant force or a resultant torque; a resultant force produces linear acceleration and a resultant torque produces angular acceleration. It follows, therefore, that two conditions must be satisfied if a body is to remain in equilibrium: first, the forces acting upon the body must balance, and second, the torques due to these forces must balance. The forces referred to throughout this chapter are assumed to act in a single plane.

75. First Condition of Equilibrium. The simplest case of equilibrium is that of a body acted upon by only two forces, for one of these must be equal and opposite to the other. A stationary ball suspended by a cord as in Fig. 73, for example, is acted on by only two forces. In the vector diagram at the right, these are shown acting upon the ball at O; the weight W of the ball is the attraction of the earth pulling downward upon it, and the force T is the tension in the cord pulling upward upon it. Since the ball is in equilibrium, the tension in the cord is equal to the weight of the ball and the forces T and W are equal.

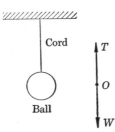

FIG. 73. Two forces producing equilibrium

When a body is in equilibrium under the action of more than two forces, the analysis can be simplified by resolving all of them into components and by considering the components rather than the forces themselves. The forces may be resolved along any directions desired, usually along the horizontal and vertical axes. When a body is in equilibrium, it must be in equilibrium in the horizontal direction, which means that the horizontal com-

124

ponents of the forces must balance. If components to the right are regarded as positive and those to the left as negative, the algebraic sum of all the horizontal components must be zero. Similarly, the body must be in equilibrium in the vertical direction, which means that the sum of all the vertical components must be zero. These statements point to a general conclusion about the equilibrium of a body under the action of forces that individually tend to accelerate it. For a body that has no linear acceleration, *the first condition of equilibrium states that the vector sum of all the forces acting on a body along any direction shall equal zero.* If the sum of the horizontal components is represented by ΣH and the sum of the vertical components by ΣV, then the first condition of equilibrium can be symbolized as:

$$\left. \begin{array}{c} \Sigma H = 0 \\ \Sigma V = 0 \end{array} \right\} \tag{67}$$

This principle is useful in determining the forces necessary to support a body in equilibrium.

Illustrative Problem

Suppose, for example, that a ball of weight $W = 10$ lb is supported from the ceiling by two cords as shown in part I of Fig. 74; the cords A and B

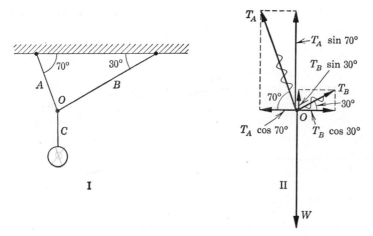

Fig. 74. Three forces producing equilibrium

make angles of 70° and 30° respectively with the ceiling and are knotted at O to the cord C which supports the weight. The tension in cord C is equal to the weight of the ball, as in the previous example, and the tensions in the other cords are to be determined.

Each cord exerts a force upon the knot O, and since the knot is at rest, it is in equilibrium under the action of three forces. These are represented in part II as follows: the weight of the ball, W, acts directly downward; the tension T_A in cord A (unknown) acts along the direction of A; and the tension T_B in cord B (also unknown) acts along the direction of B. The forces T_A and T_B will be resolved into horizontal and vertical components, and the problem solved by applying Eqs. 67. The components of the tension T_A are $T_A \cos 70°$ horizontally and $T_A \sin 70°$ vertically, and those of tension T_B are $T_B \cos 30°$ horizontally and $T_B \sin 30°$ vertically, all acting at point O. Then

$$\Sigma H = T_B \cos 30° - T_A \cos 70° = 0$$

$$\Sigma V = T_A \sin 70° + T_B \sin 30° - W = 0$$

whence $0.866T_B = 0.342T_A$ and $0.940T_A + 0.500T_B = 10$. These equations, when solved simultaneously, give the tension in cord A as $T_A = 8.79$ lb and that in cord B as $T_B = 3.47$ lb. Thus, in supporting the 10-lb weight in the manner described, the cords A and B are subjected to tensions of 8.79 lb and 3.47 lb respectively.

Sometimes the forces that produce equilibrium all pass through a common point and the first condition of equilibrium is sufficient for their determination, as in the foregoing problem.

76. Second Condition of Equilibrium. Even though the forces acting upon a body satisfy the first condition just stated, it does not necessarily follow that the body is in equilibrium. For instance, the forces may be equal and opposite, so that $\Sigma H = 0$ and $\Sigma V = 0$, thus satisfying Eqs. 67, and yet may be so applied that they exert a torque upon the body tending to set it into rotation. To counteract this tendency, it is necessary that the body be subjected to another torque just equal and opposite to the first. Hence, *the second condition of equilibrium states that, about any axis, the torques acting upon a body shall be balanced, the clockwise torques being equal to the counter-clockwise torques.* If clockwise torques are taken as positive and counter-clockwise torques as negative, the second condition of equilibrium states that the sum of all the torques, ΣT, acting upon a body shall be zero, or

$$\Sigma T = 0 \tag{68}$$

Illustrative Problem

The conditions of equilibrium are illustrated by a problem based on the bent lever ABC in Fig. 75. Part I shows the lever hinged on a pin at B, with a 50-lb force applied at A in the direction indicated, and a weight W supported at C. Calculate the value of W which is just sufficient to keep the lever stationary in the position shown, and find also the horizontal and vertical components of the thrust exerted on the weighted lever by the hinge-pin at B. The weight of the lever itself is negligible.

The problem involves only forces and their lever arms; all forces are expressed in pounds and lever arms in feet, and the units are omitted from the equations for simplicity. Show the forces acting on the lever as in part II of the figure; resolve the 50-lb force at A into a horizontal component, $50 \cos 30°$, and a vertical component, $50 \sin 30°$, and cross out the 50-lb force itself, since it is replaced by its components. Represent the horizontal and vertical thrusts of the hinge-pin by h and v respectively. Then, from the first condition of equilibrium, the horizontal forces to the right equal those to the left, and the forces acting upward equal those acting downward; thus

$$\Sigma H = h - 50 \cos 30° = 0$$

$$\Sigma V = 50 \sin 30° + v - W = 0$$

From the second condition of equilibrium, the sum of the torques due to

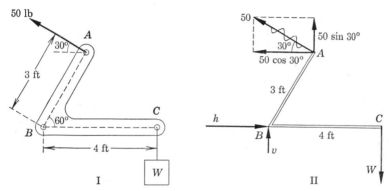

Fig. 75. Forces on a bent lever

these forces, taken about any axis, also equals zero. Moments are taken about an axis at B because two unknown forces, h and v, act through this axis and their moments are thus eliminated. The moment of the 50-lb force is computed more simply from the force itself than from its components. Hence the torque equation becomes

$$\Sigma T_B = W \times 4 = 50 \times 3 = 0$$

From the three foregoing equations, the desired results are obtained. The torque equation gives $W = \dfrac{50 \times 3}{4} = 37.5$ lb, and the other two give $h = 50 \cos 30° = 50 \times 0.866 = 43.3$ lb and $v = W - 50 \sin 30° = 37.5 - 50 \times 0.500 = 12.5$ lb.

Although it was natural in the foregoing problem to choose the hinge-pin as the axis about which torques were taken, any other axis might have been selected equally well, since the body is in equilibrium, but the same axis should be used throughout the calculation. This statement can be verified by solving the problem again, taking moments about some other axis.

77. Equilibrium Produced by Three Forces. A theorem of great value, based upon the second condition of equilibrium, states that *if three non-parallel forces acting upon a body produce equilibrium, their lines of action must pass through a common point.* This theorem can be proved by taking moments of forces about the intersection of two of the lines of action and

showing that the lever arm of the remaining force must be zero.   Fig. 76
represents a body in equilibrium under the action of three forces, shown incorrectly for this demonstration.   Since their lines of action are not parallel,

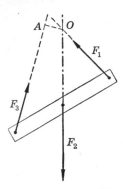

any two, if extended, will meet at some point.   Thus,
the lines of action of F_1 and F_2 meet at O.   From this
point a line OA is drawn perpendicular to the third
force F_3, meeting its line of action at A.   From the
second condition of equilibrium, $\Sigma T = 0$, the sum of
the moments of all the forces, taken about an axis
through O, equals zero.   The moments of F_1 and F_2 are
both zero, since the lines of action of these forces pass
through O, and thus their lever arms are zero.   Since
the body is in equilibrium, the moment of the remaining force F_3 about O must be zero; and since the force
F_3 is not zero, its lever arm OA is zero; that is, the line

Fig. 76.   For equilib-
rium the three forces
should pass through a
common point

of action of F_3 must pass through O.   Hence the lines
of action of three forces in equilibrium pass through a
common point.   This theorem is often useful in showing the exact direction of some unknown force.

78. Resultant of Parallel Forces.   The parallelogram and polygon constructions of §§ 12 and 13 for finding the resultant of two forces cannot be
applied where the forces are parallel; to find the resultant of two parallel
forces, it is necessary to consider what the term "resultant" basically means.
The resultant of two forces is a single force that can completely replace the
individual forces and produce all the effects that the two forces themselves
produce.

This definition will be applied to two forces acting upon a rod of negligible
weight, as shown in Fig. 77; these forces act
vertically downward, F_1 at A and F_2 at B.
Since their resultant is to be exactly equivalent to the forces themselves, its effect must
equal the joint effect of F_1 and F_2 as regards
translation of the rod.   Hence the resultant is
necessarily directed downward and its magnitude is $F_1 + F_2$; however, its line of action is
still to be determined.   The resultant F is indicated in the figure by a dotted vector drawn
through some point C, selected at random,

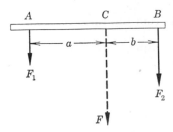

Fig. 77.   Location of the resultant of two parallel forces

which divides the line AB into two parts, a and b.   But the resultant must
also produce the same effect as F_1 and F_2 with regard to rotation of the rod;
that is, the torque due to F about any axis must equal the sum of the
torques due to F_1 and F_2 about the same axis.   Thus, about an axis
through A, $Fa = F_2(a + b)$.   Similarly, about an axis through B, $Fb =$

$F_1(a + b)$. From these equations, a relation is found between the forces and their lever arms, namely,

$$\frac{F_2}{F_1} = \frac{a}{b} \tag{69}$$

a result that would also be found by placing the torque due to F equal to the torques due to F_1 and F_2, all about an axis through C. Hence, for two parallel forces that act in the same direction, the resultant has the same direction as the forces and is equal to their sum, and its line of action divides the distance between them into two parts that are inversely proportional to the respective forces.

It is also clear that the rod in Fig. 77 would balance on a fulcrum placed at C; that is, that a force equal and opposite to F and acting along the same line would place the system in equilibrium. The foregoing principles can be extended to give the resultant of any number of parallel forces, whether or not all of them are directed the same way. The usual procedure is to determine the force which, included with the forces given, produces equilibrium; such a force is called the *equilibrant* of the given forces, and *the resultant is equal and opposite to the equilibrant and acts along the same line.*

Under certain conditions a body acted upon by several parallel forces is held in equilibrium by two or more forces instead of by a single equilibrant. These forces can also be found by applying the conditions of equilibrium.

Illustrative Problem

As an illustration, consider a rod 12 ft long supported by two cords and carrying four loads totaling 24 lb. The location of these loads is shown in Fig. 78, where the distances are indicated in feet. Find the tensions T_A and T_B in the cords; assume that the weight of the rod is negligible.

Apply the conditions of equilibrium, with forces in pounds and distances in feet. From the first condition:

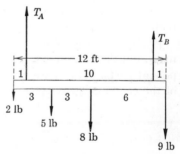

FIG. 78. Weighted rod supported by two cords

$$\Sigma V = T_A + T_B - 2 - 5 - 8 - 9 = 0$$

whence $T_A + T_B = 24$. From the second condition, with moments about an axis through the left end of the rod,

$$\Sigma T = 5 \times 3 + 8 \times 6 + 9 \times 12 - T_A \times 1 - T_B \times 11 = 0$$

or $T_A + 11T_B = 171$. These equations, when solved simultaneously, give the tensions in the cords as $T_A = 9.3$ lb and $T_B = 14.7$ lb.

It is interesting to note that this problem might have been solved by two applications of the condition $\Sigma T = 0$, without making use of the first condition of equilibrium. Thus, with moments taken about an axis through the left end of the rod, the result is $T_A + 11T_B = 171$ as before, and with moments taken about an axis through the right end,

$$T_A \times 11 + T_B \times 1 - 2 \times 12 - 5 \times 9 - 8 \times 6 = 0$$

or

$$11T_A + T_B = 117$$

From these equations the tensions in the cords are found to be $T_A = 9.3$ lb and $T_B = 14.7$ lb, as before.

If the rod in the foregoing problem were supported by props instead of by cords, and if these were located at the same places as the cords, the props would divide the load between them in the same way, each being under compression and exerting an upward force on the rod. Such upward forces are usually termed the *reactions* of the supports.

79. Center of Gravity. The attraction exerted by the earth upon an object extends to each particle of matter that the object contains, and thus its weight may be regarded as a system of parallel forces acting upon all the particles in it. When these parallel forces are replaced by their resultant, this single force is exactly equivalent to them. For a given object there is a particular point through which the resultant of the weight forces always passes, whatever the orientation of the object; this point is called the *center of gravity* of the object. Hence the weight of a body, although actually a system of parallel forces acting upon all of its component parts, can be correctly represented by a single force acting downward at the center of gravity.

Practically, the center of gravity of a body coincides with its center of mass, but deals with the weight w instead of the mass m of each of its component parts. Its location can be computed as in § 43; thus, the coordinates of the center of gravity G are

$$x_G = \frac{\Sigma wx}{\Sigma w} \qquad y_G = \frac{\Sigma wy}{\Sigma w} \qquad z_G = \frac{\Sigma wz}{\Sigma w} \tag{70}$$

These expressions are interpreted and used in the same manner as those in the section referred to above. A difference between the center of gravity and center of mass would not exist unless the body were tremendously large: so large that the weights of the particles no longer formed a system of parallel forces or that the acceleration g due to gravity varied appreciably from point to point of the body.

Illustrative Problem

A stationary truck of 150-in. wheel base weighs 2600 lb and its center of gravity is 90 in. in front of the rear axle. The truck carries a load of 3200 lb which is placed centrally with its center of gravity 30 in. in front of the rear axle. Compute the force that each tire exerts on the ground; also find the horizontal location of the center of gravity of the loaded truck.

The conditions of the problem are indicated in part I of Fig. 79. The truck is represented by the line AB in part II of the figure, and the weights of truck and load are shown, each acting downward at its own center of gravity. The upward thrust of the ground on the two rear tires is represented as a single force R, and a similar thrust at the front tires is represented likewise as F. From the first condition of equilibrium, $R + F - 3200 - 2600 = 0$, whence $R = 5800$ lb $- F$. From the second condition of equilibrium, with moments about an axis perpendicular to the paper through A, $3200 \times 30 + 2600 \times 90 - F \times 150 = 0$; from which $F = 2200$ lb. Then $R = 5800 - 2200 = 3600$ lb. But the forces exerted by the tires on the ground are equal to the reaction of the ground on the tires, and thus each front tire presses against the ground with a force of $F \div 2 = 1100$ lb, and also each rear tire presses with a force of $R \div 2 = 1800$ lb.

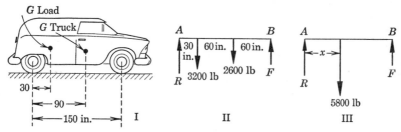

FIG. 79. Forces involved in truck problem

To find the center of gravity of the loaded truck with respect to the rear axle, use Eq. 70:

$$x = \frac{\Sigma wx}{\Sigma w} = \frac{(2600)(90) + (3200)(30)}{2600 + 3200} = 56.9$$

whence the center of gravity of the loaded truck is in front of the rear axle by a distance $x = 56.9$ in., as indicated in part III of the figure.

For bodies of simple shapes, the center of gravity can be located by inspection, since it is at the geometric center, provided the material is of uniform density throughout. Thus the center of gravity of a rod, tube, or bar, whether of circular or rectangular cross-section, is located on the axis midway between the ends; for a sphere it is at the center; and for a cone it is on the axis at a point one-fourth of the way from the base to the vertex.

When a homogeneous body is in the form of a sheet, the center of gravity is at the center of area of the sheet. For a sheet of circular shape, the center of area is located at the center of the circle; for a rectangle it is at the intersection of the diagonals; and for a triangle it is one-third of the distance from the middle point of any side to the opposite vertex. For a sheet that is not of simple shape, the center of gravity can often be located by the process of subdivision.

Illustrative Problem

A 6-in. square is cut from one corner of a square sheet as shown in Fig. 80. Find the center of gravity of the piece that remains.

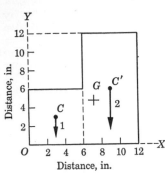

FIG. 80. Irregular sheet and its center of gravity G

In the figure, the piece referred to is shown with one corner at the origin O of the X, Y coordinate axes. This L-shaped piece is regarded as made up of two parts: a square of weight 1 centered at C and a rectangle of weight 2 centered at C'. The center of gravity of this combination with respect to the origin is located by its coordinates; these are given by Eqs. 70 as follows, with distances in inches:

$$x = \frac{\Sigma wx}{\Sigma w} = \frac{(1 \times 3) + (2 \times 9)}{1 + 2} = 7.00$$

$$y = \frac{\Sigma wy}{\Sigma w} = \frac{(1 \times 3) + (2 \times 6)}{1 + 2} = 5.00$$

Thus, the center of gravity of the L-shaped sheet has the coordinates $x = 7.00$ in., $y = 5.00$ in. This point is marked G in the figure.

The center of gravity can be determined experimentally for an irregular solid by suspending the body successively from three different points. In each test the body comes to rest with its center of gravity on a line directly beneath the point of suspension; the intersection of the three lines is the center of gravity. For a plane object, two such tests suffice. Thus, in Fig. 81 a sheet cut to represent the cross-section of a retaining wall is under test in this manner. When this model is supported at point S and displaced from its position of rest as shown, its weight W sets up a counterclockwise torque about S which rotates the model until its center of gravity G is directly below the point of suspension. After the vertical line through S is determined, the model is supported at another point and the test is repeated. The intersection of the two lines fixes the center of gravity of the model and of the cross-section that it represents.

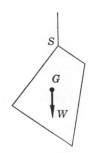

FIG. 81. Model suspended in an experiment to find its center of gravity

80. Conditions of Stability. The way in which a body is supported with respect to its center of gravity has a great effect upon the stability of equilibrium of the body. A cubical box resting on a level floor as shown in part I of Fig. 82 is in *stable equilibrium* because if one edge is raised a little and then released, the box falls back again to its original position. Tilting the box shifts the reaction R of the floor to the edge S, and the unbalanced torque set up by the weight W of the box acting at the center of gravity G produces rotation to restore the box to its initial position.   The same effect is produced in a body suspended from a point above its center of gravity, as indicated in the preceding section.

A ball resting on a level surface, as in part II of the figure, when moved to a new position on the supporting surface shows no tendency either to return to its former position or to go the other way.   Its weight W and the reaction R of the surface lie along a single line and therefore do not set up a

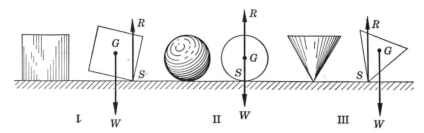

FIG. 82.   Stable, neutral, and unstable equilibrium.   The weight W of the object acts downward through its center of gravity G, and the reaction R acts upward through the point of contact S

torque; in consequence the ball is said to be in *neutral equilibrium*.   So also is a cylinder lying on its side upon a level surface.

Part III of Fig. 82 illustrates a condition of *unstable equilibrium*.   Here a cone (not rotating) is shown while momentarily balanced upon the vertex. The slightest displacement of the cone shifts its weight W to one side and sets up a torque about the vertex S which increases with the displacement and causes the cone to tip over.

81. The Balance.   The equal-arm analytical balance offers an interesting study in equilibrium.   In this instrument, shown pictorially in Fig. 4 and

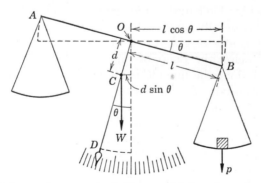

FIG. 83.   Balance of torques in finding sensitivity of equal-arm balance

diagrammatically in Fig. 83, a long slender beam AB of length $2l$ supports a scale-pan at each end and is pivoted at its midpoint O.   At this point it carries a downwardly projecting pointer OD, the lower end of which plays across a scale. The moving system of weight W is symmetrical and its center of gravity is at some point C along the pointer, a distance d below the pivot O. This distance is of importance in the operation of the balance and is exaggerated in the figure for clearness. The broken lines represent the beam and pointer when not deflected, and the solid lines show the beam deflected through the angle θ as a result of adding a very small weight p to the right-hand scale-pan. The deflecting torque about an axis through O is $p \times l \cos \theta$, and becomes smaller and smaller as θ increases. At the same time, the center of gravity is displaced, thus producing an opposing torque $Wd \sin \theta$ about the same axis; this torque becomes larger and larger as θ increases. The balance evidently comes to rest when

$$pl \cos \theta = Wd \sin \theta$$

A balance is said to be sensitive when it deflects through a large angle with a very small weight added to one scale-pan; the sensitivity is usually expressed as the deflection in scale divisions per milligram of added weight. Physically, however, the sensitivity of a balance is defined from the equation of balance that appears above. Although the ratio of the deflection θ to the load p cannot be found directly from this equation, the ratio of $\tan \theta$ to p, which is practically the same, is easily found as

$$\frac{\tan \theta}{p} = \frac{\sin \theta}{p \cos \theta} = \frac{l}{Wd}$$

and serves to express the sensitivity of the balance in terms of its constants l, W, and d.

This equation shows that for a balance to have great sensitivity the arms should have considerable length l and the beam should have a small weight W, conditions that usually imply a truss-like design to obtain the necessary rigidity; and the center of gravity of the moving system should be only a short distance d below the point of support. A small weight that can be raised or lowered along the line OC is often added to the moving system so that its center of gravity can be shifted to adapt the balance to measurements requiring more or less sensitivity.

82. Application of the Principles of Equilibrium. In applying the conditions of equilibrium to the solution of problems it is advisable to follow a definite procedure in order to avoid confusion and error. The procedure recommended is as follows:

1. Make a sketch of the device or structure; mark upon it all the known data; and assign symbols to the desired quantities.

2. Isolate some member or point of the body as the portion to be considered, and make a force diagram showing *all* the forces acting *upon* it.

3. Apply the conditions of equilibrium to this portion, by writing the

equations expressing $\Sigma H = 0$, $\Sigma V = 0$, and $\Sigma T = 0$. The moments may be taken about any one axis.

4. Solve these equations for the quantities desired.

5. Follow the same procedure for the other points or members involved in the problem.

Illustrative Problems

I. A uniform ladder 15 ft long and weighing 50 lb leans against a smooth vertical wall at an angle of 60° with level ground, and a man weighing 150 lb has climbed to a rung two-thirds the way up the ladder. With what force does the ladder press against the wall and ground? What is the smallest value for the coefficient of friction between the ladder and ground in order that the ladder shall not slip?

The ladder and the forces acting upon it are shown in Fig. 84. Herein h is the reaction by the wall upon the ladder and balances its push against the wall; it is perpendicular to the wall because that surface was assumed frictionless. Force v is the vertical reaction of the ground on the ladder, and f is the frictional force of the ground and acts in opposition to the direction in which the ladder tends to slide. Apply the conditions of equilibrium to find these three forces:

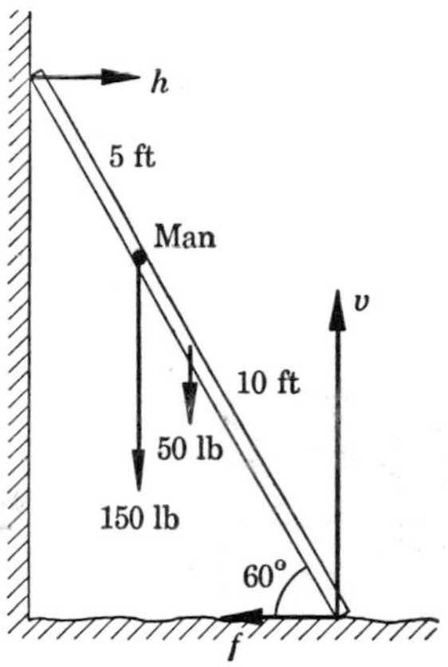

$$\Sigma H = f - h = 0$$

$$\Sigma V = v - 50 - 150 = 0$$

FIG. 84. Forces on ladder leaning against smooth wall

$\Sigma T = h\,15 \sin 60° - 50 \times 7.5 \cos 60° - 150 \times 10 \cos 60° = 0$ (about foot of ladder), whence $f = h = \dfrac{(375 + 1500) \cos 60°}{15 \sin 60°} = 72.2$ lb and $v = 200$ lb.

Hence, the ladder pushes against the wall with a normal force of 72.2 lb and pushes against the ground with a force having a horizontal component of 72.2 lb and a vertical component of 200 lb. The ratio of the frictional force to the normal force v at the base of the ladder is $\dfrac{72.2}{200}$, or 0.361. If the coefficient of friction between ladder and ground were just 0.361, the ladder would begin to slide when the man reached the position two-thirds of the way up.

Note that the push of the ladder against the ground is not directed along the line of the ladder. This push makes an angle with the horizontal given by $\tan^{-1} \dfrac{200}{72.2} = 70.1°$, whereas the inclination of the ladder from the horizontal is 60°.

II. A crane consists of a uniform boom 10 ft long weighing 300 lb, hinged on a mast at one end and supported by a cable at the other. The directions of these members are shown by the angles in part I of Fig. 85. A load weighing 600 lb is attached to the outer end of the boom. Compute the tension in the cable and also the horizontal and vertical thrusts on the hinge-pin.

Select the boom as the member to be isolated, and make a force diagram as shown in part II, wherein P is the tension in the cable, and h and v are

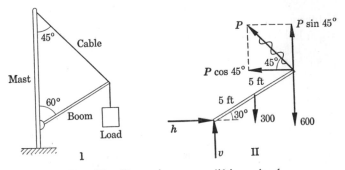

FIG. 85. Forces in a crane lifting a load

respectively the horizontal and vertical reactions on the lower end of the boom due to the thrust of the hinge-pin. The weight of the boom is considered as a single force acting at its center of gravity and P is replaced by its components. From the first condition of equilibrium

$$\Sigma H = P \cos 45° - h = 0$$

$$\Sigma V = 600 + 300 - P \sin 45° - v = 0$$

From the second condition of equilibrium, with moments taken about an axis through the hinge-pin so as to eliminate the torques due to the reactions h and v,

$$\Sigma T = 300 \times 5 \cos 30° + 600 \times 10 \cos 30° - P \sin 45° \times 10 \cos 30°$$

$$- P \cos 45° \times 10 \sin 30° = 0$$

From the torque equation, the tension in the cable is found to be $P = 672$ lb. With this value known, the force

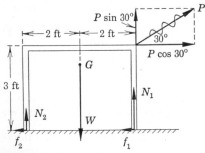

FIG. 86. Forces on a bench in uniform motion

equations give $h = 475$ and $v = 425$; thus, the horizontal and vertical thrusts on the hinge-pin are respectively 475 and 425 lb.

III. A work bench 4 ft wide and 3 ft high is dragged along a level floor at constant speed by applying a constant force P at its top edge in a direction 30° upward from the horizontal, as indicated in Fig. 86. The bench has a weight $W = 130$ lb, and its center of gravity G is on the center line. Take the coefficient of friction between bench and floor as 0.25, and determine (*a*) the value of the force needed and (*b*) the vertical reactions of the floor.

(a) The forces acting on the bench are shown in the diagram; N_1 is the total vertical reaction of the floor on the two front legs, N_2 the corresponding reaction on the rear legs, and f_1 and f_2 are the frictional forces at the respective legs. Resolve the force P into its components $P \cos 30°$ and $P \sin 30°$, and apply the first condition of equilibrium:

$$\Sigma H = P \cos 30° - f_1 - f_2 = 0$$

$$\Sigma V = W - P \sin 30° - N_1 - N_2 = 0$$

From these equations, $P \cos 30° = f_1 + f_2$, and $N_1 + N_2 = W - P \sin 30°$, whence $P \cos 30° = f_1 + f_2 = \mu(N_1 + N_2) = \mu(W - P \sin 30°)$. The required pull is found by solving for P and substituting numerical values; thus

$$P = \frac{\mu W}{\cos 30° + \mu \sin 30°} = \frac{0.25 \times 130}{0.866 + 0.25 \times 0.500} = 32.8 \text{ lb}$$

(b) Apply the second condition of equilibrium, taking moments about any axis, say one at the base of the rear legs. The torque equation, with forces in pounds and lever arms in feet, is:

$$\Sigma T = (W \times 2) + (P \cos 30° \times 3) - (N_1 \times 4) - (P \sin 30° \times 4) = 0$$

whence $4N_1 = 2W + 3P \cos 30° - 4P \sin 30°$, and numerically, $N_1 = (2 \times 130 + 3 \times 32.8 \times 0.866 - 4 \times 32.8 \times 0.500) \div 4 = 69.9$; also $N_2 = W - P \sin 30° - N_1 = 130 - 32.8 \times 0.500 - 69.9 = 43.7$. Consequently, the vertical reactions on the bench are as follows: 34.95 lb at each front leg, and 21.85 lb at each rear leg.

PROBLEMS

1. A 1-kg mass is supported by two cords a and b of lengths 75 and 100 cm respectively, which are fastened to the ceiling at two points 125 cm apart. Compute the tension in each cord.

2. The diagram shows a 1000-lb I-beam hanging at rest in a rope sling. (a) If each of the angles θ is 40°, what is the tension in each of the ropes A, B, and C? (b) For what value of θ would these tensions be equal?

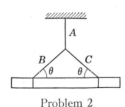

Problem 2

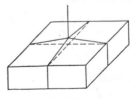

Problem 3

3. A package weighing 50 lb and measuring 12 in. along each top edge is tied with cord as shown in the diagram. When the package is held by the cord at the top central point, the knot at that point is 1 in. above the top surface of the package. Compute the maximum tension in the cord.

4. In attempting to move a car that is stuck in the mud, a man stretches a rope horizontally from the car to a tree 50 ft away and then pushes sidewise on the rope at its midpoint, as shown in the diagram. Suppose that

when he has displaced the midpoint 1 ft, he is exerting a force of 120 lb and the car is just about to move. What force is the rope then exerting on the car?

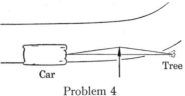

Problem 4

5. In Prob. 3 of Chap. 2, a beam is supported by two ropes. What is the tension in each rope if the beam weighs 1000 lb?

6. Two masses, A of 500 gm and B of unknown value, are joined by a cord and the combination is supported from the ceiling. One supporting cord extends from A upward at an angle of 45° from the horizontal, and the other from B upward at 60° from the horizontal. What is the value of the mass B if the cord between A and B is horizontal?

7. A uniform meter stick of 300-gm mass supports three loads: 500 gm at the 20-cm mark, 800 gm at the 60-cm mark, and 400 gm at the 100-cm mark. At what mark should a fulcrum be located so that the loaded stick will balance upon it?

8. A uniform plank 12 ft long and weighing 90 lb is supported on two props located 1 ft from each end. When a 160-lb man stands 2 ft from the center of the plank, what is the reaction at each support?

9. In the diagram, the equilateral triangle ABC represents a wire frame measuring 10 cm on each side. The frame is of negligible weight and is held at rest in a vertical plane by three forces: 200,000 dynes directed horizontally to the left midway between A and B; 500,000 dynes toward the right perpendicular to BC at its midpoint; and a force to be determined acting somewhere on the side AC. What is the magnitude, direction, and point of application of this force to keep the frame in equilibrium with AC horizontal?

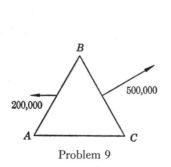

Problem 9

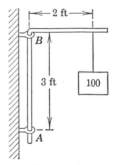

Problem 10

10. The crane in the diagram consists of an L-shaped bar supported by ring bolts at A and B; it carries a load weighing 100 lb at a point 2 ft from B, and its own weight is negligible. Construct a diagram showing the forces acting on the crane, and compute the horizontal and vertical components of the forces exerted upon it by the rings at A and B.

11. The box in the diagram represents a cover for a typewriter; it is symmetrical, measures 12 × 12 in. × 7 in. high, and weighs 1 lb. The box is hinged to a fixed support along the bottom edge *AB*, and is otherwise unfastened. How large a horizontal push *P* can be applied to the top edge *CD* as shown, without causing the box to turn on its hinges?

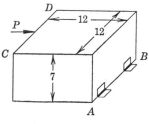

Problem 11

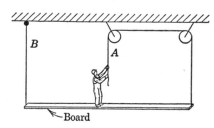

Problem 12

12. The board in the diagram weighs 30 lb and is suspended at one end by rope *B*. A man who weighs 180 lb stands at the center of the board and pulls down on rope *A* to keep the board horizontal. (*a*) What force does the man exert on rope *A*? (*b*) What is the tension in rope *B*?

13. A bridge table measures 30 in. along each edge of the top, and the legs are folded under it symmetrically. For convenience in carrying it down stairs that have a slope of 37° with the horizontal, it is held so that its upper and lower edges slope at this same angle. The table is supported by a single vertical force applied at a point on the upper edge; how far from the top corner should the point of support be located?

14. A square sheet measures 24 cm along each diagonal. How far is the center of gravity of the sheet shifted by folding one corner over so that it touches the center?

15. A block weighing 50 lb is drawn up an inclined plane at constant speed by a force parallel to the plane. If the plane is at 30° with the horizontal and if the coefficient of friction between the sliding surfaces is 0.40, what force is required?

16. A uniform ladder stands on level ground and rests against a smooth vertical wall. If the coefficient of friction between the ladder and ground is 0.35, how small can the angle between the ladder and ground be made without causing the ladder to slip?

17. A derrick has a uniform boom 15 ft long and weighing 300 lb, pivoted at the bottom of a vertical mast. A cable extends from the mast to the outer end of the boom, where a load of 1 ton is suspended, and holds the boom at 60° with the mast. What is the tension in the cable and the thrust of the boom against the mast (*a*) if the cable is horizontal? (*b*) if the cable makes angles of 60° with both boom and mast?

18. The table shown in the diagram is caused to slide along a level floor at constant speed by pushing against it with a horizontal force *P* applied centrally at one edge of the top and directed parallel to the edges as shown. If the table weighs 40 lb

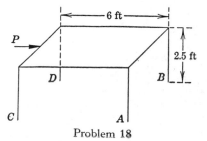

Problem 18

and the push needed is 12 lb, what is the vertical reaction of the floor at each of the legs A, B, C, and D?

19. The step ladder in the diagram has two members AB and BC, each 6 ft long; these are hinged together at the top and joined by the tie rod DE, 2 ft long, halfway between the top and the base. If the ladder is standing on a smooth floor and a 160-lb man has climbed to a position midway between D and B, what are the reactions at the floor, and what is the tension in the tie rod? The weight of the ladder itself may be neglected.

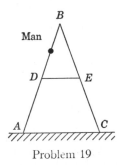

Problem 19

20. The roof truss in the diagram is subjected to vertical snow loads and a horizontal wind load of the values indicated. The truss is pinned at A and is free to roll at B. Neglect the weight of the truss itself and find the reactions at these supports.

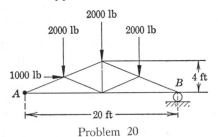

Problem 20

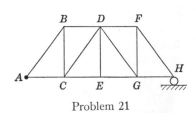

Problem 21

21. The diagram shows a model of a Howe bridge truss. The model is 12 in. long; it is fixed at A and is free to roll at H. The members are hinged at the lettered joints. The horizontal members are each 3 in. long, the vertical members are each 4 in. long, and the sloping members are each 5 in. long. A load of 8 lb is placed at point E. Calculate the forces in members AB, AC, BC, and BD.

9

HARMONIC MOTION

83. Harmonic Motion Defined. In addition to uniform motion and accelerated motion previously considered, there is another type called *periodic motion* in which a body vibrates to and fro repeatedly over the same path in equal time intervals. The most important periodic motion is that called *harmonic motion*, in which the acceleration varies continuously from instant to instant in a definite manner. Such motion may be observed in the oscillation of a weight hanging from a coiled spring, the swinging of the bob of a pendulum, and the vibration of the prongs of a tuning fork.

To investigate the characteristics of this type of motion, a weight suspended by a coiled spring may be pulled down and released, so that it oscillates up and down about its original position as a central point. In pulling the weight down, if only a small force is applied, the spring stretches only slightly, and if more force is applied, it stretches more; when the force is not too large, the stretching force and the extension of the spring vary in direct proportion. This behavior is, indeed, characteristic of elastic substances, to be studied in Chap. 10.

Whenever a force is applied to stretch the spring, there is set up within it an equal force in the opposite direction. This is the restoring force which, when the weight is released, causes the spring to pull the weight up. Since acceleration is proportional to the force that causes it, the acceleration of the weight is proportional to the restoring force, and thus varies directly as the displacement of the weight from its central position of equilibrium. When the displacement is downward, the restoring force and acceleration are directed upward, and vice versa. From such considerations, *harmonic motion is defined as a to-and-fro motion in which the acceleration of the moving body and the restoring force acting upon it are proportional to its displacement from the midpoint of its path and are directed toward that point.*

It might be remarked that to-and-fro motion is not necessarily harmonic; in fact, it is not harmonic unless it has the properties just described. In many machine parts, motion occurs back and forth repeatedly over the same path in equal time intervals but does not conform to the foregoing definition. Such motion would be classed as periodic but not harmonic.

84. Relation Between Circular and Harmonic Motion. The study of harmonic motion is much simplified by the relation that it bears to motion in a circle. If a body that is going around a circle at constant speed is viewed in the plane of the circle, it is observed to move back and forth along a line equal in length to the diameter of the circle, and this particular form of periodic motion is found to be harmonic. In fact, the projection of uniform circular motion in the plane of the circle, as in Fig. 87, is an excellent illustration of harmonic motion. It can be produced mechanically by a disk and a bar coupled by a pin-and-slot arrangement as in Fig. 88. The projecting pin near the rim of the disk engages the slot in the bar, the bar itself being supported in stationary guides to constrain its motion to the vertical direction. When the disk is driven at constant speed the pin travels uniformly in a circle, but the bar

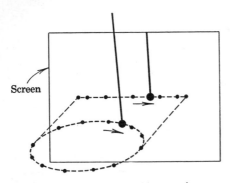

FIG. 87. Shadowgraph of harmonic motion produced by circular motion

receives only the vertical projection of this motion and consequently slides up and down the diameter of the circle with harmonic motion.

85. Amplitude, Frequency, and Related Terms. Usually when a body describes harmonic motion, there is no associated body that actually travels with circular motion as just described. It is then convenient to construct an artificial *reference circle* and to imagine a body moving uniformly around it. In Fig. 89 the path of the body describing harmonic motion is shown at the left by the line CD, and the path of the body moving uniformly in the circle is shown at the right. The up-and-down motion along CD can always be considered as the projection of the uniform motion around a reference circle of equal diameter $C'D'$. Thus, when the revolving body is at M', the vibrating body is at the midpoint M of its path; as the revolving body moves to P', the vibrating body moves to P; when the revolving body reaches D', the vibrating body reaches D, and so on. In this way the angle θ at the center O increases, sweeping out 2π radians in each revolution.

FIG. 88. Mechanical model to illustrate harmonic motion

When the body in harmonic motion moves from M to D, then from D to C, and finally from C back to M, it has completed one *vibration* (vib). In general terms, a vibration is a complete to-and-fro movement of the body over its entire path. It corresponds to a complete revolution of the body in the reference circle.

The *displacement* of a body in harmonic motion at any instant is its distance from the midposition at that instant. In Fig. 89, when the body is at P its displacement is $y = MP$.

The *amplitude* of a vibration is the maximum displacement and is represented in the figure by either *MC* or *MD*. The amplitude is equal to the radius *r* of the reference circle.

The *period* or *periodic time* is the time interval during which a vibrating body completes one vibration. In this time the body in the reference circle makes one revolution.

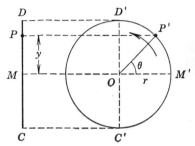

The *frequency* of vibratory motion is the number of vibrations completed per second and is therefore the reciprocal of the period. If the frequency is denoted by *n* and the period by *T*, it follows that

$$n = \frac{1}{T}$$

Fig. 89. The relation between harmonic and circular motion

The *equilibrium position* of a body in harmonic motion is the midpoint of its path. In the figure, point *M* represents the equilibrium position.

86. Sinusoidal Representation. A body having harmonic motion continually traces the same path over and over, and this fact makes it difficult to indicate clearly the direction in which the body is moving at a particular instant. To overcome this difficulty, the path of the vibration may be spread out laterally to form a curve like that in Fig. 90. This curve combines the harmonic motion up and down with uniform linear motion sideways, the two motions being at right angles. To produce such a curve, the

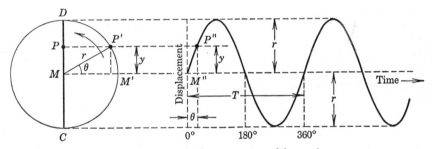

Fig. 90. Vibratory motion represented by a sine curve

vibrating body carries a stylus and the paper upon which it makes its trace is moved uniformly in a transverse direction.

In the figure the path of the body describing harmonic motion is *CD* and its midpoint is *M*. At an instant when the vibrating body is passing through *M* in an upward direction, the corresponding body moving counterclockwise in the reference circle is at *M'*; this instant is represented by *M''* at the beginning of the wavy curve. As the vibrating body passes through *P*, the corresponding point in the circle is at *P'* and the point on the curve is at P''. In a similar manner, the entire vibration can be mapped out, and the position of the vibrating body and the direction in which it is moving can be identified at any instant by a corresponding point on the curve.

The amplitude of the vibration is represented on the curve by the distance r between the extreme points and the axis; and the displacement at a particular instant is indicated by the distance y. The angle θ through which the radius MP' has rotated from its assumed datum position MM' is called the *phase angle*. At the instant represented by P, P', and P'' in the figure, the phase of the vibration is $30°$ or $\frac{1}{12}$ period. Phase angles may also be indicated on the curve as shown, since in one period T the curve advances a complete cycle, while the phase angle increases from 0 to $360°$. The displacement of the vibrating body can be expressed in terms of the angular position, since $y = r \sin \theta$. If t is the time reckoned from the instant when $\theta = 0$, the angular velocity of the radius r can be expressed as $\omega = \theta/t$, whence $\theta = \omega t$, and the displacement becomes

$$y = r \sin \theta = r \sin \omega t$$

the upward direction being positive. This is the equation of the wavy line; it indicates that the curve is a *sine curve*.

87. Velocity in Harmonic Motion. In the sine curve representing the motion of a vibrating body, the slope at any point shows how rapidly the displacement is changing at the corresponding instant, and thus the slope of the curve at that point is an indication of the instantaneous velocity. The slope varies from zero at the extreme points to a maximum where the curve crosses the axis, consequently the velocity of the vibrating body shows these same variations.

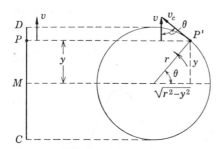

FIG. 91. Velocity in harmonic motion

In Fig. 91 a body having harmonic motion along CD is represented as the projection of a second body moving uniformly around a reference circle of radius $r = CD/2$. At a particular instant when the body in the circle is at point P', its velocity is represented by a vector v_c tangent to the circle at that point; its value is

$$v_c = \frac{2\pi r}{T}$$

where T is the period. At the instant mentioned, the body describing harmonic motion is at P, the projection of P' on the path CD, and its velocity is represented by v, the projection of v_c on that path. The angle between v_c and v equals the phase angle θ at the center, and therefore $v = v_c \cos \theta$.

But $\cos \theta = \sqrt{r^2 - y^2}/r$; hence the instantaneous velocity of the body in harmonic motion when it is passing a point distant y from the equilibrium position is

$$v = \pm \frac{2\pi}{T} \sqrt{r^2 - y^2}$$

The $\pm$ sign indicates that the vibrating body may be moving either upward or downward for any given value of the displacement. The velocity has a maximum value of $v = v_c = 2\pi r/T$ when the body is at the equilibrium position M for which $y = 0$, and is zero when the body is at the end points C and D of its path for which $y = r$.

88. Acceleration and Restoring Force in Harmonic Motion. The procedure used in the foregoing section will be followed again in finding the acceleration in harmonic motion. In Fig. 92 the body describing harmonic motion moves along CD while the body in the reference circle moves counterclockwise. At an instant when the latter is at P', its acceleration is directed toward the center and has the value

$$a_c = \frac{v_c{}^2}{r}$$

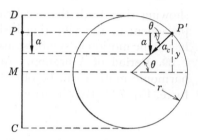

FIG. 92. Acceleration in harmonic motion

exactly as in Eq. 32. At the same instant, the body describing harmonic motion is at P, and its acceleration is represented by a, which is the projection of a_c along the straight path CD; thus $a = -a_c \sin \theta$. But $a_c = 4\pi^2 r/T^2$ and $\sin \theta = y/r$, whence

$$a = -\frac{4\pi^2 y}{T^2} \tag{71}$$

The negative sign indicates that the acceleration is always opposite in direction to the displacement.

The acceleration is zero at the instant the vibrating body sweeps through the equilibrium position M for which $y = 0$ and has its maximum value at the end positions C and D of the path, being then equal to the acceleration of the body in the reference circle, $a = a_c = 4\pi^2 r/T^2$.

A body describing harmonic motion is always being accelerated toward its midposition; it follows that such a body is acted upon continuously by a resultant force. Since this is directed toward the midposition it is commonly referred to as a restoring force. An expression for this force in terms of the mass m of the vibrating body can be obtained by applying the equation $F = ma$ to the expression for acceleration above; thus

$$F = -\frac{4\pi^2 m y}{T^2} \tag{72}$$

To state the force in terms of the weight W of the vibrating body rather than its mass, the mass m may be replaced by its equivalent, W/g, from Eq. 23.

In deriving the expressions for velocity, acceleration, and force in harmonic motion, a vertical vibration was used for illustration. The results are applicable, however, to vibrations along any direction. Since in these equations, $4\pi^2$ is a numerical constant, and T, W, g, and m are fixed for any particular vibrating body at a given place, the expressions for acceleration and force can be reduced to simplest terms by writing

$$a \propto -y$$

$$F \propto -y$$

showing that both the acceleration and force are proportional to the displacement of the vibrating body. These are basic expressions that define harmonic motion in symbols, just as the statement in § 83 defined it in words.

89. Period of Vibration. An expression for the period of vibration in harmonic motion can be obtained directly from the equation for restoring force, Eq. 72. By a rearrangement of terms, the period is expressed as

$$T = 2\pi \sqrt{-\frac{m}{F/y}} \tag{73}$$

where m, the mass of the vibrating body, represents an inertia factor that tends to lengthen the period, and F/y, the ratio of the restoring force to the displacement, is a restoring factor that tends to shorten the period. It may be noted that although F and y both vary from point to point in the path of motion, they vary in the same proportion, and their ratio F/y is constant. If the harmonic motion results from the action of a spring, the factor F/y is the quantity referred to in § 66 as the spring constant. As used here, however, this factor is negative, since F now represents the restoring force instead of the stretching force.

It is also useful to express the period of vibration in terms of the acceleration a and the displacement y. This relation is found by rearranging terms in Eq. 71, whence the period is

$$T = 2\pi \sqrt{-\frac{y}{a}} \tag{74}$$

Since the ratio y/a itself is negative, the quantity under the radical is positive, as in Eq. 73.

90. Application of Principles. The principles of harmonic motion can be demonstrated in a variety of ways. In one of these, an object is attached to a long helical spring and set into vertical vibration. From simple measurements in such a test, the frequency can be predicted, and the velocity, acceleration, and restoring force computed for any desired instant during a vibration.

Illustrative Problem

A mass of 500 gm suspended by a coiled spring extends it 10 cm. The mass is then set into vibration with an amplitude of 2 cm. (*a*) Calculate the period and frequency of vibration. (*b*) Compute the velocity and acceleration of the mass, and the restoring force acting upon it, at an instant one-sixth of a period after passing upward through the midposition. Neglect the mass of the spring.

(*a*) Initially, the spring is stretched 10 cm and the mass hangs at rest at its lower end. This position of the mass is the midpoint about which it will vibrate. Two forces act upon the mass; when at rest these are (1) its weight, $500 \times 980 = 490,000$ dynes downward (taken as negative), and (2) the upward pull of the spring, 490,000 dynes upward. When the mass is pulled down 2 cm more, the upward force of the spring is increased to $\frac{12}{10} \times 490,000 = 588,000$ dynes. In this position the resultant force on the mass is $588,000 - 490,000 = 98,000$ dynes upward. This is the restoring force F corresponding to a displacement y of -2 cm. Consequently the quantity F/y in Eq. 73 is $98,000/(-2) = -49,000$ dynes/cm. For a mass of 500 gm attached to this spring, the period of vibration, from the equation just referred to, is

$$T = 2\pi \sqrt{-\frac{m}{F/y}} = 2\pi \sqrt{-\frac{500 \text{ gm}}{-49,000 \dfrac{\text{dynes}}{\text{cm}}}} = 0.635 \text{ sec}$$

The frequency of vibration is $n = 1/T = 1/0.635 = 1.575$ per sec.

(*b*) The amplitude of vibration is specified as 2 cm, and thus the radius of the corresponding reference circle is 2 cm. As the vibrating body passes the midposition of its path this radius is horizontal, and at an instant $\frac{1}{6}$ of a period later it has rotated 60° upward from this position.

The velocity in the reference circle is $v_c = \dfrac{2\pi r}{T} = \dfrac{2\pi(2)}{0.635} = 19.80$ cm/sec,

and that of the vibrating body at the particular instant is $v = v_c \cos 60° = (19.80)(0.500) = 9.90$ cm/sec.

Similarly, the acceleration in the reference circle is $a_c = \dfrac{v_c^2}{r} = \dfrac{(19.80)^2}{2} = 196.0$ cm/sec², and that of the vibrating body at the instant mentioned is $a = -a_c \sin 60° = -(196.0)(0.866) = -169.7$ cm/sec².

Lastly, the restoring force acting upon the body at the same instant is

$$F = ma = (500 \text{ gm}) \left(-169.7 \frac{\text{cm}}{\text{sec}^2} \right) = -84,900 \text{ dynes.}$$

91. The Simple Pendulum. The *simple pendulum* consists of a concentrated mass fastened to the end of a cord of negligible weight and free to swing about a fixed point. It is closely approximated by a small metal bob attached to a thin thread. The time of vibration can be found by considering the bob to be displaced slightly and by studying the forces acting upon it; such analysis shows that the resultant force is proportional to the displacement and opposite in direction. In consequence, the vibration of the bob is harmonic, and the equations of harmonic motion can be applied to determine the period of the pendulum.

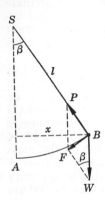

　　　A pendulum bob B is shown in Fig. 93, suspended from a support S by a thin cord of length l. As the bob swings, it will at some instant occupy the position shown, where its horizontal distance from the vertical line AS is x toward the right, taken as positive. Two forces act upon the bob: the force of gravity, W, vertically downward, and the pull P in the cord acting toward S. Their resultant F is directed toward the left (negative) and acts at right angles to the cord. The value of F can be found by completing a parallelogram as in the figure, in which the two angles marked β (beta) are equal; herefrom

FIG. 93. Forces on a simple pendulum in a displaced position

$$F = -W \sin \beta = -\frac{Wx}{l}$$

When the angle β is small, the horizontal line x may be considered to coincide with the arc AB, the force F may be regarded as horizontal, and x may be taken as the displacement of the bob. Subject to this approximation, the equation shows that the restoring force F is directly proportional to the displacement x and opposite in direction. Consequently the motion of the bob is harmonic, and the period is given by Eq. 74 as

$$T = 2\pi \sqrt{-\frac{x}{a}}$$

Reference to the figure shows that $\sin \beta$ can be expressed either as $\dfrac{x}{l}$ or as $-\dfrac{F}{W} = -\dfrac{ma}{mg} = -\dfrac{a}{g}$, where a is the acceleration of the bob and g the acceleration due to gravity. These values may therefore be equated, whence $\dfrac{x}{l} = -\dfrac{a}{g}$ or $-\dfrac{x}{a} = \dfrac{l}{g}$, and the period becomes

$$T = 2\pi \sqrt{\frac{l}{g}} \tag{75}$$

　　　The time of vibration of a pendulum is seen to be determined only by its length l and by the acceleration due to gravity at the place where the pendulum is located. By using a pendulum of known length and measuring its period of vibration, the value of g at the location can be determined with accuracy. Eq. 75 applies only to small values of the displacement angle β, which, however, need not be constant. As the vibration of a pendulum continues, the amplitude becomes smaller and smaller but the period remains practically unchanged. It is this property that makes the pendulum of value in controlling the escapements of timekeepers.

92. The Torsion Pendulum. When a weight attached to a vertical wire is twisted and released, it acts as a *torsion pendulum*, describing a series of angular vibrations analogous to the linear vibrations met with previously in harmonic motion. In Fig. 94 the forces FF act on a suspended disk at the distance R from its center O and produce a torque $2RF$. The consequent twisting of the supporting wire sets up within it an oppositely directed restoring torque which is proportional to the angular displacement, just as in linear harmonic motion a restoring force is set up which is proportional to the linear displacement. The two types of motion are closely analogous,

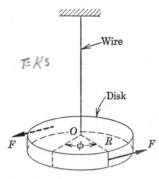

FIG. 94. A torsion pendulum

and angular harmonic motion can be taken up most simply by comparing it directly to linear harmonic motion.

In Eq. 72, $F = -\dfrac{4\pi^2 my}{T^2}$, which is a characteristic expression for linear

harmonic motion; if each linear quantity is replaced by the corresponding angular quantity, there results as the corresponding expression for angular harmonic motion:

$$L = -\frac{4\pi^2 I\phi}{T^2}$$

wherein L represents the restoring torque (this symbol being used to avoid confusion with the period T), I is the moment of inertia of the vibrating body about the axis of rotation, and ϕ is its angular displacement, that is, the twist of the wire. If the body is displaced from its rest position in a clockwise direction, the restoring torque is counterclockwise, and hence the ratio L/ϕ is negative. When this ratio is replaced by $-\tau$ (tau) and the expression rearranged, the period of angular vibration is found to be

$$T = 2\pi \sqrt{\frac{I}{\tau}} \tag{76}$$

wherein I is an inertia factor that tends to lengthen the period, and τ a restoring factor that tends to shorten it.

The torsion principle can be used to determine the moment of inertia of a body by supporting it as a torsion pendulum and measuring its period and also the angle of twist produced by a given torque.

93. The Physical Pendulum. Any body which vibrates in the manner of a pendulum but in which the mass is distributed and not concentrated as

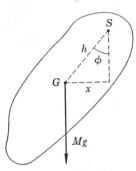

FIG. 95. Finding the period of a physical pendulum

in the simple pendulum is called a *physical* or *compound pendulum.* A rod suspended at one end or a hoop hung on a nail would vibrate as a physical pendulum if displaced and released.

It will be found that the restoring torque on such a body is proportional to the angular displacement and opposite in direction, which makes the motion harmonic, and the period can be determined from the laws of harmonic motion as in the torsion pendulum.

A body of mass M vibrating about an axis S is shown in Fig. 95 at an instant when displaced from its equilibrium position by an angle ϕ. This displacement is clockwise and is taken as positive.

The weight Mg of the body acts downward at its center of gravity G and produces a torque about the axis S which amounts to $-Mgx$; it is counterclockwise and therefore negative. This torque tends to restore the body to its position of equilibrium. If the displacement angle ϕ is small, x may be taken as the displacement of G. Under this condition the angular displacement is

$\phi = \dfrac{x}{h}$, where h is the distance between the center of suspension S and the center of gravity G. Therefore $x = h\phi$, and the restoring torque is $L = -Mgh\phi$. This equation shows that the restoring torque is proportional to the angular displacement and opposite in direction. Hence the body can be considered as having angular harmonic motion, and its period is given by Eq. 76. Since in this expression $\tau = -L/\phi$, its value for the physical pendulum is $Mgh\phi/\phi = Mgh$. Hence the period is

$$T = 2\pi \sqrt{\frac{I}{Mgh}} \qquad (77)$$

where I is the moment of inertia of the pendulum about a transverse axis at the point of suspension. This expression, like that for the simple pendulum, is valid only for small values of the displacement angle.

Illustrative Problem

Find the time of vibration of a solid disk 1 ft in diameter about a transverse axis located at its rim, as shown at S in Fig. 96.

The moment of inertia of the disk of mass M and radius r about its center C is $I_C = \frac{1}{2}Mr^2$, and hence its moment of inertia about a parallel axis at the rim is given by Eq. 45 as

$$I = I_C + Mr^2 = \tfrac{1}{2}Mr^2 + Mr^2 = \tfrac{3}{2}Mr^2$$

where the distance h in that equation is replaced by r.   Therefore the time of vibration of the disk is

$$T = 2\pi \sqrt{\frac{\tfrac{3}{2}Mr^2}{Mgr}} = 2\pi \sqrt{\frac{3r}{2g}} = 2\pi \sqrt{\frac{3 \times \tfrac{1}{2}\text{ft}}{2 \times 32 \dfrac{\text{ft}}{\text{sec}^2}}} = 0.962 \text{ sec}$$

and is independent of its mass and thickness.

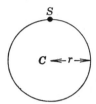

Fɪɢ. 96.   Disk with axis at rim

94. Centers of Oscillation and Percussion.   The *center of oscillation* of a physical pendulum is that point at which the concentration of the whole mass of the pendulum would cause no change in its period of vibration.   If the mass were so concentrated, the physical pendulum would reduce to a simple pendulum having the same period.   Since the period for a simple pendulum is $2\pi \sqrt{\dfrac{l = K}{g}}$ and that for a physical pendulum is $2\pi \sqrt{\dfrac{I}{Mgh}}$, it follows that the length of the equivalent simple pendulum is

$$l = \frac{I}{Mh} \tag{78}$$

This equation gives the distance between the center of oscillation of a physical pendulum and its axis of suspension.   In this expression, the symbols have the same meaning as previously.

The center of oscillation can be interchanged with the center of suspension without affecting the period.   To prove this statement, it is merely necessary to compute the equivalent length of a physical pendulum when suspended (1) at its axis of suspension and (2) at its center of oscillation, and to show that the two values found are equal.

The center of oscillation is also called the *center of percussion* because it is the point at which the pendulum can be struck without jarring the axis, for the only effect of a blow at this point is to rotate the pendulum about its axis of suspension.   When struck at any other point there is not only a tendency to rotate the pendulum but also to give the axis a motion of translation. The stinging sensation sometimes experienced in batting a ball is due to striking the ball with the bat at some point other than at its center of percussion.

PROBLEMS

1. A particle moves with harmonic motion between two points 10 cm apart and completes 20 vib in 12 sec. Determine (a) the amplitude of vibration, (b) the period, (c) the frequency, (d) the maximum velocity, and (e) the maximum distance moved during a quarter of a period.

2. A small body is vibrating in harmonic motion with an amplitude of 4 in. and a period of 2 sec. (a) How far is the body displaced from its mid-position at an instant when its velocity is half the maximum velocity? (b) What is its velocity when it is halfway between its midposition and one end of its path?

3. Refer to the preceding problem, and determine (a) how far the body is displaced from its midposition at an instant when its acceleration is half the maximum acceleration and (b) its acceleration when it is halfway between the midposition and one end of its path.

4. A 200-gm mass suspended from the bottom of a long coiled spring extends the spring 20 cm. The mass is pushed up 10 cm and released, whereupon it vibrates vertically in harmonic motion of 10-cm amplitude. At an instant when the mass is 4 cm above its lowest position, (a) what is its displacement? (b) how much upward force is exerted upon it by the spring? (c) what is the resultant force acting on the mass? and (d) what is the acceleration of the mass?

5. A weight of 20 lb hung on a vertical helical spring stretches the spring 4 in. If the weight is displaced and released, how many vibrations will it complete in 1 min?

6. A 500-gm mass is suspended by a helical spring and set into vibration. It makes 30 vib in 10 sec and the amplitude is adjusted to 2 cm. Compute the tension in the spring at an instant when the vibrating mass is (a) at its lowest position, and (b) at its highest position.

7. A 5-lb weight is hung on a long coiled spring, stretching the spring a certain amount. A 3-lb weight is added, stretching the spring 6 in. more. With what frequency will the combined weight of 8 lb vibrate when displaced and released?

8. A 2-lb weight is executing harmonic motion of 6-in. amplitude and 0.2-sec period. At an instant when the weight is 4 in. from its midposition, what is (a) its velocity and (b) the restoring force acting upon it?

9. A weight hung on a long coiled spring stretches the spring 14 cm. If the weight is pulled down and released, what is its period of vibration?

10. An object is placed on a horizontal platform and the platform is set vibrating up and down with harmonic motion having an amplitude of 3 in. How large can the frequency be and still have the object remain in contact with the platform in its downward motion?

11. A machine weighing 1 ton rests on four compression springs, each of which requires a force of 10,000 lb to compress it 1 in. If the machine is displaced slightly, with what frequency does it vibrate up and down?

12. A 500-gm mass suspended from a flat spring (Fig. 97) vibrates twice per second when pulled down and released. This mass is removed and replaced by a 900-gm mass; determine its frequency of vibration.

13. A "seconds" pendulum is one that beats seconds; its period is 2 sec. Compute the length of a simple seconds pendulum, and of one that vibrates twice as fast.

14. A certain simple pendulum has a period of 2 sec at the surface of the earth. Calculate its period at the surface of the moon, from the fact that a man who weighs 160 lb on the earth would weigh only 26 lb on the moon.

15. A small block slides back and forth inside a smooth spherical bowl, along an arc of 8-in. radius. Compute the period of vibration.

16. A straight rod 60 cm long and having a mass of 400 gm is suspended in a horizontal position from its midpoint by a vertical wire that hangs from the ceiling. The rod is displaced horizontally through an angle of 90°, twisting the wire, and it is found that forces of 3×10^4 dynes applied perpendicularly at the ends are needed to hold the rod in this displaced position. When released, the rod vibrates as a torsion pendulum; compute its period of vibration.

17. A disk 10 cm in diameter and having a mass of 200 gm is suspended in a horizontal plane by a vertical wire attached to its center, and its period of angular vibration is 2 sec. The disk serves as a platform on which objects can be placed for measuring their moments of inertia. With a certain object so placed, the combination is found to have a vibration period of 2.75 sec. What is the moment of inertia of the added object?

18. Three slender rods, each 40 cm long and each having a mass of 50 gm, are fastened together at the ends to form a triangular frame. The frame is supported on a horizontal nail at one corner and set into vibration as a physical pendulum. Determine its period of vibration.

19. A slender stick of length L is pivoted to swing as a pendulum about a horizontal axis through one end. Determine the length of a simple pendulum that has the same period as the stick.

20. A compound pendulum is made by attaching a 1-lb disk 6 in. in diameter to the lower end of a slender 8-oz rod 2 ft long, with the center of the disk at the end of the rod. The system is set into vibration about a horizontal axis at the top of the rod, the motion being in the plane of the disk. Determine the period of vibration.

10

ELASTICITY

95. Elastic Bodies. Perhaps everyone has observed the stretching of a rubber band or the bending of a piece of wood and the return of these objects to their original condition upon removal of the distorting force. These effects are evidences of the *elasticity* of matter, and the substances are said to be *elastic*. More strictly, an elastic body is one which, having had its size, shape, or proportions changed by a distorting force, returns to its original condition when the force is removed. Contrary to the usual notion, rubber is not highly elastic—not nearly so elastic as glass—for after stretching, it returns rather imperfectly to its original state.

In the foregoing chapters, it was assumed that bodies were rigid, § 42, and that under the action of applied forces the body would move as a whole, perhaps with translation, or rotation, or vibration, or combinations of these types of motion. Consideration is given here to the action of forces in distorting a body, the particles of the body moving relatively to one another through rather narrow ranges, and it is understood that the forces are applied in such a manner that the body in its entirety does not move.

96. Stress and Strain; Hooke's Law. When a load is applied to an elastic body, the body becomes distorted; that is, some portion of the body is

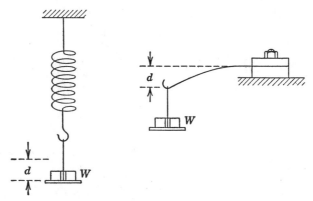

FIG. 97.   Helical and flat springs deformed by loading

displaced with respect to some other portion. As a result of this displacement, a force is developed between the molecules of the body which resists the change that the applied load has brought about, and which tends to restore the body to its original condition. The aggregate of these molecular forces just balances the applied load when the body has reached a stable condition (namely, rest) under the action of these forces. The larger the load, the larger is the deformation necessary to establish molecular restoring forces that balance the increased load. The relation between the deformation and the restoring force was first investigated by the English experimental physicist, Robert Hooke (1635–1703). He found that the force developed within an elastic body to withstand an external load is proportional to the deformation of the body under that load.

This statement can be verified by applying weights to a helical spring or a flat spring in the manner indicated in Fig. 97. If different weights W_1, W_2, W_3, $\cdots$, are placed in turn upon each spring, it is found that the steady deflections produced by them, respectively $d_1, d_2, d_3, \cdots$, are proportional to the applied weights, as shown by the straight line plotted in Fig. 98. The restoring force is, therefore, proportional to the deflection or deformation.

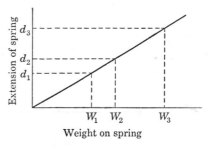

FIG. 98. Showing how stretch depends upon applied load

The restoring action set up in an elastic body when subject to deformation is customarily expressed as the force per unit area over which the force acts; the term *stress* is used for this purpose. Thus, *stress is the restoring force per unit area*, and is commonly referred to by engineers as *unit stress*. The interpretation of this quantity depends upon the particular manner in which the load is applied to the body.

The deformation of an elastic body is expressed by the change produced by the applied force in terms of some original dimension of the body; the term *strain* is used as the measure of deformation. Thus, if a sheet of rubber 10 in. square is stretched to 11 in. in both directions, it would be appropriate to reckon the strain as the ratio of change in area to original area, or

$$\frac{121 - 100}{100} = 0.21.$$

Hooke's observations can be expressed more definitely in terms of stress and strain as follows: *The stress set up within an elastic body is proportional to the strain to which the body is subjected* by the applied load, a statement known as Hooke's Law. Expressed concisely,

$$\text{stress} \propto \text{strain}$$

or

$$\text{stress} = k \times \text{strain}$$

and

$$k = \frac{\text{stress}}{\text{strain}} \tag{79}$$

where k is a constant called the *modulus of elasticity* of the material of the body.

For each material there is a limiting stress beyond which the proportionality expressed by Hooke's Law does not hold; this stress is known as the *elastic limit* of the material. If the stress is larger than this value for a specimen under test, a permanent distortion is observed, and, at a still higher value called the *breaking stress*, rupture occurs. This chapter deals with bodies that are subjected to forces which do not cause the elastic limits to be exceeded.

The deformation of a body may occur in three different ways, depending upon the manner in which the external forces are applied. In one of these, the load changes the length of the body, in another its shape, and in the third its volume. Different procedures are necessary to evaluate the stress and strain for these cases, but Hooke's Law applies equally to all three.

97. Elasticity of Length; Young's Modulus. The type of elasticity most frequently considered is that which deals with change of length under tensile or compressive loads. Fig. 99 shows a piece of wire subjected to tension by two equal and opposite forces F and F, which cause a length L of the wire to elongate an amount ΔL. The strain in the wire is defined as the elongation ΔL divided by the original length L, and the stress in the wire equals the force F divided by the cross-sectional area A of the wire. Therefore

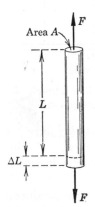

FIG. 99. Factors that determine stress and strain in a wire or rod

$$\text{strain} = \Delta L/L \qquad \text{stress} = F/A$$

consequently their ratio, which is a constant of the material of the wire, is

$$Y = \frac{\text{stress}}{\text{strain}} = \frac{F/A}{\Delta L/L} \tag{80}$$

This constant Y is called the *stretch modulus of elasticity*, also *Young's modulus* after the English philosopher, Thomas Young (1773-1829).

Young's modulus for a material is basically independent of the dimensions of the particular sample used in a test. This statement can be verified by supposing, for example, that a wire of the same material but having twice the length ($2L$) and twice the cross-sectional area ($2A$) is subjected to the same force (F) as before. The stress would then be $\dfrac{F}{2A}$, which is half of the previous value. The elongation would be doubled because of the increased length of the sample and at the same time would be halved because of its increased area; consequently, the elongation (ΔL) would remain unchanged and the strain would be $\dfrac{\Delta L}{2L}$, which is half of the previous value. Thus, the stress and strain are changed in the same proportion, and therefore their ratio remains constant. From this analysis it appears that tests on a given material can be made on rods or wires of any convenient dimensions and the results will yield the same value for its modulus of elasticity. This conclusion agrees in general with experiment, although the modulus is influenced somewhat by the shape, size, and treatment of the specimen. For most structural materials, Young's modulus applies equally to decrease of length in compression and to increase of length in tension.

In British units the stress is often measured in pounds per square inch and the strain in inches of extension per inch of original length; consequently the unit for Young's modulus becomes

$$Y = \frac{\text{lb/in.}^2}{\text{in./in.}} = \text{lb/in.}^2$$

In metric units with the stress in dynes per square centimeter and the strain in centimeters of extension or contraction per centimeter of original length, Young's modulus is in dynes per square centimeter. Since strain is a pure ratio, the unit for the modulus is the same as that for stress.

The numerical value of Young's modulus for an elastic substance is very large, since it represents the (imagined) force that would be needed to stretch a specimen of unit cross-section to twice its original length! Thus, for mild steel the stretch modulus of elasticity is 30,000,000 lb/in.^{2}, the elastic limit 35,000 lb/in.^{2}, and the breaking strength 60,000 lb/in.^{2} In designing structures, engineers allow a "unit stress" for steel of perhaps 16,000 lb/in.^{2} to give an ample factor of safety.

Illustrative Problem

The design of a steel bridge truss includes a member 15 ft long that would be subjected to a tensile force of 48,000 lb. If the stress is not to exceed 16,000 lb/in.^{2}, (a) what cross-section should be provided for this member and (b) how much would the member elongate?

(a) Both the cross-sectional area of the structural member and its elongation can be obtained from Eq. 80. Since the stress $= F/A$, it follows that the cross-sectional area is

$$A = \frac{F}{\text{stress}} = \frac{48 \times 10^3 \text{ lb}}{16 \times 10^3 \dfrac{\text{lb}}{\text{in.}^2}} = 3.00 \text{ in.}^2$$

(b) Since the modulus is $Y = \dfrac{\text{stress}}{\text{strain}}$, and the strain is $\Delta L/L$, it follows that the elongation is

$$\Delta L = 15 \text{ ft} \frac{16 \times 10^3 \frac{\text{lb}}{\text{in.}^2}}{30 \times 10^6 \frac{\text{lb}}{\text{in.}^2}} = 0.0080 \text{ ft} = 0.0960 \text{ in}$$

The small extensions which occur when metal rods are placed under tensile loads can be measured by an *extensometer;* in one type two pairs of oppositely pointed screws are pressed into the rod at places separated by a definite length, and a lever system with a short-focus microscope measures the elongation of that portion of the rod. In measuring the larger extensions of thin wires, sufficient accuracy is attained by attaching to the end of the wire a small vernier, which moves along a suitably supported scale as the wire stretches.

98. Elasticity of Shape; Shear Modulus. Often a body is subjected to a pair of equal forces which act in opposite directions but not along the same line, as in a couple, § 41. Such forces *SS* act upon the upper and lower faces of a rectangular block *abcd* in Fig. 100 and *shear* it into the parallelepiped *ab'c'd*, turning the end faces *ab* and *cd* through the small angle ϕ. Upon removal of the shearing forces the body resumes its original shape, provided the elastic limit of the material was not exceeded. This type of elasticity is termed *elasticity of shape* or of *shear* and is of importance in structural design and shafting.

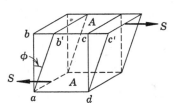

FIG. 100. Effect of shearing forces upon a cubical block

The general definitions for stress and strain apply to shear, but must be interpreted for this particular kind of distortion. The block shown in the figure may be regarded as made up of a large number of horizontal sheets of area *A*, each of which is forced to slide along slightly with respect to its neighbors under the action of the shearing forces. The area *A* is the surface that resists the shearing action caused by the force *S*, and hence the *shearing stress* equals S/A, where *A* is the area of the upper or lower face of the block. The *strain* is measured by the angle ϕ through which the end of the block is sheared and is expressed in radians. The ratio of the stress to the strain for a particular material is constant, in accordance with Hooke's Law, and is expressed as

$$E = \frac{S/A}{\phi} \tag{81}$$

This constant *E* is called the *shear modulus of elasticity* and is also known as the *coefficient of rigidity*. Since the angle of shear is simply a number, the unit in which the modulus is expressed is the same as that for stress. The stretching of a helical spring, such as shown at the left in Fig. 97, may at first sight appear to be like that of a straight wire, but actually, as the spring elongates, the wire twists, and therefore the amount of stretch is determined by the shear modulus rather than the stretch modulus of the material.

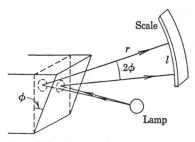

Fig. 101 indicates how the angle of shear can be measured for the block of Fig. 100. A mirror is affixed to one end face of the block and a ray of light from a lamp is reflected by the mirror upon the scale shown. As the face of the block turns through an angle ϕ the reflected ray of light turns through 2ϕ, § 371. If the scale is at a distance r from the mirror and if the scale deflection due to shear is l, the angle $2\phi = l/r$. Consequently, measurements of r and l determine the angle of shear ϕ.

Fig. 101.   Measuring the angle of shear with optical lever

Illustrative Problem

As a numerical example, suppose Fig. 100 to represent a copper alloy block of length $ad = 8$ cm, height $ab = 4$ cm, and width 5 cm, subjected to a pair of shearing forces each of 2.4×10^{10} dynes. The angle of shear is measured by the lamp-mirror-scale arrangement, and the reflected ray is observed to shift a distance of 6 mm along a scale placed 2 m from the mirror affixed to the specimen. What is the shear modulus of this alloy as given by these data?

In this test, the angle of shear is $\phi = \dfrac{l}{2r} = \dfrac{6}{2 \times 2000} = 0.0015$ radian,

and the shearing stress is $\dfrac{S}{A} = \dfrac{2.4 \times 10^{10} \text{ dynes}}{5 \times 8 \text{ cm}^2} = 6 \times 10^8 \dfrac{\text{dynes}}{\text{cm}^2}$; therefore the shear modulus of the alloy is $E = 6 \times 10^8 \div 0.0015 = 40 \times 10^{10}$ dynes/cm^2.

In practice, shear modulus is usually measured by using a specimen in the form of a cylindrical rod, fastened at one end and subjected to a known torque at the other. Under these conditions the shaft becomes twisted, the free end being displaced through some angle, which is also measured. The angular twist is directly proportional to the torque applied and inversely proportional to the shear modulus of the rod material. The shear modulus is obtained from the foregoing measurements and the dimensions of the rod by using the expression

$$E = \frac{2lT}{\pi\theta r^4}$$

derived by calculus methods from Eq. 81. In this expression, l is the length of the rod, r its radius, T the applied torque, and θ the corresponding angular twist. With the dimensions in inches, the twist in radians, and the torque in pound·inches, the modulus is in pounds per square inch.

99. Elasticity of Volume; Bulk Modulus. When a body is subjected to normal forces pressing all over its surface, it is said to be subjected to a

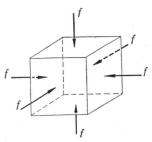

FIG. 102. Cube subjected to hydrostatic pressure

pressure, the term "pressure" being defined as the force acting per unit area. Such pressure may be applied by submerging a body in a liquid, for the force due to the liquid acts perpendicularly to each portion of the surface, as described in the following chapter. Fig. 102 represents a cube of some material subjected to hydrostatic pressure, equal forces f acting normally on all its faces.

As the pressure on a body is increased, its shape remains unchanged, but its volume decreases. A stress is set up within the material which is equal to the increase in pressure Δp. The corresponding strain is defined as the change of volume ΔV divided by the original volume V of the body; thus, strain is $\Delta V/V$. The ratio of the stress to the strain in this case is called the *bulk modulus of elasticity* and is expressed as

$$B = -\frac{\Delta p}{\Delta V/V} \tag{82}$$

in which the minus sign indicates that an increase in pressure causes a decrease in volume. The units in which the modulus B is expressed are the same as those used for the stress, since the strain is the ratio of two volumes or simply a number. This modulus is applied particularly to fluids; they offer appreciable resistance only to change of volume and so have only a bulk modulus of elasticity.

The reciprocal of the bulk modulus of a substance is known as its *compressibility*. The bulk modulus of steel is 24,000,000 lb/in.[2]; therefore its compressibility is 0.000000042—meaning that an increase of hydrostatic pressure of 1 lb/in.[2] would decrease a unit volume of steel by this amount.

100. Summary of Elastic Moduli. In the foregoing, the three moduli of elasticity were all derived from Hooke's Law, the stress in all cases being measured in force units per unit area, and the strain in all cases being a ratio of two like dimensions and therefore a number; consequently the unit in which the modulus is expressed is the same as that for stress. The expressions for elasticity of length, shape, and volume are summarized here for convenience of reference:

$$\text{Young's modulus} = \frac{\text{longitudinal stress}}{\text{change of length per unit length}} \;;\; Y = \frac{F/A}{\Delta L/L}$$

$$\text{Shear modulus} = \frac{\text{shearing stress}}{\text{angle of shear}} \;;\; E = \frac{S/A}{\phi}$$

$$\text{Bulk modulus} = \frac{\text{increase of pressure}}{\text{decrease of volume per unit volume}} \;;\; B = -\frac{\Delta p}{\Delta V/V}$$

Representative values of the stretch and shear moduli of several solids are given below in British and metric units:

ELASTICITY OF SOLIDS

Material	Young's Modulus		Shear Modulus	
	lb/in.^{2}	dynes/cm^2	lb/in.^{2}	dynes/cm^2
Aluminum.......	10×10^6	69×10^{10}	3.9×10^6	27×10^{10}
Brass...........	16×10^6	110×10^{10}	6.0×10^6	41×10^{10}
Copper (rolled)..	15.5×10^6	107×10^{10}	5.7×10^6	39×10^{10}
Glass (crown)....	9.5×10^6	65×10^{10}	3.9×10^6	27×10^{10}
Iron (cast)......	13×10^6	90×10^{10}	5.2×10^6	36×10^{10}
Steel (mild).....	30×10^6	210×10^{10}	11.6×10^6	80×10^{10}
Timber.........	1.4×10^6	9.7×10^{10}	....	....

Representative values of the bulk moduli of several liquids are given in the following table:

ELASTICITY OF LIQUIDS

Material	Bulk Modulus	
	lb/in.^{2}	dynes/cm^2
Alcohol........	16×10^4	110×10^8
Ether..........	8.7×10^4	60×10^8
Mercury.......	400×10^4	2800×10^8
Water........	31×10^4	210×10^8

101. Elasticity and Vibratory Motion. In Chap. 9 harmonic motion was defined as the motion of a body in which the acceleration and the restoring force are proportional to the displacement of the body from its equilibrium position. In this chapter it has been pointed out that an elastic body sets up a restoring force which is proportional to the displacement of its particles from their rest positions. Consequently when some part of an elastic body is displaced from its normal position, it vibrates with harmonic motion about that position upon the removal of the displacing force. This vibratory motion continues until the energy imparted to the body is dissipated in friction or otherwise. The frequency of vibration of an elastic body, as well as the velocity at any point of its path, can be computed by applying the laws of harmonic motion, as given in §§ 87–89.

In general, every mechanical system has a natural frequency with which it vibrates when it is displaced and released. Thus, a child's swing has a natural frequency approximating that of a simple pendulum. It can be forced to vibrate at other frequencies by applying regularly recurring impulses to it, and if the frequency of these impulses coincides, or nearly coincides, with its natural frequency, it vibrates with greatly increased amplitude. This effect, called *resonance*, occurs also in electric and acoustic systems and is discussed in §§ 309 and 345.

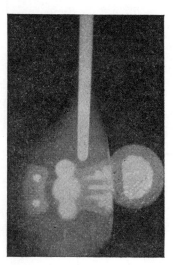

102. Elasticity and Impact. The behavior of bodies during impact, or collision, is described in § 37, where the law of Conservation of Momentum was introduced and illustrated. It was learned that the total momentum of an isolated system is unaffected by collision between its parts. Therefore, the momentum of the system before collision can be set equal to its momentum after collision, and from this equality, some unknown quantity of the system can be determined.

Fig. 103. Golf club and ball at impact. X-ray photograph taken in one-millionth of a second. (*Courtesy of Westinghouse Electric Corporation*)

If a collision is known to be elastic, this knowledge provides further information about the system. Although the time during which impact occurs is very short, nevertheless in that brief period the colliding bodies become deformed and a certain amount of energy is used to change their shape. The deformation of a golf ball when struck by a club is clearly evident in Fig. 103. If the collision is elastic, the bodies return to their original shape and the energy used to produce the deformation is restored to them. Hence, *in an elastic collision, the sum of the kinetic energies of the colliding bodies before impact equals the sum of their kinetic energies after impact.* Thus for an elastic collision, an additional equation can be stated, entirely independent of the momentum equation, and another unknown quantity can be determined.

Illustrative Problem

As an example of an elastic collision, a steel ball weighing 1 lb and fastened to a cord 27 in. long is released when the cord is horizontal; at the bottom of its path the ball strikes a steel block weighing 5 lb that is initially at rest on a level surface, as shown in Fig. 104. Find the velocity of the ball and that of the block after collision.

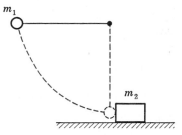

The mass of the ball is $m_1 = \frac{1}{32}$ slug; let its velocity just before collision be v_1 and after collision v_1'. The mass of the block is $m_2 = \frac{5}{32}$ slug; its velocity before collision is $v_2 = 0$ and that immediately after collision will be designated as v_2'. As the ball falls it loses potential energy and gains an equal amount of kinetic energy; therefore by Eqs. 54 and 56, $m_1gh = \frac{1}{2}m_1v_1^2$, where $h = 27$ in. $= 2.25$ ft. It follows that its velocity at impact is $v_1 =$

Fig. 104.   Impact of ball and block

$$\sqrt{2gh} = \sqrt{2 \times 32\,\frac{\text{ft}}{\text{sec}^2} \times 2.25\text{ ft}} = 12\,\frac{\text{ft}}{\text{sec}}.$$ Velocities toward the right

will be considered positive.

From the law of Conservation of Momentum,

$$m_1v_1 + m_2v_2 = m_1v_1' + m_2v_2'$$

With masses in slugs and velocities in feet per second, this equation becomes $(\frac{1}{32})(12) + (\frac{5}{32})(0) = \frac{1}{32}v_1' + \frac{5}{32}v_2'$, whence

$$v_1' + 5v_2' = 12$$

From the Conservation of Energy, for an elastic collision,

$$\tfrac{1}{2}m_1v_1^2 + \tfrac{1}{2}m_2v_2^2 = \tfrac{1}{2}m_1v_1'^2 + \tfrac{1}{2}m_2v_2'^2$$

With the same units as before, this equation becomes $\frac{1}{2}(\frac{1}{32})(12)^2 + \frac{1}{2}(\frac{5}{32})(0)^2 = \frac{1}{2}(\frac{1}{32})v_1'^2 + \frac{1}{2}(\frac{5}{32})v_2'^2$, whence

$$v_1'^2 + v_2'^2 = 144$$

The two simplified equations when solved simultaneously give the velocities after collision as $v_1' = -8$ ft/sec and $v_2' = 4$ ft/sec, showing that the ball reverses its direction and moves to the left at 8 ft/sec, while the block moves to the right at 4 ft/sec.

When colliding bodies remain distorted after impact, or when there is other evidence of wasted energy, the collision is inelastic. This type of impact can be illustrated by a device known as the ballistic pendulum, which is sometimes used to determine the speed of a bullet. The bullet is fired horizontally into a wood block, initially hanging at rest at the end of a long cord, and the resulting velocity is determined, usually by calculation based on the height to which the block swings. In this collision, energy is wasted in tearing apart the fibers of the block, and therefore the kinetic energy is not conserved. The law of Conservation of Momentum holds, however, and from it the initial speed of the bullet can be obtained.

103. Coefficient of Restitution. The extent to which a collision is elastic can be illustrated by letting a ball fall upon a fixed plate. If the ball were to rebound to its original height the collision would be perfectly elastic, and if it did not rebound at all the collision would be perfectly inelastic. Actually, neither of these extremes is realized. A collision between bodies of elastic materials, however, often approximates the elastic condition rather closely. The degree of elasticity of a collision is usually expressed in terms of a quantity called the *coefficient of restitution*. If the velocities of two colliding bodies are v_1 and v_2 before collision and become v_1' and v_2' after collision, the coefficient of restitution is defined as

$$e = -\frac{v_1' - v_2'}{v_1 - v_2} \tag{83}$$

where the numerator is the relative velocity of one body to the other after collision, and the denominator is the relative velocity before collision. For a perfectly elastic collision, $e = 1$; and for a perfectly inelastic collision, $e = 0$. In using this equation, the algebraic signs of the velocities should be substituted as well as their numerical values. Thus, in the problem of the preceding section, in which a steel ball strikes a steel block, the coefficient of restitution is $e = -\dfrac{-8 - 4}{12 - 0} = 1.000$. This value substantiates the statement that the collision is elastic. Again, in the description of the ballistic pendulum, the block and embedded bullet have the same velocity after impact; therefore $v_1' - v_2' = 0$ and so $e = 0$, as stated for an inelastic collision.

PROBLEMS

1. A bronze wire 50 cm long and 1 mm in diameter is suspended vertically from a fixed support and a mass of 15 kg is attached to its lower end. The elastic limit of the material is 38×10^8 dynes/cm^2 and its stretch modulus is 10^{12} dynes/cm^2. (a) Will the wire return to its original length when the load is removed? (b) How much does the wire stretch when the load is applied?

2. A molybdenum rod 1 ft long and $\frac{1}{4}$ in. in diameter is found to elongate by 0.0057 in. when subjected to a tensile force of 1000 lb. Compute the stress and strain, and determine Young's modulus for molybdenum as indicated by these data.

3. In a building jack, the load is supported by a steel post 3 in. in diameter and 4 ft high. Consider Young's modulus for steel in compression to have the same value as in tension, and determine (a) the amount of load that can be placed upon the post without exceeding a stress of 16,000 lb/in.² and (b) the decrease of length that this load will produce.

4. A rubber band that has a square cross-section measuring $\frac{1}{16}$ in. on each side is cut to form a straight strip. The strip is held horizontally without stretching between two fixed supports 6 in. apart. A load weighing 1 oz hung at the center of the strip causes it to stretch so that the midpoint sags $1\frac{1}{4}$ in. Compute (a) the tension in the strip and (b) the value of Young's modulus for rubber as determined from these data.

5. In the world's largest testing machine, at Lehigh University, a steel rod $7\frac{3}{4}$ in. in diameter was subjected to increasing tensile loads and finally ruptured at 3,920,000 lb. Compute the breaking stress of the specimen, based on its initial diameter.

6. An aluminum block measuring 3 × 4 cm and 2 cm high is subjected to a pair of equal and opposite shearing forces as shown in Fig. 100. If each of these forces is 3×10^8 dynes, through what angle is the block sheared?

7. To measure the shear modulus of tungsten, a wire of this material having a length of 25 cm and a radius of 1.25×10^{-3} cm is fixed at one end and twisted at the other. If the torque applied to the free end is 0.36 dyne·cm when that end is twisted through an angle of 90°, what is the value of the shear modulus?

8. A steel shaft 20 ft long and 1 in. in diameter is driven at one end and drives a load at the other. If the shaft turns at 400 rev/min, through what angle is it twisted while it is transmitting 5 hp?

9. Determine the bulk modulus of nitric acid from the information that a liter of this liquid contracts by 0.34 cm³ when subjected to a pressure of 10^6 dynes/cm².

10. A horizontal cylinder has a tightly fitting piston 9 in. in diameter. A volume of 1.5 ft³ of water is introduced into the cylinder and no air is entrapped. If the piston is pushed in $\frac{1}{16}$ in., what force is needed to hold it in this position?

11. At a depth of 3 mi in the ocean, the pressure is about 7000 lb/in.² Consider the compressibility of salt water to be the same as that of fresh water, and calculate the reduction of volume that 1 ft³ of water undergoes when the pressure on it is increased by this amount.

12. It can be shown that, for an isotropic solid, the bulk modulus B, the shear modulus E, and Young's modulus Y are related by the expression $Y = 9BE/(3B + E)$. From the values tabulated in § 100, calculate the bulk modulus of brass.

13. A straight steel wire having a length of 10 m and a cross-sectional area of 0.002 cm² hangs vertically from a fixed support, and a 4000-gm mass is attached to its lower end. If the mass is pulled down slightly and released, with what frequency does it vibrate up and down?

14. A brass wire 30 ft long and $\frac{1}{64}$ in. in diameter hangs vertically from a fixed support. If a 3-lb weight is attached to the lower end of the wire and set into vertical vibration, how many vibrations does it complete in 1 min?

15. Two blocks sliding toward each other on a horizontal frictionless surface collide head on. Block A has a mass of 1 kg and before impact is moving toward the right at 5 cm/sec; block B has a mass of 2 kg and before impact is moving toward the left at 4 cm/sec. (a) If the colliding surfaces are sticky and the blocks adhere to each other, what is their joint velocity after

impact? (*b*) If the test is repeated with clean surfaces and the collision is perfectly elastic, what is the velocity of each block after impact?

16. In the solved problem of § 102, suppose that the collision is not perfectly elastic and that the ball after impact rebounds to a position where the cord makes an angle of 45° with the vertical. (*a*) Find the velocity of the ball and that of the block after collision. (*b*) How much energy is not recovered? (*c*) What is the coefficient of restitution for the colliding bodies?

17. A block that weighs 5 lb is sliding on a smooth horizontal surface with a velocity of 2 ft/sec toward the right. Another block, which weighs 10 lb, is sliding in the same direction at 3 ft/sec, and bumps the first block from the rear. Consider the collision to be elastic and find the velocity of each block after impact. Compute also the coefficient of restitution of the colliding bodies.

18. Refer to Prob. 4 of Chap. 5, and compute the coefficient of restitution of the colliding bodies.

11

LIQUIDS AT REST

104. The Liquid Phase. Although most substances can be classified readily as solids, liquids, or gases, the lines dividing these phases cannot always be sharply drawn. Thus, tar at ordinary temperatures fractures like a solid and yet, to a slight extent, flows like a liquid. Transitions frequently occur from one phase to another, many solids becoming liquids when sufficiently heated, and liquids becoming solids when sufficiently cooled. Again, gases can be liquefied by sufficient cooling and compression, and liquids can be vaporized by heating or simply by evaporating at ordinary temperatures.

It is generally agreed that matter is composed of molecules which are in more or less violent agitation, depending upon the temperature. In a solid the molecules are generally bound closer together than in a liquid, and their motion is more restricted, consisting of vibration over narrow ranges. In a gas the molecules are relatively far apart and move about with comparative freedom throughout the entire confining space. The liquid phase is intermediate between the other two. Upon heating a solid, say a metal, the molecules become more violently agitated and less firmly bound; if the process is continued the metal melts and becomes a liquid.

Liquids have practically no elasticity of shape and conform readily to the shape of any containing vessel. This shows that liquids cannot withstand a shearing action to any great extent; indeed, an *ideal liquid* is defined as one that offers no resistance to shearing forces. A liquid, unless completely confined, has a free surface; when the liquid is at rest this surface is horizontal except at the edges, § 116. Liquids are often treated as incompressible, because a large pressure causes only a very slight reduction in volume.

PRESSURE AND FORCE DUE TO LIQUID

105. Liquid Pressure. A liquid exerts a force against any surface with which it is in contact; *the force per unit area is defined as pressure.* When a force F acts perpendicularly upon a plane area A, the corresponding pressure is $p = F/A$; hence the force can be expressed as

$$F = pA \qquad (84)$$

The idea of *pressure at a point* is often helpful in dealing with liquids. This term presupposes a small plane surface at the point in question, and is the ratio of the force ΔF exerted upon this surface to its area ΔA as the area is taken smaller and smaller, eventually dwindling to a point. To derive an expression for the pressure at a point, a horizontal surface of area

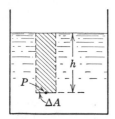

ΔA is imagined at a depth h below the surface of the liquid, as at point P in Fig. 105. This surface supports the column of liquid directly above it. The column has a volume $h\Delta A$ and a weight $\Delta F = hw\Delta A$, where w is the weight of the liquid per unit volume. Hence, the pressure at the point is $p = \Delta F/\Delta A$, or

$$p = hw \qquad (85)$$

FIG. 105. For evaluating the pressure at a point within a liquid

In British units, the pressure in pounds per square foot is the product of the depth in feet and the weight per unit volume of the liquid in pounds per cubic foot. Water weighs 62.4 lb/ft³ and so the pressure at a point 1 ft below the surface of water is 1 ft $\times$ 62.4 lb/ft³ = 62.4 lb/ft². This is equivalent to 62.4 $\div$ 144 = 0.433 lb/in.²

In metric units, the weight of the liquid per unit volume is expressed more conveniently as $\dfrac{mg}{V}$ or dg, where $d = \dfrac{m}{V}$ is the density of the liquid, §6. Hence the pressure at point P is stated as

$$p = hdg \qquad (86)$$

The pressure in dynes per square centimeter is the product of the depth in centimeters, the density of the liquid in grams per cubic centimeter, and the acceleration due to gravity, 980 cm/sec². The density of water is 1 gm/cm³ and so the pressure at a point 1 cm below the surface of water is 1 cm $\times$ 1 gm/cm³ $\times$ 980 dynes/gm = 980 dynes/cm².

The pressure at a point due to a liquid is seen to be determined completely by the depth of the point below the liquid surface and the weight of the liquid per unit volume. This pressure is not affected by the depth of liquid below the point in question nor by the size or shape of the body of liquid in which the point is located.

The foregoing expressions give the pressure due to the liquid only; if the total or *absolute* pressure is desired, the atmospheric or other pressure on the surface of the liquid should be added to the value found. Atmospheric pressure is discussed in Chap. 13; it will suffice here to give its value as approximately 14.7 lb/in.² or 1.013 $\times$ 10⁶ dynes/cm².

Because of liquid pressure, a liquid exerts a force on any surface with which it is in contact. To determine this force completely, it is necessary to know its direction, magnitude, and point of application; these properties will be considered in the following sections.

106. Force Due to Liquid; Direction.   *The force exerted by a liquid at rest is normal to any surface with which it is in contact.* To show that this statement is correct, the force may be imagined to act in some other direction, as in part I of Fig. 106, where f, the force exerted by the liquid upon the wall at P, is (incorrectly) represented as inclined to the normal. Under these circumstances f could be resolved into two components n and t, these being respectively normal and tangent to the wall. But the component t

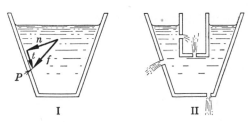

FIG. 106.   Force due to liquid is perpendicular to surface

cannot exist, for it tends to move the wall in the direction shown; if such a force existed, the wall would exert a tangential force on the adjacent layer of liquid. The liquid being unable to resist a shearing force would move in response to it, a result which is contrary to the assumption that the liquid is at rest. Hence the force f exerted by the liquid must be normal to the surface.

An experimental proof is indicated in part II of the figure, where the liquid is shown emerging normally through small openings made in various surfaces with which it is in contact.

107. Force Due to Liquid; Magnitude.   The force due to liquid pressure on any plane submerged surface can be calculated from Eq. 84, $F = pA$. For a horizontal surface, since the pressure is uniform throughout, p represents its value at any point. For any other plane surface, *the same equation can be used, provided p represents the pressure at the center of the area subjected to liquid pressure.* This statement can be proved by imagining the surface to be divided into a number of elementary areas, upon each of which the pressure is substantially uniform; the equation can then be used to find the force on each individual area, and by adding the forces thus found the total force is obtained.

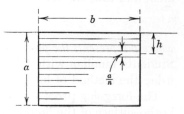

FIG. 107.   Submerged rectangular surface divided into horizontal strips for analysis

A vertical submerged rectangle of area ab is shown in Fig. 107 with its upper edge in the surface of a liquid of which the weight per unit volume is w. The rectangle is divided into n slender horizontal strips each of width

$\dfrac{a}{n}$, located at depths h_1, h_2, h_3, $\cdots h_n$, below the surface of the liquid. The total force acting on the surface is the sum of the forces on the individual strips, thus:

$$F = h_1 w \frac{a}{n} b + h_2 w \frac{a}{n} b + \cdots + h_n w \frac{a}{n} b = \frac{wab}{n}(h_1 + h_2 + \cdots h_n)$$

The quantity in parenthesis consists of n terms, each greater than the preceding by an amount $\dfrac{a}{n}$, and thus forms an arithmetical progression, the sum of the series being

$$(h_1 + h_2 + \cdots h_n) = n\frac{h_1 + h_n}{2}$$

If the number of strips is very large, it can be assumed that $h_1 = 0$ and $h_n = a$, and hence the sum of the series becomes $n\dfrac{0 + a}{2} = \dfrac{na}{2}$. Therefore the total force on the submerged surface is

$$F = \frac{wab}{n} \times \frac{na}{2} = \frac{wa^2 b}{2}$$

This value can be expressed as $F = \dfrac{wa}{2} A$, where $A = ab$ is the area of the rectangle. But the term $\dfrac{wa}{2}$ represents the pressure at the center of this area, and thus the force exerted by the liquid on the surface is

$$F = pA$$

where p represents the pressure at the center of the area in contact with the liquid. Students familiar with calculus will be able to simplify the treatment by using the method of integration.

The foregoing proof was based on a vertical rectangle with its upper edge in the surface of the liquid; the same method of treatment can be applied to surfaces of any shape, located anywhere, and inclined at any angle, provided only that the surface considered is plane, so that the liquid pressure at any point upon it varies in direct proportion to the depth.

An interesting example appears in Fig. 108, which shows a cross-section of three tanks having *bases of equal area*, the tanks being filled with water to the *same depth*. Under these conditions, the liquid is found to exert the same force on the base of each tank, thus showing that the force does not depend on the shape of the tank or the weight of liquid in it.

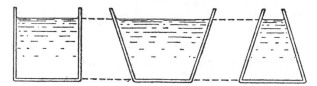

Fig. 108. The liquid exerts the same force on tank bottoms of equal area

108. Force Due to Liquid; Point of Application. Where the pressure exerted by a liquid is the same at all points of a plane surface, as in the case of a horizontal surface, then the point of application of the resultant force is the center of area of that surface. Otherwise this point of application is not at the center of area but is located at some other point called the *center of pressure.*

The location of the center of pressure for a submerged surface depends upon its shape. For a rectangle the calculation is relatively simple. In

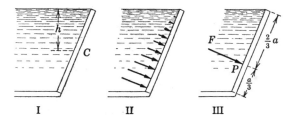

Fig. 109. Liquid exerts parallel forces on submerged rectangle; their resultant *F* acts at the center of pressure *P*

Fig. 109 the inclined surface represents a rectangle viewed edgewise with its upper edge at the liquid surface and its center of area *C* shown in part I midway between the top and bottom edges and at a distance *h* below the surface. The pressure at this point multiplied by the area of the rectangular surface gives the magnitude of the force acting upon it. This force is the sum of the component forces acting on a series of horizontal strips as indicated by the arrows in part II and as calculated in § 107. By working out a numerical example with, say, ten or more strips the student can locate approximately the center of pressure where the resultant of the component forces acts. Its accurate location is found by dividing the rectangle into an infinite number of horizontal strips and applying calculus methods; the analysis shows that the resultant acts two-thirds of the way down from the upper to the lower edge, when the upper edge of the rectangle lies in the liquid surface. The center of pressure of this rectangle is located at *P* in part III of the figure, wherein *a* is the slant height of the surface.

109. Stability of a Dam. In building tanks, dams, and other structures to confine liquids, it is necessary to know how much force the liquid exerts, in order that each surface may have the proper strength and bracing to withstand the applied load. In calculating such a force the pressure is first determined, usually by Eq. 85, $p = hw$, and the force is then found from Eq. 84, $F = pA$. A dam must be heavy enough to resist sliding along its foundation as well as to resist overturning; it is customary to build it of reinforced concrete and to design it so that the resultant of the gravitational and water forces upon it is directed through the middle third of the base.

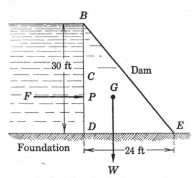

Fig. 110. Forces exerted upon a dam

Illustrative Problem

Consider a dam having a cross-section with dimensions as shown in Fig. 110, and take the width of the dam (perpendicular to the page) as 100 ft for simplicity. Determine the force F exerted by the water on the dam, and the torque tending to overturn the dam about the edge E. State the condition necessary to prevent overturning.

With the water level at the top of the dam, the center of area C of the water face is halfway along BD; that is, 15 ft below B. The water pressure at this point is $p = hw = 15 \text{ ft} \times 62.4 \text{ lb/ft}^3 = 936 \text{ lb/ft}^2$. The resultant force of the water on the dam is $F = pA = (936 \text{ lb/ft}^2)(30 \times 100 \text{ ft}^2) = 2.808 \times 10^6$ lb; it acts perpendicularly to BD at point P, two-thirds of the way from B to D.

The torque tending to overturn the dam about the edge E is the product of the force F and its lever arm PD; it amounts to $2.808 \times 10^6 \text{ lb} \times 10 \text{ ft} = 2.808 \times 10^7$ lb·ft, and its direction is clockwise in the figure.

To prevent overturning, the weight W of the dam, acting downward at its center of gravity G, must provide a counterclockwise torque about E that is greater than the clockwise torque due to the water force F.

110. Transmission of Pressure Change; Pascal's Principle.

A number of principles in the mechanics of fluids are associated with the name of the French philosopher, Blaise Pascal (1623–1662). One of these states that *an increase in pressure on the free surface of a liquid or at any point in a liquid that completely fills its container results in a like increase at every other part of the liquid.*

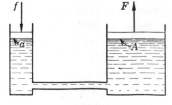

Fig. 111. Simplified sketch of hydraulic press

This principle is employed in the hydraulic press, as used for compressing goods into bales, for forming the lead sheathing upon electric cables, and the like. An elementary diagram of this device is shown in Fig. 111, which represents a liquid confined within a system having two cylinders of areas a and A respectively, each fitted with a piston. Upon applying a force f to the small piston, the pressure beneath it is increased by the amount f/a.

In accordance with Pascal's Principle, the pressure under the large piston is increased by the same amount, and therefore the force exerted by the large piston is $F = \dfrac{f}{a} A$. By this means a large force, exerted through a small distance, is obtained by exerting a small force through a large distance. The mechanical advantage of the hydraulic press can be computed as described in § 72.

Hydraulic brakes on automobiles operate on the principle of liquid pressure. A pressure or master cylinder is mounted near the fulcrum of the foot-brake pedal and is connected by copper tubing and flexible hose connections to cylinders at each of the four wheel brakes, the entire system being filled with nonfreezing liquid. When foot pressure is applied, the piston of the master cylinder is forced inward, increasing the pressure on the liquid at that point; this increase of pressure is transmitted to the four wheel cylinders and their pistons are forced outward, causing the brake bands to tighten against the wheels.

BUOYANCY AND DENSITY

111. Buoyancy; Archimedes' Principle. It is well known that a stone can be lifted more easily in water than in air; that many objects float upon water; that a swimmer does not sink in the Great Salt Lake; and that most metals float upon mercury. These illustrations show that a liquid exerts an upward force upon a body placed in it. Archimedes (c. 287–212 B.C.), Greek mathematician and inventor, determined the amount of this so-called buoyant force. The principle known by his name states that *a body submerged wholly or partially in a liquid is buoyed up by a force equal to the weight of the liquid displaced.*

This principle can be verified *experimentally* by placing an object in a vessel initially filled to the top with water and measuring the weight of the water that overflows, as well as the weight of the object and its apparent weight when immersed. Thus, if a metal block weighing 10.4 lb in air displaces 1.3 lb of water when submerged, its apparent weight in the water is found to be 9.1 lb, showing that the buoyant force of the water is $10.4 - 9.1 = 1.3$ lb. Hence, the buoyant force on the block equals the weight of liquid displaced.

Archimedes' Principle can be proved *theoretically* by calculating the buoyant force acting upon a submerged body and also calculating the weight of the displaced liquid, and showing that these quantities are equal. Thus, a block of rectangular cross-section, having a height h and having top and bottom faces of area a, is represented in Fig. 112, immersed in a liquid of which the weight per unit volume is w. On the vertical faces, the liquid exerts horizontal forces that are balanced on all sides; on the top face it exerts a downward force h_1wa, and on the bottom face an upward force h_2wa. Since h_2 is greater than h_1, the liquid exerts a net upward force on the block amounting to $h_2wa - h_1wa = hwa$. But the volume of the block,

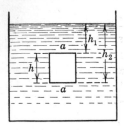

and hence that of the liquid displaced, is ha, and therefore the weight of the liquid displaced is hwa, which is identical with the buoyant force due to the liquid. Bodies of irregular shape may be considered as made up of a number of tiny blocks as described, and it follows that any body submerged in a liquid is buoyed up by a force equal to the weight of liquid displaced.

Fig. 112. Diagram used in proving Archimedes' Principle

This principle is employed in the control of submarines. In submerging the boat, sea water is admitted into tanks and the effect of the buoyant force is reduced. The boat is brought to the surface by expelling the water from these tanks with compressed air or with pumps.

112. Density and Specific Gravity. The density of a substance has already been referred to in § 6 and defined as its mass per unit volume; in symbols,

$$d = \frac{m}{V} \tag{87}$$

where in cgs units m is the mass in grams and V the volume in cubic centimeters. An associated ratio, used widely in the United States for engineering work and everyday purposes, is the so-called *weight density*, defined as

$$w = \frac{W}{V} \tag{88}$$

where W is the weight of a substance and V its volume. With the usual units of the British system for these quantities the weight density is expressed in pounds per cubic foot. The concept of weight density was used in §§ 105 and 107 in determining the pressure and force exerted by a liquid; the value of w for water is 62.4 lb/ft^3.

The specific gravity of a substance is the ratio of the density of the substance to that of water. This quantity is merely a number and tells how many times a substance is as "heavy" (dense) as water. If a substance has a specific gravity of 5, then 1 cm^3 of the substance has a mass of 5 gm, or 1 ft^3 of the substance has a weight of 5 × 62.4 = 312 lb. It will be noted that in the cgs system of units, the specific gravity of a substance has the same numerical value as its density, since the density of water is 1 gm/cm^3. Density and specific gravity of solids and liquids are independent of the size of the sample under test and depend only upon the substance of which it is made.

Values of the specific gravity of some substances are given in the accompanying table.

SPECIFIC GRAVITIES

Liquids			*Metals*	
Benzene.......	0.89	(0° C)	Aluminum, hard drawn	2.70
Glycerine......	1.26	(0° C)	Brass...............	8.25– 8.70
Mercury.......	13.596	(0° C)	Copper.............	8.80– 8.95
Oils, lubricating.	0.90–0.93	(20° C)	Iron, gray cast.......	7.03– 7.13
Turpentine.....	0.873	(16° C)	Lead................	11.34–11.36
Water, pure....	1.000	(4° C)	Platinum............	21.50
Water, sea.....	1.025	(15° C)	Silver...............	10.4 –10.5
			Steel................	7.82– 7.85
Woods			Uranium............	18.7
Balsa wood...........		0.11–0.13		
Cedar................		0.49–0.57	*Miscellaneous*	
Cork................		0.22–0.26	Diamond..............	3.5 –3.6
Lignum-vitae..........		1.17–1.33	Glass, common........	2.4 –2.8
Maple................		0.62–0.75	Ice...................	0.88–0.91
Oak.................		0.60–0.90	Kapok (in pillows).....	0.05–0.10
Pine................		0.35–0.85	Masonry..............	1.85–2.3

113. Measurement of Density. The density of a solid can usually be determined by measuring its mass and its volume separately. The mass is obtained with an equal-arm balance, and the volume is found either from the dimensions of the body or by measuring the displacement it produces when submerged in water. With the mass and the volume known, the density follows from Eq. 87. An indirect method consists of weighing the body first in air and again when submerged in water, and using Archimedes' Principle to calculate the density from the data thus obtained.

The density of a liquid can be determined by several methods. In one of these, a specific-gravity bottle of known weight is filled with the liquid and the mass is determined with an equal-arm balance. The volume of the container is usually known or can be determined by another measurement using water, and the density of the liquid can then be calculated by direct proportion. A second method for measuring the density of a liquid consists of weighing some solid body (1) in air, (2) when submerged in water, and (3) when submerged in the liquid under test; and calculating the density of the liquid by the use of Archimedes' Principle.

Illustrative Problem

To apply the principle just described, suppose that a solid object weighs 1.5 lb in air and that its apparent weight is 0.9 lb when immersed in water and 1.1 lb when immersed in gasoline; from these data determine the density of gasoline.

The buoyant force on the object when immersed in water is 1.5 − 0.9 = 0.6 lb, and by Archimedes' Principle this is the weight of the water displaced. Since 0.6 lb of water occupies a volume of 0.6 lb ÷ 62.4 lb/ft³ = 0.00962 ft³, this is the volume of the water displaced and also equals the volume of the object and that of the gasoline displaced. But the weight of the gasoline displaced is 1.5 − 1.1 = 0.4 lb; therefore the weight density of the gasoline is 0.4 lb ÷ 0.00962 ft³ = 41.6 lb/ft³.

The density of a liquid can also be determined by means of a hydrometer. Fig. 113 shows the instrument floating upright; it consists of a hollow chamber weighted at the bottom and having a graduated stem at the top. When placed in the liquid it settles until it displaces its own weight of liquid (see following section); the denser the liquid, the higher it floats. With the scale suitably calibrated, the specific gravity of the liquid can be read directly at the point where the stem projects through the liquid surface.

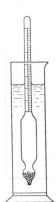

FIG. 113. Hydrometer for measuring specific gravity

Still another method for determining the density of a liquid is that of balanced columns. In this method, illustrated in Fig. 114, one arm of an inverted U-tube is dipped into water and the other into the liquid under test. When part of the air is removed from the tube through a valve at A, the two liquids rise to heights h_w and h_x, which can be measured. Since the same difference in pressure exists between the top and bottom of each liquid column, it follows that $h_w d_w g = h_x d_x g$, where d_w represents the density of water and d_x that of the liquid under test. The density of the latter can be found from this equation.

114. Stability of Floating Bodies. An upward buoyant force is experienced by a floating body as well as one completely immersed, in accordance with Archimedes' Principle. A body floating at rest, moreover, is in equilibrium, and hence the buoyant force is equal and opposite to the weight of the body itself. *A body that floats when placed in a liquid settles until it displaces its own weight of liquid.* A ship that displaces 20,000 tons of water also weighs this same amount.

The forces acting upon a ship are indicated in part I of Fig. 115, where W represents the weight of the ship, acting downward through its center of gravity G, and B represents the equal buoyant force, which acts upward through C, the center of gravity of the displaced water. In the displaced position of the ship shown in part II of the figure, its weight W acts downward at G, as before, but the upward force of buoyancy B has shifted to a parallel position through C', a new center of gravity of the displaced water. These forces constitute a couple that tends to restore the

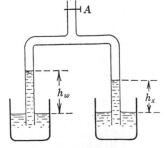

FIG. 114. Balanced-column method of measuring liquid density

ship to an upright position. The stability of a ship is determined by the position of the *metacenter M*. This point is the intersection of two lines, one drawn vertically through the center of gravity of the displaced water,

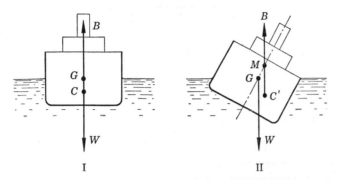

I   II

FIG. 115.   Forces on a ship in upright and listed positions

and the other being a line which was drawn vertically through the center of gravity of the ship when in an upright position.   For stability, the design should be such that the metacenter is above the center of gravity of the ship, as in the figure, although in practice the *metacentric height MG* is kept reasonably small so that the restoring couple does not cause too rapid rolling of the ship.

MOLECULAR PHENOMENA

115. Molecular Motion and Molecular Forces.   There is experimental evidence to show that the molecules of a body are in a state of eternal motion, a motion entirely erratic and irregular, and depending only upon the temperature of the substance.   The molecules themselves are too small for direct observation.   The English botanist Robert Brown (1773–1858) noted that very fine particles placed in suspension in a liquid move about in an irregular and lifelike manner.   He attributed this behavior to uneven bombardment of the particles by the moving molecules of the liquid; this hypothesis has been amply borne out by further research and mathematical study.   These erratic motions, termed Brownian movements, can be observed with a high-power microscope by viewing fine particles of insoluble carmine or some similar substance suspended in water.

There is also evidence to show that, as two molecules approach each other, a separation is reached where their combined potential energy is a minimum. In this condition, work is needed to move them nearer together or farther apart, because of the forces known to exist between them.   When molecules are very close together, these forces produce a tremendous repulsive effect, keeping the centers of the molecules at slight distances from each other. When the molecules are farther apart, the forces cause attraction; such forces are known to be very great.   It is this molecular attraction, for example, that holds a solid body together, enabling it not only to retain its shape but also to support large external loads. The attraction between molecules of the same substance is called *cohesion*, and that between molecules of unlike substances is called *adhesion*.

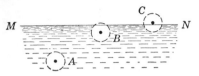

The attraction between two molecules falls off rapidly as their separation increases. It is therefore a convenient fiction to imagine a tiny sphere around each molecule, called its *sphere of action*, and to say that the molecule exerts an attractive force upon other molecules that lie within this boundary, but not upon

FIG. 116. Imaginary boundaries around molecules to represent their spheres of action

those outside of it. The sphere of action is usually considered as having a radius smaller than one-millionth of a centimeter.

116. Surface Phenomena. The theory of molecular attraction explains the interesting behavior of a liquid surface. In Fig. 116, the line MN represents a free liquid surface, and A, B, and C represent molecules of the liquid, each surrounded by its sphere of action. Molecule A, which is well within the body of the liquid, is, on the average, attracted equally in all directions by other molecules within its sphere of action, and its motion is

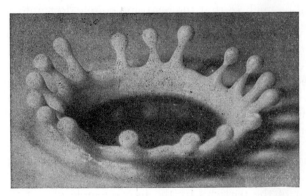

FIG. 117. Splash of a milk drop photographed with 10-microsecond exposure. (*Courtesy of Professor Harold E. Edgerton*)

unaffected. Molecule B, which is near the surface, experiences a downward force since there are more molecules in the lower half of its sphere of action than in the upper half. Similarly, molecule C, which is represented at the free surface, is acted upon by a considerable downward force. Hence a molecule which in its motion tends to rise above the surface is pulled downward. Because of these molecular forces, the surface acts like a stretched membrane, tending to shorten itself as much as possible, and assumes at each point a direction at right angles to the resultant forces acting on the surface molecules. Thus, a little mercury poured upon a level surface does not spread out into a thin film, but approaches the shape of a sphere (although slightly flattened), because a sphere has the smallest possible surface for a given volume. Fig. 117 shows an enlarged view of the splash produced by a drop of milk falling upon a surface of that liquid and reveals the rebounding droplets just before they become detached spheres.

The molecular forces in a liquid like water cause its surface to creep up the walls of the containing vessel. The adhesive and cohesive forces upon a surface molecule in this region are shown in Fig. 118. The force of adhe-

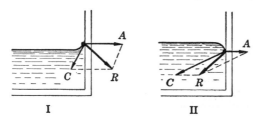

FIG. 118.   Adhesive and cohesive forces contrasted.   Adhesion predominates if the liquid surface curves upward

sion *A* exerted by the wall is perpendicular to its surface; the force of cohesion *C*, which is due to the surrounding molecules of liquid, has the general direction shown; and their resultant *R* is at right angles to the surface of the liquid.   The shape shown in part I of the figure is characteristic of liquids that wet the wall, the adhesion between the liquid and the solid being greater than the cohesion of the liquid.   Any liquid molecules near the wall that happen to rise above the free liquid surface are pulled toward the wall by the force of adhesion and are piled up along the edge.   In liquids that

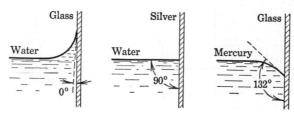

FIG. 119.   Angles of contact between liquid surface and vertical wall

do not wet the wall, like mercury, the adhesion is less than the cohesion, and the liquid surface curves downward as in part II of the figure.

The *angle of contact* at the edge of a liquid surface is defined as the angle formed by the liquid surface and a vertical wall at the point of contact, measured within the liquid.   The value of the angle of contact depends upon both the liquid and the material of the wall; it is 0° between water and glass, 90° between water and silver, and 132° between mercury and glass, for pure liquids and clean surfaces.   These values are indicated in Fig. 119.

117. Surface Tension. It has been pointed out that the surface of a liquid tends to assume the smallest possible size, acting in this respect like a membrane under tension. Every portion of the liquid surface exerts a pull upon adjacent portions or upon other objects with which it is in contact. This force acts in the plane of the surface, and its amount per unit of length is known as *surface tension*. Its value for water is about 75 dynes/cm at ordinary temperatures. Thus, if a line 1 cm long is imagined in the sur-

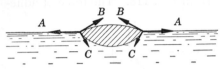

FIG. 120. Surface-tension forces determine shape of oil drop

face of water, the surface on either side of this line exerts a force of 75 dynes upon the surface on the other side. Although a liquid surface is likened to a stretched membrane, the analogy is not perfect. For instance, surface tension, being a property of the liquid, does not change when the size of the liquid surface is changed, but the forces in a stretched membrane would change under like circumstances.

The surface tension of a liquid is sensitive to the presence of molecules other than those of the pure liquid when these are at the surface. Impurities tend to lower the surface tension and allow the liquid to spread over a surface and to seep into tiny openings; these effects are often useful, as the following examples show. In a throat spray, low surface tension helps the liquid to spread and thus medicate a large area. In cleaning, the addition of a detergent to water lowers its surface tension and allows the water to enter tiny crevices that it could not reach otherwise. For a similar reason, in firefighting, firemen use so-called "wet" water containing an additive

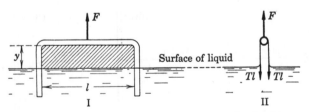

FIG. 121. Measuring surface tension of a liquid

which lowers the surface tension, to put out smoldering fires inside cotton bales.

Surface tension manifests itself not only at the free surface of a liquid but also at the boundaries or interfaces separating two liquids. As an illustration, the forces acting upon a drop of oil floating on hot water are shown in Fig. 120. The surface tension A of the water in contact with air tends to spread the oil drop, while the surface tension B of the oil in contact with air and the surface tension C of the oil in contact with water both tend to make the drop contract. Under the combined action of these forces, the drop assumes such a shape as to remain in equilibrium. At lower temperatures the surface tension of the liquids against air increases, but the increase is greater for water than for oil. Hence at ordinary room temperature the oil drop spreads into a thin film.

Some approximate values of surface tension, based on measurements at ordinary room temperature, appear in the accompanying table.

SURFACE TENSIONS OF SOME LIQUIDS

Liquid	In contact with	Dynes/cm
Benzene.........	air	29
Glycerine........	air	63
Mercury.........	air	470
Mercury.........	water	392
Olive oil........	air	35
Olive oil........	water	19
Water...........	air	75

The surface tension of a liquid can be measured by observing the force needed to pull an inverted U-shaped wire upward through the surface. In order to pull a wire of length l through the surface, it is necessary to exert some force F in excess of its weight, as indicated in part I of Fig. 121. As the wire leaves the surface a film of liquid adheres to it and exerts a downward force on the wire amounting to $2Tl$, where T represents the surface tension of the liquid, acting in each surface of the film. These forces are shown in the sectional diagram forming part II of the figure. To move the wire uniformly, the applied force must equal the downward pull; hence

$$F = 2Tl \tag{89}$$

an expression from which the surface tension of the liquid can be computed.

Surface tension can also be expressed in terms of the work done in increasing the area of the liquid surface. Thus, if the wire in Fig. 121 is pulled upward uniformly a distance y, the work done is $E = Fy$, and the increase in area of the film is $A = 2ly$, counting both sides. The work needed to produce a unit increase in area is then

$$\frac{E}{A} = \frac{Fy}{2ly} = \frac{F}{2l}$$

which, by Eq. 89, is equal to the surface tension. Hence,

$$T = \frac{E}{A} \tag{90}$$

The surface tension of water has been given before as 75 dynes/cm; it can also be expressed as 75 ergs/cm^2.

118. Capillarity. The rise of liquids in fine-bore tubes is called *capillarity*. The surface of the liquid within the tube forms a cup-shaped meniscus that is concave upward. The surface has this shape because the atmospheric pressure on its upper side is larger than the pressure within the liquid just below the surface. It is this pressure difference that causes the liquid to rise in the tube.

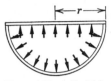

This pressure difference that exists between the sides of a curved liquid surface is related to the surface tension of the liquid and can be easily evaluated for the thin film of a soap bubble in equilibrium. Fig. 122 represents the lower half of such a bubble of radius r and shows the top of the hemispherical film closed by a flat plate. For equilibrium, $\Sigma V = 0$, whence the downward and upward forces in the figure are equal. The pressure inside the bubble exceeds that outside by some amount p, and hence the force on the plate, which is upward, has the value $\pi r^2 p$. For equilibrium, the downward force on the lower half of the bubble also equals $\pi r^2 p$, the weight of the film being neglected.

FIG. 122. Bubble with upper half replaced by flat plate

Fig. 123 shows the lower half of the bubble in perspective. The downward force acting upon it because of pressure difference is $\pi r^2 p$, as just found. The upward force upon it is due to the surface tension T acting around the circumference of the bubble on both outer and inner surfaces of the liquid film and thus amounts to $4\pi rT$, from Eq. 89, no distinction being made between the radii of the two surfaces. For equilibrium, $\pi r^2 p = 4\pi rT$; hence the pressure inside the bubble exceeds that on the outside by the amount

$$p = \frac{4T}{r}$$

FIG. 123. Half bubble held in equilibrium by surface tension acting around its perimeter

For a single spherical surface, such as that presented by a drop of liquid or an air bubble within a liquid, the pressure is half of this value, or $p = 2T/r$.

The rise of liquid in a capillary tube is caused by the atmospheric pressure forcing the liquid into the tube until the pressure due to the liquid column equals the pressure difference due to the curvature of the meniscus. Thus, in Fig. 124, the liquid rises to a height h and the pressure due to the column is hdg as given by Eq. 86; hence $hdg = 2T/r$, where T is the surface tension of the liquid, d its density, and g the acceleration due to gravity. To express the capillary rise in terms of the radius R of the tube rather than the radius r of the meniscus, the angle of contact θ between the liquid surface and the wall is introduced. Since $R = r \cos \theta$, it follows that the capillary rise is

$$h = \frac{2T \cos \theta}{Rdg} \tag{91}$$

For a liquid that does not wet the tube, the top of the meniscus is convex, θ is larger than 90°, and $\cos \theta$ is negative. The resulting negative value for

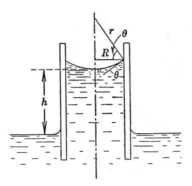

FIG. 124.   Rise of liquid in capillary tube

h in the equation indicates that the liquid, instead of rising in the tube, is depressed below the surface of the liquid outside. This result is observed with a glass tube lowered into mercury.

PROBLEMS

1. How many tons of water fall upon an acre of level ground during a 1-in. rainfall?

2. What is the liquid pressure at a depth of 10 fathoms below the surface of the ocean? Sea water weighs 64 lb/ft³, and 1 fathom = 6 ft.

3. A dam has a triangular cross-section 9 ft wide, 12 ft high, and 15 ft along the sloping side. Determine the water pressure at a point halfway down the sloping side of the dam.

4. A conical container with its axis vertical is 25 cm high and holds exactly 2 liters. In the container is ½ liter of water, covered with 1½ liters of oil that has a density of 0.9 gm/cm³. Compute the liquid pressure at the tip of the cone.

5. An open-top cylindrical tank 12 ft high has its axis vertical and is two-thirds full of water. Calculate the force due to the water on a square patch measuring 9 × 9 in. in the base of the tank.

6. Suppose the tank shown at the center in Fig. 108 has a square base measuring 2 ft along each edge, and that the tank is filled to a depth of 3 ft with 1200 lb of water. What weight of water is supported by the base, and what by the sloping walls?

7. An open-top tank that has a rectangular base measuring 3 × 4 ft and vertical walls 5 ft high is full of water. Calculate (*a*) the liquid pressure at

the base, (*b*) the force exerted by the water on the base, and (*c*) the force exerted by the water on one of the 3 × 5-ft vertical walls.

8. An aquarium has a rectangular base measuring 8 × 16 in. and vertical walls 10 in. high. When 5 gal of water are placed in the tank, what is (*a*) the water pressure at the base? and (*b*) the force exerted by the water on one of the larger walls?

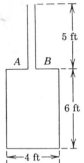

9. The diagram represents a cylindrical tank with its axis vertical; the top is closed except for a vertical pipe which extends upward. The tank and pipe have the dimensions shown, and are full of water. Compute (*a*) the force exerted by the water on the bottom of the tank, and (*b*) the pressure exerted on the water by the horizontal top surface *AB*.

Problem 9

10. A rectangular open-top tank has side walls 2 ft high, and its base measures 1½ ft along each edge. The tank when half full of water is tipped about one edge of the base until the water is just about to overflow. Assume the tank to be in this position, and determine the force that the water exerts upon the side wall beneath it.

11. A dam 20 ft long has a triangular cross-section 16 ft high with a 12-ft base. Water in contact with the vertical side extends to the top of the dam. Compute the force exerted by the water tending to slide the dam along its foundation, and the torque due to the water tending to overturn the dam.

12. Assume the 100-ft dam shown in Fig. 110 to be made of concrete weighing 150 lb/ft³, and find the torque due to the weight of the dam which tends to prevent overturning about the edge *E* by the water.

13. A rectangular tide gate 4 ft wide and 9 ft high is hinged at its top edge and hangs vertically into the sea water, the water surface on one side of the gate being below the hinge by 3 ft and that on the other side by 6 ft. Determine the net torque due to the water tending to turn the gate on its hinge.

14. The hydraulic press in the diagram has pistons with diameters of 2 in. and 10 in., and the small piston is operated by a lever as shown, pivoted at *P*. When the operator applies a downward force of 40 lb to the free end of the lever, what force is exerted by the large piston of the press?

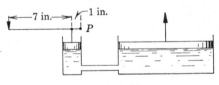

Problem 14

15. The spherical shell of a float valve has a diameter of 4 in. Compute the value of the buoyant force acting upon the shell when three-fourths of its volume is immersed in water.

16. A particular orange that is 3 in. in diameter weighs 8 oz. Will it sink in water or float? Give data to establish the answer.

17. In applying the method of balanced columns illustrated in Fig. 114 it was found that a column of carbon tetrachloride 5 cm high balanced a water column 8 cm high. (*a*) What is the density of carbon tetrachloride? (*b*) In the test described, by what percentage was the pressure of the gas in the U-tube less than atmospheric?

18. To measure the density of a liquid that does not mix with water, some of it is poured into one arm of a U-tube in which water is present. The liquids settle down to the levels shown on the scale in the diagram. Compute the density of the liquid under test.

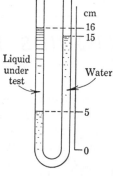

Problem 18

19. A metal sample being weighed on an equal-arm balance is balanced by 96 gm when suspended in air and by 84 gm when suspended in water. Determine the volume of the sample, its density, and its specific gravity.

20. The sample in the preceding problem is balanced by 85 gm when suspended in a liquid of unknown density. Compute the specific gravity of the liquid.

21. A metal block weighs 0.780 lb in air, and its apparent weight when suspended in water is 0.491 lb. Calculate the volume of the block, and also the weight density and specific gravity of the material of which it is made.

22. A pine plank 3 in. thick floats on fresh water. Take the specific gravity of pine as 0.60 and find how far the plank projects above the liquid surface.

23. A glass tube 20 cm long and having a mass of 3 gm is closed at one end. The tube is weighted with 10 gm of lead shot so that it will float upright. When floated in water, 5 cm of the tube project above the liquid surface. (*a*) What is the over-all cross-sectional area of the tube? (*b*) When the tube is floated in sulfuric acid of specific gravity 1.200, how much of it projects above the surface?

24. The rolling of a ship may be likened to the vibration of a torsion pendulum, the motion occurring about a horizontal fore-and-aft axis. (*a*) Suppose a ship weighing 5000 tons to have a constant metacentric height of 0.8 ft and compute the restoring couple that acts upon the ship when it is displaced through an angle of 10°. (*b*) If the ratio of the restoring torque to the angular displacement is constant, and the radius of gyration of the ship about the axis described is 24 ft, what is the period of vibration?

25. A wire shaped as in Fig. 121 and having a length $l = 5$ cm is pulled slowly upward through the surface of a liquid. Suppose the force applied to be 370 dynes in excess of the weight of the wire, and compute (*a*) the surface tension of the liquid and (*b*) the amount of work done in producing a film 2 mm high.

26. (*a*) Assume the surface tension of soap solution to be the same as that of water, and compute the amount of work done in blowing a soap bubble from zero diameter to a diameter of 5 cm. (*b*) What is the excess pressure inside the bubble when its diameter is 2.5 cm? 5 cm?

27. Calculate the excess pressure inside of (*a*) an air bubble of 2-mm radius in water and (*b*) a mercury droplet 1 mm in diameter.

28. How high does water rise in a capillary tube having an internal diameter of 2 mm if the tube is made of (*a*) glass and (*b*) silver?

29. What is the surface tension of carbon tetrachloride if a sample of this liquid exhibits a capillary rise of 1.32 cm in a glass tube of 1-mm bore? Assume the angle of contact to be zero and the specific gravity of carbon tetrachloride to be 1.6.

12

LIQUIDS IN MOTION

119. Work Done in Pumping Liquid. Liquids can be raised from one level to another by means of pumps. In this process the liquid gains potential energy with respect to its initial level, from energy supplied by the pump. An expression for this energy can be found by supposing that an

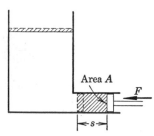

FIG. 125. Diagram used in study of work done by pump

open-top tank containing liquid is equipped at the bottom with a cylinder having a tight-fitting piston of area A, as shown in Fig. 125, and that work is done in pushing the piston inward a distance s by the application of a force F. The force required is $F = pA$, where p is the liquid pressure at the pump, and hence the work done is $E = Fs = pAs$. During this stroke of the piston the liquid pushed from the cylinder into the tank has a volume $V = As$, represented by either shaded area in the figure. Hence, in forcing this volume of liquid into a region where the pressure exceeds that of the atmosphere by p, the work done is

$$E = pV \tag{92}$$

The work done is expressed in foot·pounds if the pressure is in pounds per square foot and the volume in cubic feet.

In order that the pump indicated in Fig. 125 may force more and more liquid into the tank during successive strokes, valves are fitted into the piston or cylinder so that a new supply of liquid becomes available for each stroke. The so-called lift pump and force pump accomplish this in the manner shown in Fig. 126. In the *lift pump*, while the piston is being drawn upward, valve 1 is closed and valve 2 open, and the pressure is lowered in the cylinder and pipe below it. Liquid rises into this space because of atmospheric pressure on the water surface below. When the piston is pushed downward, valve 2 closes and the imprisoned liquid passes through valve 1 to the upper portion of the cylinder. Upon the next upstroke the cylinder fills with liquid again through valve 2, and the liquid above the piston flows out of the spout into the elevated tank U. The operation of the *force pump* can be described similarly, the liquid first being forced into the cylinder by atmospheric pressure, and then forced to any desired height. In raising water, valve 2 of either pump should be less than 34 ft above the water surface, because atmospheric pressure cannot support a column of water higher than this, § 128.

In another type known as the *centrifugal pump*, water enters at the center of a rotating wheel, or impeller, provided with radial blades. As the blades

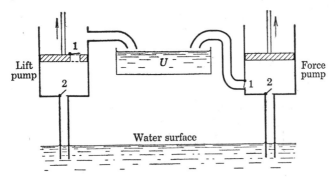

FIG. 126. Lift pump and force pump for raising liquids

rotate, the water is forced outward into the watertight housing of the pump, and thence into the discharge pipe.

120. Speed of Efflux. As liquid flows through an orifice some of its potential energy is transformed to kinetic energy, but its total energy is unchanged, if no waste occurs in the process. From this fact, the speed of efflux can be calculated. A thin layer of liquid of mass m will be considered at the liquid surface, located an average distance h above the orifice, as shown in Fig. 127. When an equal mass m of liquid has flowed from the tank, this top layer has disappeared, and the potential energy of the system is consequently reduced by an amount mgh. If the speed of efflux is v, the gain in kinetic energy is $\frac{1}{2}mv^2$, whence, by the principle of the Conservation of Energy,

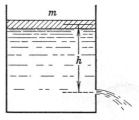

FIG. 127. Flow of liquid through an orifice

$$mgh = \tfrac{1}{2}mv^2$$

From this equality, the ideal speed of the issuing stream is found to be

$$v = \sqrt{2gh} \tag{93}$$

Since the acceleration due to gravity can be taken as constant, this expression shows that the speed of efflux depends only upon the height of liquid above the orifice and is proportional to the square root of this height. The actual efflux speeds are somewhat smaller because of friction.

121. Liquid Discharge Rate. The speed of efflux from an orifice is of value chiefly because a knowledge of this speed makes it possible to compute the *discharge rate*—that is, the volume of liquid discharged per unit time. This computation is made by simple geometry. When an incompressible liquid flows normally through an orifice of area A cm^2 at a speed of v cm/sec, the amount discharged in 1 sec would fill a cylinder A cm^2 in cross-section and v cm long. Therefore, the volume discharged per second is

$$Q = Av \qquad (94)$$

The actual discharge rate of a liquid through an orifice is smaller than given by Eq. 94 because of the contraction of the jet due to streamline flow, and also because the speed is actually less than the ideal value v, as stated

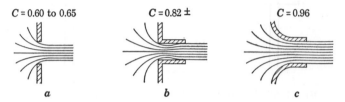

FIG. 128.   Representative orifices and their discharge coefficients

above. To find the actual discharge, the theoretical value thus obtained should be multiplied by a *coefficient of discharge C*, which corrects for both the contraction of the jet and the effect of friction. Values of the discharge coefficient, based on experiment, are given in Fig. 128 for typical orifices.

The discharge rate given by Eq. 94 applies to the flow through an orifice or to the flow past a point in a pipe line or open channel. If the liquid is taken as incompressible, then, as the stream flows from one point to another, the discharge rate is of necessity the same at both points. Expressed as an equation, this statement becomes

$$A_1v_1 = A_2v_2 \qquad (95)$$

where A represents the cross-section of the liquid at right angles to the flow and v represents the speed; the subscripts 1 and 2 refer to the two points along the stream. This expression is called the *equation of continuity*.

122. Energy of a Moving Liquid; Bernoulli's Theorem. When two points are selected in a stream of liquid, and the liquid between these points is considered, some useful observations regarding work and energy can be applied to this particular body of liquid. As the stream passes the first point, this body of liquid is pushed along by the liquid behind it and *work is done upon it*. Again, as the stream passes the second point, this body of liquid pushes on the liquid ahead of it and therefore *does work*. If it does more work than is done upon it, then the net work that it does shows how much its potential and kinetic energy is reduced as it flows from one point to the other, if no energy is wasted in friction.

Fig. 129 represents a liquid, regarded as incompressible and frictionless, flowing steadily through a tube of variable cross-section. The motion is supposed to be sufficiently slow to permit of streamline flow—that is, flow without wasteful turbulence or eddies—and for simplicity the speed at any cross-section is considered uniform throughout that section. The cross-sectional areas at sections 1 and 2 are represented respectively as A_1 and A_2, the corresponding speeds of the liquid as v_1 and v_2, in the direction of the

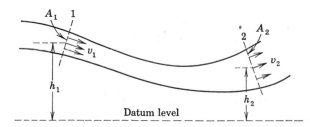

FIG. 129.   For developing Bernoulli's Theorem of liquid flow

arrows; the elevations of the centerlines of the sections above any convenient datum plane are respectively h_1 and h_2, and the pressures of the liquid, as measured by manometers, § 130, or pressure gages, are respectively p_1 and p_2.

Since the liquid is incompressible, the same mass m passes any section of the tube in a given time; the volume of this mass is $V = m/d$, where d is the density of the liquid. As this mass passes section 1 an amount of work $p_1 V$ or $p_1 m/d$ is done *upon* it by the oncoming liquid at the left, in accordance with Eq. 92; likewise at section 2 it *does* work amounting to $p_2 m/d$ on the outgoing liquid at the right. The net work done by the mass m of liquid is $p_2 m/d - p_1 m/d$, and this equals the reduction in its potential and kinetic energy as it moves from section 1 to section 2. In mathematical form:

$$\left(mgh_1 + \frac{1}{2} m v_1{}^2 \right) - \left(mgh_2 + \frac{1}{2} m v_2{}^2 \right) = p_2 \frac{m}{d} - p_1 \frac{m}{d}$$

When the terms are rearranged and each is divided by mg, the corresponding expression *per unit weight* becomes

$$h_1 + \frac{v_1{}^2}{2g} + \frac{p_1}{dg} = h_2 + \frac{v_2{}^2}{2g} + \frac{p_2}{dg} \tag{96}$$

These quantities are spoken of by engineers as follows: $h = $ *elevation head*, $\dfrac{v^2}{2g} = $ *velocity head*, and $\dfrac{p}{dg} = $ *pressure head*, and the sum of the three is called *total head*. Each term is expressed in the same unit, say, centimeters or feet.

Under certain conditions, Eq. 96 can be simplified. Thus, for horizontal flow, $h_1 = h_2$; for flow in an open channel, $p_1 = p_2$.

The law of liquid flow expressed by Eq. 96 was proposed by the Swiss scientist, Daniel Bernoulli (1700–1782). Bernoulli's Theorem states that *as an incompressible fluid flows, the total head remains unchanged.* The theorem presumes that waste of energy by friction is negligible and that no pressures are generated, as by pumps or turbines, in the region considered.

This relation shows that when a liquid speeds up in going from one position to another at the same level, then its pressure necessarily becomes less; in the notation used above, if $v_2 > v_1$, then $p_2 < p_1$, and vice versa. It should not be thought, however, that if the speed is doubled the pressure is halved.

Bernoulli's Theorem also explains in a qualitative manner a number of phenomena about the behavior of liquids which at first seem strange; just one will be cited. If two ships are steaming side by side in still water, the relative motion of the ships with respect to the water is the same as if the ships were stationary and the water were flowing with the same speed in the opposite direction. Fig. 130 shows the latter condition; as the water enters the narrowing space between the ships it speeds up, consequently the pressure there becomes less than that on the far sides of the ships. The excess pressure causes the ships to draw closer and closer together.

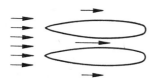

FIG. 130. Two ships headed the same way tend to move closer together

123. Application of Flow Principles. Bernoulli's Theorem, in combination with the equation of continuity, Eq. 95, becomes a powerful tool for the solution of problems involving flowing liquids.

Illustrative Problem

A horizontal tube 6 cm in diameter has a constriction 4 cm in diameter. When a liquid of specific gravity 0.7 flows through it, the pressure of the liquid in the tube is found to exceed that in the constriction by 20,000 dynes/cm². Determine the speed of the liquid in the tube.

For horizontal flow, $h_1 = h_2$ in Eq. 96, and it assumes the simpler form $p_1 - p_2 = \dfrac{d}{2}(v_2{}^2 - v_1{}^2)$. Let subscript 1 designate the tube and subscript 2 the constriction. The value of v_2 can be expressed in terms of v_1 by means of the equation of continuity, from which $\pi r_1{}^2 v_1 = \pi r_2{}^2 v_2$, where r represents the radius. Hence $v_2 = \left(\dfrac{r_1}{r_2}\right)^2 v_1 = \left(\dfrac{3}{2}\right)^2 v_1 = \dfrac{9v_1}{4}$. It follows that the pressure difference is

$$p_1 - p_2 = \frac{d}{2}\left[\left(\frac{9v_1}{4}\right)^2 - v_1{}^2\right]$$

or

$$20,000 \frac{\text{dynes}}{\text{cm}^2} = \frac{0.7 \frac{\text{gm}}{\text{cm}^3}}{2} \left(\frac{81}{16} - 1\right) v_1{}^2$$

from which the speed of the liquid in the tube becomes $v_1 = 118.6$ cm/sec.

124. Measurement of Liquid Flow. The theorem of Bernoulli provides a means for measuring the flow of a liquid through a pipe; the procedure is similar to that of the solved problem above. A horizontal section containing a constriction or throat is inserted in the pipe line and the pressures are

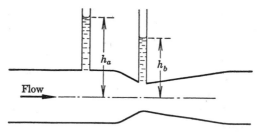

FIG. 131.   Venturi meter for measuring discharge of liquid

measured both at the throat and in the pipe by pressure gages or their equivalent.   Fig. 131 shows the arrangement using small tubes called manometers, in which the rise of liquid indicates the pressure.   The pipe on both sides of the throat flares out slowly so that the speed of the liquid can be changed without disturbing streamline flow.   This device is known as a *Venturi meter*.

Since the speed of the liquid is greater at the throat than in the pipe, the pressure at the throat is less than that in the pipe by the amount $h_a dg$ —

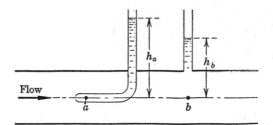

FIG. 132.   Pitot tube used in discharge measurements

$h_b dg$; consequently the liquid in the throat manometer does not rise as high as that in the pipe manometer.   From the difference in the manometer elevations together with a knowledge of the cross-sections of pipe and throat, the discharge rate $Q = Av$ can be measured.

Another device for measuring the speed of a stream, and thereby its discharge rate, is the *Pitot tube*. Fig. 132 shows a simplified form of this instrument mounted in a pipe through which liquid is flowing in the direction indicated. It consists essentially of an *L*-shaped tube, open at the ends and centered in the pipe with the opening turned upstream. Bernoulli's Theorem is applied to point *a*, inside the opening in the Pitot tube, and at point *b*, at the same level but outside the tube; a vertical manometer tube is included at the latter point to indicate the pressure in the pipe. Within the Pitot tube the liquid is at rest, and because of the impact of the current it rises to a height h_a, which is greater than h_b, the height in the manometer tube. From Bernoulli's Theorem,

$$\frac{v_a{}^2}{2g} + \frac{p_a}{dg} = \frac{v_b{}^2}{2g} + \frac{p_b}{dg}$$

Since $v_a = 0$ and $p = hdg$, it follows that the speed of the stream is $v_b = \sqrt{2g(h_a - h_b)}$.

125. Viscosity of Liquids. The property of a liquid that presents a resistance to flow is called *viscosity*. An ideal liquid is unable to resist a shearing force, and so has no viscosity, but actual liquids are viscous to some extent. If two beakers, one containing some oil and the other some alcohol, are tilted from side to side, much less mobility is observed in the oil than in the alcohol, and the oil is said to be the more viscous of the two liquids.

When a liquid flows over a flat surface, the layer of liquid particles in contact with the surface remains stationary because of adhesion, the next layer moves over the first, the third layer moves with respect to the second, and so on, the speed of each layer increasing with its distance from the solid surface. This distribution of speed causes a portion of the liquid that is cubical at one instant to become rhomboidal at a later instant, as illustrated in Fig. 133. The layer of liquid forming the lower face of the cube travels from *a* to *b* while the upper face travels from *c* to *d*. If the speed of the upper face exceeds that of the lower face by an amount *v*, and if the vertical distance between these faces is *h*, the liquid may be looked upon as shearing at the rate *v/h*, and this rate is constant as long as the shearing forces to which the liquid is yielding remain unchanged.

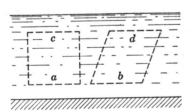

FIG. 133. Showing how a liquid shears as it flows

The shearing stress set up in the cubical portion of the liquid in Fig. 133 is measured by the force per unit area of the upper (or lower) face, and equals *F/A*. Experiment shows that in any liquid under like conditions the rate of shear *v/h* is proportional to the shearing stress *F/A*; that is,

$$\frac{F}{A} \propto \frac{v}{h} \qquad \text{or} \qquad \frac{F}{A} = \eta \frac{v}{h}$$

where η (eta) is the proportionality constant. This constant is called the *coefficient of viscosity* of the liquid; its value is given by the foregoing equation as

$$\eta = \frac{F/A}{v/h} \tag{97}$$

an expression that is similar to that for the shear modulus of elasticity, § 98. The viscosity of a liquid decreases with a rise in temperature.

The definition of coefficient of viscosity, as given by Eq. 97, can be visualized by imagining that a large flat plate is pulled along the free surface of the liquid, and that the force needed to move it with constant speed is measured. If the liquid layer is 1 cm thick and initially at rest, and if the plate is drawn with a speed of 1 cm/sec, then the force in dynes per square centimeter of surface necessary to move the plate is numerically equal to the coefficient of viscosity of the liquid. Its unit in the cgs system is the dyne·sec per cm² and is called the *poise*. Coefficients of viscosity for some liquids are given in the following table:

COEFFICIENTS OF VISCOSITY OF LIQUIDS

Liquid		Poises
Alcohol, ethyl........... at	20° C	0.012
Benzene...............	20° C	0.0065
Glycerine..............	20° C	8.3
Mercury..............	20° C	0.016
Oil, machine....	19° C	1.02
Water........	20° C	0.010
Water...............	100° C	0.0028

The usual method of measuring viscosity is to let the liquid flow through a vertical tube of small bore and to measure the rate of flow. Eq. 97 is then applied to each annular layer and the results integrated by the methods of calculus; the analysis yields the following equation for the rate of flow in cubic centimeters per second through a tube of length l cm and radius r cm:

$$Q = \frac{\pi P r^4}{8\eta l} \tag{98}$$

where P is the liquid pressure in dynes per square centimeter that would exist at the bottom of the tube if it were closed. This relation is called Poiseuille's Law after the French physiologist, Jean L. M. Poiseuille (1799–1869), and applies to small rates of flow that do not cause eddies in the liquid. A commercial instrument called the Saybolt viscosimeter measures the viscosity of a liquid by the time that it takes 60 cm³ of it to flow through a calibrated tube; water at room temperature gives a reading of about 30 sec.

PROBLEMS

1. Suppose the tank in Fig. 125 to contain oil of specific gravity 0.9 extending to a height of 12 ft above the piston, and to have a cross-section so large that the oil level does not change appreciably when a relatively small amount of oil is added. Compute the amount of work done in pumping 10 gal of oil into the tank.

2. A cylindrical open-top tank 10 ft high and having a base area of 12 ft² has its axis vertical and its base 20 ft above a constant-level reservoir. Water is to be pumped through a small pipe from the reservoir into the tank until it is three-fourths full. From a knowledge of the weight of water lifted and the vertical height through which its center of gravity is raised, determine the amount of work done, on the assumption that the supply line (a) enters the tank through the base; (b) extends to the top of the tank and that the water drops in from that level.

3. If the tank of Prob. 5, Chap. 11, springs a leak in the base, what is theoretically the speed with which water starts to squirt through the opening?

4. Refer to Prob. 9 of Chap. 11, and suppose that a small opening is made in the surface AB. Under ideal conditions, (a) with what speed does water start to flow through the opening and (b) to what initial height above the opening does it rise?

5. Equation 93 (p. 187) gives the speed of efflux through an orifice in terms of the static head h of liquid above the orifice. Express it, instead, in terms of the liquid pressure at the orifice, with other constants as needed.

6. A large tank has an orifice through which water comes out at an angle of 30° upward from the horizontal. The stream reaches an elevation 90 cm above the orifice before the water starts downward. (a) What is the speed of the stream as it passes through the orifice? (b) What is the liquid pressure at the orifice?

7. An open-top tank 300 cm high stands on level ground. The tank is full of water, which is allowed to flow out through an orifice of 2-cm² area located in the wall of the tank 50 cm from its base. Take the discharge coefficient as 1, and compute (a) the rate at which water should be added to the tank to keep it exactly full and (b) the distance from the wall of the tank at which the issuing stream strikes the ground.

8. Water is discharging from a hydrant outlet $2\frac{1}{2}$ in. in diameter at the rate of 1200 gal/min. Calculate (a) the theoretical speed of the issuing stream, (b) the height of water above the orifice that would give the same speed of efflux, and (c) the corresponding value of the pressure within the hydrant at the elevation of the outlet.

9. In a large loft bulding with a 12-ft ceiling height, water is discharging from a fire hose through a nozzle $1\frac{1}{4}$ in. in diameter at the rate of 200 gal/min. The discharge coefficient may be taken as 1. (*a*) What is the speed of the issuing stream? (*b*) If the nozzle is held 3 ft from the floor, at what angle should it be directed in order that the stream may barely graze the ceiling? (*c*) Under this condition, at what horizontal distance from the nozzle does the water strike the floor?

10. In a system of horizontal piping, a main 8 in. in diameter branches into two pipes each 6 in. in diameter. Suppose the piping to be full of flowing water, and the speed in the 6-in. pipes to be 1.5 ft/sec. Calculate the speed of the water in the 8-in. main.

11. A garden hose having an internal diameter of $\frac{3}{4}$ in. leads to a lawn sprinkler that consists simply of an enclosure in which there are 25 holes each $\frac{1}{16}$ in. in diameter. (*a*) If the water in the hose moves at a speed of 3 ft/sec, at what speed does it issue from the sprinkler openings? (*b*) How many gallons of water are discharged from the sprinkler in 1 hr?

12. Water coming from a nozzle 1 in. in diameter at a speed of 70 ft/sec is directed horizontally against a vertical wall. The water then falls vertically downward, without rebounding. Compute the force that the water exerts upon the wall.

13. Water flows down an open trough 20 ft long, inclined at 10° with the horizontal. The trough has a flat bottom and parallel vertical sides. At the upper end of the trough, the water moves at 5 ft/sec and is 1 ft deep. Find its speed and depth at the lower end, neglecting friction.

14. Water is discharging horizontally at the rate of 200 gal/min through a smooth nozzle 1 in. in diameter supplied by a hose that has an internal diameter of $2\frac{1}{2}$ in. Assume ideal conditions and calculate (*a*) the speed of the issuing stream in feet per second and (*b*) the pressure (above that of the atmosphere) within the hose.

15. Water flows through a horizontal tube 4 cm in diameter, in which there is a constriction 3 cm in diameter. When the pressure in the tube exceeds that in the constriction by 10^4 dynes/cm^2, (*a*) what is the speed of the water in the tube and (*b*) what is the discharge rate through the tube?

16. A horizontal pipe line 10 in. in diameter is conveying oil of specific gravity 0.9. At a constriction in the pipe where the diameter is 7 in., the pressure is found to be 1.5 lb/in.^{2} less than that in the pipe. Compute the discharge rate of oil through the pipe line in cubic feet per second.

17. A hydrant has a vertical body of large size with two outlets at the same elevation, each outlet having a diameter of $2\frac{1}{2}$ in. One outlet is closed, and a pressure gage connected to it reads 25 lb/in.^{2} The other outlet is wide open. Assume a discharge coefficient of 0.9 and find the rate of water discharge (*a*) in cubic feet per second and (*b*) in gallons per minute.

18. The theoretical discharge through a Venturi meter, Fig. 131, is given by the expression

$$Q = A\sqrt{\frac{2gh}{(A^2/B^2)-1}}$$

where A is the cross-sectional area of the pipe and B is that of the throat, h represents the difference $h_a - h_b$ in the manometer elevations, and g the acceleration due to gravity. Derive this expression from the equation of continuity and Bernoulli's Theorem as applied to two points below the manometers.

19. In one form of Pitot tube, the pressure difference p between the points referred to as a and b in Fig. 132 is indicated on the dial of a gage. From the gage reading, the speed of the stream is given by the expression $v = \sqrt{2p/d}$. If such a gage is held in the stream that issues from a nozzle $\frac{3}{4}$ in. in diameter and indicates a pressure difference of 18 lb/in.^{2}, what is the speed of the stream, and what is the discharge rate in gallons per minute?

20. A capillary tube 30 cm long and having a bore of 1-mm radius extends vertically downward from a large funnel. Turpentine is poured into the funnel, and the liquid surface is maintained at a constant elevation of 40 cm above the lower end of the capillary. Upon test it is found that 903 cm^3 flow out in 5 min. Compute the coefficient of viscosity of turpentine.

13

MECHANICS OF GASES

126. Gaseous Phase of Matter. The structure of a gas was described briefly at the beginning of Chap. 11, the accepted theory being that gas molecules are comparatively far apart and move about unceasingly throughout the entire space to which they are admitted. Gases differ from liquids in two respects: first, gases are very compressible; and second, they completely fill any closed vessel in which they are placed. In most other respects, however, gases resemble liquids, and since both are capable of flowing, they are designated by the common term *fluid*. Gases as well as liquids exert pressure upon surfaces with which they are in contact, and both exert upward buoyant forces in accordance with Archimedes' Principle. Flowing gases conform to Bernoulli's Theorem when their compressibility is taken into account. Gases, like liquids, have no elasticity of shape and adapt themselves to the shape of the containing vessel. Furthermore, gases show little ability to withstand shearing forces, and while they do have some viscosity, it is much less than in liquids.

The term *vapor* is applied to a gas that can be liquefied by pressure alone. Thus, at ordinary temperatures, steam and carbon dioxide are called vapors, but air, hydrogen, and nitrogen are called gases.

127. Kinetic Theory of Gases. Gases, because of their simple structure, are well adapted to mathematical study; such studies have developed into a detailed theory of gas behavior called the *kinetic theory of gases*. According to this theory the molecules of a particular gas are all alike, behave like tiny elastic spheres, are comparatively far apart, and occupy a very small fraction of the total space which encloses them. The molecules are in random motion, the amount depending upon the temperature, and continually strike against one another and against the walls of the container. Since temperature is an important concept in the study of gases, reference should be made to §§ 138 and 139.

At a given instant, some molecules are moving one way and some another, some are traveling fast and some slow, and the collective effect of these molecular speeds determines the temperature of the gas. Further, any appreciable volume contains such a large number of molecules that, in accordance with the laws of probability, some intermediate speed can be found which, if possessed by all the molecules, would correspond to the same temperature. It is known that energy is needed to raise the temperature of a substance, and hence *in a gas the temperature is assumed to be directly proportional to the mean kinetic energy of the molecules.* Consequently, the intermediate speed v is such as to impart the same kinetic energy to all molecules as that due to their individual speeds. Hence, for N molecules, each of mass m, and having speeds v_1, v_2, $\cdots v_N$,

$$N(\tfrac{1}{2}mv^2) = \tfrac{1}{2}mv_1{}^2 + \tfrac{1}{2}mv_2{}^2 + \cdots \tfrac{1}{2}mv_N{}^2$$

from which

$$v = \sqrt{\frac{v_1{}^2 + v_2{}^2 + \cdots v_N{}^2}{N}}$$

The differing individual speeds may therefore be replaced by a single speed which is found by squaring the individual speeds, taking the mean of these squares, and then extracting the square root. The result is known as the *root-mean-square* or rms speed.

Speed of Gas Molecules. The rms speed of the molecules of a gas can be found in terms of its pressure and density by summing up the impulses of the molecules against one of the confining walls; this sum calculated for unit time and unit area is equal to the pressure and leads

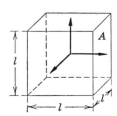

FIG. 134. Molecular speeds along three directions

directly to the desired expression. Fig. 134 shows a cubical box having a length l along each edge and a volume $V = l^3$. It is assumed to contain N molecules of gas, each having a mass m and all having the same rms speed v. The actual motions of the molecules within the box can be resolved into three components, as though one-third of the molecules were moving perpendicularly between each pair of opposite faces. Such a group of molecules moving between face A and the one opposite encounter many collisions on the way; the first of these is assumed to occur after traveling a small uniform distance x

from A. The number of molecules in a zone of this thickness is $\dfrac{x}{l} N$, one-third of which strike A with a velocity v and rebound with a velocity $-v$. Each of these molecules thus undergoes a change of momentum of $2mv$. The molecules rebounding from face A travel a distance x before collision and then back to the face, a total distance of $2x$ in a time $2x/v$, and thus strike the face $v/2x$ times each second. From Eq. 25, the force exerted on the face equals the change in momentum per second; hence the average force exerted on the face by each molecule is $(2mv)\left(\dfrac{v}{2x}\right) = \dfrac{mv^2}{x}$.

For all the molecules striking face A, the force amounts to

$$F = \frac{1}{3}\left(\frac{x}{l} N\right)\left(\frac{mv^2}{x}\right) = \frac{Nmv^2}{3l}$$

and the average pressure on the face is the force per unit area, or

$$p = \frac{F}{l^2} = \frac{Nmv^2}{3l^3} = \frac{Nmv^2}{3V} = \frac{dv^2}{3}$$

where the density of the gas is $d = Nm/V$. Herefrom, the rms speed of the molecules for a gas of density d under an absolute pressure p is

$$v = \sqrt{\frac{3p}{d}} \qquad (99)$$

A table of gas densities appears in § 133.

As an illustration, the rms speed of oxygen molecules under standard atmospheric pressure of 1.013×10^6 dynes/cm^2 is

$$v = \sqrt{\frac{3 \times 1.013 \times 10^6 \text{ dynes/cm}^2}{1.429 \times 10^{-3} \text{ gm/cm}^3}} = 4.61 \times 10^4 \text{ cm/sec}$$

which is more than a thousand miles an hour.

Molecular motion is the direct cause of the effect known as *diffusion*. This process can be demonstrated by placing two fluids in the same container with the denser one at the bottom; the motion of the molecules causes each fluid to penetrate the other, and eventually the mixture becomes uniform throughout. Diffusion is a slow process but takes place more rapidly with increased concentration and with higher temperatures.

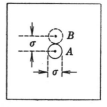

Mean Free Path. In spite of the enormous speeds of gas molecules, their advance in a given direction is fairly slow, because each molecule is continually impeded by collision with others, thus altering its speed and direction and giving it a zigzag motion.

FIG. 135. Diagram for studying collision of gas molecules

The average distance traversed between collisions is known as the *mean free path* of the molecules. This quantity will be evaluated by the aid of Fig. 135, which represents a cubical region having a volume of 1 cm^3 and containing n molecules each of diameter σ (sigma). For simplicity, the molecules are assumed to be at rest; one is shown at A in the figure. A like molecule B entering normally through one face of the cube and moving through this region will collide with A if their centers come closer together than σ; hence A is said to present a target area for collision of $\pi\sigma^2$. The probability of B colliding with A is the ratio of the target area to the total area through which B can enter, namely, 1 cm^2. When all of the n molecules in this region are considered, the probability of a collision with one of them is increased n-fold and becomes $\pi n\sigma^2$ as B moves through the region considered, a distance of 1 cm. Thus, the moving molecule is likely to make $\pi n\sigma^2$ hits per cm, and therefore the distance traveled between successive hits, or mean free path, is

$$L = \frac{1}{\pi n\sigma^2} \tag{100}$$

In this expression n is the number of molecules per cubic centimeter and can be evaluated from Avogadro's Number, § 132; σ is the diameter of the molecule, about 2 or 3 $\times$ 10^{-8} cm.

The mean free path has about the same order of magnitude for all gases at standard temperature and pressure. The approximate values $n = 2.7 \times 10^{19}$ molecules/cm³ and $\sigma = 2.5 \times 10^{-8}$ cm give the mean free path as

$$L = \frac{1}{\pi (2.7 \times 10^{19})(2.5 \times 10^{-8})^2} = 1.9 \times 10^{-5} \text{ cm}$$

128. Atmospheric Pressure. The earth is surrounded by a layer of air extending to great heights and held to the earth by gravitational attraction. This body of air, like all fluids, exerts a pressure determined by its height and density. The value of the atmospheric pressure can be measured by a mercury barometer, as in Fig. 136. In setting up this apparatus, a long glass tube sealed at one end is completely filled with mercury and inverted into a vessel of mercury as shown. The mercury in the tube thereupon settles down to a height h, leaving a vacuum above it, except for a minute amount of mercury vapor. Atmospheric pressure is commonly designated by the height of the mercury column that it supports, the value 76.00 cm at sea level and at 0° C being taken as standard. The corresponding value of the pressure is found from Eq. 86 to be $hdg = 76.0$ cm $\times$ 13.596 gm/cm³ $\times$ 980 dynes/gm = 1.013×10^6 dynes/cm², or about 14.7 lb/in.² The height of a water column supported by atmospheric pressure would be

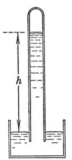

Fig. 136. Mercury barometer stands at 76 cm for standard atmospheric pressure

$$h = \frac{p}{w} = \frac{14.7 \times 144 \text{ lb/ft}^2}{62.4 \text{ lb/ft}^3} = 33.9 \text{ ft}$$

The aneroid barometer is another device for measuring atmospheric pressure. This instrument consists essentially of a small sealed metal box from which most of the air has been removed, the box having a corrugated face that moves in and out as the atmospheric pressure varies. This slight movement is magnified by a system of levers and is communicated to a pointer that sweeps across a graduated dial or faceplate.

On account of its compressibility, the air near the earth is weighed down and compressed by that above, and conversely, the strata become rarer as the elevation is increased, although this effect is somewhat offset by the contraction due to cooling. Consequently the pressure does not vary uniformly with altitude, as it would in a medium of uniform density, but changes less and less rapidly at greater heights. Fig. 137, based on actual test, shows this variation and also indicates that altitude can be estimated from a knowledge of atmospheric pressure. This fact is utilized on aircraft in the *altimeter*, a device that is essentially an aneroid barometer, calibrated to indicate altitude instead of pressure.

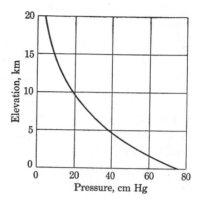

The force due to atmospheric pressure can be calculated by Eq. 84, $F = pA$, and is found to be very large, even upon a surface of moderate size. In most cases, however, both sides of an object are subjected to almost the same pressure, and therefore the object does not have to sustain a great load.

Fig. 137. Dependence of atmospheric pressure upon altitude

129. Pressure of a Confined Gas; Boyle's Law.

One of the outstanding properties of a gas is its compressibility. When some gas is confined within a closed cylinder having a tight-fitting piston, as represented in Fig. 138, and a force is applied as shown, the piston moves inward and comes to rest at some new position at which the pressure within the gas sets up a force equal to that exerted upon it by the piston. During this process the gas is compressed and its volume is reduced. The English natural philosopher Robert Boyle (1627–1691) found a very simple relation between the pressure of a gas and its volume; this relation is known as Boyle's Law and states that *the volume of a confined body of gas varies inversely as the absolute pressure, provided the temperature remains unchanged.* If p_1 and V_1 represent the pressure and volume of the gas under one condition, and p_2 and V_2 its pressure and volume under some different condition, then at the same temperature, $V_1:V_2 = p_2:p_1$, whence

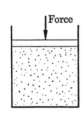

F I G . 1 3 8 . Confined gas exerting pressure and supporting piston

$$p_1 V_1 = p_2 V_2 \qquad (101)$$

An *ideal gas* is defined for the present as one that conforms to Boyle's Law.

The kinetic theory, which pictures the pressure exerted by a gas as a continual bombardment of the enclosing walls by the moving molecules, can be used to derive Boyle's Law theoretically. Since the temperature of the confined gas remains unchanged, the mean kinetic energy of its molecules is assumed to be unchanged also. In the notation of § 127, this equality of kinetic energies under the two conditions is expressed by

$$\frac{mv_1{}^2}{2} = \frac{mv_2{}^2}{2}$$

From Eq. 99, the rms molecular speed is $v = \sqrt{3p/d}$, and consequently for the two conditions, $3p_1/d_1 = 3p_2/d_2$. But the density of the gas is $d_1 = M/V_1$, and similarly $d_2 = M/V_2$, where the mass M of the gas is the same under the two conditions. Therefore by substitution, $p_1 V_1 = p_2 V_2$, as stated for Boyle's Law in Eq. 101. Thus, the product of the absolute pressure and the volume of a fixed mass of gas is constant at a given temperature.

130. Measurement of Pressure. The pressure of confined gases can be measured by *U*-shaped manometer tubes containing mercury or other liquids. Fig. 139 pictures two common types of manometers connected to

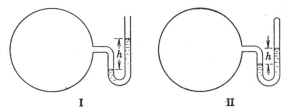

I   ·II

FIG. 139.   Manometers of open and closed types for measuring pressure

tanks of compressed gas. The pressure forces the liquid in the tube down at the near side and up at the far side. In the *open manometer* shown in part I, the difference in height h between the two columns multiplied by the weight density of the liquid shows how much the gas pressure exceeds that of the atmosphere. This pressure excess is known as the *gage pressure* to distinguish it from *absolute pressure*, which includes the pressure of the atmosphere. In the *closed manometer* shown in part II, the closed end of the tube contains air that was at atmospheric pressure when the columns were level. As the liquid in the tube is forced to the position shown this air becomes compressed and assumes a pressure given by Boyle's Law; the absolute pressure in the tank is found by adding the pressure of the air entrapped in the tube to that due to a liquid column of height h. The closed manometer is adapted to the measurement of higher pressures than the open type, but is not as sensitive, especially at high pressures.

The *Bourdon gage* is an instrument used extensively for industrial purposes, as in the measurement of steam pressures. The operating element of this device consists of a bronze tube of elliptical cross-section, the tube being curved into a circular arc. One end of the tube is fixed and the other is connected by a mechanical linkage to a toothed sector that engages the instrument pointer. When subjected to internal pressure, the tube tends to assume a circular cross-section and in so doing uncoils slightly, moving the pointer over a scale.

131. Mixture of Gases; Dalton's Law. It has been indicated that a gas upon expanding undergoes a reduction in pressure, a fact that is helpful in studying the mixture of several gases. When two or more closed vessels, originally containing different gases which do not react chemically, are joined so that each gas has access to all the containers, the molecular motion causes each gas to penetrate all of them, and eventually the mixture becomes homogeneous throughout. In this diffusion process, each of the constituent gases expands into the total available volume as though the other gases were not present, and the absolute pressure of each constituent is reduced in accordance with Boyle's Law to a lower value called its *partial pressure*. The absolute pressure of the gas mixture is found to be equal to the sum of the partial pressures of the various constituents. This relation, first established by the English chemist and physicist John Dalton (1766–1844), can be summarized as follows: *A mixture of several gases which do not react chemically exerts a pressure on the enclosing surfaces equal to the sum of the pressures that the several gases would exert separately if each were allowed to occupy the entire space alone at the given temperature.*

Illustrative Problem

Suppose 10 ft^3 of air at an absolute pressure of 60 lb/in.^{2} to mix with 30 ft^3 of nitrogen at 280 lb/in.^{2} Determine the pressure of the mixture.

The air in expanding from 10 to 40 ft^3 undergoes a corresponding reduction of pressure, and in the mixture its partial pressure is $\frac{10}{40} \times 60 = 15$ lb/in.^{2} Similarly, the partial pressure of the nitrogen is $\frac{30}{40} \times 280 = 210$ lb/in.^{2} The absolute pressure of the mixture is the sum of these partial pressures, or 225 lb/in.^{2}

132. Avogadro's Number; the Mole. The Italian physicist Amadeo Avogadro (1776–1856) suggested that, at the same temperature and pressure, *equal volumes of different gases contain equal numbers of molecules*, a statement called Avogadro's Law. Although strictly true only for an ideal gas, § 163, it applies very well to actual gases. Its agreement with the kinetic theory can be shown by considering two gases to have the same temperature and assuming their molecules to have the same mean kinetic energy. In the notation of § 127, this energy equality is expressed by

$$\frac{m_1 v_1{}^2}{2} = \frac{m_2 v_2{}^2}{2}$$

and the gas densities are given by $d_1 = \dfrac{N_1 m_1}{V_1}$ and $d_2 = \dfrac{N_2 m_2}{V_2}$, the subscripts being used to distinguish the two gases. From Eq. 99 it follows that

$$\left(\frac{m_1}{2}\right)\left(\frac{3p_1}{d_1}\right) = \left(\frac{m_2}{2}\right)\left(\frac{3p_2}{d_2}\right)$$

whence

$$\frac{3p_1 V_1}{2N_1} = \frac{3p_2 V_2}{2N_2}$$

Under like pressure-volume conditions, $p_1 = p_2$ and $V_1 = V_2$, consequently $N_1 = N_2$, and the numbers of molecules are the same, as stated in Avogadro's Law.

This law is frequently applied in Physical Chemistry to a particular quantity of a substance known as a *mole*, or gram-molecule. *A mole of any substance is a number of grams equal to the molecular weight of that substance*, that is, to the sum of the atomic weights of the atoms in the molecule. The inert gases, such as helium or neon, are monatomic, having one atom to the molecule; most other gases are diatomic. Thus, for oxygen, 1 mole = 2 × 16 = 32 grams.

The number of molecules in a mole of gas is known as *Avogadro's Number*; this number is 6.02 × 10^{23}. Hence *a mole of any gas contains 6.02 × 10^{23} molecules*. Since a mole of oxygen has a mass of 32 gm and contains 6.02 × 10^{23} molecules, the mass of a molecule of oxygen is $32/(6.02 \times 10^{23}) = 5.32 \times 10^{-23}$ gm.

A mole of any gas occupies a volume of 22.4 liters at standard temperature and pressure (0° C and 76 cm Hg). The density of oxygen under standard conditions is therefore 32/22.4 or 1.429 gm/liter, as tabulated in the following section.

133. Density of Gases. For a gas, as for any substance, density is defined as mass per unit volume. If a given mass of gas is kept at constant temperature, its volume varies inversely as the pressure, and it follows that the density of a gas varies directly as the pressure. The temperature of a gas also affects its density, for a gas at constant pressure expands when heated and contracts when cooled.

The density of air is of special importance, for it is used for reference in comparing other gases. One liter of air at standard temperature and pressure has a mass of 1.293 gm, and thus the density of air is 0.001293 gm/cm^3; this value is equivalent to a weight density of about 0.081 lb/ft^3. The specific gravity of a gas is the ratio of its density to that of a reference gas, usually air. Coal gas, which is about four-tenths as dense as air, has a specific gravity of 0.4 with respect to air.

Measurements of gas density can be made by weighing a hollow globe of known volume when filled with the gas and again when evacuated; such measurements require very careful weighing because a small volume of gas weighs so little compared with the globe. The density of any gas can be computed from its molecular weight, as was done for oxygen in the preceding section, since a mole of the gas occupies 22.4 liters under standard conditions.

The accompanying table gives the densities and specific gravities of a few common gases; these values are for standard temperature and pressure

unless otherwise noted. The values for specific gravity are stated with respect to air as unity.

DENSITY AND SPECIFIC GRAVITY OF GASES

Gas	Mass density gm/liter	Weight density lb/ft^3	Specific gravity
Air.............	1.293	0.081	1.000
Air at 20° C........	1.205	0.0755	0.932
Carbon dioxide.....	1.977	0.123	1.529
Hydrogen..........	0.090	0.0056	0.069
Helium............	0.179	0.011	0.138
Nitrogen...........	1.251	0.078	0.967
Oxygen............	1.429	0.089	1.105
Steam at 100° C....	0.598	0.037	0.462

134. Buoyancy of the Atmosphere. Archimedes' Principle, which was
considered in § 111 for liquids, applies equally well to gases, and it can be
concluded that *a body located in any fluid, whether liquid or gaseous, is buoyed
up by a force equal to the weight of the fluid displaced.* As applied to gases,
interest in this principle centers in the buoyancy of the atmosphere.

A balloon contains gas that is lighter than the surrounding air and, as a
result, is raised by the air's buoyant force. Several flights to the stratosphere have been made in specially designed balloons, for the purpose of
collecting scientific data. Such a balloon has a sealed bag and carries a
small air-tight gondola for the observers. At the start, the bag is partially
inflated with helium, and the balloon is sent aloft by releasing ballast. As
it rises, the surrounding air has less density, which tends to reduce the
buoyant force, but this effect is partly offset by the reduced atmospheric
pressure, which causes the volume of the bag to increase, even at the low
temperatures encountered. Finally a height is reached where the upward
force equals the downward force, which includes the weight of the balloon
and its load, and also the weight of the gas within it. The balloon is then
in equilibrium and does not rise higher. To descend, a valve is opened to
release some of the gas.

Illustrative Problem

One of the earliest balloon ascensions was made in 1783 at Paris by
J. A. C. Charles, famous for his work on gases, § 158. With a balloon 27 ft in
diameter, inflated with hydrogen gas, he attained a height of about 2000 ft

(0.61 km), where he remained some time before descending. Calculate the approximate weight of the balloon and its load.

At a height of 0.61 km above the earth, the atmospheric pressure is estimated to be 67 cm Hg. If temperature differences are neglected, the density of air at this level is reduced to 67/76 of its standard value, that is, to $\frac{67}{76}$ × 0.081 = 0.0714 lb/ft^3. The volume of the balloon, as calculated from its dimensions, is 10,300 ft^3, and the buoyant force upon it is therefore

$$10,300 \text{ ft}^3 \times 0.0714 \frac{\text{lb}}{\text{ft}^3} = 735 \text{ lb}$$

The hydrogen in the envelope is taken to have the same pressure as the surrounding atmosphere. Since the specific gravity of hydrogen is 0.069, its weight is 0.069 × 735 = 51 lb. Therefore the weight of the balloon and its load is 735 − 51 = 684 lb.

In precise weighing measurements it is sometimes necessary to apply corrections because of the buoyancy of the atmosphere, if the object being weighed is of different density than the weights with which it is being compared. In an equal-arm balance, the net downward force at the end of each arm is the true weight of the object there minus the buoyant force due to the atmosphere and, when the instrument is balanced, the net downward forces are equal; these facts make it possible to correct for buoyancy in weighing an object.

Illustrative Problem

Find the true density of a sample of cork if a block of this material measuring 5 × 8 × 10 cm balances 100 gm of brass weights (density = 8.5 gm/cm^3). The test is made at 20° C, at which the density of air is 0.001205 gm/cm^3.

The volume of the cork is 400 cm^3 and the buoyant force upon it is (400)(0.001205)g dynes. Similarly, the volume of the brass is 100/8.5 = 11.76 cm^3 and the buoyant force upon it is (11.76)(0.001205)g dynes. Let the mass of the cork be m gm; then

$$mg - (400)(0.001205)g = 100g - (11.76)(0.001205)g$$

whence the mass of the cork sample is m = 100.47 gm, and its density is 100.47 gm/400 cm^3 = 0.2512 gm/cm^3.

135. Bernoulli's Theorem Applied to Gases. Bernoulli's Theorem, § 122, is applicable to gases as well as to liquids, but the mathematical treatment is complicated by the fact that gases are highly compressible. This means that in Eq. 96 the density of the gas is different for different values of the pressure. Nevertheless, the general effect is the same as previously described—namely, that when a flowing stream of gas speeds up, its pressure decreases, and vice versa. Two illustrations will be cited.

A tennis ball that is set spinning when struck by a tennis racquet undergoes a curved flight as a result of the effect just described. A ball spinning in a clockwise direction while moving toward the left in still air, as indicated in part I of Fig. 140, behaves as if it were spinning on a stationary axis in a wind directed toward the right, as in part II of the figure. As the ball spins, a layer of air clings to it and is carried around with it. The velocity of the air at any point near the ball can be regarded as made up of two components, one due to the wind and the other due to the spinning of the ball. Above the ball, these components are in the same direction, while below they are opposite. It follows that the velocity is greater at the top surface than at the lower one, and according to Bernoulli's Theorem, the pressure is reduced at the top and increased below.

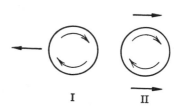

FIG. 140. Diagram for explaining curved flight of a spinning ball

Hence a force is developed that causes the ball to rise as it moves forward.

An important engineering application of Bernoulli's Theorem is the lifting effect produced upon a moving airfoil. If an airfoil section is moving to the left in still air, the effects produced are the same as if the airfoil were stationary and the air were streaming past it toward the right, as indicated in Fig. 141. The top surface of the airfoil has the greater curvature and the air that flows close to it is deflected as shown, while air at a higher level is relatively undisturbed. Therefore the stream of air entering the region just above the airfoil is forced to flow through a constricted area and its speed is increased. In accordance with Bernoulli's Theorem the pressure in this region is correspondingly lowered, and the normal atmospheric pressure upon the lower surface forces the airfoil upward.

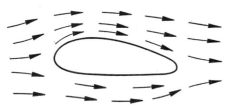

FIG. 141. Used in explaining how moving air stream above an airfoil causes lift

136. Viscosity of Gases. Molecular friction, or viscosity, is present in gases as in liquids, although to a smaller extent, as would be expected from the increased spacing of the molecules. This friction not only retards the motion of gases themselves in flowing through tubes, ducts, and the like, but also retards other bodies in moving through a stationary gas. Air friction increases with speed, and this is an important factor in airplane design, as evidenced by the streamlining of surfaces to minimize its effects.

A study of scientific interest is the motion of a sphere falling through a viscous gas, such as a raindrop falling through the atmosphere. When such a drop starts falling with constant acceleration under the action of gravity, friction at first exerts only a small drag upon it, but as it gains speed the upward force of friction becomes greater and greater, and soon equals the downward force of gravity. Thereafter the acceleration is zero and the drop descends with uniform motion. Sir George Stokes (1819–1903), British mathematician and physicist, found that for very small drops of radius r and density d the steady, or terminal, speed acquired in falling through a medium having a coefficient of viscosity η is given by the expression

$$v = \frac{2dgr^2}{9\eta} \tag{102}$$

where g is the acceleration due to gravity. When cgs units are used, the value of η obtained from this expression is in poises, § 125.

The coefficients of viscosity for some gases are given in the accompanying table. It is interesting to note that a rise in temperature causes the viscosity of gases to increase; the reverse is true for liquids.

COEFFICIENT OF VISCOSITY OF GASES

Gas		Poises
Air.............. at	0° C	173×10^{-6}
Air..............	99° C	220 "
Ammonia.........	0° C	96 "
Hydrogen.........	0° C	87 "
Mercury vapor....	300° C	532 "
Oxygen..........	0° C	189 "
Water vapor......	0° C	90 "
Water vapor......	100° C	132 "

137. Reduced Pressures. A simple device for reducing the pressure of air in a vessel to a few per cent of atmospheric pressure is called an *aspirator*. In this device, shown diagrammatically in Fig. 142, a stream of water, usually from the city mains, is admitted at W and flows through a small nozzle into the chamber C, which connects through a passage E to the vessel to be exhausted. The small size of the nozzle causes the stream to issue from it with high speed, and the pressure in the chamber C is lowered in accordance with Bernoulli's Theorem. The pressure difference causes air to be withdrawn from the vessel attached to E. This air, mingling with the water, passes out at the outlet O.

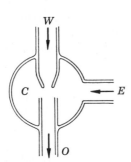

FIG. 142. Elements of an aspirator

A lower pressure than that reached by an aspirator can be obtained with a *piston pump*, operating on the principle of an ordinary force pump, but in reverse. With the ordinary pump, the amount of dead space in the cylinder when the piston has advanced to the end of its stroke would make it impossible to obtain a high vacuum; in the vacuum pump this space is reduced by covering the piston and valves with oil. Such an *oil pump* is capable of reducing the pressure inside a vessel of, say, 500-cm³ capacity to a small fraction of a millimeter of mercury in a few minutes.

Low pressures can be measured by a *vacuum gage*, a common type of which is represented in Fig. 143. This gage is actually a mercury barometer of small height mounted within an air-tight casing of glass which is attached to the system being exhausted. When the pressure is reduced to about 10 cm Hg, the column falls away from the top of the closed tube, and lower pressures can be read directly from the graduated scale.

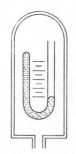

The production of incandescent and fluorescent lamps, radio and television tubes, and the like, all of which require a high degree of exhaustion, has led to highly developed techniques that result in attaining high vacua. Pressures as low as 10^{-7} mm Hg can be achieved by the modern diffusion pump. In a pump of this type, gas molecules pass by diffusion from the vessel being exhausted, enter a stream of vapor moving at supersonic speed, and are propelled away.

F I G . 1 4 3 .
Gage for moderately low pressures

It should not be thought, even with the techniques now available, that all of the gas molecules can be removed from a given space. Since under standard conditions there are 6.02×10^{23} molecules in a volume of 22.4 liters, it is apparent that even at the low pressure attained by the diffusion pump, there are still hundreds of millions of molecules present in each cubic centimeter of space.

PROBLEMS

1. Determine (*a*) the rms speed of nitrogen molecules under standard atmospheric pressure and (*b*) the ratio of the rms speed of nitrogen molecules to that of oxygen molecules.

2. Assume the diameter of the nitrogen molecule to be 3.15×10^{-8} cm and compute the value under standard atmospheric pressure of (*a*) the mean free path of nitrogen molecules and (*b*) the average number of times they collide per second.

3. Find the force exerted by the atmosphere under standard conditions upon a table top 5 ft long and 3 ft wide.

4. A storage tank used at a filling station for pumping up tires contains 60 ft³ of air at a gage pressure of 180 lb/in.² Calculate (*a*) the volume that this air would occupy at atmospheric pressure and (*b*) the absolute pressure at which this air would occupy a volume of 10 ft³.

5. A cylinder 6 in. in diameter and 9 in. high stands with its axis vertical and its top open. When a snugly fitting piston that weighs 120 lb is placed

in the top of the cylinder, how far does the piston move downward as it compresses the air in coming to rest?

6. If an automobile tire has a constant volume of 0.75 ft^3 and the gage pressure drops from 25 to 18 lb/in.^{2}, what is the volume of the air that escapes, reckoned at atmospheric pressure?

7. Oxygen for a hospital patient is drawn from a tank having a volume of 1.6 ft^3, and over a given period the gage pressure drops from 750 to 600 lb/in.^{2} Compute the volume of oxygen, reckoned at atmospheric pressure, that has been drawn from the tank.

8. A closed cylindrical tank with its axis vertical is 10 ft high. The tank is half full of water, above which air is entrapped at an absolute pressure of 30 lb/in.^{2} If a valve in the bottom of the tank is opened, what is the theoretical speed of the issuing stream at an instant when one-half of the water has flowed out?

9. A manometer of the type shown in part II of Fig. 139 is used to measure the pressure in a tank. The tube contains mercury, with the right-hand column 4 cm higher than the other and extending to a level 10 cm below the top of the closed tube. Determine (a) the pressure of the air entrapped in the closed tube, (b) the absolute pressure in the tank, and (c) the gage pressure in the tank. Express values in centimeters of mercury.

10. A tank contains 10 liters of nitrogen at an absolute pressure of 400 cm Hg. Another tank contains 6 liters of oxygen at an absolute pressure of 100 cm Hg. If the tanks are connected, what will be the resulting absolute pressure of the mixture?

11. Nitrogen at a gage pressure of 70 lb/in.^{2} is confined in a tank having a volume of 5 ft^3. How many cubic feet of air at atmospheric pressure can be pumped into the tank without increasing the gage pressure to more than 100 lb/in.^{2}?

12. A tank of compressed air has a volume of 10 ft^3, and its gage indicates a pressure of 70 lb/in.^{2} A second tank contains carbon dioxide; this tank has a volume of 20 ft^3 and has no pressure gage. When the tanks are connected, the gage indicates a pressure of 60 lb/in.^{2} for the mixture. Determine the initial gage pressure of the carbon dioxide.

13. Two containers, A and B, are joined by a short pipe in which there is a valve that is initially closed. A contains 16 gm of oxygen at an absolute pressure of 2 atmospheres, and B contains 28 gm of nitrogen at an absolute pressure of 1 atmosphere. Assume that the temperature remains constant at 0° C. If the valve is opened, (a) what is the absolute pressure of the mixed gases and (b) what is the density of the oxygen in the mixture? (c) If all of the mixture is forced into container A, what will be its absolute pressure?

14. (a) Express Boyle's Law in terms of the absolute pressure and the density of a gas instead of its absolute pressure and volume. (b) From the resulting expression, show that the rms speed of the molecules of a particular gas has a fixed value regardless of the pressure, provided the temperature is constant. (c) Use the result of Prob. 1 to determine the ratio of the average kinetic energy of the nitrogen molecules to that of the oxygen molecules in the atmosphere.

15. (a) From the atomic structure of nitrogen, as given by the symbol $_7N^{14}$, determine the mass of a neutral atom of this gas. Assume the mass of the proton and neutron to be 1.672×10^{-24} gm each, and that of the electron to be 9.11×10^{-28} gm. (b) From the foregoing result and Avogadro's

Number, compute the density of nitrogen (a diatomic gas) at standard pressure and temperature.

16. If a 1-liter flask containing air at standard atmospheric pressure were being exhausted by removing molecules at what sounds like an enormous rate of 100 million million per sec, how long a time would be required to reduce the pressure to one-half of its original value? Assume a constant temperature of 0° C.

17. What is the weight of the air at 20° C within a room that measures $20 \times 30 \times 12$ ft high?

18. (*a*) Wind speeds of 135 mi/hr were reported for hurricane "Connie" in August, 1955. Assume a temperature of 20° C, and compute the kinetic energy of 1 mi^3 of air moving at this speed. (*b*) In order to visualize the amount of this energy, suppose that all of it could be expended in elevating a large structure. How high might it conceivably raise the modern Socony Mobil building, a New York steel-encased skyscraper that covers an entire block and weighs 177,500 tons?

19. A sample of balsa wood having a specific gravity of 0.125 is balanced by 15 gm of weights on an equal-arm balance. The weights are of brass having a specific gravity of 8.48. Assume a temperature of 20° C and find the correct mass of the balsa-wood sample.

20. Droplets are formed from oil having a specific gravity of 0.9; they fall through air at 20° C for which the viscosity is 1.84×10^{-4} poise. A droplet is singled out after reaching constant speed and is observed to fall 0.5 cm in 12 sec. What is the radius of this droplet?

21. In order to measure low gas pressures, an auxiliary chamber having a volume of 50 cm^3 is placed in communication with the vessel being exhausted; this chamber is then isolated and the gas in it compressed. In such a test, the volume of the gas in the auxiliary chamber is reduced to 0.001 cm^3, at which value its absolute pressure is found to be 80 cm Hg. What is the absolute pressure of the gas in the vessel under measurement?

22. Mechanical vacuum pumps are designed to reduce gas pressures to about 0.2 micron Hg. At this pressure and at standard temperature, how many molecules remain in each cubic centimeter of space?

14

EFFECTS OF TEMPERATURE CHANGE

138. Nature of Heat. In the early days of science, heat was thought to be a weightless fluid called caloric. All substances were supposed to contain more or less of this fluid, and the passage of heat from one body to another was explained as a flow of caloric from the hotter to the colder body. Count Rumford (Benjamin Thompson, 1753–1814), a British-American scientist, was impressed by the large amount of heat produced in attempting to bore some cannon with blunt tools. Since the supply of heat appeared to be inexhaustible, he concluded that heat could not be a substance but was related in some way to motion. His investigations resulted in the present theory, confirmed by other investigators and now accepted without question, that *heat is a form of energy.*

When heat is supplied to a body, it increases the energy of that body. Since in general no change can be detected in either the kinetic or potential energy of the body as a whole, the energy supplied as heat is said to increase the *internal energy* of the body, since the energy appears to be given to the molecules of which the body is made. Molecules are known to possess kinetic energy, for there is ample evidence of their incessant motion. This property was considered earlier in connection with the kinetic theory, § 127. Some molecules also possess potential energy; this is true for the molecules of a solid or liquid that has been expanded by heating, for work must have been done upon the molecules to separate them in opposition to the forces of cohesion. Gas molecules have but little potential energy, since they are relatively far apart and in consequence have only a slight attraction for one another. The heating of a body, therefore, has a direct effect upon its internal energy, whether kinetic or potential.

It is generally known that heat flows from a hot object to a cold one, and this means that one loses and the other gains internal energy. When a body emits heat its internal energy is reduced, and when it absorbs heat its internal energy is increased. The transfer of heat from one part of an object to another is explained by change in the molecular motion. If one end of a metal rod is placed in a fire, the entire rod becomes warmer as heat is gradually conducted along it. It is supposed that the molecules of the metal in the fire are set into more rapid vibration and that these, in striking neighboring molecules, impart kinetic energy to them, and so on throughout the rod. When a gas is confined in a vessel and the vessel is heated, the gas molecules striking the heated sides of the vessel in their incessant motion rebound with greater speeds; these molecules then strike others, and so on; in this way the entire gas is heated.

139. Temperature. The transfer of heat from one body to another is determined by their temperatures. The concept of *temperature* may be de-

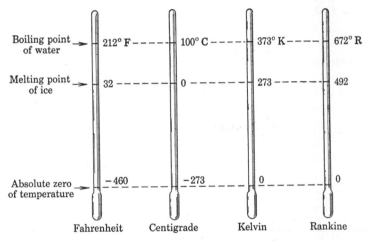

FIG. 144. Comparison of four temperature scales in general use

fined as the thermal condition of a body that determines the transfer of heat to or from other bodies. A relative idea of temperature can be gained by placing a hot object in contact with a cold one; for example, plunging a hot steel forging into cold oil. The forging becomes cooler and the oil warmer, the hot object giving up some of its energy to the cold one. This process continues until there is thermal equilibrium, in which the same temperature prevails throughout.

Terms such as cold, cool, warm, and hot, although used in everyday speech to suggest the temperature of a substance, do not allow a given thermal condition to be stated with definiteness, and this fact has led to the adoption of certain thermometric scales. Such a scale is established by selecting as *fixed points* two temperatures that can be reproduced readily, and assigning numbers to these temperatures. Thereby the zero point of the scale is determined and also the number of unit divisions between the fixed points. The unit divisions are called degrees (°) and are extended above and below the fixed points.

Four temperature scales are in common use. For each, the standard temperatures are taken as the melting point of ice and the boiling point of water, both at the standard pressure of 76 cm Hg. The *fahrenheit scale*, used largely for engineering and household purposes, was named after the German physicist Gabriel D. Fahrenheit (1686–1736), who made the first mercury-in-glass thermometer. The celsius scale, commonly called the *centigrade scale*, is due to Anders Celsius (1701–1744), Swedish astronomer, and is universally used for scientific measurements. The other two scales show *absolute temperatures*, so called because their values are reckoned from a temperature that is considered theoretically to be the lowest possible, § 174; they are used principally in thermodynamics. The one based on centigrade divisions is called the *kelvin scale* in honor of the English scientist Lord Kelvin (William Thomson, 1824–1907), and the other based upon fahrenheit divisions is called the *rankine scale* after the Scottish engineer William J. M. Rankine (1820–1872). These scales are determined by the following data and are shown aligned in Fig. 144 for comparison.

TEMPERATURE SCALES

Fixed points	Fahren-heit	Celsius	Kelvin	Rankine
Boiling point of water.......	212	100	373	672
Melting point of ice.........	32	0	273	492
Divisions between these points	180	100	100	180

It is frequently necessary to convert temperatures from one scale to another. In doing so, it should be noted that a difference of 180 fahrenheit degrees is equivalent to a difference of 100 centigrade degrees, and that the melting point of ice which serves as the usual reference temperature is marked differently on the four scales. For example, in converting a temperature of 60° F to the centigrade scale, the degrees in excess of 32° F are multiplied by 100/180, thus

$$60° F = (60 - 32)(100/180) = 15.6° C$$

The relation between fahrenheit and centigrade readings can be expressed by the proportion

$$\frac{F - 32}{180} = \frac{C}{100} \tag{103}$$

wherein the letters represent the corresponding temperatures.

Illustrative Problem

Take absolute zero to be $-273°$ C and determine its value on the fahrenheit scale.

In the proportion given by Eq. 103, C is taken as -273; hence

$$\frac{F - 32}{180} = \frac{-273}{100}$$

from which the absolute zero is found to be $-460°$ F.

A *rise* or *fall* in temperature is converted from one scale to another without reference to any fixed temperature. A rise or fall in temperature is indicated by the symbol F° or C°, so that it may not be confused with an actual scale reading, which is indicated as °F or °C. Thus a motor that heats up from 20 to 70° C experiences a temperature elevation of 50 C° or 50(180/100) = 90 F°.

140. Linear Expansion of Solids. The application of heat to solids causes practically all of them to expand. A metal rod, heated uniformly over its entire length, expands, and all linear dimensions of the rod become longer. The increase in length per unit length per degree rise in temperature is called the *coefficient of linear expansion*. This coefficient, denoted by α, has different values for different substances, and for a given substance varies somewhat over different temperature ranges. Its value for iron at ordinary temperatures may be taken as $1.2 \times 10^{-5} = 0.000012 \ \frac{cm}{cm}$ per C°; this means that a 1-cm length of iron becomes 1.000012 cm long when subjected to a temperature rise of 1 C°, and similarly a 1-in. length becomes 1.000012 in. long under the same temperature change. Some representative values of α are given in the accompanying table. The values tabulated apply to a range around 20° C except where particular temperatures are listed.

When the coefficient of linear expansion and the length of an object are known at a given temperature, it is possible to compute its length at another temperature. In most calculations, since the linear expansion coefficients are very small, it is not necessary to specify an exact value for the reference temperature. If L_c is the length at the lower temperature (cold); the increase of length due to a temperature rise t may be taken as

$$\text{Increase} = L_c \alpha t$$

Consequently, the length at the higher temperature (hot) is $L_h = L_c + L_c \alpha t$, or

$$L_h = L_c(1 + \alpha t) \tag{104}$$

The linear expansion of an object can be neutralized by the application of a suitable compressive force. In effect, such neutralization amounts to permitting the body to elongate a certain amount and then compressing it mechanically a like amount by a force determined ~~by Eq. 80~~ for Young's modulus of elasticity.

COEFFICIENTS OF LINEAR EXPANSION OF SOLIDS

Material	Per C°	Per F°
Aluminum................	24×10^{-6}	13×10^{-6}
Brass or bronze.........	18 "	10 "
Copper.................	17 "	9.5 "
Glass (soft to hard)......	8 to 9.5 "	4.5 to 5.3 "
Ice (range −10° to 0° C)..	51 "	28 "
Invar steel (36% nickel)..	−0.3 to +2.5 "	−0.2 to +1.4 "
Iron (wrought).........	12 "	6.7 "
Lead..................	29 "	16 "
Platinum...............	9 "	5 "
Pyrex glass.............	3 "	1.7 "
Silica, fused (0° to 30° C).	0.42 "	0.23 "
Silver.................	19 "	11 "
Steel..................	11 "	6.1 "
Zinc..................	26 "	14 "

Several examples of linear expansion are illustrated in Fig. 145. In part I a strip of brass B and another of steel S are joined in one line; the total ex-

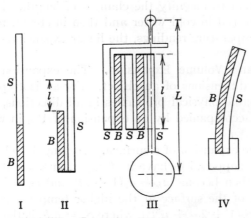

Fig. 145. Examples of linear expansion

pansion due to heating is the sum of the individual expansions of the two strips. The arrangement in part II of the figure shows these strips joined in another way to produce differential expansion. By properly choosing the lengths of the strips, the distance l between their free ends can be kept the same regardless of temperature changes. Such will be the case when the elongation $L_b t \alpha_b$ for the brass strip equals the elongation $L_s t \alpha_s$ for the steel strip over the same temperature range t. Under these conditions,

$$\frac{L_b}{L_s} = \frac{\alpha_s}{\alpha_b} = \frac{11 \times 10^{-6}}{18 \times 10^{-6}} = \frac{11}{18}$$

This principle is made use of in designing clock pendulums to keep their periods of oscillation constant. In part III of the figure is shown the left half of a clock pendulum made of steel and brass rods. In order to keep the length L of the pendulum constant at all temperatures, the lengths of brass and steel should be so proportioned that $2l\alpha_b t = (L + 2l)\alpha_s t$.

Part IV of Fig. 145 represents two strips of dissimilar metals, brass and steel, riveted or welded together side by side, their dimensions being the same at some initial temperature. The shape indicated is reached upon heating because brass expands more than steel. In thermostats and similar appliances, the bending of such a bimetallic strip is caused to make or break an electric contact and thereby control the operation of heaters or other apparatus.

A simple way of measuring the linear expansion coefficient of a metal is to use a rod of the material two or three feet long and place it within a pipe fitted with cork stoppers at each end to center the rod and to form an enclosure through which cold water or steam can be passed. The ends of the rod project slightly so that the length of the rod can be measured, and the measuring device is equipped with a micrometer for direct observation or with a lever system to magnify the changes of length. From the lengths observed with the rod in cold water and then in steam, together with the corresponding temperature readings, the linear expansion coefficient can be computed.

141. Surface and Volume Expansion. The expansion due to heating affects all of the dimensions of an object. For an isotropic body, that is, one having the same physical properties in all directions, an expansion of 1% in length is accompanied by an expansion of 1% in width and 1% in thickness.

To compute the expansion of a surface, a rectangular plate of dimensions a_c and b_c may be supposed to have its temperature raised by an amount t. The dimensions then become $a_h = a_c(1 + \alpha t)$ and $b_h = b_c(1 + \alpha t)$, consequently the area of the surface at the higher temperature is $S_h = a_h b_h = a_c b_c (1 + \alpha t)^2 = S_c(1 + 2\alpha t + \alpha^2 t^2)$, where $S_c = a_c b_c$ is the area of the plate at the lower temperature. The small second-order term $\alpha^2 t^2$ is negligible, and the final expression for the area of the plate becomes

$$S_h = S_c(1 + 2\alpha t) = S_c(1 + \alpha' t)$$

where $\alpha' = 2\alpha$ is the *coefficient of surface expansion* of the material forming the plate.

If heat is applied to a square plate of metal on which another square is marked out to form a frame of uniform width, the plate expands and the inscribed square expands proportionately. Had the inner square of metal been removed before heating, the expansion of the frame for the same temperature elevation would have been the same as though the plate were complete. To put the result in another way, the opening expands as though it were of the same metal.

The expansion of a volume can be expressed in a manner similar to that of a length or a surface. When a body of volume V_c is heated through a temperature range t, its volume becomes

$$V_h = V_c(1 + \beta t) \tag{105}$$

where β is the *coefficient of volume expansion* (sometimes called the cubical expansion coefficient) of the substance. By following the procedure ahead, it can be shown that, as a close approximation,

$$\beta = 3\alpha \tag{106}$$

It is important to remember this relation in seeking cubical expansion coefficients of solids in tables of physical constants, since usually only linear coefficients of such materials are listed.

It can be inferred from what was said about the frame above that the cavity in a hollow object expands as though it were a solid block of the same material.

Illustrative Problem

A glass flask has a volume at $0°$ C of 500 cm^3. Take the linear expansion coefficient of glass as $8 \times 10^{-6}/$C$°$ and find the volume of the flask at $100°$ C.

The coefficient of volume expansion is $\beta = 3 \times 8 \times 10^{-6}/C°$, and therefore the volume of the flask at $100°$ C, from Eq. 105, is

$$V_{100} = 500 \text{ cm}^3 \left(1 + \frac{24 \times 10^{-6}}{\text{C}°} \times 100 \text{ C}°\right) = 501.2 \text{ cm}^3$$

an increase of 1.2 cm^3.

142. Expansion of Fluids. Liquids when heated undergo only volume expansion; in general they follow the same law of expansion as solids, and Eq. 105,

$$V_h = V_c(1 + \beta t)$$

applies equally to both. The coefficients of expansion β are given for a few liquids in the accompanying table; these are average values over temperature ranges around $20°$ C. It should be remembered that when a liquid expands by heating, its container expands also, and this fact must often be taken into account.

EXPANSION COEFFICIENTS OF LIQUIDS

Liquid	Per C°	Per F°
Alcohol (ethyl).........	110×10^{-5}	61×10^{-5}
Alcohol (methyl).......	122 "	68 "
Ether (ethyl)..........	163 "	91 "
Glycerine.............	53 "	29 "
Kerosene.............	83 "	46 "
Mercury.............	18.17 "	10.09 "
Sulfuric acid..........	57 "	32 "
Turpentine...........	94 "	52 "

Illustrative Problem

A 5-gal can made of steel is filled with turpentine at 50° F. How much of this liquid overflows when the temperature rises to 90° F?

The temperature rise is $90 - 50 = 40$ F°, and the cubical expansion coefficient for steel is $3 \times 6.1 \times 10^{-6}/F°$. The volume of the turpentine at 90° F is 5 gal $\left(1 + \dfrac{52 \times 10^{-5}}{F°} \times 40 \text{ F°}\right) = 5.1040$ gal, and that of the steel can is 5 gal $\left(1 + \dfrac{18.3 \times 10^{-6}}{F°} \times 40 \text{ F°}\right) = 5.0037$ gal. The overflow is therefore $5.1040 - 5.0037 = 0.1003$ gal; this is equivalent to 23.17 in.[3]

The density of an object is affected by temperature changes, since the volume increases with temperature and the mass does not. This is particularly important in dealing with liquids and gases for their expansion coefficients are much larger than those of solids. The volumes of a fluid of mass m are $V_h = \dfrac{m}{d_h}$ and $V_c = \dfrac{m}{d_c}$ respectively at temperatures t_h and t_c, where the corresponding densities are d_h and d_c. The temperature difference $t_h - t_c$ is represented by t, as previously, and it follows from Eq. 105 that

$$d_h = \frac{d_c}{1 + \beta t} \tag{107}$$

which shows that, when the temperature of an object is raised, its density is reduced.

Gases behave in accordance with Eqs. 105 and 107 when tested at constant pressure, as was tacitly assumed in the case of liquids. The thermal behavior of gases will be considered in Chap. 16.

143. Expansion of Water and Mercury. Water and mercury are so often used for reference purposes in volume calculations that it is necessary to know exactly how they behave under changes of temperature. This information is given in the accompanying table, which shows their densities at several different temperatures.

DENSITY OF WATER AND OF MERCURY

Temperature, °C	Water, gm/cm³	Mercury, gm/cm³
0	0.99987	13.5955
2	0.99997	13.5905
4	1.00000	13.5856
6	0.99997	13.5806
8	0.99988	13.5757
10	0.99973	13.5708
15	0.99912	13.5585
20	0.99823	13.5462
25	0.99705	13.5340

In calibrating a glass flask so as to have a volume of 250 cm³ at 20° C, the amount of water that should be poured in at that temperature is 250 × 0.99823 = 249.558 gm. A mark is then placed on the glass at the liquid

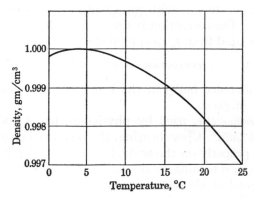

FIG. 146. Anomalous expansion of water; its maximum density occurs at 4° C

level; for accuracy, the shape of the flask should be such that the mark comes at a position where the area is small.

When water is cooled it contracts steadily until its temperature reaches 4° C. At this temperature water has its greatest density. Upon further cooling to 0° C it *expands* and its density becomes slightly less. The irregular expansion of water can be observed in the foregoing table; it is also represented in Fig. 146. This property of water is of particular importance in that it causes the freezing of lakes and ponds to begin at the surface rather than at the bottom. It is interesting to conjecture what would happen if the opposite were true!

144. Mercury Thermometry. Most temperature measurements are made with the familiar mercury thermometer, which covers the important temperature range from −20 to 500° C. In this thermometer the temperature measurement is based upon the expansion of mercury or, strictly, upon the relative expansion of mercury and glass. The thermometer, in its simplest form, consists of a glass bulb fused to the lower end of a capillary glass tube and containing mercury. Since glass softens at about 400° C and mercury boils at 356.9° C, thermometers for higher temperatures are made of borosilicate glass and filled above the mercury column with an inert gas under pressure. For low temperatures, the use of mercury is limited by its freezing point, −38.87° C. In thermometers of similar construction the range is extended downward by using toluol or pentane instead of mercury; these liquids freeze at −97 and −200° C respectively.

Most mercury thermometers are calibrated for complete immersion of the mercury, but in actual use a portion of the stem containing mercury often projects into a region that is cooler than the bulb. Under these conditions a "stem-exposure" correction should be added to the reading, since the exposed mercury does not expand as much as allowed for in the calibration. This correction can be calculated from the observed thermometer reading t by noting the length of the exposed mercury column n, in degrees, and measuring its temperature t_s with an auxiliary "stem thermometer" held near its midpoint. The correction is the amount that the exposed mercury would expand if heated from t_s to t; namely,

$$\text{correction} = n\beta(t - t_s)$$

where β is the difference between the coefficient of volume expansion of mercury and that of glass.

The *clinical thermometer*, used by physicians, has a fine constriction in the stem near the bulb. Upon heating, the mercury expands through this opening and rises properly on the scale; but upon cooling it is prevented by surface tension from returning to the bulb. This construction permits the indication to be read at any time after the thermometer is used; vigorous shaking is required to restore the mercury to the bulb.

PROBLEMS

1. (*a*) Normal body temperature is 98.6° F; express this temperature in centigrade and kelvin degrees. (*b*) The temperature of the earth's atmosphere at an elevation of 20 km above sea level is 210° K. Convert this temperature to the centigrade and fahrenheit scales.

2. Recorded temperatures in the United States range from a highest value of 134° F (in the shade) at Death Valley, California, on July 10, 1913

to a lowest value of $-70°$ F at Rogers Pass, Montana, on Jan. 20, 1954. Express these values on the rankine, centigrade, and kelvin scales.

3. (*a*) When the pressure on a block of ice is increased by 1000 atmospheres, its melting point is lowered by 8.5 C°; how much is it lowered on the fahrenheit scale? (*b*) In a pressure cooker, an increase of pressure of 1 lb/in.^{2} raises the boiling point of water by 3.4 F°. Compute the value of this temperature change in centigrade degrees.

4. Scientists have measured the frequency of rattling of a rattlesnake over a range of body temperatures and found an empirical relationship between frequency and temperature. Averaged observations on 18 snakes (Crotalus) made by L. E. Chadwick and H. Rahn fall along a straight line extending from 1038 vib/min at 8° C to 5338 vib/min at 36° C. Write an equation for the rattling frequency R in vibrations per second in terms of the temperature in degrees centigrade, which would be valid over the range of observation.

5. "We don't guarantee this one, but the story goes that you can determine the temperature [of the air in degrees fahrenheit] by finding a cricket, counting the number of times he chirps in 14 seconds, and adding 40 to that number." —Quoted from *Old Farmers' Almanac*. If the story could be relied upon, at what rate does the cricket give forth in chirps/min when the temperature is 70° F?

6. A steam pipe rising from the basement to the top of a 20-story building is 210 ft long. The pipe is of wrought iron and has four expansion joints equally spaced. Determine the expansion that each joint accommodates for a temperature variation from 60 to 212° F.

7. Steel rails are to be laid when the temperature is 35° F, the length of each rail being 40 ft at this temperature. What should be the separation between adjacent rails to allow for expansion up to a temperature of 115° F?

8. A steel tape correct at 0° C is used to measure a distance along the ground, the tape reading being 44.15 ft when the temperature is 25° C. Calculate the correct length of the distance measured.

9. Compute the force with which a steel measuring tape $\frac{1}{4}$ in. wide and 0.012 in. thick should be pulled in order to compensate for a temperature drop of 15 F°.

10. A copper rod 1.5 cm in diameter fits snugly at 20° C between a pair of fixed supports 8 cm apart. If the temperature is raised to 70° C, what force does the rod exert against the supports?

11. A copper sleeve has an internal diameter of 0.99 in. at 60° F. Determine the temperature to which it must be heated to just fit on a pin 1 in. in diameter. Assume the linear expansion coefficient of copper to have an average value of 8.9×10^{-6}/F° over the temperature range involved.

12. Iron at its melting point, 2800° F, is poured into a mold that has a volume of 100 in.^{3} In solidifying, the iron shrinks 3% in volume, and as it cools to 60° F it shrinks further. If α for cast iron has the average value of 9×10^{-6}/F° over this temperature range, what is the volume of the casting at 60° F?

13. A glass bottle is exactly filled with $\frac{1}{5}$ gal of ethyl alcohol at 40° F. Take the linear coefficient of glass to be 5×10^{-6}/F° and find the volume of liquid that will overflow when the temperature is raised to 90° F.

14. How many grams of turpentine occupy a volume of 600 cm^3 at 50° C?

15. A Pyrex glass bottle is exactly filled with 630 gm of glycerine at 0° C. Compute the mass of glycerine that will overflow if the temperature is raised to 40° C.

15

CALORIMETRY AND
CHANGE OF PHASE

145. Heat Units. Most everyone knows that it takes longer to bring a kettleful of water to the boiling point on the kitchen range than a cupful, starting with tap water of the same temperature in both instances. The reason is that more fuel or electrical energy is required. Tests with measured amounts of water and with thermometers show that the amount of energy needed is proportional to the *amount of water* and to the *rise of temperature*. In consequence, the unit of heat is chosen as the quantity of heat needed to raise the temperature of a unit mass of water through one degree.

Two units of heat are in general use: the calorie (cal) and the British thermal unit (Btu). The *calorie* is the quantity of heat required to raise the temperature of 1 gm of water through 1 centigrade degree. The *British thermal unit* is the quantity of heat required to raise the temperature of 1 lb of water through 1 fahrenheit degree. The relation between mass units given in § 6 shows that 1 lb = 453.6 gm; therefore 1 Btu = $(453.6)(\frac{5}{9})$ = 252 cal. With the units of heat established, it is a simple matter to compute the amount of heat needed to produce a given temperature elevation in any mass of water. Thus, to raise 5 kg of water from 10 to 70° C requires 5 × 1000 × (70 − 10) = 300,000 cal, and to raise 50 lb of water from 40 to 200° F requires 50 × 160 = 8000 Btu. It should be noted that the pound is used as a unit of mass in the study of heat.

Although the foregoing calculations are sufficiently exact for most practical purposes, actually the quantity of heat required to raise unit mass of water through one degree varies slightly from point to point along the thermometer scale. The *mean calorie* is defined as one one-hundredth part of the heat required to raise 1 gm of water from 0 to 100° C; experiment shows that the heat required to raise 1 gm of water from 15 to 16° C is very close to the mean value.

146. Specific Heat. While one calorie of heat raises the temperature of one gram of water through one centigrade degree, it must not be thought that the calorie raises a gram of other substances through the same temperature interval. Roughly, only $\frac{1}{11}$ cal is needed to raise 1 gm of copper through 1 C°, $\frac{1}{30}$ cal suffices for platinum, and so on. The numerical value mentioned is a characteristic of the material known as its *specific heat*.

The specific heat of a substance is the number of heat units needed to raise the temperature of a unit mass through one degree. The numerical value for any one substance is the same in both of the commonly used systems of units, and varies slightly with temperature; thus, for copper the specific heat is 0.093 cal per (gm·C°) or 0.093 Btu per (lb·F°) at 20° C, but is 0.096 at 200° C.

The specific heats of some solids and liquids are given in the accompanying table. These are average values for the temperature ranges listed.

SPECIFIC HEATS

Material	Temperature, °C	Specific heat
Alcohol (ethyl)	0–40	0.59
Aluminum	0–100	0.21
Copper	0–100	0.093
Glass, ordinary	10–50	0.14
Ice	−20–0	0.50
Iron	0–1000	0.15
Iron	0–100	0.11
Lead	0–300	0.032
Mercury	0–100	0.033
Platinum	20–100	0.032

The definition of specific heat shows that, in order to raise a body of mass m and having a specific heat c through a temperature range t, the quantity of heat required is

$$Q = mct \qquad (108)$$

This expression also shows the quantity of heat that the body emits when its temperature is lowered by an amount t. In this equation t stands for *change* of temperature, say from t_1 to $t_2°$, an interval small enough to permit the specific heat value to be regarded as constant. Thus, 50 gm of lead in being raised from 10 to 200° C absorbs $50 \times 0.032 \times 190 = 304$ cal. Again, 10 lb of iron in cooling from 800 to 30° F gives off $10 \times 0.15 \times 770 = 1155$ Btu.

The energy supplied as heat, Eq. 108, is transformed into internal energy of the body heated. Thus, the increase of internal energy of a body due to a rise of temperature depends upon its mass, its specific heat, and its temperature rise. A large mass of a substance when heated through a moderate temperature range might gain more internal energy than a smaller mass of it heated through a large temperature range.

147. Calorimetry. The measurement of heat quantities is called *calorimetry* and is carried out by mixing the substances, originally at different temperatures, and allowing the temperatures to equalize. This *method of mixtures* is based on the following principle: When two bodies, initially at different temperatures, are placed in good thermal contact, *heat is transferred from the hot body to the cold body*, the system reaching equilibrium at some temperature that is uniform throughout; during this process, *the heat given off by the hot body equals that taken on by the cold body*, provided no heat is transferred to or from the surroundings. The application of this principle makes it possible to determine some unknown factor of an experiment in which several substances at different temperatures are brought together.

The principle stated above can also be expressed as follows: In the method of mixtures, *the internal energy of the system, although redistributed among its parts, is unchanged in amount*, provided no heat is lost to or contributed by the surroundings. The internal energy values can be reckoned with respect to any desired datum. This statement leads to another approach in solving problems in calorimetry.

Illustrative Problem

Suppose it is desired to find the temperature that results when 500 gm of water at 80° C are mixed with 200 gm of water at 10° C.

The resulting temperature x is such that the heat given off by the 500 gm of water in cooling from 80° C to x equals that absorbed by the 200 gm of water in rising from 10° C to x. Thus,

$$(500)(80 - x) = (200)(x - 10)$$

from which $x = 60°$ C, the temperature of the mixture.

By the energy method, the internal energy of the system, reckoned with respect to water at 0° C, is as follows:

Before mixture: $500(80 - 0) + 200(10 - 0) = 42,000$ cal

After mixture: $(500 + 200)(x - 0) = 700x$

Since there is no change of internal energy, $700x = 42,000$ cal, whence $x = 60°$ C, as before.

One form of apparatus for measuring specific heat by the method of mixtures is shown in Fig. 147. A test sample P of known mass is heated in a steam-jacketed compartment S to a measured high temperature; the calorimeter R, a heat-insulated metal vessel containing a known amount of water at a known temperature, is pushed directly under the heated compartment and the sample is allowed to drop into it; whereupon the calorimeter is quickly moved away to prevent its absorbing heat from the jacket, and the resulting temperature of the mixture is noted. To find the specific heat of the test sample from the data thus obtained, the heat given off by

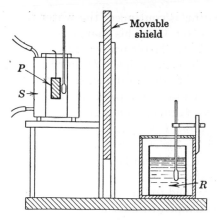

FIG. 147.   Apparatus for measuring specific heat of solids

the sample is set equal to that taken on by the water and calorimeter.   Each of these heat quantities is calculated by use of Eq. 108.

Illustrative Problem

A sample of silver having a mass of 250 gm was heated to 100° C and dropped into 465 gm of water at 19.0° C contained in a copper calorimeter of 140-gm mass; the resulting temperature was found to be 21.3° C.   Determine the specific heat c of the sample from these data.

The heat equation follows:

$$(250)c(100 - 21.3) = (465)(1)(21.3 - 19.0) + (140)(0.093)(21.3 - 19.0)$$

$$= (465 + 13.0)(2.3)$$

from which the specific heat of the sample is $c = 0.056$ cal/(gm·C°).

The product of the mass of a calorimeter and its specific heat is called its *water equivalent.*   Thus, in the foregoing illustration, the 140-gm calorimeter is equivalent to $140 \times 0.093 = 13.0$ gm of water, which means that 13.0 gm of water would experience the same temperature rise as the 140-gm copper calorimeter for a like absorption of heat.

148. Melting and Freezing.   The absorption of heat by a substance does not always result in a rise of temperature. For example, when heat is applied steadily to a block of ice at 0° C, the ice melts,

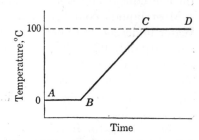

FIG. 148.   While heat is supplied to ice, temperature stays constant during change of phase

and the resulting water, if it remains in contact with the ice, stays at the temperature of 0° C until all the ice is melted.   This situation can be represented on a temperature-time chart by a horizontal line such as AB in

Fig. 148. If the heating is continued, the water rises in temperature uniformly until it reaches 100° C. This change is shown on the same chart by the sloping line *BC*. At the latter temperature, the water boils and its temperature remains constant again (line *CD*) until continued heating converts it entirely to steam. From this example, it is seen that the absorption of heat does not always cause a temperature rise, but instead may serve to change the phase of a substance from a solid to a liquid or from a liquid to a vapor. In the foregoing example, it should be noted that ice melts at 0° C and water boils at 100° C only when the pressure upon the substance has the standard value of 76 cm Hg, the boiling point especially being influenced by the pressure.

The change from the solid to the liquid phase, known as *melting*, or *fusion*, takes place at a fixed temperature for most crystalline substances, provided the pressure remains constant. In contrast, amorphous substances, such as tar and glass, pass imperceptibly from one phase to the other. During the process of melting, the heat energy supplied is used in separating the molecules against the forces of cohesion, and the melted substance has a greater internal energy than the same substance in the solid phase. The opposite of melting is *freezing*, or *solidification*. A solid that has been heated to its melting point begins to melt at this temperature upon the further absorption of heat; the corresponding liquid when cooled to this same temperature begins to freeze as more heat is emitted.

If a substance is melting while no heat is supplied to it intentionally, it is absorbing heat from the surroundings and the latter are cooled if no heat is supplied to them; for this reason melting is sometimes referred to as a cooling process. Conversely, a liquid in freezing gives up heat to its surroundings, and so freezing is sometimes called a heating process. This latter fact is reportedly utilized in fruit cellars by placing large vats of water near the fruit; should the temperature fall dangerously low, the water freezes, and the consequent emission of heat prevents freezing of the fruit.

Most liquids contract in freezing, but there are important exceptions. Water undergoes a remarkable expansion when freezing, ice at 0° C having a density only 0.91 that of water at the same temperature. This expansion accounts for the bursting of water pipes when the water in them freezes. Type metal, an alloy containing antimony as the principal constituent, also expands upon freezing (solidifying); this action fills the mold and produces a good casting.

The melting (or freezing) points of a number of substances at standard atmospheric pressure are given in the accompanying table.

The presence of impurities usually lowers the melting point of a substance. In a mixture of two metals, the melting point of the resulting alloy is lower than that of either constituent; the amount by which the melting point is lowered depends upon the constituents and their relative proportions. Ordinary solder, a tin-lead alloy, has its lowest melting point when it is 63%

MELTING POINTS

Metal	°C	°F
Aluminum...........	660	1220
Copper.............	1083	1981
Hydrogen...........	−259	−434
Iron................	1535	2795
Lead...............	327	621
Mercury............	−38.87	−37.97
Platinum...........	1755	3191
Tin................	232	450
Tungsten...........	3370	6098

tin and 37% lead by weight. The alloy having the lowest melting point is known as an *eutectic mixture* and its melting point is called the *eutectic temperature*. The solid formed on freezing at this temperature has the same composition as the liquid, and thus the liquid remains unchanged in composition as solidification progresses.

149. Heat of Fusion. The quantity of heat needed to melt a unit mass of a solid without change of temperature is called the *heat of fusion*. If the heat of fusion of a solid is represented by L, then the quantity of heat Q needed to melt a mass m at constant temperature is

$$Q = mL \tag{109}$$

This expression also gives the quantity of heat to be abstracted from a liquid to solidify it. If Q is expressed in calories and m in grams, then L is in calories per gram; if Q is in British thermal units and m in pounds, then L is in British thermal units per pound.

At standard atmospheric pressure, ice melts at 0° C; under these conditions experiment shows that 1 gm of ice in melting absorbs 80 cal from its surroundings, and conversely 1 gm of water in freezing dissipates 80 cal to its surroundings. This means that under standard pressure the heat of fusion of ice is 80 cal/gm. Since 5 C° = 9 F°, the heat of fusion of ice is also expressed as $\frac{9}{5} \times 80 = 144$ Btu/lb.

The following table gives the values of the heat of fusion for several substances, all at a standard pressure of 1 atmosphere.

The heat of fusion of ice can be measured by observing the temperature change when a measured amount of ice is dropped into a measured amount of hot water, and equating the heat given off by the water to that absorbed by the ice.

HEATS OF FUSION

Substance	Cal/gm	Btu/lb
Aluminum..........	71	128
Copper............	43.3	77.9
Ice................	80	144
Lead..............	5.4	9.7
Mercury...........	2.8	5.0

Illustrative Problem

In a particular experiment some pieces of surface-dried ice were dropped into a calorimeter containing water at 25.0° C, the mass of the water, including the water equivalent of the calorimeter, being 540 gm. After the ice had melted, the temperature was 14.5° C, and the calorimeter was found to contain 60 gm of water more than it did initially. Determine the heat of fusion of ice from these data.

The heat given off by the water was 540(25.0 − 14.5) cal; the heat absorbed by the ice in melting was 60L cal, and that absorbed by the water thus formed in rising to the final temperature was 60(14.5 − 0) cal. The heat equation therefore is

$$540(25.0 - 14.5) = 60L + 60(14.5)$$

which gives the heat of fusion of ice as $L = 80$ cal/gm.

150. Effect of Pressure on Freezing. The freezing point of a liquid is affected by the pressure to which it is subjected, but only to a small extent. For liquids that contract upon freezing, an increase of pressure raises the freezing point; for liquids that expand upon freezing, such as water, an increase of pressure lowers the freezing point. This statement is in agreement with the principle that pressure on a body tends to prevent its expansion. Consequently, for a liquid that expands upon freezing, an increase of pressure tends to prevent its solidification by lowering the freezing point.

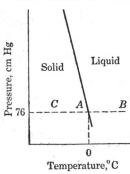

FIG. 149. Increasing pressure lowers freezing point of water

The behavior of water is represented graphically in Fig. 149, in which pressure is plotted against temperature. The curve slopes upward to the left, and a pressure increase of 100 atmospheres lowers the freezing point by less than 1 C°.

A curve such as that shown represents a state of equilibrium between the solid and liquid phases of the substance in question. A mixture of ice and water, for example, at 0° C and 76 cm Hg pressure, may be represented by point *A* on the curve. To raise the temperature of the mixture at this pressure, say to temperature *B*, it would be necessary to supply enough heat first to melt all of the ice present, and then to cause the desired temperature rise. Similarly, to lower the temperature of the mixture, say to temperature *C*, enough heat must be transferred from it first to freeze all of the water present and then to lower the temperature. In the diagram, therefore, the region to the right of the curve represents the liquid phase and that to the left the solid phase. The curve itself shows the relative conditions of temperature and pressure under which ice and water can coexist in equilibrium.

The effect of increased pressure in lowering the melting point of ice is well illustrated by a classical experiment in which a small wire, weighted at the ends, is placed across a cake of ice as in Fig. 150. The wire gradually melts its way through the ice, and as it does so, the groove formed above becomes solid ice again, leaving the cake intact. This process, known as *regelation*, is explained as follows: The pressure beneath the wire is greater than atmospheric, causing the melting point of the ice there to be slightly below 0° C. But since that ice is at 0°, it is momentarily above its melting point and a little of it melts, causing a slight reduction of temperature; the wire settles down and the water formed is squeezed into the region above it. Here the pressure is standard, and the water, which is now slightly below 0°, freezes again.

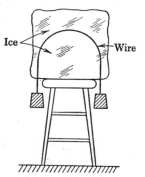

FIG. 150. Regelation experiment

During the process the heat given off by the water in freezing flows downward through the wire and serves to melt the ice below. A copper wire cuts through the ice more rapidly than an iron wire and much more rapidly than a cotton cord, if all three have the same cross-sectional area and are equally loaded.

151. Process of Evaporation. Changing a substance to the vapor phase is called vaporization. The term *vaporization* is a general one and includes: (1) *evaporation*, a conversion from a liquid to a vapor occurring only at the surface; (2) *boiling*, similar to evaporation but taking place throughout the liquid; and (3) *sublimation*, a conversion from a solid to a vapor directly without passage through the liquid phase. Boiling and sublimation are considered later in this chapter.

Evaporation goes on at all temperatures and continues until the liquid disappears or until the space above the liquid has become saturated with vapor. In the process of evaporation a liquid is gradually transformed to a vapor by loss of molecules at its surface. Since the molecules of the liquid are moving about in all directions and with various speeds, many approach the surface with sufficient speed to carry them beyond the range of attraction of the surface layer; these leave the liquid and become molecules of vapor.

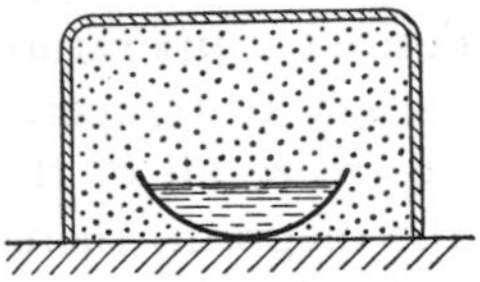

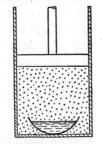

FIG. 151. Saturated vapor formed by liquid evaporating within enclosure

It will be inferred from such a conception of evaporation that the molecules which succeed in escaping through the surface are those with the higher speeds, and that consequently the average molecular speed in the liquid is lessened by evaporation; such is the case, for evaporation lowers the temperature of the liquid. Thus, water placed in a porous jar is cooled by evaporation through the walls, and a person's skin is cooled by evaporation of perspiration.

152. Saturated Vapor. A saturated vapor can be produced by allowing a liquid to evaporate into a confined space, as illustrated in Fig. 151. As the process of evaporation continues, more and more molecules leave the liquid and assume the vapor phase. These molecules of vapor are also in motion, and some of them strike the liquid surface and return to the liquid. The rate at which they re-enter increases as evaporation continues, until finally it equals the rate at which they leave the liquid surface in evaporating. In this state of equilibrium, the vapor is said to be *saturated*, and the pressure that it exerts is called the *vapor pressure* of the liquid; for water at 20° C the vapor pressure is 1.75 cm Hg. Sometimes an unconfined space may become virtually saturated, as occurs with the atmosphere on a humid day, but ordinarily the conditions necessary for the production of saturated vapor are: (1) *the presence of the generating liquid*, and (2) *a confined space*.

The value of the vapor pressure is practically unaffected by the presence of other gases, provided no chemical reactions occur. Thus, for water at 20° C, if the evaporation occurs in a vacuum, the pressure builds up to the value 1.75 cm Hg, but if the enclosure contains dry air at the standard pressure of 76 cm Hg, the pressure builds up to

FIG. 152. Pressure of saturated vapor unaffected by change of volume

an absolute value of 77.75 cm Hg, of which 76.00 cm is the partial pressure due to dry air and 1.75 cm is the partial pressure due to water vapor, § 131. Evaporation continues, regardless of other gases, until the vapor builds up a partial pressure equal to the vapor pressure of the liquid at the existing temperature.

In describing the production of a saturated vapor, no reference was made to the size of the enclosure in which the evaporation occurs. The effects mentioned take place whatever the size of the enclosure, the only difference being that the larger the enclosure, the longer the time required for saturation. The pressure of a saturated vapor is, then, independent of the volume it occupies. If the evaporation were to take place in an otherwise empty cylinder of variable volume, as in Fig. 152, the piston might be moved up or

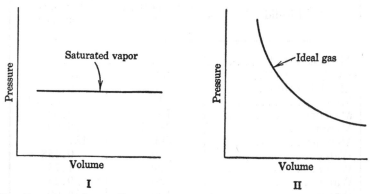

FIG. 153. Pressure-volume diagrams contrasting behavior of saturated vapor and ideal gas

down without affecting the pressure within the cylinder. These considerations show that it is impossible to change the pressure of a saturated vapor by varying the volume it occupies. If the volume is reduced, some vapor condenses to a liquid, and if the volume is increased, some more liquid vaporizes, but the pressure remains constant at a value determined by the substance and the temperature. In this respect a saturated vapor behaves quite differently from an ideal gas, § 129, the pressure of which, in accordance with Boyle's Law, varies inversely with its volume. The pressure-volume diagrams of Fig. 153 contrast the behavior of a saturated vapor in part I with that of an ideal gas in part II; the temperature is assumed constant in both.

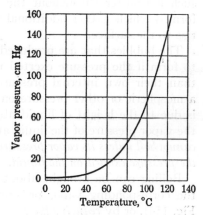

FIG. 154. Vapor pressure of water at various temperatures indicated by boiling-point curve

It is found by test that the vapor pressure of a given liquid has materially different values at different temperatures. For example, the vapor pressure of water measured at 20° C is 1.75 cm Hg, at 30° C it is 3.17 cm, at 50° C it is 9.25 cm, and at 100° C the vapor pressure is 76.00 cm Hg, or exactly 1 atmosphere. These pressure-temperature values are plotted to scale in Fig. 154.

The vapor pressures of a few liquids at several temperatures appear in the following table:

VAPOR PRESSURE OF LIQUIDS

Liquid	Temperature, °C	Pressure, cm Hg
Alcohol (ethyl)........	20	4.4
Alcohol (ethyl)........	50	22.2
Alcohol (ethyl)........	78.5	76.00
Mercury.............	20	0.00012
Mercury.............	100	0.0273
Mercury.............	356.7	76.00
Mercury.............	400	157.4
Water...............	0	0.458
Water...............	20	1.75
Water...............	50	9.25
Water...............	100	76.00
Water...............	150	357.0

153. Boiling. Evaporation has been described as a transfer of molecules from the liquid to the vapor phase at the surface of a liquid. Boiling is such a transfer throughout the liquid, bubbles of saturated vapor being formed which gather additional molecules and so increase in size as they rise to the surface.

The bubbles that are produced in the process of boiling would be unable to form if the pressure exerted upon them from the outside were greater than their own internal pressure. The external pressure consists of the atmospheric or other pressure on the liquid surface plus whatever pressure is due to the height of liquid above the bubble. The internal pressure is the vapor pressure of the liquid at its existing temperature. Hence, *a liquid cannot boil unless its vapor pressure is equal to* (or infinitesimally greater than) *the pressure exerted on the liquid.*

Boiling can be brought about either by *increasing the temperature* until the corresponding vapor pressure equals the pressure on the liquid (see Fig. 154), or by *reducing the pressure* on the liquid to the value of the vapor pressure. Water, initially at 50° C, will serve as an illustration. When heated in the open air it boils at 100° C, at which temperature its vapor pressure is 76 cm Hg. Or it may be made to boil at its initial temperature, 50° C, by lowering the pressure upon it to 9.25 cm Hg, which is the vapor pressure of water at that temperature. From these considerations it is seen that the curve in Fig. 154 can also be called a boiling-point curve, since it shows the relation between boiling point and applied pressure. The difficulty of cooking by boiling at high altitudes, where low pressures prevail, may be inferred from this curve.

Just as the freezing-point curve of Fig. 149 represents a condition of equilibrium between the solid and liquid phases of water, so the boiling-point curve of Fig. 154 represents equilibrium between its liquid and vapor phases. The region to the left of the curve represents the liquid phase and that to the right the vapor phase.

The boiling point of a liquid is influenced by the presence of impurities in it, impurities tending to raise the boiling point. Thus, a pinch of salt added to a saucepan of water raises the temperature of boiling to a higher value, an effect desired sometimes in cooking.

The following table shows the boiling points of a number of pure substances at standard atmospheric pressure:

BOILING POINTS

Substance	°C	°F
Alcohol(ethyl)..........	78.5	171.3
Copper...............	2300	4170
Helium..............	−268.9	−452
Hydrogen............	−252.7	−422.9
Iron.................	3000	5400
Lead................	1620	2950
Mercury.............	356.9	674.4
Oxygen..............	−183.0	−297.4
Sulfur...............	444.6	832.3

154. Heat of Vaporization. In the process of vaporization, work is done in separating the molecules against their attraction for one another, and it is therefore necessary to supply heat to vaporize a substance. The quantity of heat needed per unit mass of liquid to convert it to vapor without change of temperature is called the *heat of vaporization*. The equation used in § 149 for calculating heat quantities during fusion, namely,

$$Q = mL$$

applies also to heat quantities during vaporization, provided L is taken to represent the heat of vaporization. This equation shows how much heat is needed to vaporize a mass m of liquid at constant temperature, or how much heat that mass of vapor gives off in condensing under the same conditions.

The heat of vaporization depends on the temperature at which the change of phase occurs, and the temperature in turn is determined by the pressure.

The values of the heat of vaporization L for a few liquids at standard atmospheric pressure are given in the accompanying table.

HEATS OF VAPORIZATION AT STANDARD BOILING POINTS

Substance	Cal/gm	Btu/lb
Alcohol (ethyl).........	204	367
Mercury..............	68	122
Oxygen..............	51	92
Water...............	539	970

If heat is applied to water, the pressure upon it being 76 cm Hg, the water boils at 100° C, and the heat of vaporization is 539 cal/gm. If instead, water at 0° C is kept at that temperature and the pressure upon it is lowered to 0.46 cm Hg, the water boils at 0° C, and the heat of vaporization is 599 cal/gm. For water boiling at higher pressures and temperatures, the heat of vaporization is less than the values stated, and at the critical temperature, § 167, the heat of vaporization is zero.

PROPERTIES OF SATURATED STEAM

Absolute pressure, lb/in.^{2}	Temperature, °F	Btu/lb above 32° F		
		Internal energy of water	Heat of vaporization	Total
1	101.8	70	1035	1105
2	126.1	94	1022	1116
5	162.3	130	1000	1130
10	193.2	161	982	1143
14.7	212.0	180	970	1150
20	228.0	196	960	1156
50	281.0	250	923	1173
75	307.6	277	904	1181
100	327.8	298	888	1186
150	358.4	330	863	1193
200	381.8	355	843	1198
250	401.0	376	824	1200
300	417.3	394	808	1202
400	444.6	424	780	1204
500	467.0	450	754	1204

The heat of vaporization of water can be determined by passing saturated steam into cool water within a calorimeter and measuring the change of temperature. The amount of steam condensed is found by weighing the contents of the calorimeter before and after the test, and the temperature rise of the calorimeter and its contents is measured by a thermometer. If m gm of water are raised from t_c to $t_h°$ C as a result of admitting M gm of steam at $T°$ C, the heat absorbed by the water, $m(t_h - t_c)$, equals that given off by the steam, namely, $M[L + (T - t_h)]$. From this relation, the heat of vaporization L can be found readily.

Engineers frequently use "steam tables" in determining the performance of boilers. These tables include the temperature at which change of phase occurs, the internal energy of the water, the heat of vaporization, and the sum of the two preceding quantities. A few scattered entries from such a table show the variation of the heat of vaporization with the temperature at which change of phase takes place.

155. Sublimation. Under proper conditions of temperature and pressure, a substance passes directly from the solid to the vapor phase, without lique-fying as an intermediate step. This process is known as *sublimation*. Iodine crystals sublimate in this manner under ordinary room conditions, and the same is true of moth balls (naphthalene) and "dry ice" (solid carbon dioxide). Carbon behaves similarly at 3800° K.

The relation between sublimation, freezing, and boiling is illustrated for water in Fig. 155. The line FX is a redraw-ing of the freezing-point curve; BX is like-wise a redrawing of the boiling-point curve; and SX is the sublimation curve, a line rep-resenting equilibrium between the solid and vapor phases. The areas separated by these curves represent the solid, liquid, and vapor phases, as indicated.

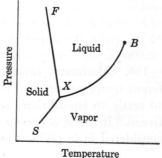

The point of intersection X of the three curves is of special interest. Every point on the curve FX represents a state of equilibrium between the liquid and solid phases; similarly every point on BX represents a state of equilibrium between the liquid and vapor phases; consequently, the intersection point X denotes a state of equilibrium among all three phases. This point, called the *triple point*, represents a condition of pressure and temperature at which water

Fig. 155. Triple-point dia-gram for water, combining Figs. 149 and 154. At triple point X water freezes and boils at same time

freezes and boils simultaneously. To reach this point the temperature is lowered sufficiently to cause freezing, and at the same time the pressure is lowered sufficiently to cause boiling. The triple point for water occurs at a temperature of $+0.0098°$ C and at a pressure of 0.46 cm Hg.

The boiling-point curve BX comes to a definite end at a point B, for which the temperature is 374° C. This is the critical temperature of water, § 167; at higher temperatures steam cannot be condensed into water, however great the applied pressure.

It might be mentioned that, although freezing normally occurs at some point on the curve FX, water that is quiescent and free from impurities can be cooled several degrees below its freezing point without solidification. This phenomenon, called *supercooling* or *undercooling*, represents a condition of unstable equilibrium. Upon dropping particles of ice into the supercooled liquid, solidification takes place immediately, and the temperature rises rapidly to the normal freezing point. Similarly, under certain conditions water can be *superheated* several degrees above its boiling point, but when boiling starts the temperature falls to the normal value. This use of the term "superheated" should not be confused with the common use of the word in connection with steam. Steam is superheated by removing it from the water and heating it; the steam then becomes a vapor that is above its liquefaction temperature and its properties resemble those of an ideal gas. In Fig. 155 the region to the right of the curves represents superheated water vapor. Supercooling and superheating are also observed with other substances.

The effect of high pressures upon the freezing point of water has been investigated by Professor Percy W. Bridgman. The upper portion of the freezing-point curve FX is found to undergo some marked changes of shape, and several varieties of ice are formed having properties different from those of ice at atmospheric pressure. For one variety the freezing-point line shifts to the right at extremely high pressures to such an extent that, at about 20,000 kg/cm^2, water freezes at 70° C.

156. Calorimetry Involving Change of Phase. When substances at different temperatures, and possibly in various phases, are mixed and allowed to settle to equilibrium, some of them may vaporize, condense, melt, or freeze. In these processes heat is either absorbed or emitted and must be considered in applying the method of mixtures.

Illustrative Problem

Suppose 4 lb of steam at atmospheric pressure, superheated to a temperature of 275° F, together with 10 lb of ice at 12° F, to be introduced simultaneously into a copper calorimeter having a mass of 5 lb and containing 70 lb of water at 60° F. The specific heats (in Btu per lb per F°) are as follows for the temperature ranges involved: steam, 0.48; ice, 0.50; and copper, 0.093. The heats of fusion and vaporization for water are respectively 144 and 970 Btu/lb. Calculate the resulting temperature of the mixture, neglecting heat transferred to or from the surroundings.

The problem will be solved by using internal energy values, calculated with reference to water at 32° F as a datum.

Before mixture, these values are as follows:

Steam:
$$4(0.48)(275 - 212) = + \; 121$$
$$4(970) = +3880$$
$$4(212 - 32) = + \; 720$$

Water:
$$70(1)(60 - 32) = +1960$$

Calorimeter:
$$5(0.093)(60 - 32) = + \;\; 13$$

$$\left.\begin{array}{r}4(0.48)(275 - 212) = + \; 121\\4(970) = +3880\\4(212 - 32) = + \; 720\\70(1)(60 - 32) = +1960\\5(0.093)(60 - 32) = + \;\; 13\end{array}\right\} = +6694 \text{ Btu}$$

Ice:
$$\left.\begin{array}{r}-10(0.50)(32 - 12) = - \; 100\\-10(144) = -1440\end{array}\right\} = -1540$$

$$+5154 \text{ Btu}$$

After mixture, this net energy value of 5154 Btu is distributed among $4 + 10 + 70 = 84$ lb of water and 5 lb of copper. Since the 5-lb copper calorimeter is equivalent to $5 \times 0.093 = 0.47$ lb of water, the 5154 Btu are imparted to 84.47 lb of water. This causes a temperature rise of $5154 \div 84.47 = 61$ F° above the datum value of $32°$ F. Thus, the final temperature is $61 + 32 = 93°$ F.

The internal energy approach is also useful in solving a problem where the resulting temperature is $32°$ F with some ice unmelted (internal energy of system above water at $32°$ F would be negative), or where the resulting temperature is $212°$ F with some steam uncondensed (internal energy of system sufficient to raise system to $212°$ F plus a surplus to vaporize part of the water). In such situations the calculation shows the amount of ice unmelted or the amount of steam uncondensed.

157. Heat of Combustion. When a substance is burned or oxidized it produces heat, and the amount of heat liberated per unit mass upon complete oxidation is called its *heat of combustion*. The heats of combustion of several fuels are tabulated in round numbers as follows:

HEATS OF COMBUSTION

Fuel	Cal/gm	Btu/lb
Coal (anthracite)...	7,600 to 8,400	13,500 to 15,000
Fuel oil...........	10,300 to 10,800	18,500 to 19,500
Gasoline..........	11,000 to 11,400	20,000 to 20,500
Manufactured gas..	5,500 to 6,400	9,900 to 11,500
Wood (various)....	4,000 to 4,500	7,000 to 8,000

The heats of combustion of carbon and of a few organic compounds are expressed below in calories per mole, § 132, but can be converted to calories per gram without difficulty. Methane (marsh gas) will be considered as an illustration. The chemical formula CH_4 indicates that the molecule of this compound is composed of 1 atom of carbon (C) and 4 atoms of hydrogen (H). Since the atomic weights of these elements are C = 12, H = 1, the compound has a molar weight of $12 + 4(1) = 16$ gm, and therefore its

HEATS OF COMBUSTION

Substance	Formula	Cal/mole
Acetylene...........	C_2H_2	312,000
Alcohol (ethyl)......	C_2H_5OH	328,000
Alcohol (methyl).....	CH_3OH	170,900
Carbon.............	C	97,300
Methane...........	CH_4	210,800

heat of combustion per gram is $210,800 \div 16 = 13,170$ cal. In engineering, heats of combustion are usually considered positive. In thermochemistry, the opposite practice is generally followed, heat evolved being regarded as negative and heat absorbed as positive. The use of signs is conventional and need cause no confusion.

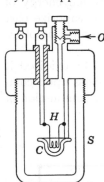

Measurements of heat of combustion are made in a special form of calorimeter such as shown in section in Fig. 156. The substance to be tested is placed in a platinum crucible C mounted within a steel bomb S lined with platinum, gold, or porcelain to prevent corrosion. Oxygen under a pressure of several atmospheres is admitted at O and the bomb is tightly sealed. It is then placed in a calorimeter containing water, and an electric current is passed through a small heating coil H which dips into the test substance. When the wire becomes incandescent, combustion takes place and the rise of temperature of the water is observed.

FIG. 156. Bomb calorimeter for measuring heat of combustion

A different procedure is used for measuring the heat of combustion of gaseous fuels. The gas is burned at a constant rate within a chamber through which water is flowing uniformly. From a knowledge of the rate of water flow and of the temperatures of the water as it enters and leaves the chamber, the energy liberated per unit volume of fuel can be determined.

In some fields of study, heat quantities are expressed in terms of the *kilogram-calorie;* this unit equals 1000 cal. Food values are stated in the larger unit for convenience; thus, the fuel value of the food consumed by the average American per day is over 3000 kilogram-calories.

PROBLEMS

1. Calculate (*a*) the number of calories needed to raise 1 liter of water from 20 to 100° C; (*b*) the number of British thermal units emitted by 1 ft³ of water in cooling from 160 to 70° F.

2. Representative heating values of gaseous fuels in British thermal units per cubic foot are as follows: natural gas, 1030; manufactured gas, 570; liquefied petroleum gas, 2850. For each of these fuels, find the number of cubic feet needed to raise the temperature of 60 gal of water from 70 to 212° F.

3. A flask containing 350 cm³ of water is placed over a Bunsen burner and the temperature of the water is raised from 24 to 100° C in 5 min. At what rate was heat supplied to the water?

4. Determine the temperature of 1 gal of water, initially at 70° F, after it has been supplied with 500 Btu.

5. A stream of water flows at a constant speed of 15 cm/sec through a metal tube that has an internal diameter of 1 cm. Surrounding the tube is an electric heater which supplies heat to the water at the rate of 120 cal/sec. Compute the temperature rise of the water.

6. A copper vessel having a mass of 215 gm and containing 500 gm of water is heated from 25 to 75° C. Determine (*a*) the quantity of heat supplied and (*b*) the increase in internal energy of the vessel and its contents.

7. How much heat is emitted by a cube of aluminum, measuring 4 cm along each edge, as it cools from 40 to 25° C?

8. It is estimated that the air in a particular room measuring 25 × 20 × 11 ft is replaced every 40 min by infiltration of outside air at an average temperature of 32° F. According to this estimate, what quantity of heat is needed to maintain an air temperature of 70° F within the room for 8 hr? Take the density of air as 0.077 lb/ft³ and its specific heat as 0.24 Btu/(lb·F°).

9. Compute the resulting temperature when 700 gm of water at 75° C are mixed with 300 gm of water at 20° C. Neglect any heat that may be transmitted to or from the surroundings.

10. A sink has two faucets. With the "cold" faucet turned on full the sink fills in 45 sec with water at 50° F, and with the "hot" faucet turned on full it fills in 30 sec with water at 150° F. With both faucets turned on full at the same time, (*a*) how long does it take to fill the sink, and (*b*) what is the temperature of the water when the sink is filled? Neglect heat wasted in heating the sink.

11. In a test to determine the specific heat of solder, a 300-gm sample of this alloy at a temperature of 95° C is dropped into a calorimeter containing 418 gm of water at 18.9° C. The calorimeter is of copper and has a mass of 130 gm. If the resulting temperature of the system is found to be 21.0° C, what is the specific heat of the solder?

12. A copper calorimeter having a mass of 70 gm contains 400 gm of water at 20° C. Into the water are placed 200 gm of aluminum at 100° C and 350 gm of iron at 80° C. Find the resulting temperature of the mixture.

13. A sample of iron having a mass of 40 gm is heated to 100° C and dropped into a cavity in a large cake of ice at 0° C. If 5.5 gm of ice are melted, what is the specific heat of the iron sample?

14. Compute the quantity of heat needed to raise the temperature of a 100-gm piece of copper, initially at 20° C, to its melting point and then to

melt it. Take 0.126 as the specific heat of copper over the temperature range involved.

15. How much heat should be removed from 10 lb of water initially at 68° F in order to lower its temperature to the freezing point and then to freeze it?

16. Water at 100° C and ice at 0° C are mixed in equal parts by weight. Compute the resulting temperature.

17. Determine the mass of ice at 0° C to mix with 250 gm of water, initially at 20° C, in order to yield a final temperature of 15° C.

18. (a) How much heat is removed from the water in forming a layer of ice 6 in. thick over the surface of a pond that has an area of 1 acre and an average depth of 5 ft? (b) As a fanciful (but informative) question, if freezing had not occurred, how much would the temperature of all the water be lowered in removing the same amount of heat?

19. The mercury column in a barometer, Fig. 136, stands at a height of 76 cm. In a test on vapor pressure, some water at 20° C is gradually introduced at the base of the column and rises to the enclosed space above. When equilibrium is reached, what is the height of the mercury column?

20. How much heat is needed to convert 1 lb of ice at 10° F to steam at 260° F? Take the specific heat of steam to be 0.48 Btu/(lb·F°).

21. Steam at 212° F is supplied to a radiator at the rate of 4 lb/hr and leaves the radiator as water at 150° F. At what rate does the radiator give out heat?

22. How many pounds of iron could be raised from room temperature of 70° F to its melting point of 2800° F by the same quantity of heat that would vaporize 1 lb of water at its standard boiling point?

23. Determine the average value c of the specific heat of water vapor over the temperature range from 212 to 401° F by comparing two processes: (1) determining the energy required to raise 1 lb of water from 32 to 212° F, to vaporize it, and to raise the temperature of the vapor to 401° F; (2) determining from a table such as that in § 154 the energy required to raise the temperature of 1 lb of water to 401° F and then vaporize it.

24. On a cold night, a certain exposed tank of water loses heat by radiation at the rate of 4.5 Btu/sec. To prevent freezing, steam at 212° F is admitted to the tank and leaves as water at 70° F. How many pounds of steam are needed per hour to offset the stated radiation loss?

25. Refer to the problem solved in § 156 and determine the final temperature and phase of the mixture upon reaching equilibrium, on the assumption that 60 lb of ice are used instead of 10 lb.

26. How many gallons of fuel oil having a heat of combustion of 19,000 Btu/lb and a specific gravity of 0.95 are equivalent in heating value to a ton of coal having a heat of combustion of 14,300 Btu/lb?

27. Calculate the amount of water needed to absorb the heat given off by the burning of a plank 12 ft long, 6 in. wide, and 2 in. thick. The specific gravity of the wood is 0.600 and its heat of combustion is 7500 Btu/lb. Assume that the water is applied to the board at 60° F and is all converted to steam at 212° F.

16

THERMAL BEHAVIOR OF GASES

158. Temperature, Pressure, and Volume Relations. This chapter deals with the manner in which gases respond to heat. For a given mass of gas of known composition, a definite relation exists between three variables: the *temperature* of the gas, the *pressure* that it exerts, and the *volume* that it occupies. If two of these variables are known, the value of the third can be determined; or if one of them is kept constant, the relation between the other two can be established. These relationships for actual gases are complicated by the interaction of their molecules, particularly near the temperatures of liquefaction. To avoid these complications the gas will be idealized in the following consideration. A provisional definition of an ideal gas was given in § 129; a fuller one will be given in § 163. Air, hydrogen, and other so-called fixed gases behave very nearly like the ideal gas over wide temperature ranges.

Constant Temperature. A mass of gas enclosed in a cylinder having a piston, as in part I of Fig. 157, occupies a volume, at some definite tempera-

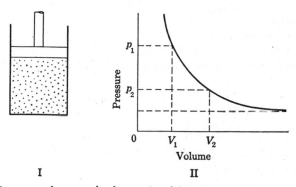

FIG. 157. Pressure of gas varies inversely with volume at constant temperature

ture, that depends upon the pressure exerted upon it. If the temperature is kept constant, *the volume of the gas varies inversely with the absolute pressure*, in accordance with Boyle's Law. This relation is given for any two conditions of pressure and volume by Eq. 101, and can be expressed in the form

$$\frac{V_1}{V_2} = \frac{p_2}{p_1} \text{ at constant temperature}$$

where V_1 and V_2 are the volumes of the gas at pressures p_1 and p_2 respectively. Graphically, this relation is represented by the hyperbola in part II of the figure. The provision made to keep the temperature constant is not shown. It might consist of a jacket surrounding the cylinder and supplied with steam at atmospheric pressure (100° C) or with a mixture of water and ice (0° C).

Constant Pressure. A mass of gas can be kept at constant pressure by enclosing it in a cylinder equipped with a freely moving piston, as indicated in part I of Fig. 158, for the slightest change of pressure causes the piston

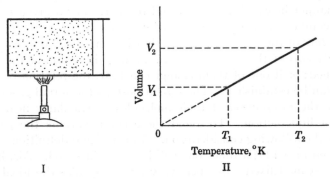

FIG. 158. Volume of gas heated at constant pressure increases with temperature

to move in or out, keeping the pressure inside of the cylinder constant at the value existing on the outside. Upon heating a gas under these conditions, it is found that *the volume varies in direct proportion to the absolute temperature*, a relation attributed to the French mathematician and physicist Jacques A. C. Charles (1746–1823). Expressed as an equation for any two conditions of volume and temperature, Charles's Law states that

$$\frac{V_1}{V_2} = \frac{T_1}{T_2} \text{ at constant pressure} \tag{110}$$

where V_1 and V_2 are the volumes of the gas at temperatures T_1 and T_2 respectively. This relation is shown in the curve forming part II of the figure. The curve if extended would meet the axis of abscissas at 0° K, but at extremely low temperatures the gas would become a liquid and finally a solid, and the gas laws would no longer apply.

Constant Volume. To keep a mass of gas at constant volume, it may be confined in a tight container, as represented in part I of Fig. 159, the container being made of some material having negligible expansion. When the temperature is raised, the pressure of the gas increases in a manner similar to that for the change of volume at constant pressure; thus

$$\frac{p_1}{p_2} = \frac{T_1}{T_2} \text{ at constant volume} \tag{111}$$

where p_1 and p_2 are the absolute pressures of the gas at temperatures T_1 and $T_2°$ K respectively. Hence, at constant volume, *the absolute pressure varies directly with the absolute temperature*, as indicated in part II of the figure.

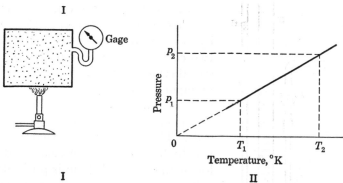

FIG. 159. Pressure of gas heated at constant volume increases with temperature

159. Coefficient of Expansion of Gases. The expansion of a gas due to a rise of temperature is similar to that of a liquid, § 142, when the gas is tested at constant pressure, as was assumed for liquids. The volume of a fixed mass of gas is found to vary with temperature in accordance with the expression

$$V_t = V_o(1 + \beta t)$$

where V_o and V_t represent the volumes of the gas at $0°$ C and $t°$ C respectively, and β is its coefficient of volume expansion. This coefficient has the value $\beta = 0.00367$ per C° for the ideal gas and has *almost exactly this same value for all actual gases*, except at very low temperatures; this value is much larger than those for solids and liquids. Expressed as a fraction, the expansion coefficient for a gas becomes $\beta = \frac{1}{273}$ per C°, which means that a given mass of gas at $0°$ C expands $\frac{1}{273}$ of its volume when its temperature is raised $1°$, and contracts by the same amount when its temperature is lowered $1°$. It should be noted that this value for β applies only when V_o is the volume at $0°$ C.

Since $0°$ C is the equivalent of $273°$ K, an increase of $\frac{1}{273}$ in the volume corresponds to an increase of $\frac{1}{273}$ in the absolute temperature. The volume of a fixed mass of gas thus varies directly with the absolute temperature, a result that establishes Eq. 110.

Similarly, the variation of pressure with temperature given by Eq. 111 is based on the expression $p_t = p_o(1 + \beta t)$, where β, the pressure coefficient, has the same value as the coefficient of expansion and is represented by the same symbol.

160. The Gas Thermometer. The gas thermometer utilizes the change of pressure caused by heating or cooling a gas at constant volume as a means for measuring temperature. The thermometer, Fig. 160, consists essentially of a thin-walled bulb B of glass or porcelain, in which the gas is confined, and to which is attached a flexible tube containing mercury. By keeping the top of the left-hand mercury column at a constant level A the volume of the gas is kept constant, and the pressure is obtained by reading the difference in height of the two columns A and C on the scale S. The gas thermometer is somewhat awkward to manipulate and is not direct-reading, but is used as a basic standard for the calibration of thermometers that serve as secondary standards. The gas in the thermometer bulb is usually hydrogen; for measurements at very low temperatures helium is preferable.

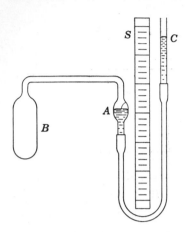

FIG. 160.   Gas thermometer for precise measurements

To show how the gas thermometer is used for temperature measurement, the pressure of the gas in the bulb will be denoted by p_1 at $t_1°$ C and p_2 at $t_2°$ C. Since the volume of the gas is constant, it follows from the foregoing that a change in temperature produces a proportional change in pressure, whence

$$(t_1 - t_o) \propto (p_1 - p_o)$$

and

$$(t_2 - t_o) \propto (p_2 - p_o)$$

The proportionality is the same in both expressions; consequently

$$\frac{t_2 - t_o}{t_1 - t_o} = \frac{p_2 - p_o}{p_1 - p_o}$$

Specifically, if the pressure of the gas is p_o when the bulb is placed in melting ice ($t_o = 0°$ C) and p_1 when the bulb is surrounded by steam at standard atmospheric pressure ($t_1 = 100°$ C); then if the pressure of the gas is p_2 at some unknown temperature $t_2°$ C, that temperature is

$$t_2 = 100 \frac{p_2 - p_o}{p_1 - p_o}$$

in terms of the observed gas pressures.

161. General Gas Law. The General Gas Law shows the relation that exists between the pressure, volume, and temperature of a fixed mass of an ideal gas when none of these quantities is kept constant. It will be derived by merging Charles's Law, Eq. 110, and Boyle's Law, Eq. 101.

A mass of gas entrapped in a cylinder with a freely moving piston is caused to expand in two steps. In the first, the gas is heated as indicated in Fig. 158, and expands at constant pressure. This process is represented in Fig. 161 by the line 1–2; this line is horizontal, since the pressure remains the same, and the volume increases from V_1 to V_2. Temperatures are not shown on this diagram, but it is known that during this process the temperature rises from T_1 to T_2, in accordance with Charles's Law, which states that

$$\frac{V_1}{V_2} = \frac{T_1}{T_2}$$

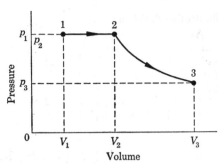

FIG. 161. Pressure-volume diagram for gas expansion at constant pressure (1–2) and at constant temperature (2–3)

In the second step the cylinder is surrounded by a jacket that is maintained at the temperature T_2 in order to keep the temperature inside the cylinder constant at this value, and then the piston is slowly drawn outward. Under these conditions, the gas expands further to a volume V_3, this time at constant temperature, as shown in Fig. 157. This process is represented in Fig. 161 by the line 2–3, and in accordance with Boyle's Law,

$$\frac{V_2}{V_3} = \frac{p_3}{p_2}$$

From these basic equations it follows that $V_2 = \dfrac{p_3 V_3}{p_2}$ and that $\dfrac{V_1}{T_1} = \dfrac{p_3 V_3}{p_2 T_2}$. Since the expansion 1–2 takes place at constant pressure, then $p_2 = p_1$; and since the expansion 2–3 takes place at constant temperature, then $T_2 = T_3$. When these values are used in the preceding equation, there results

$$\frac{p_1 V_1}{T_1} = \frac{p_3 V_3}{T_3}$$

This means that the quantity $\dfrac{pV}{T}$ is constant, a principle that is commonly stated for any two conditions of pressure, volume, and temperature as

$$\frac{p_1 V_1}{T_1} = \frac{p_2 V_2}{T_2} \tag{112}$$

This expression is known as the General Gas Law, and shows the relation between the *absolute* pressures and the volumes of a *fixed mass of gas* at different *absolute* temperatures. The form of the equation shows that any convenient unit can be used for the pressures, so long as the same unit is used for both; the same statement applies also to volumes and to temperatures. However, it is necessary to use absolute values for pressures and temperatures.

Illustrative Problem

As an application of the law, suppose that an automobile tire has constant volume of 0.9 ft^3 and that the air in it is initially at 20° C. What volume of air (reckoned at atmospheric pressure, 14.7 lb/in.^{2} and at 20° C) must be pumped into the tire to increase the pressure gage reading from 25 to 35 lb/in.^{2}? Assume all the air to be heated 7 C° during the process.

The problem will be solved by two applications of the General Gas Law. The air in the tire is initially at an (absolute) pressure of $25 + 14.7 = 39.7$ lb/in.^{2} and occupies a volume of 0.9 ft^3 at an (absolute) temperature of $20 + 273 = 293°$ K. At the final pressure of $35 + 14.7 = 49.7$ lb/in.^{2} and temperature of $27 + 273 = 300°$ K, this air may be considered as compressed into a volume V given by

$$\frac{(39.7)(0.9)}{293} = \frac{49.7 V}{300}$$

whence $V = 0.736$ ft^3.

The air to be pumped into the tire is initially at a pressure of 14.7 lb/in.^{2} and at a temperature of $20 + 273 = 293°$ K, and occupies a volume V_x to be determined. This air at the final pressure of 49.7 lb/in.^{2} and temperature of 300° K may be regarded as occupying the "left-over" volume of $0.9 - 0.736 = 0.164$ ft^3. Therefore,

$$\frac{14.7 V_x}{293} = \frac{(49.7)(0.164)}{300}$$

from which the added volume of air at its initial pressure and temperature is found to be $V_x = 0.542$ ft^3.

It is useful to express the General Gas Law in a modified form. Since $\frac{pV}{T}$ is constant, it follows that $pV = (\text{constant})T$, and the constant may be replaced by the product MR, where M is the mass of the gas and R is known as the *gas constant*. Therefore,

$$pV = MRT \tag{113}$$

where, as before, p and T represent the absolute pressure and absolute temperature of an ideal gas, and V its volume.

This law of gases confirms the theory that the temperature of a gas is directly proportional to the mean kinetic energy of the gas molecules. It was shown in § 127 that the pressure exerted by a gas is $p = Nmv^2/3V$, where N/V is the number of gas molecules per unit volume, m the mass of each molecule, and v their rms speed. It follows that $pV = Nmv^2/3$, or

$pV \propto mv^2$. But from Eq. 113, $pV \propto T$; therefore

$$T \propto mv^2 \propto \frac{mv^2}{2} \propto E_k$$

which shows that the absolute temperature T of the gas is proportional to the kinetic energy E_k of its molecules.

162. The Gas Constant. The numerical value of the *gas constant R* referred to in the preceding section can be computed readily, since

$$R = \frac{pV}{TM} = \frac{p}{T\dfrac{M}{V}} = \frac{p}{Td}$$

where d is the density of the gas. The constant R has a particular value for each gas. For example, air at 0° C and standard pressure has a density $d = 1.293 \times 10^{-3}$ gm/cm³, whence the value of the gas constant for air is

$$R = \frac{1.013 \times 10^6 \dfrac{\text{dynes}}{\text{cm}^2}}{1.293 \times 10^{-3} \dfrac{\text{gm}}{\text{cm}^3} \times 273° \text{ K}} = 2.87 \times 10^6 \frac{\text{ergs}}{\text{gm} \cdot °\text{K}}$$

Similarly in British units, the density of air, expressed to three significant figures, is 0.0807 lb/ft³ under standard conditions, whence the gas constant for air becomes

$$R = 14.7 \times 144 \frac{\text{lb}}{\text{ft}^2} \div \left(0.0807 \frac{\text{lb}}{\text{ft}^3} \times 492° \text{ R}\right) = 53.3 \frac{\text{ft} \cdot \text{lb}}{\text{lb} \cdot °\text{R}}$$

Although computed for standard conditions, these values are correct for air under all conditions of pressure, volume, and temperature.

Illustrative Problem

To illustrate the use of the gas constant, find the volume occupied by 1000 gm of air at 100° C when subjected to a pressure of 10 atmospheres. From Eq. 113,

$$V = \frac{MRT}{p} = \frac{(1000 \text{ gm})\left(2.87 \times 10^6 \dfrac{\text{ergs}}{\text{gm} \cdot °\text{K}}\right)(373° \text{ K})}{10 \times 1.013 \times 10^6 \dfrac{\text{dynes}}{\text{cm}^2}} = 106,000 \text{ cm}^3$$

By expressing the mass of a gas in moles, § 132, the gas constant R has a single value for all actual gases, although strictly it applies only to an ideal gas. From Avogadro's Law, 1 mole of any gas at 0° C and 76 cm Hg occupies a volume of 22.4 liters, and it follows that the *universal gas constant* is

$$R = \frac{1.013 \times 10^6 \, \dfrac{\text{dynes}}{\text{cm}^2}}{\dfrac{1 \text{ mole}}{2.24 \times 10^4 \text{ cm}^3} \times 273° \text{ K}} = 8.31 \times 10^7 \, \frac{\text{ergs}}{\text{mole} \cdot °\text{K}}$$

The value of the gas constant per molecule is found by dividing this result by Avogadro's Number, § 132; thus, $8.31 \times 10^7 \div (6.02 \times 10^{23}) = 1.38 \times 10^{-16}$ ergs/(molecule·°K).

163. Free Expansion. A gas is said to undergo *free expansion* when it expands without external opposition. For example, if a tank of gas under pressure is piped to a second tank from which the air has been evacuated,

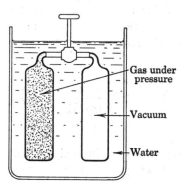

Fig. 162, and the valve between the tanks is opened suddenly, the gas expands freely into the vacuum. An experiment of this kind was conducted by the French chemist and physicist Joseph L. Gay-Lussac (1778–1850), to determine whether any temperature change occurs during free expansion. The tanks were immersed in a water bath, and the temperature of the water was observed before and after the valve was opened. In this test the temperature appeared to remain unchanged, which would indicate that the gas, taken as a whole, is neither cooled nor heated by free expansion. The experiment was not entirely convincing, however,

FIG. 162. Free-expansion experiment; temperature of ideal gas stays constant

because the bath contained so much water that a slight temperature change might readily escape notice.

In a later and more delicate experiment conducted by Joule and Thomson, the gas was allowed to escape slowly through a porous plug from a region maintained at constant high pressure to one at a constant low pressure, a thermocouple being used to detect any temperature change during the process. Although this was not a free-expansion experiment, an analysis of the results led to the conclusion that actual gases would become slightly cooled under free expansion.

As a consequence of the foregoing considerations, it is possible to define an ideal gas and to distinguish between ideal and actual gases. An *ideal gas* is one that *conforms to the General Gas Law*, and *does not exhibit cooling during free expansion*. This means that, in an ideal gas, the molecules exert no forces on one another. Further, since an ideal gas shows no temperature change during free expansion, it is evident that no energy is abstracted from it, although both its pressure and its volume are changed. This statement leads to an important principle, namely: *The internal energy of an ideal gas remains constant regardless of changes in pressure and volume, provided the temperature is not changed*; in other words, *the internal energy of an ideal gas is a function of the temperature only*.

In an actual gas, the molecules do exert slight forces upon one another, and these are forces of attraction. The kinetic theory offers a picture of what takes place when an actual gas expands through a small opening into a region of lower pressure. A molecule passing through the orifice is attracted by such other molecules as are within its sphere of action. Those ahead attract it forward, and those behind attract it backward. The predominating effect, however, is due to the molecules behind it, since the pressure—and consequently the molecular density—is greater in that region. The result is a slowing down of the molecule as it passes through the orifice, and this implies a reduction of its kinetic energy and a lowering of temperature. Thus, the theory shows that molecular attraction is responsible for the lowering of temperature of an actual gas when it expands. At ordinary temperatures, this cooling is very slight, but as the temperature is reduced the molecules come closer together (if the pressure stays unchanged) and the cooling effect is greatly increased.

164. Constrained Expansion. The expansion of a compressed gas against a back pressure is termed *constrained* to distinguish it from free expansion into a vacuum. During constrained expansion any gas, whether ideal or actual, does mechanical work. For example, Fig. 163 represents a cylinder containing gas under absolute pressure p, and indicates that the gas in expanding pushes a piston of area A back a small distance Δs. During this process, the confined gas exerts a force $F = pA$ and does an amount of work $E = F\,\Delta s = pA\,\Delta s$. The product $A\,\Delta s$ is the increase in volume of the gas and may be denoted by ΔV; whence the work done by the gas during expansion becomes

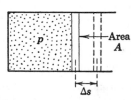

FIG. 163. For computing work done by expanding gas

$$E = p\,\Delta V \text{ at constant pressure} \qquad (114)$$

This expression is true for any change in volume that does not affect the pressure.

If no energy is supplied to the gas during this expansion, the work $p\,\Delta V$ is necessarily done at the expense of the internal energy of the gas, as a result of which its temperature falls. When an actual gas expands against a back pressure, it is cooled by doing external work, and by doing a slight (often negligible) amount of internal work in separating its own molecules.

In the commercial manufacture of ice, the refrigeration is brought about by allowing anhydrous ammonia to pass through an expansion valve into a region of reduced pressure. The evaporation of the liquid and the expansion of the vapor are both cooling processes; together they lower the temperature of the ammonia sufficiently to freeze water that is placed near by.

The compression of a gas causes it to become hotter; a familiar example is the heating of air in a tire pump. In the Diesel engine, § 176, air admitted to the cylinder is compressed, and thereby heated to about 1000° F, a temperature high enough to ignite the fuel as it is sprayed into the cylinder.

The kinetic theory again offers a picture of these processes. The gas molecules in the cylinder, Fig. 163, continually strike against the cylinder walls and piston and rebound from these surfaces. If the piston is moving outward, as during expansion, the molecules rebound from this receding surface with reduced speed. If, however, the piston is moving inward, as during compression, the molecules striking this advancing surface gain speed upon rebound. Thus, expansion lessens the speed of the gas molecules, reduces their kinetic energy, and lowers the temperature of the gas; compression produces the opposite effects.

165. Specific Heat of Gases. As with liquids and solids, the specific heat of a gas is the quantity of heat needed to raise the temperature of a unit mass one degree. For a gas, however, the specific heat is not single-valued but may have a range of values, depending upon the constraints imposed upon the gas while being heated. The quantity of heat required to raise 1 gm of gas through 1 C° is quite different if the volume is kept constant than if the pressure is kept constant, and still different if variations are allowed in both volume and pressure.

The most important values of specific heat of a gas are those at *constant volume*, c_v, and at *constant pressure*, c_p. The relation between them will be explained by considering the energy transformations during the heating process. When heat is applied to a mass of gas, the energy supplied as heat can be accounted for in one or both of two ways: (1) an increase in the internal energy of the gas due to the increased kinetic energy of its molecules and evidenced by a rise of temperature, and (2) mechanical work done by the gas in expanding. Thus, the Law of Conservation of Energy states that

$$Q = (U_2 - U_1) + E \qquad (115)$$

where Q represents the energy supplied as heat, U_1 and U_2 the initial and final values of the internal energy of the gas with respect to any desired datum, and E the work done in expansion.

This principle will be applied first to determine the quantity of heat expended in increasing the internal energy of a gas. If a mass M of an ideal gas is confined so that its volume cannot change, as in Fig. 159, and heated sufficiently to raise its temperature by an amount t, the quantity of heat supplied is Mc_vt, the subscript v signifying constant volume. Since the gas does not expand, no external work is done; therefore in Eq. 115, $E = 0$, and consequently

$$U_2 - U_1 = Mc_v t \qquad (116)$$

This equation has a wide usefulness; it states that, when a mass M of gas has its temperature raised by an amount t, the increase of internal energy amounts to $Mc_v t$. This statement is perfectly general for an ideal gas and applies to any process whatever, whether at constant volume or not.

On the other hand, if the same mass M of gas is enclosed in a cylinder with a freely moving piston, as in Fig. 158, and heated through the same temperature range t, the quantity of heat supplied is $Mc_p t$, the subscript p signifying constant pressure. In this test the gas expands at constant pressure, and does an amount of work given by Eq. 114 as $E = p\,\Delta V$, where ΔV is the change in its volume V. In terms of the General Gas Law, $pV = MRT$, the product $p\,\Delta V$ can be expressed as $MR\,\Delta t$, or $E = MRt$, where the temperature change is denoted by the single symbol t. To summarize: the heat supplied is $Q = Mc_p t$, the increase in internal energy is $U_2 - U_1 = Mc_v t$, and the work done by the expanding gas is $E = MRt$. It follows from the Law of Conservation of Energy, Eq. 115, that

$$Mc_p t = Mc_v t + MRt$$

When the product Mt is cancelled throughout and the terms are rearranged, there results

$$c_p - c_v = R \qquad (117)$$

This expression shows that the specific heat of a gas at constant pressure is larger than that at constant volume, and that the difference between these values equals the gas constant R, when all terms are expressed in the same unit. It will be shown in § 171 that the universal gas constant, given in § 162 as $R = 8.31 \times 10^7$ ergs/(mole·°K), is equivalent to 1.985 cal/(mole·°K). Eq. 117 is strictly true for an ideal gas and is very nearly true for most actual gases.

SPECIFIC HEATS

Gas	Temperature, °C	Cal/(gm·°C) or Btu/(lb·°F)		Cal / mole·°C	
		c_p	c_v	c_p	c_v
Air.................	0–100	0.242	0.173	7.01	5.01
Carbon dioxide......	0–100	0.199	0.153	8.75	6.71
Hydrogen...........	0–100	3.40	2.40	6.85	4.84
Oxygen.............	0–100	0.218	0.156	6.98	4.98
Water vapor........	100	0.48	0.34	8.65	6.13

The table on page 253 gives the specific heats of several gases at constant pressure, c_p (for atmospheric pressure) and at constant volume c_v, expressed in the units commonly used.

166. Isothermal and Adiabatic Processes. Two processes play important roles in the behavior of gases; they deal with expansion or compression under particular conditions. An expansion or contraction of a gas *without change of temperature* is said to be *isothermal*. This process has already been considered in connection with Boyle's Law; the relation between pressure and volume for an ideal gas when kept at constant temperature is shown in Fig. 157 and is given by the expression $p_1 V_1 = p_2 V_2$; or, more simply, the equation of an isothermal process is

$$pV = \text{a constant} \tag{118}$$

During an isothermal expansion, the temperature being constant, there is no change in the internal energy of the gas; and Eq. 115 becomes

$$Q = E$$

showing that *in an isothermal expansion a quantity of heat is supplied to the gas exactly equivalent to the work that it does in expanding.* This action takes place automatically if the gas is allowed to expand slowly while in good thermal contact with a source of heat maintained at the temperature of the gas. The cooling tendency during expansion is offset by a flow of heat from the source to the gas, keeping its temperature constant. Similarly, during an isothermal compression there is a continual transfer of heat away from the gas in order to keep the temperature constant, and the heat transferred is equivalent to the work done in compressing the gas. Since the heat should flow throughout the gas during these processes, isothermal changes usually take place somewhat slowly.

An expansion or contraction of a gas *without the transfer of heat* to it or from it is called *adiabatic*. Such a process would result if the gas were contained in a cylinder completely surrounded by a perfect heat insulator, so that no heat could be taken on during expansion nor given off during compression. During an adiabatic expansion, since no heat is supplied to the gas, Eq. 115 becomes

$$E = U_1 - U_2$$

showing that *the work done by the gas in expanding is equivalent to the reduction of its internal energy.* Thus, some of the internal energy of the gas is converted to mechanical work, and the temperature of the gas is lowered. Again, during an adiabatic compression, the work done upon the gas causes its temperature to rise.

To permit comparison between isothermal and adiabatic processes, an isothermal curve I and an adiabatic curve A are drawn on the same pressure-volume diagram in Fig. 164. The two curves start from point X, which represents a certain initial condition of pressure and volume of the gas under consideration. The gas, if expanded adiabatically to some lower pressure at point M, is cooler and therefore occupies less volume than if heat had been supplied to expand it isothermally to the same pressure at point N. Consequently, the curve representing the adiabatic process is steeper than for an isothermal process. Actual expansions and compressions of gases are neither isothermal nor adiabatic, but are intermediate between these processes.

The equation of the adiabatic curve can be found by considering an adiabatic expansion to be made up of very small steps, then expressing the energy relations over one such step, and summing up the result for the entire curve. The result of such a procedure shows the following relationship between pressure and volume:

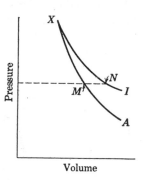

FIG. 164. Isothermal and adiabatic processes contrasted; the adiabatic curve is steeper

$$pV^\gamma = \text{a constant} \qquad (119)$$

where the symbol γ (gamma) is used to represent the specific heat ratio c_p/c_v for the gas considered.

The numerical value of γ depends upon the molecular structure of the gas. Most of the common gases, such as hydrogen, oxygen, and nitrogen, are *diatomic*—that is, they have two atoms in each molecule; the inert gases, such as helium and argon, are chiefly *monatomic*, one atom making up the molecule. It can be shown theoretically that $\gamma = 1.40$ for diatomic gases and 1.66 for monatomic gases. For air, largely composed of diatomic gases, $\gamma = 1.40$.

167. Liquefaction of Gases. In view of the fact that the molecules of a liquid are closer together than in a gas, attempts to liquefy a gas are carried out at low temperature and high pressure; both of these conditions cause the gas to contract, and thus bring its molecules closer together. The behavior of a gas as it approaches liquefaction can be studied by investigating the relation between its pressure and its volume as the temperature is held at lower and lower values. Almost a century ago, such a series of tests was carried out on carbon dioxide by Thomas Andrews (1813–1885), Irish chemist and physicist, with results as plotted in Fig. 165.

In one test, a tube containing carbon dioxide was maintained at a constant temperature of 48.1° C while the volume of the gas was reduced; during this process the pressure increased approximately in accordance with Boyle's Law, as shown by the uppermost curve in the figure. A similar test at a lower temperature, 35.5° C, showed a noticeable departure from Boyle's Law. For tests at still lower temperatures, the departure became more marked, and the curve for the test at 31.1° C shows a definite point of inflection at E. The curve for any lower temperature has a horizontal portion, signifying the presence of liquid as well as vapor, as described in § 152. In this temperature region, a curve such as $LMNP$ shows that as the volume is reduced the pressure at first increases (LM), much as for an ideal gas; next the point of saturation is reached and liquid begins to form (M); a further reduction in volume causes more and more of the vapor to liquefy, the pressure remaining constant (MN); eventually the liquefaction is complete (N); and from this point on, a great increase of pressure (NP) is required to produce a small change in volume.

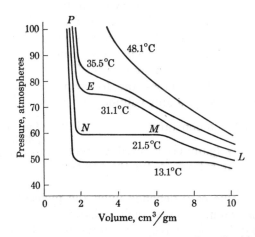

FIG. 165.   Isothermal curves for carbon dioxide

The point of inflection E on the pressure-volume curve of a substance is called its *critical point*, and the corresponding properties of the substance under test are referred to as the critical values. The *critical temperature* is that minimum temperature above which a gas cannot be liquefied, no matter how much pressure is applied; for carbon dioxide it has the value 31.1° C. The *critical pressure* is the absolute pressure (of gas and liquid) at the critical point. The *critical volume* is the volume of gas at the critical temperature and pressure which at 0° C and 76 cm Hg would have unit volume.

An experiment on critical temperature can be conducted using some liquid carbon dioxide sealed in an evacuated tube, the tube having heavy glass walls that can withstand high pressures and still allow the interior to be seen. At room temperature the liquid rests in the bottom of the tube and the space above it is filled with saturated vapor. As the tube is heated, the liquid expands and its density decreases, while the density of the vapor increases. If the amount of liquid used is in the proper proportion to the volume of the tube, the critical point is passed through; this occurs at a temperature of 31.1° C. At this point the line of demarcation between the liquid and vapor disappears and the contents of the tube present a uniform appearance throughout.   The liquid and vapor then have the same density, and the two phases cannot be differentiated.

All gases show the same general behavior with reference to liquefaction as has just been described for carbon dioxide.   The values of critical temperature, pressure, and volume are, however, quite different for different substances, as indicated in the accompanying table.

CRITICAL VALUES

Substance	Temperature, °C	Pressure, atmospheres	Volume
Air.....................	−140.7	37.2	0.0047
Alcohol (ethyl)...........	243.1	63.1	0.0071
Ammonia...............	132.4	111.5	0.0048
Carbon dioxide.........	31.1	73	0.0066
Helium.................	−267.9	2.3	0.0030
Hydrogen...............	−239.9	12.8	0.00264
Sulfur dioxide...........	157.2	77.7	0.0075
Water..................	374	217.7	0.00386

Low temperatures are needed to liquefy most gases.   For the fixed gases, the critical temperatures are so low as to require a cumulative cooling action.   This procedure was perfected by Karl R. von Linde (1842–1934), German technologist.   In liquefying air by this process, the air is compressed to about 200 atmospheres, next cooled by means of a freezing mixture, and then passed through a long tube from the end of which it is allowed to expand to a pressure of about 15 atmospheres.   The air is appreciably cooled by this expansion, and is then allowed to expand again, this time to atmospheric pressure, which results in a further lowering of its temperature.   Some of the air that has been cooled by each expansion circulates around the tube from which it issued, in order to cool the air stream before expansion cools it further.   Thus, as the system operates, the cooling action is progressively intensified, and finally the temperature is lowered sufficiently to cause the air to liquefy as it leaves the tube.   The liquid air is collected in large containers resembling thermos bottles.

By somewhat similar processes it has been possible to liquefy all known gases.   Helium was first liquefied in 1908 at −268.9° C by the Dutch physicist, H. Kamerlingh Onnes (1853–1926).   By the evaporation of liquid helium, lower and lower temperatures have been attained by many investigators; the lowest temperature reached is only a small fraction of one degree above absolute zero.

168. Actual Gases; van der Waals' Equation.   It has long been recognized that Boyle's Law, although used as a criterion for an ideal gas, is not followed exactly, even by the fixed gases. Also, the curves in Fig. 165 show how widely a gas departs from this law as it approaches the liquid phase. Numerous attempts have been made to formulate an expression that would agree more closely with the facts of experiment; one of these is due to the Dutch physicist, Johannes D. van der Waals (1837–1923). He considered that in an actual gas the attraction of the molecules for one another, which is absent in the concept of an ideal gas, would be equivalent to a slight increase in the pressure of the gas. Any given molecule is affected by a number of others within its sphere of action, and this number is proportional to the density of the gas. Further, for a given amount of gas, the number of molecules affected is also proportional to the density. Hence the correction for pressure should be proportional to the square of the density or inversely proportional to the square of the volume V. For this reason van der Waals replaced the pressure p in Boyle's Law by a term $\left(p + \dfrac{a}{V^2}\right)$, where a is a constant. He also considered that the volume, which is to be regarded as the volume into which the gas can expand, is reduced in an actual gas by the space occupied by the molecules themselves, and should be replaced by a smaller term $(V - b)$, where b is another constant.

When these corrections are applied to Boyle's Law, the relationship between the absolute pressure p and the volume V of a mass of actual gas at constant temperature becomes:

$$\left(p + \frac{a}{V^2}\right)(V - b) = \text{a constant}$$

and is shown graphically in Fig. 166. If the foregoing equation is expanded and compared with Boyle's Law, it will be found that the correction amounts to $(a/V) - pb$, the small term ab/V^2 being neglected. It is found that when p is large and V small the corrections are important. The curve conforms almost perfectly to the experimental curve $LMNP$ of Fig. 165 except that the horizontal portion is replaced by a sinuous line.

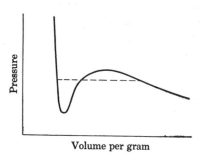

Pressure

Volume per gram

Fig. 166. Graph of van der Waals' Equation

The relation between pressure and volume can therefore be found by van der Waals' Equation for either the gaseous or the liquid phase of a substance, and the transitional region in which the equation does not apply is known to be one of constant pressure. For a fluid which satisfies the equation, it can be shown that the values of critical temperature, pressure, and volume are given respectively by

$$T_c = \frac{8a}{27bR} \qquad p_c = \frac{a}{27b^2} \qquad V_c = 3b$$

in terms of the constants a and b of the foregoing equation for that particular fluid.

169. Atmospheric Humidity. As a result of evaporation, the atmosphere always contains some moisture in the form of water vapor. This moisture does not consist of tiny particles of liquid suspended in the air, but is a vapor as truly invisible as the air with which it mixes. The amount of water vapor per unit volume is known as the *absolute humidity*, and is usually expressed in pounds per cubic foot or in grams per cubic centimeter.

Since the atmosphere is a mixture of dry air and water vapor, the total atmospheric pressure p has two components: the partial pressure due to the dry air, p_a, and the partial pressure due to the water vapor, p_w. In accordance with Dalton's Law, § 131,

$$p = p_a + p_w \tag{120}$$

Water can evaporate into the surrounding region until the partial pressure due to the vapor equals the vapor pressure of water at the existing temperature, § 152; for instance, at 20° C evaporation continues until $p_w =$ 1.75 cm Hg. At this point the surrounding region is *saturated;* that is, it

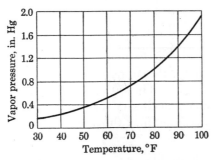

FIG. 167. Vapor pressure of water; like Fig. 154 but with British units

contains all the water vapor possible at that temperature, and evaporation ceases. Such a condition is uncomfortable in warm weather because perspiration cannot evaporate and the desired cooling effect is absent. The pressure of water vapor at saturation can be read for various temperatures from the curve in Fig. 154, but in the calculation of atmospheric humidity, pressures are usually stated in inches of mercury and temperatures in degrees fahrenheit. A similar curve in which these units are used is given in Fig. 167 for the appropriate temperature range; the data from which the curve is plotted appear in the first two columns of the accompanying table.

The other two columns show the absolute humidity at saturation and the heat of vaporization at the various temperatures.

PROPERTIES OF WATER VAPOR

Temperature, °F	Vapor pressure, in. Hg	Amount of saturated vapor, lb/ft³	Heat of vaporization, Btu/lb
0	0.0375	0.675×10^{-4}	
10	0.0628	1.10×10^{-4}	
20	0.1027	1.77×10^{-4}	
30	0.1646	2.78×10^{-4}	
35	0.2036	3.40×10^{-4}	1076
40	0.2478	4.10×10^{-4}	1073
45	0.3003	4.91×10^{-4}	1070
50	0.3624	5.88×10^{-4}	1067
55	0.4356	6.99×10^{-4}	1064
60	0.521	8.29×10^{-4}	1061
65	0.621	9.80×10^{-4}	1058
70	0.739	11.5×10^{-4}	1055
75	0.874	13.5×10^{-4}	1052
80	1.031	15.8×10^{-4}	1049
85	1.212	18.4×10^{-4}	1046
90	1.421	21.4×10^{-4}	1043
95	1.659	24.7×10^{-4}	1040
100	1.931	28.5×10^{-4}	1037

Usually and fortunately, the amount of vapor per unit volume is insufficient to produce saturation. The ratio of the amount of water vapor actually present to the amount necessary for saturation at the existing temperature is called the *relative humidity;* thus,

$$\text{Relative humidity} = \frac{\text{water vapor present}}{\text{water vapor for saturation}}$$

The relative humidity can also be expressed in terms of pressures, since the pressure due to the vapor is approximately proportional to the amount of vapor present. Hence, the relative humidity in per cent is

$$h = \frac{p_w}{p_s} \times 100 \tag{121}$$

where p_w is the pressure of the water vapor actually present in the atmosphere and p_s the pressure corresponding to saturation at the existing temperature; that is, p_s is the vapor pressure of water.

Illustrative Problem

On a particular day a test of the atmosphere at 60° F showed that the amount of water vapor per unit volume was 4.91×10^{-4} lb/ft³. What was the relative humidity at the time of the test?

The amount of vapor at saturation is given in the table as 8.29×10^{-4} lb/ft³ at 60° F; hence the relative humidity is $4.91 \times 10^{-4} \div (8.29 \times 10^{-4})$ = 0.59, or 59%.

For the stated moisture content, the pressure is given in the table as 0.3003 in. Hg, and at saturation the vapor pressure at 60° is 0.521 in. Hg. Hence in terms of pressure, Eq. 121 gives the relative humidity as

$$\frac{0.3003}{0.521} \times 100 = 58\%$$

a result that agrees sufficiently with the value above.

With a given moisture content, if the temperature of the atmosphere rises, the relative humidity is lowered, because the vapor pressure has higher values; the atmosphere feels drier, although the amount of water vapor remains the same. On the other hand, a fall of temperature increases the relative humidity for the same moisture content. If the temperature falls to a sufficiently low value, the atmosphere becomes saturated and the vapor begins to condense, forming dew; accordingly, this value of the temperature is called the *dew point.*

Condensed vapor suspended in the atmosphere is recognized as fog when at the surface of the earth, and as a cloud at greater altitudes. Upon further cooling, the water particles grow in size as more and more moisture condenses on the nuclei, and the drops so formed fall to the earth as rain. Condensation of water vapor at temperatures below the freezing point forms frost and snow.

The dew point can be measured by cooling a very small region so that it becomes saturated and observing the temperature at which the condensation occurs. The device for making this measurement is called a condensing *hygrometer;* it consists primarily of a glass or metal plate so arranged that one face can be cooled either by circulating cold water or by evaporating a liquid such as ether until dew is observed to form on the other face that is exposed to the atmosphere. The corresponding temperature of the atmosphere, which is assumed to be the same as that of the plate in contact with it, is the dew point.

The relative humidity can be calculated from a knowledge of the dew point and a reference to a vapor pressure curve like Fig. 167. The pressures read from this curve at the dew point and at the temperature of the atmosphere correspond to p_w and p_s respectively, and their ratio gives the relative humidity in accordance with Eq. 121.

The relative humidity can be determined experimentally with a *psychrometer* that consists of two suitably mounted thermometers; one thermometer bulb is exposed to the atmosphere (dry bulb) and the other is wrapped with muslin and kept moist with water (wet bulb). The drier the atmosphere, the more rapid is the evaporation of water from the muslin, and the lower is the reading of the wet-bulb thermometer. Tables are available that give the percentage humidity in terms of the dry-bulb reading and the depression of the wet-bulb temperature.

PROBLEMS

1. A 60-gal tank with its axis vertical contains air at atmospheric pressure. When 25 gal of water are pumped into the tank through a valve at the bottom, what is the absolute pressure of the confined air? Assume no change in temperature.

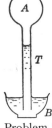

Problem 2

2. The diagram represents Galileo's air thermometer, in which an air bulb A opens into a tube T that dips into a cup B containing colored water. As the temperature rises, the air expands and pushes the water downward in the tube. The expansion may be regarded as taking place at constant pressure, since the pressure changes are slight. Also, the expansion of the glass may be neglected with respect to that of air. Assume the bulb to have a volume of 100 cm^3 and the tube an internal diameter of 1 cm, and suppose the water level to reach the top of the tube at 0° C. (*a*) How far will the liquid column be depressed when the temperature is 10° C? (*b*) Find the internal diameter of a tube to use with this bulb so that the liquid level would change $\frac{1}{2}$ cm for each C° change of temperature.

3. The gage on an oxygen tank indicates a pressure of 100 lb/in.^{2} at a temperature of 60° F; determine its reading when the temperature rises to 80° F. Neglect the expansion of the tank.

4. A cylinder with a freely moving piston contains 10 liters of air initially at atmospheric pressure and a temperature of 20° C. The temperature is raised until the volume of the air is 15 liters; then the piston is blocked so that it cannot move and the temperature is raised further, to a final value of 900° C. Compute the final value of the absolute pressure of the air.

5. To indicate the usefulness of a gas as a thermometric substance, imagine a temperature rise that would cause wrought iron to expand 1% and calculate the corresponding expansion (*a*) of mercury and (*b*) of air.

6. In a test with the air thermometer, Fig. 160, the mercury level in the open column is 5 cm below that in the other column when the bulb is at 0° C and 17 cm above when the bulb is at the temperature being measured. Determine (*a*) the value of this temperature and (*b*) the location of the mercury level in the open column when the bulb is at 100° C.

7. A quantity of oxygen initially occupies a volume of 12 liters at atmospheric pressure when the temperature is 30° C. The gas is compressed into a volume of 4 liters, at which value its gage pressure is 30 lb/in.² Compute the final temperature of the gas.

8. A tank that has a volume of 60 ft³ contains air at 70° F; its gage indicates that the air pressure is 180 lb/in.² If the valve on the tank is opened until the gage reading drops to 140 lb/in.², what is the volume of the air that escapes, reckoned at atmospheric pressure? Assume that all of the air is cooled 10 F° during the process.

9. Express the General Gas Law in terms of the density of the gas instead of the volume it occupies.

10. What mass of oxygen is contained in the tank of Prob. 3, if its volume is 2 ft³?

11. Plot a temperature-volume diagram corresponding to the pressure-volume diagram of Fig. 161.

12. An ideal gas initially occupies a volume of 4 ft³ at an absolute pressure of 100 cm Hg and a temperature of 60° C. The gas is heated in a container of negligible expansion until its absolute pressure is increased by 50%, and is then compressed at constant temperature until its volume is reduced by 50%. Show these processes on a pressure-volume diagram, and determine the final volume, temperature, and absolute pressure of the gas.

13. A certain mass of an ideal gas initially occupies a volume of 5 liters at a temperature of 0° C and at an absolute pressure of 1 atmosphere. This gas is first heated at constant pressure until its absolute temperature is doubled, next heated further at constant volume until its absolute pressure is doubled, and finally is caused to expand at constant temperature until its volume is doubled. Construct a pressure-volume diagram to represent these processes, and determine the final values of the volume, absolute temperature, and absolute pressure of the gas.

14. The rms speed of gas molecules is given by Eq. 99 in terms of the pressure and density of the gas. Apply the General Gas Law and express the rms speed, instead, in terms of the temperature of the gas and such other constants as are needed.

15. Air is pumped into a tank having a volume of 12 ft³ until the pressure gage on the tank reads 50 lb/in.² Assume the temperature to be 32° F and compute the number of pounds of air in the tank.

16. Refer to Prob. 15 and suppose the valve on the tank to be opened until the pressure-gage reading drops to 20 lb/in.² (a) How many pounds of air escape? (b) What volume would this air occupy at atmospheric pressure if no change occurs in temperature?

17. (a) A receptacle that has a volume of 15 liters contains an ideal gas at an absolute pressure of 3×10^6 dynes/cm² and a temperature of 57° C. Calculate the number of moles of gas present. (b) If the receptacle is connected to a completely evacuated chamber having a volume of 10 liters, what is the final temperature and absolute pressure of the gas?

18. A certain mass of oxygen that initially occupies a volume of 6 liters at a pressure of 1 atmosphere and a temperature of 20° C is heated and expands at constant pressure until its volume is doubled. Find (a) the mass of the oxygen, (b) its final temperature, (c) the quantity of heat supplied, (d) the increase of internal energy of the gas, and (e) the work done by the gas in expanding.

19. A mass of air occupying 224 liters at standard temperature and pressure is heated first at constant volume until its absolute pressure is doubled

and then at constant pressure until its volume is doubled. Show these processes on a pressure-volume diagram. Regard the air as an ideal gas and compute (*a*) the quantity of heat supplied in each process, (*b*) the total quantity of heat supplied, (*c*) the increase of internal energy of the air in each process, and (*d*) the total increase of internal energy. Express results in calories.

20. Refer to Prob. 19 and determine (*a*) how much of the energy supplied to the air as heat is available for mechanical work and (*b*) the amount of mechanical work that the air does in expanding. (*c*) From these values, find the amount of mechanical work that is equivalent to 1 cal, as given by these data.

21. Some air initially at an absolute pressure of 300 lb/in.^{2} expands to four times its original volume. Calculate the final value of the absolute pressure of the air on the assumption that the expansion is (*a*) isothermal; (*b*) adiabatic.

22. A cylinder contains 25 liters of air at an absolute pressure of 2 atmospheres. Determine the volume of the air when the absolute pressure is increased to 5 atmospheres, on the assumption that the compression is (*a*) isothermal; (*b*) adiabatic.

23. A quantity of hydrogen occupies a volume of 1 liter at an absolute pressure of 5 atmospheres and a temperature of 400° K. The gas is allowed to expand at constant temperature to a volume of 6 liters. Find (*a*) the mass of the gas, (*b*) its absolute pressure after expansion, and (*c*) the change in its internal energy.

24. In a Diesel engine a quantity of air, initially at atmospheric pressure and at a temperature of 70° F, is compressed to $\frac{1}{15}$ of its original volume. Consider the process to be adiabatic, and determine (*a*) the absolute pressure of the air after compression and (*b*) its final temperature. (*c*) Compute also the increase of internal energy per pound of air due to compression.

25. A room that has a volume of 9000 ft^3 is at a temperature of 70° F. A test is made in the room with a small cooled surface, and dew is observed to form on it when the temperature near by is lowered to 50° F. (*a*) What is the relative humidity in the room? and (*b*) how many pounds of water vapor does it contain?

26. (*a*) Refer to Prob. 25 and find how much additional water vapor would increase the relative humidity in the room by 10%. (*b*) What would be the new value of the dew point?

27. Suppose the temperature of the room specified in Prob. 25 to be raised by 10 F° without changing the amount of water vapor present, and determine the relative humidity under these conditions.

$$\frac{mv^2}{2} = \frac{3rTM}{2}$$

17

WORK AND HEAT

170. Laws of Thermodynamics. The recognition of heat as a form of energy implies that transformations involving heat obey the principle of energy conservation. Thus, heat can be transformed into mechanical work or mechanical work into heat, and, although during such transformations some energy may be wasted—that is, rendered unavailable for useful purposes—none is actually destroyed. This principle is made use of in previous chapters in connection with other transformations.

The science of thermodynamics is based upon two laws, the first of which deals with the quantities involved in energy transformations, and the second with the direction in which the transformations take place.

The *First Law* can be stated as follows: *Whenever heat energy is transformed into any other kind of energy, or vice versa, the quantity of energy that disappears in one form is exactly equivalent to the quantity produced in the other form.* Mathematically, this law is expressed by Eq. 115,

$$Q = (U_2 - U_1) + E$$

where Q is the energy supplied as heat, $U_2 - U_1$ the increase of internal energy, and E the mechanical work done.

The *Second Law* has been expressed in many ways and its full significance involves a thorough study of thermodynamics. For present purposes, the following statement will suffice: *Heat cannot be extracted from a body at low temperature and delivered to another at a higher temperature unless work is done to accomplish this result.* For example, in keeping a room cool by refrigeration, heat is extracted from the room and delivered to a place of higher temperature outside; hence work must be done to effect the transfer. In a steam engine, on the other hand, heat flows naturally from the high-temperature boiler to the low-temperature exhaust and does work in the process.

171. Transformation of Work into Heat. Every observer is familiar with the production of heat from other forms of energy; thus heat is produced from mechanical energy in an automobile brake, from electrical energy in an electric heater, and from chemical energy in many reactions. Heat is also produced as a by-product in most energy transformations, and in many of them a considerable portion of the heat is wasted.

The numerical relation between heat and mechanical energy, which is implied in the first law of thermodynamics, was determined about 1845 by Joule, using several independent methods. In one of these a paddle wheel was placed in a vessel containing a known amount of water and was rotated by means of descending weights. The work done in turning the paddle wheel could be readily measured; this work was converted into heat by friction in stirring the liquid, thereby raising its temperature. A measurement of the energy E supplied to the paddle wheel and the heat Q developed in the water showed that these quantities varied in direct proportion to each other; their ratio

$$J = E/Q \qquad\qquad (122)$$

is known as the *mechanical equivalent of heat*. Joule's original results have been slightly modified in subsequent investigations; the accepted values follow.

RELATION OF HEAT TO MECHANICAL WORK

Quantity of heat	Equivalent amount of mechanical work
1 cal 1 Btu 0.239 cal	4.186×10^7 ergs, or 4.186 joules 778 ft·lb 1 joule

Whenever a specified amount of work is transformed into heat, the quantity of heat produced can be found at once from the values given above. Thus, the number of heat units corresponding to 8.31×10^7 ergs of mechanical work mentioned in § 165 is

$$Q = \frac{E}{J} = \frac{8.31 \times 10^7 \text{ ergs}}{4.186 \times 10^7 \dfrac{\text{ergs}}{\text{cal}}} = 1.985 \text{ cal}$$

Illustrative Problem

The production of heat from some other form of energy is the operating principle of the electric immersion heater, which is placed in water for the purpose of heating it. If a heater rated at 100 watts is immersed in 250 cm^3 of water in a metal container, in what time does the temperature rise from 20 to 45° C? Take the water equivalent of the heater itself plus that of the container to be 18 gm, and neglect heat transferred to the surroundings.

Since 1 watt = 1 joule/sec, § 70, the electrical energy supplied in t sec amounts to $100t$ joules, and this is equivalent to $(100t \text{ joules}) \left(0.239 \dfrac{\text{cal}}{\text{joule}} \right)$

$= 23.9t$ cal. From Eq. 108, $Q = mct$,

$$23.9t \text{ cal} = (250 + 18) \text{ gm} \left(1 \frac{\text{cal}}{\text{gm} \cdot \text{C}°}\right)(45 - 20)\text{C}°$$

From this heat equation, the specified temperature rise takes place in $t = 280$ sec, or $4\frac{2}{3}$ min.

172. Transformation of Heat into Work. The transformation of heat into mechanical work, a process the reverse of that just described, is fundamental to the operation of every heat engine. This type of transformation is usually accomplished by heating a gas and causing it to do mechanical work as it expands.

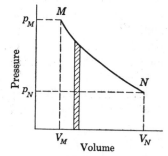

FIG. 168. Area under p-V curve represents work

The external work *done by* a gas in expanding by an amount ΔV is given by Eq. 114 as $E = p \, \Delta V$, *provided the pressure p stays constant during the expansion.* The same expression can be used to show the amount of work *done upon* the gas to compress it a like amount under the same pressure.

Usually, as a gas expands, its pressure becomes lower. Fig. 168 indicates on a pressure-volume diagram the behavior of a gas that expands from M to N, its pressure falling from p_M to p_N as its volume increases from V_M to V_N. The slope of the curve shows that the pressure is not constant and, obviously, the work done during expansion cannot be found directly from Eq. 114. Such an expansion can be considered, however, as composed of a number of smaller expansions, one of these being represented in the figure by the shaded strip, over which the pressure may be assumed to be constant. The work done in the small expansion is the product of this pressure and the increase in volume. But this pressure is represented by the height of the shaded strip, and the increase in volume by its width; hence the work done is measured by the shaded area. Since the entire area beneath the curve can be divided into similar vertical strips, each of which represents the work done during a small expansion, it is apparent that the area under the complete curve—namely, MNV_NV_M—is a measure of the work done during the entire expansion from M to N.

In general, if the expansion or compression of a gas is plotted as a pressure-volume curve, the area under this curve represents either the work done by the gas during expansion or the work done upon it during compression. Such an area can be measured with a planimeter or it can be computed by calculus if the equation of the curve is known. The work thus determined is generally expressed in mechanical units, such as joules or foot·pounds, but can be converted to heat units as shown in § 171.

When a gas is expanded and then compressed so as to return exactly to its initial condition, it is said to have completed a *cycle*. A cycle based on Fig. 168 can be imagined in which the gas is allowed to expand from M to N and then compressed so as to retrace the curve from N to M, the completed cycle representing work done *by* the gas in the first part and work done *on* it in the second. Since the two amounts are equal, the net amount of work done is zero. Naturally, there is no practical objective in carrying a gas through a cycle in which the expansion and compression curves coincide. To accomplish a useful purpose, the gas must do more work in expanding than is done upon it during compression. In the ordinary heat engine the average pressure is higher during expansion than during compression, and the cycle is represented by a loop. The area of this loop is a measure of the mechanical work that the engine delivers in return for the heat supplied.

173. The Ideal Engine; Carnot Cycle. The process of converting heat to work by an engine was idealized by the French physicist, Sadi Carnot (1796–

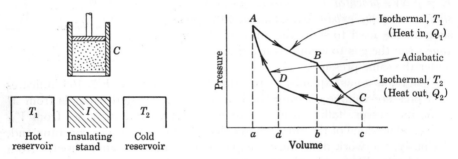

FIG. 169.   Ideal engine shown at left and its Carnot cycle at right

1832). He described an engine which has the greatest efficiency possible for any heat engine working between the same temperature limits. This *ideal engine* and its operating cycle will be explained with the aid of Fig. 169. In this description a gas will be assumed as the working substance, although it appears later that this assumption is not necessary. The engine consists of a cylinder C containing the gas; two reservoirs of heat, one at a high temperature T_1 and the other at a lower temperature T_2; and an insulating stand I. The cylinder walls and piston are supposed to be perfect insulators of heat, § 182, and the bottom, or head, of the cylinder to be a perfect conductor, through which heat flows when the inside and outside temperatures differ by the slightest amount. The engine is assumed to operate without friction.

The cycle starts with the cylinder placed on the hot reservoir and with the piston held near the bottom of the cylinder; the gas in the cylinder is at temperature T_1 and occupies a small volume at high pressure, as indicated by point A on the diagram. Then the pressure applied to the piston is gradually diminished; the gas expands, and a quantity of heat Q_1 flows into it from the hot reservoir, maintaining the temperature constant. The expansion is represented by the isothermal curve AB. Next, the cylinder is transferred to the insulating stand I and the gas is allowed to expand further. This expansion occurs without gain or loss of heat and is represented by the adiabatic curve BC; meanwhile the temperature falls until at point C it reaches the value T_2. When the gas reaches this condition, the cylinder is moved to the cold reservoir, and by gradually increasing the pressure on the piston the gas is compressed. The heat generated, Q_2, flows wastefully into the cold reservoir, and the compression of the gas at the lower temperature T_2 is represented by the isothermal curve CD. At appropriate conditions represented by point D, the cylinder is again moved to the insulating stand and further work is done on the gas, compressing it adiabatically along DA, thereby completing the Carnot cycle.

Since the mechanical work in any process is measured by the area under the corresponding pressure-volume curve, it is seen that during expansion the gas does an amount of work equivalent to the area $ABba + BCcb = ABCca$, and that during compression the work done upon it is given by the smaller area $CDdc + DAad = CDAac$. The gas, therefore, does more work than is done upon it, and the net work done by the gas during the cycle amounts to $ABCca - CDAac = ABCD$, which is the area of the closed loop.

During a cycle, the ideal engine receives an amount of energy Q_1 from the hot reservoir in the form of heat, of which an amount Q_2 is transferred to the cold reservoir, and the balance is transformed into mechanical work; the latter is represented by $ABCD$ in mechanical units or $(ABCD)/J$ in heat units. Since friction is assumed absent, the latter amount represents the mechanical output of the engine, which is consequently $(ABCD)/J$ or $Q_1 - Q_2$ in heat units. The efficiency of an engine is defined as the ratio of the mechanical work done by the engine to the energy supplied as heat; for the ideal engine this becomes

$$\text{Efficiency} = \frac{Q_1 - Q_2}{Q_1} \tag{123}$$

Further analysis, not included in this textbook, shows that the efficiency of the ideal engine is independent of the working substance used.

In the ideal engine, work is done by the gas during expansion, and a smaller amount of work is done upon it during compression. It would be possible, theoretically, to store energy during the expansion portion of the cycle and to use part of this energy for compressing the gas during the compression portion. In the actual engine this result is accomplished by using a flywheel. The ideal engine is to be considered a theoretical ideal to which the actual engine should approach as closely as possible.

Throughout the Carnot cycle the gas does not depart appreciably from a state of equilibrium. The slightest increase of external pressure during the expansion *AB* would compress the gas and cause heat to be delivered to the hot reservoir, and the slightest reduction of pressure during the compression *CD* would allow the gas to expand, removing heat from the cold reservoir. It would be possible, therefore, by slight changes of pressure during the cycle, to operate the engine in the reverse manner, abstracting heat from the cold reservoir and delivering heat to the hot reservoir. Under such conditions there would be a net amount of work done *on* the gas during the cycle rather than done *by* it. A cycle that can be reversed in this manner is called a *reversible cycle*. If such a cycle is reversed at any point and returned to its initial state, everything connected with the process is restored exactly to its original condition. In practice, this ideal is never attained, one reason being that the ever-present friction causes some dissipation of energy. Actual cycles are thus *irreversible cycles*.

174. Thermodynamic Temperature Scale. The fact that the efficiency of an ideal engine is independent of the working substance was utilized by

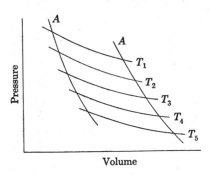

Lord Kelvin to establish a theoretical temperature scale that would not depend upon the physical properties of any particular material. He envisioned a series of one hundred ideal engines with cycles as represented in Fig. 170. All operate between the same pair of adiabatic curves *AA* and are so arranged that the first receives heat at the temperature of boiling water (100° C), while the last releases heat at the temperature of melting ice (0° C), each intermediate engine having as its hot reservoir the cold reservoir of the one preceding.

FIG. 170. A few of the Carnot cycles used in establishing thermodynamic temperature scale

Specifically, the first engine of the series takes in a quantity of heat Q_1 at temperature T_1 from its hot reservoir and rejects a smaller quantity of heat Q_2 at temperature T_2 to its cold reservoir; this quantity of heat, Q_2, serves as the heat taken in at temperature T_2 by the second engine, which rejects a still smaller quantity of heat Q_3 at temperature T_3, and so on. The series of engines is imagined to be continued to lower and lower cold-reservoir temperatures, until finally a point is reached where the last engine rejects no heat to its cold reservoir. The temperature of this reservoir is taken as zero on the temperature scale. It is further assumed that the mechanical output of each engine is the same, which means that each of the Carnot cycle loops has the same area, and also means that $Q_1 - Q_2 = Q_2 - Q_3 = Q_3 - Q_4 = \cdots$.

The thermodynamic temperature scale is now established by assuming that the temperature differences $T_1 - T_2$, $T_2 - T_3$, $T_3 - T_4$, $\cdots$, are all equal. Since both T and Q start from zero and increase by equal increments, it follows that the ratio T/Q is constant; that is

$$\frac{T_1}{Q_1} = \frac{T_2}{Q_2} = \frac{T_3}{Q_3} = \cdots \tag{124}$$

The temperature scale constructed in this manner is not dependent upon the uniformity of expansion of some thermometric substance but is based solely on thermodynamic principles; it is called the *absolute* or *thermodynamic* scale. Absolute zero on this scale is that cold-reservoir temperature at which the ideal engine would release no heat. The thermodynamic scale is followed very closely by the gas thermometer and, for engineering purposes, may be considered identical with the Kelvin absolute scale as described in § 139. Absolute zero of temperature is $-273.16°$ C or $-459.69°$ F.

175. Efficiency of the Ideal Engine. The efficiency of the Carnot engine, which was shown in § 173 to be $(Q_1 - Q_2)/Q_1$, can be expressed in terms of temperatures by making use of the thermodynamic temperature scale as defined by Eq. 124. From this proportionality, it follows that

$$\text{Carnot efficiency} = \frac{T_1 - T_2}{T_1} \tag{125}$$

where T_1 and T_2 are the respective *absolute* temperatures of the working substance as received and as released by the engine. This equation shows that the efficiency can be increased by raising the temperature at which the working substance is received or lowering the temperature at which it is exhausted. Since the efficiency depends only upon these temperatures, all ideal engines operating between the same temperature limits have the same efficiency.

Illustrative Problem

Determine the efficiency of an ideal engine supplied with saturated steam at an absolute pressure of 100 lb/in.^{2} and exhausting into the atmosphere.

The steam table in § 154 gives the supply and exhaust temperatures as 327.8 and 212° F; hence the temperature values in Eq. 125 are respectively $T_1 = 327.8 + 460 = 787.8$ and $T_2 = 212 + 460 = 672°$K. Thus, even an ideal engine operating between these temperatures has an efficiency

of only $\dfrac{787.8 - 672}{787.8} = 0.147$, or 14.7%.

176. Reciprocating Engines. The basic principles of thermodynamics will now be applied to the operation of typical reciprocating engines: the steam engine, which was the original prime mover, and two types of internal-combustion engine that are widely used today. In these engines, a piston moves back and forth within a closed cylinder, and this motion, by means of a connecting rod, rotates the crankshaft. A flywheel having a large moment of inertia is mounted on this shaft and stores up energy during each working stroke to keep the engine and its load going until the next one.

The Steam Engine. A typical steam engine, using saturated steam as the working substance, will be considered in connection with its theoretical cycle, as shown in Fig. 171. The loop *ABCD* indicates the pressure-volume relations of the steam in the cylinder between the piston and either cylinder head. At the beginning of the cycle, *A*, steam from a boiler is admitted to one end of the cylinder, the other being open to the exhaust. The piston is forced forward, while the pressure remains the same as that of the boiler, as shown by the horizontal line *AB*. At point *B*, the supply of steam is cut off, but that within the cylinder still pushes the piston forward. As the volume increases, the vapor is no longer saturated

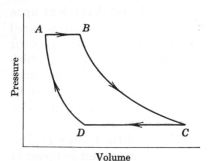

FIG. 171. Theoretical steam-engine cycle

and behaves more like an ideal gas, the pressure falling off until it reaches the pressure of the exhaust at the end of the forward stroke, *C*. The process *BC* is fairly rapid and in the theoretical cycle is represented as an adiabatic expansion.

On the return stroke, while a new supply of steam is admitted to the other end of the cylinder, the steam previously considered is exhausted at constant low pressure, as shown by the line *CD*. Near the end of the return stroke, at *D*, the exhaust valve is closed, and the steam still remaining is compressed adiabatically along *DA*, completing the cycle. Because both ends of the cylinder are used simultaneously, each stroke is a working stroke, and each corresponds to one-half revolution of the driving shaft.

Internal Combustion Engines. In the internal combustion engine, fuel is burned directly in the cylinder, and its chemical energy is in part converted to kinetic energy of the moving piston.

This type of engine, as presently used for automobile propulsion, has six or eight water-cooled cylinders, usually arranged vertically with the pistons at the bottom driving the crankshaft below. The fuel used is gasoline, which is atomized and mixed with air in a carburetor to form an explosive mixture. Mechanically operated valves control the admission of fuel to the cylinder and the exhaust of the burned gases. The first engine of this type was built by the German technician Nikolaus A. Otto (1832–1891), and the cycle is known as the *Otto* cycle.

The Otto cycle commonly consists of four strokes, as represented for the theoretical cycle in Fig. 172. At point *A*, the piston is starting downward on the first stroke (1); the inlet valve is open and fresh fuel is drawn in from the carburetor. When the piston reaches the bottom of its stroke at *B* and starts up, the inlet valve closes, and the piston compresses the mixture in the cylinder. In the theoretical cycle, this process is shown as an adiabatic compression BC. As the piston reaches the end of its upward stroke (2), the compressed mixture is exploded by an electric spark at the points of a spark plug. The extremely rapid combustion is represented from C to D as occurring at constant volume, with a large increase in pressure.

The explosion drives the piston down-ward during the next, or working, stroke (3), shown as an adiabatic ex-pansion DE. At point E the exhaust valve opens, lowering the pressure to that of the exhaust at F; on the return upward stroke (4) of the piston, FA (coincident with AB), the exhaust valve is open and the piston forces out the burned gases, leaving the cylinder ready for a new cycle. At each explosion, the heat of combustion, § 157, of the gasoline consumed is liberated, and this energy is partially converted to mechanical work. The cycle thus con-

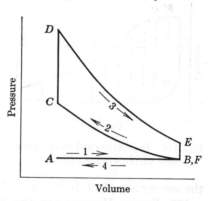

FIG. 172.   Theoretical cycle of Otto engine

sists of four strokes, one of which is a working stroke, and each stroke corre-sponds to one-half revolution of the crankshaft.

The *Diesel* engine, invented by the German engineer Rudolph Diesel (1858–1913), uses fuel oil and no spark plugs. This engine is largely used for ships and locomotives and for stationary service. Air is drawn into the cylinder and is highly compressed, thus raising it to a high temperature. Fuel oil under still higher pressure is then sprayed into the cylinder and ig-nites spontaneously as it mixes with the hot compressed air. Burning takes place without explosion, and the fuel supply is so regulated that the pressure re-mains almost constant during combus-tion. The cycle usually consists of four strokes (1–4), as in that of the gasoline engine, and is similarly lettered. The theoretical cycle, Fig. 173, is similar to the Otto cycle, but the burning of the fuel, represented by CD, occurs at con-stant pressure. One stroke out of four is a working stroke, and each stroke cor-responds to one-half revolution of the crankshaft.

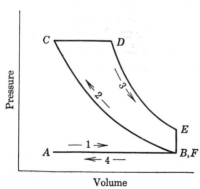

FIG. 173.   Theoretical cycle of Diesel engine

Actual engine cycles conform basically, although not exactly, to the theoretical cycles just described. A diagram of an actual cycle can be obtained by an *indicator*. This instrument is piped to the cylinder like a pressure gage and has a tracing point that moves up and down as the pressure changes. The point rests against a card which follows the forward and backward motion of the piston to a reduced scale. The vertical motion of the tracing point combined with the horizontal motion of the card results in the pressure-volume diagram of the cycle. Fig. 174 is a typical indicator diagram for a steam engine; the student should correlate the different portions of the diagram with the various steps of the cycle as described earlier in this section, and should also note the similarity between this diagram and the theoretical cycle in Fig. 171. As before, the area of the indicator card represents that portion of the energy supplied during a cycle that is available for mechanical work.

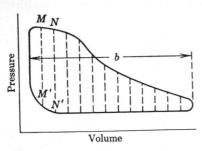

Fig. 174. Indicator card shows pressure within engine cylinder

177. Engine Horsepower and Efficiency. The horsepower of an engine can be obtained quite easily from its indicator card. Since the area of any plane figure is the product of its average height and its base, for an indicator diagram such as shown in Fig. 174 the area is the average of all the ordinates MM', NN', $\cdots$, multiplied by the base b. The average ordinate is known as the *mean effective pressure*, and represents the average difference in pressure within the cylinder on opposite sides of the piston; this pressure value will be designated as P. The base b is a measure of the volume swept out by the piston during one stroke; that is, $b \propto LA$, where L is the length of stroke and A the area of the piston. When P is expressed in pounds per square inch, L in feet, and A in square inches, the product PLA gives the work in foot·pounds for each working stroke. If there are N working strokes per minute, the work done per minute is N times PLA. Thus, the horsepower of the engine as represented by the indicator card, known as the *indicated* horsepower (ihp), is

$$\text{ihp} = \frac{PLAN}{33,000} \tag{126}$$

In practical testing, the mean effective pressure is calculated from the indicator card, and the remaining quantities are obtained by direct measurement.

The actual engine may be regarded as a heat engine combined with a mechanical engine. As a heat engine, the input is the heat absorbed from the source, which per unit time can be expressed in horsepower, and the output is the indicated horsepower. The ratio of this output to input is known as the *indicated thermal efficiency*, that is,

$$\text{Indicated thermal efficiency} = \frac{\text{indicated horsepower}}{\text{horsepower rate of absorbing heat}}$$

Because of inherent heat losses, this efficiency is less than that of an ideal engine operating over the same temperature range.

Considered as a mechanical device, the engine has for its input the indicated horsepower, and for its output the horsepower as measured by a brake, called the brake horsepower (bhp). Hence,

$$\text{Mechanical efficiency} = \frac{\text{brake horsepower}}{\text{indicated horsepower}}$$

The overall efficiency is the product of the indicated thermal efficiency and the mechanical efficiency.

For the purpose of assigning horsepower ratings to automobile engines, standard conditions have been adopted that are equivalent to a mean effective pressure of 67.2 lb/in.² and an average piston speed of 1000 ft/min. In the automobile engine the piston travels $4L$ ft for each working stroke; consequently, $4LN = 1000$. From these values, the rated horsepower per cylinder is found from Eq. 126 to be

$$\text{hp} = \frac{PLAN}{33,000} = \frac{67.2\left(\dfrac{1000}{4}\right)\left(\dfrac{\pi d^2}{4}\right)}{33,000} = \frac{d^2}{2.5}$$

where d is the diameter of the piston in inches. For an automobile engine having C cylinders, the rating is

$$\text{hp} = \frac{d^2 C}{2.5}$$

178. The Steam Turbine. The steam turbine utilizes the kinetic energy of a jet of steam, rather than the expansion of a vapor as in the cylinder of a reciprocating engine. High-speed jets are formed by passing the steam through a set of fixed nozzles; these jets impinge against a series of curved vanes or blades evenly spaced around the rim of a rotary disk and set the disk into rapid motion. Typical turbine construction is shown in Fig. 175.

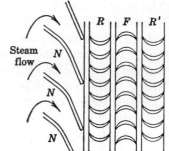

FIG. 175. Arrangement of blades in a turbine. (Optical illusion makes vertical lines appear inclined.)

The energy of the steam jets cannot be absorbed by a single row of blades without involving excessive speeds. In the arrangement shown, the steam issues from the fixed nozzles NN and impinges upon one row of rotating blades R, then it strikes a corresponding row of fixed blades F and is redirected against a second row of rotating blades R' mounted on the same rotor. In contrast, a turbine having several *stages* has a rotor consisting of a number of disks with blades, mounted on the same shaft, and the disks are separated by stationary diaphragms so that each disk is housed in a separate compartment within the casing.

The theoretical output developed by a turbine equals the reduction in kinetic energy of the steam in passing through the machine. If in t sec, W lb of steam are supplied to the blades at a speed of v_1 ft/sec and are discharged at a speed of v_2 ft/sec, then the reduction in energy, by Eq. 58, is $\dfrac{Wv_1^2}{2g} - \dfrac{Wv_2^2}{2g}$ ft·lb, and this represents the theoretical energy output of the turbine. The corresponding *power output* in horsepower is consequently

$$\text{hp} = \frac{W}{2gt} \frac{(v_1^2 - v_2^2)}{550}$$

The absence of reciprocating parts makes the vibration in the turbine less than in the steam engine, and also permits higher speeds, thereby reducing the size of the machine for a given output.

179. The Turbojet. The engine of a jet airplane is a gas-turbine system that expels a stream of exhaust gas at high velocity from the rear of the airplane, this jet being directed backward so as to drive the airplane forward by the reaction. Air is rammed into the front of the engine by the forward motion of the airplane, and is compressed adiabatically to a pressure of three to six atmospheres by a rotary compressor driven by the turbine. The air then passes to a combustion chamber, where fuel oil is sprayed into it and ignited, raising its temperature to some 1400° F and increasing its volume, at constant pressure, in direct proportion to the absolute temperature. This greatly increased volume of air, mixed with the products of combustion, is delivered to the gas turbine and expelled through a discharge nozzle at the rear. Here the gases expand adiabatically and their internal energy is largely converted into kinetic energy of the issuing jet.

In this process the air taken in at the front of the engine is discharged from the rear with greatly increased velocity; the force required to produce this velocity change equals the force of reaction. Thus, if in a time t a weight W of air has its velocity relative to the airplane raised from v_1 at the front to v_2 at the mouth of the exhaust nozzle, the force of reaction is fundamentally

$$F = \frac{W}{gt} (v_2 - v_1)$$

Values of this force up to 10,000 lb are reported for powerful turbojet aircraft.

180. Refrigeration. The manufacture of ice, the cooling of rooms, and the preservation of food in cold-storage spaces are processes that require the production of low temperatures. The articles under refrigeration must give off heat to surroundings which are at higher temperatures.

The evaporation of a liquid and the expansion of a gas or vapor are processes in which heat is absorbed. These actions can be further illustrated in the making of carbon-dioxide snow, by allowing some liquid carbon dioxide at the pressure of its saturated vapor to escape from the containing

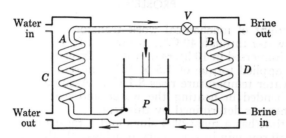

Fig. 176. Compression system of refrigeration

cylinder through a small opening into the atmosphere. The resulting evaporation and expansion take sufficient heat from the issuing stream to cause the CO_2 to solidify as snow; at atmospheric pressure its temperature is $-78°C$.

In the commercial manufacture of ice, mentioned in § 164, anhydrous ammonia circulates continuously around a closed system, such as represented in Fig. 176. The vapor is compressed in a compressor cylinder P and passes through the coils of a condenser C. In these coils, cooled by water, the vapor liquefies and the liquid flows to an expansion valve A at the freezing tank D. Here the liquid vaporizes into an evaporator or brine coil B and is thereafter drawn into the compressor to repeat the cycle. The evaporation and expansion that occur at the expansion valve absorb heat from the brine within the freezing tank, and lower its temperature. Cans filled with water are placed in the brine tank and their contents are frozen. The system may be regarded as a reversed heat engine, operating as described at the end of § 173. The working substance, or refrigerant, (ammonia vapor) absorbs heat from the cold reservoir (freezing tank); receives additional energy as heat of compression (namely, the energy supplied to drive the compressor); and gives off the sum of these heat quantities to the hot reservoir (condenser). The most effective refrigeration system is one that absorbs the most heat from the cold reservoir for a given amount of energy supplied to the compressor; the ratio of the heat absorbed to the energy supplied, both in the same unit, is called the *coefficient of performance* of the system.

The electric refrigerator for household use operates as a compression system, essentially like the ice machine of Fig. 176, but with certain modifications to adapt it to domestic use. Sulfur dioxide and ethyl chloride are commonly used as the refrigerants; the evaporator coils are located in the food compartment, and the condenser coils, which are air cooled, are outside. The compressor is driven by an electric motor, arranged with a thermostatic switch to start and stop as needed.

PROBLEMS

1. What amount of mechanical work transformed into heat would (*a*) raise 1 liter of water through 40 C°? (*b*) raise 1 ft^3 of water through 60 F°?

2. A paddle immersed in 10 liters of water is driven at a speed of 2 rev/sec by a constant applied torque of 1.5×10^8 dyne·cm. In a test of 30-min duration the water temperature rises 8.1 C°. Assume that all the energy supplied is expended in heating the water and calculate the mechanical equivalent of heat as determined by this test.

3. A wheel that has a mass of 4 slugs and a radius of gyration of 1.5 ft is turning at 450 rev/min in stationary bearings. If the wheel is brought to rest by a brake, how much heat is produced by this action?

4. An object is polished by pressing it against the rim of a polishing wheel 6 in. in diameter that is turning at 1800 rev/min. Assume the force of friction between the object and wheel to be 0.8 lb, and compute the quantity of heat developed in 1 min.

5. How long does it take a 1000-watt steam iron to convert 325 cm^3 of water at 45° C to steam at 100° C?

6. A bullet that weighs 100 grains (7000 grains = 1 lb) leaves the muzzle of a rifle at a speed of 2900 ft/sec, and in its passage through air slows down to 2000 ft/sec while covering its first 300 yd. Assume the deceleration to be constant, and determine the average rate at which heat is produced by friction during this motion. Express the result in British thermal units per second.

7. Why should the temperature of a raindrop rise while the drop falls at constant speed through air of constant temperature? If a drop falls in this manner from a height of 500 m, how much does its temperature rise if no heat is transmitted to the air?

8. A quantity of gas expands isothermally, doing 6000 ft·lb of work, and then adiabatically, doing an additional 5000 ft·lb of work. For each expansion, compute (*a*) the quantity of heat supplied and (*b*) the change of internal energy of the gas.

9. A piston that weighs 120 lb and has a circular cross-section of 80 in.^{2} is placed in the top of a vertical cylinder and released, compressing the air beneath it to a volume of 400 in.^{3} at a temperature of 100° F. If the air is then heated to 600° F, how much work does it do in expanding?

10. Verify the result of the preceding problem by computing the quantity of heat supplied to the gas and also the amount by which its internal energy is increased, during the expansion described.

11. A steam engine is supplied with saturated steam at an absolute pressure of 300 lb/in.^{2} and exhausts into the air at atmospheric pressure. Determine the maximum theoretical efficiency of the engine.

12. An ideal engine operating on a Carnot cycle has an efficiency of 15% when the hot reservoir is at 700° K. To what value should this temperature be raised in order to increase the efficiency of the engine to 20%?

13. An ideal engine operates at 480 cycles/min on a Carnot cycle with an efficiency of 25%. The engine receives 3.5 Btu/cycle from the hot reservoir at a temperature of 235° F. Find (a) the temperature of the cold reservoir, (b) the quantity of heat discharged to it per cycle, and (c) the theoretical horsepower output of the engine.

14. In a pressure-volume diagram of a Carnot cycle, as in Fig. 169, the areas under the curves, expressed in work units, are as follows: under AB 1500 ft·lb, under CD 1200 ft·lb, and under BC and DA 1100 ft·lb each. Calculate (a) the heat input per cycle, (b) the mechanical output per cycle, and (c) the efficiency of an ideal engine operating on this cycle.

15. In a particular Carnot cycle, the isothermal expansion of the gas occurs at 600° K and the isothermal compression at 450° K. If 500 cal of heat are supplied to the gas during the isothermal expansion, (a) how much mechanical work does the gas perform during the isothermal expansion? (b) how much heat does the gas reject during the isothermal compression? (c) how much mechanical work is done upon the gas during the isothermal compression? and (d) what is the efficiency of the engine operating on the cycle?

16. A reciprocating steam engine has a piston with an area of 30 in.² and a stroke of 8 in.; it operates at 400 rev/min with a mean effective pressure of 80 lb/in.² Find (a) the amount of work performed per stroke and (b) the indicated horsepower of the engine.

17. An automobile having 8 cylinders of $3\frac{1}{2}$-in. bore running at an average speed of 45 mi/hr goes 13 mi on 1 gal of gasoline. The gasoline has a specific gravity of 0.68 and a heat of combustion of 20,250 Btu/lb. If the indicated thermal efficiency is measured to be 25%, what is the indicated horsepower of the engine, and how does it compare with the rated horsepower?

18. In a mechanical refrigeration system, heat is taken from a region of low temperature at the rate of 1400 Btu/min; mechanical energy is added at a constant rate of 4 hp in driving a compressor, and the total energy is discharged as heat to a region of high temperature. For the system described, calculate (a) the rate at which heat is delivered to the high-temperature region and (b) the coefficient of performance of the system.

19. What is the hourly cost of fuel oil for heating a house that requires an average of 75,000 Btu/hr in cold weather? For the grade of oil used, take the specific gravity as 0.94, the heat of combustion as 19,000 Btu/lb, and the cost as 14.6 cents/gal.

20. A refrigeration system absorbs heat from the cold reservoir at the rate of 6000 Btu/hr and discharges heat to the hot reservoir at the rate of 7000 Btu/hr. Compute the coefficient of performance of the system and the horsepower developed by the compressor.

21. A "ton of refrigeration" is usually considered as the cooling produced by the melting of ice at the rate of 1 ton/day of 24 hr. Express this quantity in British thermal units per hour.

18

TRANSFER OF HEAT

181. Methods of Heat Transfer. Heat energy is transmitted from one place to another in several ways. One process, called *conduction*, can be explained by considering a metal rod, one end of which is in a hot furnace. The molecules of the rod at that end are in violent agitation, and in jostling their neighbors, they set them into more rapid motion; this action continues throughout the rod. A more complete explanation of the process of conduction would involve electronic motion. Good conductors of heat are also good conductors of electricity, and since the free electrons present in such conductors play an important part in the conduction of electricity, they are probably instrumental in heat conduction as well.

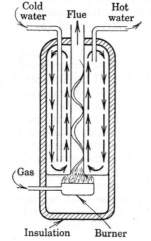

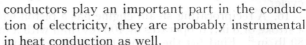

FIG. 177. Convection currents in water heater

Another way of transmitting heat is by *convection*. This is the principal way that heat is transferred through liquids and gases, for these mediums are poor heat conductors. In the process of convection, the heated fluid expands and rises, and cooler fluid takes its place. Water in a kettle on the kitchen stove is heated by convection, as is also the air in a room from a hot stove. The gas-operated water heater, Fig. 177, consists of an insulated tank of water surrounding a central flue through which the hot gases from the burner pass. The water around the hot flue is heated and expands, thereby reducing its density; and the pressure (Eq. 86) near the base of this hot-water zone is less than that due to the surrounding cold water. Therefore, the cold water forces the hot water up and flows in to take its place. In this way convection currents are set up, as indicated by the arrows in the figure, and the water becomes heated throughout the tank.

The transfer of heat by radiant energy is called *radiation*. The process involves the conversion of internal energy into radiant form at the heater, and the reversion of radiant energy into internal energy wherever the radiation is absorbed. The electric radiator operates on this principle. This appliance has a heating element mounted at the focus of a parabolic reflector;

when heated by an electric current, the element emits not only "light waves" that stimulate the eye, but also "heat waves" that do not. When a body absorbs waves of either kind its internal energy is increased, producing the various effects stated in Chap. 14. The purpose of the reflector is to concentrate the heat waves into a beam, just as a searchlight reflector does with light waves.

The process of heating a house through the use of steam radiators involves boiling water over a flame in the cellar and condensing the resulting steam in the rooms above. When a pound of water is boiled at the normal boiling point, it absorbs 970 Btu from the flame, § 154, and changes to steam at atmospheric pressure; and when that pound of steam is condensed within the radiators of the rooms, its heat of vaporization is given off and heats the neighboring air. This method of *evaporation and condensation* is also utilized in mechanical refrigeration, § 180; the refrigerant absorbs heat from the food compartment by evaporating at relatively low pressure, and delivers heat to the surroundings by condensing at higher pressures.

182. Conduction. Substances differ widely in their ability to conduct heat from one point to another; metals are relatively good conductors, while porous substances in which air is entrapped are poor conductors or good insulators. For a given material, the quantity of heat conducted per unit time along a specimen of uniform cross-section depends upon the sectional area and also upon the linear temperature distribution or gradient. The *temperature gradient* is the space rate of temperature change along the line of heat flow, and is denoted by G. If the sectional area is A, the rate of heat conduction is

$$q = kGA \qquad (127)$$

where the proportionality constant k is called the *thermal conductivity* of the substance. For steady heat flow through a uniform material of constant area, q, k, and A are constants, and G can be expressed as

$$G = \frac{t_1 - t_2}{s}$$

where $t_1 - t_2$ is the steady temperature difference over a distance s along the line of heat flow.

When the rate of heat flow q is stated in cal/sec, the temperature gradient G in C°/cm, and the sectional area A in cm², the corresponding unit for conductivity is the cal/(sec·cm·C°). With these units, k is the number of calories of heat conducted per sec through a sample of the material 1 cm² in cross-section and 1 cm long when the opposite ends are maintained at a temperature difference of 1 C°.

When heat flows through different mediums one after the other, without any leakage to or from the surroundings, the rate of heat flow is the same in each medium, although the temperature gradients are different.

Many practical calculations of heat conduction deal with large thin sheets, such as those used for insulation in the walls of frame buildings. Here the temperature gradient G is usually expressed in F°/in., the area A in ft^2, and the rate of heat transfer q in Btu/hr; with these units the conductivity k is the number of Btu conducted per hr through a 1-ft^2 section of the material 1 in. in thickness when the opposite faces are kept at a temperature difference of 1 F°. Because both the inch and the foot are used in such a calculation, the student is cautioned to include the units throughout and to use appropriate conversion factors to obtain the result sought. Average thermal conductivities of a number of substances at ordinary temperatures are listed below in metric and British units.

THERMAL CONDUCTIVITES (k)

Substance	$\dfrac{\text{Cal}}{\text{sec} \cdot \text{cm} \cdot \text{C}°}$	$\dfrac{\text{Btu} \cdot \text{in.}}{\text{hr} \cdot \text{ft} \cdot \text{F}°}$
Air.................	0.000054	0.16
Aluminum...........	0.49	1400
Brass...............	0.26	750
Cement.............	0.0007	2.1
Copper.............	0.91	2600
Cork...............	0.0001	0.29
Cotton.............	0.0005	1.5
Glass..............	0.002	5.8
Ice................	0.005	15
Iron...............	0.15	430
Silver.............	0.99	2900
Slate..............	0.005	15
Water..............	0.0015	4.3

To measure the thermal conductivity of a substance, the rate at which heat flows through a given cross-section of it under a known temperature gradient is observed. In testing metals, since their conductivity is relatively high, satisfactory precision can be attained by using specimens in the form of rods. In the usual method, the rod under test is fitted with a steam jacket at one end and with a coil of several turns of small tubing wound around the other end. Between these parts are placed two thermometers in good thermal contact with the rod and located a known distance apart. Thermometers are also used to measure the temperature of water entering and leaving the coil of tubing. The entire rod is surrounded by suitable insulation to reduce emission of heat from its surface. Steam is passed through the jacket and, when all four thermometers have attained steady readings, the test may be conducted, for then the heat supplied to the rod is conducted steadily along its length and transferred to the water.

Illustrative Problem

To determine the thermal conductivity of brass by the method described, a rod of this material 7.5 cm^2 in cross-section is fitted with thermal contacts 10 cm apart. Heat is applied to one end of the rod, and after steady conditions are reached, it is found that at the other end, 293 gm of water are heated through 4 C° in 5 min, the temperatures at the thermal contacts remaining at 60 and 80° C throughout the test.

The rate of heat flow in the rod is $q = \dfrac{(293)(4)}{(5)(60)} = 3.91$ cal/sec, and the temperature gradient along it is $G = \dfrac{80 - 60}{10} = 2.00$ C°/cm. Therefore the thermal conductivity of the rod material is

$$k = \frac{q}{GA} = \frac{3.91\ \dfrac{\text{cal}}{\text{sec}}}{\left(2.00\ \dfrac{\text{C}°}{\text{cm}}\right)(7.50\ \text{cm}^2)} = 0.261\ \frac{\text{cal}}{\text{sec}\cdot\text{cm}\cdot\text{C}°}$$

In measuring the thermal conductivities of poor heat conductors, accuracy requires that specimens in the form of sheets be used, so that the heat path is short and of large sectional area, but the test method is based on the same principle as for good conductors. Air in finely divided form serves as a good insulating substance because its thermal conductivity is very low and because circulating currents are largely eliminated. Textiles such as wool and felt are good heat insulators primarily because of the air entrapped in them. Sawdust, glass wool, loose asbestos, and similar materials are used as insulators in the walls of refrigerators, electric water heaters, frame buildings, and ice houses for the same reason.

183. Heat Conduction Through Cylindrical Walls. The escape of heat from bare steam pipes or through insulating coverings around them, and the heat transfer through boiler tubes or refrigerator piping, all illustrate the conduction of heat radially through the wall of a hollow cylinder. The wall can be imagined to consist of a series of telescoping tubes, so that the heat flow takes place

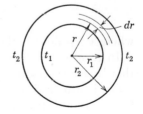

FIG. 178. For calculating heat conduction through cylindrical walls

through infinitesimal layers of slightly varying area. Consequently the inner and outer areas of any one layer may be considered the same, and the rate of heat conduction through it evaluated as in the preceding section.

A pipe, shown in section in Fig. 178, carries steam at a temperature t_1, the surrounding temperature being t_2. If dt represents the temperature difference over an annular element of radius r and infinitesimal thickness dr, then the gradient at the elementary tube becomes $G = -\dfrac{dt}{dr}$, the minus sign being introduced because an increase in the radius corresponds to a decrease in temperature. The rate of heat conduction through the element is obtained from Eq. 127 as

$$q = -k \frac{dt}{dr} A$$

where k is the thermal conductivity of the wall material and A is the area normal to the flow of heat, which for a cylinder of length l is $2\pi rl$. The temperature difference over the element is consequently

$$dt = -\frac{q\,dr}{2\pi rlk}$$

By integration, the temperature differences over all the elements of the pipe from the inner radius r_1 to the outer radius r_2 are summed up and give the temperature difference between the steam and the surroundings as

$$\int_{t=t_1}^{t=t_2} dt = -\frac{q}{2\pi lk} \int_{r=r_1}^{r=r_2} \frac{dr}{r}$$

whence

$$t_2 - t_1 = -\frac{q}{2\pi lk} \log_\epsilon \frac{r_2}{r_1}$$

It follows that the heat conducted through the wall per unit time is

$$q = \frac{2\pi lk(t_1 - t_2)}{\log_\epsilon (r_2/r_1)}$$

where ϵ (epsilon) is the base of natural logarithms.

In transferring heat through walls by conduction and transferring it farther by convection through gases or liquids in contact with the walls, cognizance is usually taken of thin films of these mediums that cling to the surfaces. Heat is transferred through these films principally by conduction, and since they have low conductivities, the temperature gradient over them is relatively large. The effects of such films can be allowed for through experimentally determined coefficients, but no corrections for them will be made in the problems on conduction in this textbook.

184. Convection. The transfer of heat by convection refers to the movement of warmed fluids, and is brought about by changes of density that accompany changes of temperature. This process is important in heating systems and ventilation. Thus, rooms are heated largely by convection; heating units are placed at certain points, and the air heated by these units is thereby set into circulation in the room. The so-called radiator (steam or hot-water) does transfer some heat by radiation, but it transfers far more by convection. The draft in a stove or in a chimney is produced by convection; within a chimney the pressure at the bottom due to the column of heated gas is less than that due to the surrounding cold air; consequently, the hot gases are forced up and out by the denser cold air.

The earth's surface is heated by radiation from the sun, and in turn heats the air in contact with it by conduction. As a result of continued heating, convection currents occur on a large scale; the air near the equator is pushed away from the earth's surface by cooler air that rushes in from the tropical belts, flowing from the north in northern latitudes and from the south in southern latitudes, and convection currents are set up that blow in these directions for long periods. These currents that flow into the equatorial belt are called the trade winds. Because of the rotation of the earth, they are deflected somewhat from the directions stated.

185. Radiation. Energy reaches the earth from the sun by radiation, that is, by waves transmitted through the intervening space. In full sunlight, the energy received above the earth's atmosphere is about 2.0 cal/min on a surface 1 cm square held perpendicular to the sun's rays; about one-third of this amount is absorbed in passing through the atmosphere. These waves are electromagnetic waves and pass through the vacuum which exists over most of the distance from sun to earth; they are similar to light and electric waves, §§ 310 and 333. Radiation impinging on a body may be reflected from it, transmitted through it, or absorbed by it. Substances that absorb radiation become heated, so the presumption is that the molecular and electronic motions within these substances are augmented by the waves.

All bodies radiate energy, whether they are hot or cold; the hotter a body, the greater is its radiation. Further, all bodies receive radiation from others. This exchange of radiant energy goes on continuously. Accordingly, when a body remains at constant temperature it has not stopped radiating, but is receiving energy at the same rate that it gives off energy by radiation. A body that is a good radiator of energy is also a good absorber of energy. A black rough surface, such as that provided by a coating of lampblack, is an excellent radiator (as well as an excellent absorber) of radiant energy; a highly polished surface has opposite characteristics.

186. Laws of Radiation. The quantitative relations that have been discovered concerning the transmission of energy by radiation are expressed in a number of laws. Some of these are discussed in this section; others are considered later in the chapter.

Stefan-Boltzmann Law. The manner in which the temperature of a source affects the radiation proceeding from it was stated empirically by the Austrian physicist Josef Stefan (1835–1893) and later deduced theoretically by his countryman, Ludwig Boltzmann (1844–1906). The relationship which they developed applies to an idealized body called a "black body," that is, a body that would absorb all of the radiant energy falling upon it and reflect none. Contrary to expectation, a black body is not one with a sooty surface, but rather an enclosure from which no energy can escape once it has been received. Such a body is closely approximated by a hollow object in which there is a small opening. Radiation entering this opening undergoes repeated reflection inside of the enclosure and very little escapes. When such a body is heated and used as a source the radiation emitted from the interior is termed "black-body" radiation.

It is found that the rate at which energy is radiated from a black body is constant if the temperature of that body is steady; this rate of emission is called *radiant flux*. The energy density, called *radiant flux density*, is the amount of flux per unit area of surface perpendicular to the flux. Both terms apply to a source emitting radiation or to a surface receiving it.

For a radiating source, the value of the flux density depends principally upon the temperature of the body and also upon its surface characteristics. The Stefan-Boltzmann Law gives the relation between the radiant flux density E and the absolute temperature T of a black body as

$$E = \sigma T^4 \tag{128}$$

where σ is a constant depending upon the units used. Experiment shows that when E is in calories per second per square centimeter and T in °K, the numerical value of σ is 1.355×10^{-12}. The equation shows how greatly the temperature of a body affects its radiation; if, for example, the absolute temperature of a body is doubled, its radiation is increased sixteenfold.

Black-body radiation is of interest historically in that it marked the inception of the quantum theory. Many effects which involve a change of energy and which appear to take place in continuous fashion in objects large enough to be observed, are believed to proceed in small but finite jumps, although it was by studying objects of atomic dimensions, where the energy values are small, that this conclusion became evident. In an investigation of the radiation from a black body, the German physicist Max Planck (1858–1947) was unable to explain his experimental results on the theory of continuous radiation, and was forced to propose a radically new theory to the effect that radiation actually consists of the emission of tiny but definite quantities of energy, each of which is now called a *quantum*.

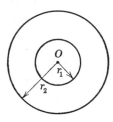

Fig. 179. Used in deriving the Inverse Square Law

This theory, which has little or no effect on classical physics, is extremely helpful in explaining many phenomena of atomic physics. Angular momentum will serve as an example. As a spinning wheel slows down, it appears to do so gradually, because of the comparative crudeness of the measurements that can be made upon it. But when a rotating molecule loses angular velocity, indirect measurements indicate that it passes abruptly from one speed to another, and that at each jump its lost energy is emitted as a quantum of radiation. The quantum theory is touched upon in the closing sections of this chapter and is considered in Chap. 40.

Inverse Square Law. The radiation received by a surface will be studied by considering a spherical enclosure, as represented in Fig. 179, with a point source of radiation located at the center O. If the source emits an amount of flux Φ and the radius of the sphere is r_1, the flux density at the surface of the enclosure is

$$E_1 = \frac{\Phi}{4\pi r_1{}^2}$$

For a sphere of different radius, say r_2, the flux density at the surface is expressed similarly, or

$$E_2 = \frac{\Phi}{4\pi r_2{}^2}$$

By division,

$$\frac{E_1}{E_2} = \frac{r_2{}^2}{r_1{}^2} \tag{129}$$

which states that the radiant flux density at any surface varies inversely as the square of the distance of that surface from a point source of radiation. This relation is commonly referred to as the Inverse Square Law.

Illustrative Problem

Estimate the temperature of the sun on the assumption that this source is a black-body radiator. Take the radius of the sun to be 433,000 mi, the average distance from sun to earth to be 92,900,000 mi, and the radiant flux density at the earth to be 2.0 cal/(min·cm²), as given at the beginning of § 185.

The radiant flux density at the surface of the sun, from Eq. 128, is 1.355 $\times$ $10^{-12}T^4$ cal/(sec·cm²), where T is its absolute temperature. At the distance of the earth from the sun, the radiation may be considered as spreading radially from a point source; hence the flux density is given by the Inverse Square Law as

$$E = \left(\frac{4.33 \times 10^5}{9.29 \times 10^7}\right)^2 (1.355 \times 10^{-12})T^4$$

But the solar constant E is known to be 2.0 cal/(min·cm²), or 0.033 cal/(sec·cm²), whence the effective temperature of the sun is $T = 5790°$ K.

Newton's Law of Cooling. The rate at which a body cools by radiation after having been heated was investigated by Newton; he found that if the temperature of the body is not much above the surroundings, the rate at which its temperature falls is proportional to the temperature elevation of the body above its surroundings. Expressed mathematically, the time rate of temperature change is

$$\frac{dT}{dt} = -K(T - T_s) \tag{130}$$

where K is a constant of proportionality, and T and T_s represent the temperatures respectively of the radiating body and the surroundings, neither of which need be an absolute value. This statement is called Newton's Law of Cooling; actually it may be regarded as an approximation to the Stefan-Boltzmann Law that was developed later.

187. Pyrometers. The measurement of high temperatures—those above 500° C—is commonly known as pyrometry. Two types of instruments for

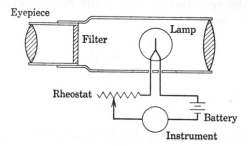

FIG. 180.   Optical pyrometer

observing such temperatures are based on radiant energy and two others are based on electrical effects; the latter are considered in §§ 229 and 302.

The *optical pyrometer* operates on the principle that the brightness of a radiating body increases as its temperature is raised, thus allowing the observer to compare the brightness of the body with that of a calibrated electric lamp. The pyrometer and its connections are shown in Fig. 180. An

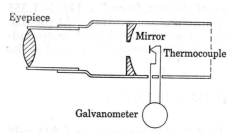

FIG. 181.   Radiation pyrometer

observation is made by focusing the telescope on the incandescent object under test, thereby bringing its image into the plane of the lamp filament, and then varying the current from a battery through the lamp until its filament appears to merge with the image of the hot body. The temperature is then determined by the current through the filament; usually the indicating instrument is calibrated in degrees. To eliminate the effect of color in the observation, use is made of a filter that permits only the red rays to reach the eye.

The *radiation pyrometer* makes use of the invisible heat rays as well as the visible light rays emitted by a radiating source. The radiation, coming from the right in Fig. 181, is focused by a concave mirror upon a tiny thermocouple, § 302, and the electromotive force generated therein is measured by a galvanometer. If the radiation proceeds from the interior of a uniformly heated enclosure, approximating a black body, the radiant flux received upon the thermocouple is found to vary as the fourth power of the absolute temperature of the source, Eq. 128. The galvanometer deflection is proportional to the amount of flux received, and the instrument can be calibrated to indicate temperatures directly.

188. Nature of Radiation. The radiation emitted by a heated body takes the form of waves in space; the lengths of these waves cover a wide range. The long ones are perceived by an observer as heat and the shorter ones as light. The energy of radiation is distributed over the range of wavelengths in a manner that depends upon the temperature of the radiating body and the nature of its surface. Fig. 182 shows the distribution of energy radiated by

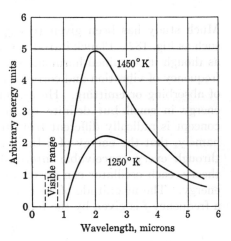

FIG. 182. Black-body radiation at two temperatures. Peak of curve shifts to shorter wavelengths as temperature rises

a black body as obtained by experiments conducted at two temperatures, namely, 1250 and 1450° K. The curves represent the relative intensities at wavelengths up to 0.0006 cm (6 microns), and the areas under them indicate the total energy radiated. The Stefan-Boltzmann Law, § 186, shows that this energy for a black body is proportional to the fourth power of the absolute temperature.

Radiation that affects the eye as light extends roughly from 0.00004 to 0.00008 cm, and is marked on the diagram as the visible range. The region to the right of this visual zone is termed the infrared, and the region to the left is termed the ultraviolet. The length λ (lambda) of the waves emitted by a source of radiation is related to the frequency f of the vibrating source and the speed of wave propagation v by the expression derived in § 328 as

$$\lambda = \frac{v}{f}$$

Increase of temperature causes not only an increase in total radiation but also shifts the peak of the radiation curve toward the shorter wavelengths. It is this effect that serves as the operating basis of the pyrometers previously described. The shift in wavelength has been formulated by the German physicist Wilhelm Wien (1864–1928), and is known as Wien's Displacement Law. It states that the product of the wavelength λ_m at which the energy density is a maximum and the absolute temperature T of the radiating body is a constant. This wavelength in centimeters is given by the equation

$$\lambda_m = \frac{0.2897}{T} \tag{131}$$

Much study has been given to experimentally obtained radiation curves such as Fig. 182. Planck introduced the idea that a radiating body behaves as though it contained harmonic oscillators, each of which responds to one frequency of vibration and corresponds to the radiations which it is capable of absorbing or emitting. He assumed these oscillators to absorb or emit energy in small but definite quantities rather than continuously. This concept is radically different from that held back to the time of Newton, namely, that the energy of a body can change from one value to another through every conceivable intermediate value. According to the newer theory, each oscillator can absorb or emit one or more of these quanta of energy. The magnitude of a quantum of energy for an oscillator that has a frequency f is given by the following equation:

$$E = hf \tag{132}$$

where E is the energy in ergs, f the frequency in vibrations per second, and h a constant that has the value 6.62×10^{-27} erg·sec. It is evident that quanta are extremely tiny grains of energy, and that the quantum is smaller for low frequencies (long wavelengths) than for high frequencies (short wavelengths). The quantity h is called Planck's Constant.

189. The Quantum Theory. The theory based upon the granular picture of energy, called the *quantum theory*, has been modified by many investigators, and now affords not only a satisfactory explanation of the radiation of energy, but also of the photoelectric effect, the structure of atoms, and all collision phenomena; these are considered in Chaps. 28 and 40.

The quantum explanation of the shape of the radiation curves for black bodies is an involved one and makes use of complicated mathematical steps. It will suffice here to give Planck's equation for the energy per cubic centimeter of the radiation associated with the wavelength interval from λ to $\lambda + d\lambda$ cm, namely,

$$E \, d\lambda = \frac{8\pi ch \, d\lambda}{\lambda^5(\epsilon^{ch/k\lambda T} - 1)}$$

where the speed c of the waves is very nearly 3×10^{10} cm/sec, § 333, and k is the gas constant per molecule, which is 1.38×10^{-16} ergs/°K, § 164.

Planck's theory was applied by the physicist Albert Einstein (1879–1955) to explain the variation of specific heats of solids with temperature, and was later modified by Professor Peter Debye to secure closer agreement with experimental results. These analyses indicate that the product of the specific heat and the atomic weight of a substance falls to zero as the absolute zero of temperature is approached and that the product has a nearly constant value at relatively high temperatures. The ultimate value averages 6.3 cal per gram-atom per °K for a large number of elements.

PROBLEMS

1. (*a*) What quantity of heat is conducted in 1 hr through a window 3 ft wide by 6 ft high in which the glass is $\frac{1}{8}$ in. thick, when the temperatures inside and outside are 68 and 20° F respectively? (*b*) How much coal would liberate this quantity of heat in burning? Use the average value tabulated for the heat of combustion of coal.

2. A cubical box that measures 3 ft along each edge is lined with cellular glass insulation 6 in. thick. The thermal conductivity of the insulation is 0.40 Btu·in./(hr·ft^2·F°). The interior of the box contains 100 lb of ice and is at 32° F. Find the rate at which the ice melts when the temperature outside the box is 80° F. Take the surface through which the heat flows to be halfway between the inside and outside of the insulation.

3. An enclosure maintained at a temperature of 85° F has one face of asbestos-cement board $\frac{1}{2}$ in. thick and one face of loosely packed mineral wool 4 in. thick, the thermal conductivities of these materials being 4.0 and 0.30 Btu·in./(hr·ft^2·F°). What is the rate of heat conduction in British thermal units per hour through a surface 1 ft^2 in area for each of these substances when the surrounding temperature is 65° F?

4. A brass rod 80 cm long is joined end to end with an iron rod 60 cm long. The free end of the brass rod is kept at the temperature of boiling water and that of the iron rod at the temperature of melting ice. The rods have the same cross-sectional area of 5 cm^2 and are covered their full length with heat insulation to prevent transfer of heat to or from the surroundings. When steady conditions are established, (*a*) what is the temperature of the brass-iron junction, and (*b*) what is the rate of heat conduction along the combination?

5. A copper-clad steel rod has a steel core 1 in. in diameter and a copper coating 0.25 in. thick. In a conductivity test, such a rod 3 ft long, covered with heat insulation over its full length, has one end kept at the temperature of melting lead and the other at the temperature of melting ice. Take the thermal conductivity of steel to be 315 Btu·in./(hr·ft^2·F°) and calculate the rate of heat conduction along the rod.

6. A glass beaker having a base 1 mm thick and 50 cm^2 in area contains 200 cm^3 of water at 100° C. The beaker is placed over a heater which keeps the lower surface of the base at a temperature of 180° C. In what time is sufficient heat conducted through the base to vaporize all the water in the beaker?

7. How much heat escapes per hour by conduction through a garage wall measuring 8 × 20 ft in area and $1\frac{3}{4}$ in. thick when the temperature inside the structure is 70° F and that outside is 40° F? The wall is made of pine wood, which has a thermal conductivity of 0.80 Btu·in./(hr·ft^2·F°).

8. The wall of the preceding problem is lined with batts of fibrous mineral wool 2 in. thick, for which the thermal conductivity is 0.27 Btu·in./(hr·ft²· F°). Calculate (a) the temperature of the interface between boards and the batts and (b) the rate at which heat escapes through the composite wall.

9. A steam pipe of 3-in. outside diameter is covered with mineral wool insulation 1 in. thick. The temperature of the insulation at its inner surface is 212° F and at its outer surface is 70° F. Take the thermal conductivity of the insulation to be 0.30 Btu·in./(hr·ft²·F°) and determine the heat loss per day by conduction through the insulation for a 10-ft length of pipe.

10. A large electrical generator operates at 145° F and dissipates heat continuously at the rate of 20 kw. It is proposed to cool this machine by circulating hydrogen through it. The circulating system, tightly closed and filled with hydrogen, would enclose the generator, extend by means of ducts to a cooling chamber, where the gas would be cooled from 145 to 70° F, and return by other ducts to the generator. Assume the pressure within the system to be maintained at 1 atmosphere and compute the rate, in cubic feet per minute, at which the hydrogen should be supplied to the generator in order to produce the desired cooling effect.

11. In an early solar engine, the sun's radiation is received by a mirror and focused upon a black liquid; here its energy is absorbed and used to generate steam to operate a small engine. If the overall efficiency of the system is 15%, what area of mirror, perpendicular to the radiation, would be required to develop an output of 1 hp? Take the solar constant at the earth's surface to be 1.333 cal/(min·cm²).

12. If the radiant flux from the sun could be utilized at an overall efficiency of 15%, how many kilowatts of electrical power could be generated from the flux incident normally upon an acre of ground? Refer to the preceding problem for the solar constant.

13. On a certain cold night the tank described in Prob. 17 of Chap. 1 is full of water at 10° C and the surroundings are at −10° C. Consider the tank as a black body and compute (a) the heat lost per second by radiation to the surroundings, (b) the heat received per second from the surroundings, and (c) the net radiation loss per second.

14. If the radiant flux density is 6 cal/(sec·cm²) at a point 20 cm from a point source of black-body radiation, (a) what is the total flux emitted by the source? (b) what is the temperature of the source? and (c) what is the flux density at a point 30 cm from the source?

15. A calorimeter is found to cool from 28.2 to 27.8° C in 60 sec in a room where the temperature is 20.0° C. As the cooling continues, how long does it take for this calorimeter to cool from 25.1 to 24.9° C?

16. A body in surroundings at 27° C is found to cool at the rate of 0.004 C°/sec when its temperature is 47° C, and it is desired to predict the rate of cooling when its temperature has fallen to 37° C. (a) Determine the result by Newton's Law of Cooling. (b) Regard the body as a black body and determine the result by the Stefan-Boltzmann Law; include the energy received from the surroundings as well as that emitted to them.

17. A source of light emits waves having a length of 0.00006 cm, which travel at 3×10^{10} cm/sec. Find (a) the frequency of the vibrating source and (b) the value of a quantum of the radiated energy.

ELECTRICITY AND MAGNETISM

19

ELECTRIC CHARGE

190. Electrostatic Attraction and Repulsion. Probably the first electrical experiment ever recorded is that due to the Greek philosopher Thales of Miletus (c. 624–546 B.C.), who observed that a piece of amber when rubbed with cloth was able to attract bits of near-by straw or feathers. Nowadays, the act of bringing about a very close contact between the amber and the cloth is said to give the amber a *charge of electricity*, and the attraction is called an *electrostatic attraction*. The term *electricity* is derived from *electron*, the Greek word for amber.

The English physician and physicist William Gilbert (1540–1603) studied electric attraction and found that many substances besides amber can be charged in the same way. An electric charge can be produced in a glass rod by rubbing it with silk. A hard-rubber rod rubbed with fur becomes highly charged; it can exert sufficient force upon a meter stick to turn it horizontally about a pivot at its midpoint.

The forces due to electric charges can be demonstrated with two pith balls, each suspended by a thread, and hung a few centimeters apart. When each ball is touched with a charged glass rod the two fly apart and remain separated; they act the same way when both are touched with a charged hard-rubber rod. But if one pith ball is touched with the glass rod and the other with the rubber rod, then they fly together. These tests reveal a difference between the electricity on the glass and that on the hard rubber. It was the American philosopher and statesman Benjamin Franklin (1706–1790) who deduced the one-fluid nature of electricity by distinguishing the two kinds as *positive* and *negative*. The charge on the glass rod is styled positive and that on the rubber rod negative. Furthermore, the tests show a fundamental fact of great importance, namely, that *like charges of electricity repel each other, and unlike charges attract each other.*

293

The presence of an electric charge on a body can be detected by an *electroscope*, the construction of which is indicated in Fig. 183. Two leaves, ordinarily of aluminum or gold foil, hang side by side from a metal rod which

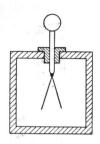

passes through an insulating bushing and terminates in a metal knob outside of the case. If the knob is touched with the charged body, the leaves acquire electricity of the same kind and repel each other, as indicated. The larger the quantity of charge, the farther the leaves stand apart.

191. Electrical Structure of the Atom. Any consideration of electrostatic phenomena involves the charges that are known to exist within the atom itself. The nucleus of the atom contains only protons which have positive charge and neutrons which have no charge, all these nucleons being held together in a compact group. Sur-

FIG. 183. A simple electroscope

rounding the nucleus are the electrons, all negatively charged. Each electron and proton has the same amount of charge, and no smaller amount has yet been observed. When the atom is in its normal uncharged condition, the number of electrons in the atom of any element equals the number of protons in its nucleus.

The planetary picture of the atom, described in § 2, was proposed by the British scientist Lord (Ernest) Rutherford (1871–1937), developed by the Danish physicist Niels Bohr, and extended by the German physicist Arnold Sommerfeld (1868–1951). This picture assumes that the electrons revolve around the nucleus in stable orbits with well-defined characteristic energies. These orbits can be arranged in groups, the so-called *shells*, in which the various orbits of a group are of similar size and possess nearly the same energy. This concept of atomic structure is useful for clarifying many facts of Physics and Chemistry.

Of all the elements, hydrogen (H) has the simplest type of atom; it is pictured as having a nucleus composed of a single proton and one orbital electron. The attraction of the positive nucleus for the negative electron accounts for the potential energy of the hydrogen atom and the motion of the electron accounts for its kinetic energy; the latter is needed for the orbit to be stable. Next in order of simplicity is the helium atom (He), composed of a nucleus and two planetary electrons, the nucleus being regarded as a stable combination of two protons and two neutrons, called an alpha particle. Both electrons are in the same shell, and this shell accommodates only two electrons.

The heavier atoms have more protons and neutrons in the nucleus and a corresponding number of planetary electrons in their shells. The number of electrons possible in a shell is given by $2n^2$, where n is the shell number; thus it takes eight electrons to fill the second shell. In progressing from one element to another the shells of the atoms are not necessarily filled.

The lithium (Li) atom, with a total of three electrons, has one of them in the second shell; beryllium (Be) has two in the second shell, boron (B) three, carbon (C) four, nitrogen (N) five, oxygen (O) six, fluorine (F) seven, and neon (Ne) eight, the last number filling the second shell. The sodium (Na) atom has a total of eleven planetary electrons, of which two fill the first shell, eight fill the second shell, the remaining one being in a third shell. A continuation of this process to include the more complex atoms leads to the so-called Periodic Table of all the elements, given in the Appendix.

Certain elements are chemically inert, and it is concluded that their atomic structures are inherently stable. Perhaps because of compactness or symmetry, such stability is associated with electron shells that are completely filled. The helium atom with its first shell complete, the neon atom with its first and second shells complete, and other atoms similarly located in the table (argon, krypton, xenon, and radon) are chemically inactive.

The ability of atoms to unite with others is determined by the outer electrons, and the tendency in combining is apparently to form arrangements in which the electron shells are completely filled. A lithium or sodium atom, with one electron in its outer shell, is in a condition that favors losing this electron, whereas a fluorine or chlorine atom, with one electron less than is needed to complete its outer shell, is in a condition that favors gaining one. When sodium (Na) and chlorine (Cl) combine to form sodium chloride (NaCl), the loosely held electron of the sodium atom joins with the electrons of the chlorine atom, thus filling the shells of both atoms. The measure of the ability of atoms to form molecules by combining in this manner is known as *valence;* thus, sodium, with one electron more than is needed to fill its outer shell, is said to have a *valence number* of $+1$, and chlorine, with one electron less than is needed to fill its outer shell, is said to have a valence number of -1. The outer electrons, which are instrumental in forming chemical compounds, are called *valence electrons*.

Some atomic quantities have been measured with great precision. For example, the hydrogen atom, which is composed of a proton and an electron, has a mass of 1.673×10^{-24} gm. Of this amount, the electron forms only a small part; its mass when at rest is 9.11×10^{-28} gm.

192. Production of Electric Charge. In the process of charging a body by rubbing it with another material, electrons are stripped from atoms at the contacting surface. Atoms of some elements release electrons with comparative ease, and others acquire them readily. A neutral or uncharged body contains equal amounts of positive and negative electricity; when electrons are added, it becomes negatively charged, and when electrons are removed, it becomes positively charged. Thus a hard-rubber rod when brought into intimate contact with fur gains some electrons and becomes negative, while the fur loses these electrons and becomes positive to an equal extent. A glass rod rubbed with silk loses electrons and becomes positive, while the silk gains these electrons and becomes negative.

Examples illustrating the production of electric charge are familiar to everyone. The effect can be observed in dry weather by passing a rubber comb through the hair or by shuffling the feet on a woolen carpet. A leather belt traveling around a pair of pulleys may acquire sufficient electricity to produce a spark to a person's finger held near it. In the process of printing, the paper usually acquires a charge when it is separated from the rollers of the printing press, and means are provided to dissipate the charge.

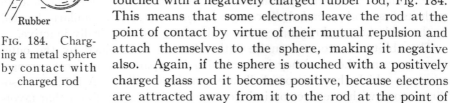

FIG. 184. Charging a metal sphere by contact with charged rod

It is possible to charge a body from another that is already charged by simply bringing the two into contact. Thus, a metal sphere gains negative electricity if it is touched with a negatively charged rubber rod, Fig. 184. This means that some electrons leave the rod at the point of contact by virtue of their mutual repulsion and attach themselves to the sphere, making it negative also. Again, if the sphere is touched with a positively charged glass rod it becomes positive, because electrons are attracted away from it to the rod at the point of contact. The positive charges are not transferred, for in solids only the electrons are mobile.

193. Insulators and Conductors. It is assumed that the metal sphere referred to in the preceding section is supported in such a manner that the charge acquired does not leak away. This can be done by suspending the sphere with a dry silk string or by supporting it on props of mica or glass. Evidently in materials like these the charges are not transferred to any appreciable extent, and for this reason they are called *insulators*. If the sphere had been suspended by a metallic wire or mounted upon a metal support, practically the entire charge might be conducted away and eventually escape to the earth. It can be concluded that metals are good *conductors* of electricity; silver and copper are the best of them.

Many substances are neither good insulators nor good conductors but may be classed in an intermediate group as fair electrical conductors—for example, the human body, a piece of damp wood, and the earth. These should not be confused with so-called *semiconductors*, a group of materials that have unusual properties and have recently found wide application, § 320.

Within conductors of electricity the atoms part quite readily with one or more of their outer electrons, and these are no longer bound to their nuclei; consequently they are free to move through the conductors. These detached particles are called *free electrons*. In a cubic inch of copper there are over 10^{24} free electrons; in insulators there are hardly any.

194. Charging by Induction. It is possible to charge a conductor from a charged body without touching the two together; the process is called *induction*. The procedure for charging a conductor by induction is as follows: (1) bring the charged body close to, but not in contact with, the conductor to be charged; (2) connect the conductor to ground; (3) break the ground connection; and (4) remove the initially charged body. In this way the conductor acquires a charge and its sign (that is, whether the charge is negative or positive) is opposite to that of the original one.

This process can be explained by reference to Fig. 185, wherein the conductor is represented as a brass tube with rounded ends mounted on a glass stem for insulation, and the charged body is a rubber rod. (1) When the negatively charged rod is held near the tube, it repels some of the elec-

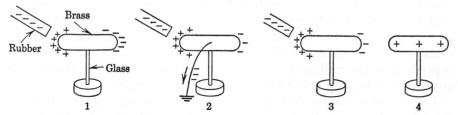

FIG. 185.   Charging a metal object by induction

trons of the tube, thus making the distant end of the tube negative, and leaving the adjacent end positive. A state of equilibrium is soon reached after which other electrons, repelled by the rod, are prevented from leaving the adjacent end of the tube by the positive charge already accumulated there. (2) When the tube is grounded, a path is provided for some electrons to escape, and they flow through the ground connection to the earth. (3) When the ground connection is broken, the body, again isolated, is found to have a positive charge, since it has lost some electrons. Finally, (4) the removal of the inducing body allows the charges on the metal tube to distribute themselves in a normal manner, and the tube becomes positive over its entire surface. In this way the tube is given a positive charge by the process of induction from a negative charge.

The attraction of light neutral objects by a charged rod mentioned in § 190 can now be explained. The rod induces a charge of opposite sign on the adjacent face of a near-by object, and hence the action between the two is one of attraction.

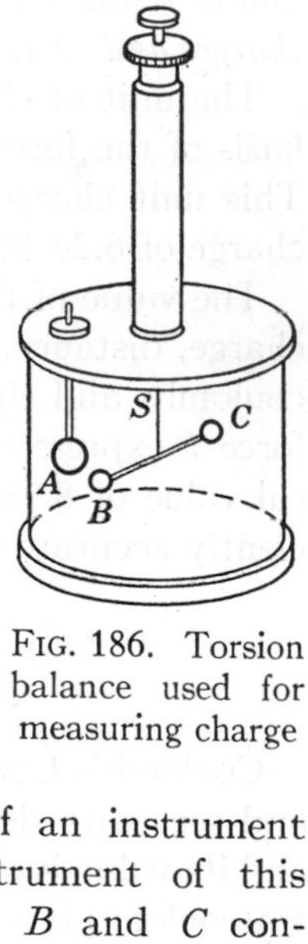

FIG. 186.   Torsion balance used for measuring charge

195. Forces Between Charged Bodies; Coulomb's Law. The first quantitative measurements of the forces between charges were conducted by the French physicist, Charles A. Coulomb (1736–1806). He made use of an instrument called a torsion balance; Fig. 186 illustrates an instrument of this type. The moving system, consisting of two spheres *B* and *C* connected by a slender rod, is suspended by a wire *S* which permits the system to swing horizontally in the same plane as a stationary sphere A. All parts are within a glass enclosure for protection against air currents.

When both spheres A and B carry charges of the same sign, the repulsion between them develops a torque that twists the supporting wire until balanced by the torsion set up within the wire. The investigations showed that the force between two charged bodies, whether of repulsion or attraction, falls off rapidly as the distance between them increases. Later investigators showed that the force of attraction or repulsion depends upon the shapes and separation of the charged bodies, and upon the amount and distribution of the charges on them. When the bodies are very small, so that the charges can be regarded as concentrated at points, the force between them varies inversely as the square of the distance from one to the other, and varies directly with the product of the charges. The force also depends upon the medium in which the charges are located; in this chapter consideration is given only to free space, that is, vacuum.

The foregoing results show that, for two point charges Q_1 and Q_2 separated by a distance r, the force that either one exerts upon the other is

$$F = k\,\frac{Q_1 Q_2}{r^2} \tag{133}$$

where k is a constant that depends upon the units chosen for the other quantities. This expression is essentially the Inverse Square Law, § 186, applied to electric charges, and is called *Coulomb's Law*. Briefly, *the force of attraction or repulsion between two point charges is proportional to the product of the charges and inversely proportional to the square of the distance separating them.*

The unit of electric charge in the mks system of units is defined on the basis of the force between moving charges, that is, electric currents, § 251. This unit charge is called the *coulomb*, and its value is equivalent to the charge of 6.24×10^{18} electrons.

The value of the constant in Eq. 133 depends upon the units selected for charge, distance, and force. When the charges Q_1 and Q_2 are expressed in coulombs and the distance r between them is in meters, then to have the force F expressed in newtons requires that the constant k have the numerical value of 8.988×10^9, which is practically 9.00×10^9. With this sufficiently accurate value, this constant for free space is

$$k = 9.00 \times 10^9 \, \frac{\text{newton} \cdot \text{m}^2}{\text{coulomb}^2}$$

Coulomb's Law is the foundation of the electrostatic system of units (esu) and serves to define its unit charge. This unit is called the *statcoulomb*, and its value is such that the constant k becomes unity. Consequently, the statcoulomb is a quantity of charge which when placed 1 cm from an equal charge is acted upon by a force of 1 dyne, the centimeter and dyne being the respective units of distance and force in the cgs system. Hence, when Q_1 and Q_2 are expressed in statcoulombs and r in centimeters, in order that the force F be in dynes, the constant for free space has the value

$$k = 1 \frac{\text{dyne} \cdot \text{cm}^2}{\text{statcoulomb}^2}$$

Since the newton equals 10^5 dynes and the meter equals 100 cm, the relationship between the coulomb and the statcoulomb is found to be

$$1 \text{ coulomb} = 3.00 \times 10^9 \text{ statcoulombs}$$

and the statcoulomb is equivalent to a charge of 2.08×10^9 electrons.

The use of several systems of units has long presented difficulties to students of Electricity and Magnetism. Each system has its merits, but the mks system appears to be gaining wider acceptance; hence it is the one featured in this book. In addition, the electrostatic system is introduced sufficiently to afford an understanding of publications in which this older system is used.

196. Effect of the Medium on Force Between Charges. The force that one charged object exerts upon another depends upon the medium in which the objects are located. Within some medium, the net force which each exerts upon the other is less than in empty space. This is so because the charged objects induce charges of opposite sign on the molecules immediately surrounding them and thus lessen the effectiveness of the charges on the objects themselves. The induced charges depend in amount upon the nature of the medium, but their effect is always to make the force between the objects less than it would be in a vacuum.

The influence of the medium can be incorporated in Coulomb's Law by modifying the constant k to include a property called *permittivity* of the medium. Its symbol for vacuum or free space is ϵ_o. Another modification makes it simpler to express derived expressions involving mks units, which expressions are more frequently used than the Law itself. This change involves the inclusion of the factor $1/4\pi$. Hence by placing

$$k = \frac{1}{4\pi\epsilon_o}$$

Coulomb's Law assumes the form

$$F = \frac{1}{4\pi\epsilon_o} \frac{Q_1Q_2}{r^2} \tag{134}$$

The value of the permittivity of a vacuum in the mks system can be derived from the value of k given in the preceding section as

$$\epsilon_o = \frac{1}{4\pi k} = \frac{1}{4\pi 9 \times 10^9} \frac{\text{coulomb}^2}{\text{newton} \cdot \text{m}^2}$$

where the fraction has the value 8.85×10^{-12}. The permittivity of air at standard pressure and temperature may usually be taken as the same as that for a vacuum. The permittivity of other mediums is considered in Chap. 25.

Illustrative Problem

As an example, compute the force that would act between two protons a billionth of a centimeter apart in air.

The charge on a proton is the same as that on an electron, namely, $1/(6.24 \times 10^{18}) = 1.60 \times 10^{-19}$ coulomb; the separation of the two protons is 10^{-11} m; the permittivity of the medium is 8.85×10^{-12} coulomb^2/(newton·m^2). Hence the force between the protons is given by Eq. 134 as

$$F = \frac{1}{4\pi 8.85 \times 10^{-12}} \times \frac{1.6 \times 10^{-19} \times 1.6 \times 10^{-19}}{10^{-22}} = 2.30 \times 10^{-6} \text{ newton}$$

197. The Electric Field. The region about a charged body is referred to as an electric field of force or, briefly, an *electric field*, because any other charge located in this region experiences a force either of attraction or repulsion. The amount of force acting upon a unit charge is taken as a measure of the strength or intensity of the field. Hence, *the intensity of an electric field at any point is defined as the force per unit positive charge placed at that point.* Specifically, if a charge Q is acted upon by a force F in an electric field, the intensity of the field is

$$\mathcal{E} = \frac{F}{Q} \tag{135}$$

where Q represents a charge placed at some point in an already existing field, and $\mathcal{E}$ the field strength at the point before that charge was introduced. More precisely, the electric field intensity is the limiting value of the ratio F/Q as the charge approaches zero.

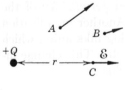

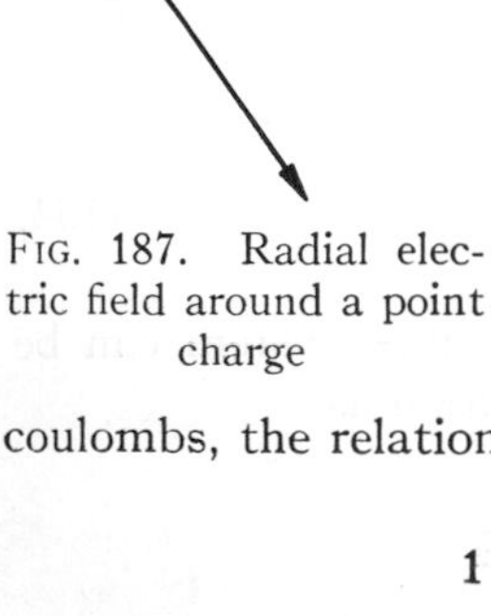

In the mks system, the unit of field intensity is the *newton per coulomb*. Thus, if a positive charge of 5 microcoulombs experiences a force of 10 newtons toward the right in a particular electric field, the intensity of that field is 2 newtons per microcoulomb or 2×10^6 newtons per coulomb directed toward the right.

Fig. 187. Radial electric field around a point charge

In the esu system, the unit of field intensity is the dyne per statcoulomb. Since the newton equals 10^5 dynes, and the coulomb equals 3×10^9 statcoulombs, the relation between the two units of electric field intensity is

$$1 \frac{\text{newton}}{\text{coulomb}} = \frac{1}{3 \times 10^4} \frac{\text{dyne}}{\text{statcoulomb}}$$

Electric field intensity is a vector quantity, § 16. The direction of the field around a positive charge is indicated in Fig. 187. The charge $+Q$ is assumed to be concentrated at a point; the direction and strength of the electric field which it produces at some other point in the region are found by assuming a point *unit positive* charge to be placed there and determining the force acting upon it. The directions of the field at four points A to D are shown in the figure by arrows all of which are radially outward from Q. The force on a unit charge at a point such as C is found from Eq. 133 to be

$$F = k \frac{Q \times 1}{r^2}$$, where r is the distance from Q to C. Hence, the field intensity

at any point distant r from a point charge Q that establishes the field is

$$\mathcal{E} = k \frac{Q}{r^2} \tag{136}$$

To summarize, the field intensity due to a point charge varies directly with the amount of charge and inversely with the square of the distance away from the charge; furthermore, it is directed radially outward from a positive charge and radially inward toward a negative one.

The value of the constant k is given in the preceding section as $k = \dfrac{1}{4\pi\epsilon_o}$ $= 9 \times 10^9$ newton·m²/coulomb², where ϵ_o is the permittivity of free space. When this value is introduced in Eq. 136, the expression for field intensity in newtons per coulomb becomes

$$\mathcal{E} = 9 \times 10^9 \frac{Q}{r^2} \tag{137}$$

where the charge Q is in coulombs and the distance r from it is in meters.

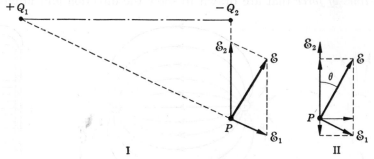

Fig. 188. Electric field due to two point charges

When the field intensity at a point is due to several point charges, its value can be obtained by determining the field intensity at the point due to each charge in turn and then by vectorial addition finding the resultant of these individual values. In part I of Fig. 188, the field intensity at point

P has one component $\mathcal{E}_1$ directed radially away from the positive charge Q_1 and another component $\mathcal{E}_2$ directed radially toward the negative one Q_2; the resultant field intensity at this point is shown at $\mathcal{E}$.

Illustrative Problem

Consider that the charges shown in part I are $Q_1 = +4$ and $Q_2 = -1$ microcoulomb, these being 12 cm apart in air, and that the point P is located 5 cm directly below Q_2. This point will then be 13 cm away from Q_1. Find the resultant field intensity.

The components of the electric field are $\mathcal{E}_1 = 9 \times 10^3 \dfrac{4}{(0.13)^2} = 2.13 \times 10^6$, and $\mathcal{E}_2 = 9 \times 10^3 \dfrac{1}{(0.05)^2} = 3.60 \times 10^6$, both in newtons per coulomb. To compute the resultant, first resolve $\mathcal{E}_1$ into a vertical component $\frac{5}{13} \times 2.13 \times 10^6 = 0.82 \times 10^6$ downward and a horizontal component $\frac{12}{13} \times 2.13 \times 10^6 = 1.97 \times 10^6$ to the right, as in part II; then subtract the first of these from $\mathcal{E}_2$, leaving 2.78×10^6 vertically; finally combine this result with 1.97×10^6 horizontally to obtain the resultant as

$$\mathcal{E} = 10^6 \sqrt{(2.78)^2 + (1.97)^2} = 3.41 \times 10^6$$

newtons per coulomb. The direction of this resultant field intensity is given by $\tan \theta = 1.97/2.78$, whence $\theta = 35.3°$ to the right of the vertical.

The concept of the electric field thus views the attraction or repulsion between two charges as caused by the presence of one charge in the electric field produced by the other. A positive charge experiences a force along the direction of the field and a negative charge a force in the opposite direction.

The electric field near a charge is represented conventionally by so-called *electric lines of force* that are drawn to show the direction and intensity of

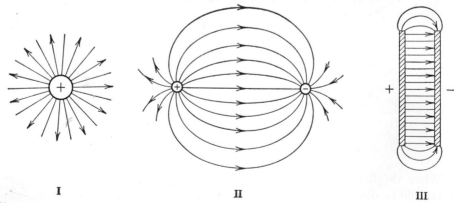

I   II   III

FIG. 189. Electric lines of force: I around isolated charge, II about unlike charges, III between parallel plates

the field at all points. Fig. 189 shows such lines for the field around an iso-lated charged sphere, that between two point charges of opposite sign, and that between two oppositely charged plates. In part I the lines are directed radially outward from the positively charged sphere; they would be radially inward to a negative charge. In part II the lines diverge from the positive point charge and converge upon the negative one. In part III the lines are parallel and equidistant between the plates, but near the edges show the characteristic shapes of the lines in part II. Maps of electric fields can be obtained experimentally by means of properly located insulating plates sprinkled with cork filings, gypsum crystals, or merely bits of hair and straw.

Electric lines of force have no physical existence, but they serve to indi-cate the configuration of an electric field. They are imagined to begin at a plus charge and to end at a minus charge, and their closeness gives a visual impression of the field strength. These lines of force associated with static charges cannot form closed loops nor end in free space; they always termi-nate on electric charges.

198. Electric Potential. · The fact that an electric field exerts a force upon a charge located within it shows that work must be done upon such a charge in moving it against this force. If the field is uniform in intensity, the work done is the product of the constant force and the distance the charge moves, provided it moves in the direction of the force. If the field is not uniform, the force varies from point to point, and the determination of work done becomes more involved.

Such determinations are simplified by introducing the idea of "electrical level," a concept called *potential*. In Mechanics, if a body is to be moved from one level to a higher one, work must be done upon it; in Electricity, if a positive charge is to be moved from one potential to a higher one, work must be done upon it. *The potential difference between two points is the work required per unit positive charge to move this charge from one point to the other.* Hence if W is the work done upon a charge Q to bring it from one point to another in an electric field, then the difference of potential between these points is

$$V = \frac{W}{Q} \tag{138}$$

When the work W is expressed in joules and the charge Q in coulombs, the unit of V is the *joule per coulomb*. This is the unit of potential difference in the mks system and is called the *volt*; it is named after the Italian physicist Alessandro Volta (1745–1827) who was an early investigator of atmospheric and muscular electricity.

In the cgs system the unit of potential difference is the erg per statcou-lomb, and is called the statvolt. Since the joule equals 10^7 ergs, and the coulomb equals 3×10^9 statcoulombs, the volt is smaller than the statvolt and the relation between them is

$$1 \text{ volt} = \tfrac{1}{300} \text{ statvolt}$$

The potential at individual points in space around a charge depends upon

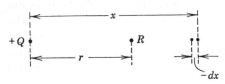

FIG. 190. For calculating electric potential at a point

their distances from the charge. In order to derive an expression for the potential at a point due to a specific charge, it is necessary to compute the work done to bring a unit positive charge from infinity where the potential may be regarded as zero up to the particular point. In Fig. 190 a unit charge is being brought from infinity at the right to a point R that is at a distance r from a point charge $+Q$. When the unit charge is at a distance x from Q, it is repelled with a force of $k\dfrac{Q}{x^2}$, and an equal force directed toward Q is required to hold it at this position. Hence, in moving it toward Q by an infinitesimal distance $-dx$ the work done is $-k\dfrac{Q}{x^2}dx$. The total work done in moving the unit charge from an infinitely great distance to point R is found by integrating this expression between the limits $x = \infty$ and $x = r$, giving

$$\int_{x=\infty}^{x=r} -k\frac{Q}{x^2}dx = \left[+k\frac{Q}{x} \right]_{\infty}^{r} = k\frac{Q}{r}$$

Consequently, the potential at a distance r from a charge Q is

$$V = k\frac{Q}{r} \tag{139}$$

When k is taken as 9×10^9 newton·m²/coulomb², as before, the potential V is in volts if the charge Q is in coulombs and the distance r in meters; it will be recalled that the joule is the work done when a force of 1 newton acts on a body while it moves through a distance of 1 meter, § 61.

Potential represents energy per unit charge, and since both energy and charge are scalar quantities, potential is also a scalar. Therefore, to find the potential at a single point due to several point charges it is merely necessary to add algebraically the individual potentials due to the several charges.

The concept of potential difference (abbreviated pd) is useful particularly because the work done in moving a charge from one point to another is independent of the path followed. The work done in transferring a unit charge between two points is equal to the potential difference $V_2 - V_1$ between them, whatever the path taken. Hence the work done in transferring any charge Q between these points is

$$W = Q(V_2 - V_1) \tag{140}$$

In units, joules = coulombs $\times$ volts.

Illustrative Problem

A charge of $+6$ microcoulombs is placed 1.2 m from a charge of $+5$ microcoulombs in free space. How much work must be done to reduce their separation 25%?

Suppose the larger charge to remain at rest; the potential that it establishes at a point 1.2 m away is $V_1 = 9 \times 10^9 \dfrac{6 \times 10^{-6}}{1.2} = 45,000$ volts, and that at $\frac{3}{4}$ of this distance is $V_2 = 9 \times 10^9 \dfrac{6 \times 10^{-6}}{0.9} = 60,000$ volts. The work needed to move the 5-microcoulomb charge from one point to the other, with a pd of 15,000 volts between them, is $5 \times 10^{-6} \times 15,000 = 0.075$ joule. The same result is obtained by supposing the 5-microcoulomb charge to be fixed and the larger charge to be moved the same distance.

It has been stated that to move a positive charge from a point of low potential to one of high potential, work must be done upon it; under the same conditions a negative charge would move of itself, if free to do so, and gain kinetic energy. The free electrons in a conductor can move whenever a pd is maintained between two points on the conductor, thus producing an electric current between them, § 216. On the other hand, if a conductor bears a charge that is not moving to produce a current, its surface must have the same potential at all points. Such a surface is called an *equipotential* surface, and it follows from the definition of potential that no work would be required to move a charge from one point to another over such a surface.

When a potential difference is established between two separate conductors an electric field exists between them, and this can be represented by electric lines of force as described in the preceding section. Each line of force extends from the conductor of higher potential to the one of lower potential; no line can begin and end on the same conductor, except under the conditions next to be described by which different parts of a conductor are maintained at different potentials.

199. Motion of Electric Charge in Solids. Most conducting solids are metals in which the atom has only a few electrons in the outer shell (see Periodic Table), a condition which favors the loss of these electrons. Moreover, some electrons serve in a dual capacity in two adjoining atoms. Under these circumstances a large number of electrons are comparatively free to move about. These free electrons are pictured as being in a state of unceasing and unordered motion, the amount of motion depending upon the temperature.

When one end of a conducting wire is maintained negative by supplying it with electrons and the other end is maintained positive by withdrawing electrons from it, the free electrons within the wire acquire a definite drift toward its positive end, and this constitutes the electric current. With current in the wire, the directed drift is superposed upon the random motion of the electrons.

Thus in solids the positively charged atoms remain fixed in position except for thermal agitation, and the *electric current is attributed entirely to a movement of electrons.* The free electrons are believed also to assist in the conduction of heat through solids.

In solids which are good insulators the electrons are not readily detachable from the atoms, and hence insulators have extremely few free electrons. If an insulator such as glass is placed in an electric field with one surface maintained positive and the other negative, there is no appreciable electron drift through it, but the electrons within the atoms shift their positions slightly with respect to the nuclei, an effect called *electric displacement.*

200. Distribution of Charge on Conductors. When a charge is given to a conductor, the charge resides on its surface. If it were possible to have a charge throughout the interior of a conductor, the forces of repulsion between the individual parts of that charge would cause them to separate from each other as far as possible and thus reach the outside surface. With the charge at rest and confined to the surface there is no electric field within the conductor itself.

The shape of a conducting body has a marked effect on the distribution of electricity over it, and in general the amount of charge per unit area is not uniform over its surface. The amount of the charge at any point on the surface can be determined with an electroscope by using a *proof plane*, consisting of a small metal disk fastened to one end of an insulating rod. The disk of the proof plane is applied to the surface point under test and then to the electroscope; the resulting separation of the leaves of the electroscope becomes a measure of the *surface density of charge.*

A charged hollow or solid sphere, when isolated so as to be uninfluenced by its surroundings, shows the same leaf separation when tested in this way for all points on the outer surface, indicating that the surface density is uniform. On an elongated conductor, such as a rod or tube, this density is found to be greater at the ends than at the middle, because the individual charges tend to repel one another to the greatest possible distance.

The distribution of electric charge can be studied further by repeating an experiment, originally conducted by the British chemist and physicist Michael Faraday (1791–1867), using a metal ice pail connected to an electroscope. When a sphere is charged from an outside source and lowered into the pail the leaves of the electroscope diverge. The sphere may then be moved around inside the pail, even touched to its inner surface and removed, without causing any further change in the deflection of the electroscope. For the behavior to be as described, the opening at the top of the pail should be as small as possible.

To explain this result, a positively charged sphere is assumed to be in the position shown in Fig. 191. The charge on the sphere attracts some of the free electrons in the metal pail to the inner surface; consequently the outer surface of the pail and the electroscope are left positive. When the sphere touches the pail the induced charge on the inside of the pail and the inducing charge on the sphere neutralize each other, leaving both sphere and inside of pail entirely without charge. The charge on the outside of the pail remains as before and, since it was as large as that on the inside before contact, it must therefore be equal to the initial amount on the sphere, and of the same sign. Consequently it may be concluded that in a region entirely surrounded by a conductor, there can be no charge on its inner walls unless the region also contains an equal and opposite charge.

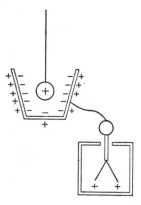

Fig. 191. Faraday's ice-pail experiment

The foregoing explains how a region can be shielded from external charges. Fig. 192 shows a metal enclosure and two external charges, as well as the electric lines of the field between them and the outside surface of the enclosure. As pointed out in § 198, no line of force can begin and end on the

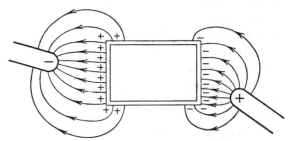

Fig. 192. Electric lines of force between two charges and hollow metal box. Box interior is shielded electrostatically

same conductor that has everywhere the same potential, and hence there cannot be an electric field in the internal space.

201. Conduction in Gases; Ionization. Electricity can be conducted through gases, but the process is different from that in solids. Conduction in gases is attributed to the presence of atoms and atomic groups that carry charges and are called *ions*. These gaseous ions, when within an electric field, experience forces and move, the positive ions in one direction and negative ions in the other; this double motion constitutes the electric current in the gas.

The flow of electricity through gases can be demonstrated by charging an electroscope so that its leaves stand apart as in Fig. 183.   When the flame of a gas jet is brought near the electroscope, its leaves fall together promptly, showing that the electroscope has lost its charge.   The molecules of the heated gases collide so forcibly with one another and with the air molecules that they knock some electrons out of the atoms, and as a result ions are formed.   If the electroscope is positive it attracts the negative ions, and if negative it attracts the positive ions.   Its charge in either case is neutralized, and the air around it is *ionized*.

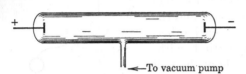

<—To vacuum pump

FIG. 193.   Gaseous discharge tube

Again, if a charged electroscope is exposed to the radiation from uranium, radium, or other radioactive substance, the electroscope loses its charge, because the radiation has ionized the air.   Ionization of the air is also produced by x-rays and ultraviolet light, as well as by cosmic radiation received by the earth from remote sources.   Practically every sample of air includes some ions.

The flow of electricity through air and other gases can be studied by the use of a glass tube fitted with sealed-in electrodes and a connection to a vacuum pump.   In the tube shown in Fig. 193, one electrode is maintained positive and the other negative; these are the *anode* and *cathode* respectively. With a large pd between the electrodes no action is observed at atmospheric pressure, but when the pressure is reduced by means of the vacuum pump, the motion of the ions produces an electrical *discharge*.   At reduced pressure this discharge may be a luminous thread of bluish color between the electrodes or a glow that fills the entire tube.   Such conduction through the tube is explained by supposing that the bombardment of positive ions knocks electrons out of the cathode, and that these electrons have sufficient energy to ionize the air within the tube by collision.   At very low pressure the discharge is in the nature of a radiation directed away from the cathode, a radiation consisting of so-called *cathode rays;* they cause certain substances upon which they impinge to glow.   These rays have electromagnetic properties by which they are recognized as a stream of high-velocity electrons.

If a pointed conductor is charged, most of the charge passes to the point, and the few ions already present in the neighboring air are accelerated so strongly that they create more ions by cumulative collision, thus permitting the electricity to escape from the conductor.   With a sufficient charge the discharge is accompanied by a glow which may be seen in the dark, and is called a *brush discharge* or *corona*.   To minimize such leakage, rounded knobs are used instead of sharp points on electrostatic apparatus.

When two electrodes, oppositely charged and located in air at ordinary pressure, are brought close to each other, the few ions already present in the air are hurled along so violently that they produce others by collision; these in turn produce still more, and by this cumulative action the air becomes highly conductive almost immediately. The result is a disruptive discharge or spark that is accompanied by a crackling noise.

Under certain atmospheric conditions the clouds gather electricity by contact with electrically charged air, and they induce charges of opposite sign on the surface of the earth below. If the intervening electric field is sufficiently intense, a disruptive discharge takes place as a stroke of *lightning*. Buildings and other structures may be protected from lightning damage by mounting on their exterior walls large pointed conductors that extend above the roof levels and are well grounded at the bottom. Such conductors, called *lightning rods*, permit a slow discharge of any charges that collect on the building or ground near by, and largely prevent the accumulation of enough charge to result in a lightning stroke. Depending upon their closeness to each other, these rods also afford more or less shielding, as described in the preceding section. In the event of a direct stroke, the lightning rods provide an easy path for the current and tend to divert it from the building.

Ionization can also occur in solids and liquids. In the solid substance sodium chloride, described in § 1, the sodium and chlorine atoms of the crystal structure carry + and − signs respectively and hence are really Na and Cl ions. In Chap. 22 it will be shown that a liquid must be ionized in order to conduct electricity.

202. Electrostatic Generators. For the operation of discharge tubes, the production of x-rays of high penetration, and the acceleration of charged particles for research on the atomic nucleus, use is often made of electrostatic generators to develop the necessary high potentials. In the modern form, the machines transport the charges on a traveling belt.

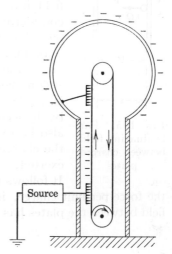

Fig 194.   Simplified electro static generator

A type of generator designed by Robert J. Van de Graaff, and developed jointly with John G. Trump, is represented diagrammatically in Fig. 194. It consists essentially of a hollow metal sphere mounted on an insulating column, within which a motor drives an endless belt of insulating material for conveying electric charges to the sphere. This sphere may be made either positive or negative; the operation will be described for the latter case.

To simplify the description, the belt is imagined to be covered with small metal disks that are insulated from each other. Two metal combs are placed at the left side of the belt; the upper one connects with the hollow sphere, and the lower one to a source having a pd of the order of 1000 volts. The belt, stretched between the motor at the bottom and an idler pulley within the sphere, is driven at high speed. As the disks pass the lower comb they pick up negative charges and carry them upward, and as they pass the upper comb the charges leave and go to the outside surface of the sphere. With continued motion of the belt the charge on the sphere becomes larger and larger and its negative potential increases accordingly. The relation between the charge and potential depends upon the diameter of the sphere, § 278. The charge can be relieved by a spark discharge to ground through the air. A unit 4 ft high can develop up to 500,000 volts with a rubber-fabric belt 10 in. wide when driven at 5000 ft/min.

203. Field Between Parallel Charged Plates. The electric field between two parallel plates is uniform, except at the edges, and the irregularities there may be neglected if the plates are large compared with the distance between them. The field intensity between the plates can be computed by considering the work done by a charge in moving from one plate to the other.

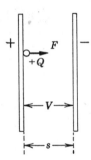

In Fig. 195, the two plates separated by a distance s are charged to a potential difference V. When a charge $+Q$ moves from the positive to the negative plate, that is, in the direction of the field, the amount of work done by it according to Eq. 138 is QV. The work done can also be expressed in terms of some force F that acts on the charge and the distance s through which this force is exerted; hence the work done is equal to the product Fs.

FIG. 195. For evaluating field between charged plates

It follows that $Fs = QV$, or $F/Q = V/s$. But F/Q, being the force per unit charge, is the field intensity, by Eq. 135; whence the field between the plates has an intensity given by

$$\mathcal{E} = \frac{V}{s} \tag{141}$$

If V is in volts and s in meters, $\mathcal{E}$ is in volts per meter. This is another name for the mks unit of electric field intensity given in § 197; hence

$$1 \text{ volt/meter} = 1 \text{ newton/coulomb}$$

204. Measurement of the Electronic Charge. An experiment that furnished an insight into the nature of electricity was the determination of the charge of the electron in 1913 by the American physicist, Robert A. Millikan (1868–1953). His method in its simplest form is to charge a tiny oil drop, place it in an electric field so directed as to urge the droplet upward against the pull of gravity, and to adjust the field strength so as to hold the droplet stationary.   Under this condition the upward force due to the field equals the downward force of gravity, a fact that permits the quantity of electricity on the droplet to be computed.

The apparatus used in the experiment is shown in Fig. 196; it consists of a closed chamber C containing near the top an atomizer A, and near the bottom a pair of parallel plates PP which can be charged from the battery B.   The air between the plates is ionized by x-rays from the tube X.   The central region between the plates is illuminated by the arc lamp Y, and ob-

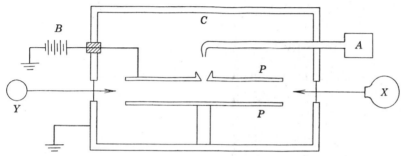

FIG. 196.   Millikan's oil-drop apparatus

servations can be made in that region by means of a telescope at the front

Oil is sprayed from the atomizer into the chamber and settles as a mist, some of the droplets falling through a pinhole into the space between the plates.   After a droplet is singled out, a preliminary measurement is made with the plates uncharged to find the time required to fall a small known distance with constant velocity.   A knowledge of this velocity makes it possible to determine the radius of the droplet from Stokes's Law, § 136, which gives the radius as

$$r = \sqrt{\frac{9\eta v}{2dg}}$$

where η is the coefficient of viscosity of the air, d the density of the oil, g the acceleration due to gravity, and v the terminal velocity of the droplet.   The mass m of the droplet can then be found from its radius and density, namely,

$$m = \tfrac{4}{3}\pi r^3 d$$

The plates PP are next connected across the battery, and the potential difference between them is adjusted to a value V such that the same droplet remains stationary at some convenient point between the plates.   The electric field strength under this condition is $\varepsilon = V/s$, where s represents the separation of the plates.   If the droplet has acquired a charge Q from the ionized air, it experiences an upward force $F = QV/s$. But this is equal to the downward force on the droplet due to gravity, whence $QV/s = mg$, from which the quantity of electricity on the droplet becomes

$$Q = \frac{mgs}{V} \tag{142}$$

The quantities in the foregoing equations should be expressed in units of the same systems, either mks or cgs.

Millikan found that the smallest charge ever acquired by a droplet has a definite value and that all others are exact multiples of this value. From these facts it is inferred that electricity consists of tiny discrete charges, and that the elementary quantity is the charge of the electron, namely,

$$e = 1.60 \times 10^{-19} \text{ coulomb} = 4.80 \times 10^{-10} \text{ statcoulomb}$$

No electrical charge smaller than this has ever been discovered.

Millikan's experiment marked an important advance in electrical science; it showed that electricity is corpuscular and not continuous in structure and established the value of the electronic charge. Furthermore, it allowed the mass of the electron to be obtained from an earlier evaluation of the ratio e/m, § 258.

PROBLEMS

1. The uncharged mercury atom has its four innermost shells filled, but the fifth has only 18 electrons and the sixth 2. List the number of electrons in its successive shells and give the total.

2. The force between two point charges is 18 newtons when they are separated by a distance of 0.5 m. What would be the force between these charges when they are (*a*) 20 cm apart and (*b*) 1.5 m apart?

3. At what separation would two like point charges each of 1 microcoulomb exert a repulsive force of 1 newton upon each other?

4. Find the force between two like point charges each of 3000 statcoulombs that are 9.49 cm apart in free space. Compare the data given with those of Prob. 3 and compare the results.

5. If the nuclei of a hydrogen atom and of a helium atom approach each other, what force does each exert upon the other when they are 10^{-6} cm apart?

6. With what force does one oxygen nucleus repel another when they are separated by a distance of 1 millimicron?

7. The electron has a mass of 9.11×10^{-28} gm, and in the normal hydrogen atom its orbital distance from the proton has an average value of 5.3×10^{-9} cm. (*a*) Compute the force of attraction between electron and proton. (*b*) How much acceleration is imparted to the electron while revolving with uniform speed in its orbit because of this force?

8. How fast does the electron of the normal hydrogen atom travel in its orbit as described in Prob. 7 and how many revolutions does it make per second?

9. Two metallized pith balls, each having a mass of 2 gm, are individually fastened to threads 50 cm long. The upper ends of the threads are fixed to a common point. When equal charges are put on the pith balls they are found to repel each other to a distance of 12 cm. Calculate the charge on each.

10. (*a*) Determine the intensity of the electric field at a place where a charge of 2×10^{-8} coulomb is acted upon by a force of 5×10^{-6} newton. (*b*) What is the electric field intensity where a charge of 60 statcoulombs is acted upon by a force of 0.5 dyne? (*c*) Compare the data given in parts *a* and *b* and compare the results.

11. A charge of $+0.1$ microcoulomb is concentrated at a point in free space. Find the electric field intensities at points 10, 20, and 100 cm away from the charge.

12. What is the electric field at a distance of 1 micron from the nucleus of a neon atom?

13. How much would an electron accelerate when it is located in an electric field having an intensity of 250 newtons/coulomb? How does the result compare with the acceleration due to gravity?

14. Make a sketch of the electric field between two equal point charges of like sign.

15. Charges of $+2$ and -1 microcoulombs are located 1.2 m apart as shown in the accompanying sketch. Calculate the electric field intensity at point *A*.

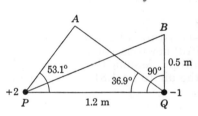

Problem 15

16. Determine the electric field intensity at point *B* for the conditions described in Prob. 15.

17. A dipole consists of equal charges $+Q$ and $-Q$ coulombs separated by a distance of 2 *s* meters. Show that the electric field intensity at a point outside the dipole distant *r* meters from its midpoint and in line with its charges has a magnitude of $\pm \dfrac{4kQrs}{(r^2 - s^2)^2}$, where $k = 9 \times 10^9$ newton·m²/coulomb².

18. For the dipole of the preceding problem derive an expression for the magnitude of the field intensity at the same distance but along its perpendicular bisector.

19. Determine the potentials at the points specified in Prob. 11. How much work is done in moving a charge of 10^{-9} coulomb from the outermost of the three points to the innermost one?

20. What is the potential at a distance of 80 cm from a charge of 6000 statcoulombs?

21. Charges of $+5$ and $+15$ microcoulombs are 2.5 m apart. (*a*) At what distance from the larger of the charges along a line connecting them is

the electric field intensity zero? (*b*) What is the electric potential at that point?

22. How much work is done in moving a charge of +3 microcoulombs from point *B* to point *A* for the conditions described in Probs. 15 and 16?

23. In a vacuum tube such as shown in Fig. 193 the electrodes are maintained at a pd of 300 volts. Assume that an electron is released at the negative electrode with no initial velocity and determine the speed with which it strikes the other.

24. What is the power required to drive an electrostatic generator if it develops a pd of 1 million volts and delivers 850 microcoulombs/sec? Neglect mechanical losses.

25. (*a*) Determine the intensity of the electric field between two large metal plates that have a uniform separation of 4 cm and a potential difference of 12,000 volts. (*b*) How much work is done in transferring a charge of 1.5 microcoulomb from one plate to the other? (*c*) What force is exerted upon this charge while in the electric field?

26. A 2000-volt source is connected across two parallel plates 5 cm in diameter and 1 cm apart. An electron is projected centrally into the region between the plates at a speed of 3×10^7 m/sec. Because of the electric field between the plates the electron is drawn toward the positive plate, but is it going fast enough to emerge from the field? Explain.

27. From the equations of § 204 derive an expression for the velocity that is imparted by an electric field to a charged particle of given radius in a viscous medium.

28. With the Millikan oil-drop apparatus, and in the absence of an electric field, a drop is observed to fall a distance of 3 mm in 50 sec. It is found that a field of 1.95×10^4 newtons/coulomb is needed to neutralize the gravitational force on this drop. Assume the density of the oil to be 0.86 gm/cm^3 and the viscosity of the air to be 1.81×10^{-4} poise. Find the number of electrons on the drop.

20

MAGNETISM

205. Magnets. A *magnet* is an object that has the property of attracting iron and steel; it can also attract a few other materials, such as nickel and cobalt, although rather feebly. Any material that a magnet can attract is known as a magnetic substance. Another property of a magnet is its ability, when freely suspended, to point in a definite direction, roughly north and south.

Magnetism was first recognized in a black mineral called lodestone—now magnetite (Fe_3O_4)—and it is believed that the word itself was derived from Magnesia, a district in Asia Minor where the ore was plentiful. It is also believed that, as far back as ten centuries B.C., Chinese sailors utilized the directional properties of a magnet by suspending pieces of lodestone for guidance in navigation.

A bar of steel can be made into a magnet merely by rubbing it with a piece of lodestone or with another magnet. It can be magnetized much more strongly, however, by placing it within a coil of wire carrying an electric current. When the bar is of hard steel, it retains its magnetism for long periods of time and is called a *permanent magnet.* Soft iron does not have such permanence. If a soft-iron bar is placed inside the coil just mentioned, forming what is known as an *electromagnet*, it becomes magnetized, but as soon as the current is interrupted it loses its magnetism except a small amount known as *residual* magnetism. The magnetizing action of the electric current is described in § 244.

206. Magnetic Poles. Experiment shows that magnetism is not exhibited uniformly over the surface of a magnet; the region where its effects are pronounced are called *poles*. A straight magnet, for example, when dipped into iron filings holds them in large clusters near its ends and shows practically no attraction at its center; thus such a magnet, as ordinarily made, has two poles. Precise tests reveal the fact that *the two poles of a magnet have exactly the same strength.*

When a bar magnet or a magnetized needle is suspended or pivoted, it rotates to a general north-and-south direction, and the same end always points northward. This fact suggested appropriate names for the two magnetic poles. The magnet pole which points to the arctic region of the earth is termed the north-seeking pole, or briefly the *north* (N) pole of the magnet; the other is termed the *south* (S) pole.

If a bar magnet is brought near another, it can be observed that the north pole of one attracts the south pole of the other, that the two north poles repel each other, and that the two south poles repel each other. In short, *unlike magnetic poles attract each other; like poles repel.*

The magnitude of the force between two magnetic poles was measured by Coulomb in 1785, using a torsion balance as in the study of electrostatic forces, but substituting magnetic poles for the electric charges. His results, later confirmed with greater accuracy, showed that the force is proportional to the strengths of the poles and inversely proportional to the square of the distance between them, the poles being assumed as concentrated at points. Thus, if two point poles have strengths m_1 and m_2, and are separated a distance r in empty space, the force between them, whether of attraction or repulsion, is given by

$$F = \frac{m_1 m_2}{\mu_o r^2} \tag{143}$$

where the constant in the denominator represents a property of the medium surrounding the poles. This constant is called *permeability;* for a vacuum it is usually designated as μ_o.

Equation 143 gives a quantitative measure of the pole strength concept. In cgs units the force F is in dynes and the separation r of the poles in centimeters; the permeability μ_o for a vacuum is taken as unity, and for air is substantially the same. With the quantities so expressed the *unit magnet pole is defined as a pole of such strength that it will exert a force of 1 dyne upon an equal pole in vacuum (or air) when placed 1 cm away from it.* There is no characteristic name for this unit of pole strength; it is merely called *unit pole.*

Illustrative Problem

As an application of the Inverse Square Law represented by Eq. 143, determine the net force between two bar magnets each 10 cm long placed in a straight line with their N poles 5 cm apart and their S poles 25 cm apart. Assume that each pole has a strength of 200 units, that it is localized in a central point on the end face of the magnet, and that the medium is air.

Between the two N poles and between the two S poles the repulsions are respectively $\dfrac{200 \times 200}{1 \times 5^2} = 1600$ dynes, and $\dfrac{200 \times 200}{1 \times 25^2} = 64$ dynes. Between each N and S pole the attraction is $\dfrac{200 \times 200}{1 \times 15^2} = 178$ dynes. Hence the net force between the magnets is $1600 - 178 + 64 - 178 = 1308$ dynes $= 0.01308$ newton.

207. The Magnetic Field. The region about a magnet where its influence can be detected as a force on another magnet is called a *magnetic field.* The force that is experienced by any given pole within the field varies in direction and in amount as that pole is moved about, and this fact indicates that the magnetic field has a certain direction and a particular intensity at every point.

The direction of a magnetic field is that of the force acting upon an isolated N *pole;* the idea of an isolated pole is convenient and implies that the companion pole of the magnet is too far away to affect the resulting action appreciably. The field is thus directed away from the N pole of a magnet and toward the S pole.

The intensity of the magnetic field at any point is defined as the force that would be exerted upon a unit N *pole placed there.* From its definition, field intensity is a vector quantity, and at any point has the same direction as the field.

The unit of field intensity in the cgs system is called the *oersted*, and is named after Hans Christian Oersted (1777–1851), the Danish physicist who discovered electromagnetism, Chap. 23. *The oersted is the intensity of a magnetic field in which a unit magnet pole is acted upon by a force of* 1 *dyne.* From this definition it follows that if at any point in a magnetic field a pole of strength m units is acted upon by a force of F dynes, the field intensity at that point in oersteds is

$$H = \frac{F}{m} \tag{144}$$

Thus, if an isolated N pole of 20 units strength placed at a point in a magnetic field is acted upon by a force of 240 dynes to the left, the field intensity there is $240 \div 20 = 12$ oersteds to the left.

The configuration of a magnetic field can be observed by placing a sheet of glass or cardboard in the region being surveyed and sprinkling it with iron filings. When the sheet is tapped, the filings align themselves with the field and form strings or chains, as represented in Fig. 197 for a bar magnet. Such tests indicate that the space around a magnet is in a peculiar magnetic condition. Faraday regarded it to be in a state of stress, whereby it is able to exert a force on any pole brought into it. He suggested the use of lines to indicate the directions of the forces on magnet poles located in a

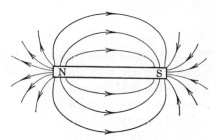

FIG. 197. Magnetic lines of force about a bar magnet

magnetic field; these lines are appropriately called *magnetic lines of force.* They are entirely fictitious but very useful in charting magnetic fields. The iron filings in the test just described assume positions that show the directions of lines of force.

Lines of force are arbitrarily taken to have the same direction as the field, and are thus directed *away from a* N *pole and toward a* S *pole*. Since a magnetic field can have only one direction at a given point, its *lines of force never cross one another*. The magnetic stresses produced by the field can be pictured by imagining that the lines tend to shorten themselves (like stretched elastic bands) and that lines extending side by side exert a sidewise thrust upon one another. The attraction or repulsion between magnet poles can then be ascribed to the interactions of lines of force in the intervening field.

Lines of force not only show the configuration of the field but are given a quantitative meaning. In a field where the lines are uniformly distributed, the number of lines of force extending perpendicularly through a unit area is taken as equal to the magnetic field intensity H in the region considered. Thus, where the lines are close together the field is strong and where they are widely separated it is weak.

208. Field Near a Magnet Pole. When the region around a magnet pole is explored it is found that the magnetic field is not uniform, but diminishes rapidly in intensity as the distance from the pole is increased. In order to determine the intensity of a field due to a pole of strength m at any point distant r from the pole, a test pole of N polarity and of strength m_1 is assumed to be placed at this point. According to Eq. 144 this pole experiences a force $m_1 H$, where H is the field intensity, as yet unknown, at the point selected. It is apparent that pole m_1 is separated from pole m by a distance r and that the force between them can also be expressed by Eq. 143 as $F = \dfrac{mm_1}{\mu_0 r^2}$, both poles being regarded as point poles located within a vacuum. Since the two foregoing expressions represent the same force, they may be equated, giving as the field intensity at the point in question:

$$H = \frac{m}{\mu_0 r^2} \tag{145}$$

This expression shows that the field intensity produced by a magnet pole varies inversely with the square of the distance from the pole; specifically, it gives the field intensity in oersteds due to an isolated pole of strength m units at a point r cm away from it.

The intensity and direction of the field due to a magnet can be obtained at any specified point by applying Eq. 145 to both of its poles, and combining the component intensities by vector addition.

Illustrative Problem

As an application of Eq. 145, compute the magnetic field intensity at points A and B due to the bar magnet shown in Fig. 198. The magnet is 6 cm long and has poles of 2000 units. Point A is 4 cm from the N pole on the axis of the magnet and point B is the same distance from the magnet on its perpendicular bisector. The surrounding medium is air.

At A the field intensity has two components, $2000 \div 4^2 = 125$ dynes per unit pole or oersteds radially away from N, and $2000 \div (6 + 4)^2 = 20$ oersteds radially toward S; these are drawn from A and extend in opposite directions and their resultant, shown by the heavy arrow, is $125 - 20 = 105$ oersteds away from N.

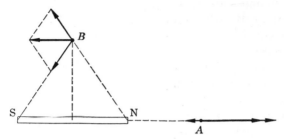

FIG. 198.   Field intensity near a bar magnet

At B the components of field intensity each have the value $2000 \div (3^2 + 4^2) = 80$ oersteds; one is directed away from N, the other is toward S, and their resultant is found by similar triangles to be $\frac{6}{5} \times 80 = 96$ oersteds parallel to the magnet and directed toward the left in the figure.

The mks units for magnetic quantities will be developed in Chap. 23. That for magnetic field intensity is called the ampere·turn per meter; one oersted is approximately equivalent to 80 amp·turns per meter.

209. Torque on a Magnet within a Field.   A bar magnet when placed in a magnetic field is subjected to forces that cause it to turn until it becomes aligned with the field.   The torque that restores the magnet to a position of equilibrium depends upon the angle between the magnet and the direction of the field.

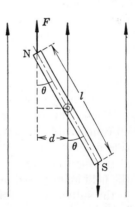

FIG. 199.   Magnet free to move in magnetic field

A magnet, of length l cm between poles, is shown in the plan view of Fig. 199 to be displaced at an angle θ from the direction of a uniform field, the field being represented by the light arrows. From Eq. 144 the N pole of the magnet is acted upon by a force in dynes amounting to $F = mH$, where m is the number of units pole strength and H is the field intensity in oersteds.   The torque due to this force about an axis through the center of the magnet is clockwise and amounts to $Fd = F\dfrac{l}{2}\sin\theta$ dyne·cm.   The force on the S pole produces a torque of the same value and direction; consequently the total torque is

$$T = 2mH\frac{l}{2}\sin\theta = MH\sin\theta$$

where $M = ml$ is a constant of the magnet called its *magnetic moment.* This torque tends to lessen the angle θ, and the magnet, because of its inertia, oscillates until friction brings it to rest in the direction of the field. While the quantities m and l are individually difficult to measure, their product M can be determined easily from the foregoing equation, since the moment of a magnet is equal to the torque needed to hold it at right angles to a field of unit intensity.

If a light magnet is mounted on a piece of cork and floated on water in a uniform magnetic field, it oscillates in the manner described but has no motion of translation. The latter fact indicates that the uniform field acts equally but oppositely upon the two poles, thus confirming a previous statement that the two poles of a magnet are equal in strength.

The idea of unit magnet pole strength used in this and preceding sections is more a mathematical concept than a tangible entity. As such it is useful in explaining magnetic fields and for indicating their relative intensities. However, the related quantity—magnetic moment—has physical significance and can be measured as just explained. The magnetic moments of an electron and of a proton are important quantities in the study of atomic structure.

210. Magnetism. An explanation of magnetism is suggested by a simple test which consists of breaking a magnet in two, then breaking one of these parts in two, and so on. As far as actual tests like this have been carried out, the parts of the original magnet are always found *to be magnets themselves;* hence it is presumed that, if the breaking process were continued until parts of microscopic magnitude were reached, each minute part would prove to be a magnet.

When a magnetic material is unmagnetized these tiny magnets point in all conceivable directions and form small stable groups that exhibit no outside magnetism. When placed, however, in a magnetic field, the magnets align themselves more and more in a definite direction as the intensity of the field is increased, and magnetic poles of increasing strength are produced in the substance. Hard steel requires a more intense field than soft iron to produce a given magnetization, because these tiny magnets turn with greater difficulty; for the same reason, upon withdrawal of the field most of them in steel retain their positions, whereas in iron most of them again assume random positions. This explains the difference in behavior of permanent magnets and electromagnets, and accounts for residual magnetism in the latter.

Again, if a piece of unmagnetized iron or other magnetic substance is placed in a magnetic field, its microscopic magnets align themselves with the field to a certain extent, and poles are *induced* in the specimen so long as it remains in the field. It is through induction that a magnet attracts a piece of unmagnetized iron, and that the iron filings line up when placed in a magnetic field.

Modern theory attributes magnetism to the **motion of electrons within the atom**, for it is known that a moving electron constitutes an electric current and that an electric current produces a magnetic effect, § 244.   In the planetary picture of an atom the electrons revolve about the nucleus and also spin about axes through their centers.   In the atoms of some elements more electrons spin in one direction than in the other, and it is believed that this unbalanced spin accounts primarily for their magnetic properties, § 266.

211. The Earth's Magnetic Field.   The orientation of a suspended magnet in a particular direction at every point on or near the earth shows that

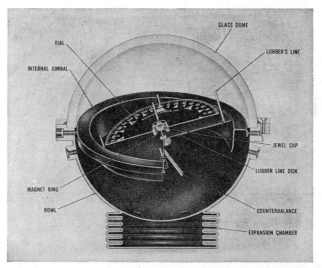

Fig. 200.   Cutaway view of magnetic compass.   (*Courtesy of E. S. Ritchie & Sons, Inc.*)

the earth is surrounded by a magnetic field.   The distribution of the field is such as might be produced roughly by a huge bar magnet within the earth, located about 17° away from its axis and having a length much less than the earth's diameter.   The two places at the earth's surface where the field is vertical are called the magnetic poles.   The latest estimate places the position of the magnetic pole in the northern hemisphere on the northwest end of Prince of Wales Island (latitude 74° N and longitude 101° W), and that in the southern hemisphere near the Mertz Glacier of the Antarctic Continent (latitude 68° S and longitude 144° E).   The magnetic equator is an imaginary line on the earth's surface connecting points where the field is horizontal.   The line is irregular and varies in latitude from 16° S in South America to 11° N in Africa.

The alignment of a pivoted magnet with the earth's magnetic field makes possible its use as a *compass* for guidance in travel and navigation.   A modern magnetic compass is shown in Fig. 200.   It has a ring-shaped Alnico magnet attached to an aluminum dial, pivoted together on a jewel bearing. The enclosing bowl and dome are filled with oil for reducing vibration, and the expansion chamber prevents the formation of an air bubble with temperature change. The lubber's line, set in the fore-aft direction of the ship, is stabilized to remain always at right angles to the dial.

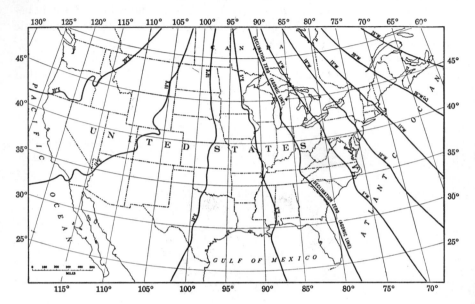

FIG. 201. Isogonic lines for the United States, 1955. (*Courtesy of U. S. Coast and Geodetic Survey*)

The magnetic polar region in the northern hemisphere is far away (1150 mi) from the north geographic pole, and, moreover, the compass is influenced by regional effects. In consequence, the compass does not point true north; the angle that it makes with the geographic meridian is called the *magnetic declination* or *variation* of the compass. A compass at New York City points about 12° west, and at San Francisco about 18° east, of geographic (true) north.

Fig. 201 shows a chart on which points of equal magnetic variation are joined by lines, the amount and direction of the declination being indicated; these lines are called *isogonic lines*. The isogonic line for which the declination is zero is called an *agonic line* and is so marked on the chart. At all places through which the agonic line passes, a compass needle points true north.

The magnetic variation at any place does not remain the same year after year, but changes somewhat over long periods of time. In addition to these so-called *secular changes*, there are fluctuations within the year and also changes of small extent throughout the day. Large erratic irregularities occur during "magnetic storms;" these are often concurrent with the appearance of sun-spots. Changes of variation are usually expressed in gammas, which are submultiples of the oersted, the gamma being 10^{-5} oersted.

The direction of the earth's magnetic field is not horizontal (except at the magnetic equator), as can readily be observed by balancing a magnetized needle on a horizontal spindle, and placing it so that its vertical plane of movement includes the direction of the field. At New York such a *dip needle* would point downward at an angle of 72.1° with the horizontal.

The horizontal and vertical components of the earth's field can be expressed in terms of the angle of dip β as

$$H_h = H_e \cos \beta \qquad \text{and} \qquad H_v = H_e \sin \beta$$

respectively, where H_e is the total intensity of the field. It is the horizontal component which is most frequently utilized in magnetic measurements. Its value in the United States ranges from 0.13 oersted at Oak Island in Lake of the Woods, Minnesota, to 0.28 oersted near Brownsville, Texas.

Much work has been done in attempting to explain terrestrial magnetism and to account for its variations, but too little is known at present about the magnetic sources within the earth and about atmospheric currents to establish a satisfying theory of the earth's magnetism.

212. The Magnetometer. It is customary to make measurements of magnetic field intensity with an instrument called a *magnetometer*. This device consists merely of a magnetic needle and some means for observing its deflection; in a simple magnetometer the needle is pivoted and carries a pointer that swings over a horizontal scale. A determination is made by comparing the field to be measured with another that is taken as a standard; the latter may be the earth's field if its value is definitely known, or else the field may be produced by an electric current, § 244.

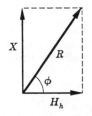

FIG. 202. Using earth's field in magnetic measurement

To measure the magnetic field X shown in the plan view of Fig. 202, the field is arranged horizontally at right angles to the earth's field of known horizontal intensity H_h. The needle of the magnetometer points in direction H_h when the unknown field X is absent, and in the direction of the resultant R of the two fields when both act upon the instrument. The angle ϕ, through which the needle deflects in moving from one position to the other, is observed. The intensity of the field under test is then

$$X = H_h \tan \phi \tag{146}$$

Another way to determine the intensity of a magnetic field in a definite plane is to allow a compass needle to swing freely in that plane and measure its rate of vibration. It can be shown in a manner similar to that for a physical pendulum, § 93, that the time of one vibration of small amplitude is

$$T = 2\pi \sqrt{\frac{I}{MH}}$$

where I is the moment of inertia of the needle about its center, M its magnetic moment, and H the field intensity sought. A common method of comparing magnetic fields is to measure the vibration time with the same compass needle successively in the two fields of intensities H_1 and H_2. The foregoing expression indicates that

$$\frac{T_1}{T_2} = \sqrt{\frac{H_2}{H_1}}$$

where the times per vibration bear corresponding subscripts.

PROBLEMS

1. Since like poles repel each other, how can the fact be explained that the N pole of a compass needle points north?

2. The bar magnets in the problem of § 206 are kept in the same alignment but are brought closer together. What is the net force between the magnets when their N poles are 2.5 cm apart?

3. Two identical magnets are arranged as in the accompanying illustration. Each is magnetized to have pole strengths of 300 units at the end points, and the distances between poles in centimeters are indicated. Compute the force between the magnets.

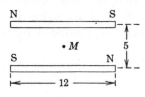

Problem 3

4. Two bar magnets are placed together center to center and held at right angles to each other. One is 8 cm long and the poles have strengths of 500 units; the other is 6 cm long and the poles have strengths of 400 units. What torque at that position is exerted between the magnets to bring them together?

5. Calculate the magnetic field intensity at a point near a bar magnet 15 cm long and having poles of 360 units strength. Choose the point to be 15 cm from each pole.

6. The magnetic field about a horseshoe magnet that has pole strengths of 600 units is to be explored in a plane perpendicular to the line joining the

poles (assumed as localized at points) and midway between them. An isolated test pole of 4 units strength, when placed at distances in this plane of 0, 2, 4, 6 and 8 cm from the line joining the poles, experiences forces of 300, 202, 107, 51 and 27 dynes. Find the magnetic field intensities at these points.

7. Choose another point from the magnet of Prob. 5, distant 5 cm from its N pole and 17 cm from its S pole, and compute the intensity of the field that the magnet produces there.

8. Determine the intensity of the magnetic field at the midpoint M between the magnets shown in Prob. 3. Reverse one magnet and solve again.

9. How far apart are the poles of the horseshoe magnet in Prob. 6?

10. A compass needle 6 cm long is mounted centrally upon a vertical pin so that it can swing in a horizontal plane. The earth's magnetic field exerts a horizontal force of 4×10^{-3} newton upon the pole at each end of the needle. Find the maximum value of the moment of the couple that acts upon the compass needle.

11. A compass needle having a magnetic moment of 100 units pole $\times$ cm is placed in several positions in a magnetic field having an intensity of 40 oersteds. Compute the torque tending to restore the needle to its equilibrium position when the needle is (*a*) at right angles to the field and (*b*) at an angle of 45° with the field.

12. The horizontal component of the earth's magnetic field has its greatest value, 0.41 oersted, near the Malay Peninsula, and the angle of dip there averages 10°. Determine the resultant field intensity and its vertical component at this location.

13. The components of the earth's field at the magnetic observatory in Cheltenham, Maryland, are 0.182 oersted horizontal and 0.540 oersted vertical. Compute the resultant field intensity and the angle of dip.

14. The compass needle of Prob. 11 vibrates 25 times in a horizontal plane every 10 sec while coming to rest in the earth's magnetic field where the horizontal intensity is 0.20 oersted. Calculate the moment of inertia of the needle about its central axis.

15. An electric current through a coil of wire produces a magnetic field that is to be measured. The coil is arranged to have its field horizontal and at right angles to the earth's field where its horizontal intensity is 0.23 oersted. If a compass needle originally aligned with the earth's field is deflected 50° when current is established in the coil, what is the intensity of the magnetic field produced by the current in the coil?

16. A pivoted magnet vibrates 40 times/min in a magnetic field where the intensity is 10 oersteds. Find the field intensity in a region wherein this magnet would vibrate 30 times/min.

21

CURRENT AND RESISTANCE

213. Electric Current. When the potential at one end of a conducting wire is different from the potential at the other, the free electrons in it undergo a drift or flow. Such a flow takes place in an electric lamp, for example, when there is a potential difference across its terminals; the flow constitutes an *electric current* through the lamp. In order for this flow to continue, the potential difference must be maintained by some electrical *source of energy*, such as a battery or generator, connected across the ends of the lamp. The source and lamp, together with the connecting wires, form a complete conducting path, or *circuit;* the part external to the source is called the *external circuit*.

The current is capable of producing a number of effects in electric circuits; the principal ones, familiar to most observers, are *heat, electrolysis,* and *magnetism*. Thus a current in an incandescent lamp heats the filament and produces illumination; a current through acidulated water (H_2O) causes the liberation of the component gases, hydrogen and oxygen, by electrolysis; a current in an electromagnet magnetizes its iron core and makes it attract pieces of iron.

214. The Simple Circuit. A circuit in which the effects of the current may be demonstrated is shown in Fig. 203. The battery B supplies current to a lamp H, an electrolytic cell E, and a coil or electromagnet M; in these circuit elements are produced respectively heat, electrolysis, and magnetism.

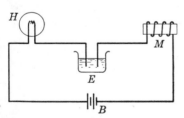

FIG. 203. Circuit to show effects of electric current

A battery or direct-current generator produces a difference of potential which establishes a current from high to low potential in an external circuit. If it is desired to have the current in the opposite direction, the terminals of the circuit must be reversed with respect to the battery or generator. For this reason, these sources of electrical energy are said to have fixed polarity, and one terminal of the source is called positive and the other negative.

From the early days of electrical science, current has been considered to traverse the external circuit from the positive terminal of the source to its negative terminal. It is now known that a current is actually a movement of electrons, and since these are negative, they travel around the external circuit from the negative terminal to the positive terminal. The *electron flow* is, therefore, opposite to the conventional direction of the *current*, making it necessary, in order to avoid confusion, to distinguish one from the other by name.

Present-day electric generating stations supply *alternating current*, which means that the flow of electrons reverses periodically through the circuits supplied by the generators. These alternating-current generators reverse their polarity at a definite rate and usually produce in every second 60 pulses of current in one direction alternately with an equal number in the other.

215. The Coulomb and the Ampere. The current in a metallic circuit is essentially a drifting of free electrons through it; quantitatively, *current* is defined as *the time rate of flow of electric charge*. The unit of current is appropriately taken as the flow of one coulomb of charge per second past some point in the circuit. Because the concept of current is so commonly used a shorter name is applied to the unit; it is called the *ampere* (abbreviated amp) in honor of the French scientist André M. Ampère (1775–1836). *The ampere is a rate of flow of electric charge of one coulomb per second.* If electricity flows at a uniform rate such that Q coulombs pass a point in t sec, the current at that point expressed in amperes is

$$I = \frac{Q}{t} \tag{147}$$

Current is measured by an instrument called an ammeter. It includes a coil, pivoted between the poles of a permanent magnet and provided with a pointer that moves over a scale. The coil is deflected by the magnetic effect of the current through it, and the size of the deflection is a measure of the current.

Electric current is sometimes confused with electric charge. The difference can be clarified through analogy with hydraulics, by considering a pump that circulates water in a pipe line, just as a battery or generator circulates charges in an electric circuit. The quantity of water is reckoned in gallons, and the rate of flow past any point in the piping is expressed in gallons per second; the quantity of electricity is reckoned in coulombs, and the rate of flow of current is expressed in coulombs per second (or amperes).

216. Electromotive Force and Potential Drop. In the study of electrostatics it was found that work is always done in moving an electric charge between two points which have different potentials, and the pd is defined as the work done per unit charge, Eq. 138. When a charge circulates around an electric circuit, *the charge does work* in traversing the circuit, as evidenced by the evolution of heat and the operation of electromechanical devices; also *work is done on the charge* as it moves through the battery or other source of electrical energy. The battery or other source is said to have an *electromotive force* (abbreviated emf), which is measured by the work done per unit charge as the charge passes through the source.

A source which can do an amount of work W upon a charge Q has an electromotive force given by

$$E = \frac{W}{Q} \tag{148}$$

As the charge moves around the external circuit and does an amount of work W in passing between two circuit points, the *potential difference* between these points is

$$V = \frac{W}{Q} \tag{149}$$

According to the Law of Conservation of Energy, the energy that the charge receives from the source must be the same as that which it expends throughout the circuit; hence it follows that the emf of the source must equal the sum of the potential drops around the circuit.

The volt, § 198, is the practical unit of both emf and potential difference. A source of electrical energy has an emf of one volt when one joule of work is done on one coulomb of charge in moving it through the source. The potential difference between two points of an electric circuit is one volt when one coulomb of charge does one joule of work in moving from one point to the other. In Eqs. 148 and 149, if W is expressed in joules and Q in coulombs, then E and V are in volts.

The difference of potential between two points in an electric circuit is measured by an instrument called a *voltmeter*, by merely connecting the instrument across the points under consideration. It operates on the same principle as the ammeter but is designed to take very little current and is calibrated to read in volts.

To give a practical idea of the volt, a few illustrations will be helpful: The familiar dry cell has an emf of 1.5 volts. Automobile engines are started by motors operated from storage batteries having an emf of 6 volts or more. Practically all electric lamps are illuminated by direct or alternating current supplied at 110 to 120 volts. Electric generating stations distribute electrical energy over moderate distances with potential differences of several thousand volts, and transmit such energy over long distances with potential differences up to 330,000 volts.

217. Electrical Energy and Power. It is apparent from the preceding section that the electrical energy supplied to a circuit by a source is given by the product of the emf E of the source and the charge Q transported around the circuit; hence $W = EQ$. This result can be expressed more usefully in terms of current rather than charge. Since the quantity of charge Q transferred is equal to the average current I multiplied by the time t of transfer, or $Q = It$, the energy supplied by the source of emf E can be expressed as

$$W = EIt \qquad (150)$$

Also, in any portion of a circuit across which the potential drop is V, the energy liberated is

$$W = VIt$$

In these expressions the energy W is expressed in joules, the emf E or potential drop V in volts, the current I in amperes, and the time t in seconds. The energy may appear in any form, such as heat, mechanical energy, or chemical energy.

The rate of expending energy in a circuit is the *power* supplied to it; this is found by differentiating the foregoing expressions with respect to time. Thus, the power supplied to the entire circuit is

$$P = \frac{dW}{dt} = EI \qquad (151)$$

and that expended in a portion of the circuit is

$$P = \frac{dW}{dt} = VI$$

In these equations the unit in which power is expressed is the joule per second, or watt. Therefore 1 watt = 1 volt $\times$ 1 amp.

218. Ohm's Law and Resistance. Experience with metallic circuits connected to an electrical source of energy shows that the current established in them is directly proportional to the emf of the source. Thus, the current I in these circuits varies directly with the emf E. By the use of a constant the relation between these quantities can be expressed as an equation, namely,

$$I = \frac{E}{R} \qquad (152)$$

where the constant R is called the *resistance* of the circuit. This relation was first given by the German physicist Georg S. Ohm (1789–1854) and is known by his name.

Ohm's Law states that the current in a metallic circuit is given by the emf in that circuit divided by the resistance of the circuit when the temperature is kept constant. If either the emf or the resistance is altered, the current automatically adjusts itself to maintain the relationship. Each of the symbols in the equation should be interpreted as applying to the entire circuit; thus R stands for all the resistance of the circuit, including the internal resistance of the source.

Ohm's Law may also be stated for part of a circuit as follows: The current in any part of a circuit is given by the potential drop across that part of the circuit divided by the resistance of that part. In symbols

$$I = \frac{V}{R} \tag{153}$$

This equation further serves to establish the unit in which resistance is expressed. Thus, if the potential drop across a resistance is one volt when the current in it is one ampere, then the resistance must have unit value; this unit is called the *ohm*. *The ohm is a resistance across which there is a potential drop of one volt when the current in it is one ampere.*

A few examples will serve to give an approximate idea of the unit of resistance. A copper wire 1000 ft long and 0.1 in. in diameter (No. 10 American wire gage) has a resistance of 1 ohm. A copper wire 2.4 ft long and 0.005 in. in diameter (No. 36) has the same resistance. An iron rod 0.75 km long and 1 cm square in section also has a resistance of 1 ohm.

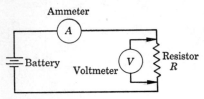

FIG. 204. Measuring resistance with ammeter and voltmeter

The resistance of a wire or device can be determined by connecting it in a circuit to a battery and using an ammeter to measure the current in it and a voltmeter to measure the potential drop across it, as shown in Fig. 204. If the current is I and the pd is V, the value of the resistance is $R = V \div I$. The instrument connections shown are also suitable for measuring the power expended in the resistance, this being the product of the ammeter and voltmeter readings, as indicated by the equation $P = VI$.

Illustrative Problem

An electric toaster takes a current of 10 amp when connected to 115-volt service mains. Determine the resistance of the toaster and the power expended.

The resistance of the toaster is given by Ohm's Law as 115 volts ÷ 10 amp = 11.5 ohms, and the power expended is 115 volts × 10 amp = 1150 watts.

219. Joule's Law of Heating. The flow of electricity through a wire or similar conductor always produces heat. The amount of heat generated in such a conductor is exactly equivalent to the energy supplied electrically, in accordance with the principle of Conservation of Energy. For a given conductor, the quantity of heat produced naturally depends upon the duration of flow and upon the value of the current. Still another factor is involved, namely, the resistance of the conductor. If the same current prevails for equal periods of time through two like-sized wires, one of copper and the ther of iron, the iron becomes hotter than the copper, showing that iron offer more opposition to electron flow than copper; hence the iron wire has the h. her resistance.

The energy supplied to a conductor across which a source maintains a pd V for a time t is given in the preceding section as $W = VIt$, where I is the current established in this conductor. If R is its resistance, then the pd can be expressed by Ohm's Law as $V = IR$. A combination of these equations shows that the energy expended in the conductor and converted into heat is

$$W = RI^2t \qquad (154)$$

This equation states that *the heat produced in a conductor is proportional to the resistance of the conductor, to the square of the current, and to the time.* This statement is known as Joule's Law of electric heating.

In Eq. 154 the heat energy is expressed directly in mechanical or electrical units; when R is in ohms, I in amperes, and t in seconds, then W is in joules. The energy can also be expressed in heat units by introducing a conversion factor, § 171. Since 1 joule = 0.239 calorie, the heat in calories is given by

$$H = 0.239RI^2t$$

If a current of 1 amp is maintained for 1 sec through a conductor of 1 ohm resistance, the amount of heat produced is exactly 1 joule, or 0.239 calorie.

The foregoing relations can be verified by using a calorimeter containing oil or other insulating liquid and immersing the conductor in it as shown in Fig. 205. The amount of current supplied to the conductor by the battery or other source is indicated by an ammeter, and the duration of flow by a stop watch. The heat liberated by the conductor can be determined by measuring the water equivalent of the calorimeter and its contents,

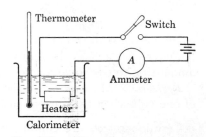

FIG. 205. Measuring the heat produced by an electric current

and observing the change of temperature that occurs during the test, § 147.

The rate at which electrical energy is converted into heat is given by $W \div t$; hence the *power* dissipated in heat is given in joules per second (or watts) by

$$P = RI^2 \cdot \qquad (155)$$

This expression applies equally well to an entire circuit or to any part of it, but the symbols must be interpreted accordingly.

Illustrative Problem

Compute the rating of an electric heater that can heat 10 liters of water from 20° to 80° C in 15 min, on the assumption that no heat is wasted. Also, what current must be supplied to this heater if its resistance is 5 ohms?

The heat needed is 10,000 × (80 − 20) = 600,000 cal, and thi amount is equal to 600,000 ÷ 0.239 = 2,511,000 joules. The power required is 2,511,000 ÷ (15 × 60) = 2790 watts; this is equivalent to a rating of 2.79 kw. From Eq. 155, $P = 2790 = 5 \times I^2$; whence the current is 23.6 amp.

220. The Practical Electrical Units. For convenience of reference the electrical quantities so far dealt with are defined below:

Charge: The *coulomb* is a quantity of electric charge that theoretically would exert a force of 9×10^9 newtons on an identical charge at a distance of one meter in free space, § 195. A coulomb is equivalent to a charge of 6.24×10^{18} electrons. The reasons for these particular numbers will be apparent after the magnetic effect of the electric current has been considered, Chap. 23.

Current: The *ampere* is a unit of current which is equal to a rate of flow of electric charge of one coulomb per second.

Energy: The *joule* is an amount of energy equal to the work done by a force of one newton exerted steadily upon a body while it moves through a distance of one meter in the direction of the force, § 61.

Electromotive Force: The *volt* is the emf of a source of electrical energy which does one joule of work on one coulomb of charge in moving through the source.

Potential Difference: The *volt* is the difference in potential between two points when a charge of one coulomb expends one joule of energy in moving from one point to the other.

Power: The *watt* is the unit of power and represents a rate of doing work amounting to one joule per second; also the watt equals a volt·ampere.

Resistance: The *ohm* is a resistance across which there is a potential drop of one volt when the current in it is one ampere.

Certain prefixes are commonly used with these units to denote large or small values of them. These include: meg = 10^6, kilo = 10^3, milli = 10^{-3}, and micro = 10^{-6}. Thus, 1 megohm = 1,000,000 ohms, and 1 microvolt = 0.000001 volt.

The relations between the practical and mks units and the electrostatic units can be found directly from the definitions in the two systems. They are as follows: 1 coulomb = 3×10^9 statcoulombs; 1 joule = 1 newton· meter = 10^7 ergs; 1 volt = $\frac{1}{300}$ statvolt.

221. Factors Affecting Resistance. The resistance of an electrical conductor opposes the flow of electrons in somewhat the same way that friction in a pipeline opposes the flow of water. As might be expected from this similarity, electrical resistance is directly proportional to the length of the conductor and inversely proportional to its cross-sectional area. Further, it is found that two conductors of the same dimensions have different resistances if made of different substances. This is ascribed to a difference in resistivity, the *resistivity* being the resistance of a sample of the substance having specified unit dimensions. Consequently, a conductor of length l, cross-sectional area A, and resistivity ρ (rho), has a resistance R given by the equation

$$R = \rho \frac{l}{A} \tag{156}$$

The reciprocal of resistivity is called *conductivity*, and its symbol is σ (sigma). Thus the resistance of a conductor can also be expressed as

$$R = \frac{l}{\sigma A} \tag{157}$$

The units of resistivity and conductivity are necessarily such that the quantities in the right-hand members of these equations yield ohms.

222. Resistivity and Conductivity. In calculating the resistance of conductors from their physical properties it is customary to make use of two systems of units. In the metric system, the length and cross-sectional area are expressed respectively in centimeters and square centimeters; to make the units balance the resistivity is in ohm·centimeters. Thus, copper has a resistivity of 1.72×10^{-6} ohm·cm, which means that a specimen of copper 1 cm long and 1 cm^2 in cross-section offers a resistance between opposite faces of 1.72×10^{-6} ohm = 1.72 microhms.

In the other system the length of the conductor is expressed in feet and the cross-section in a unit of area called the *circular mil*. One circular mil (abbreviated cir mil) is the area of a circle 0.001 in. (1 mil) in diameter. Since the area of a circle varies as the square of its diameter, a wire having a diameter of 2 mils has an area of 4 cir mils, one having a diameter of 3 mils has an area of 9 cir mils, and so on. Thus, *to find the cross-section of a wire in circular mils, the diameter should be expressed in mils and then squared.* The circular mil is a convenient unit of area for round wires because it avoids the use of the factor $\pi/4$ in the calculations.

When the length of a wire is expressed in feet and its cross-section in circular mils, the corresponding unit for resistivity in Eq. 156 is the ohm·circular mil per foot. Thus, copper has a resistivity of 10.4 ohm·cir mils per ft, meaning that a specimen of copper 1 ft long and 1 cir mil in cross-section has a resistance of 10.4 ohms.

The following table lists the resistivities of a number of common materials. The resistivity of a substance is affected somewhat by temperature changes, and the values shown apply to temperatures around 20° C. By comparing this table with that in § 182, it will be observed that those substances which are good conductors of heat usually have low resistivity and are, therefore, good conductors of electricity as well.

RESISTIVITIES OF CONDUCTORS

Substance	Microhm·cm	Ohm·cir mils per ft
Aluminum	3.21	19.3
Carbon	4000 to 7000	24,000 to 42,000
Constantan (Cu 60%, Ni 40%)	49	295
Copper	1.72	10.4
Iron	12 to 14	72 to 84
Lead	20.8	125
Manganin (Cu 84%, Ni 4%, Mn 12%)	43	258
Mercury	95.76	575
Nichrome (Ni 60%, Cr 12%, Fe 26%, Mn 2%)	110	660
Platinum	11.0	66
Silver	1.65	9.9
Tungsten	5.5	33
Zinc	6.1	36.7

Fig. 206 pictures the specimens to which reference has been made. The units of conductivity in the two systems are the reciprocals of the corresponding units of resistivity.

Wires of low resistivity (principally of copper) are used in transmitting electrical energy in order to minimize heat losses. Conductors of relatively high resistivity are used when the primary purpose of the current is to produce heat; for example, Nichrome is serviceable for electric heaters.

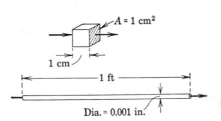

FIG. 206. Conductor dimensions on which resistivity values are based

Conductors of moderately high resistivity, combined with a low melting point, are used for electric fuses. The fuse consists of a short strip of metal, usually a lead alloy, connected directly into a circuit and is designed to melt with excessive current, thus protecting the circuit against overheating. The fusible element is suitably encased to confine the arcing that results upon opening the circuit when it melts.

The resistivities of insulators are vastly greater than those of conductors; thus, the resistivity of gutta percha is 2×10^9 ohm·cm and that of mica is 9×10^{15} ohm·cm.

223. Copper Wires. For the wiring of electric circuits and the windings of electrical apparatus, copper is used almost exclusively because of its low resistivity and moderate cost. In this country, wire sizes are standardized in terms of the American wire gage (Awg). A few entries from copper wire tables are herewith; the resistances are based on the International Annealed Copper Standard, and the current-carrying capacities are those allowed by the National Electrical Code for wires installed in conduit.

TABLE FOR COPPER WIRE

Awg No.	Diameter, mils	Cross-section, cir mils	Resis-tance, ohms per 1000 ft	Type of insulation Allowable carrying capacity, amp		
				Rubber	Thermo-plastic	Asbestos
2	258	66,400	0.156	95	120	165
3	229	52,600	0.197	80	105	145
4	204	41,700	0.249	70	90	120
6	162	26,300	0.395	55	70	95
8	129	16,500	0.628	40	50	70
10	102	10,400	0.999	30	40	55
12	81	6,530	1.59	20	30	40
14	64	4,110	2.53	15	25	30

Illustrative Problem

As a numerical example, consider an installation of lamps requiring 30 amp and located in a room 200 ft away from a source that maintains 120 volts across its terminals. What is the smallest size of rubber-insulated copper wire that can be used for the line conductors connecting the lamp load to the source, in order to keep the potential drop in them down to $2\frac{1}{2}\%$?

The first step is to find the resistance of the *line*. This can be done by evaluating the pd across it and the current in it. A $2\frac{1}{2}\%$-drop amounts to $0.025 \times 120 = 3$ volts across the two line wires, leaving 117 volts available for illuminating the lamps. The resistance of the line should be such as to give this 3-volt drop with a current of 30 amp; the resistance is given by Ohm's Law as $R = \dfrac{3 \text{ volts}}{30 \text{ amp}} = 0.10$ ohm. The next step is to find the cross-sectional area of the line wires which have a total length of 400 ft. From Eq. 156, the area is $A = \rho \dfrac{l}{R} = 10.4 \dfrac{\text{ohm} \cdot \text{cir mils}}{\text{ft}} \dfrac{400 \text{ ft}}{0.10 \text{ ohm}} = 41,600$ cir mils. From the copper wire table, the nearest standard size to this value is found to be No. 4 Awg with 41,700 cir mils; this is the proper wire size as determined by potential-drop considerations. The final step is to check the allowable current-carrying capacity of this size of conductor. The table shows that a rubber-insulated No. 4 wire is rated at 70 amp. Since the line current is less than this value, this size of wire is adequate for the installation.

224. Resistors in Series and in Parallel. There are two simple forms of electric circuit; the *series* circuit provides a single conducting path, and the *parallel* circuit provides more than one. In part I of Fig. 207, a battery supplies current to two resistors R_1 and R_2 connected in series. In part II, it supplies current to the two resistors connected in parallel or multiple.

Part I of the figure represents a frequent application where current through a device of fixed resistance R_1 is being controlled by an adjustable

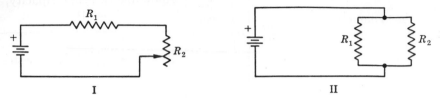

FIG. 207.　Battery supplying current to a series and a parallel circuit

resistance R_2 called a *rheostat*. Part II represents the usual connection of lamps to electric service mains; the brightness of each lamp depends upon the current through it, and either lamp can be turned off without interfering with the other.

In the series arrangement the current has the same value throughout the circuit; that is, the current is the same in the battery and in each resistor. Also, the sum of the potential drops across the several resistors is equal to the emf applied to the circuit, § 216.

In the parallel arrangement the current supplied by the battery divides between the two resistors, and the current in each is determined by its resistance. Also the pd between the terminals of resistor R_1 is the same as that for resistor R_2. In any parallel circuit the potential drop is the same across all branches and the currents in the branches add up to the value of the main current.

Actually, the connection of a single resistor to a source, whether a battery or a generator, forms a series circuit, because the source itself has resistance. Although its value is small, this so-called *internal* resistance may not be negligible. Its effect is to make the pd at the terminals less than the emf E of the source when there is current in the circuit. If the internal resistance of the source is r and the current I, then by Eq. 153 the pd within the source is Ir. When a path is traced through the source from the $-$ to the $+$ terminal, there is a rise of potential amounting to E, and also a drop of potential amounting to Ir. Hence, the potential difference across the terminals of the source is

$$V_t = E - Ir \tag{158}$$

225. Equivalent Resistances. Electric circuits usually include resistors that may be connected either in series or in parallel. To find the effect of such grouping upon the entire resistance of the circuit, consideration is given to a circuit having several resistors of resistance R_1, R_2, R_3, $\cdots$; the currents in these resistors are designated respectively as I_1, I_2, I_3, $\cdots$ and the potential drops across them as V_1, V_2, V_3, $\cdots$. Whether the component resistors are connected in series or in parallel, the rate of heat production in the entire circuit, from Eq. 155, is

$$P = R_1 I_1{}^2 + R_2 I_2{}^2 + R_3 I_3{}^2 + \cdots$$

The entire group of resistors may be replaced by an equivalent single resistor of such resistance R that the current I supplied to it is the same as the current supplied to the entire group when the pd V across this resistor is the same as that across the group. The heat produced in this equivalent

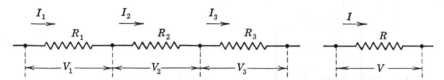

F*ig.* 208. Series connection of resistors and their equivalent resistance

resistor is RI^2. The series and parallel connection of the component resistors will be considered separately.

Series Connection. When the resistors are connected in series, as in Fig. 208, the current is the same in all of them, so that

$$I = I_1 = I_2 = I_3 = \cdots$$

Since the total rate of developing heat in the component resistors is the same as in the equivalent resistor R, it follows that

$$RI^2 = R_1 I^2 + R_2 I^2 + R_3 I^2 + \cdots$$

which shows that the equivalent resistance of the group of resistors in series is equal to the sum of their individual resistances, or

$$R = R_1 + R_2 + R_3 + \cdots \tag{159}$$

as might be anticipated.

Parallel Connection. When the resistors are connected in parallel as in Fig. 209, the potential drop is the same across all of them, so that

$$V = V_1 = V_2 = V_3 = \cdots$$

The total rate at which heat is developed in the component resistors, namely,

$$P = R_1 \left(\frac{V_1}{R_1}\right)^2 + R_2 \left(\frac{V_2}{R_2}\right)^2 + R_3 \left(\frac{V_3}{R_3}\right)^2 + \cdots$$

is the same as the rate in the equivalent resistor R; hence

$$V^2 \left(\frac{1}{R_1} + \frac{1}{R_2} + \frac{1}{R_3} + \cdots\right) = \frac{V^2}{R}$$

which shows the relation between the individual resistances R_1, R_2, R_3 $\cdots$, and the equivalent resistance R when these are joined in parallel to be

$$\frac{1}{R} = \frac{1}{R_1} + \frac{1}{R_2} + \frac{1}{R_3} + \cdots \tag{160}$$

It is an interesting fact that the group resistance is less than the lowest of the individual resistances.

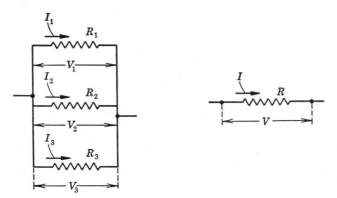

FIG. 209. Parallel connection of resistors and their equivalent resistance

The connection of *only two* resistances in parallel is of frequent occurrence in electric circuits. For two resistors R_1 and R_2 in parallel the equivalent resistance is given by Eq. 160 as

$$R = \frac{R_1 R_2}{R_1 + R_2}$$

that is, their product divided by their sum.

226. Electric Networks. The circuits that are employed in electrical work cover a variety of types; they may consist of simple series and parallel groupings like those described in the preceding section, or combinations of these groupings, or arrangements which take the forms of the letters wye (Y) and delta (Δ), or they may be repeated groupings in the form of a ladder. The term *electric network* is used for the more complicated circuits.

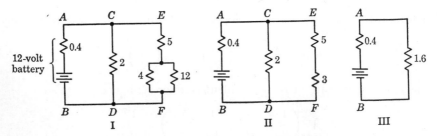

FIG. 210. Steps in simplifying a series-parallel circuit

In analyzing electric networks the plan is usually to simplify them step by step, and then solve for the unknown factors. To illustrate the procedure, consideration will be given to the circuit shown in part I of Fig. 210. It consists of the branches *CD* and *EF* in parallel, and this pair connected in series with path *AB* that includes the battery. The branch *EF* with a parallel group is simplified as shown in part II, and then the two parallel paths *CD* and *EF* are merged as shown in part III. By repeated application of Ohm's Law, it becomes possible to compute the current supplied by the battery, the current in each of the resistance elements, and the potential drop across each.

Illustrative Problem

The circuit shown in Fig. 210 is supplied with current from a battery having an emf of 12 volts and an internal resistance of 0.4 ohm; find the currents in all resistors. Their resistance in ohms are indicated on them.

The 4-ohm and 12-ohm parallel combination in part I is equivalent to a single resistance of $\dfrac{4 \times 12}{4 + 12} = 3.0$ ohms; this is in series with the 5-ohm resistor as shown in part II. The parallel combination of 8 ohms and 2 ohms is equivalent to a single resistance of 1.6 ohms as shown in part III. The total resistance of the network is therefore $1.6 + 0.4 = 2.0$ ohms.

The current supplied by the battery is 12 volts ÷ 2 ohms = 6.0 amp. The pd across the battery resistance is $6 \times 0.4 = 2.4$ volts, leaving $12 - 2.4 = 9.6$ volts across the battery terminals *A* and *B*. This pd is available to both paths *CD* and *EF*. The current in branch *CD* is $9.6 \div 2 = 4.8$ amp, and that in branch *EF* is $9.6 \div 8 = 1.2$ amp. The pd across the 5-ohm resistor is $1.2 \times 5 = 6$ volts, leaving $9.6 - 6 = 3.6$ volts across the parallel combination of the 4-ohm and 12-ohm resistors. The currents in these are respectively 0.9 and 0.3 amp.

227. Kirchhoff's Network Laws. The more intricate networks are not easily solved by the method used in the preceding section, and recourse is had to two general principles pointed out by the German physicist Gustav R. Kirchhoff (1824–1887), as follows:

1. *At any point in an electric circuit where two or more conductors are joined, the sum of the currents directed toward the junction equals the sum of the currents directed away from the junction.* This law can be rephrased to state that the algebraic sum of the currents at a junction equals zero. Currents toward the junction are regarded as positive and those away from the junction as negative; then symbolically

$$\Sigma I = 0 \qquad (161)$$

2. *Around any closed path in an electric circuit, the algebraic sum of the rises and falls of potential equals zero.* Rise of potential is considered as positive and fall or drop of potential as negative. The fact that a current *I* in a resistance *R* corresponds to a potential drop *IR* permits this law to be stated as: the algebraic sum of the emfs and potential drops in any closed

path of a circuit is zero, or symbolically

$$\Sigma E - \Sigma IR = 0 \qquad (162)$$

In applying these laws to the solution of a network, some direction should be assumed for the current in each branch, and then Kirchhoff's Laws should be expressed in as many independent equations as there are unknown currents. These equations are solved simultaneously to find the currents in the several branches of the circuit. If the result gives a negative value for any current, then its direction is opposite to that originally assumed.

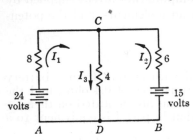

FIG. 211. Network for solution by Kirchhoff's Laws

Illustrative Problem

As an example on Kirchhoff's Laws, consider the network of Fig. 211, in which the numbers on the resistors represent their resistances in ohms. Current is supplied to the network by two batteries as shown. Find the values of the currents marked I_1, I_2, and I_3, assumed to be directed as indicated by the arrows.

From the first law, the currents at point C are related as follows:

$$I_1 + I_2 - I_3 = 0$$

From the second law, the sum of the emfs and pds around the closed paths ACD and BCD are respectively

$$24 - 8I_1 - 4I_3 = 0$$

$$15 - 6I_2 - 4I_3 = 0$$

Subtraction of the last equation from the one preceding gives

$$9 - 8I_1 + 6I_2 = 0$$

Elimination of I_3 between the first two equations gives

$$36 - 18I_1 - 6I_2 = 0$$

Addition of the last two equations shows that $I_1 = 1.731$ amp; substitution of this value in either one gives $I_2 = 0.808$ amp. Finally $I_3 = I_1 + I_2 = 1.731 + 0.808 = 2.539$ amp.

228. The Wheatstone Bridge. The Wheatstone bridge is an instrument for measuring a resistance by comparing it with standards of known value. This method, devised in 1833 by S. Hunter Christie, was brought to public attention by the English physicist Sir Charles Wheatstone (1802–1875), and has remained associated with his name. Observations are made by the "null" method which does not require the calibration of the indicating device.

The bridge consists of four resistors connected as shown in Fig. 212 to a battery B and a sensitive current-indicating device called a galvanometer, § 252. One of the resistances, X, is unknown, and the other three are known and adjustable in value. In using the bridge, resistances M and N are given suitable values, and then resistance R is adjusted until the galvanometer G shows no deflection. The bridge is then said to be balanced, and the resistance of X can be found from the known values of resistances M, N, and R.

To derive the equation of the bridge, it should be observed that, since there is no current in the galvanometer when the bridge is balanced, the current in M must be the same as that in X; this current in the upper branch of the bridge is designated I_C. Similarly, the current in N is the same as that in R; this current in the lower branch is designated I_D. The fact that there is no current in the galvanometer also shows that the potential at point C must be the same as that at point D. Hence the pd

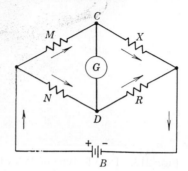

Fig. 212. Diagram of Wheatstone bridge circuit

across M is the same as that across N; also the pd across X is the same as that across R. In symbols, these statements become:

$$I_C M = I_D N$$

$$I_C X = I_D R$$

The first of these expressions is divided by the second, term by term, whereupon the resistance of the unknown becomes

$$X = \frac{M}{N} R \qquad (163)$$

and this is the equation of the balanced bridge. The resistances M and N that appear as a ratio in the equation are called the ratio arms of the bridge, and resistance R is called the rheostat arm.

Wheatstone bridges are made in various forms. In the precision type illustrated in Fig. 213, the known resistances are inside the case, and binding posts are provided at the right for external connections to the battery and galvanometer and at the left for connection to the resistance being measured. The ratio arms M and N are set by inserting plugs between metal blocks at the right, the rheostat arm R is adjustable from 10,000 to 0.1 ohm by five dials marked thousands, hundreds, tens, units, and tenths. Switches known as keys are provided at the front for closing the

FIG. 213.   Decade type of Wheatstone bridge for precise resistance measurements. (*Courtesy of Leeds & Northrup Company*)

battery and galvanometer circuits momentarily while a balance is being obtained.

229. Influence of Temperature upon Resistance.   Experimentation with metallic conductors shows that their resistance usually increases as the temperature is raised.   The relationship between resistance and temperature for a metal conductor is of the same form as that which applies to the expansion of a metal rod, § 140, but the percentage variation of resistance with temperature change is usually much greater than the corresponding percentage variation in size.   If R_{20} represents the resistance of a conductor at normal room temperature of 20° C (68° F), its resistance at temperature t is expressed by

$$R_t = R_{20}[1 + \alpha(t - 20)] \tag{164}$$

where α is a constant of the material called its *temperature coefficient of resistance*.   Numerically, α represents the increase of resistance of a 1-ohm resistance of the material when subjected to a temperature rise of 1 degree above 20° C.

The temperature coefficient is positive for metallic conductors, and for all pure metals the values have the same order of magnitude.   Certain alloys have been developed in which α is very small; these materials are useful for the resistors in Wheatstone bridges, resistance boxes, and other measuring instruments in which constancy of resistance is desired.   For practical purposes, where the temperature change involved is small, the temperature coefficient is usually considered as remaining constant at the value that it has at the reference temperature of 20° C; actually it varies somewhat with the temperature, and for accurate calculations the average value for the given temperature range should be used. Eq. 164 applies also to nonmetallic substances, including carbon, liquids, and insulating materials; for these the temperature coefficient is usually negative.

The accompanying table lists the values of the temperature coefficient for a number of materials commonly used. Unless otherwise specified, these values apply to the reference temperature of 20° C.

TEMPERATURE COEFFICIENTS OF RESISTANCE

Material	α per C°
Aluminum.............	0.0038
Carbon (0 to 1850° C) ..	−0.00025
Constantan...........	−0.00004 to +0.00001
Copper...............	0.00393
Iron.................	0.0062
Lead.................	0.0043
Manganin............	0.000002 to 0.00005
Mercury.............	0.00090
Nichrome............	0.00017
Platinum............	0.0038
Silver...............	0.0040
Tungsten............	0.0045
Zinc................	0.0037

The Resistance Thermometer. The fact that the resistance of a conductor changes with temperature is utilized in the so-called *resistance thermometer.* This device consists of a calibrated coil of wire together with suitable instruments for measuring its resistance, the coil being placed wherever the temperature is to be measured. This type of thermometer is useful over a wide temperature range, is very precise, and can be read from a remote point.

Illustrative Problem

To illustrate the measurement of temperature by a resistance thermometer, consider a coil of platinum wire to have a resistance of 8.0 ohms at 20° C and double the resistance when placed in a certain oven. Assume α to be 0.0038 per C° over the temperature range involved, and determine the temperature of the oven.

The oven temperature is given by Eq. 164 as

$$t = 20 + \frac{R_t - R_{20}}{R_{20}\alpha} = 20 + \frac{16.0 - 8.0}{8.0 \times 0.0038} = 20 + 263 = 283°\ C$$

230. Superconductivity. Certain metals exhibit a remarkable drop in resistance at very low temperatures; this effect was discovered in 1911 by Onnes and is known as *superconductivity.* As the temperature is lowered, the resistance of the specimen is observed to decrease in the manner to be expected from Eq. 164, but at a certain critical temperature—for each material a characteristic value not many degrees above absolute zero ($-273°$ C or $0°$ K)—the resistance drops abruptly to an extremely low value. The resistance of lead, for instance, becomes less than 10^{-12} of the value it has at $0°$ C. Tests with a lead ring at such low temperatures show that a current once developed in the ring persists after removal of the source of emf for many hours. Briefly, superconductivity implies the frictionless motion of electrons.

Another property of superconductors is the tendency to screen off external magnetic fields; this behavior is ascribed to frictionless currents in their surfaces at these low temperatures. Within a field of low intensity there is no penetration of the field into the interior, but in stronger fields the screening currents decay, the field does penetrate, and the metal reverts to its normal resistive state.

Superconductivity has been observed in numerous metallic elements, including tin at a critical temperature of $3.69°$ K, mercury at $4.12°$ K, and lead at $7.26°$ K, as well as in a large number of alloys. The compound niobium nitride becomes superconducting at a temperature of $14°$ K.

Recent tests at extremely high pressures have shown bismuth to become superconducting at 20,000 atmospheres with a critical temperature of about $7°$ K. Extensive research is being conducted at low temperatures to establish energy relations in superconductors and to develop a theory for their behavior.

PROBLEMS

1. (*a*) If an isolated sphere receives an electric charge of 10 microcoulombs in 20 sec, what is the average value of the current supplied to it? (*b*) What would the average current be if twice the charge were put on the sphere in half the time?

2. The current in a metallic conductor is maintained at a steady value of 0.2 amp for 35 min. (*a*) How many coulombs of charge are transferred through it? (*b*) If the pd across the ends of this conductor is 6 volts, how much work is done in transferring the total amount of charge through it?

3. The largest all-nuclear power plant presently projected in the United States is being built on a waterway 50 mi from Chicago for the Commonwealth Edison Co. and the Nuclear Power Group, Inc. This 180,000-kw station is scheduled for completion in 1960. How much electrical energy will this station be able to supply in one year?

4. The production of electrical energy in the United States in 1956 totaled close to 500 billion kilowatt·hours. Convert this figure to horsepower·years.

5. (*a*) What current does a 100-watt incandescent lamp take on 120 volts? (*b*) How much electrical energy is converted into heat and light in this lamp by the end of 1 hr?

6. The usual 100-watt incandescent lamp costs 22 cents, and the cost of electrical energy in the average home is 3 cents per kw·hr. Find (*a*) th total lighting cost for a lamp of this rating over its normal life of 750 hr and (*b*) the overall cost per hour of operation.

7. (*a*) Determine the cost of electrical energy for residential service during a 2-month period for which the watthour meter indicates the use of 450 kw·hr. (*b*) Find the average cost per killowatt·hour for the energy used during the 2-month period. The rate schedule for the locality concerned is as follows:

First 20 kw·hr (or less)	$1.60
Next 100 kw·hr	4.5 cents/kw·hr
Next 100 kw·hr	3.5 cents/kw·hr
Next 100 kw·hr	3.0 cents/kw·hr
Excess over 320 kw·hr	2.0 cents/kw·hr

8. An immersion heater takes 250 watts of electrical power. Disregard losses and calculate how long it would take to heat 1 liter of water through 50 C°.

9. A bare conductor having a length of 1000 ft and a diameter of $\frac{1}{2}$ in. has a coating of ice $\frac{1}{2}$ in. thick all around. Find the energy in kilowatt·hours that would be required to remove this coating on the assumption that only 20% of the ice need be melted to have the whole coating fall off.

10. A newly developed x-ray tube for crystallographic work takes a continuous current of 120 milliamp at 45,000 volts. How much power does this represent? and what is the equivalent resistance of the path between the electrodes of the tube?

11. It is desired to use a 40-watt, 6-volt automobile headlamp for experimental purposes on 115-volt service mains by connecting a resistor in series with it. (*a*) How much resistance should this resistor have in order that the lamp shall receive its normal current? (*b*) What power is expended in the resistor?

12. A resistor was connected in series with a 15,000-ohm voltmeter across 115-volt service mains, and the instrument was found to read 10.6 volts. Compute the resistance of the resistor.

13. Heating cable is available for the heating of soils in hotbeds and greenhouses, for de-icing of roofs, and for comparable purposes. A 60-ft length of such cable takes 400 watts on 115-volt supply circuits. (*a*) What current does this length of cable take and what is its resistance per foot? (*b*) How much heat in calories does this length of cable develop per hour?

14. A constant-temperature cabinet measures 3 × 3 × 4 ft on the outside and has walls 3 in. thick made of glass wool having a thermal conductivity of 0.27 Btu·in./(hr·ft^2·F°). A 120-volt electric heater is to be operated continuously within the cabinet to keep the interior at body temperature (98.6° F) when the surroundings are at 65° F. Take the surface through which the heat flows to be halfway between the inside and outside walls of the cabinet and determine (*a*) the current the heater should take and (*b*) its resistance.

15. Compute the resistance of a copper bus bar 5 m long and measuring 1.5 × 8 cm in cross-section. Assume the temperature of the bar to be around 20° C. Find the conductivity of copper at this temperature.

16. A 40-ohm resistor is to be wound of manganin wire having a diameter of 0.0201 in. Calculate the length of wire needed.

17. A No. 00 Awg aluminum conductor has a diameter of 0.365 in. and carries a current of 60 amp. Compute (*a*) the resistance of the wire per 1000 ft, (*b*) the potential drop over that length of conductor, and (*c*) the power loss in it due to heating.

18. For an aluminum wire to have the same resistance per mile as a copper wire, its diameter should be larger by what percentage?

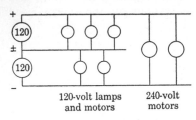

120-volt lamps and motors 240-volt motors

Problem 19

19. The three-wire distribution system for light and power service in a small factory is arranged to supply loads at 120 and 240 volts as shown in the diagram. If the load connected between the upper and neutral wires is 4 kw, that between the lower and neutral wires is 3 kw, and that between the outside wires is 6 kw, what is the current in each wire of the system, neglecting losses?

20. A load that takes 50 amp is to be located 350 ft from 240-volt constant-potential mains. Select a standard size of copper line wire such that the total potential drop between power supply and load will not exceed 3%. Determine the actual drop for the given load on the line wires selected.

21. Two 100-watt and three 40-watt lamps are operated in parallel at their rated pd of 120 volts. Find their individual resistances; thereafter determine the equivalent resistance of the group of lamps first by using Eq. 160 and then without using it.

22. The ladder circuit shown in the diagram with the resistance values

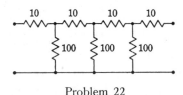

Problem 22

indicated in ohms is supplied with an emf of 150 volts at the left terminals. How much current will a 50-ohm load take when connected to the right terminals?

23. Six resistors are connected in circuit as shown in the diagram, their resistances in ohms being indicated. Find (*a*) the resistance between termi-

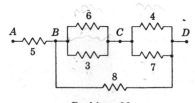

Problem 23

nals *A* and *D* and (*b*) the current and pd across each resistor when a pd of 60 volts is applied to these terminals.

24. In the diagram of the preceding problem determine
(*a*) the resistance between points B and C, and (*b*) that between C and D.

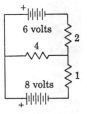

25. Two batteries supply current to the circuit shown in
the diagram in which the resistances in ohms are indicated.
Neglect the internal resistances of the batteries and compute
the currents in the three resistors.

26. If the polarity of the upper battery of Prob. 25 were
reversed, what would be the current in each resistor?

Problem 25

27. The accompanying diagram shows a network sup-
plied with current from two batteries, and the numbers on the resistors indicate their resistances in ohms. Determine the current through each resistor.

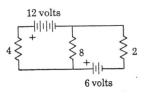

Problem 27

28. A third battery is added to the network shown in the figure of the
preceding problem by connecting a 4-volt source in series with the 8-ohm
resistor, placing the positive terminal uppermost. Calculate the current
through each of the three resistors.

29. In the circuit shown two generators, A of 600 volts and B of 570 volts,
supply electrical power to two loads through a network having the resistances indicated in ohms. Compute the current supplied by each generator
for the condition that the current in load R_1 is 400 amp and that in R_2 is
500 amp.

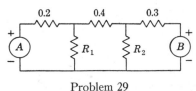

Problem 29

30. In the delta- and wye-connected trios of resistors illustrated, show
that the resistances between like-lettered terminals in the two diagrams are
the same when $a = xy/R$, $b = xz/R$, and $c = yz/R$, where $R = x + y + z$.

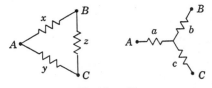

Problem 30

31. A network, arranged like the Wheatstone bridge in Fig. 212, has the
following resistances: $M = 400$, $N = 300$, $G = 800$, $X = 200$, and $R = 600$

ohms. What is the current supplied by the battery if its emf is 100 volts? *Hint.* Use the theorem of the preceding problem.

32. An iron wire that takes a current of 0.52 amp with a pd of 16 volts across its ends is practically at room temperature (20° C). When the current is increased to 1.20 amp the pd across the wire is found to be 55 volts. Find the temperature of the wire when so heated.

33. The copper field windings of a motor when idle at 50° F have a resistance of 230 ohms. In operation the winding temperature reaches 195° F. What is the resistance of the field winding at that temperature?

34. A resistance thermometer and a Wheatstone bridge are used together for the measurement of temperature. The thermometer has a platinum coil and is connected to serve as arm X of the bridge; the ratio arms M and N are set at 10 and 100 ohms respectively. At 20° C the bridge is balanced when the rheostat arm R has the value of 350 ohms; with the thermometer immersed in a freezing mixture a balance is obtained with $R = 270$ ohms. What is the temperature of the mixture?

22

ELECTRIC CELLS

231. Electrolytic and Voltaic Cells. It is generally known that electric current can be used to produce hydrogen and oxygen from dilute acid by electrolysis, or to deposit a metal coating on an electrode in a plating bath. The apparatus used in either process is called an *electrolytic cell*. In such a cell, electrical energy supplied from an outside source serves to produce the chemical changes involved, a small part being wasted as heat. Electrolytic cells are used not only for gas manufacture and electroplating, but also for the refining of metals and in many industrial chemical processes.

Other forms of cells, such as the dry cell and storage cell, can supply electrical energy; these are called *voltaic cells*. In this type, chemical energy is liberated within the cell and transformed into electrical energy, part of the energy being converted to heat. Voltaic cells are called *primary* cells if the elements need replacement after use, and *secondary* or *storage* cells if they can be charged and thus restored to their initial condition. A series or parallel grouping of like voltaic cells is called a battery.

232. Electrolytic Action. The conduction of electricity in liquids is attributed to the presence of positive and negative ions in solutions of acids, bases, or salts, and to the motion of these charges between the electrodes when there is a potential difference between them. Such solutions are termed *electrolytes*, and the process of their decomposition by electric current is called *electrolysis*.

A solution of hydrochloric acid, for example, contains two kinds of charged particles: hydrogen atoms, each having lost an electron and therefore positively charged; and chlorine atoms, each with a surplus electron and therefore negatively charged. The foregoing is described by saying that the acid *dissociates* into positive hydrogen ions and negative chlorine ions, or symbolically,

$$HCl \rightleftharpoons H^+ + Cl^-$$

The ions of a substance do not have the properties of the corresponding atoms. For example, a solution of H^+ ions affects indicators such as litmus; a solution of hydrogen gas does not.

Evidence indicates that bare H^+ ions are practically nonexistent in aqueous solutions; instead they are believed to occur in a hydrated form as *hydronium* ions, H_3O^+, each being a combination of H^+ and H_2O. To avoid complexity, however, the hydrogen ion will be represented in this book by the simpler notation H^+; hence the dissociation of water can be written as

$$H_2O \rightarrow H^+ + OH^-$$

When an acid or an alkali is added to water it is found that the concentration of one of the ions becomes much larger than the other; thus adding HCl results in a high concentration of H^+ ions and a low concentration of hydroxyl OH^- ions.

Electrolytic action in a solution of hydrochloric acid is explained in connection with Fig. 214, which shows a battery connected to the two plates that serve as electrodes in the solution. The H^+ ions are drawn to the negative plate C (cathode) and the Cl^- ions are drawn to the positive plate A (anode). The result is a drifting or migration of ions in both directions through the liquid. Each H^+ ion upon reaching plate C combines with an electron there, forming a hydrogen atom:

$$H^+ + e \rightarrow H$$

The Cl^- ions upon reaching plate A give up their electrons and become chlorine atoms:

$$Cl^- - e \rightarrow Cl$$

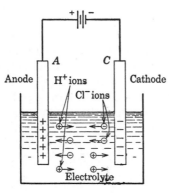

FIG. 214. Conduction by ions in an electrolytic cell

At each electrode the atoms form molecules of gas and this can be collected.

Decomposition of Water. An electrolytic cell containing a dilute solution of sulfuric acid (H_2SO_4) and having chemically inert electrodes of platinum or carbon can be used to demonstrate the electrolytic decomposition of water. The H^+ ions of the acid are drawn to the negative plate and the $SO_4^=$ ions are drawn to the positive plate. The result is again a drifting of ions in both directions through the liquid. Each H^+ ion upon reaching the cathode combines with an electron there, forming a hydrogen atom. These atoms combine into molecules and escape as gas, that is:

$$2H^+ + 2e \rightarrow H_2 \uparrow$$

When the $SO_4^=$ ions reach the anode, electrons are given to the electrode and oxygen is liberated as a gas, while more sulfuric acid is formed. That is,

$$2SO_4^= - 4e + 2H_2O \rightarrow \underbrace{4H^+ + 2SO_4^=}_{2H_2SO_4} + O_2 \uparrow$$

Thus, as much sulfuric acid is formed as is initially decomposed, and the net result is the decomposition of water into hydrogen and oxygen.

Electroplating. Next an electrolytic cell will be considered in which the electrolyte is a dilute copper sulfate solution and the electrodes are of platinum. The following equations represent the reactions that are believed to occur at the electrodes:

At cathode $\qquad Cu^{++} + 2e \rightarrow Cu$

At anode $\qquad SO_4^= - 2e + H_2O \rightarrow \underbrace{2H^+ + SO_4^=}_{H_2SO_4} + O$

These show that the copper is plated upon the cathode, and that the $CuSO_4$ electrolyte gradually changes its composition. To overcome the latter effect, copper is substituted for platinum as the material of the anode, and the anode reaction changes to

$$SO_4^= - 2e + Cu \rightarrow CuSO_4$$

while the cathode reaction remains unchanged. In this process copper is dissolved from the anode and plated on the cathode, and the electrolyte remains unchanged. Many metals can be electroplated under the general conditions just described.

233. Faraday's Laws of Electrolysis. Instances of electrolysis like the foregoing show that whenever *hydrogen or any metal is liberated in an electrolytic cell*, this action, with rare exceptions, occurs *at the cathode*, and that the liberation of other substances takes place at the anode. For electrolysis to continue, the external circuit must continuously supply electrons to the cathode and remove them from the anode; in other words, a current is necessary in the circuit containing the cell. Moreover, in forming a hydrogen or other univalent atom at the cathode one electron is required, whereas for a bivalent atom two electrons are required, and so on. Similarly, at the anode one electron is released in forming a univalent atom, and two electrons in forming a bivalent atom. Since a flow of 6.24×10^{18} electrons per sec constitutes a current of 1 amp, § 220, it follows that in an electrolytic cell a current of 1 amp maintained for 1 sec (that is, a quantity of electricity of 1 coulomb) is capable of liberating at the cathode 6.24×10^{18} hydrogen or other univalent atoms, or half this number of bivalent atoms, and so on. A corresponding liberation of atoms also occurs at the anode of the cell.

Quantitative measurements in electrolytic cells are based on two laws due to Faraday, as follows:

1. *The mass of a substance liberated in an electrolytic cell is proportional to the quantity of electricity passing through the cell.*

2. *When the same quantity of electricity is passed through different electrolytic cells, the masses of the substances liberated are proportional to their chemical equivalents.* The chemical equivalent of an element is the ratio of its atomic weight w to its valence number z; with radicals the chemical equiv-

alent is the sum of the atomic weights of the component elements divided by the valence number of the radical.

The atomic weights and usual valence numbers of several elements are given in the accompanying table.

ATOMIC WEIGHTS AND VALENCE NUMBERS

Element	Atomic weight	Valence number
Chlorine........	35.46	−1
Copper.........	63.54	+2
Gold...........	197.2	+3
Hydrogen.......	1.008	+1
Iron...........	55.85	+3
Lead...........	207.2	+2, +4
Magnesium......	24.32	+2
Oxygen........	16.00	−2
Silver..........	107.88	+1
Zinc...........	65.38	+2

In the application of Faraday's Laws of Electrolysis, it is first desirable to find the quantity of electricity that liberates 1 chemical equivalent of a substance. Silver, for example, is a univalent element which has a chemical equivalent of 107.88 gm; hence 1 coulomb of electricity deposits 6.24×10^{18} atoms. But Avogadro's constant, 6.02×10^{23}, is the number of atoms in a gram-atom of a substance, § 132; hence there are 6.02×10^{23} atoms in 107.88 gm of silver. To deposit that amount of silver therefore requires $(6.02 \times 10^{23}) \div (6.24 \times 10^{18}) = 96,500$ coulombs. This quantity of electricity, known as 1 *faraday*, liberates 1 chemical equivalent of any substance.

The mass of a substance in grams that is liberated in electrolysis can be found by simple proportion from the fact that 96,500 coulombs liberate 1 chemical equivalent w/z of that substance; thus

$$\frac{m}{w/z} = \frac{It}{96,500} \tag{165}$$

wherein the quantity of electricity is expressed as the product of the current I in amperes and the time t in seconds.

234. Single-Electrode Potentials. When a metal plate is dipped into a solution of one of its salts, a contact is established between the metallic *atoms* of the plate and the positive metallic *ions* of the solution. Two tendencies exist, either of which may determine the action that results; first, *metallic ions tend to acquire electrons and deposit themselves on the plate as* *atoms*, and second, *the atoms of the plate tend to lose electrons and go into solution as ions*. The tendency for metal to deposit on the plate is proportional to the concentration of the ions, and, theoretically, a sufficiently high concentration could always bring about deposition. On the other hand, if the ionic concentration is low, the tendency of the plate to dissolve predominates.

If a copper plate is dipped into a copper sulfate solution of ordinary concentration, a few Cu^{++} ions take electrons from the plate, forming atoms of copper which are deposited upon the plate. The action, however, stops almost immediately, because the plate becomes positive and repels the advance of other positive ions. On the other hand, if a zinc plate is dipped into a zinc sulfate solution a few atoms of the plate dissolve, leaving their electrons behind, and go into solution as Zn^{++} ions. This effect also stops promptly because the plate becomes negative, and the throwing off of further positive ions is prevented by electrostatic attraction between plate and ions. The mass of metal deposited or dissolved in these instances is very minute. The processes could be made continuous, however, by removing the charges from the plates as fast as they are formed.

The foregoing consideration shows that a copper plate placed in the solution of a copper salt assumes a higher potential than the solution, and that a zinc plate placed in the solution of a zinc salt assumes a lower potential than the solution; such potential differences are called *single-electrode potentials*. When the two solutions are in contact, the combination forms a voltaic cell with the copper positive and the zinc negative. If any small potential difference at the junction of the solutions is neglected, the emf of the cell becomes the sum of the single-electrode potentials of the two metals.

The potential of a given metal

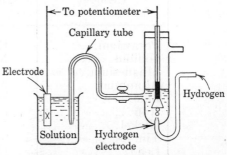

FIG. 215. Hydrogen electrode for measuring normal electrode potential

with respect to a solution of one of its salts under specified conditions can be expressed precisely. Its value is called the *normal electrode potential* if the solution is "normal"; that is, if 1 liter at 25° C contains an effective concentration of 1 chemical equivalent of the metallic ions.

Fig. 215 illustrates the apparatus for making measurements of normal electrode potential. The metal X under test is placed in a normal solution of one of its salts to form a half cell, a *hydrogen electrode* is immersed in a solution of normal hydrogen-ion content to form another, and the two are joined by a capillary. The hydrogen electrode is commonly used as a reference electrode; its potential with respect to its own solution is constant and is arbitrarily taken as zero. Hydrogen, which is nonconducting as a gas, is passed over a plate of platinum covered with platinum black. Here the gas is *adsorbed*, that is, condensed and held upon the surface; in this condition, hydrogen is conducting like a metal electrode. The normal electrode potential of the metal is found by measuring the potential difference between the electrodes, a potentiometer, § 243, being generally used for this purpose.

235. Electromotive Series; the Voltaic Cell. The relative chemical activities of the metals can be indicated by arranging them in the order of their normal electrode potentials. Under ordinary conditions, each metal in the series displaces those below it from chemically equivalent solutions of their simple salts and is itself displaced by those above it. The accompanying table indicates the more important metals and gives their normal electrode potentials with respect to the hydrogen electrode. Each value represents the emf of a cell having a hydrogen electrode and an electrode of the metal referred to.

The combination of two metals in a uniform electrolyte forms a voltaic cell; its emf can be predicted from the individual potential values listed.

ELECTROMOTIVE SERIES OF THE METALS

Element	Symbol	Normal electrode potential, volts
Potassium.........	K	-2.92
Sodium...........	Na	-2.71
Magnesium........	Mg	-1.55
Aluminum.........	Al	-1.34
Zinc.............	Zn	-0.76
Iron.............	Fe	-0.44
Nickel...........	Ni	-0.23
Tin..............	Sn	-0.13
Lead.............	Pb	-0.12
Hydrogen	**H**	**0.00**
Bismuth..........	Bi	$+0.20$
Copper...........	Cu	$+0.34$
Mercury..........	Hg	$+0.80$
Silver...........	Ag	$+0.80$
Platinum.........	Pt	$+0.86$
Carbon.......	C	$+0.90$
Gold.............	Au	$+0.98$

Thus, for a copper-zinc cell, copper has a value on the potential scale of $+0.34$ volt and zinc a value of -0.76 volt, each with respect to hydrogen; consequently the potential of copper is higher than zinc by $0.34 + 0.76 =$

1.10 volts. The simple copper-zinc cell with a solution of sulfuric acid has an emf of this value. This electrolyte contains H^+ and $SO_4^=$ ions; the H^+ ions go to the copper plate and make it positive, while Zn^{++} ions go into solution at the zinc plate and leave electrons behind, making it negative. The emf of any voltaic cell depends upon the materials used and not upon size.

236. Polarization of Cells. The current supplied by the simple voltaic cell is quickly reduced in value during even short periods of use, because of the accumulation of hydrogen on the positive plate. This action not only introduces a high resistance into the circuit, but alters the material of the electrode and sets up an opposing emf which reduces the effective emf of the cell. This effect, called *polarization*, is due primarily to the formation of hydrogen on the positive plate and to changes of concentration of the electrolyte. To offset this effect, a substance called a *depolarizer* is added to combine chemically with the hydrogen gas as it forms.

In the operation of an electrolytic cell having like electrodes, it frequently happens that the electrodes become coated with dissimilar materials. Such a cell then acts like a voltaic cell opposing the applied emf, and its own emf must be neutralized before current can be set up in it. So long as both electrodes of an electrolytic cell remain of the same substance and the electrolyte is uniform throughout, whatever electrode potential is developed at one of them will be neutralized by an equal and opposite potential at the other. The smallest potential difference applied to the cell will then set up a current in it.

237. The Dry Cell. The familiar dry cell has a positive electrode of carbon and a negative electrode of zinc, the latter serving as the container. The carbon is mounted centrally and the space between it and the container is filled with the depolarizer, which is manganese dioxide (MnO_2) mixed with carbon. The interior is moistened with ammonium chloride (NH_4Cl) as electrolyte and a little zinc chloride. The top of the cell is sealed to make it moistureproof. Fig. 216 shows a conventional diagram of the cell.

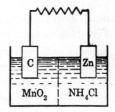

FIG. 216. Diagram of dry cell

When the cell delivers current, the zinc dissolves and forms Zn^{++} ions, leaving electrons behind. The Cl^- ions of the electrolyte migrate toward the Zn^{++} ions near the zinc electrode and the NH_4^+ ions migrate toward the carbon electrode. The formation of hydrogen gas is prevented to a considerable extent by the reduction of the manganese dioxide. The initial cell reaction is probably of the form:

$$2NH_4^+ + 2e + MnO_2 + H_2O \rightarrow 2NH_4OH + MnO$$

The complete reactions within the cell are obscure, and apparently are influenced by the conditions under which the cell is used.

This type of primary cell has an emf of about 1.5 volts and is best adapted to "open-circuit" work, that is, service in which the cell is called upon to deliver current only for short periods, its circuit at other times being open. The operation of door bells and flash lamps are typical illustrations of such service. The depolarizing action in the ammonium chloride cell is imperfect and the emf falls off with continued use; however, the cell recuperates during periods of open circuit because the layer of gas which may have been formed has an opportunity to disappear.

238. Mercury Cells. There are two cells that make use of mercury as the positive electrode; the Weston cell which dates back to 1892 and serves

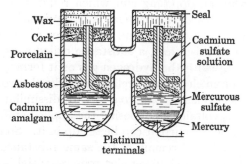

FIG. 217. Sectional view of Weston standard cell

as a standard of emf, and the other which was developed about 1942 and serves as a source of electrical energy like the dry cell.

A standard cell is designed to maintain a constant emf and is used only for comparison in measuring pds accurately, as with a potentiometer, § 243; care must be exercised to keep the current values below about a tenth of a milliampere and then only for brief periods. In the Weston cell, Fig. 217, the electrodes are placed in the opposite sides of an H-shaped glass vessel which serves as a container for the electrolyte. The positive electrode is a paste of mercurous sulfate and the negative electrode is composed of cadmium amalgam. The electrolyte is a solution of cadmium sulfate, which may be kept saturated by having crystals of cadmium sulfate present.

The emf of the saturated cell is 1.01830 volts at 20° C, and varies slightly but definitely with temperature changes. These cause slight variations in the amount of cadmium sulfate that dissolves in the solution, thereby altering the concentration, and consequently affecting the emf of the cell to some extent. In the unsaturated cell, temperature changes do not affect the concentration of the electrolyte, and their effect on the emf is so small that it is usually neglected. Each unsaturated cell made must have its emf determined by comparison with an emf of known value.

Mercury cells for supplying energy are being used where space is at a premium, ranging in capacity from the small units for pocket radio sets and hearing aids to the power units of guided missiles. These cells can withstand high pressures, operate over a wide temperature range, and can be stored for long periods. The negative electrode is zinc, the electrolyte is a concentrated solution of potassium hydroxide (KOH) nearly saturated with zincate ($Zn[OH]_2$), and the depolarizing cathode is mercuric oxide with some graphite added. The emf of each cell is 1.345 volts.

239. The Lead Storage Cell. For purposes requiring steady currents larger than can be supplied by primary cells, storage batteries are used. Typical applications include: propulsion of trucks and submarines, operation and lighting of automobiles, emergency lighting of subway cars, and stand-by service in power stations and telephone exchanges for supplying energy during short periods of power interruption.

When a storage battery is delivering current, it is said to be on *discharge*. After a period of discharge the battery can be restored to its original condition by supplying current to it in the opposite direction from an outside source; this action is called *charging*. The energy supplied to a battery during the charging process is not all delivered on discharge, usually 30 to 40 per cent being wasted in heat. The efficiency depends upon the size and construction of the battery.

The lead storage cell when charged consists essentially of a positive plate of lead dioxide and a negative plate of spongy lead, immersed in sulfuric acid as an electrolyte. As the cell discharges, Fig. 218, both plates become coated with lead sulfate and the electrolyte becomes less dense.

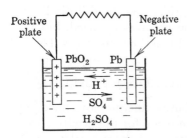

FIG. 218. Lead storage cell on discharge

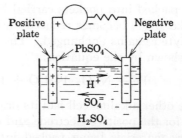

FIG. 219. Lead storage cell on charge

When the storage cell is being charged, Fig. 219, the lead sulfate on the positive plate is reconverted to lead dioxide and that on the negative plate to lead, restoring the cell to its original condition. If the cell is overcharged, hydrogen and oxygen are liberated as in the decomposition of water. This effect is known as "gassing" and indicates the completion of charge.

Since the action in the lead storage cell is reversible, the charge and discharge reactions can be combined into the single equation

$$Pb + PbO_2 + 2H_2SO_4 \rightleftharpoons 2PbSO_4 + 2H_2O$$

to provide an overall statement without reference to ions.

During discharge of the lead storage cell, the emf falls quickly from an initial value of approximately 2.1 volts and remains nearly constant at 2.0 volts throughout most of the discharge period. At the approach of complete discharge the emf falls rapidly from this value. The state of charge of the cell is tested by measuring the specific gravity of the electrolyte with a hydrometer. For an automobile battery, the specific gravity of the electrolyte is 1.285 when fully charged, and when discharged it may be as low as 1.150.

Ilustrative Problem

A 12-cell lead storage battery is charged in an emergency from 110-volt direct-current mains, the current being maintained at 10 amp for 8 hr by a rheostat connected in series in the circuit. If the average emf of the battery during the charging period is 30 volts, find the total energy supplied from the mains, the amount transformed into chemical energy, and the amount wasted in heat.

The total energy supplied from the mains is found by Eq. 150 to be 110 $\times$ 10 $\times$ 8 = 8800 watt·hr and the amount transformed into chemical energy is found similarly to be 30 $\times$ 10 $\times$ 8 = 2400 watt·hr. The difference between 8800 and 2400, namely, 6400 watt·hr, is wasted in heat.

240. Alkaline Storage Cells. Two varieties of storage cells are available which make use of potassium hydroxide (KOH) instead of sulfuric acid as the electrolyte. The first of these, devised by the American inventor Thomas A. Edison (1847–1931), employs nickel oxide for the positive electrode and finely divided iron for the negative electrode, these materials being packed into pockets carried by steel grids. As the cell discharges, the nickel oxide becomes reduced and the iron becomes oxidized, but the electrolyte remains unchanged. The chemical reactions are reversible and can be shown by the equation:

$$\text{Fe} + \text{Ni}_2\text{O}_3 \cdot 1\tfrac{1}{5}\text{H}_2\text{O} + 1\tfrac{4}{5}\text{H}_2\text{O} \rightleftharpoons \text{Fe(OH)}_2 + 2\text{Ni(OH)}_2$$

The other alkaline cell had its origin in Europe and employs nickel hydroxide for the positive electrode and cadmium oxide for the negative electrode, these materials being packed into pockets carried by steel frames. The chemical equations are also reversible and can be written as

$$\text{Cd} + 2\text{Ni(OH)}_3 \cdot 2\tfrac{1}{2}\text{H}_2\text{O} \rightleftharpoons \text{CdO} + 2\text{Ni(OH)}_2 \cdot 3\text{H}_2\text{O}$$

The average emf of either type is 1.2 volts, and the electrolyte remains unchanged in concentration. Alkaline cells are lighter than the lead-acid cells and less subject to mechanical derangement; they are not injured by freezing nor by being left in a discharged condition.

241. Cells in Series and in Parallel. Cells are frequently connected in series in order to obtain an increased emf. They are sometimes connected in parallel in order that jointly they can supply a large current to a low-resistance load without demanding an excessive current from any single cell. Cells having appreciably different emfs would not be connected in parallel in practice, because wasteful circulating currents would be set up in the cells themselves, even if the external circuit were open.

When a number of cells are connected in series, their combined emf is the sum of the emfs of the individual cells, and their total resistance is the sum of the resistances of the individual cells. In a circuit consisting of n cells, each of emf e and resistance r, connected in series to a load of resistance R, the current is

$$I_s = \frac{ne}{nr + R}$$

When a number of cells, having equal emfs and equal resistances, are connected in parallel, the emf of the combination is the same as that of any individual cell, and the resistance of the combination is that of one cell divided by the number of cells. In a circuit consisting of n like cells connected in parallel to a load of resistance R, the load current is

$$I_p = \frac{e}{\dfrac{r}{n} + R} = \frac{ne}{r + nR}$$

A comparison of the current values for the series and parallel connections of a given number of cells shows that I_s and I_p are equal when the load resistance R is the same as the resistance r of one cell. The series connection gives the larger current through the load when $R > r$, and the parallel connection gives the larger current when $R < r$. When a single cell or a battery of cells is connected to a load, the power to that load is a maximum when the internal resistance of the cell or battery is equal to the load resistance.

242. Measurement of Cell Emf and Resistance. The emf of a voltaic cell can be measured with a voltmeter connected across its terminals, but the instrument must have a high resistance in order to obtain a reasonably correct reading. If the voltmeter has a resistance R_v and the cell an internal resistance r, then the current through the circuit is the emf e of the cell divided by $r + R_v$, and that current causes a pd through the cell of

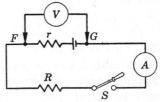

FIG. 220. Measuring internal resistance of cell

$\dfrac{er}{r + R_v}$; hence the reading is in error by that much.

The internal resistance of a voltaic cell can be measured by the ammeter-voltmeter method described in § 218. The connections are shown in Fig. 220, in which F and G represent the terminals of a cell having an internal resistance r. Across these terminals there is connected a high-resistance voltmeter V, and also a low-resistance load R in series with a switch S and an ammeter A. With the switch open, the current in the cell is very small, and the voltmeter reading V_1 may be taken as practically equal to the emf of the cell. With the switch closed, the ammeter indicates the current I in the cell, and the voltmeter reading V_2 is lower than the first reading V_1 because of the potential drop Ir in the cell. Consequently

$$r = \frac{V_1 - V_2}{I} \tag{166}$$

is the internal resistance of the cell.

243. The Potentiometer. The emf of a cell is not given exactly by the reading of a voltmeter connected across the cell terminals, because even a

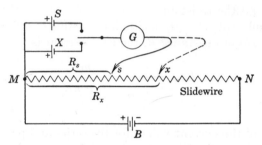

FIG. 221. Elementary circuit of potentiometer

high-resistance voltmeter takes some current. Such emfs can be compared accurately with the known emf of a standard cell by means of a potentiometer. The measurement is made when the cell is not supplying any current, and since, under this condition, *no potential drop* and *no polarization* exist in the cell, the value measured is the true emf.

The apparatus used in a potentiometer measurement is indicated in Fig. 221. A storage battery B maintains a steady current in the slidewire MN, to one end of which connections are made to a standard cell S or to the cell X under test. By means of a double-throw switch, either of these cells may be connected through the galvanometer G to a slider which can be touched at different points along the wire MN. The battery B should have a constant emf that is larger than that of either S or X.

The current I from the battery B establishes a uniform potential drop along the slidewire MN, the potential being higher at M than at N. Both cells have their positive terminals connected to M, and these terminals, therefore, have the same potential as M. When the double-throw switch is closed either way, the slider, if free from the slidewire, has a potential that is lower than that of M by an amount equal to the emf of the cell which the switch has placed into the circuit. There is some point along MN that has the same potential as the slider; this point can be found by touching the slider to different points until one is found for which the galvanometer

shows no deflection.   Under these conditions there is no current in the circuit branch containing the cell and galvanometer, and the potential drop
along the wire to the point of contact is then equal to the emf of the cell
that is in circuit.   Thus, with the double-throw switch connected to the
standard cell of emf E_s, a balance is obtained at some point s such that E_s
$= IR_s$, where R_s is the resistance of the slidewire from M to s.   Then with
the double-throw switch connected to X, another balance is obtained at
some other point x such that $E_x = IR_x$, where E_x is the emf being measured
and R_x is the resistance of the slidewire from M to x.   From these relations,

$$\frac{E_x}{E_s} = \frac{IR_x}{IR_s}$$

whence

$$E_x = E_s \frac{R_x}{R_s} \tag{167}$$

giving the unknown emf in terms of that of the standard cell and the known
resistances.

This result may be verified by applying Kirchhoff's Second Law, § 227,
around a path from M along the slidewire to the contact point, returning
through the cell S or X.   For balance at s with the standard cell there is
obtained: $-IR_s + E_s = 0$; and for balance at x with the other cell: $-IR_x$
$+ E_x = 0$.   These equations yield the same result as found previously.

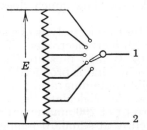

Fig. 222.   Voltage divider

Since the resistance of the slidewire is proportional to its length, the unknown emf can also be expressed as

$$E_x = E_s \frac{l_x}{l_s}$$

where l_x and l_s are the wire lengths from M to x and from M to s respectively.

The potential divider, usually called a *voltage divider*, is an arrangement
on a resistor for dividing the pd applied to the entire resistor into suitable
parts.   Fig. 222 shows a simple voltage divider with the resistor divided

into five equal parts and provided with taps. When E volts are applied to the whole resistor, the pd between terminals 1 and 2 can be varied in steps of $E/5$ volts between 0 and E. The potentiometer itself is a form of voltage divider in which a slider is used to obtain finer gradations of potential.

PROBLEMS

1. Indicate the dissociation of water into hydronium and hydroxyl ions.

2. Write the chemical equations for the electrolysis of silver nitrate $(AgNO_3)$ in a cell that has a silver anode.

3. On the basis that 1 faraday of charge liberates 107.88 gm of silver from a solution of silver nitrate, how much charge is needed to liberate 197.0 gm of gold from a solution of gold chloride $(AuCl_3)$?

4. Determine the amount of silver that would be deposited by a steady current of 5 amp when maintained for 8 hr, and state how many atoms of silver would be deposited.

5. In the electrolysis of subsurface structures, corrosion takes place where ground currents leave them to enter the soil. How much iron would be removed from a water pipe in a year at a place where the average current from pipe to soil is found to be 2.0 amp?

6. How long would a 50-lb anode of magnesium last in electrolysis if the current drain is 0.5 amp?

7. In the electrolytic refining of copper the anodes are of copper with some impurities, but only pure copper is deposited. (*a*) Compute the time taken to deposit 1 lb of copper with a current of 10 amp from copper sulfate $(CuSO_4)$. (*b*) If the pd across the cell is 0.3 volt and the cost of electrical energy is 1.2 cents per kw·hr, how much does it cost to refine 1 lb of copper?

8. Chlorine is produced by the electrolysis of a solution of sodium chloride $(NaCl)$ in cells equipped with inert electrodes. Take the density of chlorine at standard temperature (0° C) and pressure (76 cm Hg) as 3.21 gm/liter and find the volume of chlorine that is produced by 1 amp·hr of charge.

9. Sixty electrolytic cells containing acidulated water are connected in series to a 120-volt source. (*a*) Calculate the mass of oxygen liberated in these cells by a steady current of 200 amp maintained for 24 hr. (*b*) What volume would this gas occupy at standard temperature and pressure? (*c*) Determine the electrical energy required to produce the oxygen per cubic foot.

10. A metal article having a surface of 300 cm² is coated with silver in a plating bath that contains silver nitrate. The specific gravity of silver is 10.45. Compute the thickness of the plating that can be produced in 30 min by a current of 2 amp.

11. The earth-circling satellite mentioned in §47 has a gold coating to improve its ability to reflect light. The satellite is a sphere of 20 in. diameter and the coating is 1/30,000 in. thick. The density of gold is 19.3 gm/cm³. How many coulombs of electric charge would be needed to form this coating electrolytically?

12. The amount of zinc in the container of a particular dry cell is 20 gm. Determine the number of ampere·hours of electricity that the cell can deliver on the assumption that all of the zinc dissolves.

13. A lead storage cell capable of supplying 100 amp·hr at the normal 8-hr discharge rate has 1 lb of lead dioxide on its positive plates. How long would this cell be able to deliver a current of 5 amp if all of this material were converted to lead sulfate? Take valence of lead as $+2$.

14. A single lead storage cell is to be charged from the alternating-current service through a transformer and rectifier adjusted to yield a constant unidirectional pd of 8 volts. A rheostat will be used in series with the cell to keep the current through it down to 5 amp. (*a*) To which terminal of the rectifier ($+$ or $-$) should the positive pole of the cell be connected? (*b*) If the current is maintained for 10 hr, how much charge and how much energy will be supplied to the cell? (*c*) How much energy will be wasted in heating the rheostat? *Hint.* See problem in § 239.

15. Eight 6-volt storage batteries, each having an internal resistance of 0.02 ohm, are to be used for establishing as large a current as possible through a load. Should they be connected all in series or all in parallel for a load (*a*) of 0.1 ohm and (*b*) of 0.01 ohm? For each load condition give the amount of current supplied and the amount that the contrasting connection plan would yield.

16. A battery of two dry cells is connected as shown in Fig. 220. When the switch is open the voltmeter reads 3.20 volts. When the switch is closed the current indicated by the ammeter is 1.8 amp, and the voltmeter reads 2.90 volts. Find the average internal resistance of the cells.

17. A dry cell supplied current to a 3-ohm resistor for 1 hr and during this period the emf fell from 1.53 to 1.43 volts. If the current during the test dropped 10% from the initial value of 0.50 amp, by what percentage did the internal resistance of the cell increase?

18. Two storage cells connected in parallel jointly supply a current of 20 amp to an external circuit. One cell has an emf of 2.1 volts and the other of 2.0 volts, but both have the same resistance of 0.04 ohm. Determine the current in each cell.

19. Two batteries, one of 3 volts and the other of 6 volts, are connected to three resistors as shown in the diagram, the resistances in ohms being indicated. Neglect the internal resistances of the batteries and determine the current in the 2-ohm resistor by using Kirchhoff's laws.

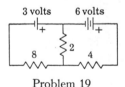

Problem 19

20. Seven dry cells, each having an emf of 1.5 volts and internal resistance of 0.1 ohm, are connected to a resistor of 2 ohms. The cells are arranged in two series groups, one of 4 and the other of 3 cells, and the two groups are connected in parallel. Compute the current through the resistor. In which direction is the current in the 3-cell group?

21. Three 12-volt storage batteries, A, B, and C, are connected in parallel to a common load of 5 ohms. The individual internal resistances of the batteries will be taken respectively as 0.05, 0.10 and 0.15 ohm, these being larger than they actually are to emphasize the result. Calculate the current supplied by each battery to the load.

22. If the batteries of Prob. 21 were disconnected from the load but left connected together, (*a*) would there be any current in the batteries if their emfs were identical? (*b*) If battery *A* had an emf 0.1 volt higher than the other two, how much current would traverse each battery?

23. An accurate form of voltage divider is shown in the accompanying diagram. The switches on the 200-ohm and 40-ohm decades have two arms apiece and each switch straddles two resistance steps to keep the input resistance the same for all switch positions. (*a*) With a pd of 100 volts across the input terminals, what is the pd across the output terminals for the switch setting shown? (*b*) Why is the input resistance constant and what is its value? (*c*) Find the resistance of the output circuit of the voltage divider for the setting shown, the input terminals being open. For part (*c*) the Δ-*Y* transformation given in Prob. 30 of Chap. 21 will be helpful.

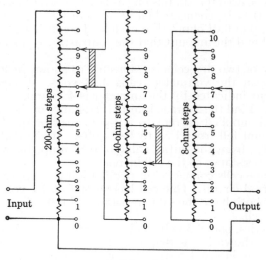

Problem 23

23

ELECTROMAGNETISM AND ELECTROMAGNETIC INDUCTION

244. Magnetic Effect of the Current. The magnetism exhibited by permanent magnets and the fields produced by them were considered in Chap. 20. Attention will now be directed to another phase of the subject—the interrelation between electric current and magnetism, called electromagnetism.

The discovery of electromagnetism was made by Oersted in 1820, through his observations that an electric current in a conductor is surrounded by a magnetic field directed circularly around the conductor. This fact can be demonstrated by mounting a single wire vertically, establishing a current in it, and moving a compass needle around the wire. At each point the needle comes to rest in a position tangent to an imaginary circle concentric with the wire and drawn through the pivot of the needle.

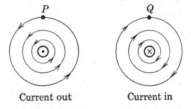

Current out   Current in

FIG. 223. Direction of magnetic field around a current-carrying wire

Fig. 223 shows two diagrams of the lines of force around a wire; the heavy circles indicate the wire in section and the light circles represent the direction of the field. When the current is directed toward the observer, as represented by a dot within the wire, the magnetic field is counter-clockwise, as shown in the left. When the current is reversed in direction, the field is reversed, as shown at the right.

A simple rule for determining the relative directions of current and field makes use of the *right hand*, the fingers being curved as though grasping the wire carrying the current, and the thumb being outstretched. *When the .humb points in the direction of the current the fingers point along the direction of the field.*

As stated in the earlier chapter the intensity of the magnetic field is a vector quantity and is represented by the symbol H. It will be found that the field intensity at any point due to an electric current depends only upon the configuration of the conductor and the current in it, and is independent of the surrounding medium, § 267. At a point near a straight current-carrying wire the magnetic field intensity is represented by a vector tangent to the concentric line of force extending through that point. Thus in Fig. 223, the field intensity at point P is directed horizontally to the left, and at point Q it is directed horizontally toward the right. With two parallel current-carrying wires influencing a region as represented in Fig. 224, the field intensity at a point has two components, H_1 due to the first and H_2 due to the second; the resultant H is obtained by the usual methods of vector addition.

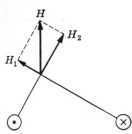

FIG. 224. Resultant of magnetic fields produced by two currents

245. Magnetic Induction. Another concept besides magnetic field intensity H is necessary in the study of electromagnetism. The reason is that the field intensity due to an electric current is independent of the surrounding medium, as just stated, whereas several effects of electromagnetism are influenced by both the field intensity and the magnetic properties of the medium. For example, the electromagnet referred to in § 205 is much stronger with the iron bar than without it, although the presence of the iron has no effect on the field intensity due to the current. The iron bar has strong poles induced in it, and this effect is added to that of the field.

The new concept combines the effect of field intensity with the effect of the magnetic medium; the quantity is called *magnetic induction* and its symbol is B. Magnetic induction is represented by lines of induction so drawn, or imagined, that the number of lines of induction extending perpendicularly through unit area equals the magnetic induction in the region considered. Collectively, lines of induction are spoken of as *magnetic flux*. The unit of magnetic flux in the cgs system is named after the Scottish theoretical physicist J. Clerk Maxwell (1831–1879); the *maxwell* is one line of magnetic induction. The unit of magnetic flux in the mks system is the *weber*, named after the German physicist Wilhelm E. Weber (1804–1891). The relationship between these flux units is

$$1 \text{ weber} = 10^8 \text{ maxwells}$$

The magnetic induction is the ratio of the amount of magnetic flux to the area through which it extends. If an amount of flux Φ (phi) is uniformly distributed and extends perpendicularly through an area A, then the flux per unit area becomes

$$B = \frac{\Phi}{A} \tag{168}$$

from which the magnetic induction B is also called *flux density*. In the cgs system the unit of flux density is called the *gauss*, after Karl F. Gauss (1777–1855), German mathematician and physicist. *A gauss is a flux density of one maxwell per square centimeter.* It is represented by a single line of magnetic flux extending perpendicularly through an area of one square centimeter. In the mks system the unit of flux density has no distinctive name; it is merely called one weber per square meter. The relationship between these flux density units is clearly

$$1 \text{ weber/m}^2 = 10^4 \text{ gausses}$$

In a region where the flux density B is uniform but the lines of induction are not perpendicular to the reference area, the component of the flux density that is perpendicular to it is $B \cos \phi$, where ϕ is the angle between the direction of the flux and the normal to the area. Hence the total flux through an area A is

$$\Phi = B(\cos \phi)A \qquad (169)$$

In the sections to follow only mks units will be used to avoid possible confusion.

The distinction between magnetic induction B and magnetic field strength H is not of real importance unless a magnetic medium is involved. Throughout the present chapter, the lines of induction that represent B and the lines of force that represent H are considered only where they extend through air, which differs but little magnetically from free space. In all such cases, B and H have the same direction at every point considered, and the lines of induction have the same configuration as the lines of force, although they may differ in number. It is important to note that lines of induction, when completed, form continuous closed loops, and that throughout their length they show, by their direction, the direction of B, and, by their closeness to one another, the magnitude of B. The effect of magnetic mediums will be discussed in Chap. 24.

246. Relation Between Current and Magnetism. The magnetic field due to the current in a wire was first investigated experimentally by Ampère and two other French physicists: Jean B. Biot (1774–1862) and Felix Savart (1791–1841). A mathematical expression, proposed by Biot, was published by Ampère for computing the magnetic flux density at any point in the field. The expression is based on

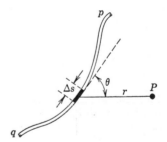

FIG. 225. For computing magnetic flux density due to current

the idea that the current in every element of the wire contributes something to the surrounding field. For the wire pq in Fig. 225, the flux density at point P due to current in the element of length Δs is given as

$$\Delta B = K \frac{I \sin \theta \, \Delta s}{r^2}$$

where I is the current, r the length of a line joining point P and the wire element, θ the angle between this line and the current in element Δs, and K a constant depending in value upon the choice of units. In the figure the direction of ΔB is perpendicular to the page. Since $\sin \theta$ is zero when $\theta = 0$, it follows that ΔB is zero at points along the tangent to the wire element.

That the flux density should vary inversely as the square of the distance from the wire element might be expected by similarity with the field intensity due to an electric charge or to a magnet pole, §§ 195 and 206. Further, it is reasonable to suppose that doubling the current or doubling the length of the element would double the flux density. Experimentation was required to show that the flux density varies as the sine of the angle θ.

The total flux density at point P in space is found by adding the individual contributions from all conductor elements. This total is expressed by

$$B = K \sum \frac{I \sin \theta \, \Delta s}{r^2} \tag{170}$$

The value of the constant K in this and the foregoing expression is chosen so that ΔB and B are in the mks unit of flux density, namely, the weber per square meter, when the current I is in amperes and the distances Δs and r are in meters. This value for a vacuum is $K = 10^{-7}$ weber/(amp·m).

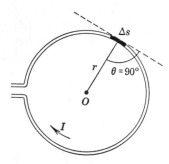

FIG. 226. For computing flux density at center of circular loop carrying current

The Biot-Ampère expression for flux density applies to circuits of all forms, and a few simple ones will be considered in the following sections.

247. Flux Density Produced by a Current Loop. The application of Eq. 170 to a circular loop of wire becomes most direct when the flux density due to current in the loop is to be found at its center. Thus in Fig. 226, the flux density at the center O due to the same current I in all wire elements Δs around the circle of radius r is equal to KI/r^2 times the summation of $\sin \theta \, \Delta s$. But the angle θ between the element and the radial line to the center is everywhere 90°; whence $\sin \theta = \sin 90° = 1$. Under this condition the summation applies only to Δs; hence for the complete loop, $\Sigma \, \Delta s = 2\pi r$. Consequently the flux density at the center of the loop is

$$B = \frac{KI}{r^2} (2\pi r)$$

where the constant K has the value 10^{-7} weber/(amp·m). The right-hand rule indicates that when the current is directed clockwise around the loop the magnetic flux is directed into the page inside of the loop and out of the page outside.

For a coil of N turns, the flux density is N times as great, provided the turns are concentrated so that the entire coil has little axial length compared with its radius. The flux density at the center of such a coil is consequently

$$B = \frac{2\pi NI}{r} 10^{-7} \qquad (171)$$

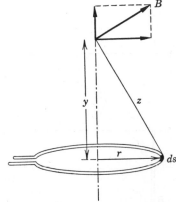

In this expression I is the current in amperes, B the flux density in webers/m², and r the coil radius in meters. The product NI is called *ampere·turns*. Since N is merely a number it does not affect the balancing of units.

The flux density at any point along the axis of a circular coil of radius r at a distance y from its plane can be found by using the distance $z = \sqrt{r^2 + y^2}$ from that point to the wire element ds instead of r in the Biot-Ampère expression for ΔB.

FIG. 227. For computing flux density along axis of circular loop

However, the result then gives the density at right angles to both line z and element ds as shown in Fig. 227, but this can be resolved into rectangular components along the axis and perpendicular thereto. For a complete loop the components at right angles to the axis cancel and the other components add up to $\frac{r}{z} B$. Hence the total flux density at a point along the axis of a coil of N concentrated turns can be shown to be

$$B' = 2\pi NI \frac{r^2}{z^3} 10^{-7} \qquad (172)$$

Illustrative Problem

Determine the flux density at the center of a flat circular coil of 50 turns formed from a wire 25 m long through which the current is 20 amp. Also determine the flux density at a point on the axis of the coil 0.1 m from its plane.

Since the length of wire is $2\pi r 50 = 25$ m, the radius of the coil is $(1/4\pi)$ m; hence Eq. 171 gives the flux density at the center of the coil as $8\pi^2 50 \times 20 \times 10^{-7} = 0.00790$ weber/m².

The distance from the axial point to the wire itself is $z = \sqrt{(1/4\pi)^2 + (0.1)^2} = 0.1278$ m, and $r^2/z^3 = 0.00634 \div 0.00209 = 3.03$. Hence the flux density at a point on the axis of the coil 0.1 m from its plane is given by Eq. 172 as $2\pi 50 \times 20 \times 3.03 \times 10^{-7} = 0.001904$ weber/m², and is directed along the axis.

248. Flux Density Produced Around a Straight Wire. The magnetic field produced by current in a straight conductor can be computed from the

Biot-Ampère expression for flux density, § 246, by the use of calculus. In Fig. 228 the vertical lines represent a portion of a wire extending indefinitely in both directions, and P designates any point in space at which the flux

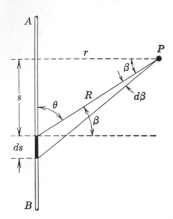

density of the magnetic field is sought. The flux at this point may be considered as made up of the contributions of successive elementary lengths, such as ds, comprising the whole wire. In terms of the symbols r, R, s, θ, and β as in the figure, the field intensity at P due to a current I in the elementary length ds is found to be

$$dB = K \frac{I \sin \theta \, ds}{R^2} = K \frac{I \cos \beta \, ds}{R^2}$$

where $\beta = 90° - \theta$.

Fig. 228. For computing flux density near straight wire

The total flux density at the point under consideration due to current in the entire wire is the sum of a series of terms like the foregoing. It is necessary first to rewrite the equation in terms of a single variable, say β; thus $s = r \tan \beta$, $ds = r \, d\beta/\cos^2 \beta$, and $R = r \sec \beta$. The equation then becomes

$$dB = \frac{KI \cos \beta (r \, d\beta)}{r^2 \sec^2 \beta \cos^2 \beta} = \frac{KI}{r} \cos \beta \, d\beta$$

The total flux density is obtained by integration; thus

$$B = \frac{KI}{r} \int_{\beta = -\frac{\pi}{2}}^{\beta = \frac{\pi}{2}} \cos \beta \, d\beta = \frac{2KI}{r}$$

When the value of the constant is introduced, namely, $K = 10^{-7}$ weber/(amp·m), the flux density in webers per square meter at point P distant r meters from a straight wire becomes

$$B = \frac{2I}{r} 10^{-7} \tag{173}$$

where I is the current in the wire in amperes.

249. The Solenoid. A coil of wire wound uniformly in a long helix is termed a *solenoid*. Fig. 229 shows in part I a solenoid wound on a straight cylindrical core. Solenoids have a wide application in electrical apparatus, and it is important to know their magnetic properties. The flux density produced by current in a solenoid can be computed from Eq. 172, which gives the density at any point on the axis of a coil having N concentrated turns. The steps in the computation are similar to those of the preceding section.

The flux density at the midpoint of a solenoid is found by summing up the contributions of the current in all the turns, stretching over the entire axial length of the solenoid, and the result is

$$B = \frac{4\pi NI}{l} \, 10^{-7} \tag{174}$$

where N is the total number of turns distributed uniformly over the axial length l of the solenoid. In mks units l is in meters, I the current in am-

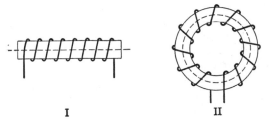

FIG. 229.   Straight and ring types of solenoids

peres, and B the flux density in webers/m^2. It is convenient to use a single symbol to express the number of turns per unit length of solenoid. If n is taken to represent this quantity, then $n = N/l$ turns per meter, and the equation becomes

$$B = 4\pi nI \times 10^{-7} \tag{175}$$

In solenoids that have a small diameter compared with the length, the flux density is reasonably uniform throughout the interior and hence the values given by Eqs. 174 and 175 can be used for this region, except near the ends.

By bending a solenoid in a circle so that the two ends touch, the winding becomes a *ring solenoid*, as shown in part II of Fig. 229. It resembles a winding that might be formed by wrapping the wire around an automobile tire, threading it repeatedly through the center opening. Such a solenoid has no ends and the magnetic flux produced by current in it is entirely within the tire itself. The fact that no outside field is produced accounts for the use of ring solenoids. The flux density in a ring solenoid is also given by Eqs. 174 and 175.

250. Force on Conductor in a Magnetic Field; Ampère's Law. Ampère also investigated the force that is exerted upon a current-carrying wire when it is located in a magnetic field. He found that when the wire is at right angles to the field the force on it is proportional to the magnetic flux density, to the current, and to the length of the wire. Thus the force on an element of the wire is

$$\Delta F = kBI \, \Delta l$$

where Δl is the length of the wire element, I the current in it, B the flux density that exists at this element, and k a constant having a value dependent upon the units selected. For a straight current-carrying wire of length l that is perpendicular to the flux of constant density, the force in mks units is

$$F = BIl \qquad (176)$$

where F is in newtons, B in webers per square meter, I in amperes, and l in

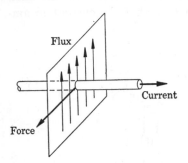

meters. The simple form of this equation without constants is the result of the coordination of the electrical and magnetic units in the mks system.

The foregoing expression is a mathematical statement of Ampère's Law and is the key equation of electromagnetism; it can be applied to all forms of circuits and is the operating principle of electric motors and electromagnetic devices. The directions of F, B, and I are mutually perpendicular; Fig. 230 pictures these directions along the three geometric axes. If the conductor of length l is not at right angles to the flux, but makes an angle ϕ with it instead, then the effective length of the conductor is $l \sin \phi$, and the force is expressed by

FIG. 230.   Direction of force on current-carrying wire in magnetic field

$$F = BIl \sin \phi \qquad (177)$$

This equation applies to any moving charge whether in a conductor or not.

The relative directions of the magnetic flux, conductor current, and force on the conductor can be visualized by reference to Fig. 231, which illustrates a current-carrying wire located in the region between the magnet poles N and S. Throughout this region the flux density B and the field intensity H have the same direction at every point, and the lines of induction and lines of force have the same configuration although they may differ in number. The magnetic lines in the figure are regarded as lines of force, because of the characteristics assigned to them of becoming as short as possible and,

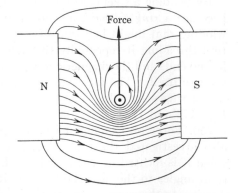

FIG. 231.   Composite field of magnet and current-carrying conductor

when in the same direction, of exerting a sidewise thrust upon one another, § 207. The lines due to the poles extend from left to right, and those due to the current in the wire are counterclockwise, since the current is directed toward the reader, as indicated by the dot within the conductor. In the space below the conductor the lines produced by the poles and those produced by the current have the same direction and the field is strong, but in the space above the conductor the fields are opposed and the resultant field is weak. The upward force on the wire can be pictured as due to the tension along the lines below the conductor and to the repulsive action between them in this region where all the lines have the same direction.

251. Force Between Conductors Carrying Current. As a result of the interaction between the electric current and the magnetic field, it follows that one current-carrying conductor exerts a force upon another, because each conductor is located in the magnetic field produced by the other. Two parallel conductors attract each other when the currents are in the same direction and repel each other when the currents are opposite.

To find the force between two conductors that are parallel over a length l and separated by a distance r, it is necessary to know the flux density produced at one wire by the current in the other. Reference to § 248 shows that the density of the flux at a distance r from a straight wire carrying a current I_1 is

$$B = \frac{2KI_1}{r}$$

where K is a constant. Eq. 176 then gives the force on the other straight wire located in this magnetic field when carrying a current I_2 as

$$F = BI_2 l$$

Hence the force between two parallel conductors is

$$F = 2K \frac{I_1 I_2 l}{r} \tag{178}$$

The force is in newtons when the currents are in amperes, the linear dimensions are in meters, and the constant K equals 10^{-7} weber/(amp·m).

The whole system of electrical units is based upon the foregoing equation, for it defines the ampere fundamentally as follows: *The ampere is that current which when established in each of two parallel conductors, infinitely long and separated by 1 meter in free space, causes the force on each conductor to be* 2×10^{-7} *newton per meter of length.*

The unit of charge, first used in Chap. 19, is derived from the foregoing definition, since the coulomb is the same as the ampere·second. With this unit of charge in Coulomb's Law for the force between charges, Eq. 134, the permittivity of free space in mks units is found to be $\epsilon_o = \dfrac{1}{4\pi 9 \times 10^9}$ coulomb^2/(newton·m^2).

The electromagnetic theory predicts that the product of the two parameters of free space, namely, the permittivity ϵ_o and the permeability μ_o, is equal to the square of the speed of light c; experiment has confirmed this prediction. With mks units the permittivity has the value given before, and the speed of light has the rounded value $c = 3 \times 10^8$ m/sec; consequently the permeability of free space becomes

$$\mu_o = \frac{1}{c^2 \epsilon_o} = \frac{4\pi 9 \times 10^9 \dfrac{\text{newton} \cdot \text{m}^2}{\text{coulomb}^2}}{\left(3 \times 10^8 \dfrac{\text{m}}{\text{sec}}\right)^2} = 4\pi 10^{-7} \frac{\text{newton}}{\text{amp}^2}$$

Since from Eq. 176 the newton in the foregoing equation can be expressed as the product $\dfrac{\text{weber}}{\text{m}^2}$ amp·m, it follows that the unit of μ_o can also be written as $\dfrac{\text{weber}}{\text{amp} \cdot \text{m}}$. The value of K in Eq. 170 and used as $10^{-7} \dfrac{\text{weber}}{\text{amp} \cdot \text{m}}$ in subsequent equations can now be evaluated as

$$K = \frac{\mu_o}{4\pi} \frac{\text{weber}}{\text{amp} \cdot \text{m}}$$

With cgs units in Eq. 178, the currents are in amperes, the linear dimensions l and r in centimeters, and the force F in dynes, the value of K is $\frac{1}{100}$ dyne/amp². Mention should be made here that there is still another system of electrical units—the so-called electromagnetic units—which is based on the same equation with K taken numerically as unity; this system is not used in this text, but its units bearing like names with prefix *ab* for the various quantities are listed in the Appendix.

Illustrative Problem

To indicate the use of Eq. 178, determine the force exerted between two parallel wires, one carrying a current of 500 amp and the other 200 amp oppositely directed to the first, when the separation between the wires is 10 cm in air.

With mks units the force per meter of conductor length is

$$F = 2 \times 10^{-7} \frac{\text{weber}}{\text{amp} \cdot \text{m}} \frac{500 \text{ amp} \times 200 \text{ amp} \times 1 \text{ m}}{0.1 \text{ m}} = 0.200 \text{ newton}$$

and is a force of repulsion. With cgs units the force per meter of conductor length is

$$F = \frac{2}{100} \frac{\text{dyne}}{\text{amp}^2} \frac{500 \text{ amp} \times 200 \text{ amp} \times 100 \text{ cm}}{10 \text{ cm}} = 20,000 \text{ dynes}$$

The two results are equivalent since 1 newton $= 10^5$ dynes.

252. The Galvanometer. The instruments ordinarily used for measuring electric currents depend for their operation on the force on conductors in magnetic fields. In the usual form of such instruments, a coil of wire is supported in a magnetic field and a current is established in it; the forces thus produced on the coil deflect it from its rest position, and the amount of deflection serves as a measure of the current. This operating principle applies to most direct-current ammeters and voltmeters used in electrical testing and also to the *d'Arsonval galvanometer* (named after the French physicist Arsène d'Arsonval), which is used for the measurement of small currents.

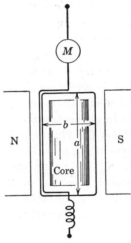

Fig. 232 shows the coil of a galvanometer suspended between the poles of a strong permanent magnet and around a central iron core. The current is conducted to the coil by a flat metal ribbon which serves as the suspension and is led out by a helix of similar material below the coil. The coil carries a mirror M so that its deflections can be read by looking through a telescope directed toward the mirror, and observing the reflections of a fixed scale.

By Ampère's Law, the force on each side of the coil of height a and width b is

$$F = BINa$$

where B is the flux density in the region between the poles (assumed uniform), I the current in the coil, and N the number of turns in the coil. These

forces act in opposite directions but combine to produce a torque in a common direction. With current directed clockwise around the coil, its right side moves forward out of the page and the left side moves backward into the page. When the coil lies in the plane of the magnet as shown, the deflecting torque is

$$T_d = 2BINa \times \frac{b}{2} = BINS$$

where $S = ab$ is the surface area of the coil face. As the coil turns in response to this torque the lever arm becomes less than $b/2$, and ultimately the coil would come to rest in a position at right angles to that shown. However, the suspension exerts a restoring torque T_r on the coil as it moves from the position shown, the value of which is proportional to the twist ϕ of the suspension, or

$$T_r = \tau\phi$$

where τ is a constant determined by the stiffness of the suspension. The coil comes to rest where $T_d = T_r$, and therefore

$$\tau\phi = BINS$$

showing that the twist ϕ for a given instrument (that is, B, N, S, and τ fixed) is proportional to the current I.

With a parallel field, as assumed in Fig. 232, this expression would be true only for small deflections. In the galvanometer as actually constructed the field is radial between curved pole pieces on the magnet and the stationary cylindrical core mounted within the moving coil; consequently the coil always swings perpendicularly to the flux. By this means the twist is made proportional to the current throughout the range of the instrument.

Another form of galvanometer, called a *ballistic galvanometer*, is designed to measure electric charge rather than a steady current. In this form the coil is wider and heavier than in the galvanometer previously described so as to make its moment of inertia greater; as a result its period of vibration is large compared with the time for the charge to pass through the coil. Thus the charge gives the coil an angular impulse before it has moved appreciably, and the angular momentum acquired turns the coil. Its greatest angular deflection is called the *throw*, and this is found to be proportional to the charge that passes through the instrument.

253. Ammeters and Voltmeters. Instruments for measuring current and potential difference in direct-current circuits are galvanometers of more substantial type in which the coil is pivoted and fitted with a pointer that moves over a suitably calibrated scale. Current is supplied to the coil through flat spiral springs which also serve to return the pointer to the zero position when the current ceases. There is no structural difference between an ammeter and a voltmeter; both instruments have permanent magnets and the pointer deflects in proportion to the current in the movable coil. The difference between them is one of electrical resistance; in this respect the instruments are designed so that when introduced into a circuit they do not change appreciably the quantities they are intended to measure.

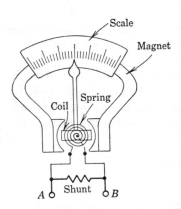

FIG. 233. Construction of direct-current ammeter

In the ammeter, Fig. 233, the coil is provided with a low-resistance bypass, called a *shunt*, connected directly across the terminals A and B, to reduce the current in the coil to a small but definite part of the entire current in the circuit. The ammeter has a very low resistance so that the potential drop across it can be kept small; naturally care must be taken to have enough resistance in the circuit associated with an ammeter so that the current is limited to a value within its range.

In the voltmeter the movable coil is connected in series with an internal resistance, so that the instrument can be connected directly across the points between which the pd is desired. A voltmeter has a high resistance so as to divert as little current as possible from the circuit to which it is connected. In a sense the voltmeter protects itself because of its high resistance, but care must be exercised not to apply pds exceeding the range of the instrument. The range of a voltmeter can be extended if desired by the use of an additional series resistance external to the instrument. Such an auxiliary resistance is called a *multiplier*.

The resistance of the shunt or series resistor for a particular instrument can be found by applying Ohm's Law and the principles of series and parallel circuits.

Illustrative Problems

I. An ammeter has a coil of 5 ohms resistance, and the pointer deflects across the entire scale with a current of 0.01 amp through the coil. Find the shunt resistance necessary to make this instrument a 10-amp ammeter, that is, one which deflects full scale when measuring a current of 10 amp.

At full-scale deflection, the potential drop across the coil is $E = I \times R = 0.01 \times 5 = 0.05$ volt, and this must also be the pd across the shunt. But the current in the shunt is $10 - 0.01 = 9.99$ amp; consequently, the resistance of the shunt should be $R = E \div I = 0.05$ volt $\div$ 9.99 amp $=$ 0.005005 ohm.

II. A voltmeter has a coil of 5 ohms resistance, and the pointer deflects full scale with a current of 0.01 amp. Find the resistance that must be connected in series with the coil to give the instrument a range of 150 volts, that is, the instrument is to deflect full scale when 150 volts are impressed across its terminals.

The current is the same in the coil and series resistance; hence the resistance of the entire instrument is $R = E \div I = 150 \div 0.01 = 15,000$ ohms. Since the coil has a resistance of 5 ohms, the series resistor must have a resistance of $15,000 - 5 = 14,995$ ohms.

254. The Wattmeter. An instrument for measuring electric power is called a *wattmeter*. Since power is the product of the potential difference and the current, § 217, a wattmeter must be designed to give the coil of the instrument a deflection that is proportional to both pd and current. The wattmeter does not have a permanent magnet like the ammeter and voltmeter described in the preceding section; instead, the magnetic field is produced by current in a winding having a few turns of large-sized wire. This winding is connected in series with the load circuit; in this way the flux density B within it is made proportional to the load current. The moving coil is connected in series with a high resistance across the circuit under measurement, and the current I in the coil is thereby made proportional to the pd across the load. Since the force on the coil according to Eq. 176 is proportional to $B \times I$, it is proportional to the product of the number of amperes in the load and the number of volts across it. Therefore, the instrument can be calibrated to read watts directly. The arrangement and connections of the wattmeter are indicated in Fig. 234; the "current coil" is shown by the fixed winding in series with the load, and the "potential coil" by the movable winding bridged across the lines.

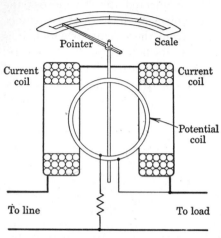

FIG. 234.   Connections of wattmeter

The metering of electrical energy for determining the cost of electric service is not accomplished by wattmeters, for these instruments indicate merely the instantaneous rate at which the energy is used; the device that is used for this purpose is called a *watthour meter*. It is similar electrically to the wattmeter, but the coil is arranged to rotate continuously at a speed dependent upon the power expended in the load circuit; the cost of service is based upon the number of revolutions indicated by the meter.

255. Induced Electromotive Force; Faraday's Law. In 1831 Faraday discovered that an emf could be induced in an electric circuit by relative motion between the circuit and a magnet. His observations provided the means for converting mechanical energy into electrical energy. The two discoveries—that of electromagnetism by Ampère and of electromagnetic induction by Faraday—form the basis of our electrical age.

The principles of electromagnetic induction will be illustrated by describing some fundamental experiments. Fig. 235 shows a bar magnet NS and a coil of wire, the coil being in a vertical plane and having its circuit closed through a galvanometer G. No action is observed as long as the apparatus remains stationary, but when the magnet is moved horizontally toward the coil, the galvanometer deflects, showing that an emf is being induced in the

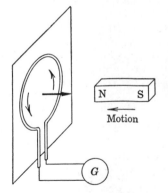

FIG. 235.   Inducing emf in coil by moving magnet

coil. This emf sets up a current in the closed circuit. The faster the magnet is moved, the larger is the deflection; if it is brought to rest, the deflection again becomes zero. Upon moving the magnet away from the coil, similar results are obtained, but the deflections are reversed, showing that the emf is now in the opposite direction. The same effects may be produced by moving the coil instead of the magnet, by using an electromagnet instead of a permanent magnet, or by turning the coil. These tests lead to the conclusion that *an emf is induced in a coil of wire whenever there is a change in the magnetic flux linked with it.*

The magnitude of the induced emf can be found by considering the energy relations in a circuit so arranged that a portion of it moves through a magnetic field. Fig. 236 is a plan view of such a circuit with the moving part located in a uniform field directed into the page. Two bare parallel rails *MN* and *PQ* in the plane of the paper are separated by a distance *l* and joined at the left by the stationary conductor *MP*. A bare wire *CD* extends perpendicularly from one rail to the other and may be moved along them without friction. An emf is induced when the wire is moved, as evidenced by the fact that a current is produced in the loop *CMPD*, and it is desired to determine the value of this emf.

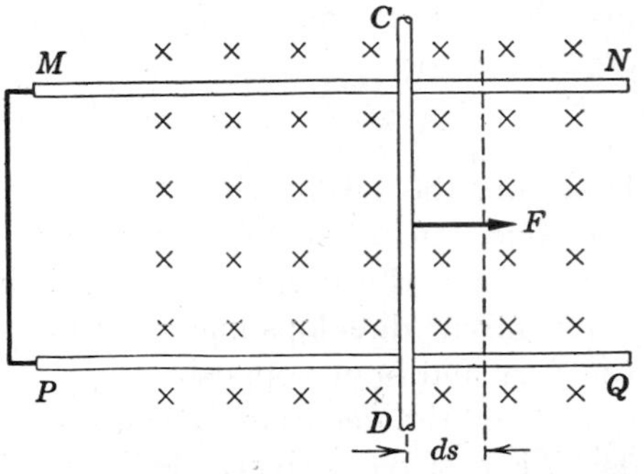

FIG. 236. For calculating emf induced in wire that moves through magnetic flux

To move the wire *CD* uniformly through the magnetic field, it is necessary that some external agent exert a force upon it, because of the current induced in the wire as soon as it moves. If this force *F* displaces the wire through a distance *ds* in a time interval *dt*, the work done by the agent on the wire is $dW = F\,ds$. During this motion of the wire perpendicularly through the magnetic flux of density *B*, the induced emf produces a current *I* in the loop circuit, and the force acting upon the wire because of its presence in the magnetic field is given by Ampère's Law as the product *BIl*. For uniform motion, the applied force *F* must have the same value in the opposite direction; in consequence, the work done on the wire during the given interval can be written as

$$dW = BIl\,ds$$

The product of *l* and *ds* is the area swept through by the wire and represents the amount by which the area of the circuit is changed. If this area is multiplied by the flux density *B*, the result is the change in magnetic flux linking the circuit, or $d\Phi = Bl\,ds$. Hence the mechanical work done on the wire becomes

$$dW = I\,d\Phi$$

The electrical energy expended in the circuit that includes the moving

$$F \frac{ds}{dt} = Ie$$

wire during the given time interval dt is expressed by Eq. 150 as

$$dW = Ie\,dt$$

where e is the emf induced in the wire by its motion through the magnetic field. According to the principle of the conservation of energy, the mechanical work done in moving the wire is equal to the electrical energy expended in its circuit; therefore the two foregoing equations represent the same energy value, or

$$I\,d\Phi = dW = Ie\,dt$$

Herefrom the induced emf in the wire is numerically $e = d\Phi/dt$. As the wire moves to the right in Fig. 236, the induced emf in it is directed from D to C, and the current produced thereby in the loop is counterclockwise. This current develops magnetic flux within the loop that is directed out of the page and hence opposite to the flux of the initial field. To indicate this opposition the negative sign is introduced, signifying that e is negative when $d\Phi/dt$ is positive. Hence the induced emf is given by

$$e = -\frac{d\Phi}{dt} \tag{179}$$

This equation expresses Faraday's Law and states that the emf induced in a circuit is equal to the time rate of change of magnetic flux in which the circuit is located. This is the operating principle of electric generators, transformers, and a host of electrical devices.

The use of mks units in Faraday's Law results in the absence of a numerical constant. Herein the magnetic flux is expressed in webers, the time in seconds, and the emf in volts. Thus, an emf of one volt is induced in a circuit when the flux linked with the circuit changes at the rate of one weber per second.

The foregoing expression applies to any circuit: for example, to a coil in which an emf is induced by motion of a magnet. For a coil wound with several turns close together, so that all are subject to the same variation of flux, equal emfs are induced in the several turns and these are added to obtain the total induced emf. Consequently, the emf induced in a coil of N turns while the flux through it is changing at the rate of $\dfrac{d\Phi}{dt}$ is given in volts by the expression

$$e = -N\frac{d\Phi}{dt} \tag{180}$$

Another way of regarding the process of induction is to consider that *an emf is induced in a circuit whenever any of its conductors cuts magnetic flux.* By a rearrangement of the preceding equations expressing work done, it will be clear that $BIl\,ds = Ie\,dt$, whence $e = Bl\,\dfrac{ds}{dt}$. But $\dfrac{ds}{dt}$ is the velocity of the conductor CD in Fig. 236, and consequently the emf induced in the circuit in which a conductor of length l cuts magnetic flux of density B with a velocity v may be expressed as

$$e = Blv \qquad (181)$$

When the flux density is in webers per square meter, the conductor length in meters, and the velocity of the conductor in meters per second, the emf is in volts. The equation applies to arrangements where the direction of motion of the conductor is at right angles to the magnetic flux; as a result the electric field is at right angles to both v and B, and hence the induced emf is also.

256. Direction of Induced Emf; Lenz's Law. Experiments on induced electromotive force, conducted by the German physicist H. F. Emil Lenz (1804–1865), led to the generalization called Lenz's Law. It states that, whenever an emf is induced in a circuit by a change of magnetic flux through it, the direction of the emf is such as to produce a current the magnetic flux of which will oppose the change. Thus, if the flux about a circuit is increased, the current induced thereby tends to decrease the flux.

To illustrate the application of this law, reference will be made to Fig. 235, which shows a magnet near a coil of wire. An emf is induced in the coil as a result of the motion of the N pole of the magnet toward it. By this motion the flux through the coil is increased. To oppose this increase, the flux produced by the current in the coil must be directed toward the magnet. By the rule described in § 244 the current to produce this flux direction must be counter-clockwise as viewed from the magnet. Thus Lenz's Law is useful in predicting the direction of the emf induced in a circuit.

257. Action of Magnetic Field on Moving Charge. It has been shown that a conductor carrying a current experiences a force when located transversely in a magnetic field; this force is given by Ampère's Law as $F = BIl$, where B is the flux density of the field, I the current in the conductor, and l its length. The corresponding equation for the force on an electric charge that moves transversely through magnetic flux is

$$F = BQv \qquad (182)$$

where Q is the charge and v its velocity. The equivalence of these expressions can be shown by supposing a charge to move with velocity v along a conductor. Then the time taken for this charge to move a distance l is $t = l/v$. The motion of this charge represents a current I in the conductor and the charge transferred during the time t is $Q = It$. Hence

$$F = BIl = B\frac{Q}{l}vt = BQv$$

The direction of the force is at right angles to both the motion of the charge and the direction of the field.

When the charge moves in a direction that makes an angle ϕ with the magnetic flux the force on the charge is

$$F = BQv \sin \phi$$

In this expression and in Eq. 182, when B is in webers per square meter, Q in coulombs, and v in meters per second, the force F is in newtons.

The sidewise thrust upon moving charges such as electrons, protons, and alpha particles is utilized in the determination of electronic mass and in the acceleration of the heavier particles for bombarding atomic nuclei.

258. Electronic Measurements; Ratio of Charge to Mass. In 1897 the English scientist Joseph J. Thomson (1856–1940) determined the ratio of

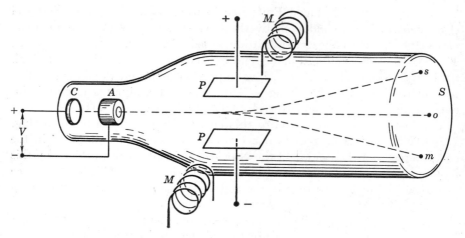

Fig. 237. Thomson's apparatus for electronic measurements

the charge of the electron to its mass. He used an evacuated tube of the form shown in Fig. 237, which contains a cathode C and an anode A near the left end, the anode being pierced by a small hole. Near the middle of the tube two parallel plates PP are arranged for establishing an electric field vertically directed in the view shown, and two coils MM for setting up a magnetic field horizontally directed. The right end of the tube has a fluorescent screen S.

When a pd V of several thousand volts is maintained across the electrodes C and A, electrons issue from the cathode and are accelerated toward the anode, but a number pass through the hole at the center. In the absence of the electric and magnetic fields, these electrons travel straight to the screen, where they produce a bright spot at o. With the plates PP charged as shown, each electron passing between them is subjected to an upward force $\mathcal{E}e$, § 197, where $\mathcal{E}$ is the electric field intensity between the plates and *e* the charge of the electron. In consequence the spot on the screen is displaced upward to some point *s*. With no electric field and the coils *MM* energized, each electron experiences a vertical force *Bev* according to Eq. 181, where *B* is the flux density of the magnetic field, and *v* the electron velocity. The current in the coils is directed so that this force acts in a downward direction, and causes the spot on the screen to be deflected to some point *m*. Finally, with both the electric and magnetic fields acting simultaneously, their strengths can be adjusted so that the upward force on the electrons due to one field equals the downward force on them due to the other, thus causing the bright spot on the screen to return to the undeflected position *o*. When so adjusted the forces balance and $\mathcal{E}e = Bev$; herefrom the electron velocity becomes

$$v = \frac{\mathcal{E}}{B}$$

As an electron of mass *m* moves from *C* to *A*, the electric field in this region does an amount of work *Ve* upon it, which appears as kinetic energy when the electron leaves the anode; whence $Ve = \frac{mv^2}{2}$. With the foregoing value for *v*, this expression may be rewritten as

$$\frac{e}{m} = \frac{\mathcal{E}^2}{2VB^2} \qquad (183)$$

which gives the desired ratio of the charge *e* of the electron to its mass *m*. The result is expressed in terms of the electric field intensity $\mathcal{E}$, the magnetic flux density *B*, and the potential difference *V* between the electrodes *C* and *A*.

With mks units in the foregoing equations, *e* is in coulombs, *m* in kilograms, *v* in meters per second, *V* in volts, *B* in webers per square meter, and $\mathcal{E}$ in newtons per coulomb or volts per meter. Results of recent measurements give the ratio *e/m* as 1.759×10^{11} coulombs/kg and the electronic charge *e* as 1.602×10^{-19} coulomb; hence the mass of the electron is found to be $m = 1.602 \times 10^{-19} \div 1.759 \times 10^{11} = 9.107 \times 10^{-31}$ kg. This is its so-called rest mass.

The energy of high-speed particles is usually expressed in terms of the pd through which the electronic charge is transferred. *The energy that an electron acquires by passing through a potential difference of one volt is called an electron·volt.* Since the transfer of a coulomb of charge through a potential difference of one volt represents one joule of energy, it follows that

$$1 \text{ electron·volt} = 1.602 \times 10^{-19} \text{ joule}$$

259. The Cyclotron. An application of electromagnetism to the problems of modern research is illustrated in a machine developed by Professor

Ernest O. Lawrence and called the *cyclotron*. Its purpose is to accelerate charged particles to very high speeds and thereby give them large amounts of energy, so that they can be used to bombard atoms in the investigation of nuclear structure and artificial radioactivity, Chap. 40.

Among the essential elements of a cyclotron are two hollow semicircular segments that face each other as in Fig. 238, the arrangement resembling a huge pillbox that has been cut in two and the halves separated. The seg-

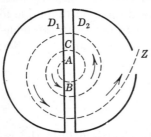

ments, called *dees*, are placed in an evacuated space within a uniform magnetic field directed at right angles to the plane of the dees, that is, perpendicular to the page in the figure. In operation, ions are released at the center of the dees, and are caused to follow the dotted path by reversing the polarity of the dees in rapid succession.

Positive ions released at point A are attracted into dee D_1 when it is momentarily negative. Each ion is continuously deflected by the magnetic field in a direction at right

FIG. 238. Path of charged particles in cyclotron

angles to its motion; hence it moves in a circular path until it emerges from that dee at B. At this instant the polarity of the dees is reversed; then the ion is accelerated by the pd that exists between the dees, and enters D_2 at a higher speed, after which it travels again in a circular path until it emerges at C. By a repetition of these events the ion travels each half-revolution with higher speed, and finally leaves the apparatus at Z, where the material to be bombarded is located.

It is necessary that the ions travel around every semicircle of the path in the same time in order that the polarity reversal rate (usually constant) of the dees may be appropriate for paths of all radii. The force exerted by the field of flux density B upon a charge Q moving with a speed v is given by Eq. 182 as $F = BQv$; this force acts continuously at right angles to the direction of motion of the charge and becomes the centripetal force of its circular motion. As in earlier chapters, this force can be expressed by $\dfrac{mv^2}{r}$, where m is the mass of the charged particle and r the radius of its path; hence

$$BQv = \frac{mv^2}{r}$$

But the speed of a particle which moves around a semicircular path of radius r in a time t is

$$v = \frac{\pi r}{t}$$

hence the time interval becomes

$$t = \frac{\pi m}{BQ}$$

which is independent of r. Thus, as the ion moves, it completes each half-revolution in the same time interval. The flux density B and the polarity reversal time t must be adjusted to values suitable for the kind of ions being accelerated.

The cyclotron is capable of developing extremely high ionic speeds without the use of unduly high potentials. The energy possessed by a particle of mass m and charge Q moving in a path of radius r is

$$E_k = \frac{1}{2} mv^2 = \frac{m\pi^2 r^2}{2t^2} = \frac{(BQr)^2}{2m}$$

The equations in this section are appropriate for quantities expressed in mks units.

Illustrative Problem

As an example, consider a cyclotron that is adjusted for the acceleration of hydrogen nuclei, and suppose the machine to have dees of 40-cm radius, upon which the polarity reverses 30 million times per second. What should be the flux density of the field and what is the energy of the issuing proton beam?

The mass of the proton is 1.672×10^{-27} kg, its charge is 1.60×10^{-19} coulomb, and the time specified for it to make a half-revolution is $1/(3 \times 10^7)$ sec; hence the flux density should be $B = \dfrac{\pi m}{Qt} = \dfrac{3 \times 10^7 \pi 1.672 \times 10^{-27}}{1.60 \times 10^{-19}} = 0.985$ weber/m^2.

The energy of a proton when it emerges at the outermost radius of the dees is $E_k = \dfrac{m}{2}\left(\dfrac{\pi r}{t}\right)^2 = \dfrac{1.672 \times 10^{-27}}{2}(3 \times 10^7 \pi\ 0.4)^2 = 1.188 \times 10^{-12}$ joule. This is equivalent to $1.188 \times 10^{-12} \div (1.602 \times 10^{-19}) = 7.42 \times 10^6$ electron·volts.

PROBLEMS

1. The two magnetic fields indicated in Fig. 224 have the intensities $H_1 = 15$ and $H_2 = 25$ oersteds, and the angle between them is 90°. Find their resultant.

2. Make up a table of the magnetic quantities referred to in §§ 208 and 245 for the two unit systems. Include the symbols for field intensity, magnetic induction and flux, and indicate the relation that exists between the corresponding units for each of these quantities.

3. A flat coil is to be designed to produce a magnetic induction of 1 milliweber/m^2 at its center with a current of 5 amp. If it is decided to make the coil 1 ft in diameter, how many turns of wire should it have?

4. It is desired to neutralize the vertical component of the earth's magnetic induction at a place where this component has a value of 7×10^{-5} weber/m^2 and is directed downward. For this purpose a flat circular coil is laid horizontally and a current is maintained through its turns. If the coil has 20 turns 1 m in diameter, what current is needed and in which direction should it be established?

5. A flat circular coil of 40 turns has a diameter of 25 cm, and a current of 0.3 amp is established in it. (a) Determine the magnetic flux density at its center produced by the current. (b) If the coil is placed vertically and in the plane of the horizontal component of the earth's magnetic field having a magnetic induction of 0.2 gauss, what is the resulting horizontal flux density at the center of the coil?

6. Derive Eq. 172 for the magnetic flux density at any point along the axis of a flat circular coil carrying a current.

7. Two flat circular coils, each of 20 turns and 40 cm radius, are placed 40 cm apart with their axes aligned. The current in each coil is 5 amp and the two currents are in the same direction. Find the flux density along the axis (a) midway between the coils and (b) at the center of one of them.

8. If an electric charge of 200 microcoulombs were whirled around a circle of 0.5 m radius 8 times/sec, what would be the magnetic flux density at the center of the circle developed by the moving charge?

9. Two long parallel wires A and B are 25 cm apart and each carries a current of 50 amp toward the right. What is the resultant magnetic flux density produced by these currents in the plane of the wires (a) at a point midway between them and (b) at a point 5 cm from A and 20 cm from B?

10. Two electrical feeders are parallel to each other and 4 in. apart over a length of 100 ft. One carries 50 amp and the other 70, and their directions are opposite. Determine the magnetic induction at points halfway between them.

11. A solenoid is formed by winding insulated wire around a cardboard mailing tube having a diameter of 4 cm. The tube is 45 cm long and the wires are placed close together over its full length which accommodates 350 turns. (a) Find the current that this winding should carry in order to have the magnetic flux density at its center amount to 0.01 weber/m^2. (b) How much magnetic flux would extend through the tube at its midsection?

12. A cylindrical frame having a diameter of 2 ft carries a winding of 420 turns wound 3 conductors to the inch. Determine (a) the flux density along the axis of the solenoid produced by a current of 85 amp through its winding and (b) the amount of magnetic flux through the solenoid at its center.

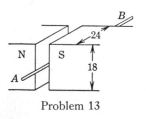

Problem 13

13. A straight conductor, located in the gap between magnet poles as in the diagram, carries a current of 30 amp directed from A to B. Each pole has the dimensions in centimeters indicated, and the magnetic flux extending from one to the other is 0.12 weber. Compute the force that the field exerts upon the conductor and state its direction.

14. When the current-carrying feeders of Prob. 9 have double the currents stated, what force per foot length does each feeder exert upon the other?

15. A galvanometer coil is 5 cm long and 2 cm wide; it is wound with 100

turns of wire. The coil is suspended by a narrow metal ribbon within the magnetic field of a permanent magnet as shown in Fig. 232. The field between the magnet poles has a flux density of 4 milliweber/m^2 and the suspension requires a torque of 5×10^{-9} newton·m to twist the coil through an angle of 1 radian. Find the steady current in the coil that would give it a 1-degree deflection.

16. The coil of a portable galvanometer has a resistance of 5 ohms and produces a full-scale deflection with a current of 10 milliamp. Compute the resistance of a shunt that can be bridged across the coil so that the instrument would yield a full-scale deflection with a current of 2 amp.

17. The coil of a voltmeter has a resistance of 10 ohms and produces a full-scale deflection when a pd of 50 millivolts is applied to it. The instrument has a resistor to make it possible to measure up to 15 volts. How can the instrument be modified so that it can measure pds up to 150 volts?

18. A triple-range ammeter, connected as shown in the accompanying figure, gives full-scale deflection with a current of 5 milliamp through its coil. The resistance in ohms of the coil and of the three shunts are indicated. When the ammeter is used with the plus terminal connected to a supply circuit, what will be the ranges of the instrument when the other lead from the supply circuit through the load is joined to terminal A, or B, or C?

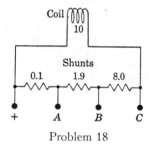

Problem 18

19. If a student, by mistake, connects the ammeter of Prob. 18 to the supply circuit and load by terminals A and B, what load current would cause the instrument pointer to deflect full scale?

20. If the magnetic flux density through the circular coil of Prob. 5 is increased from 6×10^{-5} to 7×10^{-4} weber in a period of 0.01 sec, what emf is induced in the coil?

21. A wire 12 m long is wound into a flat square coil of 20 turns and the terminals lead to an ammeter; the circuit so formed has a total resistance of 0.3 ohm. If one pole of a magnet is plunged into the coil and increases the magnetic flux through it from 10^{-5} to 10^{-4} weber in 0.25 sec, (*a*) how much is the average flux density within the coil increased? and (*b*) what is the momentary value of the current established in the coil?

22. How quickly should the wire of Prob. 13 be shifted from top to bottom of the magnetic field indicated to develop an average emf of 1 volt? What is the direction of this induced emf?

23. To measure the flux density in the gap of a large electromagnet, a ballistic galvanometer is used in conjunction with a small exploring coil that can be moved through the gap. The coil consists of 60 turns of fine wire wound on a flat circular bobbin to have an average diameter of 1 in. The coil is connected in series with the galvanometer, the total resistance of this circuit being 50 ohms. When the coil is held in the gap with its plane perpendicular to the magnetic flux and then suddenly pulled out of the gap, the observed throw of the galvanometer indicates from its calibration data that a charge of 0.002 coulomb passed through the instrument. Determine the flux density in the air gap.

24. The coil of Prob. 21 is mounted on a shaft so that it can revolve about a diagonal and is then placed in a magnetic field with the shaft perpendicular to the flux. On turning the coil the flux through it varies from 0 to 5 milli-

webers.   Determine the average value of the emf generated in each direction around the coil when it revolves at 240 rev/min.

25. Derive an equation suitable to electrostatic units for the force acting upon a charge that moves with constant velocity transversely through a magnetic field.   Name the units of the quantities represented.

26. In a test with Thomson's apparatus, the magnetic field between poles MM in Fig. 237 is maintained at a flux density of B webers/m^2 and the electric field between plates PP is absent.   Show that charged particles of mass m kg and charge q coulombs projected at right angles to the flux travel in a circle of radius r m given by $r^2 = 2m \, V/B^2q$, where V is the accelerating potential between electrodes C and A.

27. In another test with Thomson's apparatus, the electric field between the plates PP in Fig. 237 is maintained at an intensity of $\mathcal{E}$ volts/m and the magnetic field between poles MM is absent.   Show that charged particles headed for the screen while traveling horizontally a distance l m through the electric field are displaced vertically a distance s m given by $s = \mathcal{E}l^2/4V$, where V is the accelerating potential in volts.

28. A cyclotron in which the magnetic flux density is maintained at 1.2 webers/m^2 is used to accelerate helium nuclei.   The mass of the helium nucleus is 6.64×10^{-27} kg and its charge is twice that of the proton.   (a) How rapidly should the polarity of the dees be reversed?   (b) What is the energy of each particle when it reaches a path radius of 0.3 m?

24

MAGNETIC CIRCUITS

260. Effect of Iron on Circuit Behavior. Magnetic substances, particularly iron and steel, are widely used in electrical devices and machinery, because a given magnetic field develops a far greater magnetic flux in these materials than in nonmagnetic substances.

A simple way to verify this statement is to set up two identical ring solenoids, one with a wood core and the other with an iron core, both equipped with identical secondary windings and both connected as shown in Fig. 239—the primary winding P to a battery through a switch s, and the secondary winding S to a ballistic galvanometer G. With either solenoid, the galvanometer shows a momentary deflection or throw each time the switch is closed or opened, because the changing magnetic flux through the ring induces an emf in the secondary winding and produces a pulse of current through the galvanometer, §§ 252 and 255. The galvanometer cannot produce a steady deflection when the switch remains closed, because the magnetic flux associated with the secondary coil must change in order to induce an emf in it. When the switch is operated with the iron-core solenoid, the throw of the galvanometer is found to be much greater than with the wood-core solenoid; consequently the change of magnetic flux must be correspondingly greater. Evidently the same current through like primary windings produces much more magnetic flux through iron than through wood.

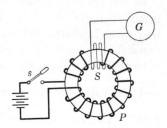

FIG. 239. Measuring magnetic induction in a ring solenoid

The large magnetic flux produced in cores of a magnetic material is attributed to the magnetization of the material, resulting from the motion of electrons within its atoms, § 191. According to the planetary picture of the atom, electrons revolve in orbits around atomic nuclei and spin about their own axes; such moving charges constitute electric currents and their paths are equivalent to turns of wire; hence magnetic effects are produced within atoms akin to the magnetism produced by current-carrying conductors as described in the preceding chapter. With magnetic substances there is evidence to show that more electrons of each atom spin in one direction than in the other, § 266, and that when exposed to an external magnetic field the magnetic moments of these atoms are oriented and produce more magnetic flux than in nonmagnetic substances.

261. Relative Permeability. When a magnetic substance such as iron is located in a magnetic field, the lines of induction inside it differ from the lines of force, because of the magnetization of the material. The relation between the flux density B and field intensity H within any magnetic substance is expressed as

$$B = \mu H \qquad\qquad (184)$$

where μ represents the *permeability* of the substance. This means that in a magnetic substance there are μ times as many lines of induction as there are lines of force. In free space the permeability is represented by μ_o, and the relation between flux density and field intensity becomes

$$B = \mu_o H \qquad\qquad (185)$$

In the cgs system the unit of flux density is the gauss and that of field intensity is the oersted. The corresponding value of the permeability of free space is unity. Thus, a field intensity of one oersted produces a flux density in vacuum (and substantially also in air) of one gauss.

In the mks system the unit of flux density is the weber per square meter and the value for the permeability of free space is $\mu_o = 4\pi 10^{-7} \dfrac{\text{weber}}{\text{amp}\cdot\text{m}}$,

§ 251. The corresponding unit of field intensity is the ampere·turn per meter. Hence a field intensity of one ampere·turn per meter produces a flux density in vacuum (and substantially also in air) of $4\pi 10^{-7}$ weber per m^2.

The relationship between the flux density units in the two systems is given in § 245 as

$$1 \text{ weber/m}^2 = 10^4 \text{ gausses}$$

and hence the relation between the field intensity units is

$$\frac{1000}{4\pi} \frac{\text{amp}\cdot\text{turns}}{\text{m}} = 1 \text{ oersted}$$

The permeability of a substance with respect to that of free space is called the *relative permeability* and is defined by the relation

$$\mu_r = \frac{\mu}{\mu_o} \qquad\qquad (186)$$

where μ is the permeability of the substance and μ_o that of vacuum. Since both μ and μ_o in a given unit system are expressed in the same units, the relative permeability of a substance is merely a number; its value for nonmagnetic substances is practically unity and for magnetic substances extends into the hundreds, thousands, and even tens of thousands. Neither

μ_r nor μ is constant for a given material but depends upon its magnetic history and the degree of magnetization.

A summary of the magnetic quantities used so far in this textbook is given below for review and reference purposes:

MAGNETIC QUANTITIES

Quantity	Sym-bol	Units		Conversion factor
		mks	cgs	
Magnetic field intensity	H	$(\text{amp} \cdot \text{turn})/\text{m}$	oersted	$1 \text{ oersted} = \dfrac{1000}{4\pi} \dfrac{\text{amp} \cdot \text{turn}}{\text{m}}$
Magnetic induction or flux	Φ	weber	maxwell	$1 \text{ weber} = 10^8 \text{ maxwells}$
Magnetic flux density	B	weber/m^2	gauss	$1 \text{ weber/m}^2 = 10^4 \text{ gausses}$
Permeability of free space	μ_o	$4\pi 10^{-7} \dfrac{\text{weber}}{\text{amp} \cdot \text{m}}$	$1 \dfrac{\text{gauss}}{\text{oersted}}$	$1 \dfrac{\text{gauss}}{\text{oersted}} = 4\pi 10^{-7} \dfrac{\text{weber}}{\text{amp} \cdot \text{m}}$

Illustrative Problem

Determine the relative permeability of a specimen of iron in which a field intensity of 1000 amp·turns/m produces a flux density of 1.5 webers/m². According to Eq. 184 the permeability μ is the ratio of B to H, and hence for the specimen mentioned its value is $1.5 \dfrac{\text{webers}}{\text{m}^2} \div 1000 \dfrac{\text{amp} \cdot \text{turns}}{\text{m}} =$ 0.0015 weber/(amp·m). The "turn" need not be included in the unit since it is a pure number. Since the permeability of vacuum is $\mu_o = 4\pi 10^{-7}$ weber/(amp·m), the relative permeability of the specimen is given by Eq. 186 as $\mu_r = \dfrac{\mu}{\mu_o} = \dfrac{0.0015}{4\pi 10^{-7}} = 1200$.

To check the result with cgs units, use is made of the conversion factors listed. Thus for the specimen of this problem the flux density is expressed as 1.5×10^4 gausses and the field intensity as $1000 \div 1000/4\pi = 4\pi$ oersteds. Since the permeability of free space in this system is 1, the relative permeability of the specimen is $1.5 \times 10^4 \div 4\pi = 1200$.

262. Magnetic Substances. A grouping of substances according to relative permeability results in three classes: *diamagnetic* substances with values less than unity, *paramagnetic* substances with values greater than unity, and *ferromagnetic* substances with values very much larger. Relative permeabilities μ_r for all known diamagnetic substances are but slightly less than unity; its value for the most diamagnetic substance, bismuth, is 0.99998. The values for paramagnetic substances are but slightly greater than unity; for example, platinum has a relative permeability of 1.00002. Iron, nickel, and cobalt are the ferromagnetic elements, and certain alloys are also ferromagnetic. Iron ceases to be ferromagnetic at 770° C.

To determine whether a substance is diamagnetic or paramagnetic, a small specimen in rod form is suspended between the poles of a powerful magnet in a region where the field is nonuniform. If the rod aligns itself with the field and is pulled toward its more intense region, then the substance is paramagnetic (or ferromagnetic); if it behaves oppositely, the substance is diamagnetic.

The accompanying table lists a number of ferromagnetic materials with their maximum permeability values, together with the flux densities that yield these values. The values are only approximate inasmuch as definite figures depend on the purity of the substance, the method of preparation, and the thermal treatment.

PERMEABILITIES OF MAGNETIC MATERIALS

	Relative permeability μ_r (maximum)	Flux density B, weber/m^2
Cobalt....................................	170	0.3
Heusler alloy (Cu 60%, Mn 24%, Al 16%)..	200	0.2
Iron-cobalt alloy (Co 34%)...............	13,000	0.8
Iron, purest commercial annealed........	6,000 to 8,000	0.6
Nickel...................................	400 to 1,000	0.1 to 0.3
Permalloy (Ni 78.5%, Fe 21.5%)...........	over 80,000	0.5
Perminvar (Ni 45%, Fe 30%, Co 25%).....	2,000	0.0004
Silicon steel (Si 4%)....................	5,000 to 10,000	0.6 to 0.8
Steel, open-hearth.......................	3,000 to 7,000	0.6
Supermendur (Fe 49%, Co 49%, V 2%).....	66,000	2.0

Certain alloys have surprising magnetic properties. Some are magnetic although composed entirely of nonmagnetic elements; a few of these were first formed by a German physicist named Heusler, one of whose alloys is listed. In contrast, steel, highly magnetic by itself, becomes practically nonmagnetic when alloyed with between 10 and 15% of manganese and 1% of carbon.

An interesting application of paramagnetic substances occurs in the measurement of temperatures near absolute zero. It is found that the factor $(\mu_r - 1)$ for such substances is inversely proportional to the absolute temperature, and the variation of this factor serves to specify a scale for these low temperatures. Measurements are made by placing a paramagnetic salt, like chromic alum or various gadolinium compounds, in the region under test within a pair of coils connected as in Fig. 239. Readings of the associated ballistic galvanometer permit the evaluation of μ_r for the salt, and from this the temperature is derived.

263. Magnetization Curves. The permeability of any ferromagnetic substance is not a constant quantity but depends greatly upon the field intensity; this dependence is usually shown indirectly by curves, called *magnetization curves*, which coordinate the flux density B with the field intensity H.

A magnetization curve can be obtained for a sample of iron or other material by arranging the specimen in the form of a ring, and using the circuit arrangement of Fig. 239. A rheostat, not shown, is connected in series with the primary coil for adjusting the current. To conduct such a test, the primary circuit is closed and the corresponding throw of the ballistic galvanometer is observed; this procedure is repeated with constantly increasing values of primary current, starting each time with the specimen demagnetized.

For each observation the field intensity inside the specimen is proportional to the primary current, Eq. 187, and the flux density is proportional to the galvanometer throw. To explain the latter fact, the emf induced in the coil at each setting is proportional to the time rate of change of magnetic flux and, equally so, to the time rate of change of flux density—that is, $e \propto \dfrac{dB}{dt}$; the current in the coil is proportional to the induced emf—that is, $e \propto i$; hence the change of flux density dB is proportional to the charge $i\,dt$, and this is the entity that the ballistic galvanometer measures, § 252.

Fig. 240 shows a typical magnetization curve for silicon steel, an iron-

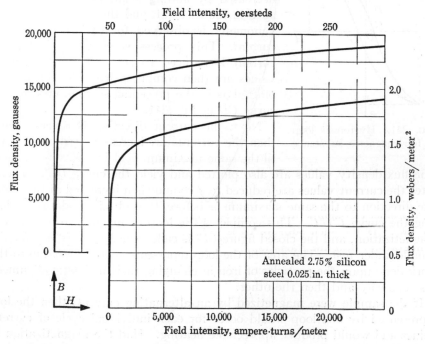

FIG. 240. Magnetization curves of silicon steel. (For mks units use lower and righ scales; for cgs units use upper and left scales.)

silicon alloy that is widely used in electrical machinery. The higher curve is coordinated to the left and top scales in cgs units (gausses vs oersteds), and the lower curve is coordinated to the right and bottom scales in mks units (webers/m^2 vs amp·turns/m). Obviously the shapes of the curves are the same since only the units are different. To find the relative permeability for a given field intensity, the corresponding value of the flux density is read from the curve, and these values are substituted in Eq. 184. Thus at a field intensity 5000 (amp·turns)/m the flux density is 1.59 webers/m^2; hence the permeability is $\mu = 1.59 \div 5000 = 0.000318$, and the relative permeability is $\mu_r = 0.000318 \div 4\pi10^{-7} = 253$. Either curve shows that for low field intensities, the flux density B increases in direct proportion to H, and that for large field intensities the specimen becomes "saturated" with flux, and the slope of the curve approaches a value that represents a relative permeability of unity.

264. Magnetic Hysteresis. Tests with the ring solenoid and ballistic galvanometer described in the last few sections can be used to obtain further information about the magnetization and demagnetization of iron. The test is started with the iron magnetized to the maximum field intensity desired. The current is then steadily decreased by adding small amounts of resistance in the rheostat, and the throw of the galvanometer is observed for each decrement of current. This process is continued until the current is reduced to zero. The flux density values are then computed from the throws and plotted as in the preceding section, yielding the curve CD in Fig. 241.

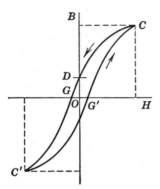

FIG. 241. Hysteresis loop of ferromagnetic substance

Next, the current direction is reversed, and then the currents are increased step by step until the same maximum field intensity is reached. The flux density values are also plotted and yield the curve DC'. Thereafter the current values are reduced to zero and then increased in the opposite direction to the same maximum as before, thus obtaining data for plotting the curve $C'G'C$. This completes the loop of magnetization and demagnetization, and the closed figure CC' is called the *hysteresis loop* for the sample under test. The area of the loop represents energy loss, due to the work done upon the particles of iron in changing their magnetic alignment first one way and then the other.

If the sample were magnetized by an alternating current, then the loss represented by one loop would occur for each individual cycle of current values and would produce appreciable heating. Had the magnetization in both directions been carried to a lesser maximum value, the hysteresis loop would have been smaller and its reduced area would represent a lower loss of energy.

In Fig. 241 the ordinate OD represents the amount of magnetism that remains when the current is reduced to zero; it is called the residual flux density. The abscissa OG represents the field intensity in a reversed direction needed to demagnetize the iron completely; it is called the coercive force. Soft iron and silicon steel not only have a high permeability but also a low coercive force and hence a low hysteresis loss; these characteristics make them suitable for use in electromagnets and electrical machinery.

265. Permanent Magnets. Magnetic materials having a large residual magnetism and a high coercive force are useful for permanent magnets. The basic component of these materials is iron, but small percentages of other elements are added to give permanence to their magnetization. The materials principally used are tungsten steel, chromium steel, and Alnico alloys, the latter containing various percentages of aluminum, nickel, cobalt, and copper.

Because a permanent magnet in serving its function is subject to demagnetizing influences due to heating, mechanical vibration, and extraneous fields, the test of its serviceability is the form of the demagnetization portion of its hysteresis loop, specifically the part in the second quadrant. The larger percentage of the total area of the loop that lies within this quadrant, the larger is the energy stored in the magnetic field of the material under test, a desired characteristic for permanent magnet materials.

In recent years permanent magnets have also been made from ultra-fine iron powder molded to shape and subjected to pressure and heat treatment. More recently a compound of manganese and bismuth has been developed that shows unusually high coercive force and is therefore most suitable for permanent magnets. The fine particles of MnBi are embedded in a plastic binder, oriented in a powerful magnetic field, and molded to shape; the resulting magnet is a nonconductor of electricity because the binder is an insulator.

Permanent magnets are widely used in electrical instruments, watthour meters, magneto generators, telephone receivers, loud speakers, and phonograph pick-ups.

266. Domain Theory of Magnetism. Reference was made earlier in this chapter to the orbital motion and axial spin of electrons within atoms, and to the development of magnetism by these moving electric charges. Studies of ferromagnetic substances indicate that one or more inner electron shells of their atoms are unfilled and that the electron spins in any one atom are unbalanced. In the iron atom, for example, the first shell contains 2 electrons and the second 8, the third shell could accommodate 18 electrons but only has 14, and the outer one has two. In all shells except the third, as many electrons spin one way as the other, but in the third, 9 spin in one direction against 4 in the other. Such an unbalanced spin causes the iron atom to be polarized and gives it a magnetic moment, § 209.

In ferromagnetic substances there are groups of millions or even billions of atoms that are aligned so that the magnetic fields developed by their spinning electrons point in a common direction; such microscopic groups are called *domains*. The motion of the electrons around their own orbits within all the atoms of a domain hardly affects its magnetic moment.

In an unmagnetized ferromagnetic substance the magnetic field of one domain differs from that of its neighbors, and since even a small specimen has a multitude of domains with fields in all directions, it has practically no resultant magnetic field.

When the substance is subjected to a weak external field the magnetic moments of the individual domains turn somewhat to bring the direction

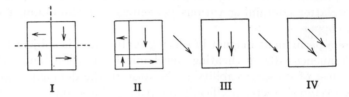

I　　　　　　　　II　　　　　　　　III　　　　　　　　IV

FIG. 242.　Behavior of domains during magnetization. (Arrows between diagrams represent direction of external field.)

of their fields nearer to that of the imposed field. Also some domains, more nearly aligned with the external field than others, acquire the moments of neighboring atoms and, in a sense, become larger at the expense of other domains. When subjected to a stronger field, there is a more gradual orientation toward the external field by expansion of domain boundaries and further alignment of their magnetic moments. These steps agree with the general shape of the magnetization curve of Fig. 240, and account for the initial sharp rise of flux density with small increases of field intensity and the subsequent markedly lessened rise as the substance approaches saturation.

The magnetic behavior of the domains during the magnetization of a ferromagnetic specimen is visualized in Fig. 242. The domains in an unmagnetized iron crystal have their fields parallel to the crystal axes as pictured in part I, and its resultant magnetism is zero. The shift of the domain boundaries is indicated in part II, the elimination of unfavorably oriented domains in part III, and the transition of domains toward the direction of the external field in part IV. Some simple domain structures of single crystals have actually been photographed.

267. Analogy Between Electric and Magnetic Circuits. Because the lines of magnetic flux form closed loops, it is customary to apply the term *magnetic circuit* to the path that flux loops follow. Magnetic circuits bear a certain similarity to electric circuits, and an expression similar to Ohm's Law can be formulated for them. The simplest approach is through the expressions derived in § 249 for a ring solenoid.

The flux density within a ring solenoid of N turns of wire carrying a current of I amp is given by Eq. 174 as

$$B = \frac{4\pi NI}{l} 10^{-7}$$

where l is the length of the ring in meters, and the constant 10^{-7} is equal to $\dfrac{\mu_o}{4\pi} \dfrac{\text{weber}}{\text{amp} \cdot \text{m}}$ as given in § 251. It follows that the flux density in webers per square meter is

$$B = \mu_o \frac{NI}{l}$$

showing that the flux density produced in free space by current through a solenoid depends upon the permeability of vacuum and the ampere·turns per unit length of the solenoid.

A comparison of this equation with Eq. 185, $B = \mu_o H$, indicates that the field intensity produced by the solenoid is

$$H = \frac{NI}{l} \tag{187}$$

showing that the field intensity depends only upon the winding and the current in it, and not upon the medium.

When the solenoid has a core of magnetic material having a permeability μ, and the flux density is uniform over its cross-sectional area A, the total flux through the core, by Eq. 168, is

$$\Phi = BA = \mu HA = \mu A \frac{NI}{l}$$

If this equation is rearranged in the form of Ohm's Law the result is

$$\Phi = \frac{NI}{\dfrac{l}{\mu A}} = \frac{\mathfrak{F}}{\mathfrak{R}}$$

where the product NI represents the agency that produces the magnetic flux, called *magnetomotive force* (mmf) and symbolized by $\mathfrak{F}$, and where the fraction $\dfrac{l}{\mu A}$ represents the opposition of the flux path, called *reluctance* and symbolized by $\mathfrak{R}$. The reluctance of a magnetic circuit depends upon its material and dimensions in the same general way that the resistance of an electric circuit depends upon these factors. Although the derivation is based upon a ring solenoid, the results are equally applicable to other shapes of magnetic circuits.

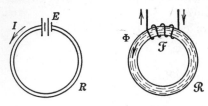

Fig. 243 illustrates the parallelism between electric and magnetic circuits. At the left is shown an electric circuit of resistance R, in which a battery of emf E sets up a current I. At the right is a toroidal core of reluctance $\mathfrak{R}$ and surrounded by a coil of wire

FIG. 243. Electric and magnetic circuits compared

carrying a current; this magnetizing agency sets up a magnetomotive force $\mathfrak{F}$ to establish a flux Φ in the toroid. The circuits are compared in parallel columns:

Electric	*Magnetic*

$$\text{current} = \frac{\text{emf}}{\text{resistance}} \qquad\qquad \text{flux} = \frac{\text{mmf}}{\text{reluctance}}$$

$$I = \frac{E}{R} \quad (152) \qquad\qquad \Phi = \frac{\mathfrak{F}}{\mathfrak{R}} \quad (188)$$

Resistance of a wire of length l, sectional area A, and conductivity σ is

Reluctance of a flux path of length l, sectional area A, and permeability μ is

$$R = \frac{l}{\sigma A} \quad (157) \qquad\qquad \mathfrak{R} = \frac{l}{\mu A} \quad (189)$$

Although the parallelism between the two circuits is seemingly exact, there are important differences which make the calculation of magnetic circuits less direct. In a metallic circuit, the resistance does not depend upon the current, except insofar as it is influenced by heating. In the magnetic circuit, on the other hand, the reluctance depends upon the magnetic flux, because the permeability is not constant. Also, in the electric circuit, the current is practically confined to the conductors, whereas in the magnetic circuit there is usually more or less magnetic leakage through the surrounding medium, for even in a vacuum there are lines of magnetic induction.

The unit for mmf in the mks system is naturally the ampere·turn, since $\mathfrak{F} = NI$ from Eq. 188. The unit of reluctance has no special name; it is obtained from the units of $\mathfrak{F}$ and $\mathfrak{R}$ in the same equation as the ampere·turn per weber. The permeability for vacuum is $\mu_o = 4\pi 10^{-7}$, and for a magnetic material of relative permeability μ_r the value of μ is $4\pi\mu_r 10^{-7}$, both in webers per ampere·meter.

Illustrative Problem

The magnetic core and winding shown in Fig. 244 has a length indicated by the dotted line of 40 cm, and a core cross-section of 10 cm². The winding consists of 200 turns and the current in it is 2.5 amp. Assume the relative permeability of the iron core to be 900 under the stated magnetization, and compute the flux established in the core.

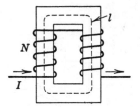

The mmf of the winding is $NI = 200 \times 2.5 = 500$ amp·turns. The length of the core is 0.40 m, the cross-sectional area is 0.001 m², and the permeability is $4\pi 10^{-7} \times 900 = 0.00113$ weber/(amp·m); hence the reluctance of the magnetic circuit is

Fig. 244. Winding on closed core

$$\Re = \frac{l}{\mu A} = \frac{0.4 \text{ m}}{0.00113 \dfrac{\text{weber}}{\text{amp·m}} \times 0.001 \text{ m}^2} = 354{,}000 \frac{\text{amp·turns}}{\text{weber}}$$

Therefore the flux in the circuit is $\dfrac{\mathscr{F}}{\Re} = \dfrac{500}{354{,}000} = 0.00141$ weber.

Rather than specifying the permeability in such calculations of magnetic circuits, it is often more direct to determine the field intensity from $H = NI/l$ and to read from the magnetization curve of the core material the value of flux density B for that particular field intensity; thereafter the flux can be obtained from $\Phi = BA$.

268. Electric Generators and Motors. The principles developed in the preceding chapter based on the laws of Ampère and Faraday, and those in the present chapter about magnetic circuits, have an all-important bearing on the operation of electrical machines. Those functioning with direct current are briefly considered here and those with alternating current at the beginning and end of Chap. 26.

Generators for the production of electrical energy and electric motors for the production of mechanical energy have magnetic circuits in which a part is arranged for rotation. The stationary part in direct-current machines is called the *field structure* and the movable part the *armature*. Each part has a winding appropriate for the emf and power of the machine as well as for the manner of connection. In series machines the two windings are connected in series and in shunt machines they are connected in parallel, the latter being the more usual. Fig. 245 shows the connections of a shunt machine; the armature A carries most of the current, and the field F in series with a rheostat R carries enough current to develop the magnetic flux necessary for generating the emf required.

Connection is made with the armature conductors through brushes that make sliding contact with a commutator, § 286; its purpose is to have all conductors on one side of the armature carry currents in one direction and all on the other side carry currents in the opposite direction. These directions are indicated in the figure by dots and crosses.

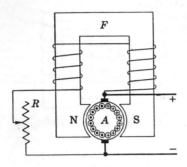

FIG. 245. Connections of shunt generator

When the machine is operated as a generator, the armature is driven by an engine or turbine, and emfs are induced in its conductors; these emfs develop currents in the two sides of the armature. These currents are directed toward the upper brush in the figure and join at that point to supply the output current. A small part of this current is used to activate the field and the rest supplies the electrical load. When the machine is operated as a motor, a small part of the incoming current activates the field and the rest is supplied to the armature. The conductors on each side of the armature receive half this current and, because of their location in the magnetic field, they are acted on by forces that collectively develop torque in the same direction, producing rotation and developing mechanical power.

Both generator and motor actions take place simultaneously in the conductors of an armature revolving in a magnetic field. As a generator, the armature is driven by the prime mover against an opposing torque that results from current in its conductors located in the magnetic field; hence more power is required to drive the generator when it delivers a greater current to the load circuits. As a motor, the armature generates a *counter emf*, and more current must be supplied when the motor drives a greater mechanical load. Thus the input to the machine accommodates itself automatically to the output required.

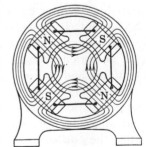

FIG. 246. Four-pole field structure

The field structure may have one or more pairs of poles; the machine in Fig. 245 has one pair and is called a bipolar machine. A typical 4-pole construction is illustrated in Fig. 246; the poles are alternately N and S, and there are four flux paths as shown by the four groups of flux loops.

The number of paths in parallel through the armature of a generator is determined by the manner in which the armature is wound. For the usual type of winding the number of parallel paths is the same as the number of poles on the machine. The emf of the machine is the same as that generated in one of the parallel paths through the armature, and the total current is the sum of the currents in these paths.

The iron structure that supports the armature coils also has emfs induced in it as a result of motion through magnetic flux. To reduce the currents produced by these emfs the structure is formed of thin laminations insulated from one another and aligned edgewise to the flux, thus lengthening the current paths and increasing their resistance. Such currents induced by flux changes in metal masses are called *eddy currents*.

Both eddy currents and magnetic hysteresis result in energy losses in the armature, as do also friction and windage due to mechanical rotation. The principal loss in generators and motors is due to the current in the windings.

269. Electromotive Force of a Generator. The emf of any direct-current generator can be computed by finding the average emf induced in each armature conductor by means of Eq. 179, and multiplying this value by the number of conductors in series in each path through the armature. When the machine is driven at n rev/sec, it completes 1 rev in $\dfrac{1}{n}$ sec, and if it has P poles the entire flux Φ webers extending from each pole is cut in $\dfrac{1}{P}$ of this time, or in $\dfrac{1}{Pn}$ sec. The average rate of cutting flux is therefore $\Phi \div \dfrac{1}{Pn}$ webers/sec, and hence the average emf induced in each armature conductor is ΦPn volts. If Z represents the total number of conductors and p the number of paths in parallel through the armature, then the number of conductors in series in each path is $\dfrac{Z}{P}$, and hence the emf of the generator in volts has an average value of

$$E = \Phi P n \frac{Z}{p}$$

For a given generator, the quantities P, Z, and p in the equation are fixed, showing that the emf is determined by the speed and flux, or

$$E \propto n\Phi$$

The emf induced in the armature conductors can be raised or lowered either by driving them faster or slower, or by increasing or decreasing the flux. In practice, the speed of a generator is determined by that of the prime mover, and the emf of the machine is adjusted by changing the flux. This is accomplished by varying the current in the field coils with a rheostat.

When a generator is producing an emf E and its armature, of resistance R_a, is supplying a current I_a, there is a small drop of potential in the armature itself amounting to $I_a R_a$. Consequently, the pd V_t across the machine terminals is smaller than the emf generated by this amount, or

$$V_t = E - I_a R_a \tag{190}$$

This equation shows that as the load on the generator increases, thereby increasing the armature current I_a, the pd across its terminals V_t falls off.

270. Torque Developed by a Motor. The fundamental principle of the electric motor is the sidewise thrust upon current-carrying conductors located in a magnetic field. The magnitude of this force on a conductor of length l m, carrying a current of I amp, and placed at right angles to a

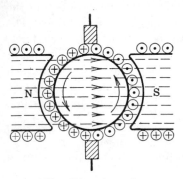

magnetic flux of density B webers/m^2 is given by Eq. 176 as $F = BIl$ newtons. The direction of the force can be determined by reference to Fig. 230. If the current in the wire is directed toward the observer, and the magnetic flux is directed from left to right, the wire is forced upward.

Fig. 247 illustrates the armature conductors within the field of a bipolar motor. A commutator (not shown) keeps the current in the right-hand belt of conductors directed toward the observer and that in the left-hand belt directed away from him. It will be seen that the conductors at the

FIG. 247. Direction of torque on motor armature

right are forced upward and those at the left forced downward. The forces on all the conductors act at a common distance from the axis of rotation and develop a torque in the same direction, counterclockwise in this case.

The torque developed by a current I in a total of Z armature conductors located at a distance r from the axis of rotation is $T = FZr = BIlZr$. The average flux density in the air gap where the armature conductors are revolving can be expressed in terms of the number of field poles P, the magnetic flux Φ per pole, the circumferential length $2\pi r$ of the air gap, and the axial length l of the poles or its equivalent, the conductor length; thus $B = P\Phi/2\pi rl$. Hence the total torque exerted on all the armature conductors is

$$T = \frac{P\Phi}{2\pi rl} IlZr = \frac{PZ}{2\pi} I\Phi$$

which shows that the torque developed by a given motor is proportional to the current in the armature conductors and to the flux from a field pole.

As the armature rotates, even though turning by its own motor action, its conductors cut magnetic flux and an emf is induced in them, exactly as in the armature of a generator. To determine the direction of this emf, the currents in the armature conductors may be supposed directed as shown in Fig. 247, driving the armature in a counter-clockwise direction. From Lenz's Law, § 256, it is found that the emf induced in each conductor is opposite to the direction of the current. As a motor rotates, therefore, a counter emf is induced in its armature that depends primarily upon the speed; its value can be calculated in the same way as for a generator. If the motor is connected across supply mains that provide a pd V_t at the motor terminals, and if E_c is the counter emf, the net potential difference acting to produce current in the armature is $V_t - E_c$. Hence the current supplied to the armature of resistance R_a is

$$I_a = \frac{V_t - E_c}{R_a}$$

This expression is analogous to Eq. 190 that applies to a generator.

Illustrative Problem

As a typical example, suppose a shunt motor operating on 230 volts to have a field resistance of 100 ohms and an armature resistance of 0.15 ohm, and to be rotating at a speed such that its counter emf is 228 volts. Find the increase in current taken when the load is increased sufficiently to lower the speed 2.5%.

The field current is $I_f = \frac{230}{100} = 2.30$ amp, and the armature current at the higher speed is $I_a = \dfrac{230 - 228}{0.15} = 13.3$ amp. At the lower speed the counter emf is 2.5% less than 228, that is, 222.3 volts; the armature current, determined as before, is then 51.3 amp. Thus the 2.5% drop in speed increases the armature current from 13.3 to 51.3 amp, a 285% increase.

The power output of a motor can be found by inserting the foregoing expression for its torque in Eq. 63, which indicates that power is equal to torque times angular velocity. For a motor turning n rev/sec the angular velocity is $2\pi n$, and hence the power output is

$$\text{Output} = T2\pi n = \Phi PnZI$$

Since the total current I_a supplied to the armature is the product of the current I in each armature conductor multiplied by the number of paths p in parallel through the armature, the output can be expressed as $\left(\Phi Pn \dfrac{Z}{p}\right) I_a$.

A comparison of this result with an expression given in the preceding section shows that the part in parentheses is the emf developed in a generator. For a motor this is the counter emf E_c, and therefore the power output of a motor is expressed simply as

$$\text{Output} = E_c I_a \tag{191}$$

The shunt motor operates at a fairly constant speed and is used industrially where heavy mechanical loads are applied after full speed has been acquired. The series motor, in contrast, is a variable-speed machine capable of exerting a large torque at low speed and less torque at higher speeds; this characteristic is desirable, for example, in railway motors.

PROBLEMS

1. A magnetic field intensity of 400 amp·turns/m develops a flux density in a malleable iron casting of 0.85 weber/m². Calculate the relative permeability of this casting at the stated magnetization.

2. A magnetic field of 0.1 amp·turn/in. in permalloy sets up a flux of 0.16 milliweber through a cross-section of 1 in.² What is the relative permeability of this material when so magnetized?

3. The magnetization curve of silicon steel is given in Fig. 240. Estimate from this curve the values of flux density for field intensities of 2500 and 25,000 amp·turns/m and determine the relative permeabilities of this steel at these magnetizations.

4. Low values of the magnetization of silicon steel cannot be read accurately from the curve of Fig. 240; some values of flux density B and field intensity H in this range follow:

B	0.25	0.50	0.75	1.00	1.25	1.50	webers/m²
H	50	75	100	190	500	2500	amp·turns/m

Plot a curve for this alloy of relative permeability as ordinates against flux density as abscissas.

5. The hysteresis loss in sheet steel may be regarded as proportional to the 1.6 power of the maximum value of the flux density reached during a cycle of current values. If this loss is 80 watts in a core that is magnetized by a 25-cycle current (that is, one that reverses 25 × 2 = 50 times each second) and reaches a flux density of 0.7 weber/m², what would be the loss when the core is magnetized by a 60-cycle current that produces a maximum flux density of 1.0 weber/m²?

6. The iron alloy called Alnico V contains aluminum (Al 8%), nickel (Ni 14%), cobalt (Co 24%), and copper (Cu 3%); it is one of the materials used for making permanent magnets. Plot the magnetization curve for this material from the following values of magnetic field intensities and magnetic inductions:

H	100	300	500	550	570	600	700	1,000	1,500	oersteds
B	100	700	2000	5000	7900	11,500	12,500	13,200	13,700	gausses

7. Determine the relative permeabilities of Alnico V from the data given in the preceding problem for magnetizations of 500 and 600 oersteds.

8. The core of a transformer forms a closed iron circuit having a mean length of 50 cm and a cross-section of 20 cm², and the magnetization curve for the iron is that shown in Fig. 240. What magnetomotive force should be provided to establish a flux of 350,000 maxwells through the core?

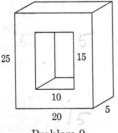

Problem 9

9. A core made up of silicon sheet steel has the dimensions in centimeters shown in the figure. A winding is placed around the core and the wire threads through the opening 140 times in the same direction. Use the data of Prob. 4 and compute the amount of magnetic flux that is developed in the core when the current in the winding is (*a*) 0.5 amp and (*b*) 2.5 amp.

10. What is the reluctance of the core of Prob. 9 when the magnetizing current is (*a*) 0.5 amp and (*b*) 2.5 amp?

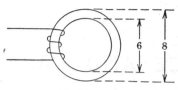

Problem 11

11. A cast-iron ring of square cross-section has the dimensions in inches shown in the sketch. It is completely wound in the manner indicated with 440 turns in all. With a current of 2 amp through the winding the relative permeability of the ring is found to be 180. Determine (*a*) the mmf applied, (*b*) the field intensity produced, (*c*) the flux density established, (*d*) the total magnetic flux developed, and (*e*) the reluctance of the core.

12. If a radial saw cut is made in the ring of Prob. 11 to form an air gap 0.05 in. long in the flux path, by how much will the flux be reduced for the same magnetization? Neglect the change in permeability introduced by the air gap.

13. The armature of a 4-pole generator has 200 conductors connected in series in each of its current paths. How much magnetic flux should extend from each N-pole of the field structure of this generator for it to develop 120 volts at a speed of 1500 rev/min?

14. A bipolar generator has square pole pieces measuring 20 cm on each edge and the flux density in the air gap between the armature core and field structure is 0.8 weber/m². The armature has a total of 240 conductors arranged in two parallel paths. Find the average emf developed by the generator when its armature rotates at 1800 rev/min.

15. In a 10-kw shunt generator, the armature has a resistance of 0.22 ohm and the field winding 160 ohms. At no load the pd at the generator terminals is 240 volts. (*a*) What is the pd at the terminals of the machine when it delivers its rated load? (*b*) What are the full-load losses in the armature and the field winding? (*c*) If all other losses in the generator amount to 450 watts, what is its efficiency?

16. The armature of a bipolar shunt motor supports 280 conductors, each 30 cm long, located 10 cm from the axis of rotation. It revolves at 1200 rev/min through a magnetic flux of 0.05 weber. Assume that the conductors move at right angles to the flux and that each carries a current of 20 amp. Compute (*a*) the torque developed by the armature and (*b*) the output of the motor.

17. A shunt motor connected to 120-volt supply mains has an armature resistance of 0.3 ohm and a field resistance of 80 ohms. When supplying power to a mechanical load, the machine is generating a counter emf of 114 volts. Compute (*a*) the armature current, (*b*) the field current, (*c*) the total current taken by the motor, and (*d*) its output.

18. The armature of a shunt motor has a resistance of 0.24 ohm and takes 15 amp from 120-volt service mains when turning at 1000 rev/min. When the load is increased, lowering the motor speed to 988 rev/min, what current will the armature take?

25

INDUCTANCE AND CAPACITANCE

INDUCTANCE

271. Mutual Induction. Important effects are developed in electric circuits when the currents through them change. A change of current produces an alteration in the magnetic field around a circuit, and the change in magnetic flux sets up emfs in suitably placed circuits near by through electromagnetic induction, § 255. Changes in current occur chiefly when a circuit is opened or closed or when the load is varied; with alternating current it is not necessary to alter the circuit conditions, for the current continually changes from moment to moment. The emfs induced in neighboring circuits by these current changes are often desired, and the circuits are designed in such situations to develop particular emfs to suit the purposes intended; in other situations the induced emfs disturb the normal operation of the neighboring circuits, and provisions are made to minimize the disturbances.

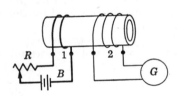

FIG. 248. Coils coupled magnetically for demonstrating mutual inductance

The effect of current changes in one circuit upon another is called *mutual induction*. To demonstrate this effect two coils of wire, wound side by side upon a cardboard tube, are connected to separate circuits, as shown in Fig. 248, in an environment that is nonmagnetic. Coil 1 is joined to a battery B in series with a rheostat R; coil 2 is joined to a galvanometer G. So long as the current in coil 1 remains steady, the magnetic flux extending through coil 2 is steady also, and the galvanometer shows no deflection; but when the current is changed by moving the slider along the rheostat, the flux through coil 2 changes and the galvanometer deflects. If, in a short interval dt, the current changes by the amount di_1, and the flux linking coil 2 changes by the amount $d\Phi$, there is induced in coil 2 an emf that is proportional to $\dfrac{d\Phi}{dt}$, as expressed by Eq. 179. Since the flux is proportional to the current that produces it, the time rate of change of flux is proportional to the rate of change of current, or $\dfrac{d\Phi}{dt} \propto \dfrac{di_1}{dt}$. Therefore the induced emf in coil 2 is proportional to the rate of current change in coil 1, or

$$e_2 = M \frac{di_1}{dt} \tag{192}$$

where M is a factor depending upon the magnetic coupling of the two coils and called the *coefficient of mutual induction*. This equation indicates that the more rapidly the current changes, the greater is the emf induced; this can be shown experimentally by moving the rheostat slider at different speeds.

Upon interchanging the battery (with rheostat) and the galvanometer, and altering the current in coil 2, an emf is induced in coil 1 that can be expressed similarly as

$$e_1 = M \frac{di_2}{dt}$$

where the coefficient M has the same value as before and $\dfrac{di_2}{dt}$ is the time rate of current change in coil 2.

The coefficient of mutual induction, also called the *mutual inductance*, is expressed in terms of a unit called the *henry;* it is named after the American physicist Joseph Henry (1797–1878). Two coils are said to have a mutual inductance of one henry when a current *change* of one ampere per second in one coil causes an emf of one volt to be induced in the other.

When the experiment with the coils is repeated with an iron core inserted in them, the results are different in two respects: first, the mutual inductance of the coils is greatly increased, and second, its value is not constant, because a given change in current does not in general cause a proportional change in the magnetic flux in the iron, § 263.

The direction of the induced emf can be found by Lenz's Law. Thus, an increase of current in coil 1 is accompanied by an increase of magnetic flux around itself and around coil 2; the latter action induces an emf in coil 2 that produces in it a current so directed as to cause a decrease of flux. In brief, an increase of current in coil 1 causes the emf induced in coil 2 to be opposite in direction to the current in coil 1. Also, a decrease of current in coil 1 causes the emf induced in coil 2 to have the same direction as the current in coil 1.

272. Self-Induction. As explained with Fig. 248, when two circuits are close together, a change of current in one of them produces an emf in the second, because of the accompanying change in magnetic flux linking the latter. A change of current in one of the coils causes a change of flux not only through the other coil but also through the very coil in which the current is changing. Hence, a change of current in any coil causes an emf to be induced in that coil; this effect is called *self-induction*. The emf induced depends upon the rate of current change and can be expressed as

$$e = -L\frac{di}{dt} \tag{193}$$

where L is a coefficient, like M in the preceding equations, that is characteristic of the coil itself and its magnetic environment. The direction of this emf can be shown by Lenz's Law to be such as to oppose the change of current that caused it; for this reason a negative sign is used in the equation and e is designated as the *counter emf of self-induction*. Similarly, L is called the *coefficient of self-induction*, or simply the *inductance*.

Inductance, like mutual inductance, is expressed in henrys. *A circuit has an inductance of one henry if a current change of one ampere per second causes an emf of one volt to be induced in it.*

A coil of many turns of wire has more inductance than the same wire when unwound so as to form only a single loop, because the emf induced depends not only upon the rate of change of flux but also upon the number of turns through which this change occurs. The inductance would also be greater if the coil were wound upon an iron core.

For some purposes it is necessary to have coils of wire with very little or no appreciable inductance, and this means, of course, that there must be very little magnetic flux around them. Such so-called *noninductive coils* are wound by arranging the wire in a long "hairpin" loop and winding the two conductors side by side until the coil has the desired resistance; when the two terminals are connected to a source of emf the flux due to current in one conductor neutralizes that due to the opposite current in the other. The resistors of Wheatstone bridges and similar instruments are wound noninductively.

273. Inductance of a Solenoid. The inductance of a coil of wire depends upon the number of magnetic lines of induction that a given current in the coil produces. This fact can be verified by considering the current in a coil of inductance L to change from one value to another, thereby inducing in its winding an emf which at any instant is given by $e = -L\frac{di}{dt}$ volts, as in the preceding section. In reality the change of magnetic flux through the coil of N turns induces an emf having an instantaneous value of $e = -N\frac{d\Phi}{dt}$ volts, § 255. Obviously, these equations express the same action in different ways, and therefore

$$L\frac{di}{dt} = N\frac{d\Phi}{dt}$$

from which $L = N\dfrac{d\Phi}{di}$. On the assumption that the flux grows uniformly with the current and that a value of flux Φ is established when the current reaches a value I, the inductance of the coil becomes

$$L = \frac{N\Phi}{I} \qquad (194)$$

where the product of the number of turns N and the number of flux loops Φ linked with them is spoken of as *flux-linkages*.

This result provides a useful definition of unit inductance, as follows: *The henry is the inductance of a circuit in which there is one flux-linkage per ampere of current in that circuit.*

The equation can be applied to a ring solenoid in which a coil of N turns is wound upon a ring-shaped core of length l and cross-sectional area A. The magnetic flux set up in this core by a current of I amp in the coil is $\Phi = \mu HA$, where μ is the permeability of the core and H the field intensity within it. The intensity is given in Eq. 187 as $H = \dfrac{NI}{l}$, and consequently the inductance, in henrys, becomes

$$L = \frac{N^2 A \mu}{l} \qquad (195)$$

This result shows that the inductance of a solenoid varies directly with the square of its number of turns, and depends upon the cross-section, length, and permeability of the core. When A and l are expressed in meters and μ in webers per ampere·meter, the inductance is in webers per ampere, or in henrys. This expression affords still another unit for permeability, namely, the henry per meter.

274. Growth and Decay of Current in Inductive Circuits. When a circuit containing inductance and resistance is connected to a unidirectional source the current does not attain its full value instantly, because the counter emf of self-induction, Eq. 193, hinders its growth. The current rises rapidly at first and then builds up more and more slowly as it approaches its final value, but the entire growth occurs in a very short time.

The effect of inductance can be illustrated by the circuit shown in Fig. 249, in which a solenoid with an iron core is shunted around a lamp and joined to a direct-current gener-

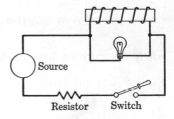

FIG. 249. Experiment to illustrate effect of inductance

ator, some resistance being included in the circuit. The coil has vastly more inductance than the lamp, but much less resistance. When the switch is closed the lamp flashes brightly and then becomes dim. The action is explained by the facts: (1) that, while the magnetic field is being established around the coil, the emf of self-induction hinders the growth of current in the coil; and (2) that, after the magnetic field has been established and the current in the coil has reached its ultimate value, the greater pd across the series resistor lessens that across both coil and lamp. Again, when the switch is opened quickly, the lamp flashes even more brightly, because the large emf induced in the coil by the rapidly decaying flux then sets up a strong pulse of current through the lamp.

Illustrative Problem

Suppose a solenoid of 5 ohms resistance and 1 henry inductance to be connected across 120-volt direct-current supply mains. At an instant when the rate of current growth is 100 amp/sec, the counter emf has a value of $e = -L \dfrac{di}{dt} = -1$ henry $\times 100 \dfrac{\text{amp}}{\text{sec}} = -100$ volts, and hence the current in the solenoid at that instant is $(120 - 100)$ volts $\div 5$ ohms $= 4$ amp. When the rate of current growth has fallen to 10 amp/sec, the counter emf is momentarily $-1 \times 10 = -10$ volts, and the current value at that instant is $(120 - 10) \div 5 = 22$ amp. The final value of the current in this circuit is $120 \div 5 = 24$ amp.

The foregoing illustration also indicates that Ohm's Law in its simple form applies only to steady currents; in a more general statement it should include the counter emf of self-induction as well as the emf E impressed upon the circuit, as follows:

$$i = \frac{E - L \dfrac{di}{dt}}{R} \tag{196}$$

This equation may also be regarded as a generalization of Kirchhoff's Law; it expresses the statements at the beginning of this section. At the instant when an inductive circuit is connected to an electrical source, all of the emf causes the current to grow, for then the current i is zero and $E = L \dfrac{di}{dt}$; when the current has reached its final value I, then $\dfrac{di}{dt} = 0$ and $I = \dfrac{E}{R}$.

Eq. 196 is a differential equation, and its solution for the current at any instant involves exponential functions. It will suffice merely to give the result, namely,

$$i = \frac{E}{R}\left(1 - \epsilon^{-\frac{Rt}{L}}\right)$$

where i is the value of the current at an instant t sec after an emf of E volts is impressed upon a circuit having a resistance of R ohms and an inductance of L henrys. In this expression ϵ is the base of natural logarithms, namely, 2.7183.

When the applied emf is withdrawn from the circuit by short-circuiting the source, the current falls to zero gradually, but in a short time. The current values during this period are given by

$$i = \frac{E}{R} \epsilon^{-\frac{Rt}{L}}$$

Fig. 250 shows a graph of current growth in an inductive circuit from the instant t_1 when it is connected to a constant source of supply, and of current decay in that circuit when the source is short-circuited at instant t_2.

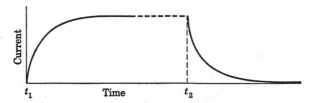

FIG. 250.   Growth and decay of current in inductive circuit

275. Energy of a Magnetic Field. When a pd is impressed upon an inductive circuit, work is done against the emf of self-induction to establish current in the circuit and create the magnetic field around it. The rate at which work is done in producing the field at any instant during the period of current growth is the product of the current i already established and the instantaneous counter emf $e = -L\dfrac{di}{dt}$. The total amount of energy that must be expended to establish the ultimate current I in the circuit can be determined by the method of integration in calculus as follows:

$$W = \int_{t=0}^{t=t} ie\, dt = \int_{i=0}^{i=I} iL\frac{di}{dt} dt = \left[\frac{Li^2}{2}\right]_0^I$$

or

$$W = \tfrac{1}{2}LI^2 \tag{197}$$

The energy of the magnetic field is expressed in joules when the current is in amperes and the inductance is in henrys. When the magnetic field is once established all further energy supplied to the circuit is dissipated in heating, for no energy is needed solely to maintain the field.

The inductance L in the foregoing equations is analogous to the mass m in the equations of Mechanics. Eq. 197 affords a statement of inductance in terms of energy: a circuit of one henry inductance and carrying a current of one ampere has $\tfrac{1}{2}$ joule of energy stored in its magnetic field.

To determine the magnetic energy stored in a substance in terms of magnetic quantities, it is convenient to consider a ring solenoid, for which the quantities needed have already been expressed. The flux density in the core is given by Eqs. 184 and 187 as $B = \mu \dfrac{NI}{l}$, and the inductance by Eq. 195 as $L = \dfrac{N^2 A \mu}{l}$. If the number of turns N is eliminated between these equations, the inductance becomes $L = \dfrac{B^2 l A}{\mu I^2}$, and hence the energy can be found by substituting this value in Eq. 197. Since the volume of a core of length l and cross-sectional area A is lA, the energy per unit volume of core material is

$$W_1 = \frac{B^2}{2\mu}$$

If B is in webers per square meter and μ in webers per ampere·meter, then W_1 is in weber·amperes per cubic meter. Since the weber is the same as the volt·second, § 255, the unit for W_1 becomes the joule per cubic meter.

276. The Induction Coil. The development of emf in one winding by a change of current in another through electromagnetic induction is the operating principle of the *induction coil.*

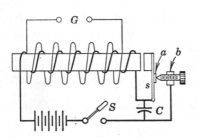

FIG. 251. Circuit of induction coil

Fig. 251 shows the two windings surrounding a straight core composed of soft-iron wires. The primary winding, represented by the heavy line, is connected in series with a battery, a switch S, and an interrupter; the secondary winding, represented by the light line, is a coil of many turns connected across a spark gap G. The interrupter is an armature mounted on a flat spring s that carries a hard metal contact a; this periodically touches a similar but stationary contact b when the spring is set into vibration. A capacitor C is bridged across the contacts in order to eliminate sparking there and to hasten the breaking of the circuit by the interrupter, § 281.

When the switch is closed, the increasing current through the primary winding establishes magnetism in the core, inducing an emf in the secondary winding. The armature is promptly attracted to the core, and the contact between a and b is broken. Current in the primary winding is thus interrupted and the magnetism in the core falls to a low value (the residual magnetism), again inducing an emf in the secondary winding. The armature is then released from the core and springs back, closing contact between a and b. This cycle is repeated as long as the switch remains closed, at a rate determined by the stiffness of the spring and the mass of the armature. The emfs induced in the secondary produce a succession of sparks across the gap.

The rate of current change is much greater when the contacts open than when they close; hence the induced emf is larger on opening the circuit than on closing it. As a result the discharge across the spark gap, except for short gap lengths, is unidirectional. The discharge shows a short bright section near the negative terminal. When the primary is supplied with alternating current, no interrupter is needed and the discharge is not unidirectional; the induction coil is then made with a closed core of laminated iron and is called a transformer, § 295.

CAPACITANCE

277. Electric Flux. The principles of electrostatics considered in Chap. 19 deal with electric charges and electric fields in free space; attention will now be given to matters involving other mediums, including such topics as electric flux, capacitance, and the energy stored in dielectrics.

The field around electric charges was pictured in § 197 as permeated with electric lines of force, drawn so as to show the configuration of the field, and the intensity at any point in the field was expressed as the force upon a unit charge placed at the point. Thus if a charge Q placed in an already existing field is acted upon by a force F, the intensity of the field there is

$$\mathcal{E} = \frac{F}{Q}$$

as given by Eq. 135. With the charge expressed in coulombs and the force in newtons, the field intensity is in newtons per coulomb.

The electric field intensity may be regarded as an agency that sets up *electric flux* in its field, just as magnetic field intensity sets up magnetic flux in a magnetic field. In free space of permittivity ϵ_0 the amount of electric flux developed by a field intensity $\mathcal{E}$ through a unit of area placed transversely to the flux is

$$D = \epsilon_0 \mathcal{E} \tag{198}$$

where D represents the density of the electric flux. If this density is the same at all points over an area A, then the total electric flux Ψ (psi) is given by

$$\Psi = DA \tag{199}$$

These expressions are analogous to those of the magnetic circuit, for in free space of permeability μ_0 the amount of magnetic flux developed by a field intensity H through a unit of area placed transversely to the flux is $B = \mu_0 H$ as given by Eq. 185, and the total magnetic flux through a transverse area A is $\Phi = BA$ as given by Eq. 168.

The foregoing equations are useful in finding the electric flux that extends from an isolated point charge. In Fig. 252 a sphere of radius r is imagined centered on a charge Q located in free space of permittivity ϵ_o. The electric flux directed outward from the positive charge must extend through the sphere and be perpendicular everywhere to the spherical surface. Over this entire surface the field intensity is given by Eq. 136 as $\mathcal{E} = kQ/r^2$, where the constant k has the value $1/(4\pi\epsilon_0)$. Thus

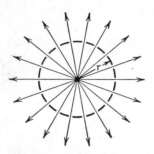

$$\mathcal{E} = k\frac{Q}{r^2} = \frac{1}{4\pi\epsilon_o}\frac{Q}{r^2}$$

Hence the flux density at the surface is

$$D = \epsilon_o\mathcal{E} = \frac{1}{4\pi}\frac{Q}{r^2}$$

FIG. 252. Electric flux from isolated point charge

Since the area of this spherical surface is $A = 4\pi r^2$, the total electric flux through it is

$$\Psi = DA = \frac{1}{4\pi}\frac{Q}{r^2}4\pi r^2 = Q \tag{200}$$

and is independent of the surrounding medium. Therefore the total flux from a point charge is numerically equal to the charge itself and hence can be expressed in coulombs. This result may be viewed as meaning that the total electric flux "outside" the sphere is the same as the charge "on" it.

278. Capacitance of an Isolated Conductor. Any conductor that is charged and isolated in space has an equipotential surface, § 198; this means that no work is done in moving a charge from one point to another on that surface. To arrive at a relationship between the potential of such a surface and the charge on it, the conductor is most conveniently assumed to have the form of a sphere. The electric flux from the charged

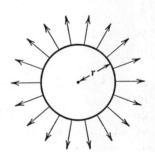

FIG. 253. Electric flux from charged sphere

sphere is shown in Fig. 253; it extends radially and has the same configuration as though its charge were concentrated at the center.

The potential at any point distant r from a concentrated charge Q in free space is given by Eq. 139 as

$$V = k\frac{Q}{r}$$

the reference potential being zero at $r = \infty$. The value of V given by this equation is also the potential of the surface of a sphere of radius r when it carries the same charge Q. The expression shows that the potential of the sphere is directly proportional to the charge on it, thus $V \propto Q$. This proportionality is equally true of any charged conductor, whatever its shape; hence the relationship between these two factors can be expressed by the equation

$$Q = CV \qquad C = \frac{Q}{V} \qquad (201)$$

where C is a constant determined by the size and shape of the particular conductor and called its *capacitance*. In this equation, when the charge is in coulombs and the potential in volts, the capacitance unit is the coulomb per volt; it is called the *farad*, derived from the name of Faraday.

To determine the capacitance of an isolated sphere, the foregoing equa-

tions are combined and solved for C; the result is $C = \dfrac{r}{k}$. In mks units the

constant k has the value $\dfrac{1}{4\pi\epsilon_o} = 9 \times 10^9 \dfrac{\text{newton} \cdot \text{m}^2}{\text{coulomb}^2}$. This unit reduces to

$$\frac{\text{joule} \cdot \text{m}}{\text{coulomb}^2} = \frac{\text{volt} \cdot \text{coulomb} \cdot \text{m}}{\text{coulomb}^2} = \frac{\text{volt} \cdot \text{m}}{\text{coulomb}} = \frac{\text{m}}{\text{farad}}$$

Hence the capacitance of an isolated conducting sphere of radius r meters is given in farads by

$$C = \frac{r}{9 \times 10^9} \qquad (202)$$

which shows that the capacitance of a spherical conductor is directly proportional to its radius.

279. Capacitance Between Parallel Plates.

An even more important concept than the capacitance of an isolated conductor is that offered by a pair of conductors, the most common arrangement being represented by two flat plates placed parallel and opposite each other. When a pd is applied across the plates, charging one positively and the other negatively, an electric field is established between them which is uniform, except near the edges, as shown in part III of Fig. 189, and its intensity is

$$\mathcal{E} = \frac{V}{s}$$

as given by Eq. 141, where s is the distance between the plates. When the applied pd is in volts and the plate separation in meters, the field intensity is expressed in volts per meter; this unit is identical with the newton per coulomb used in § 197.

The field intensity between the plates sets up electric flux extending from the charge $+Q$ on one plate to the charge $-Q$ on the other. The electric flux density developed in free space is, as before,

$$D = \epsilon_o \mathcal{E}$$

and the total flux between the plates of area A, disregarding the flux fringing at their edges, is

$$\Psi = DA = \epsilon_o \mathcal{E} A = \epsilon_o V \frac{A}{s}$$

Since all the electric flux from a charge is numerically equal to the charge itself, $\Psi = Q$ as derived in § 277, and since capacitance is expressed as the charge per unit of potential, $C = \dfrac{Q}{V}$, it follows that the capacitance of the parallel-plate arrangement in a vacuum is

$C = \mathcal{E}_o \, 4R\gamma$

$$C = \frac{\Psi}{V} = \epsilon_o \frac{A}{s} \tag{203}$$

If the dimensions of the plates and their separation are expressed in meters, and the permittivity of free space $\epsilon_o = \dfrac{1}{4\pi k} = \dfrac{1}{4\pi 9 \times 10^9} \dfrac{\text{coulomb}}{\text{volt} \cdot \text{m}}$ as in the preceding section, then the capacitance is in coulombs per volt, or farads.

280. Dielectric Substances. The effect of placing different materials in an electric field depends upon whether they are conductors or insulators. The difference can be made clear with Fig. 254, which shows a pair of

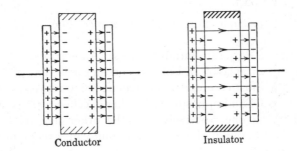

Conductor   Insulator

FIG. 254. Conductor and insulator within electric field; comparison of behavior

charged plates between which is placed a conductor in part I and an insulator in part II. With an uncharged conductor in the field the free electrons within it move from right to left and cause its surfaces to acquire charges by induction as shown. The net result is to break up the field into two parts, and to have no charge and no field in the interior of the conductor.

When an uncharged insulator is placed in the field there is no flow of electrons in it, but within each molecule there is a displacement between its positive and negative components, causing it to become a dipole. These dipoles orient themselves in the direction of the field, and thus the entire insulator becomes *polarized*. As a result, charges are developed on the surface of the insulator as shown; these induced charges produce an electric field of their own within the insulator. This field is in the opposite direction to that imposed by the charged plates and, since the extent of polarization depends upon the kind of molecules involved, the intensity of this opposing field differs from one insulator to another, but is always less than that between the plates. This result probably accounts for the fact that insulating materials are called *dielectrics*. The reduced electric field within the dielectric can also be explained by the fact that some lines of flux in the gaps between it and the plates extend from the charges on the plates to the charged ends of the dipoles at the dielectric surfaces.

It was pointed out in § 277 that the electric flux extending from a positively charged isolated sphere is numerically equal to the charge on that sphere, and that the flux as well as the flux density is independent of the medium. Since in a dielectric the electric field is reduced and the flux density is not, the equation for the flux density in free space, namely, $D = \epsilon_0 \mathcal{E}$, must be modified to be appropriate for other mediums by writing it as

$$D = \epsilon \mathcal{E} \tag{204}$$

where ϵ is the permittivity of the dielectric. Thus a lessening of field intensity $\mathcal{E}$ in the dielectric is associated with an increased permittivity ϵ so that the electric flux density D shall remain constant. The permittivity of an insulating material is therefore always greater than that for free space.

The ratio of the permittivity ϵ of a dielectric to the permittivity ϵ_0 of a vacuum is called the *dielectric coefficient* of the insulator and is symbolized by κ (kappa). Thus the dielectric coefficient is defined by

$$\kappa = \frac{\epsilon}{\epsilon_0} \tag{205}$$

and its value is equal to $4\pi 9 \times 10^9 \epsilon$ when ϵ is expressed in the same units as used previously for ϵ_0. This coefficient is a pure number and has a characteristic value for every insulating substance. Its value for air is 1.000586 at standard temperature and pressure.

281. Capacitors. Any arrangement of two conductors with a dielectric between them is called a *capacitor;* years ago the term "condenser" was used, but the newer term is more descriptive of its property, namely, capacitance. Most capacitors consist of parallel plates of metal with intervening sheets of insulating material. A capacitor can be charged by connecting its plates to the terminals of a battery or other source of direct current. The source causes electrons to leave one plate and flow to the other through the connecting wires and causes an electric displacement in the dielectric as a result of the polarization of its molecules, § 199. This process continues until a state of equilibrium is reached, during which the plates acquire the same pd as the source. Each plate then has a definite charge depending upon the emf of the battery; the larger the emf, the larger the charge.

The capacitance of the capacitor can be defined as the ratio of the charge on one of the plates to the pd between them; thus

$$C = \frac{Q}{V}$$

from Eq. 201, in which C is the capacitance in farads when the charge is in coulombs and the pd in volts. *A capacitor has a capacitance of one farad when a potential difference of one volt charges it with one coulomb of electricity.* The farad is an enormously large unit of capacitance, and for convenience smaller units are generally used; these are the microfarad and the micro-microfarad (abbreviated μf and $\mu\mu f$ respectively).

Oceanic cables have large capacitance. For example, the two coaxial telephone cables laid in 1956 joining Clarenville in Newfoundland and Oban in Scotland, each 2250 mi long, have a capacitance of 0.150 μf per mile.

The capacitance of a parallel-plate capacitor is determined entirely by the dimensions and dielectric coefficient of the dielectric, and is not affected, for instance, by the materials used for the plates, provided only that these are electrical conductors. The capacitance can be computed from Eq. 203 by replacing the permittivity ϵ_o of vacuum with the permittivity ϵ of the dielectric, and the equation becomes

$$C = \kappa\epsilon_o \frac{A}{s} \qquad (206)$$

where A is the effective area of the dielectric and s its thickness.

The dielectric coefficient κ of an insulating material is usually measured with a ballistic galvanometer by observing its throw when the capacitor is discharged, first with and then without the dielectric, and using the same charging pd in both tests. The ratio of the first throw to the second gives the value of the dielectric coefficient. Some typical values of the dielectric coefficient are given in the following table.

DIELECTRIC COEFFICIENTS

Glass, crown.......	5	to	7
Glass, flint.........	7	to	10
India rubber.......	2.1	to	2.3
Mica..............	5.7	to	7
Paper, dry.........	2	to	2.5
Paraffin wax.......	2	to	2.3
Water (pure).......		81	

Illustrative Problem

Find the capacitance of a capacitor formed of 21 square metal plates measuring 10 cm along each edge, separated by sheets of mica 0.01 cm thick. Alternate plates are connected to one terminal of the capacitor and the remaining plates are connected to the other terminal.

The 20 dielectric sheets may be regarded as a single one having an area of $20 \times 0.1 \times 0.1 = 0.2$ m^2. The permittivity of vacuum is given ahead and the dielectric coefficient of mica may be taken as 6.3. Hence the capacitance is given by Eq. 206 as $C = \dfrac{6.3}{(4\pi 9 \times 10^9)} \dfrac{0.2}{0.0001} = 1.11 \times 10^{-7}$ farad $= 0.111$ μf.

Capacitors are used to reduce arcing at contact points, to neutralize the effects of inductance, and to obtain pulses of current for various purposes. The capacitor of an automobile ignition circuit is ordinarily composed of two long strips of tinfoil separated by treated paper, and the combination is rolled into a compact cylinder. The capacitor commonly used in radio reception consists of two sets of aluminum plates separated by air, the effective area of the plates being varied by turning one set with respect to the other. Another type of capacitor used in radio circuits requiring large capacitance in limited space is the *electrolytic* capacitor; this consists of plates of like metals within a suitable electrolyte. An oxide film formed on the positive plate serves as the dielectric. Because of the thinness of the film capacitance values can reach into the hundreds of microfarads, but potential ratings are necessarily limited.

282. Energy of a Charged Capacitor. When a capacitor is connected across a source of constant emf, it charges quickly and the pd across its plates rises from 0 to the emf V of the source. At any instant during this charging period the pd v is directly proportional to the charge q that has been acquired, § 278, a relationship represented by the straight line in Fig. 255. The work done at that instant to increase the charge by an amount Δq is $v\,\Delta q$ and is represented by the area of the shaded strip. The total work done in establishing the ultimate charge Q on the capacitor can be found by summing up such values for the entire charging process.

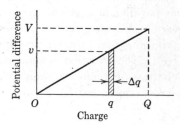

FIG. 255. For calculating work done in charging capacitor

This total is represented by the area under the complete curve, or

$$W = \tfrac{1}{2}VQ$$

This expression shows the amount of energy stored in the electric field within the dielectric. When V is expressed in volts and Q in coulombs, then W is given in joules. The energy can be expressed in terms of the capacitance of the capacitor by substituting the value of V or Q from Eq. 201; thus

$$W = \frac{Q^2}{2C} = \frac{1}{2} CV^2 \qquad (207)$$

in which C is in farads.

The energy stored in a dielectric can also be expressed in terms of field quantities rather than circuit quantities. Thus for a dielectric sheet of area A and thickness s the energy per unit volume of dielectric is

$$W_1 = \frac{\frac{1}{2}CV^2}{As} = \frac{1}{2} \frac{Q}{A} \frac{V}{s}$$

The fraction $\dfrac{Q}{A}$ is equivalent to $\dfrac{\Psi}{A}$ and represents the electric flux density D. The other fraction $\dfrac{V}{s}$ is the same as the electric field intensity $\mathcal{E}$, and this is equal to $\dfrac{D}{\epsilon}$ according to Eq. 204. By combining these results the energy per unit volume of dielectric becomes

$$W_1 = \frac{D^2}{2\epsilon}$$

and is expressed in joules per cubic meter when D is in coulombs per square meter.

283. Capacitors in Parallel and in Series. Capacitors are often connected in parallel in a circuit to increase the capacitance of that circuit, and in series to lessen the pd across each capacitor. To find the effect of such grouping upon the entire capacitance of the circuit, consideration is given to a circuit having several capacitors of capacitances C_1, C_2, C_3 $\cdots$; the charges on them are designated respectively as Q_1, Q_2, Q_3 $\cdots$ and the pds across them as V_1, V_2, V_3 $\cdots$. Whether the component capacitors are connected in series or in parallel, the total energy in their fields is given by adding the energies expressed by Eq. 207 for the several capacitors in circuit.

The entire group of capacitors may be replaced by an equivalent single capacitor of such capacitance C that the charge Q supplied to it is the same

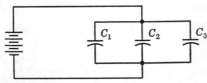

FIG. 256. Parallel connection of capacitors

as the charge supplied to the entire group when the pd V across this capacitor is the same as that across the group. The parallel and series connection of the component capacitors will be considered separately.

Parallel Connection. When the capacitors are connected in parallel as in Fig. 256, the pd is the same across each of them so that

$$V = V_1 = V_2 = V_3 = \cdots$$

Since the total energy in the component capacitors is the same as in the equivalent capacitor C, it follows that

$$\tfrac{1}{2}CV^2 = \tfrac{1}{2}C_1V^2 + \tfrac{1}{2}C_2V^2 + \tfrac{1}{2}C_3V^2 + \cdots$$

which shows that the equivalent capacitance of the group of capacitors in parallel is equal to the sum of the individual capacitances, or

$$C = C_1 + C_2 + C_3 + \cdots \qquad (208)$$

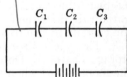

Series Connection. When the capacitors are connected in series as in Fig. 257, the momentary shift of electrons occurs in all of them, thus giving each capacitor an equal charge so that

$$Q = Q_1 = Q_2 = Q_3 = \cdots$$

FIG. 257. Series connection of capacitors

The total energy in the component capacitors is the same as in the equivalent capacitor C; hence

$$\frac{Q^2}{2C} = \frac{Q^2}{2C_1} + \frac{Q^2}{2C_2} + \frac{Q^2}{2C_3} + \cdots$$

Hence

$$\frac{1}{C} = \frac{1}{C_1} + \frac{1}{C_2} + \frac{1}{C_3} + \cdots \qquad (209)$$

which shows the relation between the individual capacitances and the equivalent capacitance when the capacitors are joined in series.

In verifying experimentally the potential distribution in circuits containing capacitors in series, it is necessary to use voltmeters that do not require current for their operation; a useful instrument for this purpose is the so-called *electrostatic voltmeter* in which the deflection depends upon the force exerted between charged plates.

PROBLEMS

1. The mutual inductance of two neighboring coils of wire is 0.02 henry. If the current changes at the rate of 130 amp/sec in the first coil, what emf is induced in the second? If the current in the second coil is then changed at half the previously mentioned rate, what emf will be induced in the first coil?

2. A coil of wire has a resistance of 5 ohms and an inductance of 0.15 henry. Determine the emfs that are induced in this coil when the current in it changes (a) at the rate of 200 amp/sec and (b) at the rate of 40 amp/sec.

3. A winding of 500 turns of wire on a cardboard mailing tube has an inductance of 40 millihenrys. How much magnetic flux is set up through the winding when the current in it is 6 amp?

4. Compute the inductance of the winding in the illustrative problem of § 267 (*a*) by using Eq. 194 and (*b*) by using Eq. 195.

5. Calculate the inductance of the ring solenoid described in Prob. 11 of Chap. 24 under the conditions there stated.

6. A long, wooden bobbin is wound full of wire of a particular size and the inductance of the winding is found to be 100 millihenrys. This wire is then removed and the bobbin is wound full of wire having twice the diameter of that used previously. What will be the inductance of the new winding?

7. Suppose that a coil having a resistance of 10 ohms and an inductance of 0.8 henry has a constant pd of 120 volts impressed upon it. (*a*) At what initial rate does the current in the coil increase? (*b*) How long does it take the current to rise to within 1% of its ultimate value?

8. The coil of Prob. 2, in series with a switch, is connected across a 12-volt storage battery. Determine how fast the current in the circuit grows at the moment (*a*) when the switch is closed, (*b*) when the current has reached $\frac{1}{3}$ of its final value, and (*c*) when the current has reached $\frac{2}{3}$ of its final value.

9. The accompanying figure shows a circuit containing a choke coil L, a resistor R, and a switch s that is initially open. Assume the coil to have an inductance of 0.5 henry and a resistance of 10 ohms, and the resistor to have

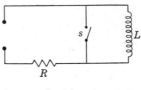

Problem 9

a resistance of 5 ohms. Compute (*a*) the current in the coil 0.10 sec after applying a pd of 100 volts to the terminals at the left and (*b*) the current in the coil 0.10 sec after closing the switch.

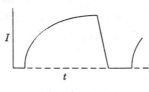

Problem 10

10. The graph shows a pulse of current in the primary winding of an induction coil during one vibration of its interrupter. Copy this graph and sketch to the same base line the companion curve of emf developed in the secondary winding of the coil.

11. The field winding of a particular generator has an inductance of 5 henrys when carrying a current of 1.8 amp. Under the condition stated how much energy resides in the magnetic field of the generator?

12. Determine the amount of energy stored in the magnetic field of the silicon-steel core of Prob. 9 of Chap. 24, when the current in the winding is 0.5 amp.

13. Two circular metal plates 50 cm in diameter are placed parallel to each other and 1 cm apart in air. Assume that the plates have a pd of 3000 volts and that edge effects are negligible. For the region between the plates, calculate (a) the intensity of the electric field, (b) the electric flux density, and (c) the total amount of electric flux.

14. Two metal spheres, one 15 and the other 20 cm in diameter, are isolated from each other in space. They are charged separately to 0.02 and 0.05 microcoulomb respectively. The spheres are then brought into contact, so that they assume the same potential. If care is taken so that no charge is lost and the spheres are again separated, what charge will each one have?

15. A ballistic galvanometer is used to measure the capacitance of a capacitor. The galvanometer is first calibrated and found to produce a throw of 235 divisions on its scale for a charge of 0.001 coulomb. Then the capacitor is charged to 240 volts and discharged through the galvanometer; the throw is found to be 370 divisions. Compute the capacitance.

16. How much charge resides on the terminal of an electrostatic generator of the type described in § 202, on the assumption that this terminal is a sphere 0.8 m in diameter and has a potential of 1 million volts?

17. A parallel-plate air capacitor is to be designed for a capacitance of 400 $\mu\mu$f. If the plates are separated $\frac{1}{16}$ in., what surface area should be provided for the dielectric?

18. A capacitor is formed of plates of metal foil and a dielectric of paper having a dielectric coefficient of 2.4. The paper has an effective area of 1.5 m^2 and a thickness of 0.08 mm. Find the capacitance of the capacitor.

19. Two parallel metal plates separated in air by a distance of $\frac{1}{4}$ in. have a capacitance of 200 $\mu\mu$f. A plate of glass $\frac{1}{4}$ in. thick is inserted between the plates and the capacitance increases to 1200 $\mu\mu$f. Determine the permittivity of this specimen of glass.

20. How much energy is stored in a tantalum electrolytic capacitor rated at 25 μf and charged to a pd of 15 volts, and how much charge does it take?

21. Refer to the glass-plate capacitor of Prob. 19 and determine (a) the size of the plate, (b) the amount of energy that is stored in it with 20,000 volts across the terminals, and (c) the electric flux density in the glass when so charged.

22. The submarine cable referred to in §§ 281 and 312 has two copper conductors—a central one of 0.160 in. diameter and a concentric tube of 0.620 in. inside diameter—insulated from each other by polyethylene-butyl having a dielectric coefficient $\kappa = 2.27$. The capacitance in microfarads of such a cable is given by

$$C = \frac{\kappa l}{K \log_{10}(r_2/r_1)}$$

where r_1 and r_2 are the inside and outside radii of the dielectric expressed in a common unit, l is its length in meters, and K a numerical constant having the value 4.15×10^4. This equation is analogous to that for heat conduction through a cylindrical wall, § 183, and can be derived from Eq. 206. Compute the capacitance per mile of the coaxial cable.

23. Two capacitors having capacitances of 3 and 6 μf are connected in series across a 120-volt direct-current source. Determine the charge on each capacitor and the pd across each.

24. The accompanying figure shows four capacitors with their individual capacitances in microfarads marked upon them. When they are connected as shown to a battery having an emf of 250 volts and the switch is closed, what is the charge on a plate of each capacitor, and what is the pd across the two plates of each?

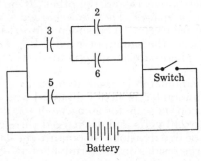

Problem 24

25. A 3-μf capacitor is needed for a certain test, but only 2-μf capacitors are on hand. How few of these would be needed and how would they be connected to obtain the desired capacitance?

26

ALTERNATING CURRENTS

284. Generation of Alternating Electromotive Force. The principle utilized in the conversion of mechanical into electrical energy is Faraday's Law of electromagnetic induction, § 255. Its application is the basis of operation of all types of electric generators, that is, the production of emf in conductors by their motion through magnetic flux. Most generators are of the alternating type, producing emfs that set up currents which traverse the

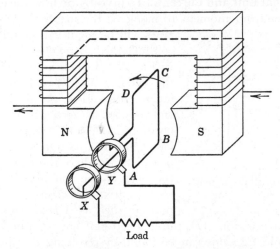

FIG. 258. Elementary alternating-current generator

circuit first in one direction and then the other, reversing direction many times a second.

The simplest way to generate alternating emfs is to rotate a coil between the poles of an electromagnet, placing the axis of rotation in the plane of the coil and at right angles to the flux. Fig. 258 shows a simple *alternator* wherein the coil $ABCD$ rotates between the magnet poles N and S of the field structure. The ends of the coil are joined to *slip rings*, and *brushes* X and Y press against them, so that the coil, while rotating, may remain connected to the load circuit and supply electrical energy to it.

At an instant during rotation when the coil is in the position shown, no emf is generated, since at this instant neither coil-side AB nor CD is moving across the magnetic flux extending from N to S. Also at this instant the rate of change of magnetic flux through the coil is zero. As the coil rotates in a counterclockwise direction from this position, AB moves upward and CD downward through the flux, setting up small emfs directed from A to B and from C to D; these add together and make brush Y positive and brush X negative. The emf keeps increasing in magnitude until the coil is horizontal, at which instant the conductors have their greatest velocity at right angles to the flux; also the rate of change of magnetic flux through the coil is a maximum. As the coil turns farther, the emf becomes smaller, finally reaching zero again when the coil-sides AB and CD have interchanged places from their initial positions. During the second half-revolution the same effect is produced, but the emf is in the opposite direction because AB is then moving downward and CD upward through the flux. This action continues and results in an alternating emf which sets up alternating current in the external circuit.

285. Sinusoidal Emf and Current. To investigate how the emf of a simple alternator varies from moment to moment, the magnetic flux between the poles will be regarded as uniform and the coil imagined to revolve at constant speed.

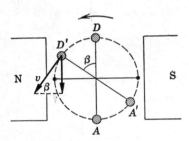

FIG. 259. Coil rotating in magnetic field

In Fig. 259 the coil is viewed end-on, with the ends A and D of its two conductors facing the reader. As already stated, the emf induced is zero when the coil passes position AD, and reaches a maximum value, say E_m, as it passes the axis of the poles NS, for there the conductors forming the sides of the coil move at right angles to the flux. At some intermediate coil position such as $A'D'$, making an angle β with the initial position AD, the induced emf has a value between these extremes of 0 and E_m; this can be found by resolving the linear velocity v of the conductor into two components. The effective component is the one that is perpendicular to the flux, namely, $v \sin \beta$; it follows that the emf at that position becomes $e = E_m \sin \beta$. If t is taken as the time in which the coil turns through the angle β, its angular velocity is $\omega = \beta/t$; consequently, the instantaneous emf generated in it may be written as

$$e = E_m \sin \omega t \qquad (210)$$

This equation shows that the emf generated by a coil rotating at constant speed in a uniform field can be represented by a sine curve plotted with respect to time.

When such an alternating emf is generated in a circuit, and when no other emfs are acting in it, the current established undergoes similar variations, and the instantaneous current i is related to the maximum value I_m in the same way, that is,

$$i = I_m \sin \omega t \tag{211}$$

Hence a sine curve, as shown at the left in Fig. 260, may be used to represent either the alternating emf of the generator or the alternating current in the circuit.

During the time that the coil rotates through 360°, it generates a complete *cycle* of emf or current values, and the curve of emf has a positive lobe from 0 to 180° and a negative lobe from 180 to 360°. The time required to complete one cycle is known as the *period*, and the number of cycles completed per second is called the *frequency*. For a coil rotating in a bipolar field and driven

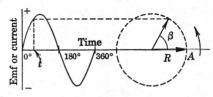

FIG. 260. Sine curve of emf or current and rotating vector

at 3600 rev/min (60 rev/sec), the period is $T = \frac{1}{60}$ sec, and the frequency is $f = 1/T = 60$ cycles/sec. The frequency and the angular velocity of the coil are related by the expression

$$\omega = 2\pi f$$

where the angular velocity ω is expressed in radians per second.

A sine curve can be constructed by considering a point that rotates uniformly around a circle, and projecting its successive positions upon the vertical diameter of the circle, § 84; the projections determine the corresponding ordinates of the curve. It is usual to represent an alternating emf or an alternating current with the aid of a radius extending to such a rotating point. The radius is a vector having a length equal to the maximum value of the sine curve, and is assumed to turn counterclockwise, making one revolution per cycle. The rotating vector R in Fig. 260 represents the sine curve shown at the left; its vertical projection after a rotation of β from the zero position at A gives the value of the emf or current at instant t, as shown.

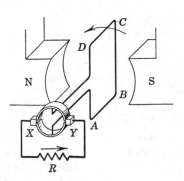

FIG. 261. Elementary direct-current generator

286. The Direct-Current Generator. To convert the simple alternating-current generator described thus far into a direct-current generator of rudimentary form requires only that the slip rings be replaced by a *commutator* for reversing the connections between the coil and the external circuit at the instants when the emf reverses in the coil. The construction is represented in Fig. 261, in which the commutator is shown as a split metal tube, one part connected to conductor AB and the other to conductor CD of the coil.

Fig. 262 illustrates the action of the commutator by showing both the emf developed in the coil at different positions and the emf available at the brushes. As the coil moves from the position shown, the performance during the first half-revolution, represented between 0 and 1 in the figure, is the same as that of the alternator; this produces the positive lobe of the emf curve. During this time, conductor AB has been connected to brush Y

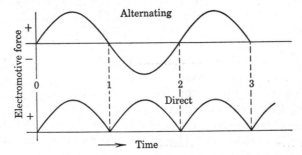

FIG. 262. Alternate half-cycles reversed by commutator

and conductor CD to brush X. At the instant represented by 1 the commutator interchanges these connections, joining AB to X and CD to Y; consequently during the second half-revolution, from 1 to 2 in the figure, another positive lobe is produced with the direct-current generator, instead of the negative lobe produced by the alternator. Therefore, as the coil is rotated, it supplies a pulsating but unidirectional current to the load circuit.

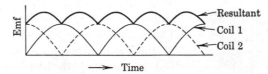

FIG. 263. Emf fluctuations smoothed out by using two coils

The generator in practical use has a large number of armature coils and a correspondingly large number of commutator segments. The advantage of this construction appears in Fig. 263, which shows the effect of connecting in series two coils so located that, when one coil generates its maximum emf, the emf in the other is zero. The instantaneous values of these emfs are added, and their resultant is represented by the heavy line in the diagram. It will be seen that the fluctuation is less in the resultant emf than in the emfs of the individual coils. By the use of a large number of coils, the fluctuation is practically eliminated.

287. The Alternating-Current Generator. The modern alternator is a development of the simple machine described in § 268, and is generally designed so that the armature is stationary and the field coils rotate. This arrangement provides more room for the armature windings that must be well insulated for the high emfs generated in them. The stationary member is called the *stator* and the rotating one the *rotor*.

The emf generated in the armature depends upon the length of the armature conductors, the peripheral speed of the rotor, and the flux density of the magnetic field, as expressed by Eq. 181. In brief, the emf depends upon the time rate of change of magnetic flux through the armature circuit.

The *synchronous speed* of an alternator is the speed at which the generated emf has its rated frequency. In a 2-pole machine a cycle of emf values is produced in each revolution of the rotor. In a 4-pole machine two cycles are produced in one revolution. In general, a machine having P poles produces $P \div 2$ cycles/rev. If the machine is driven at a speed of n rev/sec, the frequency in cycles per second is

$$f = \frac{Pn}{2} \qquad (212)$$

The standard frequency in the United States is 60 cycles/sec.

288. Effective Values. It is natural to inquire how a definite numerical value can be given to an alternating current, when it actually has all values from zero up to the maximum value corresponding to the highest point on the sine curve. Such an evaluation is made possible through the heating effect of the current. A test is made with a direct current of 1 amp through a resistor immersed in water and the heat produced in a given time is measured. The test is repeated with alternating currents of different magnitude until a value is found for which the same amount of heat is produced in the resistor over the same period. This alternating current is then said to have an *effective value* of 1 amp. Thus, in a particular conductor, *one ampere of alternating current produces the same amount of heat in a given time as one ampere of direct current.*

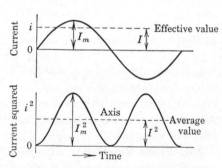

FIG. 264. Used in determining effective value of alternating current

Since the heating effect is known to be proportional to the square of the current, § 219, the effective value of an alternating current can be calculated from the sine curve by squaring the successive ordinates over a cycle, taking the average of these values, and extracting the square root. The effective value, being the root of the mean square of the instantaneous currents, is also called the root-mean-square (rms) value of the current. This process is indicated in Fig. 264, wherein the instantaneous values of current i are plotted as a sine wave at the top, and the corresponding values of current squared i^2 are plotted below; the latter curve is observed to be a sine curve also, but one having doubled frequency and having its axis displaced by an amount equal to the amplitude. The height or ordinate of this axis is the average of the i^2 values, and the square root of this ordinate gives the effective current I.

A definite relation exists between the effective value of a sinusoidal alternating current and its maximum or *peak* value I_m; it can be determined easily from the procedure represented in the figure. Since the average of the current squared values is $\frac{1}{2}I_m{}^2$, the effective current is the square root of this amount, or

$$I = \frac{I_m}{\sqrt{2}} \tag{213}$$

Alternating emfs are related in the same manner. The maximum value of a sinusoidal emf is represented by E_m, and therefore the effective value is

$$E = \frac{E_m}{\sqrt{2}}$$

Illustrative Problem

A 60-cycle alternating current of sinusoidal wave shape has a maximum value of 25 amp. Find the effective value of this current, and also its momentary value at an instant 0.002 sec after passing in a positive direction through the zero value.

The effective value of the current is $25/\sqrt{2} = 17.68$ amp. Since the angular velocity $\omega = 2\pi f = 2\pi 60 = 377$, the instantaneous current value for $t = 0.002$ sec is given by Eq. 211 as $i = 25 \sin (377 \times 0.002) = 25 \sin (0.754 \text{ radian}) = 25 \sin 43.2° = 25 \times 0.685 = 17.13$ amp.

Whenever alternating quantities are expressed it is understood that effective values are meant; thus, an alternating current of 10 amp means an effective current of 10 amp (its maximum or peak value is 14.1 amp if sinusoidal). Alternating-current ammeters and voltmeters are calibrated to indicate effective values.

289. Phase Relations. It must be recognized that when two alternating quantities are active in a single circuit their sine curves may not rise and fall together. The time separation between the curves is usually expressed as an angular difference called *phase difference*. The term is applied to alternating emfs or currents, or to a combination of them.

Phase difference will be explained by supposing that two alternators which develop emfs of the same frequency are connected in series to a load circuit. If the emfs pass through the zero value at the same instant, rise together, pass through the maximum positive values together, and so on, they are said to be *in phase*, as illustrated by curves A and B in part I of Fig. 265. The resultant emf curve R is obtained by adding the ordinates of curves A and B point by point.

When the two emfs do not rise and fall together, they are *out of phase* with respect to each other. Part II of the figure represents the condition when one machine is generating its maximum positive emf at the instant when the other has its maximum negative value. The curves *A* and *B* are displaced from each other by 180°, indicating that the two emfs are in op-

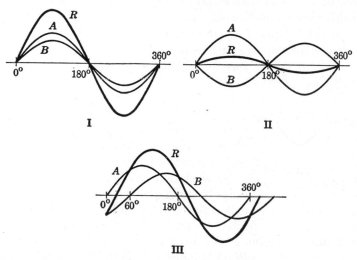

FIG. 265.   Phase relations between two emfs shown by sine curves

position and partially annul each other; the resultant emf is their difference as indicated by curve *R*. In part III, the emf *A* of one generator reaches its maximum emf value somewhat before *B*, the phase difference shown being 60° with *A leading B*, or *B lagging A*. The resultant emf is shown by *R*.

The phase relations shown above can be represented more simply by replacing the sine curves by appropriate vectors. These vectors are commonly drawn to represent the *effective values* of alternating quantities rather than the maximum values. The vector diagrams in Fig. 266 correspond respectively to the sine curve diagrams shown in Fig. 265. The vectors *A* and *B* represent two individual emfs and *R* represents the resultant. If *A* and *B* are in phase, the resultant *R* is their numerical sum. This condition is represented by drawing *A* and *B* along the same line, and adding them; part I of the

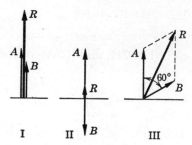

FIG. 266.   Phase relations shown by vectors. These correspond to the curves of Fig. 265

figure shows this addition. If the individual emfs are in opposition, as shown in part II, their resultant is the difference between them. If they are out of phase, as in part III, the resultant can be obtained by the Parallelogram Method; its magnitude and phase are correctly represented by R in the figure.

290. Circuits Containing Resistance Only. The current due to an alternating emf in a circuit containing only resistance is determined by Ohm's Law, § 218. At an instant when the emf is zero, the current is also zero; when the emf has its maximum positive value, the current also has its maximum positive value, and so on. Thus, *the current is in phase with the emf*, as represented in Fig. 267 by the curves I and E. Also, if a part of any alternating-current circuit contains resistance only, the potential difference across that part of the circuit is in phase with the current in that part.

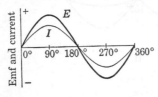

FIG. 267. Phase relations in circuit having resistance only

At high frequencies, and particularly with conductors of large cross-section, it is found that a conductor presents more resistance to an alternating current than to a direct current. The increase is due to emfs which are set up by variations of flux within the conductor itself; these crowd the current toward the surface, giving rise to the so-called *skin effect*, which renders the inner portion of the conductor less effective than the outer portion.

291. Inductive Circuits. Whenever the current in a circuit containing inductance is changing, an emf is induced in it which depends upon the inductance of the circuit and upon the rate of change of current, § 272. This emf, called the emf of self-induction, has a value at any instant given by the expression $e = L\dfrac{di}{dt}$, where L is the inductance of the circuit, and $\dfrac{di}{dt}$ is the instantaneous rate of current change. With an alternating current in such a circuit, the emf of self-induction can be found by expressing the instantaneous current as

$$i = I_m \sin \omega t$$

as in Eq. 211, and differentiating it with respect to time; thus

$$e_L = L\frac{dI}{dt} = L\frac{d}{dt}(I_m \sin \omega t) = \omega L I_m \cos \omega t$$

This equation for the emf of self-induction represents a cosine curve; it has the same shape as the sine curve of current.

To discover the phase relation between e_L and i, it will be noted first that any value of time t which would make $\sin \omega t$ a maximum in the equation for current, would make $\cos \omega t$ zero in the equation for emf, and vice versa. By Lenz's Law, the emf of self-induction is directed in such a way as to oppose the change of magnetic flux that produces it, which means that this emf opposes any change of current; thus, when the current is increasing,

this emf is opposite in direction to the current, and when the current is decreasing, this emf has the same direction as the current. Therefore, the emf
of self-induction e_L lags the current i by 90°.

Evidently an inductive alternating-current circuit contains two emfs in
series: E from the alternator that supplies the circuit, and e_L resulting from
the inductance of the circuit. If a circuit is imagined to contain inductance
only, its resistance being negligible, then the current adjusts itself to such
a value that the applied pd is equal and opposite to the emf of self-induction;
hence

$$E = -e_L = -\omega L I_m \cos \omega t$$

and its maximum value E_m occurs when $\cos \omega t = 1$. Hence $E_m = \omega L I_m$
and, expressing both emf and current in effective values, $E = \omega L I$. The
angular velocity ω is given in § 285 as $\omega = 2\pi f$, and it follows that the current in amperes established in an inductance of L henrys
by a pd of E volts of frequency f cycles/sec is

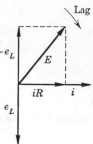

$$I = \frac{E}{2\pi f L}$$

in a circuit of negligible resistance. The quantity $2\pi f L$
is called the *inductive reactance* of the circuit; in symbols

$$X_L = 2\pi f L \tag{214}$$

where the inductive reactance X_L is expressed in ohms
when the inductance L is in henrys. Thus, inductance
in a circuit not only causes the current to lag the pd applied, but also reduces its value. This characteristic of
choking down the current accounts for nicknaming a
coil having inductance a *choke coil*.

Fig. 268. Vector
diagram for circuit
comprising induct-
ance and resistance

When the circuit has both resistance and inductance the current at any
instant can be expressed as the resultant of the two emfs E and e_L divided
by the resistance of the circuit, or

$$i = \frac{E + e_L}{R}$$

but this must be viewed as a vector equation. It can be rewritten as $\vec{E} =$
$\vec{iR} - \vec{e_L}$, which means that the pd impressed upon the circuit is the vector
sum of iR and $-e_L$. These components are shown in Fig. 268 in which the
current is taken as the datum or reference phase. The potential drop iR
due to resistance is in phase with i; the emf of self-induction e_L lags i by
90° as shown; $-e_L$ is equal and opposite to e_L and therefore leads i by 90°;
and finally the resultant of iR and $-e_L$ gives the pd E. It will be observed
that the current in the circuit lags the emf of the source included in the
circuit or the pd applied to the circuit.

292. Capacitive Circuits. A capacitor that is connected across a source of alternating emf becomes charged alternately in opposite directions, and electrons surge to and fro in the connecting wires. An alternating-current ammeter placed in such a circuit shows a steady deflection, and this fact gives rise to the expression that alternating current "flows through" a capacitor; actually in the dielectric and molecules are polarized first one way and then the other, and the effect is equivalent to an alternating displacement current, §§ 199 and 281.

The current in a circuit containing only capacitance can be derived from Eqs. 201 and 211 in a manner similar to that followed in the preceding section. Only the key equations are included here for guidance in the derivation:

$$de_C = \frac{i\,dt}{C}$$

$$e_C = \int \frac{i}{C}\,dt = \frac{1}{C} I_m \int \sin \omega t\,dt = -\frac{I_m}{\omega C} \cos \omega t$$

$$E_m = \frac{I_m}{2\pi f C}$$

where C is the capacitance and e_C the pd applied to the capacitor; the other symbols have the same significance as before. Hence the current in a capacitive circuit is

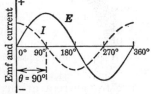

FIG. 269. Phase relations in circuit having capacitance only

$$I = 2\pi f C E$$

The current I in the capacitor leads the emf E of the source by $\theta = 90°$, for when this emf starts to decrease from its maximum value the capacitor begins to discharge in the opposite direction. These relations are shown in Fig. 269, the current changing from positive to negative at the instant the emf recedes from its maximum positive value.

The capacitive circuit presents a reactance somewhat similar to the reactance of a choke coil; it is called *capacitive reactance*. Its value is

$$X_C = \frac{1}{2\pi f C} \tag{215}$$

and is expressed in ohms when the capacitance C is in farads and the frequency f is in cycles/sec.

293. Alternating-Current Series Circuits. In general, circuits used with alternating currents may include all three circuit elements—resistance, inductance, and capacitance. Consideration will be given to a series circuit in which both the inductance and capacitance are lumped rather than distributed through the circuit. When an alternating pd is applied to such a circuit, the current established in it is the same at all parts of the circuit, and the vector sum of the pds across these parts is equal to the pd applied.

The diagram of Fig. 270 shows these pds plotted with respect to the current as datum phase. The pd across the resistance R is *in phase* with the current and is shown as IR; that across the inductance L *leads* the current by 90° and is shown as IX_L; and that across the capacitor C *lags* the current by 90° and is shown as IX_C. The net reactive pd is the difference between the capacitive drop and the inductive drop, and will be either $IX_C - IX_L$ or $IX_L - IX_C$, depending on which is the

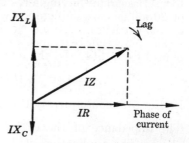

FIG. 270. Vector diagram for generalized series circuit

greater. This reactive drop is added at right angles to the resistance drop to obtain the total pd across the entire circuit; it is shown as IZ. It is called the *impedance drop* and is equal to the pd E that is applied to the circuit.

The total opposition to the establishment of current in an alternating-current circuit can be expressed in a manner similar to Ohm's Law for a direct-current circuit; thus

$$Z = \frac{E}{I} \qquad (216)$$

where Z is called the *impedance* of the circuit. Its value can be obtained from the figure as

$$Z = \sqrt{R^2 + (X_L - X_C)^2} \qquad (217)$$

When the resistance R and the two reactances are in ohms, the impedance is also in ohms.

The current in the series circuit is given by the general equation

$$I = \frac{E}{\sqrt{R^2 + (X_L - X_C)^2}}$$

and lags the emf E of the source by an angle

$$\theta = \tan^{-1} \frac{X_L - X_C}{R} \qquad (218)$$

It is interesting to note from Eqs. 216 and 217 that, in circuits having a large inductance, X_L is large and the current is correspondingly small, but that in circuits having a large capacitance, X_C is small and the current is correspondingly large.

Illustrative Problem

As an example, consider a 20-volt, 1000-cycle source to supply current to a series circuit having a resistor of 200 ohms resistance, an inductive coil of 20 millihenrys inductance with negligible resistance, and a capacitor of 0.36 μf capacitance. Find the impedance of the circuit and the current in it.

The inductive reactance of the circuit is $X_L = 2\pi1000 \times 0.020 = 125.6$ ohms by Eq. 214, and the capacitive reactance is

$$X_C = 1 \div (2\pi1000 \times 0.36 \times 10^{-6}) = 442.3 \text{ ohms}$$

by Eq. 215; consequently the net reactance is $442.3 - 125.6 = 316.7$ ohms. The impedance of the entire circuit is $Z = \sqrt{(200)^2 + (316.7)^2} = 374.6$ ohms. The application of 20 volts to this circuit establishes a current of $20 \div 374.6 = 0.0534$ amp $= 53.4$ milliamp. It leads the emf of the source by the angle $\theta = \tan^{-1}\dfrac{316.7}{200} = 57.7°$.

If the capacitor were removed from the circuit, the current would be $20 \div \sqrt{(200)^2 + (125.6)^2} = 0.0846$ amp. If, instead, the inductive coil were removed, the current would be $20 \div \sqrt{(200)^2+(442.3)^2} = 0.0412$ amp.

An alternating-current circuit in which there are several paths connected in parallel can be handled by calculating the current in each path separately as above, and then adding these currents vectorially to find the total current.

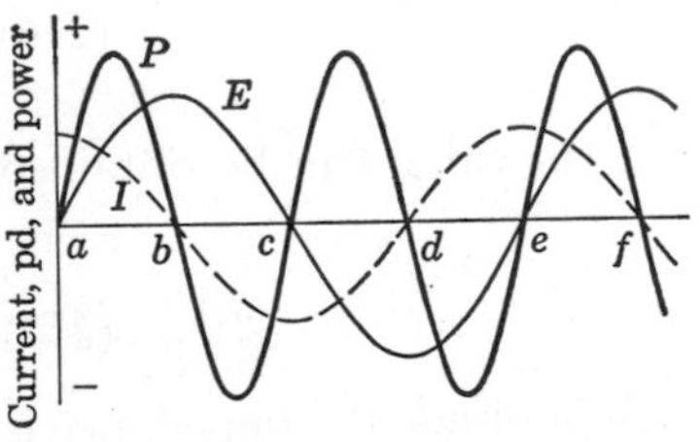

294. Power and Power Factor. The power developed in a direct-current circuit is the product of the pd applied and the current established, § 217, but in an alternating-current circuit this statement applies only to instantaneous values. Hence it is desirable to set up a method for

Fig. 271. Curves of pd, current, and power in a capacitor

determining the power in terms of effective values of pd and current.

In a purely capacitive circuit the current I leads the applied pd E by 90°, as shown in Fig. 271. When their instantaneous values are multiplied point by point the power curve P is obtained. Since this curve is plotted with power as ordinates and time as abscissas, the area under it represents energy. From a to b along the time axis, the values of E and I are both positive, and hence the power curve over this period has a positive lobe, representing energy stored in the capacitor. From b to c the pd is positive but the current is negative, and the power curve has a negative lobe, representing energy returned to the circuit as the capacitor discharges. During the second half of the cycle from c to d to e, the situation is the same; consequently, the power curve is alternately positive and negative, and since the lobes have the same area, the net energy expended in the circuit is zero. A similar result is obtained for an inductive circuit of negligible resistance; in this case I lags E by 90°. Evidently, a current that is 90° out of phase with the applied pd represents no power expenditure.

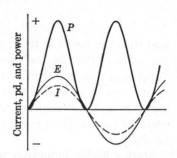

FIG. 272. Curves of pd, current, and power in a resistor

In a circuit containing only resistance, the curves of current I and pd E are in phase, as shown in Fig. 272, and whether both instantaneous values are positive or both negative their product always has a positive value. The power curve P is similar to that shown in Fig. 271 but is entirely above the axis, and the area between it and the axis represents energy that is dissipated as heat.

For circuits in which the current is neither in phase nor 90° out of phase with the applied pd, the power curve has larger positive lobes than negative ones, as shown in part I of Fig. 273; the difference between their areas represents the energy used. The amount can be determined most readily by representing the effective values of E and I as vectors and computing the component of current that is in phase with the pd. Thus in part II of the

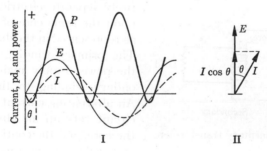

FIG. 273. Curves of pd, current, and power in circuit having inductance and resistance

figure, the current I lags the applied pd E by the angle θ; consequently the component of current in phase with E is $I \cos \theta$. Therefore, the rate at which energy is expended in the alternating-current circuit is

$$P = EI \cos \theta \tag{219}$$

This equation differs from the expression for the rate at which energy is expended in a direct-current circuit by the cosine of the phase angle between emf and current. This quantity is appropriately called the *power factor* (abbreviated pf) of the circuit. From the preceding equation,

$$\text{Power factor} = \cos\theta = \frac{P}{EI} \tag{220}$$

and thus the *power factor of a circuit can be defined as the ratio of the power to the product of the pd and current;* that is, the ratio of the true power to the "apparent power." Reference to Fig. 270 shows that the power factor of a circuit can be expressed also as the ratio of its resistance R to its impedance Z. For a circuit containing resistance only, the phase angle is 0, so that $P = EI$ (as for direct currents) and the power factor has its maximum value of unity.

Both a highly inductive and a highly capacitive circuit have a low power factor; in the first the current lags and in the second the current leads the applied pd by a large angle. Low power factor is a disadvantage, because on the usual electric supply circuits it necessitates a relatively large current in order to supply a given amount of power, and the large current causes more energy to be wasted in heat. The rating of electric machines is based on their ability to dissipate the heat produced in them, and consequently alternating-current machines are rated in kilovolt-amperes (kva) instead of in kilowatts.

295. Transformers. A transformer is used to change an alternating pd from one value to another. It consists essentially of two coils of wire, entirely separate electrically but wound upon the same core of laminated iron, as represented in the diagram, Fig. 274. The primary winding is connected to the power supply mains and the secondary winding to the load circuit. An alternating current in the primary circuit sets up an alternating flux in the core, and the continual building up and collapsing of this flux induce an

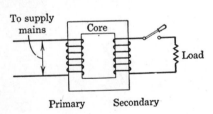

To supply mains Core Load

Primary Secondary

FIG. 274. Elementary transformer

emf in the secondary coil. The value of this emf depends upon the number of turns N_2 of the secondary coil and upon the rate of change of flux $\frac{d\Phi}{dt}$ through its turns, in accordance with Eq. 180 which gives $E_2 = -N_2\frac{d\Phi}{dt}$. These same flux variations also affect the primary coil of N_1 turns and induce in it an emf $E_1 = -N_1\frac{d\Phi}{dt}$. This emf, by Lenz's Law, opposes the impressed pd in somewhat the same manner as does the counter emf of a motor. These expressions may be combined, yielding

$$\frac{E_1}{E_2} = \frac{N_1}{N_2} \quad \frac{I_1}{I_2} \tag{221}$$

which shows that the emfs in the transformer coils are directly proportional to the numbers of turns on their windings.

When the secondary winding is not connected to a load, the transformer takes very little current from the supply circuit, for the emf induced in the primary coil is very nearly equal to the pd of the supply mains; for practical purposes they are often taken as equal. Upon connecting a load to the secondary winding, the emf induced in that coil sets up a current. This current opposes the magnetizing effect of the primary current and reduces the flux in the transformer core slightly. As a result, the counter emf induced in the primary winding is lessened, and more current is taken from the supply mains. In this manner the input to a transformer automatically accommodates itself to the output.

The efficiency of transformers is very high, as might be expected from the absence of moving parts, and values from 95 to 99% are usual. Since most transformers have but little effect upon the power factor of the circuits to which they are connected, the efficiency can be expressed as the ratio of the output kva to the input kva, or

$$\text{Efficiency} = \frac{E_2 I_2}{E_1 I_1} \tag{222}$$

If the efficiency is assumed to be 100%, then $E_2 I_2 = E_1 I_1$, and Eq. 222 becomes

$$\frac{I_1}{I_2} = \frac{N_2}{N_1} \tag{223}$$

showing that the primary and secondary currents, I_1 and I_2, are inversely proportional to the numbers of turns on their respective coils. The rating of transformers in kilovolt·amperes may be taken for practical purposes to represent either the input or the output.

Illustrative Problem

As an example, suppose that a 10-kva transformer with 900 primary turns and 90 secondary turns is connected across 2200-volt alternating-current supply mains and that it is delivering its rated load. Find the currents in its windings.

The secondary emf is found from Eq. 221; thus $E_2/2200 = 90/900$, whence $E_2 = 220$ volts. At full load, $E_1 I_1 = E_2 I_2 = 10,000$ volt·amp; hence the primary and secondary currents are respectively 4.55 and 45.5 amp.

The transmission of electrical energy over long distances is accomplished with high pds, because a given amount can be transmitted in a given time with a correspondingly small current, thus reducing heating loss in the transmitting lines, and permitting the use of relatively small line wires. Transformers step up the pd to a high value at the alternator end of a line and step it down at the other end to values suitable for the apparatus to be operated.

Transformers for electric welding have massive secondary windings of one turn or a few turns in order to produce large currents, and the parts to be welded form a part of the secondary circuit.

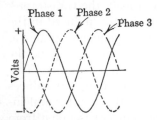

FIG. 275. Emf curves of three-phase alternator

296. Polyphase Generators. The simple alternator shown in Fig. 258 generates a single alternating emf and is called a *single-phase* machine to distinguish it from the more usual type of alternator that generates three alternating emfs at the same time, and is called a *polyphase alternator*. The three-phase alternator has three like sets of coils, symmetrically placed on the armature so as to produce three equal emfs that are 120° apart in phase, as shown in Fig. 275.

There are two ways in which the windings of a three-phase machine are usually connected. In one of these, called the Y-connection, one end of each winding is joined to a common point, and the three line wires are connected to their other ends, as shown at the left in Fig. 276. With this connection the current in any line A, B, or C, is the same as that in the corresponding phase winding 1, 2, or 3; and the pd acting between any two lines

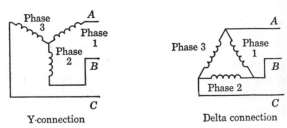

FIG. 276. Methods of connecting windings of three-phase alternator

is $\sqrt{3}$ times the emf generated in one of the phase windings. For instance, the pd between A and B is found by combining the emfs generated in windings 1 and 2; these differ in phase by 120°, but one is reversed with respect to the other and so must be subtracted vectorially from it.

The other method of connecting the armature windings of a three-phase alternator is to arrange them in a closed triangle, from the corners of which the line wires are brought out. This so-called delta (Δ) connection is shown at the right in the figure. The pd acting between any two lines AB, BC, or CA is the same as the emf generated in one of the phase windings 1, 2 or 3, and the line currents are $\sqrt{3}$ times the currents in the phase windings.

The total power developed in a three-phase alternator is the sum of the amounts of power developed in its phase windings. Expressed in terms of the line values, which can be directly measured, the power developed with equal loads on all three phases is

$$P = \sqrt{3}\, EI \cos \theta$$

where E represents the pd between any pairs of lines, I is the line current, and θ is the phase angle between the pd and current.

297. The Induction Motor. The alternating-current motor most widely used is the *polyphase induction motor* invented by Nikola Tesla. It consists essentially of a stationary field structure called a *stator* and a rotating member called a *rotor*. The rotor winding is usually formed of heavy copper bars welded to end rings and resembles a squirrel cage; it is not connected to the supply circuit. The windings on the stator are distributed uniformly around the inner periphery of the machine, and are connected to a polyphase supply circuit.

As the current in each phase winding of the stator varies between a maximum positive and a maximum negative value, the magnetic flux associated with it changes accordingly, and since the currents in the several phases rise and fall at different times, Fig. 275, the net effect on the rotor is the same as if the flux through it were rotating mechanically. This so-called *rotating field* induces currents in the rotor bars and these currents, in reacting with the flux, develop forces which cause the rotor to follow the rotating field.

The speed of the rotor is slightly less than the synchronous speed of the rotating field, the difference being called the *slip* of the motor. As the load on the motor is increased, the machine slows down a little, thereby increasing the slip and causing larger currents to be induced in the rotor; these larger currents set up a greater torque, enabling the motor to drive the increased load. The polyphase induction motor has characteristics similar to those of the direct-current shunt motor, § 270.

The polyphase induction motor, operating close to synchronous speed, would continue to rotate if one phase of the supply were disconnected, for the alternations of flux at the poles still energized would be properly timed to give unidirectional torque. Such a machine would not start on a single phase, but there are specially designed motors which start and operate on single-phase supply lines.

298. Alternating-Current Measurements. The usual measurements in alternating-current circuits are those of current, difference of potential, and power. Other measurements include inductance, capacitance, and frequency; wave forms of alternating currents can also be determined.

The *iron-vane* instrument makes use of the fact that iron is attracted by a coil carrying current regardless of the direction of current, and hence is attracted steadily with alternating current. In an ammeter of this type the current in a stationary coil causes the attraction of a soft-iron vane, which, as it moves, swings a pointer over a scale. An instrument of similar construction is used as a voltmeter, the coil having a high resistance in series with it to permit direct connection across a supply circuit.

The *dynamometer* type of ammeter has two current coils in series, one of which is stationary. The other coil carries a pointer and is pivoted at right angles to the field of the first, being normally held in this zero position by a spring. An alternating current through the instrument reverses simultaneously in both coils, and the resulting torque on the moving coil is, there-

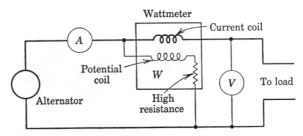

FIG. 277. Measuring power factor in single-phase circuit

fore, always in the same direction. When a high resistance is connected in series with the coils, this type of instrument can be used as a voltmeter.

The power delivered to a load connected in an alternating-current circuit cannot be measured with a voltmeter and an ammeter, because of phase difference between the applied pd and the current produced. Instead, the instrument used is the wattmeter, § 254, which operates with alternating as well as with direct current. The torque producing the deflection is proportional to the instantaneous values of current and pd, and the deflection is proportional to the power delivered.

The power factor of a load circuit can be determined by measuring the power with a wattmeter W, the current with an ammeter A, and the potential difference with a voltmeter V, connected as shown in Fig. 277; and dividing the watts by the volt-ampere product.

Measurements of inductance and capacitance are made with a form of Wheatstone bridge, § 228, in which the arms contain standards of inductance and capacitance, the battery is replaced by a source of alternating emf having appropriate frequency, and the galvanometer is replaced by a detector of alternating current. A telephone receiver can be used as the detector if the current is of audio frequency.

299. The Cathode-Ray Oscilloscope. The instrument for determining the wave form of alternating currents and transient effects is called an *oscilloscope;* it makes use of a *cathode-ray tube* that is somewhat similar to the evacuated tube used in Thomson's experiment for determining the charge-to-mass ratio of the electron, § 258. The appearance of the cathode-ray tube is shown in Fig. 278 wherein the cathode C is a filament, § 303, the anode A is a disk pierced by a hole, and the pairs of plates P_1 and P_2 are arranged in planes at right angles to each other. When the filament is heated and a pd is maintained between it and the anode, a stream of electrons or *cathode rays* passes through the hole. The rays, focussed by applying particular potentials to additional electrodes not shown, travel a straight path and impinge upon a fluorescent screen S, there producing a tiny luminous spot. When the plates P_1 are charged, the electric field established between them acts on the electron beam and deflects it upward or down-

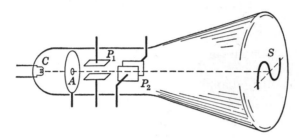

FIG. 278. Cathode-ray oscilloscope

ward; when a field is established between plates P_2, the electron beam is deflected to one side or the other. If the pds on the deflecting plates vary, the electron beam is deflected accordingly, and the spot on the screen moves about, tracing a luminous line that reveals the character of these potential differences.

When the oscilloscope is used to show the wave form of an alternating emf, one pair of plates, P_2, is periodically charged at a uniform rate from a capacitor and then suddenly discharged. Each time, the luminous spot sweeps horizontally across the screen during the charging period and, at discharge, it retraces quickly to the starting point. The alternating emf is applied to the other pair of plates, P_1, thereby producing vertical displacements of the spot. The combination of the two displacements gives a picture showing the wave shape. The rapidity of the sweep motion is adjusted to the frequency of the alternating emf in order to produce a steady image of its wave shape on the screen.

To show that the vertical deflection of the electron beam is proportional to the pd V that is applied between the plates P_1, reference will be made to some principles developed in Chap. 19. The work done on an electron of charge e in moving it from C to A may be expressed as eV', where V' is the potential difference between these electrodes. This work appears as kinetic energy of the electron as it leaves A; whence $eV' = \frac{1}{2}mv^2$, where m is the mass of the electron and v is its velocity along the tube axis. The plates P_1 are assumed to have a length l and a separation s. The time t required for the electron to travel the length l of the electric field between the plates is $\dfrac{l}{v} = \dfrac{l}{\sqrt{2eV'/m}}$. While in this field, the electron experiences a vertical force $F = e\mathcal{E}$, where the electric field is $\mathcal{E} = \dfrac{V}{s}$. Finally, the electrons have a vertical acceleration $a = \dfrac{F}{m} = \dfrac{eV}{ms}$, and in time t move vertically a distance $d = \frac{1}{2}at^2$. Hence the electrons are displaced by an amount

$$d = \frac{1}{2}\,at^2 = \frac{1}{2}\frac{eV}{ms}\frac{l^2m}{2eV'} = \frac{l^2}{4sV'}\,V$$

Consequently the displacement of the electron beam on emerging from the plates is proportional to the pd V between them, and since the beam is straight after leaving plates P_1, the displacement of the spot on the screen is proportional to the pd applied across these plates.

PROBLEMS

1. A single coil of wire as shown in Fig. 258 has the dimensions $AB = 20$ cm and $BC = 10$ cm. If the coil makes 60 rev/sec in a magnetic field that has an intensity of 5 milliwebers/m², what is the maximum value of the emf generated in the coil?

2. The coil of Prob. 1, moving as described, is connected through slip rings to a resistor of 0.07 ohm resistance. If the resistance of the coil itself is neglected, what is the maximum value of the current set up in the circuit, and what torque is required to turn the coil, neglecting friction, at the instant it is generating its maximum emf? Show that the mechanical power needed at that moment to turn the coil is equal to the instantaneous electrical power developed in the circuit.

3. What are the synchronous speeds of the following machines that supply 60-cycle emfs: (*a*) a turbo-alternator that has 2 field poles and (*b*) a water-wheel generator that has 36 poles?

4. A sinusoidal emf has a maximum value of 160 volts. Find the instantaneous emf values at 15° intervals for the first quarter of a cycle. Plot one lobe of the emf curve and draw a line across it to indicate the effective value.

5. The effective value of a 60-cycle sinusoidal current in a circuit is 75 amp. (*a*) What is the peak value of this current? (*b*) What is the instantaneous current in the circuit $\frac{1}{400}$ sec before reaching this peak value?

6. An electric water heater is immersed in 5 liters of water and an alternating current of 8 amp is maintained through it for 10 min. This particular heater has a resistance of 15 ohms. Assume that all the heat produced is used in heating the water and compute the resulting rise in temperature.

7. A 400-cycle pd of 100 volts is applied to a reactor having negligible resistance and the current through it is found to be 0.7 amp. Calculate the inductance of the reactor.

8. A solenoid has an inductance of 75 millihenrys and a resistance of 150 ohms. Find its reactance and impedance to a current having a frequency of 1000 cycles/sec.

9. A 60-cycle emf of 120 volts is impressed upon a series circuit containing a 20-ohm resistor and a reactor of unknown inductance and resistance. When a voltmeter is connected across the resistor the pd is found to be 50 volts, and when connected across the reactor the pd is found to be 100 volts. Determine the constants of the reactor.

10. How much capacitance should a capacitor have to pass a 1000-cycle current of 0.1 amp with an impressed pd of 100 volts?

11. A telephone set includes a ringer and a 2-μf capacitor. Determine the reactance of the capacitor for a current at $16\frac{2}{3}$ cycles/sec used for operating the ringer, and at 1000 cycles/sec, taken as the average frequency of the voice currents.

12. Two alternating emfs of the same frequency supply current to a reactive circuit that has an impedance of 50 ohms at that frequency. One has an effective value of 120 volts and the other of 60 volts, and their positive peak values are 45° apart in phase. What is the current in the circuit?

13. A series circuit, consisting of a resistor R, a choke coil L, and a capacitor C, is connected to a 60-cycle source of alternating current as shown in the accompanying figure. With $R = 25$ ohms, $L = 0.1$ henry, and $C = 50$ μf, the current in the circuit is 3.5 amp. What would be the reading of a voltmeter when connected across (*a*) terminals 1 and 2, (*b*) terminals 2 and 3, and (*c*) terminals 3 and 4?

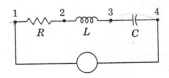

Problem 13

14. In the preceding problem, what would be the reading of a voltmeter when connected across (*a*) terminals 1 and 3, (*b*) terminals 2 and 4, and (*c*) terminals 1 and 4?

15. In a series circuit like that pictured above, the values of resistance, inductance, and capacitance are so adjusted that with a 1000-cycle 0.2 amp current through the circuit the pd across each of these circuit elements will be 100 volts. What is the pd between (*a*) terminals 1 and 3, (*b*) terminals 2 and 4, and (*c*) terminals 1 and 4? (*d*) What are the values of R, L, and C?

16. (*a*) If the capacitance of the circuit of Prob. 15 is decreased, without making any other changes, would the current increase or decrease? (*b*) If only the frequency of the emf applied to this circuit is increased, would the current increase or decrease?

17. A series circuit has a resistance of 10 ohms, an inductance of 10 microhenrys, and a capacitance of 10 μμf. (*a*) Find the current in the circuit produced by an emf of 10 millivolts at a frequency of $10^8/2\pi$ cycles/sec. (*b*) What are the pds across the circuit elements?

18. The circuit described in the preceding problem is energized by an emf of 100 millivolts at 10^8 cycles/sec. Calculate the current in the circuit.

19. Determine the current in the circuit of Probs. 17 and 18 for the same conditions as in the latter except that the frequency of the applied emf is 10^7 cycles/sec.

20. When an inductive circuit is tested with direct current, a pd of 120 volts produces a current of 2.1 amp. When tested with 60-cycle alternating

current, the same pd produces only 1.3 amp. What are the power factor and inductance of the circuit?

21. A circuit has two branches in parallel; one has a capacitance of 10 $\mu\mu$f, and the other an inductance of 10 microhenrys and a resistance of 1000 ohms. If the emf applied to the circuit is 1 volt at 10^7 cycles/sec, what is (a) the current in each branch and (b) the total current in the circuit?

22. (a) How much energy is expended in the entire circuit of Prob. 13 during a period of 10 min? (b) How much power does this represent?

23. Determine the rate at which electrical energy is being supplied to an inductive load when a 60-cycle pd of 240 volts is applied to it. The load has a resistance of 25 ohms and an inductance of 0.04 henry.

24. What is the power factor of the circuit described in Prob. 9?

25. A fluorescent lamp unit of two 4-ft tubes and ballast takes a current of 0.85 amp on a 115-volt supply circuit and draws 88 watts. What is the power factor of this lighting unit?

26. A 25-kva overhead transformer has its primary winding connected to 2400-volt supply mains and has its two secondary windings connected in parallel to provide 120 volts for lighting service. The iron losses of the transformer are 115 watts and the heating losses in its windings at full load are 375 watts. Assume the transformer to be delivering its rated load and compute the currents in the primary and secondary windings.

27. A 500-kva three-phase transformer for electric network systems is connected as shown in the diagram to 13,200-volt supply mains and delivers its rated output at 120 and 208 volts. The iron losses are 1900 watts and the copper losses at full load are 5900 watts. Assume the same non-inductive load on all three phases and determine the currents in the primary and secondary windings.

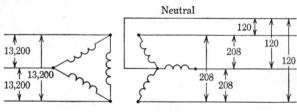

Problem 27

28. Two three-phase generators supply the same power to two separate but identical balanced loads each of 90% power factor. One generator has its armature Y-connected and the other Δ-connected. If the current in each of the line wires from generator to load is 50 amp and the pd between line wires is 120 volts, (a) what are the currents in the phase windings of the two generator armatures and the pds across them? (b) How much power is supplied by each machine?

29. A three-phase 60-cycle magnetic air circuit breaker, rated at 48,000 volts and 50,000 kva, can interrupt the current in 3.5 cycles. What is the value of the current per phase at the rated capacity, and what is the average rate of its decay?

30. A three-phase generator at the Gallatin Station of the Tennessee Valley Authority has the highest emf and the largest output of any electrical generator in the United States. This machine is rated at 24,000 volts and 250,000 kva; it has a bipolar field winding revolving at 3600 rev/min.

FLIGHT INSTRUCTION   PASSENGER & CHARTER FLIGHTS

 COMPLETE SHOP FACILITIES

VALLEY AIRMOTIVE CORP.
LOGAN CACHE AIRPORT

PHONE 752-5131   P. O. BOX 281

LOGAN, UTAH

Customer's
Order No. _____   Date 6-26 _____ 196 5

M _A Lin Matleson_

Address _____

SOLD BY	CASH	C. O. D.	CHARGE	ON ACCT.	MDSE. RETD.	PAID OUT
H.T.	✓					

QUAN.	DESCRIPTION	PRICE	AMOUNT
	Flite to		
	Cedar city	30.00	
	Pd in Full		
	Thanks very much		
	Roy		

ALL claims and returned goods MUST be accompanied by this bill

6798   Rec'd by _____

®M

What is the frequency of its emf, and the line current at full noninductive load?

31. A typical air conditioner to cool an entire house in the 1200 to 1700 sq-ft class delivers 2.75 so-called "tons of cooling," one ton being equivalent to 12,000 Btu/hr (see Prob. 21 of Chap. 17). The single-phase motor for driving the compressor of such a unit operates on 230 volts and has a nominal rating of 3 hp. However, because the cool gas in a hermetic refrigerant system flows over the windings of the motor, this machine has a maximum output of 4.9 hp. Under these conditions, if the motor has an efficiency of 80% and a power factor of 95%, what current does it take?

32. The deflecting system of an oscilloscope has plates 2.5 cm long. If the electric field between the horizontal plates is 52,000 volts/m, and if the electrons forming the cathode ray enter the region between the plates horizontally at a speed of 2.7×10^7 m/sec, at what angle to the horizontal does the ray leave this region?

27

THERMOELECTRICITY
AND THERMIONICS

THERMOELECTRICITY

300. The Seebeck Effect. Two different metals when placed in contact with each other are found to assume slightly different potentials. This phenomenon, discovered in 1800 by Volta, is now explained as a transfer of some of the free electrons, present in all metals, across the junction of the two metals. Thus, if more electrons pass from the first metal to the second than pass the other way, then the second metal becomes negative and the first positive. The pd between the metals, spoken of as *contact potential difference*, depends in amount upon the specific metals that are joined and upon the temperature of the junction. This contact pd explains three thermoelectric effects which have been known for many years.

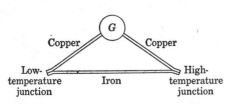

FIG. 279. Thermoelectric circuit

The most important of these thermoelectric effects was discovered by the German physicist Thomas J. Seebeck (1770–1831); this is the production of an emf in a so-called *thermocouple* formed of two wires of different metals when their junctions are at different temperatures. Fig. 279 shows a loop circuit of an iron wire and a copper wire, with the latter divided so as to include a galvanometer for indicating the emf that is developed. At each junction the contact emf is directed from copper to iron, and when the two junctions are at the same temperature their emfs are equal and opposite, and there is no current in the circuit. But when one junction is kept at a constant low temperature and the other junction is raised to a higher temperature, the contact emfs at the two junctions are unequal and a current is established in the circuit (clockwise in Fig. 279) which causes the galvanometer to deflect and indicate the thermo emf produced. As the high-temperature junction is heated more and more, the thermo emf increases to a maximum value, then diminishes to zero, reverses in direction, and then increases again. The values for an iron-copper thermocouple are plotted in Fig. 280.

The emf of a thermocouple formed of two specific metals depends upon the temperatures of the junctions, and is always the same for any given temperatures, provided the metals retain their purity and crystalline structure. With one junction held at the reference temperature of 0° C, the temperature of the other for which the thermo emf of a couple has a maximum (or minimum) value is called the *neutral point*, and the temperature at which this emf reverses is called the *inversion point*. The slope of the thermo emf curve at any temperature is called the *thermoelectric power* of the thermocouple; this is an incorrect use of the term "power." For the iron-copper couple the neutral point is 205° C, and the inversion point 480° C; the thermoelectric power ranges from 13.7 microvolts per degree at 0° C to zero at 205° C.

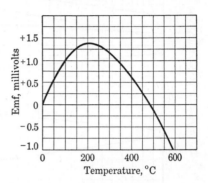

FIG. 280.   Thermo-emf diagram of iron-copper couple

Other pairs of metals have their own characteristic neutral and inversion temperatures as well as thermoelectric powers.

The emfs produced by couples formed of any two metals can be computed from the values of their thermoelectric powers with respect to some metal chosen as a standard, such as lead or platinum. For this purpose graphs of thermoelectric power against temperature are useful. Fig. 281 shows such graphs for a few metals against lead; they are straight lines over the temperature range shown. Since the ordinates represent emfs per degree and the abscissas represent degrees, the area between the graph of any metal and the zero horizontal axis represents the product of these coordinates, namely, the emf of that metal with respect to lead, for the range between specified junction temperatures.

Illustrative Problem

As an example, determine from the graphs of thermoelectric power the emf developed by a thermocouple of iron and copper with the junctions at 20 and 200° C.

The thermoelectric powers of these metals at the stated temperatures as shown by their graphs are tabulated below:

	° C	Microfarads/° C
Iron............	20	15.4
	200	5.3
Copper.........	20	3.0
	200	5.0

The total emf produced by a thermocouple of iron and lead with its junctions at the stated temperatures is equal to the area between their graphs

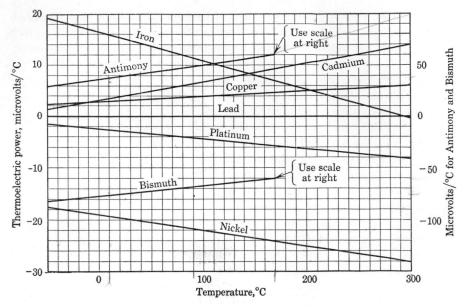

FIG. 281.   Thermoelectric powers of several metals against lead

over the designated temperature range, or $\dfrac{15.4 + 5.3}{2}\ 180 = 1863$ micro-

volts. Similarly the total emf produced by a thermocouple of copper and lead is 720 microvolts. Consequently the emf of an iron-copper couple at the same temperatures is $1863 - 720 = 1143$ microvolts.

A multiplicity of couples formed of two metals and placed close together is used in the measurement of radiant heat energy; such a compact group is called a *thermopile.* A typical thermopile is one constructed of short lengths of bismuth and antimony connected in series alternately, and put together in zig-zag fashion so that every other junction can be exposed to the radiation while the intermediate ones are shielded from it.

The *thermo-milliammeter*, which utilizes a thermocouple in contact with a hot wire, is used for measuring small alternating currents. Heat is evolved in the wire by the current being measured and causes the thermocouple to generate an emf, thereby producing a deflection in a calibrated instrument connected across the couple. Increased sensitivity is secured by placing the wire and couple in a vacuum.

301. Peltier and Thomson Effects. The second thermoelectric effect, an inversion of the Seebeck Effect, was discovered by the French physicist Jean C. A. Peltier (1785–1845). He found that when two dissimilar metals are connected in series with a source of emf which establishes a current in the circuit, one junction becomes heated and the other cooled.

The heat generation at the warm junction is brought about by the current doing work in opposing the contact emf there and is distinct from the heating of both metals due to their resistance—the so-called RI^2 heating. The cooling at the other junction occurs where the current has the same direction as that in which the emf would of itself set up a current. Under this condition the electrons receive energy from the source of emf as in a voltaic cell, but in the thermoelectric circuit, this energy is supplied by the internal energy of the metal at the junction, as evidenced by a lowering of the temperature. The RI^2 heating often masks the heat absorption at the cool junction.

The extent to which the junctions are heated or cooled by a given current depends solely upon the metals used. For an iron-copper junction near room temperature the heating due to the Peltier Effect amounts to about 4 calories per hour per ampere of current. At ordinary temperatures when a current traverses the iron-copper circuit of Fig. 279 in a clockwise direction, the left junction becomes heated and the right junction cooled. A comparison of the two effects for any pair of metals shows that the hot and cold junctions are interchanged for the same direction of current.

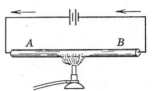

Fig. 282. Experiment to show Thomson Effect

An analysis of these thermoelectric effects prompted William Thomson, later Lord Kelvin, to predict by thermodynamic principles that an emf must exist between different parts of the same metal if they are at different temperatures. He demonstrated that when a uniform metal bar is heated at the middle and a current is established in it from end to end by an external source, the heat is conducted unequally along the two halves. In a copper bar, Fig. 282, the region A where current is directed from a colder to a hotter part is found to be cooler than it would be if there were no current, and the region B where current is directed from a hotter to a colder part is found to be warmer; thus, in copper, B is warmer than A. The same is true for cadmium, silver, and zinc, but the opposite is true for iron and nickel, to mention but a few metals. This effect and the emf involved are named after Thomson. Lead shows no appreciable Thomson Effect, and this accounts for its frequent use as a reference metal (see Fig. 281).

302. Thermocouples in Pyrometry. The emf of a thermocouple varies in a known manner with the temperature difference between its junctions. Consequently, if the temperature of one junction is kept constant, that of the other junction can be measured by observing the emf produced. When so used, a thermocouple is called a thermoelectric thermometer or a *pyrometer*, the latter word referring to measurements of high temperatures, such as those of furnaces and molten metals.

The basis of thermoelectric thermometry is the Seebeck emf, actually the algebraic sum of the Seebeck emfs at the junctions and the Thomson emfs in the dissimilar metals of a couple. For any given thermocouple the relationship between its emf E and the temperature difference between the reference junction at $0°$ C and the hotter junction at $t°$ C is given approximately by

$$E = at + bt^2$$

where a and b are constants that depend on the metals used; this is the equation of a parabola. The thermoelectric power of the couple is then expressed as

$$\frac{dE}{dt} = a + 2bt$$

and this is the equation of a straight line.

Several combinations of metals are used for pyrometers. One of the most satisfactory for the temperature range from 0 to $1500°$ C has one metal of platinum and the other of an alloy of 90% platinum and 10% rhodium. A less expensive couple that is serviceable for the range between -200 and $+350°$ C has one metal of copper and the other of constantan (copper 60%, nickel 40%).

Illustrative Problem

For a platinum-platinum rhodium couple with one junction at $0°$ C and the other at the melting point of aluminum ($660°$ C) the emf is 5.83 millivolts, and with the latter junction at the melting point of nickel ($1453°$ C) the emf is 14.97 millivolts. From these values find the constants a and b of the foregoing equation for the thermocouple.

The specified values of emf provide the expressions:

$$5.83 = 660a + (\ 660)^2 b$$
$$14.97 = 1453a + (1453)^2 b$$

The simultaneous solution of these equations gives the values of the constants as $a = 7.60 \times 10^{-3}$ and $b = 1.86 \times 10^{-6}$.

THERMIONICS

303. Thermionic Emission. The electric incandescent lamp, § 359, was developed by Edison in 1880 and immediately found application in artificial lighting throughout the world. In further experimentation on such a lamp equipped with a separate electrode he made a discovery three years later which remained practically unused for two decades before its importance was realized. This discovery, now called the Edison Effect, was the real beginning of the present scientific field of Electronics.

In the experiment Edison connected a galvanometer between the filament and the separate electrode or plate to indicate any possible current between them, and found that there was a current when the connections were such as to make the plate positive as in Fig. 283, but not when negative. This current is now explained by the emission of electrons from the heated filament into the space surrounding it and the attraction of these electrons by the nearby plate.

The emission of electrons from the surface of a metal is comparable in many respects to the escape of molecules from a liquid during the process of evaporation. The situation is a little different, however, because an electron about to leave the metal induces a positive charge on the region behind it and this causes it to be attracted back into the metal. This action is largely responsible for the so-called *potential barrier*, somewhat like surface tension, that must be overcome before the electron can leave the surface. With the metal heated, the electrons have increased kinetic energy and more of them can cross the potential barrier. For each metal, a definite amount of energy is needed to release an electron from the surface; this energy is known as the *work function* of the metal.

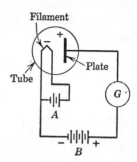

FIG. 283.　Diode and its circuit

The emission of electrons by a hot body, called thermionic emission, is the operating principle of most electron tubes. The simplest of these is the two-element tube, or *diode*. This device consists of a bulb or tube having a filament like that of an incandescent lamp and a separate metal plate, as shown in Fig. 283. The tube is evacuated and the filament is heated to incandescence by battery A. Electrons emitted from the filament are attracted to the plate when it is maintained positive by battery B as indicated, and the galvanometer deflects. If the plate were made negative by reversing battery B, the electrons evaporated from the filament would be repelled by the plate and, since no electrons are emitted from the cold plate, the galvanometer would not deflect. Hence, the electrons can flow only from filament to plate or, what corresponds to the same thing, the current as conventionally directed can be only from plate to filament. Consequently this electron tube, containing the plate as anode and the heated filament as cathode, acts as a rectifier.

The number of electrons emitted per unit of time depends upon the material of the cathode and its temperature. The English physicist Owen W. Richardson (1879–1945) expressed the rate of electron emission per unit area at absolute temperature T as

$$J = AT^2 \epsilon^{-\frac{b}{T}} \tag{224}$$

where J is the current per unit of surface area of the heated body, T is in °K, ϵ is the base of natural logarithms, and A and b are constants. With the current density J in amperes per square meter, the value of A for pure metals is 6.02×10^5. The value of b depends upon the material and includes its work function; the values for three of the usual cathode materials as found experimentally are: molybdenum 50,900, thorium 38,900, and tungsten 52,400; these correspond to °K.

The current from plate to cathode of an electron tube as expressed by the foregoing equation is the so-called *saturation current* that results when the plate potential is high enough to produce an electric field between the electrodes sufficiently strong to sweep all the electrons from the region as fast as emitted. With lower pds between the electrodes, many of the emitted electrons accumulate around the filament as a cloud and form a negative *space charge;* this causes some emitted electrons to be forced back into the cathode and reduces the net rate of emission, as a result of which the current is less than the saturation value.

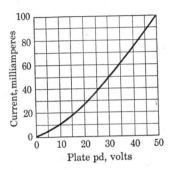

FIG. 284. Characteristic curve of thermionic rectifier

In most types of electron tubes it is not expedient to measure the saturation current because its value is so large as to change the emitting conditions or to damage the tube.

The current through a diode at low pds is usually indicated by a curve such as Fig. 284, which shows the lower portion of the current-potential characteristic curve of a thermionic rectifier tube used in radio receiving sets for supplying direct currents to their other tubes. The equation of this lower portion is of the form

$$I = KE^n \tag{225}$$

where K and n are constants determined by the geometry of the tube electrodes. An appropriate value of n for a diode with plane parallel electrodes is 1.5.

304. Tube Rectifiers. The electron tube with a cathode and one or more plates as anodes is widely used for rectifying alternating currents. For single-phase circuits the diode with one anode eliminates alternate half-cycles and is called a *half-wave rectifier*, and the diode with two anodes utilizes both half-cycles and is called a *full-wave rectifier*.

The circuit of the full-wave rectifier is shown in Fig. 285; it includes an iron-core transformer T with three windings. The primary winding joins to the source of alternating current, the secondary winding 1-2 connects with the two anodes P_1 and P_2, and the tertiary winding supplies current to heat the filament F. Mid-taps 3 and 4 on the secondary and tertiary windings lead to the load circuit. At an instant when terminal 1 of the secondary winding is positive, the current is directed from P_1 to F, to 4, through the load, to 3 and back to 1. When terminal 2 is positive, the path of the current is from P_2 to F, to 4, through the load, to 3 and back to 2.

Thus throughout a cycle the current through the load is in one direction, but it does pulsate between zero and a maximum value. To make the current steadier in value, use is made of an *electric filter*, consisting of choke coils connected in series with the load and capacitors connected in parallel with it. High alternating pds can be rectified similarly, the tube for this purpose being often called a *kenotron*.

Gases and vapors are used in some types of rectifier tubes in order to obtain large currents. The gas atoms are bombarded by the electrons emitted from the cathode and become ionized when electrons are knocked out of them. These gas ions are positively charged and tend to neutralize

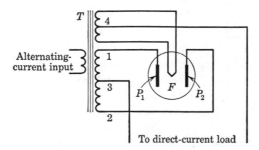

Fig. 285.   Full-wave electron-tube rectifier

the space charge about the cathode, thereby increasing the emission of electrons from this electrode. The Tungar rectifier and the mercury-vapor rectifier are examples. The first contains argon or other inert gas at low pressure, a cathode of tungsten coiled into a closely wound spiral, and an anode of graphite having a relatively large area. The other contains electrodes of mercury and graphite, and current is set up between them through mercury vapor whenever the mercury electrode is sufficiently negative.

305. Three-Element Electron Tubes. An important development in electron tubes was the addition of a third electrode for controlling the number of electrons passing between the other two. The introduction of this electrode in the form of a *grid* between the filament and plate was made in 1906 by the American inventor Lee De Forest. The resulting three-element tube, or *triode*, is exceedingly useful in serving a number of functions in the communication arts.

The effect of the grid is like that of a shutter which, opening and closing, controls the flow of electrons going through it from filament to plate. This control is accomplished by changing the potential of the grid. When the grid is positively charged, it attracts electrons and increases their flow to the plate, for most of them pass right through the relatively large openings of the grid structure. When the grid is negatively charged it repels the electrons and fewer reach the plate.

Fig. 286 is a diagram of a triode and its circuits. The filament F is heated by battery A, the potential of the plate P is provided by battery B, and the circuit of the grid G leads to the terminals TT'. When a small alternating emf is applied to these terminals, the grid is made alternately positive and

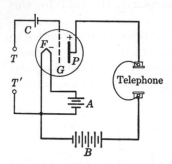

negative and the electron flow is increased and decreased accordingly, thereby varying the direct current in the plate circuit and causing corresponding responses in the telephone receivers, § 306. Actually, the grid is not made positive with respect to the filament, but only more or less negative. This is done by inserting a battery C in the grid circuit to provide a potential *bias* so that the grid is still negative for the highest positive potential applied at terminals TT', and consequently there is no current in the grid circuit. Thus, the grid serves as a gate-valve to control the plate current while taking practically no power itself.

FIG. 286. Triode and its elementary circuit

The cathode of the tube is usually a thin nickel sleeve coated with barium oxide, or with barium and strontium oxide, or other material having a low work function; a heating coil of tungsten wire is mounted within but separated from the sleeve. This construction makes it possible to heat the cathode with alternating current without introducing disturbing effects.

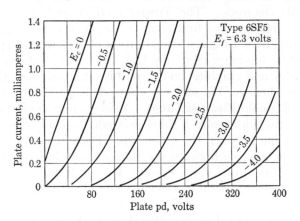

FIG. 287. Characteristic curves of a triode

The behavior of a *triode* is best portrayed by a family of curves of plate current plotted against plate potential. Fig. 287 shows such plate characteristic curves of a typical vacuum tube used in radio sets and each curve represents a particular grid potential E_c from 0 to -4 volts. The heater of the cathode takes 0.3 amp at a potential difference $E_f = 6.3$ volts.

As previously mentioned, the space near the cathode has a negative charge because of the presence of electrons. The more negative the grid, the more it assists this space charge in limiting the electron flow. The curves show, for example, that with the plate potential maintained at 200 volts, the plate current is 0.9 milliamp with −1.5 volts on the grid, 0.31 milliamp with −2.0 volts on the grid, and 0.1 milliamp with −2.5 volts on the grid. This illustrates the large variation in plate current that can be obtained by relatively small changes of grid potential.

The *amplification factor* of a tube is defined as the ratio of a change in plate potential to a change in grid potential in the opposite direction such that the plate current remains unchanged. An illustration will clarify the meaning of this factor.

Illustrative Problem

For the triode having the characteristics shown in Fig. 287 assume −2.5 volts on the grid and +300 volts on the plate, both with respect to the cathode; for these conditions the plate current is 0.9 milliamp. Again, with −1.0 volt on the grid and +150 volts on the plate, the plate current is also 0.9 milliamp. Thus, an increase of 1.5 volts on the grid yields the same output with a decrease of 150 volts on the plate. The ratio of 150 to 1.5 shows the amplification factor to be 150 ÷ 1.5 = 100.

Two other operating factors of a triode can be obtained from its plate characteristic curves; these are called the plate resistance and the transconductance. The *plate resistance* is the ratio of a small change in plate potential to the corresponding change in plate current (the grid potential being unchanged); it is found by drawing a tangent to the curve at the operating point and measuring its slope with respect to the line representing current. The *transconductance* of a triode is the ratio of a small change in plate current to the corresponding change in grid potential which caused that current change (the plate potential remaining unchanged). The relationship between the three factors of a tube for the same operating condition is

$$\text{Transconductance} = \frac{\text{amplification factor}}{\text{plate resistance}}$$

306. Amplifiers in Telephony. The transmission of speech by telephone was first accomplished by Alexander G. Bell (1847–1922), American inventor and physicist. The elements of telephonic communication consist of a *transmitter* for producing a variable current having the same characteristics as the sound waves of the voice that impinge upon it, and a *receiver* for converting this so-called "voice current" into sound waves to reproduce the original sounds.

The transmitter consists of carbon granules confined between two electrodes, one being rigid and the other flexibly mounted on the diaphragm against which the voice is directed. Variations of air pressure on the diaphragm cause changes of resistance of the granules because their contacting areas are altered.

The receiver comprises a small electromagnet combined with a permanent magnet, and a thin diaphragm of magnetic material. Variations of current in the electromagnet cause variations in the attraction of the diaphragm, thereby setting it into vibration to produce sound. Without the permanent magnet, the diaphragm would produce sounds of double pitch, for the diaphragm would be attracted once for the positive half-cycle of alternating current and once for the negative, thereby producing two complete vibra-

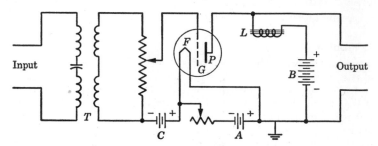

FIG. 288.   Telephone repeater element

tions of the diaphragm for each current cycle. With the magnet present, the resultant flux from both permanent magnet and electromagnet does not change in direction but only in magnitude, and hence the diaphragm is attracted only once for each current cycle.

The simplest connection for demonstrating the transmission of speech is a series circuit including a transmitter, a receiver, and a battery. A sound impressed upon the transmitter causes its diaphragm to be moved with varying amplitudes and frequencies. Each push against the diaphragm lowers the resistance of the transmitter, causes a larger current in the circuit, and produces in the receiver an increased pull upon its diaphragm. The action of the transmitter is therefore to alter or "modulate" the current to conform to the incident sound waves. Thus the modulated voice-current is a mixture of currents of a wide range of frequencies.

Electron tubes are extensively used in telephony for the amplification of current. A typical triode circuit is shown in Fig. 288. The voice current to be amplified is received by the input transformer T at a repeater station, and a portion of the emf developed in its secondary winding is impressed between the filament F and the grid G. The battery A provides current to heat the filament, and the battery C maintains the grid negative to prevent current in the grid circuit. The battery B provides the potential for the plate P of the tube. The choke coil L offers high impedance to the high-frequency voice current and very little circulates through the battery.

Small variations in the voice current in the input transformer cause proportional variations in grid potential, and these in turn produce similar but amplified current variations in the output circuit at the right. The additional energy is supplied by the battery in the plate circuit.

Additional grids are used in electron tubes to improve their characteristics for various purposes. Thus, to lessen the capacitance between the grid and plate a so-called *screen grid* is placed between the plate and the regular grid, then called the *control grid*, and is given a suitable potential to shield the latter electrostatically from the plate. In this way the "feedback" of energy from the output to the input circuit of the tube is minimized.

The gain in power due to an amplifier is expressed in terms of a unit named after Bell and called the *decibel* (abbreviated db). One decibel represents a ratio between two power values of $10^{0.1}$ to 1. When the gain of an amplifier is N db, the ratio of the output power P_2 to the input power P_1 is $10^{0.1N}$, or

$$\frac{P_2}{P_1} = 10^{0.1N}$$

Herefrom, the gain in decibels becomes

$$N = 10 \log_{10} \frac{P_2}{P_1} \tag{226}$$

The decibel scale is also used in the measurement of sound and noise levels, § 351.

Illustrative Problems

As examples of the decibel scale in expressing amplification, suppose the input to an amplifier is 5 microwatts, and the gain is first 10 db and then 50 db. Determine the output power for both gains.

A gain of 10 db means a power ratio $P_2/P_1 = 10^{0.1 \times 10} = 10$; consequently there is a 10-fold increase and the output is 50 microwatts. Similarly, a gain of 50 db signifies a 10^5-fold power increase to 0.5 watt.

Again, suppose the input and output powers of an amplifier to be specified as 5 and 200 microwatts respectively. Find the amplifier gain.

The gain in decibels is given by Eq. 226 as $N = 10 \log_{10} \frac{200}{5} = 10 \log_{10} 40 = 10 \times 1.602 = 16.02$ db.

307. Gas Triodes for Power Control. The use of gases in triodes renders them capable of handling much higher currents than is possible with the vacuum type. An important feature of the gas tube is the delay in establishing the plate current until the positive plate potential reaches the critical value at which the particular gas ionizes. But after the current is once started, its value is not affected by changes in grid potential as in vacuum triodes, but continues until either the plate potential falls almost to zero or the current becomes too low to maintain ionization.

The *thyratron* is a three-element tube containing mercury vapor and is used for controlling currents of the order of amperes by varying the conditions of its grid potential. With a definite pd between cathode and plate, ionization of the vapor begins at some particular grid potential. With the grid more negative than this critical value, no ionization takes place, but otherwise a current is established, provided the plate is positive with respect to the heated cathode. After the plate current is once started, the grid cannot stop or control it. However, if the current stops sufficiently long for the vapor to de-ionize, the grid again resumes control.

With alternating potentials on both plate and grid, the latter electrode can regain control once each cycle and delay establishment of current in the plate circuit as long as the grid is sufficiently negative. Therefore, the phase relation between these two potentials fixes the point in each cycle at which current is established and thereby determines the average amount of current in the plate circuit. The thyratron is useful chiefly in controlling contactors, solenoids, magnetic brakes, and rectifiers.

308. X-Rays and Their Production. A discovery in science of far-reaching importance was made in 1895 by the German physicist Wilhelm K. Röntgen (1845–1923). While experimenting with vacuum tubes he discovered an

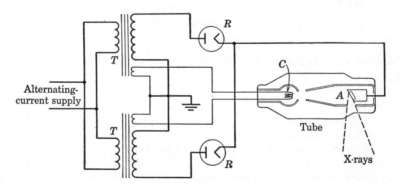

Fig. 289. Hot-cathode x-ray tube and its connections

invisible radiation capable of affecting photographic plates. He called the radiation *x-rays*, because of their unknown nature. These rays, also spoken of as Röntgen rays, are now known to be similar in character to light, but the waves are much shorter in length.

X-rays are produced copiously when cathode rays strike metals of high atomic mass, and are more penetrating when the speed of the electrons constituting the cathode rays is high. Nowadays the electrons are derived from a heated cathode and are speeded toward the target anode by large pds maintained between these electrodes.

The basic circuit of an x-ray tube is shown in Fig. 289. The anode *A* of the tube is a target of tungsten and the cathode *C* is a filament of tungsten wire. These electrodes are supplied with high-potential direct current through a pair of diode rectifiers RR from the transformers TT. The cathode is heated by current supplied by tertiary windings on the transformers.

When different substances are interposed between a photographic plate or film and a source of x-rays, the radiation penetrates them to different extents, largely according to their densities, and the plate or film, upon development, shows the shadows of the objects interposed. When the hand is so placed near an x-ray tube, the plate is affected less behind the bones than behind the flesh, because the bones are more opaque to the radiations. A print made from such a "radiograph" gives shadows of the bones and a faint outline of the flesh. Broken bones and foreign objects in the body can be located accurately in this manner.

A new technique has recently been developed for making x-ray pictures without photography. A metal plate coated with selenium is uniformly charged and then, with the object under examination placed between the tube and plate, exposure is made to x-rays. Every area on the plate thereby loses charge in proportion to the transparency of the object to the rays. The result is a latent image of the object on the plate, and the pattern is brought out by spraying the plate with a powder. The powder gathers more thickly on the still heavily charged areas than in those lightly charged, and thus is produced a so-called "xeroradiographic portrait." Such portraits give more detail and show greater contrast than ordinary radiographs. The lack of permanency can, of course, be met by taking a photograph of the portrait to any desired size; thereafter the powder can be brushed off and the plate used again.

Direct observations with x-rays are made with a screen coated with certain crystals, such as platinobarium cyanide or calcium tungstate, which fluoresce under the action of x-rays. If the hand is interposed between the x-ray tube and such a *fluoroscope* screen, the shadow of the bones can be plainly seen.

Physicians use x-rays not only in making examinations but also for their curative action. Animal tissue undergoes a change in structure when exposed to x-rays and is destroyed by prolonged exposure. In x-ray therapy, the rays are concentrated upon abnormal or diseased tissue that is to be destroyed.

When a gas is exposed to x-rays it becomes ionized, and the amount of ionization produced serves as a measure of the intensity of the rays. Such a measurement is carried out with an ionization chamber and a charged electroscope. The chamber consists of a closed metal box, having a window of thin celluloid or aluminum, and containing an insulated metal electrode to which the electroscope is connected. When the rays are admitted through the window, and a pd is maintained between the electrode and the box, the ions produced by the x-rays separate; those of one sign gather on the electrode, while those of the other sign collect upon the chamber. The rate at which the electroscope discharges is an accurate measure of the intensity of the x-rays.

The radiation from an x-ray tube covers a wide range of frequencies, the range extending to higher frequencies as the pd between the target and cathode is increased. It will be shown in § 441 that there is an upper limiting frequency f_m and that this is determined by the applied pd V according to the relation

$$Ve = hf_m \tag{227}$$

where the product Ve represents the energy with which the electrons strike the target, and h is Planck's constant, § 188. In this expression e is the charge of the electron, namely, 1.60×10^{-19} coulomb, and the constant h has the value 6.62×10^{-34} joule·sec. With the pd expressed in volts the maximum frequency of x-rays becomes

$$f_m = 2.41 \times 10^{14} V$$

In general, the higher the frequency, the greater is the penetrating power of the x-rays. Equipments have been developed for high-speed x-ray photography, and for locating defects in thick metal objects.

PROBLEMS

1. From the graphs of thermoelectric power given in § 300 determine the emfs developed by a thermocouple of antimony and bismuth between the temperatures (a) of 10 and 90° C and (b) of 10 and 170° C.

2. What emf is developed by a copper-nickel thermocouple when one junction is at 0° C and the other is (a) at 100° C and (b) at 200° C?

3. A platinum-platinum rhodium thermocouple with one junction at 0° C develops 9.11 millivolts with the other junction at the melting point of silver. Estimate the temperature at which silver melts from the data given in the problem of § 302.

4. A thermopile for use in fire protection is designed to develop 120 millivolts when the exposed surface reaches 150° C while the other remains at the room temperature of 20° C. How many junctions of antimony and bismuth would be needed?

5. Determine the rate of electron emission in amperes per square centimeter from a tungsten filament that has a temperature of 2347° C.

6. The work function of a metal can be derived from a knowledge of the value of constant b in Richardson's equation, for this constant by theoretical analysis is found to be the ratio of the work function to the gas constant per molecule. Refer to § 162 for the latter constant and determine the work function of molybdenum and tungsten in electron·volts.

7. In a triode having the characteristic curves shown in Fig. 287 the grid potential is varied from -0.5 volt to -2.0 volts while the plate current is maintained constant at 1.10 milliamp. Determine the amplification factor of the tube under these conditions.

8. For the triode of the preceding problem estimate the plate resistance of the tube (a) when the plate and grid potentials are respectively 210 and

−2.0 volts and (*b*) when these potentials are respectively 210 and −1.5 volts.

9. Determine the transconductance of the triode of Probs. 7 and 8 with 120 volts on the plate and a change of grid potential from −0.5 to −1.0 volt; express the result in microamperes per volt.

10. The input to a telephone repeater is 10 microwatts and its output is 3.2 watts. Calculate the repeater gain.

11. A magazine writer in giving an idea of a microwatt of power expressed its magnitude as equivalent to the power developed by a flea having a mass of 1 mg and jumping 50 cm high every 5 sec. How close is this illustration to the correct value?

12. Each of the transatlantic telephone cables mentioned in § 281 has a total of 51 electron tube repeaters placed about 43 mi apart. Each repeater provides 65 db of amplification at the highest transmission frequency. What is the ratio of the power output of each repeater to its input?

13. A public address system has a rated output of 20 watts. If the input to the system is 5 milliwatts, what is the gain of the amplifier unit?

14. Determine the limiting upper frequencies for the radiation from x-ray tubes that are operated with pds between cathode and target of 50,000 and 150,000 volts. Refer to § 188 or 328 for the relation between frequency and wavelength, assume the velocity of wave propagation as 300,000 km/sec, and compute the wavelengths of the radiations that correspond to the limiting frequencies.

28

ELECTRICAL RADIATION

309. Resonant Circuits. Mechanical impulses that are suitably timed and impressed upon an elastic system can set it into a sustained mechanical vibration at its natural frequency, as explained in Chap. 9. The same is true of a corresponding electrical system that receives suitably timed electrical impulses. The electrical system must have both inductance and capacitance, for the energy of vibration is stored periodically in its magnetic field and its electric field.

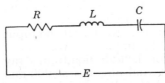

FIG. 290. Series alternating-current circuit

An alternating-current circuit containing an inductor and a capacitor, and subjected to an alternating emf of frequency f cycles/sec, has an inductive reactance $X_L = 2\pi f L$ and a capacitive reactance $X_C = \dfrac{1}{2\pi f C}$, as given by Eqs. 214 and 215. With the inductance L in henrys and the capacitance C in farads, these reactances are expressed in ohms. When the inductive and capacitive reactances of a circuit are equal to each other, the circuit is said to be in *resonance;* thus the resonant condition is

$$2\pi f L = \frac{1}{2\pi f C}$$

The frequency at resonance is obtained herefrom as

$$f = \frac{1}{2\pi\sqrt{LC}} \tag{228}$$

and is called the *natural frequency* of the circuit.

In a series circuit having a resistance R, an inductance L, and a capacitance C, as shown in Fig. 290, the impedance is

$$Z = \sqrt{R^2 + (X_L - X_C)^2}$$

as given by Eq. 217. When the inductive reactance equals the capacitive reactance, $X_L = X_C$, the impedance of the circuit in ohms reduces to $Z = R$. Hence at resonance the current established in a series circuit by an impressed emf E has its greatest value, amounting to $I = E/R$, and is in phase with that emf. Resonance is sought for in tuning radio circuits and is obtained by altering either the inductance or capacitance, usually the latter, to favor currents having a particular range of frequencies.

A quite different result is obtained when the inductive and capacitive reactances are balanced in a parallel circuit, such as in Fig. 291. While relatively large currents are set up in the re-

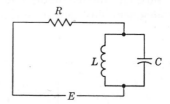

actor L and in the capacitor C, respectively $I_L = E/(2\pi fL)$ and $I_C = 2\pi fCE$, at resonance these are equal and substantially in phase opposition; consequently the current in the main circuit through R is practically zero. Thus parallel resonance gives maximum impedance and is utilized in communication circuits when currents over a definite frequency range are to be suppressed, as in electric filters for rectifiers, § 304.

Fig. 291. Alternating-current circuit with inductance and capacitance in parallel

310. Electromagnetic Radiation. In an alternating-current circuit having capacitance and inductance that are distributed rather than localized, it is found that some energy is emitted in the form of radiation whenever the current in the circuit changes. The discovery of this *electromagnetic radiation* and its transmission through space was made about 1887 by the German physicist Heinrich R. Hertz (1857–1894), who also showed that the radiations behave as waves. The Italian scientist Guglielmo Marconi (1874–1937) made use of this discovery to bring about radio communication.

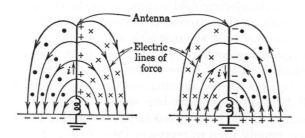

Fig. 292. Electric and magnetic fields set up by antenna current. (Direction of magnetic field is indicated by dots and crosses.)

The radio waves are launched at the transmitting or broadcasting station from an aerial wire system or *antenna*, and are received at similar antennas connected to resonant circuits tuned to receive them.

At the transmitting station a high-frequency source is joined between the antenna and ground, and this forces electrons up and down, charging the upper end of the antenna alternately $+$ and $-$. The antenna and ground together act like the plates of a capacitor and the region between them is under electrostatic stress. The antenna current is made as large as possible by adjusting the inductance or capacitance of the transmitting circuit so as to give resonance at the frequency desired. The region around the antenna may be pictured as shown in Fig. 292; at the left the antenna current i is upward and at the right it is downward. The electric field is directed from the antenna to ground, or vice versa, as depicted by the lines of electric flux, and the magnetic field encircles the antenna as indicated by the lines of magnetic flux shown sectionally by dots and crosses.

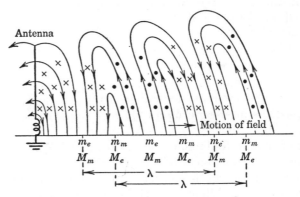

Fig. 293. Electromagnetic waves spreading out from transmitter antenna. (Locations of maxima and minima are represented respectively by M and m with subscripts for electric and magnetic fields.)

The charges surge up and down the antenna as the current reverses, and since the lines of the electric field terminate on the charges themselves, the ends of these lines at the antenna also move up and down. At the same time, the variations of both the magnetic and electric fields that accompany current changes during each cycle move away from the antenna. Fig. 293 shows the composite field in cross-section; the lobes embracing the electric lines are concentric with the antenna and the magnetic lines are horizontal circles, both expanding outward into space. The electromagnetic waves travel in space with the same speed as light, namely, 300,000 km/sec; the symbol c is commonly used to represent this speed.

The length of a wave, marked λ in the figure, depends upon the frequency of the source in the antenna circuit; the higher the frequency, the shorter the wavelength. The relation between frequency f and wavelength λ is

$$\lambda = \frac{c}{f} \tag{229}$$

where c is the speed of propagation. If this speed is in kilometers per second and the frequency is in kilocycles per second, then the wavelength is in meters. Light and radio waves differ only in wavelength. The wavelengths of visible light extend over a narrow range, from 75 to 37 millionths of a centimeter. Those of radio waves extend over a very wide range, from a few kilometers to a fraction of a centimeter.

Illustrative Problem

The tuned circuit of a radio transmitter is composed of a coil having an inductance of 0.06 millihenry in series with a variable capacitor. What should be its capacitance to make the circuit resonant for waves 500 m long?

For 500-m waves the frequency of the resonant circuit should be 300,000 km/sec ÷ 500 m = 600 kilocycles/sec (abbreviated kc). The required capacitance, by Eq. 229, is therefore

$$C = \frac{1}{(2\pi 600 \times 10^3)^2 (0.06 \times 10^{-3})} = 1.175 \times 10^{-9} \text{ farad} = 0.001175 \text{ } \mu\text{f}$$

311. The Electron-Tube Oscillator. The rapid to-and-fro motion of electrons in a radio antenna was set up formerly by high-frequency alternators and electric arcs, but now electron tubes are used for this purpose. The output and input circuits of the tube are coupled in such a way that some energy from the plate circuit is fed back to the grid circuit, thereby maintaining electrical oscillations in the associated resonant circuit.

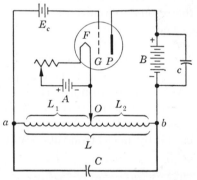

A form of electron-tube oscillator devised by Ralph V. L. Hartley is shown in Fig. 294; the capacitor C and reactor L constitute the resonant circuit. The filament F, heated by battery A, is connected at one terminal to the middle of the reactor. The potential of plate P is supplied by battery B. A capacitor c,

FIG. 294.   Electron-tube oscillator

bridged across this battery, offers a path of low impedance to the high-frequency currents generated so that they can by-pass the battery. The potential of grid G is biased by battery E_c to permit selection of the operating condition that results in minimum loss in both circuits.

When the filament and plate circuits are closed, the electrons emitted from the cathode are drawn to the plate, establishing a unidirectional current in the plate circuit and developing a magnetic field in coil L_2. The growing flux about this half of the reactor cuts the turns of the other half, inducing an emf in L_1 exactly as in a transformer. The momentary direction of the counter emf in L_2 is such as to make the midpoint O positive with respect to b. Similarly the emf induced in L_1 is such as to make point a positive with respect to O, and therefore positive to b also. Hence, as the current in the plate circuit grows, it is aided by the positive potential pulse imparted to the grid by L_1. As the plate current reaches a limiting value and no longer continues to rise, the emf induced in L_1 becomes less, and very soon falls to zero.   Under these conditions the plate-circuit current decreases, because the positive potential which was available at the grid is now lacking.   As the plate current falls in value, the emf induced in L_1 is reversed in direction and increased in magnitude.   This reversal of the pd across L_1 aids the reduction of the plate current until it vanishes.   When this occurs the emf induced in L_1 is again zero and the plate current begins to rise, because the negative grid potential necessary to keep the plate current zero no longer exists.   Once more the current rises in the plate circuit and produces an emf in L_1 directed to make G positive, thereby aiding the current to grow, and this continues until the steady value is reached.   This cycle of events is repeated over and over again.

There is no need to supply energy from an outside source to initiate the oscillations just described; merely closing the circuits is sufficient to produce a potential pulse that starts the action.   The oscillations are maintained, however, at the desired strength by energy supplied from the battery in the plate circuit.   Their frequency is controlled by the constants L and C of the resonant circuit, and can be adjusted to a particular value over a range extending from a few cycles per second to several million per second.

Apart from their use in radio communication, electron-tube oscillators are used for a variety of industrial and investigational purposes in scientific and technical work.   One important application is in connection with the acceleration of atomic particles for nuclear research—for example, to provide the rapid polarity reversal of the dees in a cyclotron, § 259.

312. The Radio Transmitter.   The oscillations produced in a resonant circuit by an electron tube oscillator can be transferred to an antenna circuit

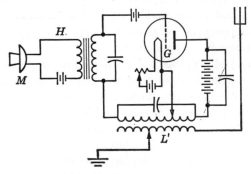

FIG. 295.   Radio telephone transmitter

so that corresponding electromagnetic waves can be radiated into space. This transfer of energy is made through a suitable coupling device, such as the coil L' in Fig. 295, which shows the circuits of a radio telephone transmitter.   The inductance of this coil plus that of the antenna, together with the capacitance of the aerial with respect to ground, also forms a resonant circuit, and this is attuned to the frequency of the oscillator for maximum transfer of energy.

The electromagnetic waves set up by the oscillations in the antenna may be used for radio telegraphy by modulating the generated waves to conform to the dots and dashes of the telegraph code, or for radio telephony by modulating them to conform to the characteristics of sounds to be transmitted. The frequencies of audible sounds range from about 16 to upward of 10,000 cycles/sec, and the usual method of modulation is really a superposition of such audio-frequency waves on the radio-frequency waves

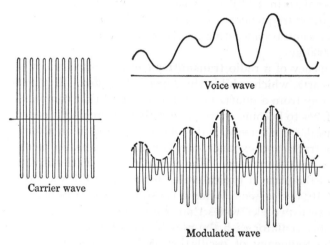

Voice wave

Carrier wave

Modulated wave

Fig. 296. Carrier current modulated for radio telephony

generated by the oscillator. This process of modulation is analogous to the superposition of the speech waves on the direct current used in wire telephony.

Modulation can be accomplished by inserting a telephone transmitter or microphone in a local circuit coupled to the grid circuit of the electron-tube oscillator, as shown, an arrangement that is effective in low-power circuits. The speech waves impinging upon the microphone M are converted into corresponding current variations in the local circuit H, and these voice currents impress suitably varying potentials upon the grid G by means of the transformer. A capacitor is shunted around the secondary winding of this transformer to by-pass the radio-frequency currents.

The grid is subjected to two sets of potential variations, one being the very rapid radio-frequency oscillations or *carrier wave* shown at the left in Fig. 296, and the other being the relatively slow audio-frequency variations as shown by the *voice wave* at the right. As a result the oscillations generated by the tube, which are constant in frequency, are varied in amplitude in accordance with the sound wave, as shown by the *modulated wave* at the right bottom of the figure. This procedure is known as *amplitude modulation* to distinguish it from another procedure to be considered in § 314.

Analysis of a carrier wave that is modulated by a sinusoidal audio wave shows that it is equivalent to three separate waves, the carrier itself and two *sidebands*, one on either side of the carrier. Each sideband has a width that corresponds to the modulation frequency and provides one communication *channel*. In transmitting the complicated waves of speech a side band should be wide enough to carry the speech component of the highest frequency to be accommodated. For example, the coaxial transatlantic cables referred to in § 281 are designed to provide 36 channels each 4 kc wide on carrier frequencies ranging from 20 to 164 kc. Bandwidths for high-fidelity radio broadcasting are 10 kc and those for the video television channels 6000 kc.

The frequency of a radio transmitter can be controlled by utilizing crystals, like quartz, which exhibit the *piezoelectric effect*. If a plate is cut in a particular way from a quartz crystal, it is found that compressing the plate causes its faces to become charged, and then stretching it causes this charge to be reversed. Conversely, if the plate is located in an alternating electric field, it contracts and expands periodically and sets up mechanical vibrations of constant frequency. The vibration rate varies inversely with the thickness of the plate, a typical value for a 1-mm thickness of quartz being about 3×10^6 cycles/sec. When a crystal plate of appropriate thickness is placed between two electrodes that are connected to the grid circuit of an electron-tube oscillator with the plate circuit tuned to the frequency of the crystal, the frequency of oscillation is kept constant regardless of load changes.

313. The Radio Receiver. The function of a radio receiver is to absorb energy from the electromagnetic waves that pass its antenna, to amplify

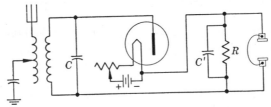

FIG. 297. Simple electron-tube receiver

the weak current set up in the antenna circuit, to rectify or *demodulate* the carrier for obtaining the currents of audio frequency it conveys, and to amplify these currents sufficiently for operating the telephone receiver or loudspeaker. To receive waves from a particular station, the receiver is tuned by adjusting the capacitance or inductance of its antenna and associated circuits to the frequency of that station. When so tuned, the waves from other stations transmitting at different frequencies also develop currents in this receiver but, since resonance does not prevail for them, the currents are usually too small for their signals to be heard.

Demodulation is often accomplished by a diode used as a rectifier or detector. Fig. 297 shows such a tube coupled to the antenna of a radio receiver without amplifiers. Variations of potential across capacitor C act upon the diode, and impulses are passed along to the output circuit consisting of the telephone headset. The capacitance of C' is selected to make its reactance low at the carrier frequency and high at audio frequencies; in this way the carrier by-passes the headset.

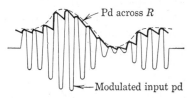

FIG. 298. Carrier wave demodulated by diode

The process will be explained by reference to Fig. 298, which shows the modulated input potential from capacitor C as the light line. With each positive lobe of this potential curve the other capacitor, C', becomes charged and its potential rises to a value slightly less than the peak value because of the pd through the tube itself caused by the charging current. During the following negative lobe some of this charge leaks through the resistor R and the potential on C' falls somewhat. This process is continued and the heavy wavy line shows the output potential. This is unidirectional and has the general characteristics of the modulated carrier as shown in Fig. 296; its radiofrequency ripple does not affect the headset.

In order that an electron-tube detector may operate to the best advantage, it is necessary that the input pd be reasonably large. Since the energy ordinarily received in an antenna is insufficient to develop an adequate pd, it is customary to amplify the received radio-frequency impulses before applying them to the detector. The process is termed *radio-frequency amplification* and is accomplished by one or more electron tubes connected somewhat like that in Fig. 288.

With one or more stages of radio-frequency amplification applied ahead of the detector tube of a receiver, the output of the detector may still be too weak to actuate the sound-reproducing devices. The output may then be increased by means of *audio-frequency amplifiers* which usually have two stages of amplification. The second stage often employs a tube of larger capacity, a so-called *power tube*, in order to yield the desired volume of sound from the loudspeaker.

314. Frequency Modulation. A later method of modulating carrier waves is that devised by the American inventor Edwin H. Armstrong (1890–1954) and called *frequency modulation*. In this method the frequency rather than the amplitude of the carrier wave is modulated by the sound being transmitted, and the amplitude of the radio wave has a constant value determined only by the power radiated by the transmitter. Broadcasting stations using frequency modulation operate at much higher frequencies than those using amplitude modulation; they are of the order of 10^8 cycles/sec, or 100 megacycles/sec (abbreviated 100 mc). An advantage of frequency modulation is the elimination of the disturbance called *static* which produces extraneous noises in amplitude-modulated receivers.

The basic principles of frequency modulation are: (1) the frequency of the carrier is varied over a range which is proportional to the intensity of the sound, and (2) the rate at which this variation takes place is equal to the frequency of the sound. Fig. 299 represents a frequency-modulated carrier wave on a time axis. The frequency (and therefore wavelength) of the carrier varies with the intensity of the sound being carried, and the frequency range expands and contracts at a rate which depends upon the pitch

FIG. 299.   Frequency-modulated carrier wave

of that sound. Thus, loud sounds produce a wide change of carrier wavelength, and high-pitched sounds produce a rapid stretching of the wave pattern.

Illustrative Problems

As numerical examples of the principles of radio frequency modulation, a transmitter is assumed to be operating at a carrier frequency of 45 mc. If in transmitting a 1000-cycle tone of certain intensity the frequency variation is 10,000 cycles/sec (0.01 mc) above and below the normal carrier frequency, what is (a) the *range* of frequency variation in transmitting a tone of double the initial intensity, and (b) the *rate* of frequency variation in transmitting a 4000-cycle tone that is as intense as the initial tone?

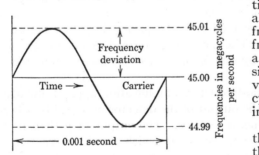

FIG. 300. Illustrating frequency modulation. Ordinates signify frequencies and not amplitudes

The conditions are depicted by the sine curve of Fig. 300, in which the ordinates show a frequency variation of the carrier from 44.99 to 45.01 mc to represent the initial sound intensity, and in which the full abscissa indicates the time of sweeping through one complete set of frequency values. The latter is seen to be 0.001 sec, which means that 1000 such sets of values are swept out per second, a rate that corresponds to a 1000-cycle tone.

(a) For a tone of twice the initial intensity, the variation of the carrier frequency is doubled, extending the range from 44.98 to 45.02 mc, but the rate of variation remains unchanged at 1000 per sec. Of course, the amplitude of the radiated wave remains the same throughout.

(*b*) For a 4000-cycle tone of the same intensity as the initial tone, the variation of the carrier frequency extends over the original range from 44.99 to 45.01 mc, but the rate is 4000 per sec.

The reception of frequency-modulated signals requires the use of specially constructed receivers. In addition to amplifiers and a detector, such a receiver includes two tubes, called a *limiter* and a *discriminator*. The first sets an upper limit to the plate current at a value which corresponds to a low signal potential on the grid of the tube, and eliminates any amplitude variations in the incoming signals due to static or other causes. The second tube transforms the frequency-modulated signals to corresponding amplitude-modulated ones of audio frequency.

315. Photoelectric Emission. Experiments made in 1888 showed that freshly polished zinc when initially charged loses its charge when illuminated, but only when the charge is negative. These experiments were made by the German scientist Wilhelm Hallwachs (1859–1922) using an electroscope for measurement and light from an arc lamp; he concluded that the incidence of light upon the zinc caused the escape of negative electricity. Subsequently this effect was recognized as the emission of electrons and called *photoelectric emission*. Such emission occurs from a number of metals, and the electrons emitted are called *photoelectrons* to indicate that they originate as a result of illumination.

The radiant energy known as light covers a visual range extending from red through the various colors to violet, and this range is bordered by infrared at one side and by ultraviolet at the other. The oscillations that give rise to visible light are extremely rapid, extending from 4×10^{14} vib/sec for red to 8×10^{14} for violet; the wavelengths are correspondingly short and extend from 0.000075 cm for red to 0.000038 cm for violet, as computed from Eq. 229. The vibration frequencies of infrared light are lower than for red, and those of ultraviolet are higher than for violet.

Investigation of photoelectric emission shows that with incident light of a given frequency, a variation of light intensity does not cause a change in speed of the electrons emitted, but does change the number expelled per unit of time. On the other hand, raising the frequency of the incident light increases the speed of emission, and lowering the frequency decreases the speed of emission down to a limiting frequency, characteristic of the metal used, at which the photoemissive effect disappears.

Einstein found that in order to explain these facts it was necessary to apply the quantum theory, § 189, to photoelectric emission, and to suppose that light in space is itself made up of discrete quanta of energy. His photoelectric equation states that the maximum kinetic energy of the electrons emitted from a metal is

$$\tfrac{1}{2}mv_m{}^2 = hf - w \qquad (230)$$

where m is the mass of the electron, v_m is the maximum speed of the electrons, h is Planck's constant, f is the frequency of the incident light, and w is the work function of the metal. Each quantum of incident radiation, called a *photon*, is entirely absorbed by a single electron, an amount w being used to pull it out of the metal and the rest appearing as kinetic energy. The energy of a photon is dictated by its frequency and is given by the product hf. When the energy values in the foregoing equation are in joules, the value of h is 6.62×10^{-34} joule·sec.

The low-frequency limit, or threshold value f_o, is obtained when $hf_o = w$; this limit varies with the material. The threshold wavelength at ordinary temperatures for cesium is 0.000068 cm, sodium 0.000058 cm, and potassium 0.000044 cm, all in the visible range. Other metals show emission only for ultraviolet light. The foregoing facts have an important bearing upon the theory of light and radiation, § 442. It is of interest here to observe that the number of electrons which are emitted per second is proportional to the intensity of light which causes emission.

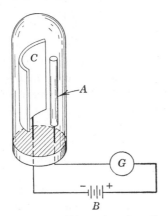

FIG. 301. Photoelectric cell and circuit

The photoelectric cell is an electron tube that consists of a light-sensitive surface, most often of cesium, constituting the cathode, and a small wire or plate constituting the anode, both within an evacuated tube. The circuit of such a cell appears in Fig. 301, its anode wire A and semi-cylindrical cathode C being connected to a battery B and a galvanometer G. When light falls upon the cathode surface, the electrons emitted are drawn to the anode; this flow constitutes a current in the circuit and produces a deflection of the galvanometer. Experiment shows that, over considerable ranges, the current is directly proportional to the illumination at the cell. The currents developed by photoelectric cells are of the order of microamperes for the usual range of illumination, but these can be amplified by using triodes.

Photoelectric cells are usually of the vacuum type, but some are filled with argon at pressures lower than 1 mm Hg. Greater currents can be obtained with gas-filled tubes, because of the ionization of the gas molecules by collision, but the response is not quite as rapid as with the vacuum type. Photoelectric cells are used particularly for color analysis and comparison, control of street lights and electric signs, counting operations, and for talking motion pictures.

316. Television. During the last decade great progress was made in the development of electrical means for seeing at a distance, and the word "television" no longer needs introduction. The fundamental principles of television involve: (1) scanning the scene to be transmitted spot by spot in an orderly fashion; (2) establishing a current that varies with the light intensities of these spots; (3) amplifying these so-called *video* currents and transmitting them over wire lines or by radio waves; (4) receiving these currents or waves and converting them into corresponding light fluctuations; and (5) arranging these light patches upon a screen to form an image of the original scene. It is necessary to scan the entire scene repeatedly, at least 20 times per second, in order that the successive images may merge and produce a steady result like that of motion pictures.

In the television system devised by Vladimir K. Zworykin, a narrow electron beam is used to scan an image of the scene in a photoelectric tube of special design called an *iconoscope*. This is an evacuated glass tube arranged as illustrated in Fig. 302. The electrons are emitted by a heated cathode *C*, controlled and focussed by passing them through the grid *G* and the anodes A_1 and A_2, and then directed upon

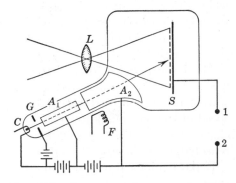

FIG. 302. Iconoscope for converting light image into video current

the screen *S*. The screen consists of a thin sheet of mica having a metal film on one side and a tremendous number of tiny photosensitive particles resembling a mosaic on the other.

The scene to be transmitted is imaged upon the mosaic by a lens system *L* as shown, and as a result its particles are illuminated to various intensities. Each particle may be regarded as a tiny photoelectric cell that also forms a capacitor with the metal film on the other side of the mica sheet, and therefore each one acquires a charge by photoelectric emission that depends upon the intensity of light upon it. The electron beam is deflected from one side to the other along a line, and then deflected from line to line by means of a magnetic field that is symbolized by *F* in the figure. In this way the entire image is scanned and the charges on the particles of the mosaic are released in succession, thereby establishing a current in the output circuit 1-2 that fluctuates in accordance with the light elements of the screen image. Improvements in the design of the iconoscope have resulted in tubes called the image orthicon and the vidicon. The video current from any of these tubes is amplified by electron tubes and transmitted or broadcast by methods already described in this chapter.

The television receiver comprises electrical receiving and amplifying tube circuits, together with a large vacuum tube resembling the cathode-ray oscilloscope described in § 299. The intensity of the electron beam in the tube is controlled by the video current that represents the incoming picture signals. This beam is moved from side to side and from line to line by applying appropriate potentials to its deflecting plates as previously explained, or by using a magnetic field for its deflection. With proper synchronization of the scanning operation to that at the transmitter, an image of the original scene is produced upon the fluorescent screen of the receiving tube.

317. Radar. The method of locating objects by radio waves is known as *radar*, a contraction of *ra*dio *d*etection *a*nd *r*anging, and is particularly adapted to aerial and marine navigation. Aerial navigators use radar, when vision is obstructed, to determine altitude, to locate mountains, and to avoid aircraft in flight. Marine navigators use the system at night or in fog to locate coastlines, icebergs, buoys, and ships. Radar is a vital component of the air defense system of the United States.

The basic principle of radar is the scanning of a region with a narrow beam of waves from a station of known position and the detection at that station of the reflected waves from the object being located. Since the speed of the waves is known, it is only necessary to measure the time that elapses between the transmission of the radio pulses and the arrival of the reflected waves in order to locate the object which caused the reflection.

Radar equipment includes an antenna, the transmitter and its modulator, the receiver and its indicator, and the usual power supply system and auxiliary circuits. The antenna is a short conductor which usually has a parabolic reflector to focus the radio waves into a narrow beam, just as the parabolic reflector of a searchlight does with light. The antenna assembly can be rotated continuously up to speeds of 20 rev/min.

The transmitter has an oscillator of special design to generate the very short waves needed in radar; the frequencies range upward of 1000 mc. These short waves are called *microwaves* and are produced by oscillators employing resonant metal cavities instead of oscillatory circuits as the field storing element; some of these microwave tubes are known as magnetrons and klystrons and receive their energy directly from the stream of electrons. More recently the interchange of energy between a "slow" electromagnetic field and an electron stream, traveling either with or against the electrons, is utilized for generating microwaves in the so-called traveling-wave tube. Currently, research is being conducted on a solid-state device for producing microwaves; it employs a crystal containing a paramagnetic salt and operates through electron spins. Its use as an amplifier will also be important.

The modulator causes the transmitter to radiate its signals in short pulses, usually of 1 microsec or less, with a recurrence rate of about 1000 pulses/sec. The pulses are of high intensity; in fact, the power transmitted in each pulse may be of the order of several kilowatts. When the transmitter is active, the power is conveyed to the antenna through an electronic switch consisting of a needle spark gap within an enclosure containing gas under pressure. When a pulse is sent out from the antenna, the high potential used causes a spark at the gap and short-circuits the receiver, thus protecting it from damage; when the pulse ends, the gas de-ionizes in a few microseconds and the receiver is ready for any returning signal.

The receiver amplifies and rectifies the signal pulse and impresses it upon the cathode-ray oscilloscope of the indicator. Radial scanning is employed, in which the bright spot starts from the center of the oscilloscope screen and spirals outward in a direction to match that of the radio beam from the antenna, and then returns quickly to the center. When the echo signal is received, the rectified pulse from the receiver is impressed on the grid which controls the intensity of the electron beam in the oscilloscope. This beam is synchronized with the antenna and a corresponding trace is made on the screen. The persistence of the luminescent screen is such that the repeated scannings produce a picture of the region about the radar station, obstacles appearing as bright spots on a dark background.

Since the time required for the microwaves to reach an obstacle and return to the radar is determined by the distance of the obstacle, the distance of a bright spot on the oscilloscope from the center of its screen bears a fixed relation to the distance of the obstacle. The range of the obstacle may be measured by a control on the set which moves an expanding circle on the screen to the position of the white spot which corresponds to that of the obstacle. The bearing or direction of the obstacle is determined generally by reference to a line from the center to the top of the screen; this line may represent either the lengthwise axis of the ship or the true north-south direction. Bearings from that line are read on a graduated circle around the edge of the screen.

The radar technique is applied in determining the speed of automobiles on a highway for traffic control purposes. The method utilizes the Doppler Effect, § 347, for detecting the difference in wavelength between the incident beam and that reflected from an approaching or receding car. The receiving instrument consists of an indicator that reads speeds directly in miles per hour and a graphic recorder that makes a permanent record. If V is the speed of the car in miles per hour and f the frequency of the incident beam in cycles per second, then the change of frequency in the same units is found to be practically $2Vf/c$, where c is the speed of light in miles per hour. Thus with microwaves having a frequency of 2450 mc there is a change of frequency of $7\frac{1}{3}$ cycles/sec for each mile per hour of vehicle speed.

PROBLEMS

1. A series circuit has a resistance of 20 ohms, an inductance of 0.1 milli-henry, and a capacitance to render the circuit resonant at a frequency of 1 megacycle/sec. Assume that a pd of 10 volts is applied to the circuit and determine (*a*) the capacitance of the circuit, (*b*) the current established at resonance, (*c*) the total reactance of the circuit when the operating frequency departs 2% from the resonant frequency, and (*d*) the current in the circuit at that operating frequency.

2. If the resistance of the circuit of Prob. 1 were reduced to 10 ohms, (*a*) what would be the current at resonance and at an operating frequency that is 2% different from the resonant frequency? (*b*) Plot the current values for the circuits of both problems and determine which circuit would show the steeper curve of current against frequency and which therefore can be more sharply tuned. Explain.

3. A microwave oscillator, developed at the Bell Telephone Laboratories and called a reflex klystron tube, oscillates at 60,000 megacycles/sec and has an output of 20 milliwatts. How long are the waves that it produces? For an electric circuit to be resonant at the frequency stated, how small would the product of its inductance and capacitance have to be?

4. A radio transmitting antenna has a capacitance to ground of 500 $\mu\mu f$ and its circuit has an inductance of 30 microhenrys. Determine (*a*) the natural frequency of the antenna circuit and (*b*) the resonant frequency of the antenna circuit when a capacitor of 1000 $\mu\mu f$ is joined in series with it.

5. A triode has a grid bias such that within the limits of its operation the plate current varies linearly with the pd on the grid. The plate resistance, plate current, and amplification factor are respectively 10,000 ohms, 1.00 milliamp, and 10. A sinusoidal signal having a peak value of 1 volt is impressed upon the input terminals of the tube. Assume the sinusoidal component of the output current to lie equally above and below the steady value of 1.00 milliamp. Calculate (*a*) the peak value of the sinusoidal current in the output circuit that has a load of 20,000 ohms resistance and (*b*) the rms value of the total current in that circuit.

6. Make a sketch similar to Fig. 300 showing the solutions of parts (*a*) and (*b*) of the solved problem in § 314, and include a graph for the initial conditions.

7. What wavelength is associated with a quantum that has 1 electron·volt of energy?

8. Ultraviolet light of 0.2293 micron wavelength falls upon a photoelectric surface of sodium. Find the maximum value of the kinetic energy possessed by the photoelectrons.

9. From the threshold wavelengths of cesium and potassium given in § 315, determine the threshold frequencies and work functions for these elements.

10. The television picture is virtually a checkerboard with minute squares that constitute the individual picture elements, and all of them are scanned 30 times/sec. In present practice there are 525 horizontal scanning lines that form an equal number of picture elements vertically, and for the usual picture proportions each line may be regarded as having $\frac{4}{3}$ that many picture elements horizontally. The condition for which alternate elements are light and dark results in the highest possible modulation frequency. How wide a frequency band is needed for a television video channel?

11. A traffic control radar equipment operating on 2200 megacycles/sec gives an indication for an automobile speeding along a highway that the frequency change between incident and reflected beams is 500 cycles/sec. How fast is the car traveling?

12. A pulse of radar waves lasting 0.8 microsec is transmitted from a ship's antenna at a frequency of 2000 mc. The radar echo is received at the same antenna 25 microsec after transmission. (*a*) How many waves does the pulse contain? (*b*) How far from the ship is the obstacle that caused the echo?

29

SOLID-STATE ELECTRONICS

318. Crystal Structure. Most solids are crystalline in structure and are usually composed of a multitude of individual crystals held together tightly. The distinction between crystalline and noncrystalline solids was made in § 1; further consideration of crystals is given here as an introduction to solid-state electronics. This new branch of Physics, already industrially important, deals with effects produced in certain solids when activated by electric fields, magnetic fields, or light.

The crystalline structure of solids is characterized by atomic patterns that are repeated regularly in three dimensions. The repeat unit of a crystal is called a *unit cell*, and all the unit cells of a particular crystal are identical in atomic composition, orientation, and dimensions. The corners of an array of unit cells stacked together to form a perfect crystal are called the points of a *space lattice*. Additional points of the lattice framework are sometimes located at the centers of the faces or at the center of the body of the unit cell, Fig. 303.

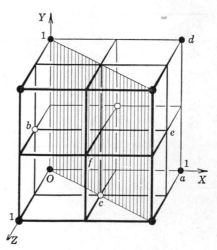

FIG. 303. A unit cell of cubic crystal system

Most perfect crystals have their atoms (or ions) symmetrically disposed with respect to certain axes and planes, but few crystals are perfect. The imperfections are usually due either to an excess or a deficiency of one of the kinds of atoms present or to disorder within the structure. The faces of the crystal itself or those obtained through cleavage are planes that contain relatively large numbers of atoms. Crystals of any one kind as found in nature are not necessarily identical in exterior form.

Any crystalline solid can be described in terms of the shape of its unit cell and the locations of the atoms in it. Crystals are classified into systems according to the relative lengths of their axes of symmetry and the angles between them. The following table lists the seven crystal systems and gives the characteristics of their axes and lattices. Atoms are located at the cor-

CRYSTAL SYSTEMS

Name	Lengths of Axes	Angles Between Axes	Additional Lattice Types
Cubic.........	Equal	90°	{ Face-centered { Body-centered
Hexagonal.....	Two equal	120° between equal axes, others 90°	....
Rhombohedral	Equal	Equal, but not 90°	....
Tetragonal....	Two equal	90°	Body-centered
Orthorhombic	Different	90°	{ Face-centered { Base-centered { Body-centered
Monoclinic....	Any	Two 90°	Base-centered
Triclinic......	Any	None 90°	....

ners of the unit cells, and also elsewhere in them as indicated in the last column. Thus in all there are 14 distinct types of space lattice, as first enumerated by the French scientist Auguste Bravais (1811–1863).

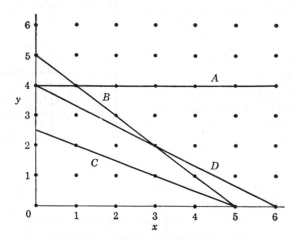

Fig. 304. Lines connecting atoms in crystal

The positions of lattice points can be specified by using XYZ coordinates. The left lower back corner of a unit cell is chosen as the origin and the relative distances to the other points are measured along the crystal axes. Thus in Fig. 303 with the origin O designated as 000, the location of the corner atom a is $x = 1$, $y = 0$, $z = 0$ and written as 100; similarly the face-centered atom b is designated $0\frac{1}{2}\frac{1}{2}$, and the base-centered atom c by $\frac{1}{2}0\frac{1}{2}$. When the unit cell has a body-centered atom instead of face-centered atoms, the location of that atom is designated $\frac{1}{2}\frac{1}{2}\frac{1}{2}$. The structure of sodium chloride (NaCl) is cubic and based on a face-centered lattice with Na ions at the corners and Cl ions at the mid-points along the edges of the unit cell, or vice versa (see Prob. 3).

Crystal faces or atomic planes are designated by indices that are determined by the intercepts of the planes on the three axes. The scheme is best described for just two dimensions. The lettered lines in Fig. 304 are drawn through dots that represent atoms (but not through the origin) and are listed in the first column of the following table. The second column gives the intercepts of these lines on the X and Y axes, the next column gives ratios of the reciprocals of these intercepts, and the last column gives the indices found by reducing each pair of ratios to its equivalent and smallest integers.

Line	Intercepts x, y	Reciprocals	Indices
A.............	∞, 4	$1/\infty$, $1/4$	0, 1
B.............	5, 5	$1/5$, $1/5$	1, 1
C.............	5, $2\frac{1}{2}$	$1/5$, $2/5$	1, 2
D.............	6, 4	$2/12$, $3/12$	2, 3

Extension of the method to the Z axis permits any plane to be designated by three integers, usually shown in parentheses. If the lines in the figure represent traces of planes that are perpendicular to the page, then the designation for the z direction is 0 for all four. For example, such a plane that includes line B would be specified as (110); again the plane shown shaded in the cube of Fig. 303 is specified as (101). Parallel planes have the same designation.

The atomic structure of a surface was actually photographed recently by means of a so-called field ion microscope developed by Professor Erwin W. Müller at Pennsylvania State University. The picture in Fig. 305 made by him shows the tip of a single-crystal tungsten wire with the (011) crystal plane near the center and a (123) plane at the rim. The tip has a diameter of 10^{-4} mm and was cooled by liquid hydrogen to obtain the low temperature needed for good resolution of detail. The picture was taken with helium ions produced under an electric field intensity of 4×10^8 volts/cm, and the surface of the tip was imaged on a fluorescent screen that was negatively charged. The flat crystal faces, developed by the evaporation of tungsten during the process of degassing by heating, appear dark in the picture, and the rings of bright spots are the intersections of the curved surface of the tip with the atomic planes. The spots themselves are caused by the individual atoms of tungsten.

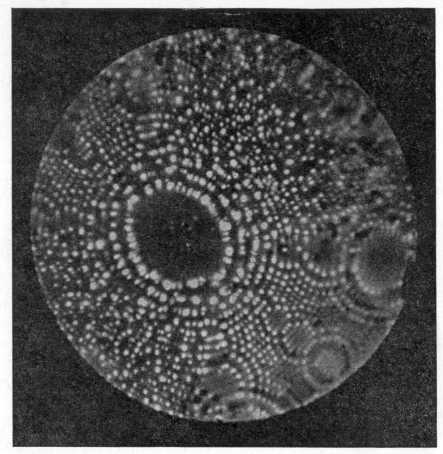

FIG. 305.   Magnified surface of tungsten.   (Scale 1 in. = 10^{-6} cm.)   (*Courtesy of Professor Erwin W. Müller*)

319. The Hall Effect.   An introduction to solid-state electronics necessitates not only an acquaintance with the elements of crystal structure but also with modern views of electrical conduction in solids.   These are based on the interpretation of a discovery made by the American physicist Edwin H. Hall (1855–1938).   He found that when a current-carrying conductor is placed in a magnetic field directed perpendicularly to the direction of the current, an electric field is developed at right angles to both current and magnetic field.   Specifically, with a conductor carrying a current I due to the electric field $\mathcal{E}_x$ set up by an outside source directed along the x axis, and placed in a magnetic field of density B in the y direction, as shown in the perspective view in part I of Fig. 306, the charge carriers are deflected sideways and build up charges along the sides of the conductor; as a result a transverse electric field $\mathcal{E}_z$ is developed in the z direction.   This electric field

rises in intensity until its effect on the charge carriers is just equal and opposite to the effect of the magnetic field on them. Thereafter there is no further accumulation of charge along the sides of the conductor, and the direction of current through it is the same as it would have been without the
magnetic field.

In the consideration of electrical conduction through metals thus far the
carriers of charge have been the free electrons, and their motion is opposite
to that of the conventional current direction. Thus, when the electric field
$\mathcal{E}_x$ and the current it produces are directed to the right as shown in part I of

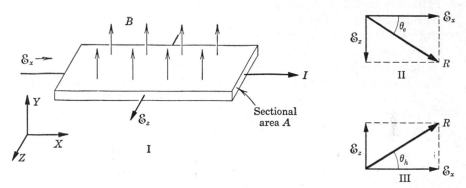

FIG. 306. The Hall Effect. Vector diagrams of parts II and III are in plane of
conductor in part I; Hall angles for electronic and hole conduction are shown as θ_e
and θ_h respectively

Fig. 306, the electrons with their negative charges travel to the left. The
magnetic field directed upward deflects the electrons toward the reader,
causing the front edge surface of the conductor to assume a lower potential
than the rear one; hence the transverse electric field $\mathcal{E}_z$ is directed toward
the front as shown. The resultant of the transverse field $\mathcal{E}_z$ and the longitudinal field $\mathcal{E}_x$ is designated as R in part II; the angle it makes with the longitudinal electric field is called the *Hall angle*.

In some substances the transverse field was found to be directed opposite
to that expected of electronic carriers. This result showed that electronic
motion alone could not account for all the phenomena of electric conduction. The deficiency of an electron at any place, technically called a *hole*,
can lead to a transportation of charge similar to that conveyed by positive
carriers. Thus the motion of holes toward the right in Fig. 306 causes them
to be deflected toward the reader, thereby producing an electric field $\mathcal{E}_z$ directed as shown in part III. Distinction is made between the effects of the
two types of carriers by designating the Hall angle θ_e for electrons and θ_h
for holes.

The idea of holes shifting their positions can be appreciated from certain
games that contain blocks within a frame that has one more space than the

number of blocks, and which are played by shifting the blocks to obtain some definite order. Shifting a block from one space to the next can also be viewed as shifting the vacant space by the same amount in the opposite sense, and so the space can be regarded as moving. Similarly it may be thought that in a crystal lattice, if an electron is missing from one of its usual positions and a neighboring electron is caused to take that position, then in effect the hole left by the electron has moved; and further, since a shifting of electron positions means a transfer of negative charge, it follows that a shifting of holes means a transfer of positive charge. This concept is extremely useful in explaining the action of semiconductors, § 320.

The balancing of the transverse forces due to both the magnetic and electric fields on the charge carriers makes it possible to determine their mobility and concentration. The following analysis applies to conduction in metals either by electrons or holes.

The force on an electron moving along the conductor with velocity v through the magnetic field of density B is $F = Bev$, § 257, where e is the electronic charge. The force on the electron exerted by the electric field of the Hall effect is $\mathcal{E}_z e$, according to Eq. 135. Hence in the steady state

$$\mathcal{E}_z e = Bev$$

In mks units the electronic charge is 1.60×10^{-19} coulomb, the electric field intensity is measured in volts per meter, the magnetic flux density in webers per square meter, and the velocity of the carriers in meters per second. Herefrom, the velocity of the carriers is expressed as the ratio of the electric field intensity to the magnetic flux density, or

$$v = \frac{\mathcal{E}_z}{B} \tag{231}$$

The *mobility of charge carriers* along a metal expresses the ease with which they can be moved by an electric field applied in that direction; the term is defined as the velocity of the carriers per unit electric field and is given by

$$\mu = \frac{v}{\mathcal{E}_x} \tag{232}$$

With $\mathcal{E}_x$ also expressed in volts per meter, the mobility μ is in meters squared per volt·second.

The *concentration of the carriers* is defined as their number per unit volume of conductor. If e is the electronic charge and n the concentration, then the charge per unit volume is ne. When the carriers move through a conductor of cross-section A and travel a distance l in a time t, the current is

$$I = \frac{neAl}{t} = neAv$$

where v is the velocity of the charge carriers. Hence the concentration of the carriers is given by

$$n = \frac{I}{Aev} \tag{233}$$

When the current I is in amperes, the cross-section A in square meters, and e and v are in the same units as before, then the concentration n is the number of charge carriers per cubic meter.

The extent of the Hall effect in a conductor is usually expressed by the so-called *Hall coefficient* defined as the reciprocal of the charge per unit volume. Its value is

$$R_H = \frac{1}{ne} = \frac{Av}{I} = \frac{\mathcal{E}_z}{JB}$$

where $J = I/A$ is the current density in the conductor. The value of R_H at room temperature for copper is about 6×10^{-5} and for silicon about 1000 cm^3/coulomb. The Hall effect is important because it affords information on the conductive process; specifically, its coefficient provides the data for calculating the number of electronic carriers.

Finally, the *conductivity* of the conductor material is the product of the mobility μ of the carriers and their collective charge per unit volume (ne). Thus the conductivity σ, the reciprocal of the resistivity ρ as described in § 221, is

$$\sigma = ne\mu \tag{234}$$

and its unit is $\dfrac{1}{\text{ohm} \cdot \text{meter}}$ in the mks system.

In certain materials the carriers are both electrons and holes, and it can be shown that their effect on conductivity is additive. Therefore

$$\sigma = n_e e \mu_e + n_h e \mu_h$$

where the subscripts distinguish between the two kinds of carriers.

320. Semiconductors. Solid substances are classified on the basis of their electrical behavior into conductors, insulators, and an intermediate class called *semiconductors*. The conductivities of semiconductors range from 10^{-9} to 100 per ohm·cm, whereas good conductors are of the order 10^5, and good insulators range from 10^{-14} to 10^{-22} in the same units. All metallic conductors have positive temperature coefficients of electrical resistance, § 229. The conductivity of semiconductors is also affected by temperature, but the important characteristic is that the *resistance increases as the temperature is lowered*, a behavior that is contrary to that of most conductors. Further, the resistance variation with temperature change is markedly greater than with metallic conductors.

Because of their peculiar electrical properties, semiconductors have found wide application in electrical communication circuits. The important semi-conductors at present include cuprous oxide (Cu_2O), germanium (Ge), in-dium antimonide (InSb), lead telluride (PbTe), selenium (Se), silicon (Si), and silicon carbide (SiC). Of these the best understood are germanium and silicon. The crystals of these elements are cubic, as in Fig. 303, with face-centered atoms (shown by circles) and additionally (but not shown) with atoms at the centers of four alternate cubes that have one-half the edge lengths of the large unit cell illustrated. It will be found upon constructing a model of these crystals that each atom has four nearest neighbors which are equally distant from it. This crystal structure is typical of four-valent atoms and is the same as that of carbon (C) in diamond.

The electrical properties of all crystalline solids can be explained in terms of a unified concept called the *energy band theory.* According to this theory the electrons of a crystal have different states of motion that can be grouped into ranges of energy called *bands;* no electron can have an energy value in the gaps between bands. Depending on the number of electrons per unit cell, some of these bands are empty, some filled, and some are only partially occupied; those that are full have the lowest energy values.

The band occupied by the valence electrons is called the *valence band.* In metals the valence band is not completely filled, and therefore conduction can take place by the transfer of an electron from one state of motion to an-other within the band. In insulators the valence band is filled and the ener-gies of the nearest empty band are so high that transitions of electrons from one band to another across the gap cannot occur except under unusually high electric fields. In semiconductors the valence band is filled at zero tempera-ture and no conduction can take place. However, when thermal energy is supplied to the electrons, they cross the gap from the valence band into the neighboring empty one, and conduction is made possible; hence this band is called the *conduction band* for semiconductors. The size of the gap is char-acteristic of the type of crystal; it can be lessened locally by the presence of an impurity or a growth fault in the crystal.

The energy level diagram of allowed states in a semiconductor is pictured in Fig. 307 with the valence band below and the conduction band above. A certain minimum amount of energy is needed to jolt an electron out of the valence band into the conduction band, a jump that corresponds to releas-ing an electron from its ties with a particular atom and permitting it to roam throughout the lattice. With germanium this amounts to 0.72 electron·volt and with silicon to 1.12 electron·volts.

In the presence of an electric field, electrons move in one direction and holes in the other. A semiconductor in which conduction takes place chiefly by electrons is said to be of the *n*-type, meaning that most carriers are nega-tive, and one in which conduction takes place chiefly by holes is of the *p*-type, meaning that most carriers are positive.

The mobility of the charge carriers depends upon the semiconductor material and upon the nature of the carrier. Expressed in meter squared per volt·second, the mobilities of electrons and holes in germanium around room temperature are respectively 0.37 and 0.18, and the corresponding mobilities for silicon are 0.13 and 0.05.

The conductivity of semiconductors can be vastly improved by adding small amounts of certain impurities. When impurities with five valence electrons per atom, such as phosphorus, arsenic, antimony, and bismuth, are added to germanium, four of them fit nicely into the electronic structure of the crystal but the fifth is extra, and little energy is needed to jolt it into the conduction band. Such impurities are said to be of the *donor* type, and the excess electrons become free for conduction purposes. In contrast, when impurities with three valence electrons, such as boron, aluminum, gallium, and indium, are added to germanium, the fourth electron per atom is missing, thus leaving holes in the electronic structure of the crystal. Again little energy is needed to cause neighboring electrons to occupy these holes, and the result is that in the valence band where these electrons came from there

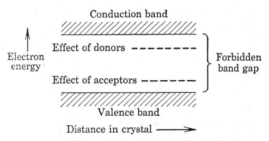

FIG. 307. Energy level diagram of semiconductor

are holes free to move throughout the lattice. Impurities that produce a deficiency of electrons are said to be of the *acceptor* type. The lesser energy values needed for the freeing of carriers because of the presence of either kind of impurity is indicated by the dotted lines in Fig. 307. The presence of donor atoms in an *n*-type semiconductor introduces energy levels occupied by the additional electrons below the bottom of the conduction band; that of the acceptor atoms in a *p*-type semiconductor introduces empty energy levels above the top of the valence band.

Relatively few electrons and holes are available for conduction in pure germanium at room temperature, and the addition of traces of the elements mentioned increases the number of carriers of one type or the other and causes a tremendous rise in conductivity. The effect of adding impurities to semiconductors is similar to the addition of an acid or salt to water in increasing the number of ions available for conduction in electrolytes, § 232.

The combination of *p*-type and *n*-type material is pictured in Fig. 308 and shows a single-crystal semiconductor which is hole-conducting (*p*-type) at the left of the central line and electron-conducting (*n*-type) at the right. With impurities present there is generally an excess of either donor electrons or acceptor holes, yielding a majority of one type of carrier and a minority of the other, as suggested by the + and − signs in the figure. Most of the electrons and holes stay on their respective sides of the *n-p* junction; their first tendency to diffuse across it and combine places charges on the initially neutral halves—the *n*-side, positive and the *p*-side, negative—until an electric field is produced just sufficient to balance this diffusion flow of the free charges.

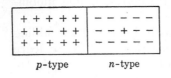

p-type   n-type

Fig. 308.   Junction of two types of semiconductors

When a battery is connected across the two crystal parts of Fig. 308 so as to make the *p*-region positive and the *n*-region negative, electrons and holes flow toward each other across the central line. In this flow they combine, each electron filling one hole, and the resulting current is large. If the battery is reversed so as to make the *p*-region negative and the *n*-region positive, the electrons and holes flow away from each other, and leave the region near the junction devoid of charge carriers. In consequence this central region becomes an insulator and hardly any current crosses the junction. This action accounts for designating this region at the junction a *barrier layer;* it should not be visioned as an obstacle which the carriers have difficulty in crossing, but rather as a region where at times there are no carriers.

The barrier layer serves an important function in rectifying devices. Use was made of them in the early days of radio broadcasting as detectors, the usual form being a fine wire called a catswhisker in contact with a crystal such as the sulfide of lead known as galena (PbS). Subsequently crystals of silicon were found useful for the detection of microwaves in radar.

321. Metallic Rectifiers and Varistors. Semiconductors in combination with metals find a variety of applications in electric circuits. When a semiconductor is in contact with a metallic conductor in a circuit that includes a battery, the polarity and pd of the battery as well as the barrier layer at the interface determine the value of the current established. With the battery connected one way the current is much greater than with the battery reversed. The direction that provides the larger current is called the *forward direction*, and the other is called the *reverse direction*. This almost unilateral behavior provides the basis for rectification.

The development of semiconductors for rectifying alternating currents for small power purposes resulted first in the copper-oxide and later in the selenium rectifier. Such devices are styled *metallic rectifiers* to distinguish them from electron-tube rectifiers, § 304. They are used for charging storage batteries and for various purposes in communication circuits and industrial electronics. Currently progress is being made with germanium and with silicon alloy rectifiers for similar purposes.

Fig. 309 gives a schematic section of several rectifiers; the location of the barrier layer is indicated for each and the forward direction of current is shown by arrows. A number of such units are connected in series to suit the pd of the circuit in which they are used; the selenium type requires fewer for a given pd than the copper-oxide type, and hence has the advantage of

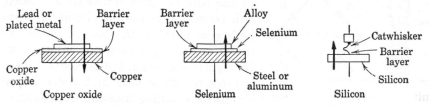

FIG. 309. Semiconductors that serve as rectifiers

smaller size and lesser weight. The germanium rectifier is now widely used to serve the same purpose as the diode electron tube, and is generally known as a germanium diode.

The variation of current with the pd applied to a semiconductor device is shown by a volt-ampere characteristic such as Fig. 310, the forward direction being to the right. The current is not proportional to the pd in either direction, as evidenced by the shape of the curve, and hence the resistance of the device varies from one operating condition to another. Such a nonlinear circuit element is called a *varistor*. Its resistance is defined differently for direct and alternating currents; the direct-current resistance at any operating point such as P is the ratio of the abscissa E to the ordinate I, and the alternating-current or so-called dynamic resistance is the ratio of dE to dI at that point. The dynamic resistance of the varistor biased to potential E is the reciprocal of the slope of the curve at point P.

For full-wave rectification of alternating currents four varistors are used

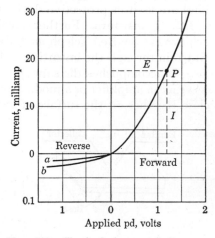

FIG. 310. Typical characteristic curve of varistor. Note change of current scale at bottom for reverse direction; curve a is for room temperature, b for elevated temperature

and connected to the direct-current load as shown in Fig. 311. Each of the varistors A to D is depicted as a transverse line for the cathode and a solid triangle for the anode, the triangle pointing in the forward direction of current. During intervals when the upper transformer terminal is positive the current path extends through varistor A, the load, and varistor B; during intervals when the lower transformer terminal is positive the current path extends through varistor C, the load, and varistor D; thus the current through the load is always in one direction.

An application of varistors for the protection of a circuit makes use of two varistors connected in parallel with the polarities opposed; when so connected the volt-ampere characteristic curve of the pair becomes symmetrical. Such a pair connected across the circuit presents a high resistance to the low potentials normally applied and does not interfere with its regular operation, but presents a low resistance to abnormally high potentials and shunts the resulting transient current around the circuit for its protection.

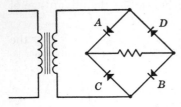

FIG. 311.   Connection of four varistors to form full-wave rectifier

A modification of the silicon rectifier makes use of silicon carbide (Carborundum) crystals mixed with a binder and fired to form ceramic-like rods or disks. The individual crystals actually form a multitude of rectifier units connected in series and in parallel with random polarity and so constitute a varistor with a symmetrical characteristic. Only large pds pass appreciable currents, and consequently rectifiers of this kind are used in protective devices such as lightning arresters.

322. Transistors. Further development in the use of semiconductors was achieved at the Bell Telephone Laboratories by John Bardeen and Walter H. Brattain through the invention in 1948 of the crystal device called a *transistor*. It accomplishes the same purposes as the triode electron tube and can serve as an amplifier or a modulator. The early form had two point contacts close together on the surface of the crystal and a third at its base, as indi-

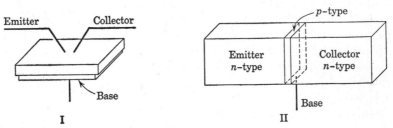

FIG. 312.   Point-contact and junction forms of transistor

cated in part I of Fig. 312. One of the point contacts is called the *emitter* and the other the *collector*, and the semiconductor can be of either the n-type or p-type.

The later form was devised at the same laboratories by William Shockley and is called the junction transistor. It consists either of a thin section of p-type semiconductor between two parts of n-type as shown in part II of the figure and called an n-p-n transistor, or arranged the other way round and called a p-n-p transistor. Each actually has two junctions located very close together, and it is desirable that all three parts be of a single crystal in order to avoid discontinuities of crystal structure at the boundaries, and thereby to facilitate movement of the charge carriers.

The operation of the device can be explained in connection with Fig. 313, which shows an *n-p-n* junction transistor, say of germanium. A battery is connected to the input circuit between the emitter and the base; its emf is directed to give the emitter a forward potential bias. A battery of higher emf is connected to the output circuit between the base and collector and gives the latter a reverse potential bias. Electrons from the emitter diffuse across the emitter junction and enter the base region at concentrations controlled by pd between emitter and base. The base layer is so proportioned that practically all of the injected electrons are drawn across to the collector junction by the attraction of the positively biased collector before they find their way to the base terminal or are lost by combining with holes. The emitter current also includes holes injected from the base. The fraction of

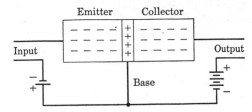

Fɪɢ. 313.   Circuits of transistor

the emitter current that crosses the collector junction is known as the *alpha* of the transistor; its value may reach 0.99.

If the emitter current is varied by a signal pd introduced at the input terminals, there will be a corresponding variation in the collector current. By making the impedance of the output circuit much larger than that of the input circuit, with virtually the same current in both, a considerable gain can be obtained in power. For example, if the impedance of the input and output circuits are respectively 200 ohms and 2 megohms, then the power gain is about 10,000. The additional energy, of course, is supplied by the battery in the collector circuit.

Transistor junctions can be made in several ways; the principal methods are: (1) growing the crystal with appropriate change of impurity, (2) diffusing the impurity into the crystal, and (3) alloying the impurity with the crystal.

In the growing process a single crystal "seed" of the semiconductor material is dipped into its melt that contains either donor or acceptor impurity, and is slowly withdrawn at such speeds as 1 mm/min, all within a purified hydrogen atmosphere and under appropriate temperature control. When a junction is to be formed the opposite type of impurity is added to the melt and the growing process is continued. Soon thereafter more of the first type of impurity is added and the growing is continued again. As a variant, the melt is formed with both donor and acceptor impurities that have different tendencies to segregate between solid and liquid, depending upon the rate of growth of the crystal. Changing the rate of growth suddenly by suitable modulation of the oven temperature produces a reversal of the impurity segregation.

In the diffusion process there are several techniques. One is to expose a section of a *p*-type semiconductor crystal to the vapor of an *n*-type diffusant (or vice versa) at a high temperature. Another is to deposit the donor or acceptor material on the semiconductor and then diffuse it in a similar manner; for example, a phosphorus additive to silicon at a temperature of about 1200° C produces an *n*-type junction.

In the alloying process, say indium with *n*-type germanium, a small piece of the impurity is placed on a single germanium crystal and the temperature is raised above the melting point of indium. Germanium is slightly soluble in liquid indium and enough germanium can be dissolved to leave a depression in its surface and hold the molten alloy there. Upon cooling slowly, the germanium recrystallizes as *p*-type, while the alloy solidifies and later forms the contact. The *p-n* junction is located at the depressed interface between the original germanium crystal and the recrystallized germanium.

Recently success has been obtained in raising the frequency range of junction transistors by reducing the width of the central *p*-type layer to less than 0.0005 cm and adding another electrode to this base layer. By placing a potential bias between the two base electrodes of this so-called *tetrode* transistor, the action is limited to a very small area near one of them. As a result the base resistance and diffusion capacitance are reduced and operation at very high frequencies is improved. Still another successful fabrication method makes use of base wafers with graded impurity concentration; this arrangement produces an electric field in the base which speeds up the minority carriers.

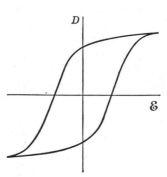

FIG. 314.   Hysteresis loop of ferroelectric substance

Transistors have found wide application in the communication and kindred arts. The fields of use include radio, television, hearing aids, telephone switching, ballistics, and electronic computers.

323. Ferroelectricity. A number of crystals exhibit dielectric properties that are somewhat analogous to the magnetic properties of ferromagnetic substances; because of this analogy such crystals are classified as *ferroelectric*, but they have nothing to do with iron. These materials have astonishingly high dielectric coefficients, § 280, relative to vacuum (or air). Just as a ferromagnetic substance yields a hysteresis loop when magnetic flux density is plotted against magnetic field intensity over a cycle of values, § 264, so a ferroelectric substance yields a hysteresis loop when dielectric displacement is plotted against electric field intensity over a cycle of values. Fig. 314 illustrates the general shape of a ferroelectric loop, in which the ordinates represent the dielectric displacement D and the abscissas the electric field intensity ε.

By definition, a ferroelectric crystal is one that exhibits spontaneous electric polarization; this means that the centers of positive and negative charge do not coincide even in the absence of an electric field. Spontaneous polarization exists only in a definite temperature interval, the extent and location of which vary for different materials.

In a ferroelectric crystal not subjected to an external electric field, there are numerous regions that are polarized in different directions; these regions are called ferroelectric domains by analogy with ferromagnetic domains. The characteristic property of a ferroelectric substance is that the direction of polarization of the domains can be changed by applying an electric field. The opposition to orientation of the domains by such a field gives rise to the hysteresis loop.

Spontaneous polarization is accompanied by spontaneous mechanical strain, a behavior characteristic of the piezoelectric effect, § 312. All ferroelectric substances are piezoelectric, but only few piezoelectric crystals are ferroelectric; for example, quartz is piezoelectric but not ferroelectric.

The important ferroelectrics are Rochelle Salt ($NaKC_4H_4O_6 \cdot 4H_2O$), potassium dihydrogen phosphate (KH_2PO_4), a substance abbreviated as KDP, and barium titanate ($BaTiO_3$). Rochelle Salt is ferroelectric only between the temperatures of -18 and $+23°$ C, but beyond this range the crystal is piezoelectric. KDP is ferroelectric below $-150°$ C and is piezoelectric above and below this temperature. Barium titanate has three ferroelectric phases, one below $-80°$ C, another below $5°$ C, and a third below $120°$ C. All three of these crystals can be grown from their solutions.

The dielectric coefficients of ferroelectric crystals are generally high and are even higher at the transition temperatures. For example, with the electric field directed along the most favorable axis, the dielectric coefficient of barium titanate has peak values of about 3500 at $-80°$ C, 5500 at $5°$ C, and almost 10,000 at $120°$ C; above each of these transition temperatures the coefficient shows a rapid decrease, thus at $80°$ C its value is about 3500. Along the least favorable axis the values are still in the hundreds.

A study of the domain structures of ferroelectric crystals can be made with the polarizing microscope, § 436, since the materials are transparent and the refractive indices differ along the different axes. More detailed study is made possible by x-ray diffraction, § 429, and more recently by diffraction of neutrons.

Uses of ferroelectricity are foreseen in electronic and acoustical applications. As storage elements for computers, estimates indicate that ferroelectric substances could store over 2000 bits of information per square inch of material only a few mils thick, through potential pulses shorter than 1 microsec.

324. Photoconduction. The incidence of light upon a semiconductor can also cause electrons to be jolted out of the valence band into the conduction band. The resulting increase of charge carriers produces an increase of conductivity or, its equivalent, a decrease of resistivity. This response to radiant energy is called *photoconduction*. The difference between photoconduction and photoemission in the photoelectric effect, § 315, is that in photoconduction the electrons absorb sufficient energy from the light quanta or photons to enable them to cross the gap between the valence and conduction bands, whereas in photoemission they absorb enough energy to be liberated completely from the cathode into the surrounding vacuum where they can be collected by a suitable anode.

In pure photoconductors, radiant energy of proper wavelength liberates electrons and holes in equal numbers as long as the irradiation continues. The amount of energy associated with a photon of wavelength λ can be obtained by combining Eqs. 132 and 229, and is given by

$$E = \frac{hc}{\lambda}$$

where h is Planck's constant and c the speed of light. The values of these factors are respectively 6.62×10^{-34} joule·sec and 3×10^8 m/sec. For a wavelength of 1 micron $= 10^{-6}$ m, the energy is found to be 1.986×10^{-19} joule, or 1.24 electron·volts. Hence the threshold wavelength (least energy) for a given excitation process is

$$\lambda_m = \frac{1.24}{E_d} \tag{235}$$

in microns, where E_d is the energy difference between the edges of the valence and conduction bands of a pure semiconductor, or between an impurity state and either band edge, expressed in electron·volts.

The sensitivity of a photoconductor is the ratio of the number of carriers that pass through the semiconductor to the number of photons absorbed, both per unit time. Its value depends upon the mobility of the carriers, the electric field applied to the semiconductor, and the effective lifetime of the carriers before they recombine or are trapped. The lifetimes of free electrons and holes are independent of one another and quite different; their values are important characteristics of photoconductors.

In pure germanium and silicon, photoconduction extends through the entire visible spectrum and into the near infrared region; with impurities the response goes farther into the far infrared region. At present the most sensitive and most rapid detectors of infrared radiation are photoconductive cells with lead salts; at room temperature lead sulfide (PbS) is effective between 1 and 3 microns, and at the low temperatures produced by dry ice or liquid air lead telluride (PbTe) is effective between 2 and 5 and lead selenide (PbSe) between 3 and 7 microns. In addition to studies on these lead salts, investigations are being conducted on the corresponding salts of cadmium and zinc, and also on "intermetallic" compounds that consist of two or more elements with a metallic character. Photoconductors are currently in use or are being developed for use in photocells for the measurement of light intensity, automatic headlight dimmers on automobiles, streetlight control, light amplification, and television camera pick-up.

Another photoeffect of semiconductors is the development of an emf upon exposure to light in devices called *photovoltaic cells.* Unlike photoelectric and photoconductive cells, photovoltaic cells do not require an external source of emf for their operation. They are typified by the barrier-layer cells of selenium and cuprous oxide, and are used principally for the measurement of light intensities, § 365. Recent progress in the direct conversion of light energy into electrical energy has resulted in the "solar battery" for operation in sunlight. It consists of series-connected wafers of silicon with a small amount of arsenic impurity (n-type), all covered with a very thin layer that has boron impurity (p-type); so far, 100 watts have been developed per square meter of silicon surface.

Still another photoeffect of present-day interest is *electroluminescence,* whereby a substance emits light due to the action of an electric field. The better substances for this effect are compounds in the sulfide phosphor family that have been specially treated, and the electric fields are alternating. The emission of light is cold and occurs from a multitude of tiny bright spots; the color can be changed by varying the frequency.

PROBLEMS

1. Specify (a) the positions of atoms marked d, e and f in Fig. 303 and (b) the plane that passes through atoms a, d and e.

2. Name the indices which specify three mutually perpendicular faces of a cubic crystal and give a sketch for each.

3. The unit cell of sodium chloride is shown in the diagram in which the dots represent the Na^+ ions and the circles the Cl^- ions, or vice versa. In this crystal the shortest distance between any two ions is 2.83×10^{-8} cm.

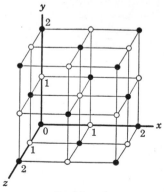

Problem 3

Find the distance between adjacent planes designated as (100) and between those designated as (120).

4. Estimate the number of electronic carriers that are present per cubic centimeter in silicon at room temperature.

5. Show that Eq. 234 for conductivity is consistent with Ohm's Law.

6. Show that for small values of the Hall angle the mobility of charge carriers can be expressed as the ratio of this angle to the magnetic flux density.

7. If 10^{-3} mg of antimony is melted together with 50 gm of germanium, how many atoms of antimony will exist as an impurity in a cubic centimeter of the ingot? Take the density of germanium as 5.36 gm/cm^3. The atomic weights of germanium and antimony are respectively 72.60 and 121.76.

8. Specify the positions of the four interior atoms of the unit cell of germanium (or silicon) and make a sketch of their locations.

9. Calculate the conductivity of the ingot mentioned in Prob. 7 on the assumption that the donor electrons from the antimony atoms are all effective in conduction and that their mobility is 0.36 m^2/(volt·sec).

10. Estimate the direct-current and dynamic resistances of the varistor having the characteristic curve shown in Fig. 310 for the operating condition represented by point P.

11. The accompanying diagram shows the elementary circuit for three-phase power conversion to direct current with six selenium rectifiers. If an output of 25 kw at 120 volts is required, what is the effective value of the si-

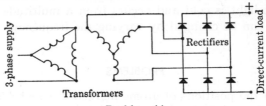

Problem 11

nusoidal currents in the secondary windings of the transformer? Neglect losses. *Hint.* Sketch the three half-waves of current to proper phase and estimate the average value of their sum.

12. What are the threshold energy values for photoconduction in lead sulfide, lead telluride, and lead selenide?

30

WAVE MOTION

325. Some Types of Waves. In the study of wave motion it will become apparent that waves are of many kinds and of common occurrence. Water waves sweep across the surface of the ocean; distortional waves surge to and fro within vibrating bodies; sound waves carry tones and noises through the air; and electromagnetic waves provide radio and television programs, and transmit light and x-rays.

Probably everyone has thrown a stone into quiet water and watched an ever-widening circular wave spread over the surface from the point of impact. The water does not move as a whole, but some particular configuration of the surface does. To set up such a configuration the individual particles of water move in transmitting the wave, but their motion takes place over rather short paths. Another example of wave propagation is the motion of a disturbance along a rope stretched horizontally. If the rope is pulled taut and the hand is moved up suddenly and then back again, a wave starts along the rope. When launched in this way, the wave consists practically of only one crest, and is called a *single-pulse wave*. If the hand is moved up and down repeatedly, going through the same motion each time, a train of waves is set up in the rope. These waves repeat themselves in equal intervals of time and are called *periodic waves*. Unless specially mentioned, all the waves to be studied herein are of this kind.

The motion of the prongs of a tuning fork sets up periodic waves in the surrounding air. Each forward movement of a prong compresses the air in front of it, and each backward movement rarefies the air. These conditions are transmitted outward from the fork as a wave disturbance comprising so-called *condensations* and *rarefactions*. Upon entering the ear, these waves produce the sensation of sound, and the waves themselves are called sound waves.

Waves can be produced by vibrations other than those of material particles. The current in the antenna circuit of a radio station sets up a magnetic field and an electric field in the region around it. As the current oscillates, these fields continually rise and fall, and in so doing set up electromagnetic waves that spread outward from the antenna. These waves are not transmitted by motion of air particles but by changes in the magnetic and electrical conditions of space.

Most waves can be classified as either longitudinal or transverse. A *longitudinal wave* is one in which the vibrating particles move forward and backward parallel to the direction in which the wave is propagated. The sound wave produced by the tuning fork already alluded to is longitudinal. A *transverse wave* is one in which the particles vibrate at right angles to the direction of propagation. The wave moving along the rope previously mentioned is transverse. Electromagnetic waves of all types act as transverse waves in which the vibration of physical particles is replaced by variations in electric and magnetic fields.

The progress of a wave involves two distinct motions. The particles of the medium that conveys the wave vibrate to and fro with harmonic motion, their locations at successive moments depending upon the period, amplitude, and phase of vibration. The wave itself, in a homogeneous medium and for moderate particle amplitudes, moves forward with constant speed, which means that the configuration advances equal distances in equal periods of time. The terms mentioned have been used in the study of harmonic motion; their definitions are restated below, together with those of some other terms commonly used in wave motion.

The *period* of a vibrating particle is the time in which it completes one vibration, and the *frequency* is the number of vibrations completed per second. The *amplitude* of vibration is the maximum displacement from the undisturbed position. Two particles vibrating with the same frequency have definite *phase relations*. They are in phase when they pass through corresponding points of their paths at the same instant. Otherwise, they are out of phase; for the particular condition in which they reach their maximum displacements in opposite directions at the same instant, they are in phase opposition. The *wavelength* is the distance measured along the direction of propagation between two points that are in phase on adjacent waves.

326. The Mechanism of Wave Propagation. The process by which a wave advances through a medium will be explained by reference to a mechanical model, Fig. 315. The medium is pictured as a long coiled spring with small masses distributed along its length, the small masses A, B, $C \cdots$ representing the vibrating particles. The spring is fastened at the far end, and particle A at the near end is given harmonic motion along the path 0–1–2–0. As a result, the particles are set into vibration one after another, and a wave travels along the spring.

During the time that particle A is moving up to position 1, particle B is pulled upward by the spring tension, and proceeds in that direction, as shown in part I of the figure. Because of its inertia, B continues to move upward when A reverses its direction. As A moves to 2, a downward force acts on B which soon arrests its upward motion and causes it to move down. The same behavior is repeated at the lower end of the path, and it follows that B has the same kind of motion as A, but reaches a corresponding point

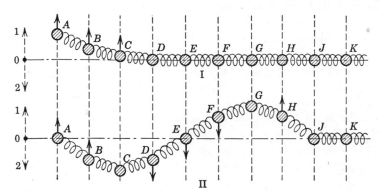

FIG. 315.   Mechanical wave model and transverse wave

of the path a little later than A does. As a consequence of the inertia of the particles and the elasticity of the spring, similar motion is imparted successively to all parts of the spring, and the particles reach their maximum displacements in the sequence $A, B, C \cdots$, causing the wave to advance toward the right. At the instant when A has been given one complete vibration the wave has advanced to J, and the wave along the spring has a crest at G and a trough at C, as indicated by the displacements in part II of the figure.

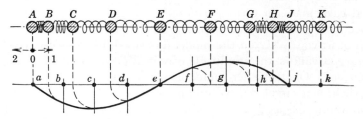

FIG. 316.   Longitudinal wave in wave model. Lower curve shows this wave in transverse form

The same model also serves to illustrate the motion of a longitudinal wave, as represented in Fig. 316. Motion of A toward the right compresses the spring and motion toward the left extends it, giving B the same kind of motion as A, except for a slight lag in phase. Similarly, B produces a corresponding motion of C, and so on. There results a series of condensations, in which the particles are close together, separated by rarefactions in which they are farther apart; both configurations move to the right and constitute the advancing wave. In the condensations, the particles move in the same direction as the wave, while in the rarefactions they move in the opposite direction. The wave in the spring has advanced to J at the instant shown in the figure.

In a longitudinal wave, the wave form is not apparent, but may be made so by laying off the displacements of the particles at right angles to the direction in which they actually occur. Such a construction is shown at the bottom of the figure. In this diagram the normal rest positions of the particles are indicated by corresponding lower-case letters and the displacements along the axis are shown turned through 90° by means of arcs centered at these points.

From the behavior of the mechanical wave model, some general inferences can be made. Wave motion is not due to bodily transfer of the medium through which the wave advances. It is caused by vibrations of individual particles over short ranges about normal rest positions, all the particles having the same kind of motion, but with a progressive change of phase along the direction of propagation. Moreover, mechanical wave motion requires that the transmitting medium possess both elasticity and inertia; for electromagnetic waves these properties are replaced by their electrical equivalents, permittivity and permeability, §§ 196 and 206.

327. Energy Transmission by Waves. Waves transmit energy along the direction of propagation. This fact can be illustrated by the mechanical model of Figs. 315 and 316 which shows waves progressing to the right. For either type of wave, each section of the spring exerts a force on the masses at its ends, and the masses at the right move in the direction of this force, but those at the left move in opposition to it. Each spring section thus *does work on the mass ahead of it* and *has work done upon it by the mass behind it*, § 61, and each mass, in turn, performs a similar action on the adjoining spring sections. Hence, a continuous transfer of energy takes place in the direction of wave travel. In the model described, if no energy were wasted as the wave advances, the amplitude of vibration would be the same for all of the masses. On the other hand, in a wave that spreads out as it advances, such as a circular wave on the surface of water, the amplitude of vibration diminishes as the wave progresses, since the energy is distributed over a larger and larger circle. The energy of a wave can be transformed in various ways; for example, that of a sound wave can be converted into mechanical energy in setting the ear drum into vibration.

When a wave encounters a medium of a different character, some of its energy is *reflected* back into the initial medium, and the rest is *transmitted* into the second medium; also, as the wave advances, part of its energy is *absorbed*. For a light wave which impinges upon a sheet of glass, most of the energy is transmitted to the region beyond the glass, part being returned by reflection at the surfaces and a small portion being absorbed within the glass itself. When a light wave strikes black velvet, no light is reflected from it nor transmitted through it; the energy is absorbed by the velvet and its temperature is raised.

328. Equations of Wave Motion. The relationship between the frequency of vibration of the source, the speed of propagation of the wave, and the wavelength in the medium, § 188, is applicable to all wave motion.

A vibrating body completes one vibration in the periodic time T, and the wave meanwhile advances uniformly a distance equal to its wavelength λ; hence the speed of the wave is $v = \lambda/T$. But the period T is the reciprocal of the frequency f, and thus the speed is

$$v = f\lambda \tag{236}$$

The speed v of the wave is determined completely by the properties of the transmitting medium. For a given speed it follows that whenever f changes a corresponding change takes place in λ to satisfy the equation.

To consider the relation between wave propagation and the motion of the particles in the transmitting medium, a source is imagined to vibrate with frequency f and to have an amplitude r; its displacement at any instant is given by the expression

$$y_s = r \sin 2\pi ft$$

where t is the time reckoned from the instant when the vibrating source passes through the midposition of its path in a positive direction. A particle in the medium at a point distant x from the source duplicates the displacement of the source, but first the wave must reach that point, and part of the time t in the equation is taken up in this manner. The time occupied by the wave in traveling a distance x at a speed v is x/v, and consequently the displacement of a particle in the medium at a distance x from the source is

$$y_p = r \sin 2\pi f\left(t - \frac{x}{v}\right) \tag{237}$$

in which t is still reckoned from the instant when the vibrating source passes the midposition of its path. This equation is valid for a wave that is propagated along a single line, such as one set up in a stretched cord; for a wave that spreads out, like a water wave or sound wave, the displacements are naturally reduced as the wave advances.

The wave equation, Eq. 237, shows how the displacement of the vibrating particles varies with respect to their locations and also with respect to time. If a particular value for t is selected and the values of y for different values of x are plotted, a sine wave is obtained which represents a snapshot of the wave in space; if this process is repeated for a slightly greater value of t, it will be found that the whole wave profile has moved away from the source. The equation therefore represents a traveling wave.

To learn how the displacement of a particle of the medium varies from moment to moment, a particular value for x is selected to represent the distance of the particle from the source, and then y is plotted against t. This also yields a sine curve and represents the harmonic vibration of the particle in the medium with respect to time.

329. Wave in a Stretched Rope. The speed of a transverse wave in a stretched rope is determined by the mass of the rope per unit length and the force or tension with which the rope is stretched. To show how these quantities are related, consideration will be given to a long taut rope that is subjected to a blow at one place, thereby producing a dent having the shape shown in Fig. 317. The displacement sets up a distortional wave that tra-

FIG. 317. For calculating speed of wave in a rope

vels along the rope with a speed v, substantially retaining the shape of the dent in its forward motion. To keep this dent stationary in space, the rope can be imagined to be propelled with the same speed v in the opposite direction. With this artifice, successive sections of the rope move around the curve; perhaps the reader has observed the maintenance of such shapes in the movement of belts between pulleys. The force acting upon the curved section of the rope can be evaluated if the dent, or a small part of it, is regarded as circular, for the force then becomes the centripetal force of circular motion.

In part I of the figure, the short central portion of the dent Δl is considered as a circular arc of radius r subtending an angle $\Delta\theta$ at the center. If this portion of the rope has a mass Δm, the centripetal force acting upon it is $F = \dfrac{\Delta m v^2}{r}$, and is provided jointly by the forces SS, each representing the stretching force in the rope. These forces are laid off from a common point P in part II of the figure, and since $\Delta\theta$ is very small, it follows as a close approximation that $F:S = \Delta l:r$, whence

$$\frac{\Delta m v^2}{rS} = \frac{\Delta l}{r} \qquad \text{or} \qquad v^2 = \frac{S}{\dfrac{\Delta m}{\Delta l}}$$

If the mass of the rope per unit of its length, namely, $\dfrac{\Delta m}{\Delta l}$, is designated as

m_1, the expression for the speed of the rope and its equivalent, the speed of the wave along the rope, becomes

$$v = \sqrt{\frac{S}{m_1}} \qquad (238)$$

In metric units, S is expressed in dynes, m_1 in grams per centimeter, and v in centimeters per second. In British units, S is in pounds, m_1 in slugs per foot, and v in feet per second.

Illustrative Problem

Suppose a distortional wave to be established in a 40-ft rope that weighs 5 lb and that it is stretched with a force of 50 lb. Find the speed of the wave, and the time in which it travels the length of the rope.

The mass of the rope is $\frac{5}{32}$ slug, and the mass per unit length is $(\frac{5}{32})/40 = \frac{1}{256}\ \frac{\text{slug}}{\text{ft}}$. Since the slug as a unit of mass can be expressed as $\frac{\text{lb} \cdot \text{sec}^2}{\text{ft}}$, § 34, the wave speed is

$$v = \sqrt{\frac{50\ \text{lb}}{\dfrac{1}{256}\ \dfrac{\text{lb} \cdot \text{sec}^2}{\text{ft}^2}}} = 113.1\ \frac{\text{ft}}{\text{sec}}$$

The time taken for the wave to travel 40 ft is 40 ft ÷ 113.1 ft/sec = 0.354 sec.

330. Propagation of Sound. The longitudinal waves transmitting sound do not pass through a vacuum. This fact can be demonstrated by operating an electric bell within a transparent chamber from which the air has been exhausted; the hammer can be seen striking the bell but no sound can be heard. The physical medium required for the propagation of sound may be a solid, liquid, or gas. Consideration will first be given to propagation within a liquid, and the analysis will show that the velocity is determined by the elasticity and density of the medium. The expression for this velocity is found by comparing the pressure of the medium and the velocity of the particles within a condensation with the same properties in the undisturbed medium, and evaluating the force that produces the change of motion.

Fig. 318 pictures a longitudinal wave, represented by vertical lines, advancing with a velocity v toward the left through a liquid medium. The liquid is assumed to have a constant cross-section. Rarefactions are shown at R and R', and condensations at C and C'; at point N just ahead of the foremost condensation the medium is as yet undisturbed by the wave. It will be remembered that in a condensation the vibrating particles are moving in the same direction as the wave; consequently the medium at C has some velocity v' toward the left when that at N is at rest, as indicated at the top of the figure. Also, it is evident that the pressure is greater at C than at N, since C is at a condensation. In what follows, the conditions at these two points will be considered in further detail.

It will be imagined that the liquid as a whole is moving with the same velocity v as the wave but in the opposite direction, so that the rarefactions and condensations remain stationary with respect to the surroundings. If t is the time in which the liquid stream flows from N to C, then in this time interval a certain mass m of liquid passes N at a velocity v and an equal mass passes C at a reduced velocity, namely, $v - v'$, as indicated at the bottom of the figure; the reduction of velocity will be called $-\Delta v$. Since the mass m of liquid undergoes a velocity reduction $-\Delta v$ in time t, it has an

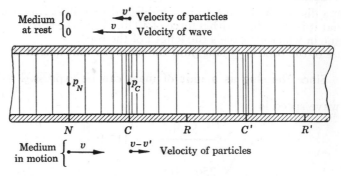

FIG. 318. For determining velocity of longitudinal wave in a fluid

average negative acceleration equal to $-\Delta v/t$. The reduction in velocity can be attributed to the fact that the pressure at C is greater than that at N. If these pressures are denoted respectively by p_C and p_N, and the cross-sectional area of the liquid by A, then the backward force acting upon the liquid at C is $p_C A$, and is greater than that urging it forward at N, namely, $p_N A$. The resultant force acting on the liquid under consideration is $p_C A - p_N A$ or $A\,\Delta p$, where Δp represents the pressure difference $p_C - p_N$. Then, from Newton's Second Law,

$$A\,\Delta p = m\left(\frac{-\Delta v}{t}\right)$$

The mass m can be evaluated by considering the liquid passing point N, where the density of the undisturbed medium is d. The volume of liquid passing this point in time t is Avt by Eq. 94, and hence its mass is $m = Avtd$. If this value is substituted in the foregoing equation there results:

$$A\,\Delta p = Avtd\left(\frac{-\Delta v}{t}\right)$$

whence

$$vd = \frac{-\Delta p}{\Delta v} \quad \text{or} \quad v^2 d = \frac{-\Delta p}{\Delta v/v}$$

The equation will be modified further by expressing the denominator in terms of volume V rather than velocity v. The liquid which at N would occupy a volume $V = Avt$ is compressed by an amount $-\Delta V = At(-\Delta v)$ upon reaching C. In consequence $\dfrac{-\Delta V}{V} = \dfrac{At(-\Delta v)}{Avt} = \dfrac{-\Delta v}{v}$, and

$$v^2 d = \frac{-\Delta p}{\Delta V / V} = B$$

where B is the bulk modulus of elasticity of the liquid, § 99. Hence the velocity of the liquid and consequently that of the wave become

$$v = \sqrt{\frac{B}{d}} \tag{239}$$

In metric units, B is expressed in dynes per square centimeter, d in grams per cubic centimeter, and v in centimeters per second. Similarly, in British units, B is in pounds per square foot, d in slugs per cubic foot, and v in feet per second.

The foregoing treatment may also be applied to the transmission of sound along a solid rod. The result will be the same as that just obtained except that B becomes Young's modulus of the medium rather than its bulk modulus.

331. Velocity of Sound in Gases. The method used in the preceding section for finding the velocity of a sound wave in a liquid which resulted in the equation $v = \sqrt{\dfrac{B}{d}}$ can also be used when the medium is gaseous. In order to interpret the elastic modulus B, it becomes necessary to inquire how the volume V of the gas is affected by changes in the pressure p. If the temperature remains constant during compression and expansion, then in accordance with Boyle's Law, § 129, a change of pressure Δp causes a change of volume ΔV such that

$$pV = (p + \Delta p)(V + \Delta V)$$

The small $\Delta p\, \Delta V$ product is negligible, whence $p\, \Delta V = -V\, \Delta p$, or $p = \dfrac{-\Delta p}{\Delta V / V} = B$. Hence if the compressions and expansions are isothermal the velocity of the wave is $v = \sqrt{p/d}$.

In the passage of a sound wave, the medium undergoes compression and expansion at a rapid rate, up to thousands of times each second. Although the gaseous medium is warmed in the condensations and cooled in the rarefactions, very little heat is conducted between these regions, and the compressions and expansions are found to be adiabatic rather than isothermal, throughout the audible range of the ear. In an adiabatic process, the pressure change Δp corresponding to a given volume change ΔV is γ times as great as for an isothermal process, where γ represents the ratio of the specific heats c_p/c_v, § 165. Hence, for such a process

$$\frac{\Delta p}{p} = \gamma \frac{\Delta V}{V}$$

and the modulus of elasticity B in Eq. 239 should be replaced by γp. Consequently the velocity of a sound wave in gases becomes

$$v = \sqrt{\frac{\gamma p}{d}} \tag{240}$$

the units being the same as before; see also § 353. For air under standard pressure and at a temperature of 0° C the value of γ is 1.40 and the values of p and d are given in Chap. 13; from these it is found that sound travels at a velocity

$$v = \sqrt{1.40 \times 1,013,000 \, \frac{\text{dynes}}{\text{cm}^2} \div 0.001293 \, \frac{\text{gm}}{\text{cm}^3}} = 33,130 \text{ cm/sec}$$

The velocity or speed of sound in the atmosphere is unaffected by changes in the barometric pressure because the density is changed in the same proportion, thereby leaving the ratio p/d unchanged. Changes in the temperature of the atmosphere, however, affect the density without markedly influencing the pressure, and hence cause a change in the speed of the wave. An inspection of the General Gas Law, Eq. 113, shows that the density of a gas varies inversely with its absolute temperature T. From this fact, and from Eq. 240, it follows that $v \propto \sqrt{T}$. Consequently, for two temperature conditions 1 and 2, the ratio of the speeds of sound becomes

$$\frac{v_1}{v_2} = \sqrt{\frac{T_1}{T_2}} \tag{241}$$

For calculations in which the effect of temperature is of no interest, the speed of sound in air may be taken in round numbers as 1100 ft/sec.

Values of the speed of sound in several mediums are given in the following table.

332. Water Waves. In surface waves, like those observed on water, the particles transmitting the disturbance move longitudinally as well as transversely. When the liquid is deep, the speed of wave propagation depends upon the gravitational force on the liquid and upon its surface tension; it can be shown by extended analysis that the equation for the speed is

$$v = \sqrt{\frac{g\lambda}{2\pi} + \frac{2\pi T}{\lambda d}}$$

SPEED OF SOUND

Medium	Tempera-ture, °C	Speed	
		meters/sec	feet/sec
Air................	0	331.3	1,087
Aluminum.........	..	5,100	16,700
Copper............	..	3,970	13,000
Hydrogen..........	0	1,286	4,220
Iron and steel.......	..	4,900 to 5,100	16,000 to 16,700
Lead..............	..	1,230	4,040
Water.............	15	1,450	4,760

where g is the acceleration due to gravity, T the surface tension, d the density of the liquid, and λ the wavelength. For long waves in shallow liquids the speed of the wave is found to depend upon the depth h rather than the wavelength λ, and is expressed by the equation

$$v = \sqrt{gh}$$

indicating that the speed is independent of the surface tension of the liquid.

333. Electromagnetic Waves. Although many waves are transmitted by the mechanical vibration of physical particles, there are others in which the propagation is due to periodic variations in electric and magnetic fields; these are called electromagnetic waves. In the study of Electricity and Magnetism, the relation that exists between the speed of electromagnetic waves in free space and its permittivity ϵ_0 and permeability μ_0 was stated in § 251. Expressed in equation form, the speed is

$$c = \frac{1}{\sqrt{\epsilon_0 \mu_0}}$$

Similarly, in any other medium of permittivity ϵ and permeability μ the speed of propagation of electromagnetic waves is given by

$$v = \frac{1}{\sqrt{\epsilon \mu}} \tag{242}$$

With mks units in these equations the permittivity is expressed in coulombs per volt·meter and the permeability in newtons per ampere². The numerical values of the constants for free space in these units are $\epsilon_0 = \dfrac{1}{4\pi 9 \times 10^9}$

(very nearly) and $\mu_o = 4\pi 10^{-7}$. Hence

$$c^2 = \frac{4\pi 9 \times 10^9}{4\pi 10^{-7}} \frac{\text{volt} \cdot \text{m}}{\text{coulomb}} \frac{\text{amp}^2}{\text{newton}} = 9 \times 10^{16} \frac{\text{m}^2}{\text{sec}^2}$$

and the speed of the waves becomes $c = 3 \times 10^8$ m/sec, which corresponds to 186,000 mi/sec. These values apply to a vacuum, but can also be used for air without appreciable error. The coincidence of this speed with the measured speed of light led Maxwell to conclude initially that light is propagated by electromagnetic waves.

The various kinds of electromagnetic waves are listed in the order of their wavelength ranges in the accompanying table. These waves are all of the same character and differ only in frequency and wavelength.

THE ELECTROMAGNETIC SPECTRUM

Type of Wave	Wavelength
Radio, low frequency.............	30,000 to 600 m
Radio, broadcast frequency........	600 to 200 m
Radio, high frequency.............	200 to 0.3 m
Radio, microwaves...............	30 to 0.08 cm
Infrared light...................	0.08 to 7.5×10^{-5} cm
Visible light....................	7.5×10^{-5} to 3.8×10^{-5} cm
Ultraviolet light.................	3.8×10^{-5} to 0.1×10^{-5} cm
X-rays........................	10^{-6} to 10^{-10} cm
Gamma rays...................	3×10^{-9} to 5×10^{-11} cm

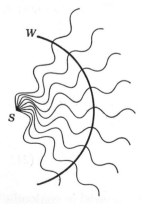

FIG. 319. Wave from point source and trace of spherical wave front

334. Wave-Front Construction; Huygens' Principle. In the passage of waves within the same or different mediums, or in the reflection of waves at boundaries, a useful concept is that of *wave front*, defined as a surface of which all points are vibrating in phase. Fig. 319 illustrates a wave spreading outward from a source S, and the line W represents a wave front connecting particles of the medium which are momentarily at their greatest distances in a positive direction from the undisturbed positions. In a homogeneous medium the wave front from a point disturbance is spherical; however, at considerable distances from the source, small portions of such a wave front may be regarded as plane. By studying the changes in wave front that occur as a wave advances, it is possible to predict the effects that are produced when a wave encounters an obstruction or enters another medium. This study is greatly assisted by use of a principle accredited to the Dutch scientist Christian Huygens (1629–1695).

Huygens' Principle states that *every point on a wave front acts as though it were itself a center of disturbance, sending out little wavelets of its own, always away from the source, the collective effect of which constitutes a new wave front.*

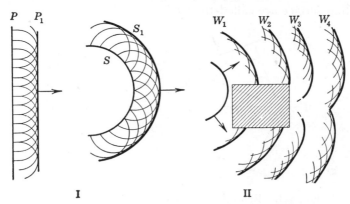

FIG. 320.   Progress of wave shown by Huygens' construction

These wavelets may be represented by arcs of equal radius drawn from various points on a given wave front as centers, the radius representing the distance the wavelets advance in some specified time. A line or surface tangent to these arcs on the side toward which the wave is advancing shows the new shape and location of the wave front at the end of the time interval selected.

This construction is applied in part I of Fig. 320 to a plane wave front P and to a spherical wave front S, both advancing toward the right to new positions at P_1 and S_1 respectively. The progression of a wave around an obstruction is illustrated in part II of the figure. The same procedure is followed in constructing the successive wave fronts W_1 to W_4, but the time intervals between them are purposely made different.

335. Law of Reflection.   The behavior of a wave upon striking a plane reflecting surface can be determined by Huygens' construction. In Fig. 321, a plane wave front represented in cross-section by the line AB is shown impinging upon the surface MN, through which it cannot pass. If this surface had not been present, the wave would have advanced without change in direction, and in a certain time interval would have reached the position CD. The presence of the reflecting surface, however, causes a change in the direction of the wave front. In the particular time interval, different points on the wave front proceed as follows: B advances directly to D; A cannot advance to C and travels an equal distance above the surface to some point on the arc CQ of radius AC; and any other point E advances without obstruction to F and, being unable to continue to G, travels an equal distance to some point on the arc of radius FG. The line DH tangent to the arcs is a cross-section of the wave front at the end of the specified time, the wave being reflected back into the region above the surface MN.

The line AB represents the incident wave front and DH represents the reflected wave front. The angles i and r that these wave fronts make with the reflecting surface are called the angles of incidence and of reflection re-

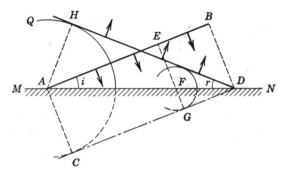

Fig. 321.   Reflection of plane waves at plane surface

spectively. To show the relation between these angles, it is helpful to draw the radius AH to the point of tangency H. Since $BD = AC = AH$, the right triangles ADH and DAB are equal, and consequently the angles i and r are equal. These angles are also coplanar, since the points A, B, D, and H lie in the same plane. These facts are embodied in the *law of reflection* which is symbolized

$$i = r \tag{243}$$

and states that, *when a wave incident upon a plane surface is reflected, the angles of incidence and of reflection are equal and lie in the same plane.*

336. Law of Refraction. A wave that enters another medium obliquely undergoes an abrupt change in direction if the velocity of the wave in the second medium is different from that in the first. This phenomenon is called *refraction.* In Fig. 322, the incident wave front AB, moving with velocity v_1 in medium 1, encounters the interface MN at an angle of incidence i. Here the wave is partly reflected back into medium 1 and partly transmitted through medium 2, the latter traveling with velocity v_2. In the time required for B on the wave front to advance in the first medium a distance BD to the interface at D, point A does not advance an equal distance to C, but travels a distance $(v_2/v_1) \times AC = AH$ in the second medium to some point on the arc centered at A. Any other point E advances to F in the first medium and then travels a distance $(v_2/v_1) \times FG$ in the second medium to some point on the arc centered at F. The line DH drawn tangent to these arcs represents the refracted wave front at the end of this time interval, and the angle r which it makes with the interface is called the angle of refraction.

It was discovered by Willebrod Snell (1591–1626), Dutch astronomer and mathematician, that the ratio of the sine of the angle of incidence to the sine of the angle of refraction is constant for given homogeneous mediums. The relation between these angles is found by drawing the radius AH to the point

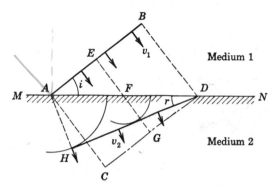

FIG. 322. Waves undergoing refraction at plane surface. Direction of wave changes abruptly at interface MN

of tangency H and comparing the triangles ABD and AHD. Since $\sin i = BD/AD$ and $\sin r = AH/AD$, it follows that

$$\frac{\sin i}{\sin r} = \frac{BD}{AH} = \frac{BD}{(v_2/v_1)BD}$$

or

$$\frac{\sin i}{\sin r} = \frac{v_1}{v_2} \tag{244}$$

This relation expresses the *law of refraction*, which states that, when a wave travels obliquely from one medium into another, the angles of incidence and refraction lie in the same plane and are so related that the *ratio of their sines is the same as the constant ratio of the respective wave velocities in these mediums*.

337. Interference of Waves. Two waves moving simultaneously through the same region advance independently, each producing the same disturbance of the medium as though it were alone. The combined action of both waves can be pictured by adding the ordinates of the component waves algebraically, point by point.

Two waves of the *same frequency, in phase with each other* and moving in the *same direction*, produce *reinforcement*. This result is shown in part I of Fig. 323, in which the individual waves are represented by A and B. The resultant wave R is in phase with the component waves and has an amplitude equal to the sum of their amplitudes.

Two waves of the *same frequency, in phase opposition* and moving in the *same direction,* produce *interference;* if, further, they have equal amplitudes, the result is a complete annulment. An annulment is represented in part II of the figure, the amplitude of the resultant R of the individual waves A and B being zero at all points. In the wave-front constructions in Figs. 321 and 322 the multiplicity of wavelets, typified by the two arcs in each diagram, also interfere with each other, and it can be shown that these wave-

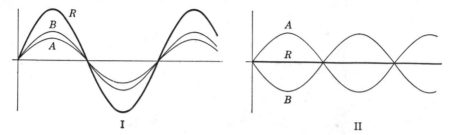

FIG. 323.   Interfering waves A and B and their resultant R; part I shows reinforcement and part II annulment

lets annul one another except at the outermost points where the envelope representing the new position of the wave front is located.

Two waves of *slightly differing frequencies* produce a type of *pulsating interference* which is particularly noticeable with sound waves. The resulting sound is alternately loud and soft, giving pulses or throbs which are spoken of as *beats.* The effect is most pronounced when the individual waves have equal amplitude. For example, two such waves A and B originate from vibrating sources at M in Fig. 324, and the frequency of the source generating

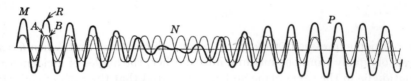

FIG. 324.   Production of musical beats by interfering sound waves. At the instant shown the sound is loud at M and P and weak at N

A is 1 vib/sec greater than that of B. Each source sets up a train of waves; these are indicated in the figure at a particular instant by their transverse representations, and their resultant is shown by wave R. At the instant shown, the sources are vibrating in phase, and the waves produce reinforcement at M and P and an annulment at N. At an instant $\frac{1}{2}$ sec later, the sources will be in phase opposition, and the waves A and B will be displaced with respect to each other by one-half wavelength from the positions shown, producing annulments at M and P and a reinforcement at N. At another instant $\frac{1}{2}$ sec later still, the sources once more vibrate in phase, and the relative positions of the waves are again as shown in the figure. These changes continually recur as long as the sources are kept in vibration. An observer at any point along the path *MNP* will notice a reinforcement and an annulment of sound each second, that is, he will hear 1 beat/sec. If the difference in frequency of the sources were d vib/sec, then at a given point, a reinforcement would change to an annulment and back to a reinforcement again in $1/d$ sec, and the observer would hear d beats/sec.

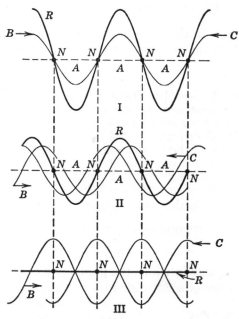

FIG. 325. Waves B and C moving in opposite directions produce the standing wave R. The stationary nodes are at N

338. Stationary Waves. Two waves of *equal frequency and amplitude*, moving in *opposite directions* through the same medium, produce a standing or *stationary wave*. Such a wave has stationary *nodes*, or points of zero displacement, with intermediate *antinodes* at which the displacement varies between its widest limits. In Fig. 325, B and C represent two such waves, B moving to the right and C to the left. In part I the component waves coincide, yielding a resultant R of double amplitude. In part II, representing the situation $\frac{1}{8}$ of a period later, both B and C have advanced $\frac{1}{8}$ wavelength in their respective directions; and in part III, for an instant $\frac{1}{8}$ period later still, a similar advance has occurred, bringing the component waves into opposition. As the waves progress, the nodes N of the resultant remain fixed in space $\frac{1}{2}$ wavelength apart, and the intervening antinodes A undergo a maximum variation of displacement.

The production of stationary waves can be demonstrated with a rope that is fastened to a wall at one end and moved transversely with appropriate frequency at the other end. The outgoing waves are reflected at the wall with little reduction of amplitude, and consequently the two wave trains set up a stationary wave in the rope. Fig. 326 illustrates the appearance

FIG. 326.   Appearance of stationary wave in stretched rope

when the rope vibrates in three segments with nodes at N, the rope whipping back and forth at the antinodes A.

Illustrative Problem

In an experiment devised by Franz E. Melde, stationary waves were produced in a string fastened to one prong of a vibrating tuning fork. Assume that the string is 90 cm long and has a mass of 0.1 gm, and that the fork is kept vibrating electrically at 264 vib/sec. Suppose the string to extend along the direction of the prong, and find the force with which it should be stretched in order that it may vibrate in three segments.

Since the length of each segment is 30 cm, the wavelength is 60 cm, and consequently the velocity of propagation is $264 \times 60 = 15,840$ cm/sec. The required stretching force in the string is found by Eq. 238 to be $S = m_1 v^2 =$
$$\frac{0.1 \text{ gm}}{90 \text{ cm}} \left(15,840 \frac{\text{cm}}{\text{sec}}\right)^2 = 279,000 \text{ dynes.}$$

Another interesting way in which the production of stationary waves can be illustrated makes use of a flat dish with mercury and a tuning fork with

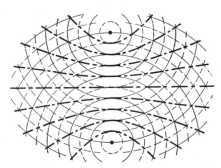

FIG. 327.   Interference pattern produced by surface waves on mercury

a stylus on each prong. When the fork is set into vibration and each stylus is brought in contact with the mercury, circular waves proceed along its surface outward from the points of contact. These are represented at some particular instant by the concentric circles in Fig. 327, the full lines representing the crests and the dotted ones the troughs. At points where full lines intersect or dotted lines intersect, the waves from the two sources meet in phase, and the disturbance of the surface by one source is reinforced by that of the other. Between these points, however, are intersections of full lines with dotted lines; these represent the meeting of a crest from one source with a trough from the other and are, therefore, points where interference occurs. The surface of the mercury is thus divided into regions of maximum disturbance (shown by the heavy lines), separated by lanes where the surface remains almost perfectly at rest.

PROBLEMS

1. The diaphragm of a loudspeaker vibrates back and forth and sets up a sound wave in the surrounding air. Consider the speed of the wave to be 1100 ft/sec, and compute its wavelength when the diaphragm vibrates 200 times a second.

2. A long cord, fastened to a fixed support at one end, is stretched horizontally and its free end is attached to a vibrator that moves up and down with a frequency of 2 vib/sec and an amplitude of 20 cm. As a result, a transverse wave travels along the cord at 120 m/sec. (*a*) What is the displacement of the vibrator from its midposition at an instant 0.1 sec after it passes through this position in an upward direction? (*b*) What is the displacement of a point on the cord 500 cm away from the vibrator at the same instant?

3. A catgut string 1.5 ft long weighs 0.1 oz and is stretched with a force of 75 lb between fixed supports at its ends. Find the speed of a transverse wave set up in the string.

4. If the cord in Prob. 2 has a length of 1000 cm and a mass of 1.5 gm, what stretching force is required (*a*) to produce the wave speed specified? (*b*) to produce double this speed?

5. A 25-ft rope weighing 0.5 lb is fastened to a wall at one end and is stretched horizontally with a force of 2 lb. A vibrator moves the free end of the rope up and down 20 times a second. Calculate the speed and wavelength of the transverse wave set up in the rope.

6. A rope having a mass per unit length of 2 gm/cm is fixed at one end and knotted at the other to a rope having a mass per unit length of 0.5 gm/cm. The ropes are subjected to a tensile force of 500,000 dynes and the free end is set into vibration at the rate of 10 vibrations every 4 sec. A wave (No. 1) travels from the vibrating source to the knot; at that point a wave (No. 2) is reflected back toward the source and a wave (No. 3) is transmitted onward in the larger rope. Determine the frequency, speed, and wavelength of each wave.

7. Find the time in which a longitudinal wave travels 1 km in sea water, on the assumption that the bulk modulus is the same as that of pure water.

8. A source of sound in air above a pool of water emits a wave having a frequency of 440 cycles/sec and a speed of 1100 ft/sec. State the frequency of the wave within the water, and calculate its speed and wavelength.

9. The heating effect of air friction in airplane travel is evidenced by a recent report which states that an airplane flying at Mach 2 in rarefied air at an elevation of 35,000 ft and a temperature of $-65°$ F will reach a skin temperature of $220°$ F. The "Mach number" is the ratio of the speed of an object to the speed of sound in the atmosphere through which it is moving. Compute the speed of the aircraft to which reference was made.

10. A steel rail is struck at a distant point and an observer with his ear to the rail hears two sounds, one transmitted through the rail and one through the air. If these sounds are 1.4 sec apart, how far from the observer was the rail struck? Take the speed of sound in steel as 16,000 ft/sec.

11. Give a consistent set of units for the quantities in the expression for for the speed of a wave on the surface of deep water.

12. A speech delivered in an auditorium is broadcast by radio at the

same time. Who will hear a given syllable first: a person in the auditorium 40 ft from the man giving the speech, or a person 500 mi away sitting 10 ft from his radio set? Compute the time of speech transmission in each instance.

13. What wavelength is used for the carrier frequency (*a*) in radio broadcasting at a frequency of 880 kilocycles/sec? (*b*) in video telecasting at a frequency of 67 megacycles/sec?

14. Our nearest star, α in the Centauri group, is 2.54×10^{13} mi distant from the earth. If this star is observed on Jan. 1, 1960, when did the star emit the light by which it is seen?

15. Moving machinery is made to appear stationary by a stroboscope: a device which illuminates the moving object by regularly recurring flashes of light of very short duration. A motor under observation in this manner has a spot painted conspicuously on its pulley, and is driven at 1800 rev/min. When illuminated by 1800 flashes/min the spot appears stationary and the motor seems at rest. With what velocity does the motor seem to rotate when the flashing rate is (*a*) 1795 flashes/min? (*b*) 1810 flashes/min?

16. A spoked wheel appears on a television screen; a person spins it and allows it to slow down. Explain why the wheel seems to turn one way at times and oppositely at other times while coming to rest.

17. An airplane in horizontal flight passes over an observer on the ground. At an instant when the observer hears the airplane directly above him he sees it along a line known to be inclined 20° from the vertical. Determine the speed of the airplane.

18. A man standing in a canyon with vertical parallel walls fires a rifle. If he hears the first echo after 1 sec and the next one $1\frac{1}{2}$ sec later, how wide is the canyon?

19. Two plane mirrors are placed edge to edge with their reflecting surfaces at right angles. A beam of light is directed upon one mirror at a point 4 cm from the meeting edges at an angle of incidence of 30° and is reflected by both mirrors, the incident and emergent beams being in the same plane. Sketch the path of the light, and compute the distance between the incident beam and the emergent beam.

20. A narrow beam of light directed downward at 40° with the vertical enters a tank of water within which its velocity is reduced to $\frac{3}{4}$ of its value in air. Determine the direction of the beam in the water.

21. A beam of light directed 55° from the vertical in air enters a horizontal plate of lucite, within which its direction is found to be 33° from the vertical. What is the velocity of light in lucite?

22. Two tuning forks placed side by side are set into vibration and produce 54 beats in 20 sec. One fork has a frequency of 264 vib/sec. Find two possible frequencies for the other fork.

23. With what frequency should the string of Prob. 3 be set into vibration in order that it may vibrate in 2 segments?

24. Refer to Prob. 5 and determine the distance between nodes in the stationary wave set up in the rope by reflection at the wall.

25. Two cords, each 100 cm long, are tied together and fastened between supports 200 cm apart. One cord has a mass of 1 gm and the other a mass of 4 gm. A transverse wave having a frequency of 20 cycles/sec is initiated in the cords and the stretching force is adjusted until a stationary wave is established with 2 nodes and 3 antinodes between the end supports. Compute the value of the stretching force, and make a sketch of the standing wave.

31

SOUND PRODUCTION

339. Characteristics of Sound. The term *sound* is used in two senses: subjectively, it signifies the auditory sensation experienced by the ear, and objectively, it signifies the vibratory motion which gives rise to that sensation. It is used in the latter sense in Acoustics, the subject that deals with the motion of vibrating bodies, the production and propagation of sound waves in different mediums, and the effect of discontinuities in the mediums. Some of these topics common to sound, light, and other types of waves are considered in the preceding chapter on Wave Motion; others, together with some of their applications, are discussed in this and the following chapter.

A variety of terms is employed in ordinary language to convey impressions of sounds; these include howl, whistle, squeal, rustle, rumble, and hum. Most of these are classed as *noises*, in contrast with sounds that are called musical *tones*. The distinction is based largely upon the regularity of vibration of the source and the degree of damping, as well as upon the ability of the ear to recognize components that have a musical sequence. The sound made by a stick when dropped upon a table top is definitely a noise, but when a number of sticks of appropriate lengths are dropped in suitable order the effect of musical tones may be produced. The complicated sounds of speech are formed by grouping the more-or-less sustained tones of vowels and the impulsive launching and quenching of these tones by the consonants.

The ear can distinguish tones that differ in *pitch*, in *loudness*, and in *quality*. Each of these characteristics is associated primarily with a single property of the sounding body or of the waves which it produces. Thus, *pitch is determined chiefly by the frequency of vibration, loudness by the intensity of the sound, and quality by the overtones present.* In Fig. 328 are several curves depicting both the shapes of sound waves and the characteristics of the vibrations which produce them. The sine curves A and B differ in frequency, B producing the tone of higher pitch. Curves A and C differ only in amplitude, A producing the louder sound. Curves A and D differ in shape, D having components of higher frequency that are not present in A; the curves represent sounds of different quality.

In general, the pitch of a tone is determined by the number of condensations and rarefactions received per second, and corresponds to the vibration frequency of the sounding source, although it is known that pitch is influenced somewhat by the intensity of the sound and by the presence of overtones. The relation between pitch and frequency can be shown experimentally by means of a siren consisting of a disk with regularly spaced holes through which air is blown gently. As the disk revolves the air stream is

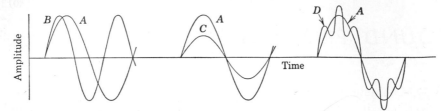

FIG. 328. Comparison of sound waves. *B* represents a higher pitch than *A*; *C* is softer than *A*; and *D* has a different quality

interrupted, and the resulting puffs in the medium become condensations and rarefactions, which are received by the ear. The rise in pitch with increased speed of the disk can be exhibited strikingly in this manner.

340. Intensity of Sound. The intensity of a sound is defined as the time rate of transfer of vibratory energy per unit of sectional area of the sound wave. To show that this intensity is dependent upon the amplitude and frequency of vibration of the sound, consideration will be given to a plane wave in which the vibrating particles have harmonic motion, and specifically to a layer of the medium that is thin enough so that all of the particles in it may be assumed to have equal displacements. If the layer has a thickness x and the medium a density d, then the medium in unit area of this layer has a mass $m = xd$. Furthermore, if the vibrating particles in this layer have a frequency f, a maximum displacement r at one moment, and a maximum velocity v' at another, then as explained in §§ 65 and 87, the maximum energy of the particles in the layer under consideration is

$$E_k = \frac{1}{2} m(v')^2 = \frac{xd}{2} (2\pi f r)^2$$

The energy of the layer is all of kinetic form as the particles sweep through their equilibrium positions and all of potential form when they have their maximum displacements; at other times they have some of each kind of energy, but the total is always as just expressed if losses are neglected. In consequence, the total energy per unit volume of the medium is

$$\frac{E_k}{x \times 1} = 2\pi^2 f^2 r^2 d \tag{245}$$

and may be termed the *energy density* of the wave. When metric units are employed this equation gives the energy in ergs per cubic centimeter. If the velocity of wave propagation is v cm/sec, the time rate of transmission of energy per unit of area of the wave front is v times the foregoing energy density, and this product becomes a measure of the physical intensity of the sound wave. Therefore, the *intensity* of the sound in ergs per second per square centimeter is

$$I = 2\pi^2 v f^2 r^2 d \tag{246}$$

This result shows that the intensity of a sound in a given medium is proportional to the square of the frequency of vibration as well as the square of the amplitude.

Eq. 246 for intensity was derived for a plane wave, but may also be applied to a spherical wave at a great distance from its source. At any distance from a point source, the intensity of the wave varies inversely as the square of that distance, in accordance with § 186. Reference to that section shows that intensity and flux density both express energy per unit time per unit area; hence the Inverse Square Law may be expressed as

$$\frac{I_1}{I_2} = \frac{R_2^2}{R_1^2} \tag{247}$$

where R_1 and R_2 represent any two distances from the source, and I_1 and I_2 the values of the intensity at these positions. It follows that the amplitude of vibration r varies inversely as the distance from the source.

As a sound wave advances, variations in pressure occur at all points in the transmitting medium. The greater the pressure variations, the more intense the sound wave; it can be shown that the intensity is proportional to the square of the pressure variation regardless of the frequency. Thus, by measuring pressure changes, the intensities of sounds having different frequencies can be compared directly, and instruments that make such measurements are preferred to those that measure amplitude.

341. Quality of Sound. The tones produced by tuning forks have wave shapes approximating the sine waves A, B, and C of Fig. 328 and are often referred to as pure tones. The tones produced by most sources can be represented by composite waves, in which the sound of lowest pitch, called the *fundamental*, is accompanied by overtones having frequencies 2, 3, 4, $\cdots$ n times that of the fundamental. Hermann L. F. Helmholtz (1821–1894), German physiologist and physicist, showed that the quality of a tone depends upon the number of overtones present, and upon their frequencies and intensities relative to the fundamental. It is this characteristic that distinguishes tones of like pitch and loudness when sounded on different types of musical instruments.

It is possible to produce a tone of any desired quality by combining pure tones in suitable proportions. Even the complicated vowel sounds can be duplicated by combining the pure tones of particular organ pipes. For example, Fig. 329 represents the compounding of three sine curves of different frequencies, the resultant curve at the bottom being obtained by adding the ordinates of the three at many points along the time axis. The resultant

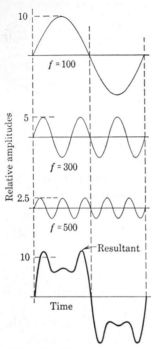

can also be expressed as the sum of three terms, each having the form given by Eq. 237; for the amplitudes and frequencies noted in the figure the equation of the resultant is

$$y = 10 \sin (2\pi 100t) +$$

$$5 \sin (2\pi 300t) + 2.5 \sin (2\pi 500t)$$

in which y is the instantaneous displacement of the resultant at any time t, reckoned from the origin.

The reverse process, namely that of resolving a sound wave into its components, can also be carried out. Curves of sound wave shapes can be obtained by an oscilloscope, § 299, actuated by a microphone. The sound waves striking the microphone set up corresponding electrical vibrations, and these are rendered visible upon the fluorescent screen of the instrument.

A mathematical analysis for determining the relative amplitudes and phases of the component pure tones is based upon a general principle stated by the French mathematician Jean B. J. Fourier (1768–1830), to the effect that any periodic function can be represented by a trigonometric series, the terms of which have frequencies

FIG. 329. Three component sine curves of a sound wave and their resultant

that are exact multiples of the fundamental frequency. By Fourier's analysis, any periodic wave form can be resolved mathematically into component sine curves, of definite amplitudes and phases, and having frequencies in the proportion 1, 2, 3, $\cdots$ n. Machines are available for determining the sinusoidal components of complicated wave shapes; they are called harmonic analyzers.

VIBRATING SYSTEMS

342. Strings. The bowing of a stretched string sets up disturbances which travel to its ends as waves and are there reflected. At either end of the string the incident and reflected waves have the same frequency and essentially the same amplitude and, since they move in opposite directions, they establish a stationary wave, § 338, forming nodes at intervals of one-half wavelength from that end of the string. The same effect is produced at the other end. As the reflected waves travel from end to end of the string repeatedly, the nodes produced by reflection from both ends coincide only for definite wavelengths. If the string were set vibrating with a multitude of frequencies at the same time, most of these vibrations would annul one another, and only a few would persist. These are called *free vibrations;* they are the ones for which the length of the string is an exact number of half wavelengths.

The free vibrations of a string are transverse and set up in the surrounding air condensations and rarefactions which proceed away from the string as a

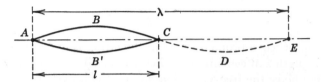

FIG. 330.   Loop formed by stretched string vibrating in fundamental mode

longitudinal sound wave. The tone heard by an observer has the same frequency as the vibration of the string.

The simplest mode of vibration of a string is that for which the ends of the string are the only nodal points, and the center is the only antinode. This condition, producing the fundamental tone of the string, is pictured in Fig. 330. Herein $ABCDE$ represents a sine wave of length λ, and AC represents the string of length l. During its vibration, the string travels periodically from its extreme upper position ABC to its extreme lower position $AB'C$, and forms a single loop which can be observed by the blurred pattern

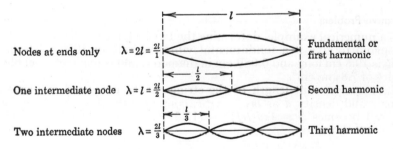

FIG. 331.   Three modes of vibration of a string

it makes. Thus, for the fundamental mode of vibration the string forms one loop and its length is a half wavelength.

The string may also vibrate at particular higher frequencies, depending upon the number of nodes between its ends. Fig. 331 illustrates the simpler modes of vibration, in which the string forms one, two, and three loops. The corresponding tones are called *harmonics.* In general, if the string of length

l vibrates in n loops, the wavelength of the nth harmonic is

$$\lambda = \frac{2l}{n} \qquad (248)$$

All harmonics may exist in a vibrating string.

The frequency of vibration of the string is obtained by combining Eq. 248 with the equation for the velocity of wave propagation, namely, $v = f\lambda$, where f is the frequency of vibration. Thus, the frequency of a vibrating string is

$$f = \frac{nv}{2l} \qquad (249)$$

If the velocity of wave propagation v in the string is in centimeters per second and its length l in centimeters, then f is in vibrations per second. For any vibrating body the free vibration having the lowest frequency is called the *fundamental* or *first harmonic*, a vibration having twice the frequency of the fundamental is called the *second harmonic*, and so on. To express the vibration rate of a string in terms of its physical constants, the foregoing equation may be combined with Eq. 238. The result gives the frequency in vibrations per second as

$$f = \frac{n}{2l} \sqrt{\frac{S}{m_1}} \qquad (250)$$

where n is the number of loops in the string of length l cm, S the stretching force of the string in dynes, and m_1 the mass of the string per unit of length in grams per centimeter.

Illustrative Problem

As a numerical example, determine the tensile force needed in the c' string of a piano to give it a fundamental vibration rate of 1056 vib/sec. The string is 19.3 cm long and 0.089 cm in diameter, and is made of steel having a density of 7.8 gm/cm^3.

The mass per unit length of the string can be expressed in terms of its radius r and density d as $m_1 = \pi r^2 d$; consequently the stretching force in Eq. 250 becomes $S = 4\pi d(lrf)^2 = (12.57)(7.8)(19.3 \times 0.0445 \times 1056)^2 = 8.07 \times 10^7$ dynes.

To verify Eq. 250 experimentally, use is made of a sonometer in which a string is mounted over a sounding board. One end of the string is rigidly fastened, and the other end passes over a pulley and carries a weight to provide the stretching force. By bowing the string at chosen places and by touching it lightly at appropriate points, the string can be set into vibration in a number of ways as illustrated by Fig. 331. The stretching force can be varied by altering the weight, and the length can be varied by shifting the movable bridges on which the string rests.

343. Rods and Plates. Rods and tubes can be set into longitudinal vibration by stroking them lengthwise with a small rosined pad. Free vibrations are thus produced, the possible modes of vibration depending upon the manner in which the rod is supported.

When the rod is supported at one end, the fundamental mode of vibration is characterized by a node at that end and an antinode at the other. This longitudinal vibration is shown at the top of Fig. 332 in the usual transverse fashion with a node at the left and an antinode at the right. The curves between these points form a half loop and the length of the rod is a quarter

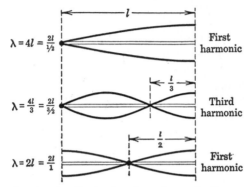

FIG. 332. Representing longitudinal vibration of a rod. In upper diagrams the rod is supported at left end; in lower diagram, at center of rod

wavelength; thus a full wavelength would extend over four rod lengths or $4l$. The next higher mode of vibration introduces an intermediate node, located two-thirds the way out from the fixed end as shown at the center of the figure, the wavelength being $4l/3$. The bottom diagram shows a rod supported at the center so as to form two half loops; the corresponding wavelength is $2l$. In general, if there are n loops, the wavelength of the vibration is $\lambda = \dfrac{2l}{n}$. Theory shows that these results are true only when the wavelength is very large in comparison with the thickness or width of the rod.

The frequency of longitudinal vibrations in a rod of length l cm for the fundamental mode is obtained from Eqs. 239 and 249 as

$$ f = \frac{n}{2l} \sqrt{\frac{Y}{d}} \tag{251} $$

where Y is Young's modulus of elasticity of the rod in dynes per square centimeter and d is its density in grams per cubic centimeter. A rod fixed at one end or at the center can give forth only the odd harmonics.

Transverse vibrations in a straight rod or bar are more complicated than longitudinal vibrations. It appears that when a transverse wave approaches the free end of the rod, reflection does not take place at exactly the end but at a place slightly farther away. As a result, the nodes within the rod are displaced from their normal positions, and the frequencies of the overtones are not exact multiples of the fundamental frequency. Again, if a rod, originally vibrating with two nodes, is imagined to be bent at the center until it assumes a U-shape, the nodes approach each other in the process and become so close together that the rod vibrates practically as two separate bars, each fixed at one end. Fig. 333 illustrates such a bent bar with a stem attached to the center to form a tuning fork, the nodes being indicated by *NN*. Transverse motions of the prongs *PP* cause an up-and-down motion in the stem *S*, and this motion can be arranged to impart vibration to a sounding board or to a column of air to intensify the sound produced by the fork. Tuning forks are usually made of steel, aluminum, or magnesium.

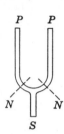

Fig. 333. Location of nodes in a tuning fork

The vibrations of plates can be investigated experimentally by supporting them horizontally at the center or edge, sprinkling fine sand upon them, and setting them into vibration by mechanical or electrical means. The sand particles will be seen to hop about and accumulate in places of least motion, thereby indicating a series of nodal lines. The diaphragms of telephone transmitters and receivers can be tested similarly.

A bell may be regarded as a combination of a plate and a cylinder, with relatively more metal near the center. Many overtones accompany the fundamental tone of a bell when it is struck, and it is the aim of bell-founders to attain certain relationships between the frequencies of the principal overtones.

344. Air Columns. Disturbances in air or other gaseous mediums are propagated as condensations and rarefactions in all directions in open space. When the medium has the form of a column within a rigid tube, a disturbance produced at one end travels to the other end, is there reflected, travels back to the initial end, is reflected again, and so on. The outgoing and reflected waves set up stationary waves in the gaseous column and one or more nodes are formed within the tube.

Fig. 334 illustrates how an air column can be set in vibration by a jet of

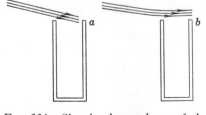

Fig. 334. Showing how column of air can be set in vibration

air impinging against one side of the tube at *a*. The condensation so produced travels down the tube, is reflected at the bottom, and returns to the upper end again; there it pushes the air jet aside as shown at *b*. The resulting rarefaction starts down the tube, is reflected at the bottom, and retraces its path; upon arrival at the top of the tube, the condition represented at a is restored. This process is repeated over and over again. The closed end of the tube becomes a node, the open end becomes an antinode, and the tube length constitutes a quarter wavelength for the fundamental mode of vibration.

A somewhat similar behavior is observed for a tube open at both ends; each condensation is reflected as a rarefaction and both tube ends become antinodes. When only one node is formed between these ends, the air col-

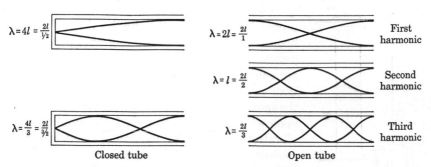

Closed tube   **Open tube**

Fig. 335. Harmonics of air columns in closed and open tubes. Closed tubes sound only the odd harmonics

umn vibrates in its fundamental manner, and the tube length constitutes a half wavelength.

Some harmonics produced by air columns and the relation between the wavelength λ and the length l of the column are indicated in Fig. 335. The frequencies of the various harmonics are given by

$$f = \frac{v}{\lambda} = \frac{nv}{2l}$$

where v is the speed of the sound wave in the gaseous medium and n is the number of loops formed by the vibrations. This equation is the same as Eq. 249. For closed tubes $n = \frac{1}{2}, \frac{3}{2}, \frac{5}{2}, \cdots$, while for open tubes $n = 1, 2, 3, \cdots$.

This equation is not quite correct, because reflection does not occur exactly in the plane of the open end but somewhat beyond it. With cylindrical tubes having a radius that is small in comparison with the wavelength, the plane of reflection may be taken as lying outside the tube by a distance about $\frac{6}{10}$ of the radius of the tube.

Illustrative Problem

As an example, determine the frequency of the fundamental tone of a tube 12 ft long and 6 in. in diameter. Assume the speed of sound in air to be $v = 1100$ ft/sec.

If the end correction is neglected, the frequency with the tube closed is $f = (\frac{1}{2} \times 1100 \text{ ft/sec}) \div (2 \times 12 \text{ ft}) = 22.9$ vib/sec; with it open, $f = (1 \times 1100 \text{ ft/sec}) \div (2 \times 12 \text{ ft}) = 45.8$ vib/sec. The end correction is

0.6 × 3 in. = 1.8 in. or 0.15 ft. The effective tube length is 12.15 when closed and 12.30 ft when open; hence, the corrected vibration frequencies are 22.6 and 44.7 vib/sec.

345. Resonance. The production of sound by some vibrating systems, such as strings, rods, and air columns, has been considered in the three preceding sections. These systems were assumed to be set into vibration without constraint to produce free vibrations, that is, vibrations having fre-

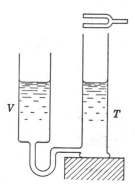

quencies determined entirely by the constants and properties of the vibrating bodies themselves. Such bodies may also be set in motion by periodic impulses imparted by outside agents; then the bodies are said to execute *forced vibrations*. When conditions are so adjusted that the forced vibrations have the same frequency as the free vibrations of the body upon which they are impressed, the amplitude of the vibrations is markedly increased, an effect known as *resonance*. When the impressed vibration has a different frequency from that of the free vibrations of a body, the received impulses sometimes help and sometimes hinder the free vibrations, and as a result do not affect the free vibrations appreciably.

FIG. 336. Acoustic resonance of air column with tuning fork

To demonstrate the phenomenon of resonance, a tuning fork may be held over an air column, as shown in Fig. 336. The level of the water in the cylindrical tube T can be varied by raising or lowering the communicating vessel V. Upon sounding the fork and altering the height of the air column, resonance is established when the sound is loudest. This experiment affords a simple means of determining the velocity of sound in air; in such a test a tuning fork of known frequency is used and the length of the column at resonance is measured.

Illustrative Problem

For example, a tuning fork vibrating 440 times per sec is held above an air column of adjustable length. Resonance is observed when the column is 17.9 cm long and again when it is 56.7 cm long. Compute the speed of sound from these data.

By using an air column sufficiently long to resonate at two lengths there is no need to make the end correction because it is the same for both. Since the difference between the two lengths is one-half wavelength, the wavelength is 2(56.7 − 17.9) = 77.6 cm. Therefore, by Eq. 236, the speed of sound in air is found to be $\dfrac{440}{\text{sec}} \times 77.6$ cm = 34,100 cm/sec.

There are many applications of the phenomenon of resonance. Mechanical resonance was considered previously in connection with the vibration of a swing, § 101. Electrical resonance is utilized in the tuning of a radio receiver by adjusting the inductance or capacitance of its circuits for the same frequency as that of the radiation from the desired broadcasting station, § 312. Acoustical resonance is utilized in the mounting of tuning forks on top of wooden boxes closed at one end and open at the other; the length of such boxes is about one-quarter wavelength of the sound emitted by the fork so as to produce a loud response. Resonance is sometimes avoided to prevent free vibrations from building up excessive amplitudes; for example, appropriate bracing is used in narrow suspension bridges to prevent setting up destructive vibrations at high wind velocities.

346. Measurement of Speed of Sound. The speed of a sound wave in the atmosphere can be determined by observing the motion that produces a distant pulse of sound, and measuring the time which elapses before the sound reaches the ear, as well as the distance between source and observer.

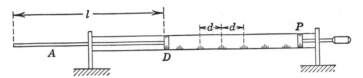

FIG. 337.   Kundt's method for measuring speed of sound

Since the time required for light to travel that distance is insignificant, the speed of sound can be computed directly, although the result is subject to considerable personal error. The distance to a lightning flash may be estimated in this way by counting seconds until its thunder is heard and by allowing 5 sec to the mile for the thunder to reach the ear.

A better method for measuring the speed of sound was devised by August A. E. Kundt (1839–1894), a German physicist. Longitudinal vibrations are set up in a metal rod placed so as to develop stationary waves in air or other gas within a glass tube. Lycopodium powder or cork filings, spread over the interior of the tube, permit the location of the nodes and antinodes to be determined. The tube is shown in Fig. 337; a rod A, clamped at the center and terminating in a disk D, projects into one end and a plunger P is provided at the other.

In conducting the experiment, the rod is set into longitudinal vibration and the plunger is moved until the powder shows distinct patterns along the tube. At the nodes the powder is lumped together, and at the antinodes it assumes sharply defined ridges across the tube. A node is formed at the plunger and an approximate node is formed at the disk. The rod has a length l, and its pitch f is measured by comparison with a siren or equivalent means. When producing the lowest tone, the sound wave in the rod has a wavelength $\lambda = 2l$, and a speed $v = f\lambda = 2fl$, as explained in § 343. If the average distance measured between successive antinodes is d, the sound wave in the gas has a wavelength $2d$, and a speed $v = 2fd$.

SOUND EFFECTS

347. Doppler's Principle. A person standing near a railroad track can observe a distinct lowering of pitch in the whistle of a train as the train passes him. This observation illustrates a principle applicable to all wave motion; it was developed by the Austrian physicist Christian Doppler (1803–1853). Applied to sound, this principle states that the frequency of the sound heard differs from the frequency of the vibrating source from which it originates whenever the observer or the source moves. This difference is quite marked even when the speed of motion is only a few per cent of the speed of sound: 1100 ft/sec in air.

The tone heard by the observer has an *apparent frequency that can be obtained by dividing the speed with which the waves pass him by the wavelength of these waves.* In applying this principle to the various situations, the frequency of the source will be represented by f, the apparent frequency of the sound heard by p, the speed of the source by S, the speed of the observer by O, and the speed of wave propagation by V.

Source Moving. The apparent frequency of the sound heard by a stationary observer when the source moves can be found as follows: in one second the source emits f waves, and these spread out into the surrounding medium; in the region in front of the source these f waves are crowded into a distance equal to $V - S$. Hence the wavelength in this region is reduced to $\dfrac{V - S}{f}$ and the apparent frequency of the sound heard by the observer in front of the source is raised to the value $V \div \dfrac{V - S}{f}$. Thus when the source moves toward a stationary observer the apparent frequency is

$$p = f\left(\frac{V}{V - S}\right) \tag{252}$$

Similarly, when the source moves away from the observer, the apparent frequency is

$$p = f\left(\frac{V}{V + S}\right)$$

Observer Moving. The apparent frequency of the sound heard by a moving observer when the sounding source is stationary can be worked out as a problem in relative motion, § 20, since there is no change of wavelength. The velocity with which the waves pass an observer approaching the source is $V + O$, and the wavelength of these waves is V/f. Hence the apparent frequency is

$$p = f\left(\frac{V + O}{V}\right) \tag{253}$$

Illustrative Problems

Suppose a whistle to be moving with a speed of 60 ft/sec toward a stationary observer, while emitting a sound of frequency 400 vib/sec. What is the apparent frequency of the tone heard by the observer?

In one second the whistle produces a train of 400 waves, the first of which advances 1100 ft while the last is just being emitted from the source at a point 60 ft ahead of its location when the first wave was emitted. This train of waves occupies a length of (1100 − 60) ft; therefore, the wavelength of the sound is (1100 − 60) ÷ 400 = 2.6 ft. The apparent frequency is equal to the wave speed divided by the wavelength, that is, 1100 ÷ 2.6 = 423.1 vib/sec.

Suppose that the 400-cycle whistle of the preceding problem is stationary, and that the observer is approaching it with a speed of 60 ft/sec. What is the apparent frequency of the tone heard by the observer?

The velocity with which the waves pass the observer is (1100 + 60) ft/sec, and since the wavelength of the sound in air is 1100/400 ft, the apparent pitch of the sound heard by the observer becomes (1100 + 60) ÷ (1100/400) = 421.8 vib/sec. It is interesting to note that the increase in apparent frequency with the observer advancing toward the source is different from that obtained with the source approaching the observer at the same speed.

Any problem in which both the source of sound and the observer are specified as moving should be solved separately for each motion. The apparent frequency is changed in the proportion $\dfrac{V}{V \mp S}$ by motion of the source, and in the proportion $\dfrac{V \pm O}{V}$ by motion of the observer.

348. Musical Scales. The charm of music is based upon the blending and the succession of sounds to give satisfying auditory sensations. The characteristics of the ear impose certain physical restrictions on the frequencies of the sounds to be combined to secure harmonious effects. The ear would interpret quite differently a frequency increase of 50 vib/sec in an initial sound having a pitch of 200 vib/sec than a like increase in a sound having a pitch of 400 vib/sec, but would give the same interpretation to an increase of 100 vib/sec in the sound of higher pitch. Thus, the ear recognizes two sounds to have the same tonal interval as two others, if the *frequency ratios*, rather than the frequency differences, are the same for the two pairs.

Further, two simultaneous sounds that have nearly the same frequency produce pulsations in sound intensity. Thus, tuning forks that execute 200 and 205 vib/sec set up 5 beats/sec if sounded together, § 337. But if the frequency difference of two sounds is large, the beat frequency will be perceived as a new tone, called a *combination tone.*

The complete sequence of tones used in music constitutes a scale, and the tones are designated as notes of the scale. The scale is divided into octaves; a note having twice the frequency of another is said to be an octave higher.

Experience shows that tones having frequency ratios of 2 to 1, 3 to 2, 4 to 3, 5 to 3, 5 to 4, and 6 to 5 produce pleasing effects; musical scales are based upon these ratios. The scales are formed by using three combinations called *triads*, each of which is a chord formed of three tones. In such a chord, the octave of a tone may accompany or replace the fundamental without altering the nature of the chord.

The major scale of eight notes beginning with middle C as the basic note includes notes D, E, F, G, A, and B of successively higher pitches in reaching the octave c. The frequencies of these notes are determined by the major triads CEG, FAc, and GBd, which notes have frequency ratios of 4:5:6, and also by the pitch of some one note regarded as standard. Based upon the present standard concert pitch of 440 vib/sec for A in the treble clef, the notes of the major scale have the following frequencies and intervals:

Major Scale

	C	D	E	F	G	A	B	c	d
Triads	4		5		6				
				4		5		6	
					4		5		6
Name	do	re	mi	fa	sol	la	si	do	re
Frequency	264	297	330	352	396	440	495	528	594
Intervals		$\frac{9}{8}$	$\frac{10}{9}$	$\frac{16}{15}$	$\frac{9}{8}$	$\frac{10}{9}$	$\frac{9}{8}$	$\frac{16}{15}$	

The intervals $\frac{9}{8}$ and $\frac{10}{9}$ are called full tones, and the interval $\frac{16}{15}$ is called a half tone. A study of the frequencies tabulated reveals that the tones of a triad as well as their harmonics do not produce disturbing beat notes. For example, the third harmonic of C coincides with the second of G, the fifth of C coincides with the fourth of E, the sixth of E coincides with the fifth of G, and so on.

The minor scale is built upon three minor triads for the same notes as the major scale, but having frequency ratios of 10:12:15. The notes of this scale have the following frequencies and intervals over the range of values previously tabulated:

Minor Scale

	C	D	E	F	G	A	B	c	d
Triads	10		12		15				
				10		12		15	
					10		12		15
Frequency	264	297	316.8	352	396	422.4	475.2	528	594
Intervals		$\frac{9}{8}$	$\frac{16}{15}$	$\frac{10}{9}$	$\frac{9}{8}$	$\frac{16}{15}$	$\frac{9}{8}$	$\frac{10}{9}$	

The intervals have the same values as before, but have a different sequence. As a result, three additional notes are needed to produce the minor scale; these are below E, A, and B of the major scale.

To accommodate different instruments and voices, it is desirable to have sufficient tones to permit changing the key-note from *C* to some other note. If, for example, the successive notes were to be determined for the key of *D*, the same procedure followed above would indicate the successive frequencies for the major scale to be 297, 334, 371, 396, 445, 495, 557 and 594 vib/sec. These frequencies agree with those previously found for notes *G* and *B* as well as for the key-note, and approximate them for notes *E* and *A*; but two are quite distinct and these notes are designated as *F* sharp and *c* sharp.

Similar computations for other keys in both scales reveal the necessity of having a large number of separate notes if it were desired to render a selection in any key. To avoid this situation and yet provide sufficient flexibility in musical instruments, like the piano and organ, that produce sounds of fixed frequency, a scale has been developed that has 12 intervals and has the same frequency interval between consecutive notes. This so-called *tempered scale* has a frequency interval of the twelfth root of 2, namely, 1.0595. The equal temperament scale is now universally used, and only persons with well-trained ears can detect the slight errors of pitch from the natural scales.

349. Vocal Organs. The organs of speech are composed of the vocal cords, through which the lungs force streams of air, and of the resonating chambers formed by the throat, mouth, and nasal cavities. Fig. 338 shows a sectional view of these parts of the neck and head. The larynx is the valve at the entrance of the windpipe and consists of a framework of cartilages connected by ligaments, including two fibrous bands called the *vocal cords*. These form a straight slit (*glottis*) from 11 to 15 mm long, and when the breath passes through it the cords are set into vibration and send puffs of air to the chambers above it. The vibration rate is determined principally by the size of the glottis opening and, to some extent, by the tension of the vocal cords.

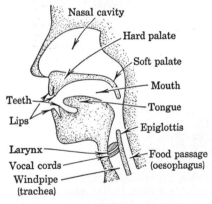

FIG. 338.   The vocal organs

The lips, tongue and teeth modify the shape of the vocal passages; certain tonal characteristics are impressed by this action upon the air puffs and they emerge from the mouth as speech or tonal sounds. When relaxed, the vocal cords are farther apart and form a V-shaped aperture; in this condition the passage of air to and from the lungs occurs without the emission of sound, as in normal breathing.

The sounds of speech are complicated tones that have many harmonics. As with musical tones, the quality is determined by the relative intensities of these harmonics. The wave in Fig. 339 was produced by the vowel "o" as in *tone*. Measurements of the power of speech sounds show that the average power for conversational speech is about 10 microwatts. Talking as loudly as possible raises this average to about 1000 microwatts, and talking as softly as possible without whispering lowers the average to about 0.1 microwatt.

The pitch of the voice in singing ranges generally from about 80 to 300 vib/sec for bass voices, and from about 250 to 850 vib/sec for soprano voices, but these ranges are extended considerably by many individuals.

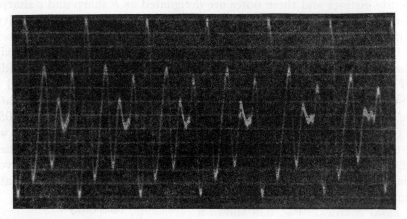

FIG. 339. Wave shape produced by the vowel "o" as in *tone*. (*Courtesy of Bell Telephone Laboratories*)

PROBLEMS

1. A circular saw has 120 teeth around its rim. Find the frequency of the sound produced when the saw is cutting wood while rotating at 750 rev/min.

2. A low tone and a high tone sounded on a pipe organ have frequencies of 33 and 4224 cycles/sec. If the amplitudes of vibration of these tones are in the proportion 100:1 respectively, in what proportion are their intensities?

3. A source emits sound energy at the rate of 0.01 watt. Determine the intensity of the sound wave at a place 5 m away from the source.

4. Suppose that the wave referred to in the preceding problem is set up in air at 0° C and that the source has a frequency of 550 vib/sec; compute the amplitude of vibration of the air particles at the place specified.

5. A sounding source radiating uniformly in all directions produces a wave that has an intensity of 0.4 erg/(sec·cm²) at a distance of 100 cm from the source. At what rate in microwatts is the source emitting sound energy?

6. Construct to scale the sine curves represented by the equations $y_1 = 50 \sin (2\pi 500t)$ and $y_2 = 20 \sin (2\pi 1500t)$ and their resultant, all in a single diagram.

7. A brass wire 60 cm long is stretched with a force of 4×10^6 dynes and set into vibration in its fundamental mode. The wire has a mass of 4.2 gm. (a) Calculate the frequency of the tone produced. (b) If this wire is sounded

together with a piano string vibrating at 66 vib/sec, how many beats are produced in 10 sec?

8. In a sonometer test, a wire 18 in. long is stretched so that it vibrates in its fundamental mode with a frequency of 132 vib/sec. What stress is set up within the wire if it is made of steel having a specific gravity of 7.8?

9. A stretched string 25 cm long vibrates in its fundamental mode with a frequency of 256 vib/sec, and sets the air around it into vibration. Determine the speed and wavelength (*a*) of the wave in the string and (*b*) of the wave in the air at a temperature of 0° C.

10. Refer to Prob. 3 of Chap. 30, describing a catgut string under tension, and find the frequencies of the fundamental and second harmonic produced when this string is set into vibration.

11. An aluminum rod 3 ft long is clamped and set into longitudinal vibration. Compute the frequencies of the two lowest harmonics that the rod produces, when clamped (*a*) at the middle; (*b*) at one end.

12. A tube 4 ft long is open at both ends. When the air within the tube is set into vibration, what are the frequencies of the three lowest harmonics produced? Neglect the end correction. Sketch the standing waves within the tube and label the nodes and antinodes.

13. Repeat the preceding problem with the tube closed at one end.

14. A pipe 30 cm long and open at both ends is sounded when filled with air and again with hydrogen. Neglect the end correction and take the temperature to be 0° C. Find the frequency of the fundamental tone produced in each gas.

15. How long a tube open at both ends would have its air column vibrate in its fundamental mode at 200 vib/sec? Take the diameter of the tube as 2 in. and include the end correction.

16. Enrico Caruso's voice was reported so powerful that he could shatter a glass tumbler by setting it into violent vibration at its natural frequency. As an approximation to this feat, compute the frequency of the tone which, if intense enough, would shatter a glass tube 6 in. high, closed at one end. Take the diameter of the tube to be $1\frac{1}{2}$ in. and include the end correction.

17. Find the length of a resonating box, closed at one end, that would reinforce the tone produced by a tuning fork having a frequency of 396 vib/sec. Disregard the end correction.

18. The experiment illustrated in Fig. 336 is conducted with a tuning fork vibrating 264 times a second, and resonance is observed when the air column is the tube in 11.9 in. long. (*a*) As the water is lowered, what will be the length of the air column when resonance occurs again? (*b*) Estimate the diameter of the tube.

19. In Kundt's method for measuring the speed of sound, the metal rod when stroked emits a tone of the same pitch as that produced by a siren having 100 holes and driven at 798 rev/min. The tube contains air at standard temperature and pressure, and the powder heaps within it are found to be 10.2 cm apart. From these data, compute (*a*) the speed of sound in air and (*b*) the ratio γ of the specific heat of air at constant pressure to that at constant volume.

20. An automobile is moving along a straight highway with its horn sounding steadily at 300 vib/sec. Calculate the lowering of frequency of the sound heard by an observer standing near the highway as the car approaches and passes him.

21. A man running away from a dentist at a speed of 30 ft/sec emits a shriek having a frequency of 500 vib/sec. What is the frequency of the tone heard by the dentist if he is chasing the man at 10 ft/sec?

22. Derive the equation used in radar traffic control and given in § 317, namely: Frequency change $= 2Vf/c$, where V is the speed of the automobile, f the frequency of the incident radar beam, and c the speed of light.

23. A Diesel engine is hauling a freight train at 30 mi/hr and its horn is sounding steadily with a frequency of 400 vib/sec. Compute the apparent frequency of the sound heard (*a*) by a man standing near the track ahead of the train, (*b*) by a man standing near the track behind the train, (*c*) by a man running on the ground alongside the track at 10 mi/hr and following the train, (*d*) by a man sitting in the train, and (*e*) by a man running along the top of the train at 10 mi/hr toward the engine.

24. The standard piano keyboard has 88 keys, with middle *C* (264 vib/sec) near the center. The lowest note is *A* in the fourth octave below middle *C*, and the highest is exactly four octaves above middle *C*. Determine the frequencies of the lowest and highest tones produced by the instrument.

32

SOUND RECEPTION AND CONTROL

350. The Ear. In the process of hearing, the acoustic waves enter the auditory canal of the outer ear and fall upon the eardrum; the vibration of this membrane is transmitted through the middle ear to the inner ear and received by nerve endings, which in turn send nervous impulses to the brain that cause the sensation of hearing.

The principal parts of the ear are illustrated in Fig. 340, the inner ear being much enlarged with respect to the outer ear, and the sectional view of

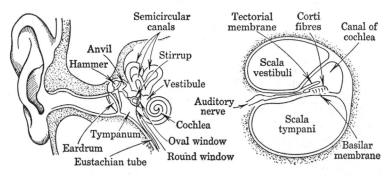

FIG. 340.   The organs of hearing and associated parts

the end-organ (cochlea) being further magnified.   The cavity beyond the eardrum, called the *tympanum*, connects with the upper part of the throat through the *Eustachian tube* which opens when swallowing occurs, equalizing the pressure with that of the outside air.   The tympanum houses the three tiny bones of the middle ear, the *hammer, anvil* and *stirrup*, and the base of the latter bone is applied to a membrane that covers an oval window called the *fenestra ovalis*.   Another membrane at that side of the tympanum covers a round window called the *fenestra rotunda*.   Both of these membranes transmit incoming vibrations to the inner ear.   This part of the ear, encased in solid bone, can be subdivided into three sections: the semicircular canals (which do not contribute to the process of hearing but serve as an organ of balance), the vestibule, and the *cochlea*.   The latter has the form of a spiral of nearly three turns, and is the organ where the vibrations are translated into nerve impulses.

The cochlea is divided along its length into three parallel canals, as shown in the sectional view at the right, but the upper two, separated by a very thin flexible membrane, act mechanically as though they were one. The *scala vestibuli* and *scala tympani* have at their ends the oval and round windows respectively for communication with the tympanum, and are separated by a bony projection for about half their length and by a flexible membrane, called the *basilar membrane*, for the other half. The terminal organs of hearing are the *Corti fibres* which are nerve terminals in the form of rods with

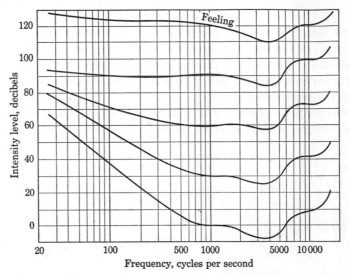

FIG. 341. Equal-loudness contours for the normal ear. The top and bottom curves represent the thresholds of feeling and audibility respectively

small hairs that extend from one side of the basilar membrane into the canal of cochlea. Opposite them is a soft loose membrane called the *tectorial membrane*. In receiving sound, these two membranes move relatively to each other and stimulate the hair-like nerve endings, thereby causing the sound to be heard. That the cochlea is very small can be judged from the facts that the length is about 35 mm when straightened out and that the average cross-section of either canal is about 1 mm^2. It is believed that the cochlea is responsive to different frequencies along the different parts of the length of its basilar membrane, so that its behavior may be likened somewhat to that of a harp. The reception of a complex sound on this basis would signify the agitation of certain of the resonating elements of the cochlea and the transmission of a corresponding pattern to the brain.

The range of sounds that can be heard varies with the individual, but the average range extends from about 20 to 20,000 vib/sec. If the ear is tested with tones of any one frequency and the intensity is changed, it will be found that the auditory sensation ceases when the intensity has been reduced to a sufficiently low level called the *threshold of audibility;* also that the sound produces the sensation of feeling and begins to be painful when the intensity has been increased to an appropriately high level called the *threshold of feeling.* Such a procedure carried out over a wide frequency range and a wide intensity range gives valuable information about the response of the ear.

Fig. 341 shows the results of such tests on normal ears. The curves, called *equal-loudness contours,* are plotted with frequencies as abscissas (on a logarithmic scale) and intensity levels as ordinates, the latter being more closely related to loudness than sound intensities themselves, § 340. Each curve represents the sounds of different frequencies that seem of equal loudness to the average ear. The chart indicates that at low intensity levels the tones of higher frequency sound louder than those of lower frequency, and that at high levels the tones of all frequencies sound almost equally loud.

351. Intensity Levels. As the intensity of a sound wave is increased, the sound becomes louder, but there is no proportionality between wave intensity and loudness sensation. For this reason another concept has been found useful, that of *intensity level,* which is defined in such a way as to make its value roughly proportional to the sensation of loudness. A scale of such intensity levels is extensively used in acoustical measurements.

Just as ground elevations are measured from sea level as a datum, so intensity levels are measured from that of a particular sound intensity chosen arbitrarily as a reference standard, namely, 10^{-10} microwatts/cm^2. This value corresponds to the zero level in Fig. 341. If the reference intensity is taken as I_r and the intensity of a sound under consideration is taken as I, then the intensity level of that sound can be expressed by the logarithmic equation

$$N = 10 \log_{10} \frac{I}{I_r} \tag{254}$$

where the coefficient 10 is introduced to have the intensity level given in the customary unit called the decibel, § 306. The more intense the sound, the higher is the number of decibels which expresses its intensity level. The meaning of 1 db can be appreciated by letting $N = 1$ and solving for I/I_r; the result is $10^{0.1} = 1.26$, showing that a 1-db rise in the intensity level corresponds to a 26% increase of sound intensity.

Illustrative Problem

As an example, if the intensity of a sound is doubled and then doubled again, by how many decibels has its intensity level been increased?

By Eq. 254 the change in intensity level for the first doubling of the sound intensity is $N = 10 \log_{10} \frac{2}{1} = 3.01$ db, and the change for the second doubling is also 3.01 db; hence the total change in intensity level is 6.02 db.

352. Sound Recording and Reproduction. The first sound recorder was devised by Edison and consisted of a diaphragm with a stylus projecting at the back, and a cylinder of tinfoil that could be moved while in contact with the stylus. Speech was recorded by speaking in front of the diaphragm and causing the stylus to produce indentations in the moving cylinder. Upon returning the cylinder to its initial position and moving it as before, the diaphragm was set into vibration by a needle that followed the indentations, and the original sounds were reproduced. The invention led to the development of the dictating machine which employs cylinders of hard wax, and of the phonograph which operates with records in the form of disks.

In the ordinary phonograph record, the groove, when magnified, appears as a wavy line and represents a composite wave that is usually the resultant of many individual waves superimposed upon one another. In electrical reproduction of a phonograph record, the motion of the tracing point causes an iron armature to move within a coil of wire. The resulting disturbance of the magnetic flux induces an emf in the coil and sets up an electric current which is amplified by electron tubes and operates a loudspeaker.

Another means for recording sound makes use of a magnetized tape in a so-called tape recorder. The speaker talks into a microphone, and the voice current, suitably amplified, is passed through the coil of a small electromagnet. Traveling beneath the magnet is a plastic tape coated with fine particles of magnetic iron oxide; the variations in the voice current produce corresponding changes in the magnetization of the oxide film. In reproducing the sound, the tape is driven under a similar electromagnet, and the variations in magnetism induce corresponding emfs in its coil; these produce a small varying current which is amplified and supplied to a loudspeaker. The record can be "erased" by passing the tape through an alternating magnetic field of high frequency, and the tape used again.

The sound record of a talking motion picture usually consists of a narrow strip or "sound track" which extends along one edge of the film and is crossed by lines of varying intensity. To make the record, the sounds are picked up by a sensitive microphone and cause corresponding variations of the electric current in the microphone circuit. This current, suitably amplified, is caused to control a neon lamp, the intensity of which responds instantly to current changes. The light from the lamp is passed through a narrow transverse slit upon the moving film, and produces a series of lines of varying degrees of darkness in the finished film. In reproduction from the film, a steady light shines through a similar slit upon the sound track, the transmitted beam varying continually in intensity. This beam strikes a photoelectric cell, § 315, and causes proportional changes in the current through it. The varying current, properly amplified, operates a loudspeaker and reproduces the original sound.

353. Ultrasonic Vibrations. Investigations of longitudinal vibrations have been extended into the so-called *ultrasonic frequency* region beyond the upper limit of hearing, and the resulting short waves have found a variety of applications. Such vibrations can be produced by a quartz crystal mounted between metal electrodes, making use of the piezoelectric effect described in § 312. The crystal has a natural frequency determined by its elasticity and density. When an alternating emf of this same frequency is impressed upon the electrodes, the crystal is set into mechanical vibration, which it communicates to the surrounding medium.

Ultrasonic vibrations can also be produced by slight periodic changes in length of an iron or nickel rod that is magnetized by a high-frequency alternating current through a solenoid around the rod; the variation in length due to magnetization is called *magnetostriction*. A more recent method for producing ultrasonic vibrations makes use of ferroelectric substances, § 323, that can be set into vibration by alternating electric fields. One of these is barium titanate; it can be easily molded and shaped to focus the waves, and thereby obtain high intensities in small zones.

Because of their relatively short wavelength, ultrasonic waves do not spread much by diffraction, § 425, but remain localized in narrow beams; this property makes them suitable for under-water communication between ships. The transmitting crystal is supported outside of the ship's hull and sets up a longitudinal wave in the water. This wave acts upon a similar crystal at the receiving station, setting it into vibration and causing it to generate an emf of the same frequency between its electrodes. The water wave corresponds to the carrier wave in radio telephony, § 312, and the same methods of modulation and reception are used for both.

Ultrasonic waves are used for locating hidden flaws in metals by the impulse-echo method, in which a quartz crystal is used both to transform electrical energy into acoustic energy and vice versa. Used in this way, the device is called a *transducer*. A high-frequency emf is applied to the crystal and sets it into mechanical vibration; as a result an ultrasonic wave is sent into the test object. The applied electrical impulse is highly damped and consists of only two or three oscillations. When these have been completed, the high-frequency oscillator is blocked and the quartz crystal, now coupled to an amplifier unit, stands by to receive the echo as the ultrasonic wave is reflected from the surfaces of the test object or from faults within it. The crystal is set into mechanical vibration by the reflected wave and generates a pulse of emf, which is indicated on the screen of an oscilloscope. This cycle is repeated automatically several hundred times a second and results in a continuous picture on the screen; this shows the location of the flaws in the metal with respect to its surfaces.

The impulse-echo method is used at sea for depth sounding and for determining the range and bearing of under-water objects. The system known as "Sonar" has been effectively used in naval operations to locate enemy submarines. This system utilizes crystals of ammonium dihydrogen phosphate and operates on frequencies from 10 to 30 kilocycles per sec.

Illustrative Problem

In a test with a depth-sounding instrument on board ship a signal was sent downward and its echo from sea-bottom was received $\frac{1}{80}$ sec later. Take the speed of the waves in sea water to be 1500 m/sec, and determine the depth in fathoms at the place of observation.

The depth is $\frac{1}{2}$ (1500)($\frac{1}{80}$) = 9.38 m. Since 1 fathom is 6 ft = 6 $\times$ 30.48 cm, the depth is 9.38 $\times$ 100 $\div$ (6 $\times$ 30.48) = 5.13 fathoms.

Chemical and biological effects are produced in many substances by exposure to strong beams of ultrasonic radiation; for example, particles of colloidal material in liquids are shattered and form extremely fine emulsions. An ultrasonic oscillator immersed in oil sets the liquid into violent agitation; a glass rod held between the fingers and dipped into the oil becomes agitated so much that the fingers may be burned by friction.

In medicine, ultrasonic radiation is used as an adjunct in the treatment of arthritis, neuritis, and other inflammations. The ultrasonic waves do not travel through a vacuum, and transmission through air is ineffective in these treatments; for this reason a coupling agent, such as oil or water, is placed between the ultrasonic source and the skin over the region to be treated. At a frequency of 800 kilocycles/sec and an intensity up to 3 watts of ultrasonic energy per square centimeter of area, the waves may reach a layer of tissue 2 to 6 cm deep.

The passage of ultrasonic waves through a liquid sets up planes of condensation and rarefaction which may be so close together that the medium acts as a diffraction grating, § 428, causing incident light perpendicular to the direction of wave propagation to be spread into spectra of several orders. This phenomenon has been used to measure the moduli of elasticity of liquids and solids.

In gases, calculations show that as the frequency of ultrasonic waves is increased, say to the order of 10^8 vib/sec, bringing the wavelength close to the mean free path of the molecules, the compressions and rarefactions become more and more nearly isothermal. Under these conditions the speed of the waves is given by the expression $v = \sqrt{p/d}$, as explained in § 331.

Industrially, ultrasonic waves are being used as a tool for a number of processes, such as cleaning and degreasing of metals parts, drilling very hard and brittle materials, tanning of leather, and emulsification of seemingly immiscible liquids.

ROOM ACOUSTICS

354. Reverberation. Almost everyone has noticed the persistence of sound, particularly in a large empty hall. This effect is caused by echoes repeated in rapid succession, and is called *reverberation*. It may be explained by considering the effect of sustaining a tone within a room from which no acoustic energy escapes. When the source is set into vibration, the sound waves emitted travel to the walls and other surfaces, and are then reflected back and forth from one surface after another. If none of the acoustic energy were absorbed, the resulting sound intensity would increase indefinitely. Absorption does take place at the surfaces, however, and as a result, the intensity reaches a steady value when the rate of energy absorption equals the rate of emission. After this condition has been attained and the vibrating source is stopped, the sound dies away slowly as the acoustic energy within the room is absorbed. The intensity I at an instant t sec after stopping a sound is given in terms of the maximum intensity I_o by the equation:

$$I = I_o \epsilon^{-kt} \tag{255}$$

where ϵ is the base of natural logarithms and k is taken as a constant for the room under consideration.

The time in which a sound diminishes until it can no longer be heard has been appropriately termed *reverberation time*. Wallace C. Sabine (1869–1919), an American pioneer in acoustics, regarded the reverberation time more definitely as the *interval during which the intensity of the sound diminishes to one-millionth of its initial value*. In accordance with this definition, the reverberation time is obtained from Eq. 255 by taking I_o/I as 10^6, giving

$$t = \frac{1}{k} \log_\epsilon \frac{I_o}{I} = \frac{2.303}{k} \log_{10} 10^6 = \frac{1}{k} (2.303 \times 6)$$

This reverberation time can also be defined as the time in which the intensity level of a sound falls 60 db by absorption.

355. Absorption. The slowness with which sounds die away is due to incomplete absorption at the reflecting surfaces; the greater the sound absorption at these surfaces the shorter the reverberation time. Since an open window returns none of the sound energy that reaches it, the opening acts as a perfect absorber; this idea makes it possible to express the *absorbing power* of room surfaces in terms of equivalent areas of open windows. The absorbing power of the room, including furnishings and audience, is found by adding a number of terms for the various surfaces, each term consisting of the area s multiplied by an appropriate *absorption coefficient* β, thus

$$a = \beta_1 s_1 + \beta_2 s_2 + \beta_3 s_3$$

although a more exact appraisal of the absorbing power of a room takes account of the manner in which its various absorbing surfaces are distributed.

Absorption coefficients have been measured for many materials, and are expressed as fractions of the "absorption" at an open window of equal area. A felt surface is a good absorber because it contains many tiny channels in which the air vibrations are damped out and their energy dissipated as heat; its coefficient $\beta = 0.70$ indicates that 1 ft^2 of felt is equivalent to 0.70 ft^2 of open window space in quenching reverberation. On the other hand, glass and metals are poor absorbers. Absorption coefficients vary somewhat with the frequency of the sound and with the condition of the surface. Some values of absorption coefficients and absorbing power appear in the accompanying tables.

ABSORPTION COEFFICIENTS

Open window.........	1.00
Acousti-Celotex.......	0.80
Brick wall............	0.03
Carpet, felt lined......	0.40
Draperies, cotton......	0.50
Felt.................	0.70
Glass...............	0.025
Linoleum............	0.03
Plaster, smooth........	0.03
Wood paneling........	0.06

ABSORBING POWER (EFFECTIVE FT^2)

Audience, each person........4.0
Upholstered chairs, each......2.8
Wood seats, each............0.3

A number of chambers have been built for acoustic research that are echoless and noiseless. In one of them constructed recently the surfaces are lined with 2-ft wedges of glass fiber, placed side by side and pointing into the chamber, for absorbing sounds generated within it; the wedges are inside of double-thick walls of concrete for keeping out extraneous noises. The sound-absorbing wedges are illustrated in Fig. 342.

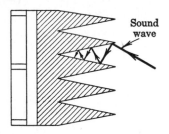

Sound wave

FIG. 342. Wall section of anechoic (echo-free) chamber

356. Acoustics of Rooms. The suitability of large rooms for lecture purposes and for the presentation of music depends primarily upon two factors—reverberation and interference. Reverberation can be controlled by selecting wall and ceiling materials that absorb sound energy to the desired extent. Interference causes variations of intensity from point to point within the room; excessive interference can be avoided by a proper choice of dimensions and shape in designing the room.

In an auditorium where the reverberation time is too long, speakers find it necessary to talk very slowly to prevent confusion between a syllable being spoken and the echoes of the preceding one. If the reverberation time is too short, the sounds die away so quickly that the room would be judged "too dead." Values of 1 sec for a small auditorium and about 2 sec for a large one are considered acceptable. The reverberation time of a room is given in § 354 as $t = \dfrac{1}{k}(2.303 \times 6)$. The factor $\dfrac{1}{k}$ in this equation is determined by the constants of the room and can be evaluated as follows:

In a small room the sound reflections at the walls follow one another more rapidly than in a large room, consequently the reverberation time depends upon the volume of the room. For a similar reason this time varies inversely with the speed of sound. Also, it is influenced by the absorbing power of the surfaces of walls and ceiling, of fixtures and draperies, and of the audience itself. If the volume of the room in cubic feet is represented by V, the velocity of sound in feet per second by $v = 1100$, and the absorbing power of the room in effective square feet by a, these effects can be incorporated in the foregoing equation by taking $\dfrac{1}{k} = K\dfrac{V}{va}$, where K is another constant.

Theory and experiment show that this constant has the value 4 for the units employed; consequently, the reverberation time in seconds becomes

$$t = 4\,\frac{V}{1100a}\,(2.303 \times 6)$$

or

$$t = \frac{V}{20a} \tag{256}$$

Illustrative Problem

As an example, compute the reverberation time in an auditorium measuring $60 \times 90 \times 20$ ft. The absorbing materials consist of 9100 ft^2 of plaster, 7000 ft^2 of wood, 400 ft^2 of glass and 300 ft^2 of drapery. Assume the room to have 800 wooden seats and an audience of 500 persons.

The absorbing power of the room and audience, based on the coefficients listed in § 355, is:

Plaster.	9100×0.03	273
Wood.	7000×0.06	420
Glass.	400×0.025	10
Drapery.	300×0.50	150
Seats.	800×0.3	240
Audience.	$500 \times (4.0 - 0.3)$	1850
Absorbing Power		2943 effective ft^2

Hence, by Eq. 256, the reverberation time is

$$t = \frac{60 \times 90 \times 20}{20 \times 2943} = 1.83 \text{ sec}$$

This value appears rather high for an auditorium of this size, and could be reduced by the use of more highly absorbing materials.

The second factor involved in the acoustics of an auditorium is that of interference produced by reflection of the sound waves from the walls, ceiling, and other surfaces. As a result, the waves tend to reinforce one another at certain regions and to annul one another at other places. Tests by Sabine showed regions within an auditorium where the intensity of sound was greater than near the source, and others where it was almost zero. In particular, large curved surfaces tend to focus the sound at definite spots. If such a surface is to be used in the architectural design of a room, it should be so shaped that the point of focus lies outside the room, thus avoiding the effects observed in so-called "whispering galleries."

PROBLEMS

1. From the values for speech power in § 349, compute the range of intensity level for the average voice.
2. A scale of sound levels for typical noise sources shows the automobile horn at 120 db and the airplane test chamber at 140 db. Determine the relative intensity of noise in the test chamber with respect to that of the automobile horn.
3. Two sound waves A and B in air have frequencies of 264 and 528 vib/sec respectively. Measurements at a point near the sounding sources show the intensity level of A to be 2.5 db above that of B. What is the ratio of the intensity of A to that of B? of the amplitude of A to that of B?
4. An observer outdoors is 40 ft from a steady source of sound and finds that the intensity level at his position is 30 db. Compute the intensity level 20 ft farther from the source.
5. A machine is tested in a factory where the background noise level is 70 db above the reference standard; with the machine running, the noise level is 75 db. What would be the noise level for the machine when tested in a quiet place?
6. The development of the jet airplane has resulted in sound levels considerably higher than those previously created by any machine; values of 160 db and higher are now being recorded. (*a*) For an intensity level of 160 db, at what rate in horsepower is energy dissipated as sound through a square foot of wave front at the point of measurement? (*b*) With a 160-db sound level existing on a uniform spherical wave front 4 ft from a point source, at what rate in horsepower is sound radiated by the source?
7. Tests on an air-raid siren showed the sound level of its signal to be 130 db at a point 100 ft away and to decrease by 8 db each time the distance from the source was doubled, the Inverse Square Law not applying because the wave front is not spherical. In a particular district, a signal of at least

98 db is desired; find the distance from the siren at which this level will be obtained.

8. A logarithmic scale similar to that for sound intensity level is used for comparing the brightness of stars. It is based on a brightness ratio of 100 to 1 for the brightest stars (first magnitude) to those that are just visible to the unaided eye (sixth magnitude), and with successive magnitudes such that the logarithms of their relative brightnesses differ by equal amounts. What is the brightness ratio of a star of the fifth magnitude to one of the sixth?

9. An ultrasonic wave having a frequency of 4 megacycles/sec passes into an aluminum bar and is reflected from the far end. Calculate the distance between nodes in the standing wave that is set up within the metal.

10. A particular transducer for detecting flaws in metals allows 0.002 sec for ultrasonic waves to travel through the specimen and echo back again. What maximum length of brass rod can be tested end-on with the apparatus? Take the specific gravity of brass to be 8.5.

11. If the reverberation time of an auditorium is 1.5 sec, in what time interval does the intensity of a sound diminish by absorption to one-half of its initial value?

12. Calculate the reverberation time of an auditorium in which the intensity level of a sound diminishes by absorption from 80 to 40 db in 1.2 sec.

13. A sound wave in a room undergoes repeated reflections at Acousti-Celotex walls, and at each reflection 80% of the energy of the incident wave is absorbed. If the wave has an initial intensity of 100 ergs/(sec·cm^2) and if no energy is transmitted through the walls, what is the intensity of the wave after five successive reflections?

14. In the auditorium described in the solved problem of § 356, the reverberation time is to be reduced to 1.4 sec by covering part of the plaster with Acousti-Celotex. How many square feet should be covered in this manner?

15. A basement restaurant, without windows, measures 25 × 40 ft and is 12 ft high. The floor is covered with linoleum; the walls are of plaster, except for a wainscot 4.5 ft high of paneled wood. What is the reverberation time of the empty room if the ceiling is covered (*a*) with plaster? (*b*) with material having an absorption coefficient of 0.5?

33

SOURCES AND ILLUMINATION; SPEED OF LIGHT

357. Some Properties of Light. Of all the radiations that abound in space those of light are undoubtedly the most important. Light radiations differ from the others of the electromagnetic spectrum given in § 333 only in wavelength. The term *light* is generally applied to a broader range of wavelengths than affects the eye, for it includes the longer waves of infrared and the shorter waves of ultraviolet radiation which border the visible range. The emission of all radiations and their absorption by matter are described in terms of tiny quantities of energy called quanta, § 188, and their transmission from place to place in terms of electromagnetic waves.

Our everyday experiences with the behavior of light have to do largely with reflection and refraction; we see our images by reflection in mirrors or in other highly polished surfaces, and we observe the bending of rays of light by refraction as they slant from one medium to another. The latter is usually accompanied by the splitting up of white light into the component colors of the spectrum, an effect called dispersion. Three other effects can be observed with simple facilities. The colors seen in soap or oil films are due to the interference of waves of light that are reflected from both faces of such films. On looking at a distant light source through a piece of silk, a series of bright spots is seen instead of a single one; this effect, called diffraction, is caused by the spreading of light waves that pass through the tiny spaces between the silk fibers. Passing light through a crystal like tourmaline or a film like polaroid changes its character through polarization, a change that can be evidenced by the quenching action produced with another specimen placed crosswise to the first.

These and other effects of light are considered in the chapters that follow; the present one deals with light sources, brightness, illumination, and the speed of light.

358. Rays and Waves. It is generally stated that light travels in straight lines within a uniform medium. This statement is true to a close degree of approximation, as can be shown in many ways. For example, the shape of the shadow which an object casts when illuminated by a distant source is determined by the shape of the object. The straight-line transmission of light is made use of by practically everyone in sighting along edges and surfaces to verify their straightness or flatness.

The direction or path of propagation of light may be represented by a straight line, called a *ray*. This practice will be used frequently in the study of light; thus, the radiation from a point source is often represented by rays diverging from this spot. When such divergent rays enter the eye, § 412, they are rendered converging and brought to a focus upon the retina; the image there formed stimulates the nerve endings, and the resulting sensation is that of "seeing" the spot from which the rays appear to diverge.

Many of the effects of light can be explained in simple terms upon the hypothesis that light travels in straight lines. This hypothesis is the basis of Geometric Optics, a branch of the subject in which descriptions can be given adequately with rays of light; fundamentally this statement holds because of the shortness of light waves. The wave properties of light often provide a more satisfactory explanation of the various effects, and in some phenomena like diffraction and polarization, the wave theory alone can be relied upon. In the following chapters either rays or waves will be used, whichever provides the more simple and straightforward analysis for the particular phenomenon involved.

SOURCES, BRIGHTNESS, AND ILLUMINATION

359. Sources of Light. The production of light is attributed physically to actions taking place within the atoms or molecules of the glowing source. When an atom in its normal state is excited by collision with another atom or by other means, the energy it receives causes the electrons to assume higher energy levels, § 390. The subsequent falling of electrons to lower energy levels is accompanied by loss of energy through radiation, and if its frequency is within the proper range the radiation stimulates the eye to produce vision.

Our great natural source of light is the sun. Its radiation is described in § 386, and curves are given in Fig. 182 which show that most of the energy falls outside the visible range. In a sense, the moon is also a natural source of light, but strictly speaking, it is merely a reflector of sunlight. Artificial sources of light, in the order of their development through the centuries, include the torch, the oil lamp, the candle, the gas lamp, the electric arc lamp, the incandescent electric lamp, vapor lamps, the fluorescent lamp, and luminous gas tubes.

Arc Lamps. The electric arc consists of a pair of carbon rods connected in series with a resistor to the supply mains. The arc is started by bringing the carbons into contact and then separating them. As the carbons burn away during operation, they are fed toward each other manually or automatically to keep the gap between them fairly constant. With direct current, most of the light comes from a crater that is formed in the tip of the positive carbon; its temperature is about 3600° K. The use of the arc lamp is practically confined nowadays to picture projectors and searchlights.

Incandescent Lamps. The incandescent lamp consists essentially of a conducting filament enclosed within a glass bulb and heated so intensely by the electric current that it emits light. The original lamp of this type, brought out by Edison in 1880, used a filament of carbonized bamboo, mounted within an evacuated bulb to prevent oxidation. About 1910, when it became possible to draw tungsten into thin wires, lamp filaments were made of this metal and operated in a vacuum. The principal drawback was a gradual blackening of the bulb due to deposition upon it of tungsten evaporated from the hot filament. Subsequent improvement brought about the gas-filled tungsten lamp, in which the bulb is filled with an inert gas, such as nitrogen, under a pressure of about an atmosphere. The presence of the gas retards the evaporation of the filament, as desired, but produces an undesirable cooling of the filament through convection currents. To offset the latter effect, the filament is arranged in the form of a closely wound helix; practically all of the incandescent lamps used today have such filaments, operating at temperatures upward of 2600° K.

In lamps used for the projection of motion pictures, the filament is concentrated into a small space and aligned in one plane; to make them so compact the coiled filament is again coiled. Other special-purpose incandescent lamps include miniature lamps for low-potential circuits, sealed-beam lamps for automobiles, photoflood lamps for photography, infrared lamps for heating and drying, and series lamps for street lighting.

Vapor Lamps. The mercury vapor lamp contains mercury and a little argon; it has two main electrodes, each consisting of a coiled tungsten wire coated with barium oxide, and a starting electrode that is connected with a resistor to control the starting current. When the lamp is connected to the alternating-current service, an electric field is established between the starting electrode and one of the main electrodes, and electrons are emitted from the latter whenever it has a sufficiently high negative potential. This stream of electrons ionizes the argon, and a blue glow fills the tube. The discharge serves to heat the mercury vapor to the point of ionization, and conduction is established between the main electrodes; the starting electrode then becomes inactive. Such mercury vapor lamps give off light of a greenish color and are used for street and industrial lighting.

The sodium-vapor lamp contains some metallic sodium and a little neon gas; it has two electrodes, one a molybdenum anode and the other a coiled-filament cathode. When the lamp is started, the neon ionizes and develops enough heat to vaporize the sodium. This lamp emits the orange-red glow of neon during the first few minutes of operation and thereafter the characteristic yellow light of sodium vapor; it is used for highway lighting.

Fluorescent Lamps. Fluorescence is a property of many crystalline substances that causes them to glow when stimulated by radiation like ultra-violet light and x-rays or by exposure to speeding particles like electrons and alpha particles. With some substances the light is emitted only while stimulated and with others it persists for a short time afterward; these effects

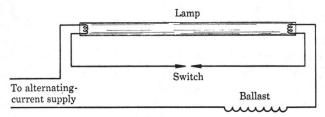

FIG. 343. Fluorescent lamp circuit. The ballast is a reactor for limiting current while starting lamp

are called *fluorescence* and *phosphorescence* respectively. Among fluorescent substances may be mentioned fluorspar, willemite, some lubricating oils, alcohol solutions of chlorophyll, and uranium glass; among phosphorescent substances zinc sulfide and calcium sulfide glow for several hours after the exciting radiation is removed. These materials, when stimulated by radiation, emit light of longer wavelength than that to which they were exposed.

The fluorescent lamp utilizes this fact. The fluorescent material or *phosphor* is applied in a thin layer on the inner walls of long tubular glass bulbs containing argon gas and mercury vapor. A lamp has two coiled filaments of tungsten wire, one at each end, and these are connected to the alternating-current supply circuit as shown in the simplified diagram of Fig. 343. In starting the lamp the filaments are momentarily connected in series and become heated; they then serve alternately as cathodes for the emission of electrons to ionize the gas in the tube. Shortly afterward the connection between the two filaments is broken automatically at the switch and thereafter they serve as the tube electrodes. Between them the applied potential difference produces a gaseous discharge that is rich in ultraviolet radiation; this energizes the phosphor, which in turn becomes a brilliant source of visible light, the color depending upon the phosphor used. The operating temperature is relatively low, the glass tube itself being about 45° C. The materials of some phosphors are: calcium tungstate for blue, zinc silicate for green, cadmium borate for pink, magnesium tungstate for blue-white, and calcium halo phosphate for white light.

Luminous-tube Lighting. Long tubes containing gas at low pressures are widely used in display lighting; neon produces an orange-red light, argon and mercury a blue light, and helium a pinkish-white light. The units are operated through step-up transformers. When the circuit is closed an initial potential difference up to 15,000 volts is impressed upon the electrodes of the tube and the gas becomes ionized at the electrodes, the ionization almost instantly extending throughout the tube as a result of the collision of electrons and ions with the atoms of the gas.

360. Vision. The ability of our eyes to afford a picture of our surroundings in form, color, and motion is, of course, of incalculable importance. Although adaptable in seeing things near and far, the eye is, nevertheless, limited to seeing within a narrow range in the gamut of waves that travel through space. This visible range is given in the table of electromagnetic waves in § 333 as extending over wavelengths from 0.000075 to 0.000038 cm; it corresponds to the color range of the spectrum from red to violet. The eye cannot see the neighboring wavelengths of the longer infrared nor the shorter ultraviolet radiations. Furthermore, the eye is not equally sensitive to the radiations within the visible spectrum. Under good lighting the eye is most sensitive to yellow-green light having a wavelength of 0.0000555 cm, and

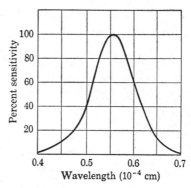

FIG. 344. Relative sensitivity of eye at average illumination

under subdued lighting it is most sensitive to blue-green light having a wavelength of 0.0000505 cm. Experimentation with many persons shows the relative sensitivity of the average eye under good lighting to be as plotted in Fig. 344. This graph, called the *luminosity curve,* shows that the sensitivity of the eye is a maximum (designated arbitrarily as 100%) at the wavelength of 0.0000555 cm, and falls off rapidly for the longer and shorter waves.

The interpretation of the luminosity curve will be considered further. All sources of electromagnetic waves radiate energy, and the amount radiated per unit time is called *radiant flux.* If this radiant flux lies in the visual range, the sensation produced upon the eye is one of *brightness;* the larger the flux, the greater the brightness as measured upon a suitable scale. With equal amounts of radiant flux at different wavelengths in this range, the brightness sensation differs from one wavelength to another, and this is the significance of Fig. 344. Thus radiant flux of wavelength 0.000050 cm is only 40% as effective in evoking the sensation of brightness as the flux of wavelength 0.0000555 cm.

The foregoing consideration shows the need of another term, *luminous flux,* defined as the radiant flux evaluated in terms of its capacity to produce the brightness sensation. The unit of luminous flux is called the *lumen*, and is defined in the next section. It is found that a luminous flux of 680 lumens is equivalent to 1 watt of radiant flux at the wavelength 0.0000555 cm for which the eye is most sensitive. For radiant flux of wavelength 0.000050 cm the luminous flux is equivalent to only 40% of 680 or 272 lumens per watt.

361. Luminous Intensity and Luminous Flux. The luminous intensity of a source of light is expressed in terms of a source selected as a standard; originally the flame of a spermaceti candle burning at the rate of 120 grains per hour was selected for this purpose. This source was regarded as having an intensity of one "international candle" when viewed in a horizontal plane. Subsequently the flame of a specified oil lamp and later the light from calibrated incandescent lamps were used as standards.

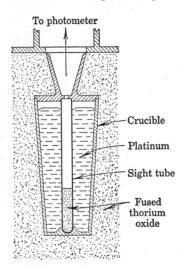

To photometer

Crucible

Platinum

Sight tube

Fused thorium oxide

FIG. 345. Primary standard of luminous intensity

The present primary standard of luminous intensity was developed by the National Bureau of Standards. It consists of a glowing enclosure operated at the temperature of solidifying platinum, 2046° K, and arranged as shown in cross-section by Fig. 345. The platinum, contained in a crucible of fused thorium oxide surrounded by heat insulation, is placed in an alternating magnetic field and melted by the currents thereby induced in it; this method of heating is used because of its violent stirring action. A sight tube, also of fused thorium oxide and containing some of this material in a finely ground state, extends into the molten metal and serves as a black-body radiator, § 186. The brightness within this tube is taken as 60 candles/cm^2 when the metal, in cooling slowly, reaches its solidifying temperature. The new *candle* is therefore one-sixtieth of the luminous intensity of one square centimeter of a hollow enclosure at the temperature of solidifying platinum. This candle is a somewhat smaller unit than the obsolete international candle.

The amount of luminous flux that issues from a source having a luminous intensity of 1 candle can be found by imagining a sphere centered on the source to be illuminated by it. A solid angle of such a sphere is depicted in Fig. 346; its size is so chosen as to embrace unit area at unit distance. This particular angle is called a *steradian;* if the radius of the sphere is 1 ft the unit area is 1 ft^2, and if the radius is 1 m the area is 1 m^2, as shown. *The amount of luminous flux that radiates from a one-candle source throughout a solid angle of one steradian is defined as one lumen.*

Since the total area of the spherical surface is 4π times the square of its radius, it follows that the total luminous flux from a source having a luminous intensity of 1 candle is 4π lumens. A source that produces I candles uniformly in all directions has a total luminous flux output in lumens given by

$$F = 4\pi I \qquad (257)$$

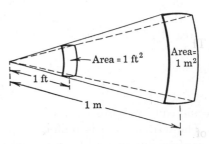

For example, if a 100-watt tungsten lamp had a uniform luminous intensity of 130 candles in all directions, the luminous flux from it would be $4\pi130 =$ 1630 lumens. Because the filament of

FIG. 346. Solid angle extending to unit area at unit distance

an actual lamp is not symmetrical in all planes, and because of the presence of its base for connection purposes, the light flux cannot be the same in all directions.

362. Efficiency of Light Sources. Electric lamps are commonly rated in terms of their power input in watts, and their outputs are stated in lumens. The efficiency, instead of being expressed numerically by a percentage as with machines, is given more usefully as the ratio of the output in lumens to the input in watts. Data on some modern 110- to 120-volt lamps are listed in the following table. The incandescent lamps are of the tungsten gas-

EFFICIENCIES OF ELECTRIC LAMPS

Incandescent			Fluorescent		
Input to lamp, watts	Output, lumens	Efficiency, lumens per watt	Input to bulb, watts	Output, lumens	Efficiency, lumens per watt
40	465	11.6		*Warm white*	
60	835	13.9	20	1030	52
100	1630	16.3	30	1930	64
200	3700	18.5	40	2600	65
300	5700	19.0		*Blue*	
500	9900	19.8	20	460	23
750	15,600	20.1		*Green*	
1000	21,500	21.5	20	1300	65

filled type for direct or alternating current. The fluorescent lamps are for alternating current, and the tube lengths are 2, 3, and 4 ft respectively for the 20-, 30- and 40-watt sizes. The efficiencies of high-intensity mercury vapor lamps (250- and 400-watt sizes) and of sodium vapor lamps (180-watt size) are approximately 40 and 50 lumens per watt respectively.

363. Illumination of Surfaces. The illumination of a surface is defined as the amount of luminous flux it receives per unit area. For a surface of area A which receives a total flux F, the illumination is

$$E = \frac{F}{A} \tag{258}$$

and can be expressed in lumens per square foot or lumens per square meter. The illumination is uniform when the flux distribution is uniform. For a surface illuminated by a single lamp the illumination is uniform only when all portions of the surface are equally distant from the source.

The amount of illumination produced by a light source upon a given surface is determined by the luminous intensity of the source, its distance from the surface, and the direction of the rays. Upon increasing the intensity I of the source, the light flux falling upon the surface increases proportionately. Upon increasing the distance r from the source, the illumination of the surface varies inversely with the square of the distance in accordance with the Inverse Square Law, § 186. When both of these factors are considered, the illumination is found to vary as I/r^2, or $E = kI/r^2$, where k is a proportionality factor. Illumination is frequently expressed in foot-candles; *one foot-candle is the illumination of a surface one foot away from a uniform point source of one candle.* With this unit the factor k becomes unity, and the expression can be written

$$E = \frac{I}{r^2} \tag{259}$$

giving the illumination produced by a source having a luminous intensity of I candles upon a surface at a distance of r ft. The numerical value of illumination is the same whether expressed in foot-candles or in lumens per square foot.

Illustrative Problem

To prove this equality by a numerical illustration, consider a surface that is everywhere 6 ft away from a 200-watt lamp which has a luminous intensity of 294 candles in all directions.

The illumination of the surface as given by Eq. 259 is $E = 294/6^2 = 8.17$ foot-candles. To compute the illumination in lumens per square foot it is necessary to determine the total light flux issuing from the lamp and the total area over which it spreads uniformly. The total flux emitted is $4\pi294 = 3700$ lumens, and the spherical surface of 6-ft radius has an area of $4\pi(6)^2 = 453$ ft^2; consequently the illumination computed from Eq. 258 is $E = \dfrac{4\pi294}{4\pi36} = 8.17$ lumens/ft^2, the same as before.

The recommended values of illumination have been rising steadily over the years; a few of the values currently regarded by illuminating engineers as suitable for particular locations are listed in the accompanying table.

ILLUMINATION VALUES

Location	Foot-candles	Location	Foot-candles
Auditoriums......	20–30	Homes..........	5–50
Cafeterias........	30	Laboratories......	50
Classrooms.......	50	Libraries.........	50
Corridors........	10	Offices..........	30–100
Drafting rooms...	100–150	Show windows....	200
Factories........	50–70	Sports areas......	20–200
Flood lighting.....	10–20	Stores..........	20–100

In calculating the illumination from a single source by Eq. 259, it is supposed that all parts of the surface are at the same distance r from the source. This expression is, therefore, true only for a spherical surface with the source at the center, as shown in part I of Fig. 347. It can also be used without appreciable error for a flat surface having dimensions that are small compared with the distance to the source, provided the light flux is approximately perpendicular to the surface, as shown in part II of the figure. In brief, the equation $E = I/r^2$ applies to normal illumination. If a flat surface receiving the light flux F under normal illumination is inclined so that its normal N makes an angle i with the light rays, as indicated in part III of the figure, then the light flux intercepted by the surface is reduced from F to $F \cos i$, and the illumination is lowered in the same proportion. A source of intensity I at a distance r produces upon such an inclined surface an illumination

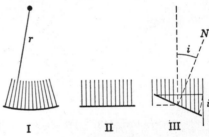

Fig. 347.　Normal and oblique illumination of surfaces

$$E = \frac{I \cos i}{r^2} \tag{260}$$

provided the surface dimensions are small in comparison with the distance to the source.

364. Photometric Measurements. The eye is not capable of comparing the intensities of two light sources by viewing them directly, but can determine quite accurately whether two surfaces side by side are equally bright. This is the operating principle of the visual *photometer*. In this device, two lamps are placed a suitable distance apart with a screen between them, each side of the screen being illuminated normally by one of the sources. The screen of the Bunsen photometer consists of a small sheet of paper with a waxed spot near the center, and is provided with a pair of mirrors so that an observer can see both sides at the same time. The screen is moved laterally until both sides appear equally bright, and the distances from it to the lamps are measured. Then from Eq. 259 it follows that

$$\frac{I_1}{r_1{}^2} = \frac{I_2}{r_2{}^2} \tag{261}$$

where I_1 and I_2 are the luminous intensities of the sources in candles, and r_1 and r_2 are their respective distances from the screen. From this equation, the intensity of either lamp can be computed if that of the other is known.

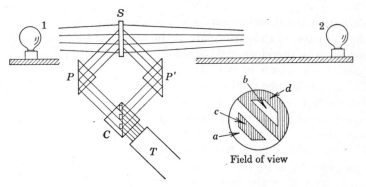

FIG. 348. Arrangement of Lummer-Brodhun photometer

The Lummer-Brodhun photometer has an improved optical system. Its elements, shown in Fig. 348, comprise a white opaque screen S, an observing telescope T, reflecting prisms P and P', and a compound glass cube C. The latter element consists of two prisms cemented together, one having a design etched in its principal face to give the field of view the appearance shown. The paths of light along which both sides of the screen can be observed in the telescope are also indicated in the figure. From the side illuminated by source 1, the rays pass to P and are reflected to C, the light passing through to the telescope without obstruction except where the cube is etched. From the other side, illuminated by source 2, the rays pass to P' and are reflected to C, where the light is reflected at the etched portions into the telescope. The field of view is thereby illuminated at zones a and b by lamp 1 and at zones c and d by lamp 2. When the screen is so placed as to to be equally illuminated by the sources, the pattern vanishes and the field

appears uniform throughout. This arrangement, whereby a zone illuminated by one source is completely surrounded by another illuminated by the
other source, makes it easy for the eye to judge equality of illumination, and
permits the luminous intensities of the light sources to be compared with
precision.

The procedure for determining the candle power of a lamp by comparison
with the primary black-body standard, § 361, utilizes a photometer to compare the illumination on two sides of a screen. One of these is illuminated
by the lamp under test. The other receives the radiation from the primary
standard after it passes through an aperture of known size placed near it, a
lens being used to form an image of the source upon the screen. The illumination of this image may be found by the equation $E = I/r^2$, in which I
is taken as the product of the brightness of the source (60 candles/cm^2) and
the area of the aperture in square centimeters, and r as the distance from
the aperture to the screen.

Illustrative Problem

Suppose that equal illumination is produced when a lamp under test and
the aperture of the primary standard are respectively 125 cm and 340 cm
distant from the screen, the aperture having a radius of 0.85 cm. Determine the luminous intensity of the test lamp.

If I is the luminous intensity of the lamp under test, then the illumination
it produces at 125 cm is $I/(125)^2$. The illumination produced by the primary
standard at 340 cm is $60\pi (0.85)^2/(340)^2$. An equality of these illumination
values results in $I = 18.4$ candles as the luminous intensity of the lamp under test.

Difficulties are encountered when it is attempted to compare the intensities of two lamps that have different colors, since the eye cannot judge accurately the equality of illumination of two surfaces unless their colors match
approximately. Lamps of different colors can be compared by means of a
so-called *flicker photometer* which has a rotating prism or other optical arrangement to enable the observer to view first one side of the screen and then
the other alternately in rapid succession. Upon increasing the frequency of
alternation, a value can be found for which the flicker due to color difference
disappears, the colors of the two sources appearing to blend into a single resultant hue. If the frequency is not too high, however, the flicker due to
illumination difference remains. The photometer screen is then moved until this flicker also disappears, yielding a brightness equality, whereupon the
intensity of the test lamp can be computed in the usual way.

The photoelectric cell, § 315, is now usually employed in photometric
measurements instead of the eye. Cells are now available which, when used
with suitable filters, have the same sensitivity characteristics as the normal
eye, § 360. The cell is exposed to each lamp in turn and the corresponding
currents in the cell are indicated by a microammeter. Since the current is

proportional to the illumination at the cell, the luminous intensity of one lamp can be expressed definitely in terms of the other regarded as a standard.

Measurements of total luminous flux are made by placing the lamp under test within a large sphere, called a *sphere photometer*, and observing the illumination which it produces at the inner surface. The walls of the photometer chamber are painted dull white in order to scatter the light in all directions. While direct illumination of the surface by the light source may have different values at various points, the illumination produced by reflection is uniform over the surface and is proportional to the flux emitted by the source. This illumination is measured at a small translucent window in the spherical shell that is shielded against direct radiation from the source, the readings being made with a photoelectric cell.

If two lamps tested in a sphere photometer are found to emit luminous fluxes F_1 and F_2, and produce illumination values E_1 and E_2 respectively, it follows that

$$\frac{E_1}{E_2} = \frac{F_1}{F_2}$$

Therefore, by Eq. 259, the ratio of their luminous intensities is

$$\frac{I_1}{I_2} = \frac{E_1}{E_2}$$

showing that the luminous intensity of a lamp is proportional to the illumination which it produces on the window of the instrument.

365. Measurement of Illumination. Since the object of artificial lighting is to produce adequate illumination, it is essential to have convenient means for measuring this quantity. One instrument for this purpose is the *illuminometer;* it is virtually a portable photometer for comparing the illumination of the surface under measurement with that produced by a small incandescent lamp of known intensity. The lamp is mounted within a light-tight enclosure and can be moved until it produces the same illumination as that existing upon the surface. Its value is then known to be $E = I/r^2$, where I is the luminous intensity of the standard lamp, and r its distance from the surface. Since each position of the standard lamp corresponds to a particular value of illumination, a

Fig. 349. Foot-candle meter for measuring illumination. (*Courtesy of Weston Electrical Instrument Corporation*)

scale can be provided on the instrument to give the result in foot-candles directly.

Another device for measuring illumination is the photovoltaic cell, § 324, which generates an emf under exposure to light. In the usual form a plate of copper is coated with a semi-transparent layer of copper oxide and electrons pass from the copper oxide to the copper; the cell develops an emf that is proportional to the illumination. The current is indicated on a microammeter, the scale of which usually is calibrated directly in foot-candles. No external source of emf is necessary. Fig. 349 is an instrument of this type. Exposure meters used by photographers also make use of photovoltaic cells.

366. Illumination of Rooms. For correct interior lighting a sufficient amount of light should be provided to give the desired value of illumination, and the lighting units should be so designed and placed as to make it reasonably uniform, without glare.

The three basic methods of lighting are the so-called direct, indirect, and semi-indirect methods. With direct lighting, the lamps project light directly upon the desired working surfaces. With indirect lighting, the lamps are concealed entirely, and the illumination is produced by reflection from the walls and ceiling of the room. With semi-indirect lighting, the illumination is produced in part by light reflected from the walls and ceiling, and in part by direct transmission, usually through translucent glassware. In all of these methods, a large amount of light is absorbed by the walls and ceiling, particularly if these are dark-colored, making it necessary to generate more luminous flux at the lamps than is received at the plane of utilization.

The usual procedure for determining the proper lamps to be installed involves three steps: (1) a calculation of the amount of luminous flux that should reach the working plane in order to produce the desired illumination; (2) the application of a *coefficient of utilization* suitable for the installation to obtain the amount of luminous flux to be generated in the lamps; and (3) a determination of the size and number of lamps to be used.

The coefficient of utilization gives the amount of light that reaches the working plane expressed as a fraction of that produced by the lamps; its value varies with the type of lighting unit, the room proportions, and the color of walls and ceiling. Such coefficients have been determined for a wide variety of conditions and their values can be obtained from lamp manufacturers.

Illustrative Problem

The procedure can be illustrated by laying out the fluorescent lighting for a room, measuring 30 × 40 ft and having a ceiling height of 15 ft, to provide an illumination of 20 foot-candles. Assume a coefficient of utilization of 0.39 as appropriate for the proportions of the room and the percentage of reflectance from walls and ceiling.

The ceiling of the room can be divided suitably into 12 squares, each 10 ft on a side; a luminaire at the center of each square would afford reasonably uniform illumination. The desired illumination is equivalent to 20 lumens/ft², and since the area to be illuminated is $30 \times 40 = 1200$ ft², it follows that the working plane is to receive $1200 \times 20 = 24,000$ lumens. To provide this amount of luminous flux requires that the lamps develop $24,000 \div 0.39 = 61,500$ lumens. Thus each of the 12 luminaires would have to produce 5125 lumens. Reference to the table of lamp efficiencies shows that each luminaire should have 2 fluorescent lamps rated at 40 watts each.

SPEED OF LIGHT

367. Measuring the Speed of Light. The speed of light is so extremely great that early attempts to measure it were entirely unsuccessful. It is recorded that Galileo conducted an experiment in which two men, stationed

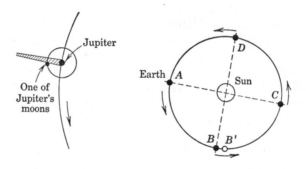

FIG. 350.   Measuring speed of light by Roemer's method

some distance apart, flashed signals to each other with lanterns, a new signal being sent out at the instant one was received. It was hoped that after sending a number of such signals, the speed of light could be found by dividing the total distance the light traveled by the total elapsed time. It is easy to recognize now that altogether too much time was lost between the receipt of a signal and the sending of a new one; hence the method was bound to fail. Some decades later significant results were achieved by astronomical methods.

The first successful measurement of the speed of light was made by the Danish astronomer Ole Roemer (1644–1710), from observations on the revolution of one of the moons of the planet Jupiter. This method is illustrated in Fig. 350, which represents Jupiter and the earth in their orbits about the sun. Roemer found that the time interval between two eclipses of the satellite (about 40 hr) was the same when measured with the earth at A or at C, but that the interval was lengthened when the earth was at B and shortened when at D. These variations, he judged correctly, were not due to irregular motion of the satellite, but were caused by the fact that it takes time for light to travel. Thus, if the earth were at B at the beginning of a measurement, it would move away to some position B' during the 40-hr interval between eclipses, and the light would have to travel the additional distance BB' to mark the conclusion of the test, thereby increasing the elapsed time.

From measurements made with the earth at A, Roemer predicted the time at which the moon in question would emerge from behind Jupiter for a particular transit when the earth had moved to C about 6 months later, on the supposition that the speed of light is infinite. He found this event to occur many minutes later than predicted on this assumption, and considered the difference between the observed and calculated times to represent the time required by the light to traverse the diameter of the earth's orbit. From more recent measurements the time difference is approximately 1000 sec and the diameter of the earth's orbit is 186,000,000 mi, thus giving 186,000 mi/sec as the speed of light.

368. Terrestrial Methods. A terrestrial method for measuring the speed of light was devised by the French physicist, Jean B. L. Foucault (1819–1868). He directed a narrow beam of light upon a plane mirror rotating at high speed, and the reflected beam flashed around accordingly. A distant mirror received a momentary flash of light and reflected it back to the rotating mirror, from which it was reflected to the observer. During the time interval in which the light beam traveled

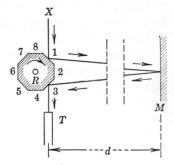

FIG. 351.   Measuring speed of light by Michelson's method

the measurable distance to the distant mirror and back, the rotating mirror turned through some definite angle, and from observations of these quantities the speed of light was computed.

The rotating-mirror method was improved by the American physicist Albert A. Michelson (1852–1931). The essential parts of the apparatus are indicated in Fig. 351. Light from an intense source X strikes one face of an octagonal mirror R, and is reflected to a distant plane mirror M; the ray that returns strikes another face of the octagonal mirror and is reflected into the observer's telescope T. When the octagonal mirror is set into rotation in a clockwise direction, flashes of light strike the distant mirror and the reflected beam falls to the left of the telescope, since the mirror will have turned through a small angle. If the rotation of the octagonal mirror is increased, a speed is reached such that in the time required for the light to travel to the mirror M and back again, mirror face 2 advances to the position shown at 3. Under this condition the light is reflected into the telescope again for observation. If n represents the speed of the mirror in revolutions per second, then the time required to turn through one-eighth of a revolution is $\frac{1}{8}$ of $1/n$ sec. In this time the light travels to mirror M and back, a distance $2d$; consequently the speed of light becomes

$$V = \frac{2d}{\dfrac{1}{8n}} = 16\ nd$$

In Michelson's experiment, the revolving mirror was located at the observatory on Mt. Wilson, California, and the stationary mirror was at Mt. San Antonio, the distance between them (about 22 mi) being measured with great precision by the U. S. Coast and Geodetic Survey. The speed of the revolving mirror was determined by comparison with an electrically operated tuning fork, the fork in turn being calibrated against a free pendulum, which finally was compared with a standard astronomical clock. The speed of light so determined becomes 299,776 km/sec when reduced to a vacuum. Later tests using an evacuated tube 1 mi long gave results agreeing substantially with this value.

The latest determination of the speed of light was made by electrical means using an instrument devised by the Swedish scientist Eric Bergstrand and called a geodimeter. Pulses from oscillators having modulating frequencies close to 10 mc were sent over an accurately measured distance (about 11 km) in Wiltshire, England. The result was reported in 1956 by the British Ordnance Survey Office as 299,792.4 km/sec. In general calculations the speed of light is rounded out to 300,000 km/sec and to 186,000 mi/sec.

The speed of light in the atmosphere is so nearly the same as in a vacuum that the values for the latter apply without appreciable error. In other mediums, the speed is less than in a vacuum and, moreover, is different for different wavelengths, blue light traveling slower than red light.

So great is this speed that the light emitted by the sun reaches the earth in only 8.3 min, whereas a jet airplane traveling at 1000 mi/hr would require over 10 years for the same distance. The light from the stars takes years to reach the earth; for the nearest of them, α in the Centauri group, the time is about 4.3 years; the distance to this star is conveniently expressed as 4.3 light-years. The great spiral galaxy in Andromeda is over a million light-years distant. The light we now see from most of the stars left them centuries ago.

PROBLEMS

1. Two beams of monochromatic light are combined; the energy of one having a wavelength of 5×10^{-5} cm is 8 watts and the energy of the other having a wavelength of 6×10^{-5} cm is 12 watts. For the combined beam find the radiant flux and the luminous flux.

2. Determine the luminous intensities of 40-watt and 60-watt incandescent lamps on the supposition that the luminous flux from them is distributed uniformly in all directions.

3. Operating an incandescent lamp at a pd 10% above its rated value increases the input current 5% and the output lumens 35%, although such use decreases the life of the lamp. How does this change of pd affect the efficiency of the lamp?

4. The illumination at a particular area on a horizontal workbench is 25 foot-candles and this is to be increased fourfold by means of a supplementary incandescent lamp. Assume this lamp to produce 5700 lumens and to radiate uniformly in all directions; compute the height at which it should be placed vertically above the area mentioned.

5. A 120-volt incandescent lamp is supported at the center of a spherical enclosure 5 ft in diameter. When supplied with its rated current of 1.25 amp, the lamp is found to produce an illumination of 34.4 foot-candles on the inner surface of the enclosure. Find the output of the lamp in lumens and its efficiency in lumens per watt.

6. A two-lamp combination of 40-watt warm-white fluorescent lamps with their ballasts takes a current of 0.85 amp on 120 volts. The ballast of one lamp has inductive reactance only and the other has both capacitive and inductive reactance in series, an arrangement that improves the power factor of the circuit to an over-all value of 90%. The power loss in the ballast is 18 watts. What is the light output per watt of electrical power supplied to the bulbs?

7. A desk measuring 3×5 ft is illuminated by a single incandescent lamp placed 5 ft above its center. Compare the direct illumination at the center of the desk surface with that at one corner.

8. Two lamps are mounted upright at opposite ends of a photometer bench 4 m long; their luminous intensities in a horizontal direction are 40 and 300 candles. (*a*) At what position along the bench between the lamps will a screen be illuminated equally on both sides? (*b*) What is the illumination on the screen at this position, assuming it to be placed transversely to the bench?

9. The diagram shows a simple form of photometer. The sources S_1 and S_2 illuminate the wall W, upon which a rod R casts shadows at regions a and b. In a particular test these regions are found to be equally illuminated for $S_2 = 66$ candles when the rod is 1.0 ft from the wall and sources S_1 and S_2 are respectively 5.0 ft and 4.1 ft from the rod. Calculate the luminous intensity of source S_1.

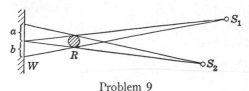

Problem 9

10. The luminous intensities of two lamps are compared by causing each in turn to produce normal illumination upon a photovoltaic cell and observing the corresponding current produced by the cell. When a standard lamp of 130 candles is placed 1.5 m from the cell the current is 8.0 microamp, and when a test lamp of unknown intensity is placed 1.2 m from the cell the current is 6.2 microamp. Compute the luminous intensity of the test lamp.

11. An illumination meter, such as that shown in Fig. 349, has two parallel-connected photovoltaic cells, each of 1.45 in. diameter. Together, the

cells produce a current of 1.5 microamp per foot-candle of illumination. (a) Determine the sensitivity of the device in microamperes per lumen. When illuminated by a lamp held 3 ft vertically above the cells the meter receives a current of 22 microamps; (b) what is the luminous intensity of the lamp in the direction in which it is held?

12. A room that measures 24 × 16 ft is to be lighted with 115-volt incandescent lamps. The walls and ceiling are such as to have a coefficient of utilization of 0.5. Lay out a plan of illumination for this room to provide 45 lumens/ft² and specify the number and size of lamps required.

13. An indoor sports area at Union College measuring 200 × 200 ft is illuminated by 35 luminaires each having 14 fluorescent lamps 8 ft long. Each lamp produces 6000 lumens when operated on 400-cycle alternating current supplied at 600 volts. Each luminaire has capacitive and inductive ballasts so that the current it takes, 2.3 amp, is practically at unity power factor. (a) Assume that the coefficient of utilization is 0.63 and calculate the illumination produced. (b) What is the over-all efficiency of this lighting installation in useful lumens per watt?

14. The great spiral galaxy in Andromeda is reported by astronomers to be about 450 kiloparsecs distant from the earth. The parsec is defined as the distance at which the radius of the earth's orbit subtends one second of arc. Estimate the distance to this galaxy in light-years.

15. An early terrestrial method for measuring the speed of light was devised by Fizeau; he sent a beam of light through an opening between the teeth of a gear wheel placed transversely to the beam, and adjusted the speed of the wheel so that the beam, after reflection from a distant fixed mirror, would pass through the next adjacent opening between the gear teeth. If a gear with 200 teeth were used, how rapidly should it rotate in order for the reflected light to be received as indicated from a mirror 10 mi away?

16. In some tests made by Michelson light was reflected back and forth in an evacuated tube about 1 mi long, and its speed was measured with the aid of a 32-sided mirror. In one test the length of the light path was 12.811 km, and the speed of the mirror was 731.22 rev/sec for the outgoing beam to be reflected from one face and the returning beam from the next. Determine the speed of light from these data.

17. (a) A workman carries a stovepipe along level ground at a speed of 1.5 m/sec while it is raining. If the drops fall vertically with a speed of 4 m/sec, at what angle should he incline the pipe to the vertical in order that the drops entering at the top will follow its axis, and emerge at the lower end?

(b) A star directly overhead is to be observed through a telescope. Knowing that the telescope is actually moving at 18.5 mi/sec because of the earth's motion around the sun, and assuming that this motion is at right angles to an imaginary line joining star and observer, find the angle at which the telescope should be inclined in order that the star can be seen centrally through it.

34

REFLECTION AND REFRACTION

REFLECTION

369. Regular and Diffuse Reflection. The behavior of waves upon striking plane surfaces has been considered in Chap. 30, wherein Huygens' construction is used to determine the location of the resulting wave fronts. To apply this procedure to the reflection of light, a source S of luminous flux is located in front of the plane mirror M in Fig. 352. At some particular in-

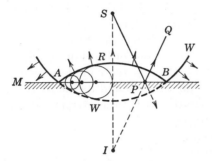

Fig. 352. Reflection of spherical wave at plane surface

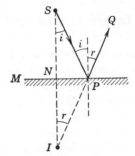

Fig. 353. Reflection of ray at plane surface

stant the wave front originating at S would have advanced to position WW had it not been for the reflecting surface. When points A and B on the wave front have reached the positions shown, each of its intermediate points has reached the reflecting surface and returned to some position along the arc of a secondary wavelet. Several of these wavelets are represented by the circles in the figure. A curve tangent to the circles shows the position of the reflected wave front R; the reflected wave appears to have come from I, and this point is said to be the *image* of S. By symmetry, the image I is located on a line through S normal to the mirror surface, and is as far back of the mirror as the object is in front of it. Thus a ray of light SP upon striking the mirror is redirected along PQ as though it had come from the image I.

These rays, together with the normal connecting the source S and the image I, are transferred to Fig. 353 for clearness. Since the source and image are equally distant from the mirror, $SN = NI$, and the triangles SNP and INP are similar, the side NP being common. It follows that angle i at

S and angle *r* at *I* are equal, and these in turn are equal to the angles similarly marked at *P*. Thus, as stated in the law of reflection, § 335, the angle of incidence *i* between the incident ray and the normal is equal to the angle of reflection *r* between the reflected ray and the normal, both angles being in the same plane.

Reflection of light from a smooth surface, like that of a mirror, takes place along a definite direction determined by the direction of the incident ray, and is called *regular* or *specular*. Reflection from a rough or mat surface, like that of plaster or blotting paper, occurs in a great many directions for any one direction of the incident beam, as indicated in Fig. 354, and is said to be *diffuse* or *scattered*. It is by diffuse reflection that nonluminous objects become visible. The law of reflection is evidently true for each tiny element of the reflecting surface in diffuse reflection.

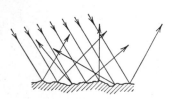

FIG. 354. Reflection of parallel beam from rough surface

370. Images Formed by Plane Mirrors. The image of a point object formed by reflection in a plane mirror is located the same distance behind the reflecting surface that the object is in front of it. For an extended object, each image point is similarly located and the complete image can be constructed readily. Fig. 355 shows an object *O* and its image *I* formed by reflection in the mirror *M*. Rays are drawn for the extreme object points toward the mirror and redirected to an eye at *E*, the angles of incidence, as at *i* and *i'*, being made equal respectively to the angles of reflection, as at *r* and *r'*. The rays from each object point enter the eye as a diverging pencil, and the image is at the point where the prolongations of these rays intersect.

In drawing a ray from an object point to the mirror and thence to the eye so that the angles of incidence and reflection become equal, the procedure is (1) to locate the corresponding image point as far back of the reflecting surface as the object point is in front of it; (2) to draw the line from that image point to the eye and determine its intersection with the mirror; and (3) to draw the ray from the object point to this mirror point and redirect it from there to the eye.

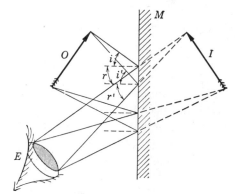

FIG. 355. Seeing image of object in plane mirror

Two plane mirrors that are inclined to each other yield multiple images of an object placed between them. These images can be located and **the** rays drawn by the procedure just described.

371. Rotation of Reflected Ray. The rotation of a plane mirror upon which a ray of light falls causes the reflected ray to rotate also; the rotation of the reflected ray is found to be *twice* that of the mirror. This fact is used in amplifying the deflections of galvanometers and other sensitive instruments, and is mentioned in § 252. In Fig. 356 an incident ray of light from a source S falls upon a plane mirror M at an angle i with the normal N; it is reflected along Y at an equal angle r, and the angle $SOY = i + r = 2i$.

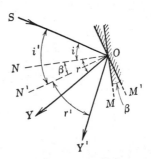

Upon rotating the mirror through an angle β to M', the normal undergoes an equal rotation to N'; the angle of incidence increases to $i' = i + \beta$, and the angle of reflection r' increases equally, the reflected ray being rotated to the position shown at Y'. The angle $SOY' = i' + r' = 2i'$, which may be written $2(i + \beta)$. The reflected ray, therefore, rotates through an angle

$$YOY' = SOY' - SOY = 2(i + \beta) - 2i = 2\beta$$

which is twice the rotation of the mirror.

FIG. 356. Effect of turning mirror on direction of reflected ray

This fact is made use of in the sextant, a portable instrument for determining latitude by observing the angle between the sun and the horizon. It consists essentially of two mirrors—the movable index glass M and the fixed horizon glass m shown in Fig. 357, both supported perpendicularly to a metal framework which also carries the telescope and a scale. Mirror m is clear over half its surface so that the observer's eye at E can see the horizon beyond B directly, that is, without reflection at mirror m. Mirror M is carried by an arm that is pivoted at P and fitted with a vernier V at its other end to enable the position of the index glass to be read accurately on scale S. When the two mirrors are parallel, the observer can also see the horizon via the path $AMmE$, and the image blends with the direct one obtained along BE; the vernier for this position of mirror M reads zero. In viewing the sun at an angle θ degrees above the horizon, the arm carrying the mirror is turned through an angle $\theta/2$ so that the rays from the sun coming along the line CM are reflected along the line Mm, and again reflected into the telescope by the silvered portion of the horizon glass m. The image of the sun is then aligned with the image of the horizon, and the altitude of the sun is twice the angle through which the vernier arm is turned.

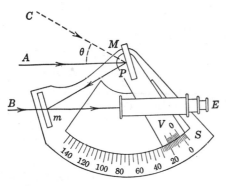

FIG. 357. Principal parts of a sextant

372. Spherical Mirrors. Curved mirrors are used to deviate a beam of light and at the same time to render it more or less converging than it was before incidence. Spherical mirrors are classified as *concave* and *convex*, depending on whether the reflecting surface is on the inside or outside of the spherical shell.

Fig. 358 shows a concave and a convex mirror *M M*, with the center of each spherical surface, called the *center of curvature* of the mirror, designated by *C*. The line *XX* connecting the middle point of the mirror surface and

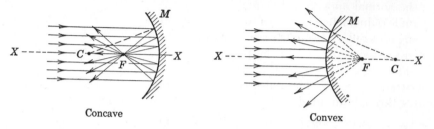

Fig. 358.   Reflection of parallel light from spherical mirrors

the center of curvature is called the *principal axis* of the mirror. A parallel beam of light incident upon each mirror along its principal axis is shown before and after reflection.

Most spherical mirrors used for optical purposes are comparatively flat, that is, the dimensions of the mirror are small in comparison with the radius of the surface; such mirrors are said to have a small *aperture*. With such a mirror, a bundle of rays parallel to the principal axis converges through a

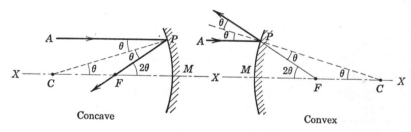

Fig. 359.   Location of focus of spherical mirrors

common point *F* after reflection if the mirror is concave, or diverges as though originating from a common point *F* if the mirror is convex. The point *F* is the *principal focus* of the mirror, and its distance from the mirror is called its *focal length*. The concentration of parallel rays from the sun at the focus of a concave mirror can be shown experimentally by their ability to melt a bit of wax or scorch a piece of paper placed at that point.

The principal focus of a spherical mirror is located on the principal axis half way between the center of curvature and the mirror surface. This relation can be proved by reference to the diagrams for a concave and a convex mirror in Fig. 359. In either, an incident ray AP, parallel to the principal axis XX, strikes the mirror M at point P and is reflected along the line PF. The angle of incidence between the ray AP and the normal PC is indicated by θ, and the angle of reflection, equal to the angle of incidence, is similarly lettered. Further, the angle made by the normal at C with the principal axis is equal to θ, since AP and XX are parallel. The angle between the reflected ray and this axis at F is 2θ, for the same reason. For mirrors of slight curvature, the angles θ are small, and the surface PM may be considered perpendicular to the principal axis. Hence the figures CPM and FPM are virtually triangles, and therefore

$$PM = CM \tan \theta = FM \tan 2\theta$$

But the tangents of small angles may be set equal to the angles themselves; thus $(CM)\theta = (FM)2\theta$, or $CM = 2FM$. If the focal length FM is represented by f and the radius of curvature by r, then

$$f = \frac{r}{2} \tag{262}$$

showing that the focal length of a spherical mirror is equal to half its radius of curvature. This relation is restricted to mirrors that are only slightly curved, but most spherical mirrors are of this type.

373. Images Formed by Spherical Mirrors. The images produced by spherical mirrors may be larger or smaller than the object, and may be either real or virtual. An image is called *real* if the rays after reflection actually

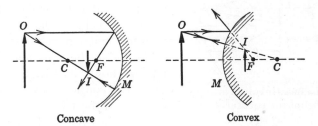

Concave   Convex

FIG. 360.   Location of images formed by spherical mirrors

pass through it, and *virtual* if they only appear to do so. Both types present the same appearance to the eye, but a real image can be received upon a screen, whereas a virtual image cannot.

A graphical method of image location, using rays of light, is indicated in Fig. 360 for a concave and a convex mirror of small aperture. In either mirror, two particular rays are drawn from an object point O to the mirror M and are there reflected; one ray parallel to the axis passes through the principal focus F after reflection if the mirror is concave, or its prolongation does so if the mirror is convex; the other ray through the center of curvature C strikes the mirror normally and is reflected back upon itself. The intersection of these reflected rays (or their prolongations) is the corresponding image point I. Any other point of the image may be found in the same way. The figure shows the entire objects and images sketched in position by symmetry; the image formed by the concave mirror is real, inverted, and reduced, and that formed by the convex mirror is virtual, erect, and reduced.

Concave mirrors can produce images which are real or virtual, erect or inverted, magnified or reduced, depending upon the position of the object. Convex mirrors always produce virtual, erect, and reduced images of real objects. Although two rays are sufficient to locate the image of a point, it must not be inferred that only two are effective in forming the image. All other rays from the object point that strike the mirror contribute to the image as well; consequently the larger the mirror, the brighter the image.

The image of an object can be located analytically by means of the equation

$$\frac{1}{p} + \frac{1}{q} = \frac{2}{r} = \frac{1}{f} \tag{263}$$

in which p is the distance from the object to the mirror, q the distance from the image to the mirror, r the radius of the mirror, and f its focal length.

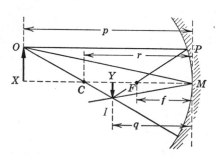

FIG. 361. Distances involved in applying the mirror equation

The equation can be made to apply to both concave and convex mirrors by considering distances back of the mirror to be negative; thus, r and f have *negative* values for a *convex* mirror. A negative value for q signifies that the image is behind the mirror and is, therefore, virtual.

To derive the equation, the concave mirror shown in Fig. 361 will be regarded as considerably flatter than depicted and the triangles formed by the rays will be evaluated. The object and image are located respectively at O and I as in the previous figure, and the same two rays are shown joining their head-ends, one to P and through F, and the other through C and back upon itself. An additional ray is shown between these points; it extends from O to M and is reflected by the mirror along MI, the incident and reflected rays making equal angles with the axis XM. These three rays form two pairs of similar triangles. From one pair, OXC and IYC, it follows that

$$\frac{OX}{IY} = \frac{XC}{CY} = \frac{p - r}{r - q}$$

and from the other pair, OXM and IYM,

$$\frac{OX}{IY} = \frac{p}{q}$$

Hence $\dfrac{p}{q} = \dfrac{p-r}{r-q}$, or $qr + pr = 2pq$. If this expression is divided by pqr, there results

$$\frac{1}{p} + \frac{1}{q} = \frac{2}{r}$$

and the focal distance $f = r/2$, as before. The relation between the object distance p, the image distance q, and the radius r applies to any spherical mirror, whether concave or convex, provided it has a small aperture.

The magnification produced by a mirror (or lens) of all lines transverse to its principal axis is called the linear or *lateral magnification*. Its value for the mirror of Fig. 361 can be found from the similar triangles OXM and IYM. The size of the image IY is to the size of the object OX as the image distance q is to the object distance p, the signs being neglected. Hence, for any spherical mirror

$$\text{Magnification} = \frac{IY}{OX} = \frac{q}{p} \tag{264}$$

Illustrative Problem

For example, an object is placed 12 cm in front of a convex spherical mirror of 15-cm radius. Locate and describe the image, and find its size for an object 3.0 cm high.

Solve Eq. 263 for the reciprocal of q and substitute numerical values as follows:

$$\frac{1}{q} = \frac{2}{r} - \frac{1}{p} = \frac{2}{-15} - \frac{1}{12} = -\frac{13}{60}$$

from which $q = -60/13 = -4.62$ cm. Consequently, a virtual image will be formed 4.62 cm behind the mirror. The right-hand diagram in Fig. 360, if drawn to scale, would serve as a graphical solution of this problem, and would show further that the image is erect. The height of the image, from Eq. 264, is $(4.62/12) \times 3.0 = 1.150$ cm.

374. Spherical Aberration. The foregoing treatment of spherical mirrors applies to those of small aperture, the incident light rays being only slightly inclined to the principal axis. When such is not the case, the images formed are confused and imperfect. Thus, rays issuing from a point source on the axis do not come to a focus at a common point; instead, the rays reflected from the outer parts of the mirror cross the axis nearer to the mirror than those reflected from the central portion. This imperfection is called *spheri-*

cal aberration, and is illustrated in Fig. 362, where the symbols C and M have the same meaning as before. The rays from the source P reflected from this wide-aperture mirror intersect as shown and generate a bright surface called the *caustic* of the mirror. A

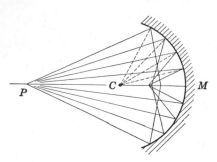

similar effect can be observed on the surface of milk in a glass when illuminated obliquely by a distant source, the glass acting as the reflector and the milk as a screen.

It is possible, of course, to design a reflecting surface of such shape that rays from a definite object point will be brought to a common focus. For an object point at infinity, the mirror would be a paraboloid; this form of mirror is often used with searchlights

FIG. 362. Spherical aberration of a mirror

and automobile headlights. The lamp is placed at the focus, and the light initially directed toward the mirror is reflected in a parallel beam.

REFRACTION

375. Refractive Index. The phenomenon of refraction is described in § 336, where it is shown that a plane wave undergoes an abrupt change of direction upon passing obliquely into another medium wherein it travels with a different speed. This result can be represented more simply with rays of light than by progressive positions of the wave front. *The ray is deviated toward the normal when the speed of the waves is reduced, and deviated away from the normal when the speed is increased.*

In Fig. 363 a ray of light passes from medium 1, where its speed is V_1, into medium 2, where its speed is V_2. The angle of incidence is i and the angle of refraction is r, both with respect to the normal N. In this case $V_2 < V_1$ and therefore the ray is deviated toward the normal, making $r < i$. Some of the incident light is reflected at the interface, but the reflected ray is omitted in the figure for clearness.

The ratio of the light speeds V_1/V_2 in two contacting substances is a constant for those mediums known as the *refractive index* of the second medium relative to the first; it is represented by the symbol μ_{12}, the order of the subscripts indicating the direction of light travel. This concept can be combined with that expressed in Eq. 244, and the law of refraction expressed mathematically is as follows:

$$\frac{\sin i}{\sin r} = \frac{V_1}{V_2} = \mu_{12} \qquad (265)$$

The (absolute) refractive index of a substance is its index with respect to a vacuum; the index against air has practically the same value. Thus, if the speed of light is V_s in a particular substance, V_o in a vacuum, and V_a in air, the index of the substance is

$$\mu = \frac{V_o}{V_s} = \text{approximately } \frac{V_a}{V_s}$$

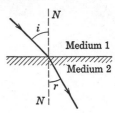

Medium 1

Medium 2

The refractive index of a substance can be measured fundamentally by passing a narrow beam of light into it in the manner suggested in Fig. 363, observing the angles of incidence and refraction, and applying Eq. 265. Methods are available for measuring precisely the index of refraction of all kinds of substances.

FIG. 363. Refraction of ray at plane interface

The refractive index of a substance varies somewhat with the wavelength of light, § 383; the following list gives a few representative values as measured with yellow light of wavelength approximately 0.00006 cm. It is natural that glass, being a synthetic product, should vary considerably in refractive index, depending upon the ingredients used; the table indicates the range of values to be expected.

INDICES OF REFRACTION

Gases and Vapors	
Air	1.0002918
Carbon dioxide	1.0004498
Mercury vapor	1.000933
Liquids	
Carbon disulfide	1.6276
Water	1.3330
Solids	
Diamond	2.417
Glass (crown)	1.48 to 1.61
Glass (flint)	1.53 to 1.96
Ice	1.31
Rock salt	1.5443

A medium with a large index of refraction causes light to have a lesser speed through it than through one of low index. Thus for ice the refractive index is $\mu = 1.31$; this means that the speed of light in vacuum (or air) is 1.31 as great as in ice; also that it takes the same time for light to travel through 1 cm of ice as it takes to travel through 1.31 cm of air. *Thus, μ indicates numerically the equivalent air distance of 1 cm of a substance having that refractive index.*

376. Refraction in Parallel-Sided Plates. A ray of light in passing through one or more parallel-sided slabs and emerging into the original medium is displaced laterally but is not deviated. This result is shown in Fig. 364, where a, w, and g represent any three different mediums such as air, water, and glass.

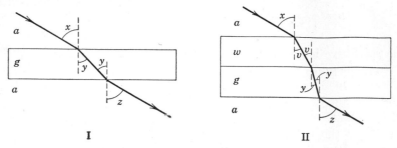

FIG. 364.   Ray of light through parallel-sided plates

With a single slab, as in part I of the figure, and with the angles of incidence, refraction, and emergence marked x, y, and z respectively, the law of refraction gives for the two surfaces of the glass:

$$\frac{V_a}{V_g} = \frac{\sin x}{\sin y} = \mu_{ag} \quad \text{and} \quad \frac{V_g}{V_a} = \frac{\sin y}{\sin z} = \mu_{ga}$$

When these equations are multiplied member by member it is seen that, since the product of the first members is unity,

$$\frac{\sin x}{\sin y} \times \frac{\sin y}{\sin z} = 1$$

whence angles x and z are equal, making the incident and emergent rays parallel. It appears further that the product of the two indices of refraction is unity, whence

$$\mu_{ag} = \frac{1}{\mu_{ga}} \tag{266}$$

showing, for example, that the refractive index of glass with respect to air is the reciprocal of the index of air with respect to glass.

When the same procedure is applied to two slabs, as indicated in part II of the figure, it is found that the angle of incidence x and the angle of emergence z are equal, and also that

$$\frac{V_a}{V_w} \times \frac{V_w}{V_g} \times \frac{V_g}{V_a} = 1$$

It follows that $\mu_{aw} \times \mu_{wg} \times \mu_{ga} = 1$, whence

$$\mu_{wg} = \frac{1}{\mu_{aw} \times \mu_{ga}} = \frac{\mu_{ag}}{\mu_{aw}} \tag{267}$$

showing that the relative refractive index of any substance g with respect to another substance w is equal to the absolute index of substance g divided by that of substance w.

377. Deviation by a Prism. Prisms are often employed in optical devices to deviate a beam of light. In a triangular prism, the amount of deviation depends upon the angle of the prism, upon its refractive index, and also upon the angle of incidence. It can be shown, either by experiment or by calcu-

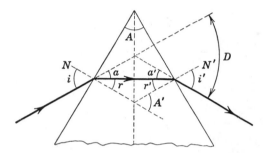

Fig. 365. Ray passing symmetrically through prism

lation, that for such a prism the deviation has a *minimum* value when the ray passes *symmetrically* through it as shown in Fig. 365.

To prove this relation analytically, the deviation of the beam is expressed in terms of the angles of incidence and refraction, and the result is differentiated and equated to zero. The incident beam strikes the left face of the prism at an angle i with the normal N, is refracted at an angle r with this normal, proceeds through the prism, and emerges from the right face making angles of incidence r' and refraction i' with the normal N'. From geometric considerations the angle A of the prism is equal to the angle A' between the two normals, and since the latter angle is the exterior angle of a triangle of which r and r' are the opposite interior angles, it follows that $A = r + r'$. The angle of deviation between the incident and emergent rays is the sum of the deviations produced at the two faces individually, or

$$D = a + a' = (i - r) + (i' - r') = i + i' - A$$

If μ is the index of refraction of the prism relative to air, it follows from the law of refraction that $\sin i = \mu \sin r$ and $\sin i' = \mu \sin r'$, so that the deviation is

$$D = \sin^{-1}(\mu \sin r) + \sin^{-1}[\mu \sin(A - r)] - A$$

In order to find the relation between the angles r and r' which will make the deviation a minimum, this expression is differentiated with respect to r

and the result is equated to zero. Thus,

$$\frac{dD}{dr} = \frac{\mu \cos r}{\sqrt{1 - \mu^2 \sin^2 r}} - \frac{\mu \cos (A - r)}{\sqrt{1 - \mu^2 \sin^2 (A - r)}} = 0$$

whence

$$\frac{\cos^2 r}{\cos^2 r'} = \frac{1 - \mu^2 \sin^2 r}{1 - \mu^2 \sin^2 r'}$$

and it follows that the angles r and r' are equal.

Whether demonstrated experimentally or analytically, it is found that the deviation is a minimum for a ray that passes symmetrically through the

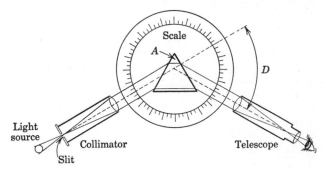

FIG. 366. Deviation of light measured with spectrometer

prism. For such a ray, $r = r'$ and $a = a'$; hence the angle of minimum deviation is

$$D_m = a + a' = 2a = 2(i - r)$$

The index of refraction μ of the material constituting the prism can be expressed in terms of the prism angle A and the angle of minimum deviation D_m by stating the angles of incidence and refraction in terms of these quantities, and applying Eq. 265. Thus, the angle of refraction is $r = \dfrac{A}{2}$, and the angle of incidence is $i = \dfrac{D_m}{2} + r = \dfrac{D_m + A}{2}$. From the law of refraction, the refractive index of the prism material is

$$\mu = \frac{\sin \frac{1}{2}(D_m + A)}{\sin \frac{1}{2}A} \tag{268}$$

An accurate determination of the refractive index of a substance can be made from measurements of A and D_m taken on a prism of that substance. For liquids, a hollow glass prism is used to hold the liquid; the faces of the prism, being parallel-sided slabs, produce no deviation and thus do not influence the result. The measurements are made with a spectrometer, the essential parts of which are shown in Fig. 366. The test is conducted simply with light of a single wavelength, corresponding to a particular color of the spectrum. The light enters the instrument through a narrow slit, is formed into a parallel beam by a lens, and falls upon the prism. Here it undergoes refraction and upon emergence is received by a suitably placed telescope, in which the observer sees an image of the slit. The prism and telescope are turned by trial until the angle of deviation D is observed to be a minimum; the value of this angle is read from the circular scale. The angle A is usually measured optically by reflecting light from one face of the prism, as from a plane mirror, and then rotating the prism until the second prism face occupies the same position; the angle A is found by subtracting the angle of rotation from 180°.

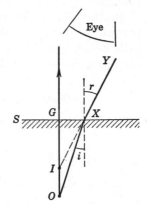

FIG. 367. Effect of refraction on apparent depth

378. Apparent Depth of a Submerged Object. Refraction causes an object which is immersed in a medium of higher refractive index than air to appear nearer the surface than it actually is. Point O in Fig. 367 represents a stone in water a distance GO below the surface S, and light rays extend upward from it to the eye, as shown. For the ray OXY, the angle of incidence i is equal to GOX and the angle of refraction r is equal to GIX; therefore

$$\frac{\sin GOX}{\sin GIX} = \frac{1}{\mu}$$

where μ is the refractive index of water. For small angles the sine may be equated to the tangent, whence this index is

$$\mu = \frac{\tan GIX}{\tan GOX} = \frac{GX}{GI} \div \frac{GX}{GO} = \frac{GO}{GI}$$

Herefrom the apparent depth GI of the object when viewed from above is the ratio of the actual depth GO to the refractive index of the medium.

379. Atmospheric Refraction. Most persons have noticed the apparent quivering of an object when observed across the top of a hot radiator. This effect is due to the lowering of the refractive index of air by heating it, and the mixing of the warm with the colder air in the process of convection produces a continually changing refraction of the transmitted light rays.

Light from outer space encounters air of increasing density and increasing refractive index as it approaches the earth. Consequently, a beam of light slanting downward through the atmosphere is bent more and more toward the vertical as it advances. For this reason, the stars are not seen in their true directions unless exactly overhead. The same phenomenon also explains the fact that the entire disk of the sun or moon may be seen for a short time when it is geometrically below the horizon where it would not be visible at all except for atmospheric refraction.   This effect is pictured in Fig. 368.

Another illustration of atmospheric refraction is the *mirage,* an effect reported by observers in desert lands but not restricted to such regions.   With little circulation the air heated by the earth remains adjacent to it, so that the refractive index of the atmosphere is smaller near the earth than farther

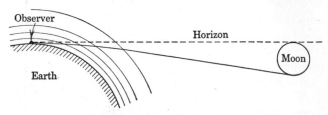

FIG. 368.   Illustrating atmospheric refraction

up.   The situation is just the opposite of that pictured in Fig. 368, and a bit of skylight reaches the observer from a place below and some distance ahead, giving him the impression that he sees this light by reflection in water.   Automobilists in driving along straight smooth highways on hot sunny days frequently comment upon such imaginary puddles.

380. Total Reflection.   A ray of light in a medium of high refractive index and directed toward one of lower index, passes into the second medium with

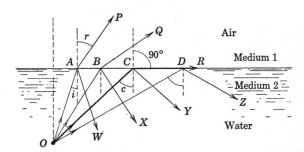

FIG. 369.   Refraction and total reflection of light rays

refraction, provided the angle of incidence is not too large.   If the ray is inclined more and more, however, a position will be reached in which it does not enter the second medium, but experiences *total reflection* at the surface of separation.

A source of light O is imagined to be located in water of refractive index μ and to emit light rays in various directions as indicated in Fig. 369.   The light emitted along OA is mostly refracted into the air along AP in such direction that $\dfrac{\sin i}{\sin r} = \dfrac{1}{\mu}$, but a small part is reflected along AW. Similarly, the light emitted along OB is partly refracted along BQ and partly reflected along BX.

The ray OC strikes the surface S at such an incident angle c that the refracted ray CR grazes the surface, the angle of refraction being 90°; the reflected part travels to Y. Any ray such as OD for which the angle of incidence is greater than c does not emerge into the air but is totally reflected along some line DZ.

The angle c is called the *critical angle* of incidence for total reflection; it is the angle of incidence in the more highly refractive medium for which the angle of refraction in the other medium is 90°; its value is evidently given by

$$\sin c = \frac{1}{\mu} \qquad (269)$$

In general, total reflection occurs at the boundary separating any two mediums having different refractive indices, when a ray in the medium of higher index is directed toward the other medium at an angle of incidence greater than the critical angle. For this general case, it can be shown in the same manner that the critical angle c is given by the relation

$$\sin c = \frac{\mu_2}{\mu_1} \qquad (270)$$

when $\mu_2 < \mu_1$.

The principle of total reflection is frequently used in optical instruments. Fig. 370 shows three positions of a prism, having two 45° angles, in the path of the light rays forming an image. In the first position, the prism acts like

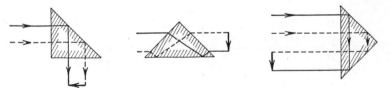

FIG. 370. Prism of 45–45–90° used for total reflection

a plane mirror tilted downward; when rotated into the second position it inverts the image; and when turned to the third position it displaces the rays and reverses their direction.

381. Refractometers. A number of instruments called *refractometers* have been designed for the rapid and precise measurement of refractive index. In one of these, shown in Fig. 371, a glass hemisphere of high refractive index is arranged with its plane face horizontal to receive the specimen under test, and a beam of light is caused to enter the hemisphere radially from below. The direction of the entering beam is adjusted so that when it impinges upon the specimen it undergoes total reflection, The reflected beam emerges radially and is received by a telescope that can be moved along a scale for reading its position. In testing a liquid, a few drops of it are placed upon the hemisphere and the telescope is moved to the position which indicates the critical angle of total reflection. In testing a crystal, a few drops of a liquid of higher refractive index (like monobromonaphthalene) are placed between the hemisphere and the lower face of the crystal to provide optical contact and the same procedure is followed; the film of liquid has parallel faces and thus does not affect the result. Even crystals that are more or less opaque can be measured in this way.

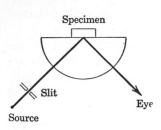

FIG. 371. Scheme of refractometer utilizing total reflection

Illustrative Problem

As an experiment with such an instrument, a piece of lucite (methyl methacrylate) is placed upon the hemisphere with an intervening layer of liquid. The refractive index of the hemisphere for sodium light is 1.9180, and the observations of the critical angle are 51° 50′ for the lucite, and 59° 54′ for the liquid, these angles being measured away from the vertical. Determine the refractive indices for both.

The refractive index of the lucite specimen is 1.9180 sin 51° 50′ = 1.5080 and that for the liquid is 1.9180 sin 59° 54′ = 1.6594.

Another instrument, the Pulfrich refractometer, is illustrated diagrammatically in Fig. 372. It consists of a right-angle prism P upon which the

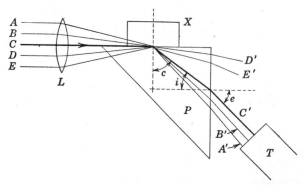

FIG. 372. Sectional view of Pulfrich refractometer

specimen X is placed, a lens L for converging a beam of monochromatic light along the interface, and a telescope T that is moved around a graduated quadrant (not shown) to obtain the direction of the emergent rays. The prism has a known refractive index, which is higher than that of any material to be tested. Rays such as A and B are refracted to positions A' and B' respectively in the telescope, giving a band of light which is terminated sharply by the limiting ray CC' that makes grazing incidence. Rays such as D and E are totally reflected along D' and E' and do not enter the telescope, which is set on the boundary of the refracted beam.

The refractive index μ_x of the test specimen can be found in terms of the angle of emergence e and the refractive index μ_p of the prism by applying the law of refraction. Since the critical angle c is complementary to the angle of incidence i on the vertical face of the prism,

$$\frac{1}{\mu_p} = \frac{\sin i}{\sin e} = \frac{\sin (90° - c)}{\sin e} = \frac{\cos c}{\sin e}$$

from which

$$\cos c = \frac{\sin e}{\mu_p}$$

Also for grazing incidence at the horizontal face of the prism, by Eq. 270,

$$\sin c = \frac{\mu_x}{\mu_p}$$

But $\cos^2 c + \sin^2 c = 1$, and consequently

$$\frac{\sin^2 e}{\mu_p{}^2} + \frac{\mu_x{}^2}{\mu_p{}^2} = 1$$

from which the index of refraction of the specimen becomes

$$\mu_x = \sqrt{\mu_p{}^2 - \sin^2 e}$$

To measure the refractive index of liquids by this method, a short glass tube of large bore is cemented edge-on to the prism. The liquid under test is poured into the cup so formed and the measurement is made as for a solid.

382. Loss in Reflection and Absorption. The amount of light that is reflected from a transparent substance depends upon the angle of incidence and the refractive index of the substance. The French physicist Augustin J. Fresnel (1788–1827) first derived an expression for the ratio between the intensity of the reflected beam and that of the incident beam. For natural (unpolarized) light perpendicularly incident within a medium of refractive index μ_1, upon a transparent substance of refractive index μ_2, the ratio of the intensity I of the reflected beam to the intensity I_o of the incident beam is given by

$$\frac{I}{I_o} = \left(\frac{\mu_2 - \mu_1}{\mu_2 + \mu_1}\right)^2 \tag{271}$$

For light reflected in air against glass of refractive index 1.5, the ratio of intensities is $(0.5/2.5)^2 = 0.04$, showing that 4% of the incident light is reflected where there is perpendicular incidence upon an air-glass boundary.

The amount of absorption of light in its passage through a transparent substance depends upon the nature of the absorbing medium and its thickness. If the entire medium is regarded as made up of a number of equally thin layers, each one absorbs the same fraction of the light entering it. Thus, if 100 lumens impinge upon the first layer and if each absorbs $\frac{1}{10}$ of the light which reaches it, the amount incident upon the second layer is 90 lumens, upon the third layer 81 lumens, upon the fourth layer 72.9 lumens, and so on.

It has been established by experiment that for light of a given color an infinitesimally thin layer cuts down the intensity by an amount which, expressed as a fraction of its value, is directly proportional to the thickness of the layer. If I is the intensity at a particular layer of infinitesimal thickness dx and $-dI$ is the change of intensity in this layer, then the foregoing statement can be expressed mathematically in the form

$$-\frac{dI}{I} = k \, dx$$

where k is a constant of the material called its *absorption coefficient*. This expression is integrated to obtain the intensity of a light beam after passing through a thickness x of a medium in terms of the intensity I_0 of the entering beam. The result is

$$I = I_0 \epsilon^{-kx} \qquad\qquad (272)$$

where k is the absorption coefficient and ϵ the base of natural logarithms.

PROBLEMS

1. An object placed between two plane mirrors mounted parallel to each other forms a series of images behind each one. For a lamp placed 2 ft from mirror A and 4 ft from mirror B, locate the first two images behind each.

2. What height should a vertical plane mirror have for a man 6 ft tall to see his full image in it when standing erectly? Explain.

3. The location of an object between two plane mirrors placed at right angles to each other is indicated in the diagram. Locate the image formed by reflection at both mirrors and show the rays by which the end-points of the object would be seen by an observer at E as a result of such reflection.

Problem 3

4. A lighted candle is placed between two plane mirrors that touch each other at an angle of 60°. How many images of the candleflame can an

observer see? Make a diagram showing only the ray that is reflected three times at the mirrors on its way from source to eye.

5. Two flat glass plates of negligible thickness meet at an angle α at edge A as shown in the diagram. A ray of light incident at angle i upon one plate is partially reflected, and the transmitted ray is partially reflected from the other plate. Show that the two reflected rays meet at an angle 2α, and that these rays meet at a distance from the point of incidence B equal to $AB \sin(i - \alpha)/\cos \alpha$.

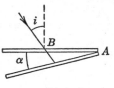

Problem 5

6. For a concave spherical mirror of 12 in. focal length, find analytically two locations of an object for which the image will be 3 times as high as the object. Verify the results graphically with diagrams drawn to scale.

7. An object is placed at various distances in front of a concave spherical mirror having a radius of 40 cm. Determine the image locations for the object when held at the following distances in centimeters from the mirror surface: ∞, 60, 30, 20, 10, 4, and 0.

8. An object is placed 1 ft away from the surface of a polished metal sphere 2 ft in diameter. (*a*) Locate the image analytically. (*b*) Verify the result graphically by a diagram drawn to scale. (*c*) Describe the image fully. (*d*) Determine the height of the image for an object 6 in. high.

9. To determine the focal length of a convex mirror, an object O is placed in front of its vertex V, and a plane mirror P is placed between them, as in the diagram. Each mirror forms an image of the object, and the plane mirror is moved along axis OV while looking from side to side until these images coincide. In a test, coincidence results when $OP = 20$ cm and $PV = 15$ cm. Compute the focal length of the convex mirror.

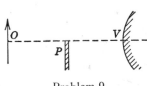

Problem 9

10. Determine the index of refraction of lucite from the data given in Prob. 21 of Chap. 30.

11. Compute (*a*) the refractive index of water with respect to flint glass of absolute index 1.70 and (*b*) the refractive index of the glass with respect to water.

12. A ray of light slanting downward 40° from the horizontal passes through water and then enters a level plate of crown glass having a refractive index of 1.60. Find the direction of the ray in each medium.

13. A beam of light is incident upon a flat plate of glass 1 in. thick at an angle of incidence of 60°. Assume the refractive index of the glass to be 1.60 and determine (*a*) the angle of refraction within the glass, (*b*) the velocity of light in it, and (*c*) the lateral displacement of the beam in passing through the plate.

14. It is found by experiment that a 60° flint-glass prism produces a minimum deviation of 50° 30′ for yellow light. Determine (*a*) the index of refraction of the glass for this light and (*b*) the angle that the light rays make in air with the normals to the incident and emergent faces of the prism.

15. A prism has an apex angle of 45° and a refractive index of 1.80. At what angle of incidence should light be directed upon the prism in order that it may undergo minimum deviation in passing through it?

16. A prism of 60° angle is found to produce minimum deviation for

yellow light when the ray strikes it at an angle of incidence of 52°. For the
light used, determine (*a*) the angle of minimum devi-
ation and (*b*) the refractive index of the prism material.

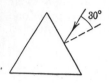

17. A narrow beam of parallel light is incident upon
an equilateral prism in the direction shown in the accompanying sketch. The prism is of glass having a
refractive index of 1.5 and is located in air. (*a*) Make a
sketch of the path of the ray through the prism. (*b*)
Compute the angle between the emergent ray and the
normal to the surface at the point of emergence.

Problem 17

18. Carry out the same objectives as in Prob. 17 for a ray entering a
right-angled glass prism having a refractive index of 1.5, the direction of
the incident ray being shown in the sketch.

19. The general equation that relates the angle
A of a prism with the angles of incidence *i* and
emergence *e* of a light beam is

$$\mu^2 \sin^2 A = \sin^2 i + \sin^2 e + 2 \sin i \cdot \sin e \cdot \cos A$$

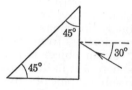

where μ is the refractive index of the prism. (*a*)
Show that this expression reduces to Eq. 268 when
the angle of deviation is a minimum. (*b*) Solve
Prob. 17(*b*) by means of the general equation.

Problem 18

20. How thick does the glass plate of Prob. 13 appear to be when viewed
in a direction normal to its surfaces?

21. Lithium fluoride has a refractive index of 1.39 and rock salt 1.54.
Which of these materials could be used in a right-
angled prism to reflect light rays as shown in Fig.
370? Explain.

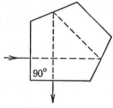

22. The penta prism shown in the sketch deflects
rays of light through an angle of 90° by two reflections from silvered surfaces. Give the values of the
four angles of the prism not marked and indicate
how its action differs from that of a right-angled
prism that deflects rays through 90° by total reflection.

Problem 22

23. A ray of sodium light is incident upon the glass
hemisphere of Fig. 371 from below. As the angle of
incidence is increased the light reflected into the eye becomes intense when
the incident angle reaches 35°. The test is repeated with a drop of liquid
placed centrally upon the flat surface; intense reflection then occurs when
the incident angle reaches 55°. For sodium light, determine the index of
refraction of the glass and of the liquid.

24. A beam of light having an intensity of 80 lumens/ft² is incident
normally upon a parallel-sided slab of plastic material that has a refractive
index of 1.5. If 10% of the light entering the slab is absorbed in passing
through it, (*a*) what intensity is lost in reflection? and (*b*) what is the intensity of the emerging beam?

35

DISPERSION, SPECTRA, AND COLOR

DISPERSION AND SPECTRA

383. Dispersion. White light, such as that produced by the glowing carbons of an arc lamp, is in reality composed of many colors blended together. When a narrow slit is illuminated by such white light and the issuing beam is refracted through a prism, the colors are spread out into a brilliant array, merging imperceptibly into one another and forming a *spectrum*. Although there are hundreds of distinct hues in the spectrum, they may be

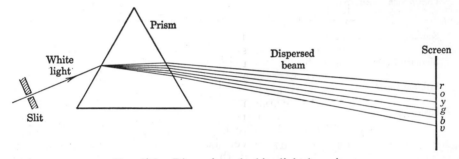

FIG. 373.   Dispersion of white light by prism

grouped broadly into six principal colors. These are red, orange, yellow, green, blue, and violet, in the order of increasing deviation, and are indicated by their initial letters in Fig. 373. Passing the light through a second prism, identical with the first and arranged to produce deviation in the same direction, gives a spectrum of greater length. If the second prism is opposed to the first, the colors are recombined almost perfectly into white light.

The spreading out of a light beam into its component colors is called *dispersion*. To obtain a sharply defined spectrum by the dispersion of light through a prism it is customary to place a lens in the light path; in effect this lens yields a series of colored and overlapping images of the illuminated slit. Color is determined by the frequency of vibration and the associated length of the light wave, the wavelength being greatest for red and least for violet.

The deviation produced by a prism is greater for light of the shorter wavelengths. No simple relation exists between deviation and wavelength, however, and prisms of different substances spread out the component colors of white light to somewhat different extents. If two such prisms are arranged one above the other in such a manner that their spectra match exactly at two colors, say at the extremes of the red and violet portions, it is found that the intermediate colors do not register point by point. A few substances exhibit what is known as *anomalous* dispersion; prisms of such substances do not disperse white light in the regular color sequence. Thus, fuchsine deviates red and orange light more than blue and violet, and absorbs the middle portion of the spectrum.

The spectrum extends at both ends into regions which are invisible to the eye, the infrared being beyond the red and the ultraviolet beyond the violet of the visible spectrum.

384. Emission Spectra. A glowing object emits light, and the spectrum it produces is termed an *emission* spectrum. Its appearance depends prima-

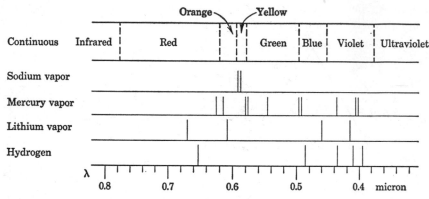

FIG. 374. Continuous spectrum and several bright-line spectra

rily upon the composition and phase of the luminous object. Incandescent solids, liquids, and gases under high pressure produce *continuous spectra* extending from color to color without interruption. Such a spectrum is represented at the top of Fig. 374.

Luminous gases and vapors under moderate or low pressure produce *bright-line spectra*, each spectrum consisting of lines of definite wavelength. The principal lines in the visible spectra of a few substances are shown in the figure above the wavelength scale; each line is an image of the slit through which the light passes. Sodium vapor gives two bright lines in the yellow region; they are so close together that unless the slit is very narrow they merge as one line. Mercury vapor yields several bright lines in the green and blue regions. The line spectra of lithium vapor and hydrogen are also shown. Thus each spectrum is characteristic of the radiating gas or vapor.

In a quantitative study of the spectrum, it becomes necessary to refer to

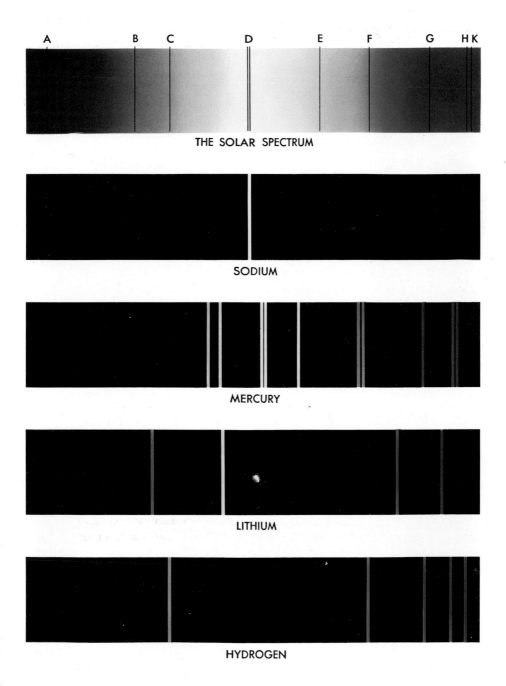

THE SOLAR SPECTRUM

SODIUM

MERCURY

LITHIUM

HYDROGEN

THE SOLAR SPECTRUM AND A FEW BRIGHT-LINE SPECTRA

each particular part of it with definiteness. This is done by specifying any hue by the vibration rate f of the light source, or the corresponding wavelength λ, the relation between these quantities being given by Eq. 236, namely,

$$c = f\lambda$$

where c is the speed of light. The wavelengths may be designated in centimeters, in microns (that is, thousandths of a millimeter), or in terms of the *Angstrom unit*, named in honor of the Swedish physicist Anders J. Ångström (1814–1874).

$$1 \text{ cm} = 10^4 \text{ microns} = 10^8 \text{ Angstrom units}$$

For example, the green line of the mercury spectrum has a wavelength λ = 0.00005461 cm = 0.5461 micron = 5461 Angstrom units. The wavelengths in Fig. 374 are expressed in microns.

The number of lines in a bright-line spectrum depends not only upon the nature of the source, but also upon the amount of energy with which its atoms are excited in order to produce glowing. Atoms may be excited by imparting energy to them, usually by heating in a flame or by supplying electrical energy in an arc or spark, or in a discharge tube, § 201. The excitation produced by heating a substance in a Bunsen or in a hotter flame is not as intense as by heating it in an electric arc, and additional lines appear when excited in the latter manner, extending its spectrum over a wider range. When the excitation is produced by a disruptive discharge or spark, formed between electrodes made of the material under investigation, the potential needed is much higher than for the electric arc. As a result the excitation is increased, and the lines of the spark spectrum extend over a wider range than those of the arc spectrum. Intense excitation of gases at low pressure can be obtained within a discharge tube energized by an induction coil or electrostatic generator.

385. Absorption Spectra. When the light from a glowing solid or other source yielding a continuous spectrum is passed through an absorbing medium before being dispersed, the spectrum is usually crossed by dark spaces which show that radiations of particular wavelengths have been absorbed. If the absorbing material is solid or liquid, these dark spaces appear as broad, structureless bands. If it is gaseous, they consist of dark lines that occupy the same positions as some of the bright lines in the corresponding bright-line spectrum.

The production of a dark-line spectrum is illustrated by a well-known experiment showing the reversal of the sodium lines. An arc lamp is arranged to project an intense beam of light upon a prism, the beam being directed through a cloud of glowing sodium vapor produced by heating common salt in a Bunsen flame. A narrow slit is provided near the prism in the light path. In conducting the experiment, the glowing sodium vapor is first used alone; the resulting spectrum consists of the two bright yellow lines characteristic of sodium. Upon starting the arc lamp and shining its rays through the sodium vapor, a continuous spectrum is formed, having two dark lines at exactly the positions previously occupied by the bright lines. This reversal of the lines can be explained by supposing that the sodium vapor, which emits these particular lines when excited, responds to the corresponding frequencies of vibration, and absorbs the energy of these particular vibrations from the beam proceeding from the arc. This vapor, considered as a source, has low luminosity compared with the arc because of its relative coolness, and hence the spectral lines that it produces are dark in comparison with the rest of the spectrum.

The absorption spectrum of a gas may also take the form of fluted bands, which under sufficient dispersion are found to consist of closely spaced dark lines arranged in an orderly manner. *Band spectra* are emitted only by molecules, and may be contrasted with *line spectra*, since these are emitted only by single or uncombined atoms. From the study of band spectra much has been learned about the structure of molecules and the forces acting within them. Bands occasionally appear in bright-line or emission spectra, but less commonly than in absorption spectra, because the intense excitation used in producing emission spectra is likely to break up the molecules into their component parts.

386. The Solar Spectrum. The spectrum produced by passing sunlight through a prism appears continuous from a casual inspection; a more critical examination, however, shows that it is crossed by numerous dark lines. No doubt the radiation from the sun comprises all wavelengths throughout the

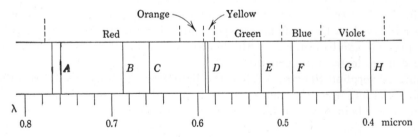

FIG. 375. Location of Fraunhofer spectral lines

visible range, but in passing through its outer atmosphere, which is relatively cool, certain wavelengths are absorbed; therefore the spectrum observed is in reality an absorption spectrum of that atmosphere. The dark lines indicate which gases are present around the sun and also reveal its own composition. The first careful study of these absorption lines was made by the German optician and physicist Joseph von Fraunhofer (1787–1826), who assigned letters to several of the more conspicuous ones. These lines are shown in Fig. 375, where their locations are indicated to scale. They are located in definite color zones, as shown at the top of the preceding color plate. The accompanying table gives additional data for some of the lines more commonly used:

FRAUNHOFER LINES

Designation	Color	Wavelength, microns	Produced in the Spectrum of
A........	Red	0.7630	Oxygen
C........	Red	0.6563	Hydrogen
D........	Yellow	0.5896, 0.5890	Sodium
F........	Blue	0.4861	Hydrogen
K........	Violet	0.3934	Calcium

387. Variation of Refractive Index. Lights of different color travel with different speeds in a transparent medium, a fact that explains why a beam of light comprising many colors is dispersed in passing through a prism. This is illustrated in Fig. 376, where the angles of refraction are different for the several colors, although the angle of incidence is the same for all. In consequence, the refractive index of the medium has a definite value for each color. The accompanying table lists the indices of refraction of a few common materials for light of particular wavelengths corresponding to the C, D,

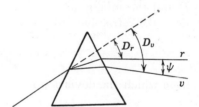

Fig. 376. Deviation and dispersion of light by prism. Angles are exaggerated for clearness

and F Fraunhofer lines. The index for the D line is often used as a reference value because this line is near the middle of the visible spectrum.

VARIATION OF REFRACTIVE INDEX WITH COLOR OF LIGHT

Material	Index of Refraction		
	C line	D line	F line
Carbon disulfide (20° C)..........	1.6182	1.6276	1.6523
Crown glass, sample..............	1.5145	1.5172	1.5240
Flint glass, sample...............	1.6221	1.6270	1.6391
Water (20° C)...................	1.3312	1.3330	1.3372

388. Dispersion by a Prism. The amount of dispersion is expressed quantitatively by the angular separation of particular colors of the spectrum. Thus the angle ψ (psi) in Fig. 376 indicates numerically the dispersion of white light produced by a prism from the red to the violet region. This angle is clearly the difference between the deviations of the violet and red components of the incident light beam. If these deviations are called D_v and D_r respectively, the dispersion becomes

$$\psi = D_v - D_r$$

The deviation produced by a prism is definitely related to the angle of the prism by Eq. 268, which gives the refractive index as

$$\mu = \frac{\sin \frac{1}{2}(D_m + A)}{\sin \frac{1}{2}A}$$

where A is the prism angle and D_m the angle of minimum deviation of the ray through the prism. When the prism angle is small, the sines of the angles may be replaced by the angles themselves, and when the rays pass through the prism with approximate symmetry the difference between the deviation D and the minimum deviation D_m may be neglected. With these restrictions the refractive index becomes

$$\mu = \frac{\frac{1}{2}(D + A)}{\frac{1}{2}A}$$

from which the deviation is

$$D = A(\mu - 1) \tag{273}$$

This expression shows that, for a prism of small angle, the deviation is directly proportional to the angle of the prism and to the amount by which the refractive index exceeds unity. The equation can be used for prism angles up to 30° without exceeding about 5% error in the deviation.

The dispersion between any two colors can be found for a small-angle prism by using the foregoing equation to compute the respective deviation values. The dispersion between violet and red is $D_v - D_r = A(\mu_v - 1) - A(\mu_r - 1)$, or

$$\psi = A(\mu_v - \mu_r) \tag{274}$$

The amount of dispersion depends not only upon the angle of the prism but also upon the *dispersive power* of the material of which it is made. Dispersive power is the ratio of the dispersion which a small-angle prism would produce to the deviation of the median ray of the spectrum. The dispersion is commonly taken between violet and red, and yellow is considered as the middle color of the spectrum; whence the dispersive power δ (delta) is the ratio of ψ to D_y, or

$$\delta = \frac{\mu_v - \mu_r}{\mu_y - 1} \tag{275}$$

The fact that the prism angle has been eliminated shows that the dispersive power is a property of the substance and not of the shape of a dispersing agent.

When more definite values of deviation, dispersion, or dispersive power are needed, these quantities may be calculated with reference to particular Fraunhofer lines in the desired regions of the spectrum. For example, crown glass, having the indices listed in § 387, has a dispersive power over the region from blue to red (F line to C line) of

$$\delta = \frac{1.5240 - 1.5145}{1.5172 - 1.0000} = \frac{0.0095}{0.5172} = 0.0184$$

Deviation of light without dispersion can be produced by an achromatic prism formed of two prisms so placed as to deviate the light individually in opposite directions; the two prisms have different dispersive powers and their angles are so proportioned that the dispersion due to one annuls that due to the other.

Illustrative Problem

What angle should a flint-glass prism have to achromatize a 12° crown-glass prism between the C and F spectral lines? What is the resulting deviation of the prism combination for the D line?

The dispersion produced by a 12° crown-glass prism between the stated spectral lines is 12° (1.5240 − 1.5145) = 0.114°, as found from Eq. 274 and the refractive indices listed. To annul this dispersion with a flint-glass prism, its angle should be 0.114°/(1.6391 − 1.6221) = 6.7°. The deviation produced by the prism combination for the D line is 12° (1.5172 − 1) − 6.7° (1.6270 − 1) = 2.01°.

389. Spectrum Analysis. The detailed study of emission and absorption spectra is termed spectrum analysis or *spectroscopy;* it has played an important role in gaining knowledge of the structure of atoms and molecules. The widest application of spectroscopy is the identification of the elements present in a sample of unknown composition by the recognition of their characteristic spectra. Spectra disclose not only what elements are present but show whether the atoms are parts of molecules or exist by themselves, and in addition furnish evidence as to the conditions of ionization, temperature, and pressure under which they exist.

Analysis of the light from the sun and stars reveals the presence of the same elements as occur upon the earth; helium derives its name from having been first discovered in the atmosphere of the sun (Greek, *Helios*). In the spectra of certain stars, the expected lines appear, but are displaced slightly from their normal positions. This displacement indicates an apparent change in frequency, as explained by Doppler's Principle, § 347, and reveals the fact that there is relative motion between the star under examination and the earth. A shift toward the red end of the spectrum, for example, means an apparent increase in wavelength or lowering of frequency, and shows that the star and earth are receding from each other.

Many kinds of instruments are used for the examination of spectra; it will suffice to describe briefly one type for each of the ultraviolet, visible, and infrared ranges.

A spectrograph for the visible and ultraviolet regions is arranged as in Fig. 377. It consists of an equilateral prism of quartz mounted between two quartz lenses L_1 and L_2, together with an adjustable slit and a photo-

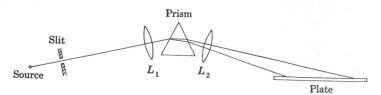

FIG. 377.   Diagram of quartz spectrograph

graphic plate holder. Light coming through the narrow slit is made parallel by a collimating lens L_1, and after dispersion by the prism is brought to a focus upon the sensitized plate by a camera lens L_2 (see Chap. 36). The plate is inclined considerably to the dispersed beam in order to accommodate the different focal lengths of the lens for radiations of wavelengths from 0.2 to 1 micron. The exposure time is suited to the intensity of the source and to the width of the slit. Provision is often made for photographing a scale calibrated in wavelengths next to the spectrum, so that the wave-

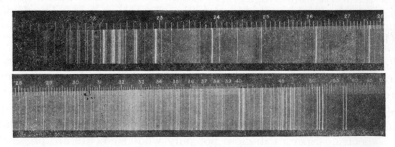

FIG. 378.   Arc spectral lines of copper in visible and ultraviolet regions

lengths of its individual lines can be read directly. A spectrogram of a copper arc showing the lines down to 0.215 micron appears in Fig. 378.

A precision spectroscope for the visible region is illustrated in Fig. 379. It consists of a glass prism mounted on a table which can be rotated over a small angular range, two glass lenses L_1 and L_2 that serve the same purposes as in Fig. 377, a slit of adjustable width, and either a telescope for visual observation of the spectrum or a camera for making a spectrogram. The prism has the following angles: $a = 90°$, $b = 75°$, $c = 135°$, and $d = 60°$. Its action can be explained by drawing the line ac and dropping a perpendicular to this line from b; this divides the prism into two 30–60–90°

prisms and one 45–45–90° prism, the latter serving as a mirror by total reflection. A little study will show that the incident and emergent beams are
at right angles to each other, and that for all positions of the prism the center of the emergent beam has minimum deviation. A calibrated scale is

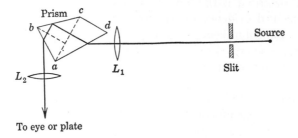

FIG. 379. Plan of spectroscope having constant-deviation type prism

fitted to the prism table for reading directly the wavelength of the spectral
line that appears at the center of the field of view.

Fig. 380 illustrates a spectrometer for the infrared region. It consists of
a rock-salt prism and a mirror M mounted on a table so that the two can
be rotated as a unit, a concave spherical mirror C_1 for forming the incident

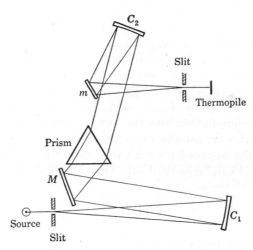

FIG. 380. Arrangement of an infrared spectrometer

radiation into a parallel beam, another concave mirror C_2 for focusing the
emerging radiation upon the receiving slit by way of the plane mirror m,
and a thermopile behind the slit for developing an electric current that can
be measured. The prism table is moved by a drum carrying a scale, so
that the wavelength of the radiation falling upon the thermopile can be read
directly. The range of a typical instrument of this type is from 0.38 to 17

microns. A study of the distribution and intensity of the radiation emitted by a black body over this range of wavelengths led to the quantum theory, § 189.

390. Spectral Series. The definiteness of the spectral lines of the elements has long been regarded as the key to an understanding of atomic structure. Much experimental evidence on spectra has been accumulated and correlated with the quantum theory, as a result of which it is now known that the atom has definite energy levels, and that it assumes a higher energy level upon absorbing energy and a lower one upon emitting energy through radiation.

Johann J. Balmer (1825–1898), a Swiss physicist, found that the spectral lines of atomic hydrogen form a *series* that can be expressed by the equation

$$\lambda = 0.3646 \frac{N^2}{N^2 - 4}$$

where λ is the wavelength of the lines in microns, and N is an integer having values greater than 2. For the four most prominent lines in the visible portion of the spectrum, the measured wavelengths are 0.6563, 0.4861, 0.4340 and 0.4102 micron. The foregoing equation gives these values when N is taken successively as 3, 4, 5, and 6. For progressively shorter wavelengths, the values of N become larger and larger, the limiting value being for a wavelength of 0.3646 micron in the ultraviolet region.

Other spectral series for hydrogen have been found beyond the visible region of the spectrum. The American physicist Theodore Lyman (1874–1954) discovered a simple equation for the lines in the extreme ultraviolet, and the German spectroscopist Friedrich Paschen (1865–1947) originated a similar equation for a series of lines in the near infrared region. Later three other series extending farther into the infrared zone were established. Lines of the various series are usually expressed in terms of the number of waves per centimeter, the so-called *wave number*, rather than the wavelength, and when so expressed can be merged into the single equation

$$\nu = 109,737 \left[\frac{1}{k_2{}^2} - \frac{1}{k_1{}^2} \right] \tag{276}$$

where ν (nu) is the wave number or the reciprocal of the wavelength in centimeters, and k_2 and k_1 are integers having the following values:

Lyman series $k_2 = 1$ $k_1 = 2, 3, 4, \cdots$

Balmer series $k_2 = 2$ $k_1 = 3, 4, 5, \cdots$

Paschen series $k_2 = 3$ $k_1 = 4, 5, 6, \cdots$

When these integers are applied, the limiting wave numbers of hydrogen are found to be 5,334 and 12,193 for the Paschen series, 15,241 and 27,434 for the Balmer series, and 82,303 and 109,737 for the Lyman series. Expressions similar in character to the foregoing equation have been developed for many other elements.

The mathematical relationship between the wave numbers of spectral lines, as expressed by Eq. 276 for hydrogen, was explained on a physical basis by Professor Bohr in 1913. He applied the planetary picture of the atom, comprising a positively charged nucleus with external electrons revolving about it in shells or orbits, and postulated that an electron could occupy any one of a definite number of orbits or *stationary states* without radiating, each of these representing a definite energy value. For the hydrogen atom, with its single planetary electron, the normal state corresponds to the electron residing in its innermost orbit. When this atom receives energy, the revolving electron moves to a larger orbit in opposition to the attractive force of the nucleus. When the atom loses energy by radiation, the electron falls to definite inner orbits, and the amount of energy radiated is given by

$$E_h - E_l = hf \qquad (277)$$

where E_h represents the higher energy level of an outer orbit, E_l represents the lower energy level of the inner orbit, h is Planck's constant, § 188, and f is the frequency of the radiation given off. Each spectral line produced by an excited atom, therefore, corresponds to a specific change of energy as the electron falls from some definite outer orbit to a particular inner one. The spectral lines of any series are produced by the electrons of excited atoms falling back to a common inner orbit.

The relation between the wave number ν, the wavelength λ (cm), and the frequency f of the radiation is indicated by Eq. 236 as

$$\nu = \frac{1}{\lambda} = \frac{f}{c}$$

where c is the speed of light in centimeters per second. When this expression is combined with Eq. 277, the wave number becomes

$$\nu = \frac{1}{hc}(E_h - E_l)$$

which has the same form as Eq. 276. If now corresponding terms are compared, it appears that the energy levels of the hydrogen atom are given by

$$E_h = 109,737\,\frac{hc}{k_2{}^2} \qquad \text{and} \qquad E_l = 109,737\,\frac{hc}{k_1{}^2}$$

From the numerical values $h = 6.62 \times 10^{-27}$ erg·sec and $c = 3.00 \times 10^{10}$ cm/sec, it follows that the entire numerator for either expression becomes a constant having the value 21.8×10^{-12} ergs. If the symbol A is used to represent this value, the energy levels of hydrogen can be expressed by

$$E = \frac{A}{k^2} \tag{278}$$

where k represents successive integers that have the values of k_2 and k_1 previously tabulated for the three spectral series.

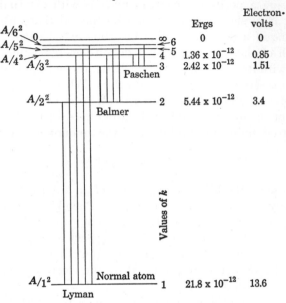

FIG. 381.   Energy levels of the hydrogen atom

Fig. 381 represents the energy levels of the hydrogen atom by horizontal lines for values of k up to 6.   If such an atom changes its energy from level 3 to level 2, it radiates energy amounting to

$$E = \frac{A}{2^2} - \frac{A}{3^2} = 21.8 \times 10^{-12} \left(\frac{1}{4} - \frac{1}{9} \right)$$

or 3.03×10^{-12} ergs, and produces only the spectral line having the wave number $109{,}737 \times (\frac{1}{4} - \frac{1}{9}) = 15{,}241$ waves/cm; it is represented by the heavy vertical line in the figure.   This wave number gives close agreement with the wavelength of the red line, $\lambda = 0.6563$ micron, found by experiment.   The vertical lines connecting levels $A/2^2$, $A/3^2 \cdots A/6^2 \cdots$ with level $A/1^2$ represent the energy changes that produce the spectral lines of the Lyman series; those connecting $A/3^2$, $A/4^2 \cdots A/6^2 \cdots$ with $A/2^2$ likewise correspond to the spectral lines of the Balmer series; and similarly for the Paschen series.

The values of energy given at the right of the figure are the energies necessary to pull an electron out of the atom from the corresponding shell.

391. Resonance and Ionization Potentials. The emission of the line of lowest wave number in a spectral series involves the least energy. As more energy becomes available from the source of excitation, additional lines appear; thus, the number of lines of a series that are present in the spectrum of an element is a measure of its energy of excitation. All the lines of a series are present when the energy is just great enough to cause an electron to leave the atom, an action that constitutes ionization. These energy values may be expressed in ergs, as in the preceding section, but are more commonly stated in electron·volts, § 258. Since 1 electron·volt is 1.60×10^{-12} erg, the expression for the energy levels of the hydrogen atom becomes

$$E = \frac{13.60}{k^2}$$

in electron·volts.

The energy required to excite the first line of a spectral series, expressed in electron·volts, is called the *resonance potential* for that series. The energy required to excite all the lines of the series is called its *ionization potential*, for it corresponds to the complete removal of an electron from an atomic system. Resonance and ionization potentials can be determined experimentally with gaseous discharge tubes and such measurements confirm the atomic energy levels computed theoretically. Values of these potentials for a few atoms are given in the accompanying table.

RESONANCE AND IONIZATION POTENTIALS

Atoms	Electron·volts to Produce First Spectral Line	Electron·volts to Cause Ionization
Helium....................	19.74	24.54
Hydrogen (Lyman series)....	10.20	13.60
Mercury...................	4.67	10.42
Potassium.................	1.58	4.33
Sodium...................	2.09	5.13

COLOR

392. Characteristics of Color. The term *color* is used in two senses. Physically, color of light is determined by the spectral distribution of energy in the light beam—that is, by the frequencies of its component waves and their intensities. Physiologically, color refers to the sensation produced by these waves upon entering the eye; our sense of sight combines the component waves proceeding from a given point and evokes a single resultant effect of color.

Three characteristics of color can be distinguished: hue, saturation, and brightness. Hue, such as red or green, is indicated by the dominant wavelength of a limited spectral distribution curve shaped like Fig. 344 but narrower. Saturation, or purity, of color indicates the amount of dilution of the hue with white light; thus pink is a mixture of saturated red and white. Brightness is determined by the intensity of a light beam or the brightness of an illuminated surface. The latter characteristic applies to light in general and was considered in Chap. 33. The others—hue and saturation—and their associated concepts of wavelength and purity are of chief importance in the study of color.

393. Mixture of Colored Lights; the Additive Process. When a spectrum is produced by passing white light through a prism, and then all the colors of the spectrum are caused to overlap, their effects are added together and produce the sensation of white light. This result can be observed by allowing the composite beam to enter the eye directly, or by projecting it upon a white screen. However, it is also found that by combining only the yellow and blue-violet portions of the spectrum, a white light is produced which the eye cannot distinguish from the other. There are several pairs of colors that yield white light when added; they are called *complementary colors*. Yellow and blue are complementary, as are also red and blue-green.

Furthermore, the light from a sodium vapor lamp appears much like that of illuminating gas, but the former has primarily the yellow spectral lines, whereas the latter has the continuous spectrum of glowing carbon. Evidently a particular color sensation can be produced in a variety of ways, and the composition of a light beam cannot be determined by its appearance but only by an analysis of its spectrum. Such analysis makes it possible to match many colors by the addition of red, green, and blue-violet lights in suitable proportions; these three are called the *additive primary colors*.

394. Specification of Color. A particular color can be specified in terms of three properly chosen components by stating the relative proportions of the components that should be added to match it. For this purpose the International Commission on Illumination has adopted red, green, and blue-violet, closely approximating the primary colors mentioned above. If the relative proportions of these components are designated as r, g, and b in per cent, then for a given light beam $r + g + b = 100$. The composition of any color can be plotted in terms of two of them, for the third is naturally the proportion to bring the total percentage to 100.

In Fig. 382 the abscissas represent percentages of red and the ordinates the percentages of green, and the curve itself is the locus of the spectrum colors with their wavelengths noted alongside in microns. The marks are spaced 0.01 micron apart, except in the two end spaces. The straight line that connects the ends of the locus represents colors not in the spectrum; they include purple and magenta. The complete loop is called a *chromaticity diagram*.

The point C near the center of the loop represents the composition of white light. This particular white is specified by the Commission as the spectral distribution from a standardized source, the light from which is equivalent to average daylight. A straight line from C to any point on the locus represents a color having the dominant wavelength indicated at its extremity, and a purity varying from zero at C to saturation at the locus. A straight line from a point on the locus, through C, and extending to the loop on the far side represents a pair of complementary colors of varying purities.

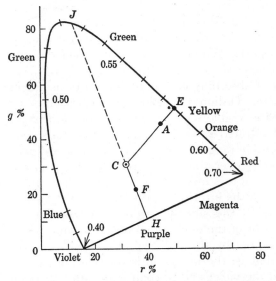

Fig. 382. Chromaticity diagram. The two end spaces of the scale around the loop are not subdivided; that at the left extends from 0.40 to 0.47 and that at the right from 0.62 to 0.70

To specify the composition of a color represented by an interior point such as A, a line is drawn from C to A and extended to the locus at E; this color (A) has a dominant wavelength designated at E of 0.576 micron and a purity given by the ratio CA/CE. For another color such as F, the extension of the line through it from C meets the closing line of the spectral loop, along which line there is no wavelength scale. The procedure then is to extend the line in the opposite direction to meet the locus at J; this color (F) is specified as complementary to one having a dominant wavelength at J of 0.525 micron and a purity indicated by the ratio CF/CH. The foregoing description explains how a color can be matched by a mixture of the three component colors.

395. Selective Absorption; the Subtractive Process. The light incident upon a nonluminous object is partly *reflected* and partly *absorbed*, and the remainder is *transmitted*. The color of the object depends upon the composition of the incident light and the extent to which the various component colors are reflected, absorbed, and transmitted.

A sheet of ordinary glass held in front of a source of white light appears colorless by light transmitted through it, because it transmits practically all of the light falling upon it. In contrast, a sheet of red glass appears red because the red-yellow range is transmitted, whereas the green-violet range has been subtracted by absorption. Similarly, a blue-violet transmitting medium absorbs the red-green range, and one of green absorbs both the red-orange and blue-violet ranges. In these three illustrations the light absorbed is a blue-green called cyan, a yellow, and a purple called magenta. These are the *subtractive primary colors;* they are the complements of the additive primary colors. When filters or pigments of the subtractive primary colors are superimposed, they produce black.

The property of absorbing certain colors and transmitting others is called *selective absorption*. Ordinary uncolored glass transmits the entire range of wavelengths of the visible spectrum, but is comparatively opaque to most ultraviolet and infrared radiation, and thus exhibits selective absorption outside of the visible range. For example, the glass of a greenhouse transmits radiant energy over the entire visible and near-infrared region to the plants within, where it is largely converted into heat and chemical energy. The radiation from the interior is principally in the far-infrared region (so-called radiant heat), and since glass does not transmit these longer wavelengths, the interior of the enclosure remains warm.

The light given out by the ordinary incandescent electric lamp is redder than sunlight, that is, the spectrum is relatively more intense toward the red than toward the violet end as compared with that of sunlight. The incandescent *daylight lamp* has an envelope of blue glass which, by selective absorption, removes some of the radiation from the red end of the spectrum, and the transmitted light, although somewhat dimmed, conforms more closely to sunlight in the relative proportions of the component colors.

The principles of selective absorption are applied in germicidal lamps that are used for sterilizing food and food containers, and also articles subject to mold and fungus growths. This source consists of a long closed tube containing inert gas and mercury vapor, and having coated electrodes at its ends. An electric discharge is maintained within the tube and produces radiation mostly in the ultraviolet region. The tube is made of special glass which absorbs the radiations not desired, and transmits most of the radiation in the region of 0.254 micron that has been found effective in destroying micro-organisms.

396. Color by Reflected Light. Opaque bodies are seen by light diffusely reflected from them. When an object is examined in white light containing all wavelengths of the visible spectrum, and the object reflects no light, then it appears black; if it reflects all of the light incident upon it, it appears white; if it reflects only part of the light, but reflects all wavelengths in equal proportions, it appears gray.

Most objects that appear colored when viewed by reflected light do so because of selective absorption. Reflection is not strictly a surface phenomenon, as the light seems to penetrate a short distance beneath the surface before reflection. With paints the dyed particles, such as oxides of lead, titanium, or zinc, are suspended in a colorless liquid such as linseed oil; these particles behave like tiny filters through which the light passes on incidence and reflection.

The color circle on the plate facing page 602 is helpful in visualizing the mixing of pigments; complementary colors are located diametrically opposite each other. A surface painted cyan (blue-green) absorbs the complementary red and reflects blue and green. Similarly, a surface painted yellow absorbs blue-violet and reflects hues from red to green. If cyan and yellow paints are mixed, the only color reflected by both is green. This result is quite different from that produced by mixing lights of yellow and blue, § 393.

An object has its true color when examined by light that contains all the wavelengths of the visible spectrum. If certain colors are absent from the incident light, the apparent color of the object may be quite different from its true color. Thus, dark blue cloth appears nearly black when examined under an incandescent electric lamp, because of the deficiency of blue in the incident light. Again, a red object appears black under a mercury vapor lamp, because of the deficiency of red in the incident light.

A few instances occur in which bodies exhibit a *surface color* which is apparently due to *selective reflection*, like the luster of metallic surfaces. Gold exhibits a yellow surface color, but this is not because the other colors are absorbed; in fact, the surface color itself is the one that is absorbed most strongly. This can be shown by passing white light through a sheet of gold foil, for it will be found that the transmitted light is bluish green, the yellow and orange having been absorbed.

397. Color Photography. The art of color photography depends upon the fact that any color occurring in nature can be matched by merging the additive primary colors in appropriate amounts. Latent images are formed on a light-sensitive emulsion separately for the red, the green, and the blue portions of the subject being photographed, each showing the variations in the intensity of the light of that particular color emitted or reflected by the subject. Positives of the images, dyed the appropriate colors, can be combined in proper register to form a natural color photograph. One way of doing this by the additive process would be to dye the positive of each picture the respective primary color and then to throw pictures of the three positives in proper register from separate projectors upon a screen. Such a procedure would be unwieldy, and other methods are commonly used. One of these will suffice for illustration; it utilizes the subtractive process.

The colors are separated by using emulsions that are sensitive to different parts of the spectrum, and arranging them in three separate layers. A cross-section of the film is illustrated in Fig. 383. The top emulsion is sensitive to blue-violet light only; the green and red light pass through without affecting it. A filter between the top and middle emulsions passes red and green but prevents any blue-violet light reaching the two lower emulsions. The middle emulsion is sensitive to blue-violet and green light, but blue-violet cannot reach it; the red light passes through without affecting it. The bottom emulsion is sensitive to blue-violet and red light, but the blue-violet was cut off by the filter. Exposure of the film thus produces three separate latent

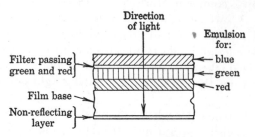

FIG. 383.   Cross-section of Kodachrome film

images: by blue-violet light in the top, green in the middle, and red in the bottom emulsion.

By rather complex processing operations the filter and the minute silver particles in the emulsions are bleached out and the film yields three negatives (the image being least transparent where most light reaches the film), each in a dyed gelatin complementary in color to the light that produced the original latent image. Thus the top layer appears as a yellow positive and subtracts blue-violet light, the middle layer appears as a magenta positive and subtracts green, and the bottom layer appears as a cyan (blue-green) positive and subtracts red; these elements of the resulting transparency are illustrated on the plate facing this page.

In projection, white light is passed through the film and falls upon a screen where it produces the results indicated. From left to right with light projected upward, white is produced by unobstructed passage through the film. Red is produced by light filtered through layers of magenta and yellow dye, the magenta absorbing green and the yellow absorbing blue-violet. Green is produced by the cyan layer absorbing red, and the yellow layer absorbing blue-violet as before. Blue-violet is produced by the cyan layer absorbing red, and the magenta layer absorbing green. Black is produced by the absorption of all colors by heavy dye deposits in all three layers. Intermediate colors are obtained by partial absorptions in the various layers. This method is used in the Kodachrome and Ektachrome processes to reproduce the original colors.

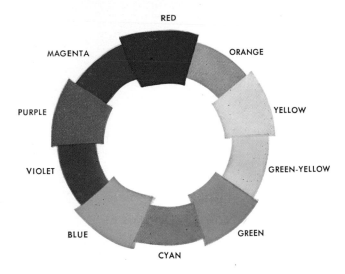

COLOR WHEEL

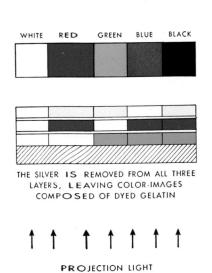

THE SILVER IS REMOVED FROM ALL THREE
LAYERS, LEAVING COLOR-IMAGES
COMPOSED OF DYED GELATIN

PROJECTION LIGHT

KODACHROME REPRODUCTION

To produce a picture upon paper instead of a transparency, three separate negatives are made, one by the light of each of the primary colors. Images from these are dyed in complementary colors, the red-filter negative image being dyed cyan, the green being dyed purple, and the blue-violet being dyed yellow; these are then transferred in register to a sheet of white paper. The picture is observed by light transmitted through the dyes to the paper, and reflected by it back through the dyes.

398. Colors of the Rainbow and Skylight. The rainbow is caused by the dispersion of sunlight within raindrops. The light that falls upon a drop is

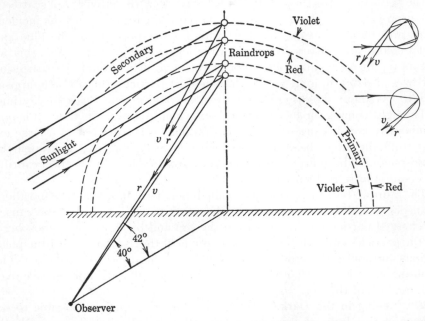

FIG. 384. Primary and secondary rainbows. Incident rays from the sun are pictured in perspective as horizontal

refracted at its front surface, partly reflected at the rear surface, and refracted again upon emergence. Much of the light is scattered in various directions, but the rays near the path of minimum deviation from a series of drops merge into a fairly intense beam along the directions shown in Fig. 384. The dispersion resolves the incident white light into the spectral colors and the observer sees the emergent rays directed at like angles from a multitude of drops; the collective result is a circular band of color ranging radially from red to violet. Under appropriate climatic conditions two concentric rainbows can be seen; the principal one is called the primary and the other the secondary rainbow.

In the primary rainbow there is one reflection inside a drop as indicated in the detail at the center right in the figure, and the angle between the inci-

dent and emergent rays is about 40° for violet and 42° for red. The observer sees the red rays outermost since they reach him from drops higher than those from which the violet rays come. In the secondary rainbow there are two internal reflections as indicated in the detail at the upper right, and the angle between the incident and emergent rays is about 50° for red and 54° for violet. The observer sees this rainbow outside the primary one and with the violet rays outermost.

The light from the sky is due to the scattering of sunlight by the molecules of air, as well as by dust and other impurities contained in the atmosphere, as the sun's rays pass through it. It is known that the intensity of scattered radiation varies directly as the fourth power of the frequency of the incident light, and for this reason the short waves, corresponding to the blue and violet colors, are scattered more than the longer waves of red light; this accounts for the prevailing blue color of the sky. The size of the scattering particles also has an influence; with large dust particles the sky may appear yellow. Without the atmosphere, the sky would appear black in daytime.

The light coming directly from the sun when it is near the horizon is predominantly red, because the blue portion has been scattered to a large extent from the direct beam in traversing relatively long paths through the atmosphere. The reflection of such light from clouds yields the beautiful effects at sunrise and sunset.

The aurora borealis, popularly called northern lights in the northern hemisphere and aurora australis in the southern, is believed to be caused by charged particles emanating from the sun and reaching our atmosphere. As the particles enter the earth's magnetic field they spiral toward the polar regions and ionize the atoms and molecules of the upper atmosphere. The resulting electrical discharge, § 201, produces a brilliant luminescence over wide regions of the sky.

399. Seeing in the Dark. Strange as it may seem, it is possible to see objects in the dark. A device for doing this was developed during World War II and is called a sniperscope. It consists essentially of an infrared light source and an image tube having a light-sensitive cathode. The device can be attached to a rifle and project upon objects in front of it a beam of infrared radiation from which all visible light has been filtered out. The rays after reflection are caught upon a cesium cell, which is sensitive to infrared light and which forms the cathode of the image tube. The radiation impinging upon the cell causes it to liberate photoelectrons and these are focused on a fluorescent screen to form a visible image (see part II of Fig. 414).

Objects can also be detected by the infrared radiations which they emit as a result of their own temperatures, particularly if those temperatures are high, as in the exhaust of an airplane. For this purpose, use is made of photoconductive cells, § 324, for these are sensitive to wavelengths as long as 7 microns. Applications of infrared radiation for detection and communi-

cation are limited by atmospheric conditions, chiefly because of absorption by water vapor and carbon dioxide.

PROBLEMS

1. What knowledge is gained from the facts (a) that the background of the solar spectrum is continuous? and (b) that some of the dark lines crossing this spectrum correspond to wavelengths of 0.3934, 0.6563 and 0.7630 microns?

2. White light in a narrow beam is directed upon a flat plate of crown glass at an angle of incidence of 50°. Find the angle between the C and F lines of the refracted beam within the glass.

3. A beam of white light passes through a 60° flint-glass prism so that the deviation for the D spectral line is a minimum. Determine the dispersion in the emergent beam between this line and the F line.

4. Compute the angle of a crown-glass prism that would yield a dispersion of $\frac{1}{6}°$ between the C and F spectral lines when white light passes through the prism with minimum deviation for the D line.

5. When a beam of white light is passed through a flint-glass prism of 12°, what would be (a) the minimum deviation for the D spectral line? and (b) the dispersion between the C and F lines? (c) If these rays proceed to a screen 2 m distant from the prism, how far apart are they at the screen?

6. Compare the dispersion between the C and F spectral lines produced by a small-angled hollow prism filled with carbon disulfide with that produced by the same prism filled with water, the angle of incidence being the same in both cases.

7. (a) Determine the angle of a crown-glass prism that can annul the dispersion due to a 10° flint-glass prism between the C and F spectral lines. (b) When the two prisms are put together as an achromatic prism, what deviation will the D spectral line have?

8. It is desired to combine a 10° flint-glass prism with a crown-glass prism so that when light is passed through the combination the D spectral line is not deviated. Compute the angle of the crown-glass prism needed and also the dispersion between the C and F lines due to the combined prisms.

9. A beam of ultraviolet light is passed through a 60° prism of fused quartz. For the three wavelengths of 0.3610, 0.2750, and 0.2140 microns the refractive indices of this substance are respectively 1.475, 1.496, and 1.534. (a) If the light of the intermediate wavelength passes symmetrically through the prism, what is the angular dispersion between the outer spectral lines? (b) What is the dispersive power of fused quartz over this wavelength range with respect to the intermediate spectral line?

10. An astronomer photographs the spectrum of a star and finds that the wavelength of the hydrogen F line measures 0.4856 micron. What is the relative velocity of earth and star?

11. Determine to four significant figures the corresponding frequencies and wave numbers of the sodium spectral lines.

12. Calculate the wave numbers of the first three lines of each of the three spectral series of hydrogen.

13. Two projectors, each with a colored filter, throw beams of light upon a white screen. What hue will result on the screen where the beams overlap

when (a) one filter is green and the other purple? and (b) when one filter is yellow and the other red?

14. Refer to the chromaticity diagram of Fig. 382 and specify the composition of the color represented by (a) the point ½ in. vertically above C and (b) the point ½ in. vertically below C. (c) Designate the wavelengths of the complementary colors represented by a horizontal line through C.

15. The phosphors in fluorescent lamps, § 359, are excited by ultraviolet radiation, principally the mercury line of 0.2537 micron wavelength, and produce radiation in the visible range. Determine the frequency and wave number for this spectral line and also for the limiting values of the visible range.

16. Phosphors that give three primary colors suitable for the screens of color television receivers, together with the locations of these colors on the chromaticity diagram, are as follows:

Red	Manganese activated zinc phosphate	$r = 0.67$	$g = 0.33$
Green	Manganese activated zinc ortho-silicate	0.22	0.70
Blue	Silver activated zinc sulfide	0.16	0.08

Colors of all hues and purity within the triangle determined by these points can be reproduced by these phosphors. Compare this area with the area of the entire chromaticity loop.

36

LENSES

400. Types of Lenses. A transparent material shaped to converge or diverge a beam of light transmitted through it is called a lens. It is usually a circular disk of glass that varies in thickness from the center to the rim, one or both surfaces being spherical. If a lens is thicker at the center than at the rim, it converges a parallel beam of light and is called a *converging* or *positive lens*. If it is thinner at the center than at the rim, it diverges such a beam and is called a *diverging* or *negative lens*.

The development of a lens from a prism can be shown with the aid of Eq. 273, which states that the amount of deviation D produced by a prism of angle A is equal to $A(\mu - 1)$, provided the prism angle is small. A parallel beam of monochromatic light is incident upon the prism shown in part I of Fig. 385. The three rays depicted are parallel upon emergence, each being

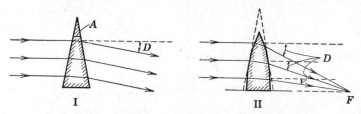

FIG. 385. Development of a lens from a prism

deviated by the same angle D from the initial direction. To converge the beam at some point F requires that the upper ray be deviated more and the lower one less than the center one, as shown in part II of the figure. Since the refractive index μ of the prism is the same for all the rays, the only way to change D is to make a corresponding change in A. Thus, the prism angle should be larger for the upper ray and smaller for the lower ray, as indicated. To bring all possible rays of the incident beam to the same point of convergence, the angle of the prism should change continuously from top to bottom; that is, one or both faces should be curved. When modified in this way the prism may be regarded as a semi-section of a lens by which a cylindrical beam of parallel light is brought to convergence.

Fig. 386 shows the basic shapes of converging and diverging lenses. From left to right they are called double-convex, plano-convex, concavo-convex, double-concave, plano-concave, and convexo-concave. The center line XX

for any lens is called its *principal axis;* it is a line that passes through the centers of curvature of the lens surfaces.

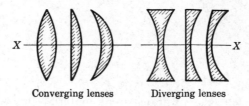

Converging lenses   Diverging lenses

FIG. 386.   Positive and negative lenses

401. Focal Length and Conjugate Distances. When a parallel beam of light is incident upon a lens along its principal axis, the point of convergence or of divergence of the beam after passing through a lens is called the *principal focus* of the lens.   In Fig. 387 the two upper diagrams show such parallel

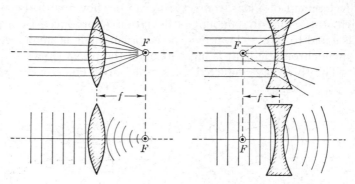

FIG. 387.   Foci of converging and diverging lenses

rays of light refracted in passing through a double-convex and a double-concave lens.   The rays converge to point F for the lens at the left and diverge from point F for the lens at the right; the distance from the principal focus F to the lens of either type is called the *focal length* of the lens, the symbol for which is f.   Should parallel light be incident upon these lenses from the right, instead of from the left as shown, the focal points would be on the other side of the lenses at the same distances f from them.

In the simpler theory of lenses the thickness of a lens is assumed to be negligibly small in comparison with its focal length, and this assumption applies to this chapter except § 410.   With *thin lenses*, therefore, distances may be measured to either lens surface.   In diagrams, it is customary to show the lenses with appreciable thickness in order to indicate their shapes more clearly, and particularly to show whether they are converging or diverging. In drawing lines to represent rays of light in such diagrams, the procedure is to deviate the lines at the transverse plane which actually shows the position of the ideally thin lens, instead of showing the refraction that occurs at each surface. The upper diagrams of Fig. 387 indicate this procedure.

The lower diagrams of the figure show the same results using wave fronts instead of rays of light. Plane waves normal to the principal axis are incident upon a double-convex lens at the left, and, because the retardation is greater at the center than near the edge of the lens, the waves converge upon the principal focus at *F*. With the double-concave lens at the right, plane incident waves diverge after refraction through the lens as though they had originated at *F*. The figure represents the behavior of all six types of lenses; the diagrams at the left typify converging lenses, and those at the right diverging lenses.

Consideration will next be given to the image formed of an object by a converging lens. When the object is placed at some point along the principal axis of the lens and at a distance *p* from it, the image is

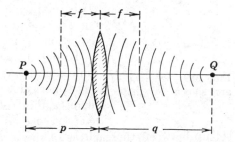

Fig. 388.   Conjugate distances of lens

formed at another point along this axis at a distance *q* from the lens. The relation between these distances and the focal length *f* of the lens is given by

$$\frac{1}{p} + \frac{1}{q} = \frac{1}{f} \tag{279}$$

as demonstrated in the sections to follow. Fig. 388 shows a spherical wave issuing from the point source at *P*, falling on the lens of focal length *f*, and converging to form an image at *Q*. Since the equation is symmetrical in *p* and *q*, it follows that object and image may be interchanged; that is, if the object is located at *Q*, the image is formed at *P*. For this reason the distances *p* and *q* are called *conjugate distances* of the lens.

For every value of the object distance *p* there is a particular value of the image distance *q*. If the foregoing equation yields a negative value for *q*, then a virtual image is formed and its location at *Q* is on the same side of the lens as *P*. If the object is at infinity, then *p* = ∞ and the image distance *q* becomes equal to *f*.

402. Relation between Focal Length and Radii of Curvature. The focal length of a lens can also be expressed in terms of its physical constants, specifically its radii of curvature and its refractive index. The expression can best be derived by using wave fronts rather than rays, but it is necessary first to establish a geometrical relation dealing with the segment of a circle. The distance between the arc and its chord, measured along the radius perpendicular to the chord, is called the *sagitta* of the arc, and is shown as *s* in

Fig. 389. In the diagram the radius OM of length r is intersected by the chord from L perpendicular to OM. If the chord has a length $2y$, then $r^2 = y^2 + (r - s)^2$, or $y^2 = 2rs - s^2$. For chords that are short in comparison with the radius, s^2 is negligibly small with respect to $2rs$, and consequently the length of the sagitta becomes

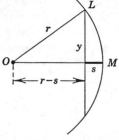

$$s = \frac{y^2}{2r} \qquad (280)$$

FIG. 389. Sagitta of arc shown by heavy line

This relation between the radius and semi-chord of an arc and its sagitta is helpful in developing the equation for lenses.

To derive the relation between the conjugate distances of a lens and its radii of curvature, a diverging spherical wave front will be considered to fall upon a thin converging lens and to be brought to convergence after refraction. A relationship will be set up between the sagittas of the incident and emergent wave fronts and of the two surfaces of the lens, and this will then be converted to semi-chords and radii by means of Eq. 280.

Light issues from a point source at P on the principal axis PQ of the converging lens shown in Fig. 390, and this lens produces an image of the source at Q. The lens has surfaces of radii r_1 and r_2, as shown, and the distance from its axis to its edge E is represented as y. Incident and emergent wave

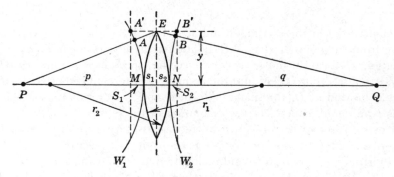

FIG. 390. Determining relation between conjugate distances and surface curvatures of lens

fronts, W_1 and W_2, are shown just touching the lens surfaces at M and N, and the extreme rays PE and EQ are drawn to the edge of the lens, intersecting these wave fronts at A and B respectively.

Basically all rays of the light wave require the same time to travel from an object to its image. Hence the ray from any point on the wave front W_1 advances to the corresponding point on W_2 in the same time. This means that at the edge of the lens the distance AEB, entirely in air, is traversed in the same time as the distance at the center MN, entirely in the lens of refractive index μ. From the definition of refractive index, it follows that

$$AE + EB = \mu(MN)$$

The extreme rays are assumed to make small angles with the principal axis, so that points A' and B' on the wave fronts at a distance y from the axis can be substituted for A and B without appreciable error. With this approximation, the lens surfaces and the wave fronts can be represented by arcs having the same semi-chord y. The sagittas of these arcs are marked in the figure as s_1 and s_2 for the lens surfaces, and S_1 and S_2 for the wave fronts. With these substitutions the foregoing equation becomes $A'E + EB' = \mu(MN)$, or

$$S_1 + s_1 + s_2 + S_2 = \mu(s_1 + s_2)$$

whence

$$S_1 + S_2 = (\mu - 1)(s_1 + s_2)$$

Each of the sagittas may be expressed in terms of the semi-chord and radius in accordance with Eq. 280, giving

$$\frac{y^2}{2p} + \frac{y^2}{2q} = (\mu - 1)\left(\frac{y^2}{2r_1} + \frac{y^2}{2r_2}\right)$$

where p is the object distance PM, q is the image distance NQ, and r_1 and r_2 are the radii of the left and right lens surfaces, all as shown in the figure. Then each term is divided by $y^2/2$, and the relation between the conjugate distances becomes

$$\frac{1}{p} + \frac{1}{q} = (\mu - 1)\left(\frac{1}{r_1} + \frac{1}{r_2}\right) \tag{281}$$

Finally, when the object distance is infinitely great, the image is formed at the focus; this means that $q = f$ when $p = \infty$, and Eq. 281 becomes

$$\frac{1}{f} = (\mu - 1)\left(\frac{1}{r_1} + \frac{1}{r_2}\right) \tag{282}$$

This equation expresses the relation between the focal length of a lens and its physical constants. Eqs. 281 and 282 are the fundamental equations for lenses and apply to all forms of thin lenses, but for correctness the distances p, q, and f should be such that the rays to the rim of the lens subtend small angles at both object and image.

Opticians express the focal power of spectacle lenses in terms of a unit called the *diopter*, found by taking the reciprocal of their focal lengths in meters. As examples: the focal power of a lens of 1 meter focal length is 1 diopter, that of a lens having a focal length of 20 cm is $1/0.20 = 5$ diopters. Thus, the shorter the focal length of a lens the greater is its focal power.

403. Image Constructions. It is frequently desired to verify the solution of a lens problem by constructing graphically the image which the lens produces of a given object. Such construction requires a knowledge of the focal length of the lens, and this may be procured by applying Eq. 282 if the surface radii of the lens and its refractive index are known.

The procedure is illustrated in Fig. 391, wherein a number of rays are shown extending from the head-end of the arrow as object O to various points on the lens and thereafter refracted to a common point which forms

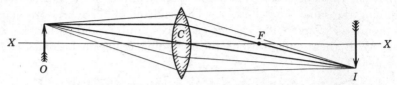

FIG. 391.   Rays extending from object, through lens, to image

the image I of that object point. A similar diagram can be drawn for any other point of the object. Thus, every portion of the lens contributes its share to the production of each part of the image. A fragment of a broken lens, having portions of its refracting surfaces in good condition, can produce a clear image, but not as bright as with the entire lens.

Only two rays are necessary to locate a point of an image, and it is natural to choose the two that can be drawn most conveniently. These are shown in heavier lines than the others in Fig. 391. One is drawn from the head-end of the object parallel to the principal axis XX as far as the lens, and thereafter through the principal focus F, as described in § 401. The other

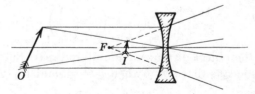

FIG. 392.   Image construction for diverging lens

is drawn from the same point of the object straight through the center C of the lens; it is undeviated because planes tangent to the lens surfaces where this ray meets them are parallel and the lens merely acts as a parallel-sided slab of glass. The intersection of these lines (or their prolongations backward) locates the image of the head-end of the object.

The procedure is the same whatever the shape of the lens and location of the object. For converging lenses the focal point used is on the side of the lens opposite the object, while for diverging lenses the focal point used is on the same side. If the construction is carried out for both ends of a straight object, the entire image can be definitely located with four rays. Fig. 392 illustrates the image construction for a diverging lens; the object is inclined to the axis. The horizontal rays from the object O appear after refraction to come from F, but they do not actually do so; in consequence the image I is virtual.

404. Application of Lens Formula. The relation between the conjugate distances, the focal length, and the surface curvatures of a lens, as expressed by Eqs. 279, 281 and 282, applies to all types of thin lenses, provided correct signs are chosen for the various quantities involved. The combined equa-

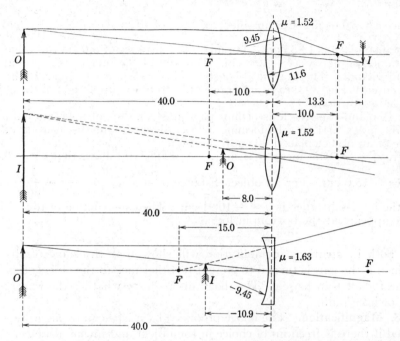

FIG. 393. Image constructions for verifying analytical solutions of lens problems

tion and the rules governing the choice of signs are as follows:

$$\frac{1}{p} + \frac{1}{q} = \frac{1}{f} = (\mu - 1)\left(\frac{1}{r_1} + \frac{1}{r_2}\right)$$

Focal length (f) is taken *positive* for *converging* lenses and *negative* for *diverging* lenses.

Radius (r_1 or r_2) is taken *positive* for *convex* surfaces and *negative* for *concave* surfaces.

Object distance (p) or image distance (q) is *positive* when object or image is *real*, and is *negative* when object or image is *virtual*. The significance of a virtual object is considered in § 406.

The following examples illustrate the application of these rules in locating the image I of an object O formed by a lens having its foci at $F F$, as shown in Fig. 393.

Illustrative Problems

I. A double-convex lens of crown glass has radii of 11.6 and 9.45 cm, and a refractive index of 1.52. Calculate the focal length and determine where images are located when the object is first 40 cm and then 8 cm from the lens.

Since $r_1 = 11.6$ cm, $r_2 = 9.45$ cm, and $\mu - 1 = 0.52$, it follows that

$$\frac{1}{f} = 0.52 \left(\frac{1}{11.6} + \frac{1}{9.45} \right) = 0.100$$

whence $f = 10.0$ cm. For an object distance of 40 cm, $\dfrac{1}{40} + \dfrac{1}{q} = \dfrac{1}{10}$, and the image distance q is 13.33 cm. For an object distance of 8.0 cm the value of q is obtained similarly as -40.0 cm. The first of the images is real, and the second virtual. The graphical constructions are shown to scale at the top and center of Fig. 393; rays are drawn only from the upper end of the object to avoid confusion.

II. A plano-concave lens of flint glass has a radius of 9.45 cm and a refractive index of 1.63. Determine its focal length, and the location of the image of an object placed 40 cm from the lens.

Here $r_1 = -9.45$ cm, $r_2 = \infty$, and $\mu - 1 = 0.63$; it follows that $f = -9.45/0.63 = -15.0$ cm. For an object distance of 40 cm, $\dfrac{1}{q} = \dfrac{1}{-15} - \dfrac{1}{40}$; therefore the image distance is $q = -10.91$ cm. The construction of this virtual image appears at the bottom in Fig. 393.

In both illustrations, computation will show that the same results are obtained if the lens is turned to present its other face to the object; this fact is true for all thin lenses. The diagrams indicate whether the images are erect or inverted.

405. Magnification. The image produced by a lens can be made any size desired if there is freedom of choice in the object and image distance. The diagrams of Fig. 393 indicate that, when the image is farther from the lens than the object, the image is larger than the object, and vice versa. The ratio of image size to object size, as measured transversely to the principal axis, is called the lateral magnification of the lens. When these sizes are equal the lateral magnification is unity.

Fig. 394 shows two locations of a lens between object and screen, and only the rays through the lens centers are indicated. In position L_1 the lens produces an image $A'B'$ that is larger than the object AB, whereas in position L_2 it produces a reduced image $A''B''$. The two triangles formed at the center of the lens by the object and its image in either position are similar; consequently the ratio of image size to object size is the same as the ratio of image distance to object distance. Thus, the lateral magnifications for the two lens positions become

$$M_1 = \frac{A'B'}{AB} = \frac{q_1}{p_1} \quad \text{or} \quad M_2 = \frac{A''B''}{AB} = \frac{q_2}{p_2} \tag{283}$$

The magnification produced by a lens of focal length f can also be expressed as the ratio $(q - f)/f$ by merging Eqs. 279 and 283.

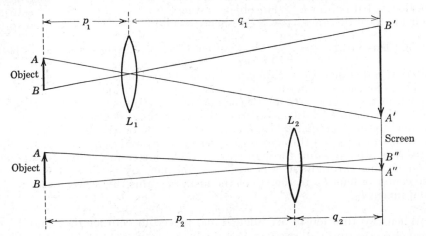

FIG. 394. Magnification produced by lens in two positions

406. Lens Combinations.

In many optical instruments the image formed by one lens serves as the object for another. The computation or construction for the location and size of the final image is carried out for the first lens and then for the second, as described previously. If the second lens is interposed between the first lens and the image the first produces by itself, then that image serves as a *virtual object* for the second lens; in the calculation for the final image the object distance for the second lens is regarded as negative.

Illustrative Problem

Consider an object such as a lamp placed 15 cm in front of a converging lens having a focal length of 10 cm, and suppose that the rays to the image are intercepted by a second converging lens having a focal length of 8 cm and located 14 cm from the first lens. Locate the image produced by the lens combination.

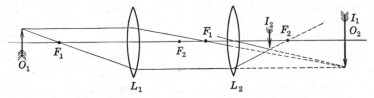

FIG. 395. Construction of image formed by a pair of lenses

Fig. 395 shows the lens positions and image constructions to scale. An image I_1 is formed of object O_1 by lens L_1, the foci being located at points F_1. Since the focal distance $f_1 = 10$ cm, and the object distance $p_1 = 15$ cm, an application of Eq. 279 for the first lens shows that the image distance $q_1 = 30$ cm. The second lens is less than this distance from the first, and consequently the image serves as a virtual object O_2 for lens L_2, which has its foci located at points F_2. The object distance $p_2 = -(30 - 14) = -16$ cm, and the focal distance $f_2 = 8$ cm; hence applying the same equation to the second lens yields $\dfrac{1}{8} = \dfrac{1}{-16} + \dfrac{1}{q_2}$; from which the image is found to be located at a distance $q_2 = 5.33$ cm to the right of lens L_2.

The construction lines for the graphical determination of the image I_2 are shown in the figure only for the head-end of the object. The intermediate image I_1 is found by two rays from the tip of the object O_1; one of these is parallel to the principal axis and passes through F_1 on the far side of the lens, and the other passes through the nearer focus F_1 and is parallel to the principal axis after passing through lens L_1. The latter ray converges upon F_2 after passing through the second lens. Another ray is shown passing from the center of lens L_2 to the tip of the image I_1; this ray serves to locate the final image I_2.

———————

When two thin lenses are aligned and placed in contact they may be regarded as the equivalent of a single thin lens. To find the focal length of the combination their individual focal lengths are represented by f_1 and f_2 and use is again made of Eq. 279. An object distant p from the first lens produces an image at a distance q_1 on its other side, so that $\dfrac{1}{p} + \dfrac{1}{q_1} = \dfrac{1}{f_1}$.

This image serves as a virtual object for the second lens at a distance $-q_1$ from it, and the final image is located at a distance q from the lenses, so that $\dfrac{1}{-q_1} + \dfrac{1}{q} = \dfrac{1}{f_2}$. When these equations are added and the result compared with that for the equivalent single lens of focal length f, namely, $\dfrac{1}{p} + \dfrac{1}{q} = \dfrac{1}{f}$, it follows that

$$\frac{1}{f} = \frac{1}{f_1} + \frac{1}{f_2} \tag{284}$$

This equation applies only to thin lenses that are in contact. It can be modified to suit two thin lenses that are a distance s apart by subtracting the term $s/f_1 f_2$ from the right-hand member.

The foregoing equation can be expressed in simple form when each term is expressed in diopters, for then the focal power of a combination of two lenses is seen to be the sum of the focal powers of its components. Thus, a converging lens of $+5$ diopters combined with a diverging one of -2 diopters results in an equivalent converging lens having a power of $+3$ diopters.

407. Spherical and Chromatic Aberration. Rays of light parallel to the principal axis of a lens that pass through it near the rim are not brought to a focus at exactly the same point as those that pass through the center of the lens. This imperfection, called *spherical aberration*, is not due to inaccuracies in the spherical surfaces of the lens. The effect with a converging lens is exaggerated in Fig. 396. The parallel rays from a distant source intersect at various points along the principal axis from F to F'. A screen placed at these points shows a blurred image of the source, but a position can be found between them where blurring is least. The figure shows this position to be at C; the rays there constitute a *circle of least confusion*. The amount of spherical aberration produced by a lens is usually measured by

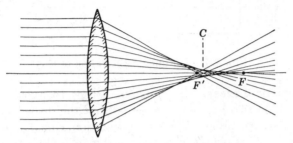

FIG. 396.   Spherical aberration of lens

the axial distance FF' between the intersections of the central and marginal rays.

Spherical aberration can be reduced in designing lenses by choosing appropriate radii for their surfaces. Minimum aberration occurs when the deviation of light rays is the same at both refracting surfaces. It can be shown that a lens of refractive index μ has minimum aberration for parallel incident light when the surface radii are in the proportion:

$$\frac{r_1}{r_2} = \frac{\mu + 4 - 2\mu^2}{\mu + 2\mu^2}$$

In a good photographic lens this aberration is less than $\frac{1}{2}\%$ of its focal length. A plano-convex lens when used with light incident upon the curved face gives relatively little spherical aberration.

So far in this chapter, no mention has been made of the influence of the color of light upon the behavior of a lens. The dispersion of white light, already explained for prisms, § 388, also occurs in lenses with the result that the component colors of a beam are brought to a focus at different points. Since the refractive index is greater for the violet end of the spectrum than for the red end, it follows from Eq. 282 that the focal length of a lens is less for violet light than for red. This dispersive effect produced by a lens is called *chromatic aberration*.

Fig. 397 shows a parallel beam of white light incident upon a converging lens. All pencils of the beam are dispersed in the same manner as the two shown, and their collective effect is a convergence of the several colors at individual points along the principal axis from the focus of violet light at F_v

to the focus of red light at F_r. The color distribution can be observed by moving a screen along the axis; at F_v a concentric color pattern appears with violet at the center, and at F_r with red at the center.

Curved mirrors produce spherical aberration, § 374, but not chromatic aberration; the latter fact gives such mirrors a distinct advantage over lenses in particular applications.

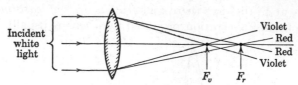

FIG. 397.   Chromatic aberration of lens

408. Achromatic Lenses. In designing lenses to avoid dispersion, the plan is to combine two (or more) lenses so that the dispersion produced by one is annulled by the other. Such a combination, called an *achromatic lens*, usually employs lenses placed in contact and made of substances having different dispersive powers. The principle will be explained for an achromatic doublet having a converging component lens of crown glass and a diverging component of flint glass, which is to be achromatized over the color range from violet (*v*) to red (*r*).

For violet light, the focal length f_v of the two lenses in contact is given by

$$\frac{1}{f_v} = \frac{1}{f_{vC}} + \frac{1}{f_{vF}}$$

where the subscripts C and F denote the crown-glass and flint-glass lenses respectively. Similarly for red light

$$\frac{1}{f_r} = \frac{1}{f_{rC}} + \frac{1}{f_{rF}}$$

To achromatize over this color range, the focal lengths f_v and f_r of the doublet should be equal; consequently

$$\frac{1}{f_{vC}} + \frac{1}{f_{vF}} = \frac{1}{f_{rC}} + \frac{1}{f_{rF}}$$

By the use of Eqs. 275 and 282 this relation can be reduced to the form

$$\frac{\delta_F}{f_F} = -\frac{\delta_C}{f_C} \tag{285}$$

where δ_F and δ_C are the dispersive powers of flint and crown glass respectively. This expression is the condition for achromatism.

It is also possible to make an achromatic lens of two components that have the same dispersive power. This is done by using lenses of the same kind of glass and placing them coaxially a distance apart equal to one-half the sum of their focal lengths. The Huygens eyepiece, Fig. 398, illustrates this construction. It consists of two plano-convex lenses, one having a focal length about three times that of the other, with both plane faces directed toward the eye. The lens nearer the eye, called the *eye lens*, has the shorter focal length, and the other, called the *field lens*, is twice that distance from the eye lens. At the field lens the violet light is deviated more than the red, as shown by the rays marked *v* and *r*, but the eye lens receives the first of these rays at a point nearer the center and, for this reason, deviates it less than the other. With lenses of correct proportions and spacing the total

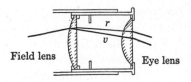

FIG. 398. Cross-section of Huygens' eyepiece

deviation can be made the same for both colors, rendering the eyepiece achromatic.

409. Astigmatism. In addition to spherical and chromatic aberration, there are several other defects of a spherical lens that cause indistinctness in the image. An important one of these is called astigmatism; because of this defect, rays of light that pass through the lens obliquely from an object point remote from the principal axis do not converge upon a common image point.

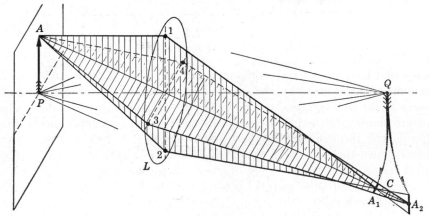

FIG. 399. Astigmatic focal lines produced by lens

Fig. 399 is a perspective view of a long slender object *AP* sending rays through a converging lens *L* to form an image at the right. Rays from point *P* on the axis, if they are continued through points 1 to 4 on the lens, would converge upon emergence to point *Q*. In contrast, rays from point *A* off the axis, and going through the same points on the lens, are seen to converge upon the zone A_1A_2. The rays through points 1 and 2 along the vertical diameter of the lens meet at A_1, and those through points 3 and 4 along the horizontal diameter meet at A_2. A screen placed at either of these positions receives light from all points of the lens and linear patches of light called *focal lines* are produced. The focal lines A_1 and A_2 are at right angles to each other, and somewhere between them the patch of light would be roughly circular in shape. This is the nearest approach to a point image that the lens can produce of the head-end of the object. Astigmatism can be corrected by the use of two lenses with appropriate separation.

Rays of light that are incident obliquely upon a spherical mirror behave similarly upon reflection. The amount of astigmatism of a lens or mirror for any object point is indicated by the distance between its focal lines as measured along the middle ray from that point.

410. Thick Lenses. The lenses considered thus far were assumed so thin that no appreciable error is introduced in calculations for focal lengths or conjugate distances by reckoning these quantities to either lens surface. For

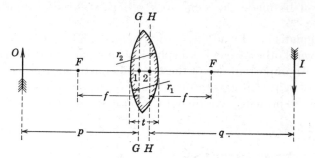

FIG. 400. Principal points and planes of thick lens

lenses that have thicknesses comparable to their focal lengths such calculations may also be made by the usual equations if, instead of reckoning distances to the lens surfaces, the distances are reckoned to two different but definite points. In the usual case where the rays re-enter the same medium after passage through the lens, these points are called its *principal points*, and planes drawn through these points perpendicular to the principal axis are called its *principal planes*. The distance of each principal point from its associated lens surface depends upon the thickness of the lens, its refractive index, and both radii of curvature; the methods used in determining such distances are explained in books on lens design.

Fig. 400 shows a double-convex lens of thickness t with principal points at 1 and 2, and principal planes at G and H. The object and image distances, p and q, extend respectively from O and I to the nearer principal point. The focal distance f, from either of these points to the principal focus F, is called the *equivalent focal length* of the lens. When p, q and f are measured in this way, Eq. 279, namely, $\dfrac{1}{p} + \dfrac{1}{q} = \dfrac{1}{f}$, applies also to thick lenses. Eq. 282 is sometimes generalized so that the equivalent focal length of a thick lens can be computed from its dimensions. The general equation proves to be

$$\frac{1}{f} = (\mu - 1) \left(\frac{1}{r_1} + \frac{1}{r_2} - \frac{(\mu - 1)t}{\mu r_1 r_2} \right) \tag{286}$$

which reduces to the simpler form when $t = 0$.

The procedure in constructing graphically the image produced by a thick lens is illustrated in Fig. 401. A ray from the head-end of object O is drawn

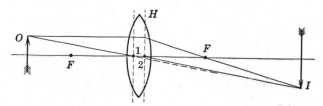

FIG. 401. Construction of rays for thick lens

to the first principal point, 1, and upon emergence is continued in a parallel direction from the other principal point, 2. The other ray is drawn parallel to the principal axis as far as the second principal plane, H, where it is shown refracted to pass through the focus F. The intersection of these rays at I locates the head-end of the image. This procedure assumes the same medium on both sides of the lens.

PROBLEMS

1. An incandescent lamp is mounted with its axis vertical and a screen is placed horizontally 32 in. below it. The manufacturer's imprint giving the rating of the lamp is etched on the glass, and this serves as a convenient object when the lamp is illuminated. If an image of this imprint is produced on the screen by a reading glass held 5 in. from the lamp, what is the focal length of the reading glass?

2. A lens is observed to converge the sun's rays to a point 15 cm from the lens. This lens is then used to form an image of a nearby object. How far from the object should a screen be placed to receive a sharp image when the lens is placed (*a*) 30 cm from the object? (*b*) 60 cm from the screen?

3. If the reading glass of Prob. 1 is held 10 in. from the lamp described, at what distance from the lamp will its imprint be focused?

4. Two segments are laid off on a circle of 12-in. diameter; the chord of one of them is 5 in. long and that of the other is 8 in. long. For each segment compute (*a*) the true value of the sagitta and (*b*) the approximate value of the sagitta as given by Eq. 280.

5. A thin plano-convex lens of flint glass has a focal length of 20 cm and the radius of its curved surface is 15 cm. (*a*) Determine the refractive index for the glass of which the lens is made. (*b*) If this lens was ground from a disk 3.5 cm in diameter, what is its axial thickness?

6. The lens of Prob. 5 is placed under water and a beam of parallel light is incident upon it axially. At what distance from the lens will the beam be brought to a focus?

7. An object is placed at the following distances in front of a converging lens of 15-cm focal length: 60, 40, 30, 20, 15, 12, 10, 5, and 0 cm. Determine analytically the corresponding image locations, and plot a graph showing the relation between object distances as abscissas and image distances as ordinates.

8. Verify the image locations for the lens of Prob. 7 by diagrams drawn to scale for an object distance (*a*) of 60 cm and (*b*) of 12 cm. Describe each image.

9. A thin double-concave lens is to be constructed of glass having a refractive index of 1.65 for light of a particular wavelength, and its focal points are to be 3 in. from the lens. If the surfaces are to have equal curvature, what should their radii be?

10. An object is located a distance *a* outside of the principal focus of a converging lens, and the image is a distance *b* outside of the other principal focus of the lens. Show that the focal length of the lens can be expressed as $f = \sqrt{ab}$.

11. A disk of glass having a refractive index of 1.55 is ground to form a lens with one concave surface of 6-cm radius and one convex surface of 8-cm radius. This lens is used to form an image of an object placed 20 cm from the lens. Find (*a*) the focal length of the lens and (*b*) the location of the image. (*c*) Confirm this location graphically.

12. Where should an object 1 in. long be placed with reference to a converging lens of 4-in. focal length in order to produce an image 10 in. from the lens and on the same side as the object? How long will the image be?

13. Compare the sizes of the images produced by the reading glass of Probs. 1 and 3 in its two positions.

14. Where should an object be placed with respect to the lens of Prob. 9 in order that the image may be ¼ as high as the object? Verify the analytical solution by a diagram drawn to scale.

15. Between an object and a screen that are 50 cm apart is placed a lens that has two convex surfaces of 6-cm radius and a refractive index of 1.60. Determine (*a*) the two positions at which the lens yields distinct images of the object on the screen and (*b*) the relative sizes of the two images.

16. Determine the focal length of a lens to be placed in contact with that in Prob. 5 to yield a combination having a focal power of 7.5 diopters. If the supplementary lens is of the same type and material, what is the radius of its curved surface?

17. Two identical converging lenses of 30-cm focal length are placed in contact and an object is mounted coaxially with the lenses and 40 cm from them. (*a*) Locate the image. (*b*) Move one lens 10 cm farther from the object and determine the distance that the image is shifted.

18. Two converging lenses, *A* of 20-cm focal length and *B* of 15-cm focal length, are arranged coaxially a distance *x* apart as shown in the diagram. Determine the location of the final image formed by the lens combination of an object 50 cm from *A* when the separation is (*a*) *x* = 30 cm and (*b*) *x* = 40 cm.

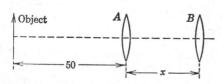

Problem 18

19. Replace lens B of Prob. 18 by a diverging lens of the same focal length and determine the location of the final image for a lens separation of 25 cm. Compare the size of this image with that of the object. Verify the results graphically.

20. Place the converging lens B of Prob. 18 a distance $x = 10$ cm from lens A and make an optical diagram of the images and the rays leading to them. Verify the result analytically.

21. An object O, a converging lens L of 30-cm focal length, and a plane mirror M are arranged as in the diagram. Locate the image of the object as formed by light reflected by the mirror back through the lens. Could this image be projected on a screen placed at the left of the lens?

22. An object 2 cm high is placed 40 cm in front of a converging lens having a focal length of 15 cm, and a concave mirror of 20-cm radius is placed 30 cm

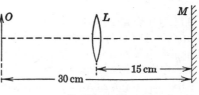

Problem 21

beyond the lens. Determine the location of the final image that is formed after light from the object has been reflected by the mirror and passed through the lens a second time. Describe the image and give its height.

23. A converging lens is to be designed for a focal length of 6 in. and for minimum spherical aberration with parallel incident light. If the index of refraction of the lens is 1.60, what should be the radii of its surfaces?

24. Light is incident upon a converging lens of flint glass; one lens surface is plane and the other has a radius of 10 in. How far apart are the principal foci for the C and F spectral lines?

25. A converging crown-glass lens is to be combined with a diverging flint-glass lens in contact with it to form an achromatic combination having a focal length of 8.25 in. Use the data of § 387 and calculate the focal lengths of the component lenses.

26. An achromatic lens is formed of a converging crown-glass lens and a diverging flint-glass lens cemented together, the contacting surfaces having radii of 5.0 cm. Determine the radii of the exposed surfaces to give the combination a focal length of 18 cm.

27. A plano-convex lens has a thickness of 0.9 cm and its curved surface has a radius of 12 cm; the glass has a refractive index of 1.55. One of the principal planes of the lens is at the curved surface and the other is $\frac{1}{3}$ of the lens thickness away and toward the plane surface. This surface receives rays from an object 35 cm distant. For this thick lens compute (a) its diameter, (b) its focal length, and (c) the location of the image with respect to the object. Make an optical diagram.

37

OPTICAL INSTRUMENTS

411. Optical Aids to Vision. When objects are viewed at such close range that the eye, even while exerting its greatest effort, cannot focus their images sharply, or when the objects are so remote that their details are indistinguishable, optical instruments can be used to supplement the abilities of the eye. Such instruments employ mirrors or lenses of appropriate design and location and have a variety of forms. They include magnifying glasses and microscopes, astronomical and terrestrial telescopes, transits and levels for surveying, and binocular field and opera glasses, as well as low-power telescopes for such instruments as photometers, sextants, refractometers and spectroscopes, already described. The essential elements of some magnifying instruments and their magnification will be considered in this chapter; the factors governing their resolving power will be deferred to the next chapter.

412. The Eye. The human organ of vision consists of the eyeball cushioned in a bony socket, a muscular system for moving it, and lachrymal

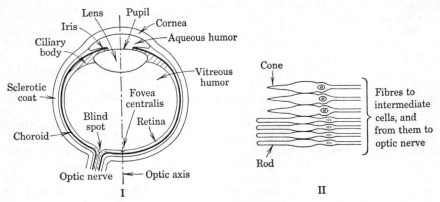

Fig. 402. Horizontal section of right eyeball and section of retinal surface

glands and ducts for moistening its anterior portion. The eyeball comprises a lens system for producing images of objects under observation, a *retina* for the reception of the images and their conversion into nervous impulses, and the *optic nerve* for transmitting these impulses to the brain to produce the sensation of vision.

The eyeball has two coatings outside of the retina, as illustrated in part I of Fig. 402. The outermost is the white fibrous envelope which, because of its toughness, is called the *sclerotic* coat. Its front portion, transparent and more curved than the "white of the eye," is called the *cornea* because of its horny texture. The inner layer or *choroid* is composed of numerous blood vessels that nourish the eye, and pigment cells that shield the retina from stray light. This dark coat extends forward to the colored *iris* diaphragm which, by involuntary muscular control, regulates the amount of light admitted through its circular aperture or *pupil.*

Within the eye is the *crystalline lens* comprising flexible layers of different refractive indices. The chamber in front of the lens contains a weak salt solution called the *aqueous humor,* and the chamber in back of it contains a gelatinous substance called the *vitreous humor.* The dimensions and refractive indices of the optical parts of the normal eye vary from person to person; approximate values are given in the accompanying table.

CONSTANTS OF THE EYE

Parts of the Eye	Radius in mm		Thickness along Axis in mm	Index of Refraction
	Front	Back		
Cornea..............	7.8	7.3	0.5	1.351
Lens				
for near objects.......	6.0	5.5	4.0	} average
for distant objects.....	10.0	6.0	3.6	} 1.437
Aqueous humor				
for near objects.......			3.2	} 1.337
for distant objects.....			3.6	}
Vitreous humor.........		12.0	15.9	1.337

The ability of the eye, not possessed by any other optical instrument, to focus automatically upon objects located at different distances is called *accommodation.* This result is accomplished by changing the shape of the lens, chiefly the curvature of its front surface, through the action of the muscles of the *ciliary body.* It is believed that in accommodating for a near object these muscles contract and relax the ligaments around the rim of the lens, thereby allowing the lens to thicken by its own elasticity. When the eye is focused for parallel rays, that is, upon remotely distant objects, it is said to be unaccommodated. The faculty of accommodation diminishes with increasing age.

The end organs of sight on the retina are microscopic elements called *rods* and *cones,* shown greatly enlarged in part II of Fig. 402. At the central point of the retina, the *fovea centralis,* only cones are present, and this is the place of acutest vision. Beyond the center the proportion of cones to rods decreases and in the peripheral portions there may be but one cone to ten rods. It is believed that only the cones are responsive to color. No sensation of vision is produced by light which falls upon that part of the retina known as the *blind spot*, where the optic nerve enters the eyeball.

Important properties of the eye are the quickness of perception upon exposure to light and the persistence of vision for a time after its removal; upon these properties depend the operation of television receivers and of motion pictures. With the latter a continuous impression results from the projection of 20 or more images per second, each "frame" of the film being held stationary while being projected.

413. Some Defects of Vision and Their Correction. In the passage of light through the cornea, aqueous humor, lens, and vitreous humor to the

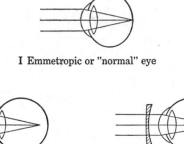

I Emmetropic or "normal" eye

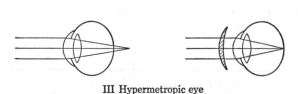

II Myopic eye

III Hypermetropic eye

FIG. 403. Correction of myopia and hypermetropia by spectacle lenses

retina of the eye, the greatest deviation occurs at the front surface of the cornea where the refractive indices of the adjacent mediums of the lens system differ most. In the diagrams of Fig. 403, which show parallel beams of light entering the pupils of typical eyes, all the refraction is indicated for simplicity as occurring at this surface.

Diagram I represents an eye which, when relaxed, forms an image of a distant object upon the retina; it is called a normal or *emmetropic eye*. Nearer objects are focused upon the retina by making the lens system more converging through accommodation.

Diagram II represents at the left a nearsighted or *myopic eye* that is relaxed; the rays from a distant object focus in front of the retina, usually because the eyeball is too long. Such an eye can see only near objects distinctly. A diverging lends, as shown at the right, is needed to lessen the high focal power of the eye and permit distant objects to be seen clearly.

Diagram III represents at the left a farsighted or *hypermetropic eye;* the rays from a distant object focus behind the retina. A converging lens, as shown at the right, is needed to increase the focal power of the eye and permit near objects to be seen distinctly.

If the lens system of the eye is more converging in one plane than in another, an object point is imaged along two focal lines as with an astigmatic pencil of light through a lens, § 409. This defect of vision is called astigmatism and is generally due to unequal curvature of the front surface of the cornea. It is corrected by cylindrical lenses so arranged that the convergence produced by eye and spectacle lens together is the same in all planes.

414. The Camera. A picture of an object can be produced on a photographic plate or film merely by interposing a screen having a tiny aperture. Rays of light from each object point proceed through the aperture in straight lines to a corresponding point on the plate as illustrated in part I of Fig. 404.

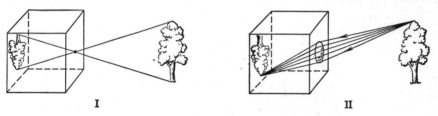

FIG. 404. Action of photographic camera

This arrangement is termed the *pinhole camera.* If the aperture is made larger to let more light fall upon the plate, a diverging pencil proceeds from each object point and produces a patch of light upon the plate; these patches overlap and yield a blurred picture. Thus, brightness of the picture is attained at the expense of definition.

With a lens placed in the aperture, all the rays from each object point passing through the lens are brought to a focus upon a corresponding image point, as shown in part II of the figure. The usual photographic camera makes use of this arrangement, and includes facilities for varying the distance between lens and plate to permit focusing objects at different distances, and for regulating the aperture of the lens by stops to adjust for different lighting conditions and speed.

The brightness of the image upon the plate depends upon the aperture of the lens or objective, that is, upon the diameter of the opening in the diaphragm placed at the lens. This diameter is expressed as a fraction of the focal length of the objective; thus a lens set at $f/8$ is "stopped" down to a diameter one-eighth of its focal length. If the stop is changed to $f/4$, the aperture diameter is doubled and four times as much light reaches the plate; the corresponding exposure time is one-fourth the previous value.

The better-made objectives for cameras are corrected for spherical and chromatic aberration, astigmatism, and other defects; with proper focusing they yield sharply defined pictures. An example of such lenses is the so-called *anastigmat* lens; Fig. 405 shows a section of the well-known Tessar anastigmat objective formed of four lenses, the two inner ones having lower indices of refraction than the others.

FIG. 405. Anastigmat lens

415. Projection Apparatus. A *projector* for lantern slides or motion picture films consists optically of a *condensing lens* for illuminating the glass slide or film, and a *projection lens* for forming an enlarged image of that object upon the screen. A typical arrangement is illustrated in Fig. 406, wherein the condenser C consists of two plano-convex lenses, and the projection lens P consists of two lenses also, although shown as one for simplicity of ray construction. The lantern slide or film frame O is placed upside down in order to have the image I erect. In projecting objects that cannot be inverted,

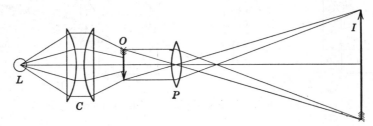

FIG. 406. Optical system of projector

such as cells of liquids for demonstrating capillarity and electrolysis, it is customary to place an erecting prism just beyond the projecting lens. The lateral magnification I/O is equal to the ratio of image distance to object distance, and depends upon the focal length of the projection lens. The source of illumination L may be an incandescent lamp with its filament concentrated in a small flat zone, or an arc lamp.

Illustrative Problem

A motion picture projector in an auditorium throws a picture upon a vertical screen distant 75 ft horizontally from the projection lens that has a focal length of 6 in. Find the magnification produced.

It is necessary first to find the object distance for an image distance of 75 ft by Eq. 279. Thus, $\dfrac{1}{p} = \dfrac{1}{f} - \dfrac{1}{q} = \dfrac{12}{6} - \dfrac{1}{75} = \dfrac{1}{0.503}$; whence $p = 0.503$ ft. The lateral magnification, by Eq. 283, is then $q/p = 75/0.503 = 149$.

In projecting television pictures for a large audience, an optical system devised by the Estonian astronomer Bernard Schmidt has been found effective. It makes use of a large concave mirror for projecting the images on a screen and a ring-shaped lens for compensating the spherical aberration of the mirror. In this way a wide-angle system of large aperture (equivalent to about $f/0.9$) can be realized at far less expense than with an all-lens system.

The arrangement is indicated in Fig. 407. The television receiving tube, § 316, is shown at C with its fluorescent screen facing the spherical mirror M, both being aligned vertically; a plane mirror is used to redirect the image upon a vertical screen S. Light from an object point O is collected by the spherical mirror and focused at I on the screen, only the extreme rays being shown. In the path is a nonspherical ring-shaped lens, usually molded of a transparent plastic material, that corrects for the spherical aberration of the curved mirror. Such Schmidt rings or corrector plates are also serviceable with telescopes.

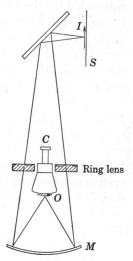

416. Astronomical Telescopes. There are two types of astronomical telescopes, the refracting instrument and the reflecting instrument, the designations referring to the kind of objective used.

The *refracting telescope* consists of two lenses or lens systems: the objective is a carefully corrected achromatic lens of large diameter, and the eyepiece is a doublet like the Huygens eyepiece. The objective

Fig. 407. Elements of the Schmidt reflection system

has a long focal length and produces a real image of the object, whereas the eyepiece has a relatively short focal length and produces a virtual image of the first one for visual inspection. The optical arrangement is shown in Fig. 408; the dotted lines represent rays from the head-end of the distant object converging upon image I_1 by action of the objective. These rays continue and are deviated by the eyepiece, so that they appear to come from the head-end of image I_2.

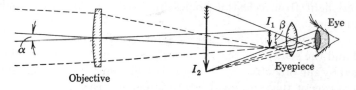

Fig. 408. Refracting astronomical telescope

To evaluate the magnification of the telescope, little help is afforded by the image-object ratio used in expressing lateral magnification, § 405, because of the inaccessibility of the object. A more direct approach is to express the magnification in terms of the *visual angles* that the object subtends at the eye with the instrument and without it, the ratio between these angles being the *angular magnification.* The angles are determined by the extreme rays from the object and image through the lens centers, and are shown by the full lines in the figure.

Without the telescope, the distant object produces an image on the retina subtended by the visual angle α, and with the telescope the larger retinal image is subtended by the angle β. Consequently the angular magnification of the instrument is $M = \beta/\alpha$. Since image I_1 is located at the principal focus of the objective of focal length F, and since this image is practically at the principal focus of the eyepiece of focal length f, it follows that $\alpha = I_1/F$, and $\beta = I_1/f$; consequently the angular magnification of the telescope is

$$M = \frac{F}{f} \tag{287}$$

The *reflecting telescope* has a large mirror for collecting light, and uses a lens system as eyepiece. Fig. 409 shows such a telescope of the Newtonian type, in which a small plane mirror (or a prism) on the axis shifts the real image

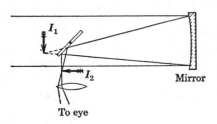

formed by the concave mirror from position I_1 to position I_2 for the eyepiece to enlarge. In the Cassegrainian type, also widely used, the rays from the objective are doubled back by a convex hyperbolic mirror on the telescope axis and pass through a central hole in the mirror itself to the eyepiece.

FIG. 409. Reflecting astronomical telescope

Refracting telescopes are in use that have objectives up to a diameter of 40 in.; some reflecting telescopes are much larger. The 100-in. telescope at Mount Wilson Observatory in California has a mirror of 42.3-ft focal length. The largest is a 200-in. mirror at Mount Palomar Observatory, also in California; this telescope can receive and record light from celestial bodies hundreds of millions of light-years distant in space.

When a telescope is used for making photographic records, the eyepiece is removed and the sensitized plates are located at the place where the images are formed by the objective. The optical arrangement is then the same as in the camera except that the focal length is much greater.

Telescopes that yield erect images are called *terrestrial telescopes.* Several methods can be used for inverting the image produced by the astronomical telescope, such as inserting a lens between objective and eyepiece, introducing an erecting prism as described in § 380, or employing a diverging instead of a converging lens as eyepiece.

417. The Magnifying Glass. In viewing an object, the visual angle it forms at the eye determines the *apparent size* of the object. In the upper part of Fig. 410 the angle α is the visual angle subtended by the object O at the distance d, and also by the inverted retinal image I. An object twice as long and located twice as far away would have the same visual angle and produce the same retinal image, consequently it would have the same apparent size. As the object is brought nearer to the eye its visual angle and apparent size increase, but a limit is reached by the accommodation of the eye. This limiting distance for the normal eye at middle age is about 10 in. or 25 cm, and is spoken of as the *minimum distance of distinct vision.*

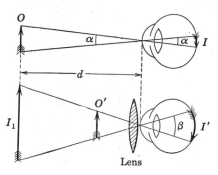

FIG. 410. Increasing visual angle with simple magnifier. The lens enlarges the retinal image from I to I'

The visual angle of an object can be increased by bringing the object nearer to the eye and interposing a converging lens to yield a virtual image of the object where it can be accommodated easily. In the lower part of the figure the object O, initially at the minimum distance of distinct vision d, is moved nearer the eye; when it reaches position O' the lens produces an erect image I_1 at this same distance d, and the visual angle has been increased by this shift from α to β. Thus the lens used as a magnifier has an angular magnification of $M = \beta/\alpha$.

The lateral magnification of the lens is the ratio of the size of the image I_1 to the size of the object O, that is, $M = I_1/O$. With small angles $\alpha = O/d$ and $\beta = I_1/d$, and hence the magnification (either lateral or angular) is

$$M = \frac{\beta}{\alpha} = \frac{I_1/d}{O/d} = \frac{I_1}{O}$$

The magnification of the **magnifying glass** can be expressed in terms of its focal length by applying the procedure of § 405. The object O is located at a distance p from a converging lens of focal length f. With p numerically less than f, a virtual image I_1 is formed on the same side of the lens at a distance q from it such that

$$\frac{1}{p} = \frac{1}{f} + \frac{1}{q}$$

Consequently the magnification is

$$M = \frac{I_1}{O} = \frac{q}{p} = q\left(\frac{1}{f} + \frac{1}{q}\right) = \frac{q}{f} + 1$$

For the eye accommodated to the minimum distance of distinct vision ($q = 25$ cm), the lens of focal length f cm has a magnification of

$$M_e = \frac{25}{f} + 1 \tag{288}$$

For the relaxed or unaccommodated eye the image is formed at infinity, and the object is at the focus of the lens. Then the angle subtended at the unaided eye by the object at the distance of distinct vision is $\alpha = O/25$, and that subtended by the image formed by the lens with the object at the focus is $\beta = O/f$; whence the magnification β/α becomes $(O/f) \div (O/25)$ or

$$M = \frac{25}{f} \tag{289}$$

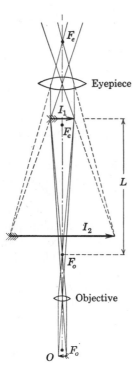

FIG. 411. Optical diagram of microscope

Thus, for a magnifying glass having a focal length of 15 cm the magnification ranges from 2.67 as given by Eq. 288 to 1.67 as given by Eq. 289, depending upon the degree of accommodation.

Oculists use the lens system of the eye as a magnifier to produce an enlarged image of the retina for examination. For this purpose an *ophthalmoscope* is used, consisting essentially of a concave mirror with a hole at the center; the observer reflects light upon the retina and then views it at close range through the hole.

418. The Compound Microscope. An instrument for obtaining greater magnification than can be provided by the magnifier described above is called a *compound microscope*, because it comprises two lenses or lens systems; the first lens, or *objective*, forms a real enlarged image of the object under observation, and the second lens, or *eyepiece*, forms an enlarged virtual image of this image just as in the magnifying glass. Such microscopes are used chiefly in biological, chemical, and metallographic investigations.

Fig. 411 illustrates in convenient proportions the construction of images formed by the microscope. The object O is just outside the principal focus F_o of the objective, and this lens produces a real image of the object at I_1. This image falls between the eyepiece and its principal focus F_e, and the eyepiece forms an image of I_1 at the minimum distance of distinct vision. The final image I_2 is virtual and much larger than the object.

The magnification produced by the objective is commonly stated in terms of the *optical tube length*, which is taken as the distance between the upper focus of the objective and the image I_1 formed by this lens; this distance is marked L in the figure. Since the image I_1 is close to the focal point F_e of the eyepiece, the lateral magnification due to the objective of focal length F can be found as in § 405; its value is approximately $M_o = \dfrac{L}{F}$, with L and F expressed in the same unit.

The magnification produced by the eyepiece of focal length f cm is given by Eq. 288 as $M_e = \dfrac{25}{f} + 1$. The total magnification of the microscope is the product of M_o and M_e, or

$$M = \frac{L}{F}\left(\frac{25}{f} + 1\right) \tag{290}$$

Microscope objectives are highly corrected for spherical and chromatic aberration over the entire aperture; Fig. 412 shows a section of a typical objective having six lenses. Eyepieces, such as the Huygens eyepiece shown in Fig. 398, are usually rated by angular magnification.

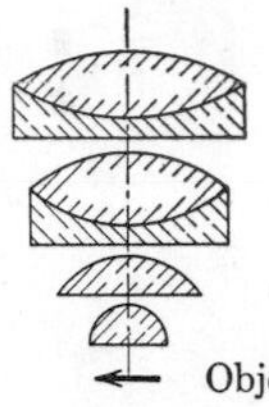

To obtain maximum illumination in high-power microscopes, their objectives are designed to use a liquid, such as cedar oil, that has about the same refractive index as glass, between the object and the lowest lens of the objective. This lens is hemispherical like that shown in Fig. 412, but the one above it has its lower surface concave instead of plane. An objective of this type, called an *oil-immersion* objective, permits rays over a wide angle to be collected by the lower lens without introducing spherical aberration, and to be refracted for normal incidence upon the one above.

← Object

Fig. 412. Microscope objective

Microscopes of high magnification enable an observer to recognize objects down to about 0.3 micron in size; smaller particles (to about 0.005 micron) can be discerned by scattered light against a dark background, the particles being illuminated by rays that are too oblique to enter the objective. When so used the instrument is called an *ultra microscope*. Minute organisms, colloidal particles, and Brownian movements, § 115, can be rendered visible in this way; the method is also used in the Millikan oil-drop experiment, § 204.

419. Binocular Vision. Vision in three dimensions is based primarily upon the fact that both eyes give their impressions simultaneously, each eye viewing the scene from a slightly different angle than the other. The familiar *stereoscope* simulates this effect upon a flat surface. In this device two photographs taken from slightly different positions are viewed at the same time, the arrangement being such that the right eye sees only the scene as photographed from the right, and the left eye sees it from the left. As a result the objects in the scene stand out in correct perspective, giving "depth" to the picture.

Numerous optical instruments employ binocular vision. In the *opera glass* the eyepieces are diverging lenses; each is placed so as to intercept the rays to the image that would be formed by the objective, thereby producing an erect virtual image of the object for observation. This construction has the advantage of providing a relatively short tube length for a given magnification. Short tube length is secured in the *prismatic field glass* by the use of two total-reflecting prisms (as shown at the right in Fig. 370) that double back the rays twice between the objective and the converging eyepiece and yield an erect image. A *binocular microscope* is illustrated in Fig. 413.

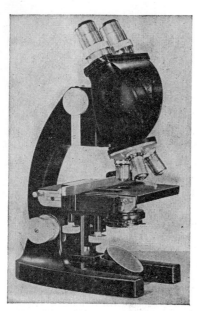

FIG. 413. Binocular microscope. (*Courtesy of Bausch & Lomb Optical Company*)

420. The Electron Microscope. An entirely new approach to the problem of high magnification applies the deflecting action of electric and magnetic fields upon charged particles. The experiments of H. Busch in 1926, using cathode rays in axially symmetrical fields, showed that such fields could focus a beam of electrons very much as a lens focuses a beam of light. For this reason such symmetrical fields are spoken of as electrostatic and magnetic *electron lenses*, and the subject itself, dealing with the study of such lenses and their application, is termed *electron optics*. Its principles are utilized in an arrangement styled the electron gun for accelerating electrons to high velocities for experimental purposes, in television apparatus for electronically reproducing distant scenes, and in the electron microscope for achieving very high magnification.

The law of refraction has its counterpart in electron optics. An electron that moves in an equipotential region is not acted upon by any forces and naturally its path is straight, but when it travels from one such region to another that has a different potential, the path changes abruptly.

In part I of Fig. 414 an electron beam travels from a region of constant potential V_1 to another of value V_2. The latter region is assumed to be more highly positive than the first, and hence an electron changes its direction toward the normal NN in crossing the potential boundary, because the component of its velocity along the normal is increased while the component along the separating plane remains unchanged. If the electron velocities in regions 1 and 2 are respectively v_1 and v_2 and their unchanged velocity component is v_x, then $\sin i = \dfrac{v_x}{v_1}$ and $\sin r = \dfrac{v_x}{v_2}$, where i and r are respectively the angles of incidence and refraction of the electron beam at the plane separating the two equipotential regions. Consequently

$$\frac{\sin i}{\sin r} = \frac{v_2}{v_1}$$

The work done on an electron in crossing the boundary is

$$e(V_2 - V_1) = \tfrac{1}{2}mv_2{}^2 - \tfrac{1}{2}mv_1{}^2$$

where e represents the charge of an electron and m its mass. The work done

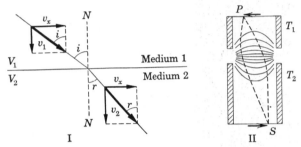

FIG. 414.   Electronic refraction and an electrostatic electron lens

upon the electron initially in bringing it into the zone of potential V_1 is eV_1 $= \tfrac{1}{2}mv_1{}^2$; it follows that $eV_2 = \tfrac{1}{2}mv_2{}^2$, and by division $V_2/V_1 = v_2{}^2/v_1{}^2$. This result is merged with the earlier one to yield

$$\frac{v_2}{v_1} = \sqrt{\frac{V_2}{V_1}} = \frac{\sin i}{\sin r}$$

showing that the ratio of electron velocities in the two regions is proportional to the square root of the potential ratio and to the inverse ratio of sines of the angles that the electron beam makes with the normal to the interface of the potential regions.

Although the abrupt bending of an electron beam as described is analogous to the refraction of light on entering a medium of greater refractive index, in practically all arrangements applying electron optics the potential regions change gradually, and consequently the electron paths shift gradually from one region to another. Thus, part II of Fig. 414 shows a simple arrangement, consisting of two cylindrical tubes T_1 and T_2 charged to different potentials, which is equivalent optically to a converging lens and serves as an electron microscope of low power. The curved lines are sections of symmetrical equipotential surfaces which spread into the tubes, the potential gradient being greatest at the midplane of the gap where these surfaces are closest. To explain the action, a light image is imagined to be projected from above onto the semi-transparent photoelectric surface P, causing it to release electrons from each spot in proportion to the intensity of light incident upon it. The beam of electrons from each spot diverges and reaches the electrostatic lens between the tubes; this converges the beam upon a particular spot on the fluorescent screen S at the lower end, as shown for the head end of the object.

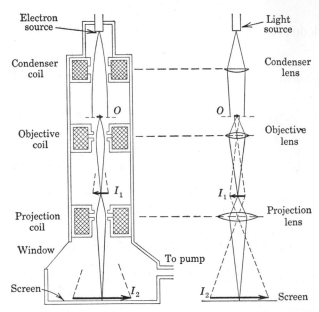

Electron source

Light source

Condenser coil

Condenser lens

O

O

Objective coil

Objective lens

I_1

I_1

Projection coil

Projection lens

Window

To pump

Screen

I_2

I_2

Screen

FIG. 415.   Magnetic electron microscope and its optical counterpart

In this way an inverted image is produced on the screen in a manner analogous to the formation of an image on a photographic film with a camera lens. The magnification can be made quite large and the focusing more precise by placing near the electron-emitting surface several anode rings that are charged to appropriate potentials.

Magnetic lenses are more powerful than those of the electrostatic type just described, but their action is more difficult to visualize. An electron slanting into a uniform magnetic field has two component motions: the one parallel to the field remains unchanged in direction, while the other crosswise of the field becomes circular, as in the cyclotron, § 259. The combination of these motions causes the electron stream to move along a helical path in such a manner that electrons issuing from a particular object point meet at a corresponding point on a screen to form the image. An electron microscope using magnetic lenses is illustrated in Fig. 415, together with its optical equivalent; the object on a transparent film is shown at O, an intermediate image at I_1, and the final image at I_2. Such an instrument has possibilities of magnifications upwards of 20,000 diameters.

The resolving power of any optical instrument is limited by the wavelength of light, § 427. Since the equivalent wavelength of an electron, § 443, is very short, resolution of detail by the electron microscope is very good; in fact, it is much superior to that afforded by the optical microscope.

PROBLEMS

1. A nearsighted person cannot see distinctly beyond a distance of 40 cm from the eyes. Determine the focal length in centimeters and focal power in diopters of spectacle lenses needed to enable this person to see distant objects distinctly. Disregard the fact that such lenses are a short distance from the eyes.

2. A farsighted person wears spectacle lenses having a focal power of 2.5 diopters. With these lenses, objects 25 cm from the eyes can be seen distinctly; without them, what is the shortest distance at which objects can be seen distinctly by this person?

3. The objective lens of a small folding camera has a focal length of 12 cm. Its diaphragm has a number of stops, the first four being marked $f/4.5$, $f/5.6$, $f/8$ and $f/11$. Compute (a) the diameters of these apertures and (b) their relative exposure times referred to the shortest exposure time as unity.

4. An aircraft camera for aerial mapping has a focal length of 6 in. and takes pictures measuring 9×9 in. Determine the ground area encompassed by each print when the camera is carried by an airplane flying horizontally at an altitude of 5000 ft.

5. Light from glowing hydrogen vapor passes through a prism, falls normally on a converging lens, and continues to a photographic plate, where it produces a photograph of the spectral lines. The C line is sharply focused at a place on the plate which is 10 in. from the camera lens; how far should the plate be from the lens at the F line in order that it also may be sharply focused? Assume that the lens is of flint glass having refractive indices as tabulated in § 387, and that the beam incident upon it is practically parallel.

6. A camera has a lens of 10-cm focal length and produces upon the film an image of an object 6 ft high. (a) Determine the height of the images that result when the object is at distances of 25 m and of 5 m. (b) What would be the corresponding results for a lens of 5-cm focal length?

7. A camera lens of 10-cm focal length has a diameter of 1.8 cm. If an exposure meter indicates that the time for photographing a certain scene is $1/100$ sec with an $f/8$ aperture, what should be the exposure time with the lens wide open?

8. Show that the exposure time for taking pictures of distant objects with camera lenses varies as the square of the ratio of their focal lengths to their apertures.

9. The lens of a camera, adjusted to photograph an object 10 ft from the objective, has placed next to it a supplementary lens called a portrait attachment. If objects 3 ft from the lens can then be focused upon the film, what is the focal length of the attachment?

10. In the focal-plane shutter used in many cameras a curtain with a horizontal slit is located directly in front of the film, and is swept rapidly

downward during exposure. A picture of a racing car taken with such a camera having a lens of 6-in. focal length showed that vertical lines on the car were displaced 10° in the photograph; such distortion is due to the fact that the lower parts were photographed later than the upper parts. The shutter moved downward 4 in. in 0.025 sec, and the car was 50 ft from the camera. What was the speed of the car?

11. The transparencies in the standard 2 × 2 in. color-film slides measure 1 3/8 × 15/16 in. The pictures are to be viewed on a wall 15 ft from a projector lens that has a focal length of 6 in. What is the size of the picture?

12. A simple astronomical telescope is made up of two converging lenses having focal powers of +1 and +10 diopters. How far apart should the lenses be placed, and what is the magnification of the telescope?

13. The largest refracting telescope, that at the Yerkes Observatory in Wisconsin, has a diameter of 40 in. and a focal length of 65 ft. Compute its magnification when used with an eyepiece of 1-in. focal length. What would be the *f*-number of the objective lens?

14. The light that enters the objective of a telescope is collected by the eyepiece within a small circle called the "exit pupil." This circle is the image of the objective as formed by the eyepiece. If the focal lengths of objective and eyepiece are respectively 35 in. and 0.5 in., and the instrument is focused for viewing distant objects, (*a*) how far is the exit pupil behind the eyepiece? (*b*) what is the diameter of the exit pupil if that of the objective is 2.5 in.?

15. In a telescope for terrestrial use, the inverted image formed by the objective is made erect by placing a converging lens at a distance twice its focal length behind the image formed by the objective. This additional lens forms its image at an equal distance beyond that lens, which image serves as an object for the eyepiece. Suppose such an erecting lens of 4-in. focal length to be used in the telescope of Prob. 14; construct an optical diagram of the instrument and compute the distance between the objective and the eyepiece.

16. The mirror of a reflecting telescope serviceable for amateur use has a diameter of 6 in. and a focal length of 4 ft. What magnification does the instrument afford when equipped with eyepieces that have focal lengths of 28 mm and 0.25 in.?

17. A certain converging lens yields a magnification of 5 diameters when used as a simple magnifier to produce a virtual image 25 cm from the lens. What magnification would it yield if it were arranged to produce a real image 25 cm from the lens?

18. The glass of a plano-convex lens has a refractive index of 1.6 and its curved surface has a radius of 7.5 cm. Determine the magnification of this lens when used as a simple magnifier for an image located (*a*) at the distance of distinct vision and (*b*) at a great distance.

19. A compound microscope has an objective lens of 16-mm focal length and an optical tube length of 16.0 cm; the eyepiece is used as a simple magnifier and gives a magnification of 10 diameters. The focusing of the instrument is such that the final image is 25 cm away from the eyepiece. Compute (*a*) the total magnification of the microscope and (*b*) the distance of the object from the objective.

20. To make a photomicrograph, the position of the microscope eyepiece is changed so that the final image will be real instead of virtual, and this image is recorded on a plate in a light-tight enclosure. Suppose the micro-

scope of Prob. 19 to be arranged in this manner and the final image to be 25 cm behind the eyepiece. Construct an optical diagram of the instrument and compute the total magnification from the object and image positions.

21. Tiny objects are to be observed by a crude microscope made up of two spectacle lenses. The focal length of the lens serving as objective is 4 cm and that of the other serving as eyepiece is 10 cm. Compute the magnification due to each lens and that due to both for an object located 5 cm from the objective.

22. Determine the exit-pupil diameter of prism binoculars that are rated as 7 × 50, meaning that the over-all magnification is 7 and the free diameter of the objective lenses is 50 mm. See Prob. 14.

38

INTERFERENCE AND DIFFRACTION

INTERFERENCE OF LIGHT

421. Interference and Reinforcement. The wave character of light leads to the consideration of some important effects in physical optics. The superposition of two light waves upon arriving simultaneously at a given point does not necessarily produce more illumination than one of them would alone; indeed, it may produce less. This variation is due to interference, § 337. Actually the total illumination at a point depends upon the wave-

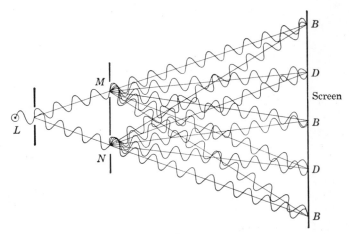

FIG. 416. Reinforcement and annulment of light waves

lengths, amplitudes, and relative phases of the waves arriving there. With monochromatic light, waves of equal amplitude reinforce one another if they arrive in phase agreement, but annul one another if they arrive in phase opposition. When they annul and produce zero illumination at certain points there are other points where the illumination is increased, since the total energy of the waves remains unchanged. With white light, in which many colors are blended, the annulment of one color at a particular point still leaves illumination by the other colors.

Interference of light was originally demonstrated and explained by the English physicist Thomas Young (1773–1829), using two shields and a screen arranged as in Fig. 416. Monochromatic light from a lamp L is directed upon a small opening in the first shield; this serves as a point source for illuminating two pinholes M and N in the second shield. From these apertures waves spread out in all directions, a few of which are indicated in a single plane. Waves leaving apertures M and N in phase agreement and proceeding to the screen reinforce one another and produce brightness at certain places BBB; and annul one another and produce darkness at other places DD. *Reinforcement occurs when the two waves arrive at the screen in phase agreement*, both waves having traveled the same distance or either having traveled one or more complete wavelengths farther than the other. *Annulment occurs when the two waves arrive at the screen in phase opposition*, one wave having traveled an odd number of half wavelengths farther than the other. The result on the screen is an interference pattern of so-called *fringes* that are alternately bright and dark. The figure shows a sectional view of only the zone containing the interference pattern; this region is very small and is greatly exaggerated for clearness.

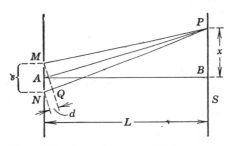

FIG. 417.   Interference of light passing through two slits

The factors that determine the spacing between fringes will be investigated with the aid of Fig. 417, which represents a sectional view of two parallel-sided slits M and N separated by a distance s, and a screen S which is distant L from the plane of the slits. The line AB is drawn perpendicular to the screen from A, midway between the slits, to B, at the center of the interference pattern. Rays are shown from the apertures to some point P on the screen at a distance x from B. Light waves issuing from the slits travel different distances in reaching P. By drawing MQ so as to make $QP = MP$, the difference in path may be expressed as $d = NQ$. A line connecting points P and A is practically perpendicular to MQ, and hence the angles NMQ and PAB are equal. Since these angles are small, d/s, which is approximately the sine of the first, can be equated to x/L, which is the tangent of the second, giving the simple relation

$$\frac{d}{s} = \frac{x}{L} \tag{291}$$

For different positions of point P along the screen the condition for reinforcement or annulment can be expressed in terms of the wavelength λ of the monochromatic light and some integer n as

$$d = \frac{n\lambda}{2}$$

reinforcement occurring when $n = 0, 2, 4, \cdots$ and annulment occuring when

$n = 1, 3, 5 \cdots$. With this value for d in Eq. 291 a rearrangement of terms gives the distance of the fringe from the center of the pattern as

$$x = \frac{n\lambda L}{2s} \tag{292}$$

This expression shows that the spacing of the fringes varies directly as the wavelength λ and the screen distance L, and varies inversely as the distance s between the slits. That the distance between fringes is very small will be evident from a numerical example.

Illustrative Problem

Suppose that green light from a mercury vapor lamp is directed upon two slits 1 mm apart and that the screen is 1 m away. Determine the fringe spacing on the screen for this light of wavelength 0.5461 micron.

With respect to the center of the interference pattern the first dark line is located at a distance $x = \dfrac{5461 \times 10^{-8} \text{ cm} \times 100 \text{ cm}}{2 \times 0.1 \text{ cm}} = 0.0273 \text{ cm}$, the first bright line at 0.0546 cm, the second dark line at 0.0819 cm, and so on.

When white light is used instead of monochromatic light, each color produces its own interference fringes, those for red light being spaced about twice as far apart as those for violet light, and the resulting pattern shows

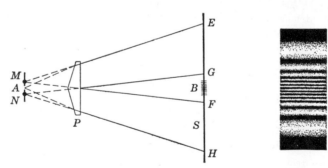

Fig. 418. Interference fringes produced by biprism

the combined effect of all colors. Such brilliantly colored designs may also be observed by looking at a distant white-light source through a piece of silk or a fine-mesh screen, their apertures acting as closely spaced sources that send out the interfering waves.

The Biprism. In order to show the interference effects described, the phase relation of the waves should remain unchanged, that is, the waves should be *coherent* as they emerge from the slits. This condition requires that *the slits receive light from the same point of the source.* Several methods have been devised for accomplishing this result conveniently. In one of these, the pair of apertures is replaced by a thin prism having an angle of almost 180° and known as a *biprism*. Such a prism, shown at *P* in Fig. 418, refracts the light from a narrow slit *A* so that it appears to come from two virtual sources *M* and *N*. The screen *S* is illuminated by source *M* over the region *EF* and by source *N* over the region *GH*. The interference fringes occur near *B*, at the center of the overlapping region *GF*: these may be observed with a low-power telescope.

The pattern at the right is an enlargement of the interference fringes produced by parallel white light through a biprism. The broader shadings at top and bottom are diffraction bands, § 425.

422. Thin Films. Colors are frequently observed in films such as soap bubbles, thin layers of oil or water, and coatings of oxide on heated metal. Such films are usually observed by reflection, and the colors are due to interference of light waves reflected at the front and rear surfaces. Fig. 419 represents a film of refractive index μ, illuminated by a beam of monochromatic light incident upon the surface in the direction *A*. The eye receives light reflected partly at *B* (ray 1) and partly at *C* (ray 2). In order to compare the optical paths of these rays a line *FG* is drawn perpendicular to the direction in which they approach the eye. The only differ-

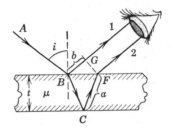

Fig. 419. Interference by reflection from both sides of film

ence in path occurs between the point *B* common to both rays and the line *FG*; the second ray travels farther than the first by an amount $2a - b$, where a represents the distance *BC* or *CF*, and b represents the distance *BG*. The distance $2a$ within the film is equivalent to an air distance of $2\mu a$, and hence the equivalent light path of ray 2 exceeds that of ray 1 by the amount $2\mu a - b$. For normal incidence, the distance a is the same as the thickness t of the film and the distance b becomes zero, whence the optical path difference is $2\mu t$. For incidence at angle i this path difference can be shown to be $2t\sqrt{\mu^2 - \sin^2 i}$.

It might be expected that, as the film thickness t approaches zero, the two rays would come into phase and reinforce each other, since their optical paths would then approach equality. However, experiments with soap bubbles show that a black spot appears where the film becomes so thin that it is about to rupture, showing that interference of light rather than reinforcement occurs when the film has negligible thickness. To explain this effect it will be recognized that one reflection takes place within a medium (air) of low refractive index at the boundary of a medium (soap film) of higher index, and the other reflection takes place oppositely. Under these circumstances, there is always a *phase shift* equivalent to a path difference of a *half wavelength* between the two reflected waves due to reflection, in addition to the phase displacement due to difference in optical path.

To summarize, the retardation of ray 2 in Fig. 419 with respect to ray 1 for perpendicular incidence amounts to $2\mu t$ due to path difference, plus $\lambda/2$ due to reflection. Consequently, the total retardation of ray 2 with respect to ray 1 is

$$\text{Retardation} = 2\mu t + \frac{\lambda}{2} \qquad (293)$$

When the retardation amounts to an odd number of half wavelengths, interference and darkness occur; when it amounts to an even number of half wavelengths, maximum reinforcement and brightness occur. Thus, for the first reinforcement $2\mu t + \dfrac{\lambda}{2} = 2\dfrac{\lambda}{2}$; whence the minimum thickness of film is $t = \lambda/4\mu$.

With illumination of thin films by white light, a thickness that results in interference for one colored component does not yield interference for components of other wavelengths; consequently a residual color will appear. Thick films do not appear colored, because so many wavelengths satisfy the conditions for reinforcement, namely, $t = \dfrac{\lambda}{4\mu}, \dfrac{3\lambda}{4\mu}, \dfrac{5\lambda}{4\mu} \cdots$, that the reinforced waves upon merging after reflection produce the effect of white light.

An interesting experiment on the interference produced by films utilizes a plano-convex lens of large radius and an optically flat plate placed together so that a wedge-shaped film of air is formed between them. When the apparatus is illuminated by monochromatic light and examined by reflection, the observer sees an interference pattern that consists of a series of bright and dark rings concentric around the point of contact. This phenomenon was first described by Newton and the rings are called by his name. The effect is due to the interference of light reflected from both surfaces of the air film between the convex and plane surfaces.

Illustrative Problem

As an exercise dealing with Newton's experiment, show that the bright rings in the interference pattern have radii that are proportional to the square roots of the successive odd integers.

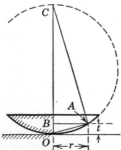

In Fig. 420 the lens is shown resting on a flat plate, both of glass. At the point of contact O there is interference, because the air film has zero thickness and the light waves reflected from its upper and lower boundaries differ in phase by $\dfrac{\lambda}{2}$, as explained. At point A where the film has a thickness $t = \dfrac{\lambda}{4}$ there is reinforcement, because the light re-

FIG. 420. Newton's ring experiment

flected at the plate underneath is retarded with respect to that reflected at the lower face of the lens by an amount $\dfrac{\lambda}{4} + \dfrac{\lambda}{2} + \dfrac{\lambda}{4} = \lambda$. Reinforcement also

occurs where the thickness is $t = 3\dfrac{\lambda}{4}, \, 5\dfrac{\lambda}{4}, \, \cdots$, or in general $(2n - 1)\dfrac{\lambda}{4}$,

where n is an integer and $2n - 1$ designates an odd number.

With the construction lines shown in the figure, the right triangles OAB and ACB are similar, whence $AB:OB = BC:AB$. If R represents the radius of the lens and r the radius of a bright ring of the interference pattern, then $r:t = (2R - t):r$. Since t is negligibly small compared with $2R$, the radius of the bright ring becomes $r = \sqrt{2Rt} = \sqrt{2R(2n - 1)\lambda/4}$, which shows that

$$r \propto \sqrt{2n - 1}$$

Thus the bright fringes have radii proportional to the square roots of the successive odd numbers.

The interference patterns due to thin films under monochromatic light are widely used to detect slight surface irregularities in lenses, optical plates, and mirrors.

423. Nonreflecting Glass. Lenses and other optical parts are often coated with thin transparent films in order to minimize reflection from the surfaces. The films are formed of such materials and thicknesses that the light reflected from the film annuls the light reflected from the glass. To produce light interference the two reflected waves should have (1) *equal amplitudes and* (2) *opposite phase.*

The requirements for meeting the first condition can be determined from Eq. 271, which gives the intensity of a reflected beam from an interface between two transparent mediums of indices μ_1 and μ_2 when the beams are perpendicular to the surface.

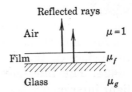

FIG. 421. Annulling reflection from glass

Since the intensity of a wave is proportional to the square of its amplitude, § 340, the ratio of the amplitude of the reflected wave to that of the incident wave becomes

$$\frac{A}{A_o} = \frac{\mu_2 - \mu_1}{\mu_2 + \mu_1}$$

In Fig. 421, if μ_f and μ_g represent the refractive indices of film and glass respectively, then the reflected rays have equal amplitudes when

$$\frac{\mu_f - 1}{\mu_f + 1} = \frac{\mu_g - \mu_f}{\mu_g + \mu_f}$$

or

$$\mu_f = \sqrt{\mu_g} \tag{294}$$

This indicates that the films should have relatively low indices of refraction.

The second condition for interference of the two reflected rays, with monochromatic incident light, requires that the equivalent air thickness of the film be an odd number of quarter wavelengths, as explained in the preceding section. For the minimum thickness t and for a wavelength λ, it follows that

$$\mu_f t = \frac{\lambda}{4}$$

Ordinary window glass ($\mu_g = 1.52$) can be rendered nonreflecting for yellow light ($\lambda = 0.589$ micron) by coating it with a film having a refractive index of $\sqrt{1.52} = 1.23$ and a thickness $0.0000589 \div (4 \times 1.23) = 0.000012$ cm. Such thin films can be produced by evaporation, and the index of refraction of the film substance can be lowered to the desired value by decreasing its density through control of the evaporation conditions. Films of the metallic fluorides, such as magnesium fluoride, have been found to stick firmly to the glass and to possess mechanical strength. Glass plates with such films on both sides show very little reflection of white light and transmit well over 98% of the incident beam.

Film coating finds an important application in lenses for cameras, picture projectors, telescopes, and other optical instruments. Most of these are combination lenses having several glass-air surfaces, reflections at which not only reduce the amount of light transmitted but also scatter light over the field of view, thus lessening the clarity of the image. Such internal reflections also produce so-called ghost images of any bright concentrated light sources that may be in the field of view. These objectionable effects are largely overcome by surface coatings.

424. The Interferometer. A precision measuring instrument based on light interference is called an *interferometer*. With it determinations can be made of wavelength in terms of a standard of length, or of small distances in terms of known wavelengths. The essential parts of the instrument devised by Michelson are arranged as in Fig. 422; they comprise two plane mirrors A · and B arranged in perpendicular planes, a glass plate M that has its upper face silvered lightly, and a telescope T for observing the interference effects. The silvered plate is set at 45° to the axes BX and TA, and mirror A is carried on a platform that can be moved by an accurately threaded screw.

Monochromatic light from the source X is formed into a parallel beam by a lens L and projected upon the plate M where it divides into two beams, 1 and 2; these advance to the mirrors A and B respectively and return to M, and then proceed to the telescope. Ray 1 passes through the half-silvered plate M three times, while ray 2 passes through it only once; to equalize the two paths, a second plate N of the same thickness and inclination is placed on the axis BX. If the waves after recombination at M are in phase, the field of the telescope appears bright, and if they are in opposition, the field appears dark

To begin a measurement, light of wavelength λ is directed upon the half-silvered plate and the distances to mirrors A and B are adjusted so that the field of the telescope is dark. If the movable mirror is now advanced slowly, a movement of $\lambda/4$ causes a change of path of $\lambda/2$ and the field appears bright; a further movement of $\lambda/4$ makes it dark again, and so on. A finely divided scale is provided for measuring the distance through which this mirror is moved; consequently the wavelength of the incident light can be determined directly from the number of light annulments. Thus, if n suc-

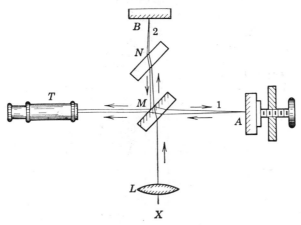

Fig. 422. Plan of Michelson interferometer

cessive interferences are observed while the mirror is moved a distance l, the wavelength is found to be

$$\lambda = \frac{2l}{n} \tag{295}$$

Small distances can be measured by the same procedure when light of known wavelength is used.

The mirrors are not generally set at right angles to each other as stated previously, but depart very slightly from this condition. When the mirrors are so placed, the field of the telescope is crossed by straight lines that are alternately dark interference fringes and bright reinforcement fringes. The movement of mirror A can be observed by counting the fringes as they sweep past the cross-hair of the telescope.

Michelson used the interferometer to calibrate the standard meter in terms of the wavelength of the red line in the cadmium spectrum; such a measurement definitely fixes the length of the standard in terms of an unvarying unit. The diameters of some of the larger stars have been determined by applying interference methods to telescope measurements.

DIFFRACTION OF LIGHT

425. Diffraction. Although it is commonly said that light travels in straight lines, careful observation shows that it bends slightly around the edges of an obstruction. The spreading of a beam of light into the region behind an obstacle is known as *diffraction*. Because of diffraction, a parallel beam of monochromatic light passing through a slit toward a screen ordinarily produces on it a bright band somewhat wider than the slit itself, and

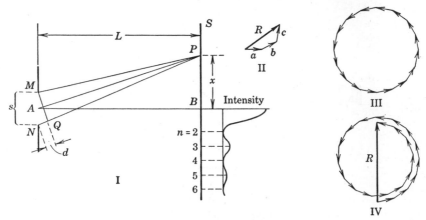

FIG. 423.   Diffraction of light through a slit

furthermore this band is bordered by a few narrower bands that are alternately dark and bright.

The phenomenon of diffraction can be explained with the aid of Fig. 423, which shows a single slit MN of width s located a distance L from a screen S. The line AB is drawn perpendicular to the screen from the middle of the slit, and P represents any point on the screen distant x from the center of the pattern at B. The line MQ is drawn at right angles to a line connecting A and P to show the difference in path length of the extreme rays NP and MP; this difference NQ is marked d. If the path difference of the rays from the slit edges is one wavelength of light ($d = \lambda$), then P is a point of darkness rather than brightness. This can be proved by imagining the slit to be composed of a series of parallel and much narrower slits extending uniformly from M to N, and investigating the combined effect of the wavelets from them in producing illumination at the reference point.

The amplitude of the wavelets at P coming from the uppermost of these tiny slits can be represented by vector a in part II of the figure; the amplitude of the wavelets at the same point from the next lower slit is then represented by vector b slightly out of phase from a, because they travel farther from this slit to reach the reference point. Similarly, the amplitude of those from the third slit is represented by c, and so on. The resultant amplitude for the three slits so far considered can be found by placing the individual vectors end to end and drawing the closing line R of the figure as shown. If this process were continued for all the tiny slits extending from M to N, the extreme vectors would again be in phase, and the resultant of them all would be zero, as shown in part III; that is, point P is dark when $d = 2\dfrac{\lambda}{2}$. This position of the reference point shows the location of the first dark band above or below the screen center and marks the limit of the central bright band (where $n = 2$ in part I). However, brightness on the screen occurs again when the point P is so located that $d = 3\dfrac{\lambda}{2}$, the resultant R being shown to larger scale in part IV of the figure, and darkness when so located that $d = 2\lambda$, and so on. In general, for annulment or reinforcement, the path difference for the extreme rays of the slit is

$$d = n\frac{\lambda}{2}$$

interference occurring for the even values of n and reinforcement for the odd values. The locations of the fringes on the screen above and below the center of the pattern at B are found as in § 421 to be given by

$$x = \frac{n\lambda L}{2s} \tag{296}$$

annulment occurring when $n = 2, 4, 6 \cdots$ and reinforcement occurring when $n = 3, 5, 7 \cdots$. The diffraction pattern consists of a central band having a width $2x = 2\left(\dfrac{2\lambda L}{2s}\right) = \dfrac{2\lambda L}{s}$, bordered on each side by narrower bands, alternately dark and bright, which become less distinct as the distance from the center is increased. The relative light intensities at different points on the screen are indicated by the curve in the lower portion of part I of the figure.

Eq. 296 shows that the narrower the slit, the wider the spacing of the bands forming the diffraction pattern. If, however, the width of the slit is reduced to the same order of magnitude as the wavelength of light, it will be apparent from the construction in Fig. 423 that no points of annulment appear on the screen and the result is merely a spreading of light over its surface by diffraction. In Young's experiment, for example, in addition to the interference effects described in § 421, some light reaches all parts of the screen through each slit by diffraction.

The diffraction pattern produced by light through a circular hole consists of a round patch of light, surrounded by a few rings that are alternately dark and bright. This result may be thought of as a development of that just described by imagining the circle to be divided with parallel lines into three zones and by disregarding the outer ones because of their relatively small area. Thus a circular aperture may be considered equivalent to a slit of reduced width, and hence its diffraction pattern has a proportionately wider spacing. Mathematical analysis shows that the central diffraction disk produced by a round hole of diameter s is 1.22 times as wide as that for a parallel-sided slit of width s.

426. Diffraction by a Lens. Because of diffraction, parallel light passing through a circular hole produces a spot of light somewhat larger than would

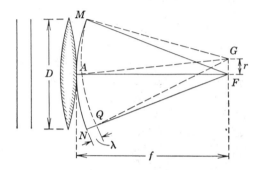

FIG. 424.   Diffraction diagram for lens

be indicated by the rectilinear propagation of light. For the same reason, parallel light passing through a lens produces at the focal plane a small disk of light rather than an ideal point of light such as indicated by the geometrical lens constructions of Chap. 36. This result is not due to any imperfection of the lens but is a consequence of the nature of light itself. The smallness of the disk image determines the ability of the lens to register detail in the object under observation.

Fig. 424 represents a lens of diameter D and focal length f which converges plane incident waves upon its principal focus. By diffraction, the light passing through the lens spreads beyond the region bordered by wave front MAN and the focus F. By analogy with the diffraction at a slit, annulment of light of wavelength λ may be expected at a point such as G, the location of which is determined by rotating the figure MNF to the position MQG, making $NQ = \lambda$. The distance FG then represents the radius r of the disk image of an infinitely distant point source. The angle between the curves MN and MQ may be regarded as equal to that between their radii, and hence, as a close approximation

$$\frac{\lambda}{D} = \frac{r}{f}$$

As stated in the foregoing section, the central diffraction disk for a circular aperture is 1.22 times as wide as that for a slit of the same width as the aperture; consequently the disk image has a diameter $d = 1.22 \times 2r$ or

$$d = \frac{2.44f\lambda}{D} \tag{297}$$

and subtends an angle d/f at the lens.

The diffraction pattern produced by a lens of an object point consists of the central bright disk surrounded by alternate dark and bright rings. The registration of minute detail implies a small diffraction pattern, and Eq. 297 indicates that such a pattern can be realized with a lens of large size compared with its focal length. Aside from the lens constants, the smallness of the disk image involves the wavelength and is therefore limited by the wave character of light.

427. Resolving Power. The ability of a lens to disclose detail in an image is spoken of as its *resolving power*. If two object points subtend too small

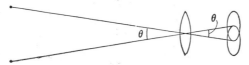

FIG. 425. Overlapping disk images formed by lens of two objects

an angle at the lens, their image disks merge and cannot be resolved. Resolving power is measured by the *smallest angle* between two object points at which these points can be recognized as separate. Users of optical instruments find that they can distinguish two points as separate when their disk images overlap by not more than the radius of one of the disks. This limit is pictured in Fig. 425, greatly magnified. The angular separation of the object points is clearly the same as that between the disk images and, at the limit of resolution, is one-half of the angle subtended by a single disk image at the lens. From the preceding section, this limiting angle of resolution of a lens becomes

$$\theta = \frac{d}{2f} = \frac{1.22\lambda}{D} \tag{298}$$

This equation shows that the limit of resolving power of a lens is inversely proportional to its diameter, which means that the larger the lens, the smaller is the diffraction pattern and the clearer the image.

Illustrative Problem

The objective lens of the Yerkes telescope has a diameter of 1.02 m. Calculate the distance at which this lens can distinguish two point sources 10 cm apart as separate ones.

If the average wavelength of light is taken as 0.6 micron, the limiting angle of resolution of the lens, from Eq. 298, is $\theta = \dfrac{1.22(6 \times 10^{-5} \text{ cm})}{102 \text{ cm}} =$

7.18×10^{-7} radian. This angular separation for sources that are 10 cm apart means that they can be distinguished at a distance of $10/(7.18 \times 10^{-7})$ $= 13.9 \times 10^6$ cm; this is equivalent to 86.3 mi.

Two objects 1 in. apart can be resolved by the eye at a distance of about 100 yd; this indicates that the limiting angle of resolution of the eye is about 1 minute of arc. Rays entering the eye with this angular separation fall upon adjacent cones at the central part of the retina.

428. The Diffraction Grating. The principles of interference and diffraction are applied to the measurement of wavelength in the *diffraction grating*. As constructed for use with transmitted light, the grating is essentially a

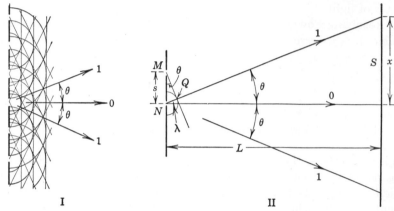

Fig. 426. Diffracted wave fronts produced by grating

transparent plate upon which there are many opaque lines, usually several thousand to the centimeter, all parallel and evenly spaced. A parallel beam of monochromatic light incident upon the grating sets up secondary wavelets at the slits between the lines, in accordance with Huygens' Principle, § 334, and these spread throughout the region beyond the grating. At points where these wavelets arrive in phase there is reinforcement and the fringes are bright, and where they arrive in opposite phase there is annulment and the fringes are dark.

In Fig. 426, the wavelets through the slits of a grating are represented by arcs in part I, the distances between them being the wavelength of the incident light. Straight lines drawn tangent to these wavelets connect only points that are in phase agreement, and consequently these lines represent wave fronts which advance in the directions of the arrows. One of these, joining wavelets that have advanced equal distances, continues along line 0 without change of direction. Two other wave fronts, each joining wavelets from successive slits that have advanced distances of λ, 2λ, 3λ, $\cdots$, are shown deflected through rather large angles θ and travel along the directions 1, 1.

Part II of the figure is a plan view showing two of the grating slits, M and N, separated by a distance s, and a screen S placed at a distance L from the grating. The waves advance along the directions indicated and produce on the screen bright lines that are parallel to the slits of the grating. The wavelength λ is the radius of the wavelet at N; its value can be determined by noting that the angle between the wave front MQ and the grating also equals θ, whence

$$n\lambda = s \sin \theta = s \frac{x}{\sqrt{L^2 + x^2}} \qquad (299)$$

where x is the distance along the screen from the center bright line to similar lines produced by the diffracted wave fronts along the directions 1, 1. The

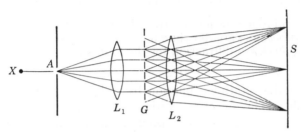

FIG. 427.　Formation of diffracted images with lenses

equation shows that the extent to which a wave is diffracted by a grating depends upon the wavelength of the light used and the slit spacing of the grating. The angle of diffraction is large when the light has a long wavelength (red) and when the slits are close together.

The experimental arrangement of the diffraction grating is represented in Fig. 427. A narrow slit A, illuminated by monochromatic light from the source X, is placed at the principal focus of the converging lens L_1, from which a beam of parallel light is directed normally upon the grating G. A second converging lens, L_2, receives the parallel bundles of rays after diffraction and forms images of the illuminated slit upon the screen S, as shown. The upper and lower ones shown are called the *first order* diffracted images; images of higher order are formed beyond these. The order of an image equals the number of wavelengths in the path difference between rays from adjacent slits.

With a white-light source the image at the center of the pattern is white, because the length of the paths to that point are the same for all the color components of white light. The diffracted waves form spectral bands at each side, because the component colors have different wavelengths and their images are spread out along the screen in accordance with Eq. 296. Each diffraction spectrum has the same color sequence as a prismatic spectrum, but is reversed, the red light being diffracted through a larger angle than the violet because of its greater wavelength.

Illustrative Problem

Light from magnesium vapor passes through a narrow slit and falls normally upon a diffraction grating that has 4000 lines/cm. The spectrum of magnesium includes three green lines having wavelengths of 0.5167, 0.5173, and 0.5184 micron. Calculate the angular position of the middle spectral line for the various orders as observed on a spectrometer.

The grating space $s = \dfrac{1 \text{ cm}}{4000} = 0.00025 \text{ cm} = 2.5$ microns, and the angular positions, reckoned from the normal to the grating surface, are found from the following relations: $\sin \theta_1 = \dfrac{\lambda}{s} = \dfrac{0.5173}{2.5} = 0.2069$ for the first-order spectrum, $\sin \theta_2 = \dfrac{2\lambda}{s} = 0.4138$ for the second-order spectrum, and similarly for the third- and fourth-order spectra. There are no spectra of higher order, because $n(\lambda/s)$ becomes greater than unity for values of n larger than 4. The corresponding angles of diffraction for the four orders are 11.9°, 24.4°, 38.4° and 55.9°.

Many diffraction gratings function by reflection rather than by transmission of light. The reflection grating is made by ruling lines with a diamond point on a polished surface, speculum metal (Cu 68%, Sn 32%) often being used for this purpose.

429. Diffraction of X-rays. To test the wave character of x-rays, the suggestion was made by the German physicist Max von Laue that crystals might be used as natural diffraction gratings with such rays, because of the close and symmetrical spacing of their atoms. The experiment was successful and furnished the key to both the nature of x-rays and the structure of crystals. Today x-ray diffraction techniques provide the all-important experimental means for studying the sub-microscopic structure of matter in the solid state, and the changes in structure produced by such mechanical processes as hardening, annealing, and rolling of metals.

In most diffraction measurements on crystals it is customary to use monochromatic x-rays, that is, waves having a common wavelength, usually between 0.07 and 0.20 millimicron. When a narrow beam of such rays is directed upon a crystal and a photographic plate is placed behind it, most of the radiation passes right through, but some is scattered by the atoms of the crystal. The scattered wavelets from the host of atomic planes annul one another in certain directions and reinforce in others; the latter produce spots on a photographic plate. The result is a symmetrical pattern which indicates that crystals are periodically arranged groupings of atoms, § 318, and that the atomic planes are inclined in various directions and form a three-dimensional diffraction grating.

Fig. 428 illustrates the characteristic pattern of a hexagonal crystal. It is a photograph of a single crystal of ice taken with the special exposure facilities available in the precession camera.

FIG. 428.   Crystal diffraction pattern of ice.   The x-ray beam transmitted directly through the crystal is blocked off at the center.   (*Photograph by Professor I. Fankuchen*)

Analysis of the diffraction patterns produced with crystals can be made with diffractometers; the arrangement of such instruments is shown in Fig. 429.   The x-rays are collimated by lead screens into a fine beam which strikes the crystal face at the glancing angle θ.   With appropriate angles of incidence the intensity of the scattered x-rays become a maximum at an

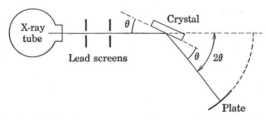

FIG. 429.   Analyzing the structure of crystals with a diffractometer

equal angle.   Thus the diffracted wavelets scattered from the atoms appear as a reflected ray from parallel crystal planes.   The ray is received on a photographic plate displaced at an angle 2θ from the incident beam, § 371.

In Fig. 430 the atoms in a crystal are represented by the small circles separated by a distance d, and a beam of x-rays from the source X is shown meeting the horizontal atomic planes at the small angle θ.   Reflection at an equal angle occurs at innumerable planes, each reflected ray being retarded more than the one next above it by an amount $MB + BN = 2d \sin \theta$. If this retardation amounts to an integral number n of wavelengths λ, the reflected rays from the atomic planes reinforce each other and intense reflection occurs when

$$2d \sin \theta = n\lambda \tag{300}$$

This relation was first developed by the British physicists Sir William H.

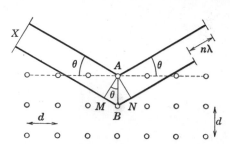

Bragg (1862–1942) and his son Sir William L., and is known as Bragg's Law of crystal diffraction. With it either the atomic spacing of the crystal or the wavelength of the x-rays can be determined by experiment if the other of these quantities is known.

It has been found possible to produce x-ray spectra independently of crystals, by using a ruled diffraction grating of the reflection type and directing a narrow beam of x-rays upon

Fig. 430.   Diffraction of x-rays from atomic planes of a crystal

it so that they almost graze the surface. The diffracted images are received upon a photographic plate and from this record the wavelength can be determined accurately.

As an application of Eq. 300, a beam of monochromatic x-rays will be considered to impinge upon a crystal that has a primitive cell with atoms at the corners and body center. Such rays having a wavelength of 0.1542 millimicron are incident upon the cubic lattice faces of cesium chloride (CsCl), and the smallest glancing angle ($n = 1$) for reinforcement is found to be 10.78°. The equation gives the spacing between successive planes of Cs atoms (or Cl atoms) in the crystal as

$$d = \frac{n\lambda}{2 \sin \theta} = \frac{1.542 \times 10^{-8}}{2 \sin 10.78°} = 4.13 \times 10^{-8} \text{ cm}$$

An independent evaluation of this spacing can be made from the density of this substance, 3.97 gm/cm^3, and its molecular weight, 168.37. From Avogadro's Number, § 132, there are 6.02×10^{23} molecules in 168.37 gm of CsCl; this gives 3.58×10^{21} atoms of cesium (and an equal number of atoms of chlorine) per gram. Hence there are $3.58 \times 10^{21} \times 3.97 = 14.21 \times 10^{21}$ Cs atoms per cm^3. Since the crystal structure is a multitude of cubes with atoms at the corners, there are $\sqrt[3]{14.21 \times 10^{21}} = 2.42 \times 10^7$ Cs atoms in a row 1 cm long. Consequently the spacing between such atoms and also between rows of them is $1/(2.42 \times 10^7) = 4.13 \times 10^{-8}$ cm, a result that verifies the value found above by Bragg's Law.

X-ray diffraction can be applied also to crystal specimens in powder form, because the vast number of small crystals which make up the specimen have a random orientation and make every conceivable angle with the incident beam. The powder technique serves mainly for the identification of crystals rather than for the analysis of their structure.

PROBLEMS

1. Monochromatic light from two narrow slits 1.6 mm apart falls upon a screen placed 1.2 m away and parallel to the plane of the slits. Assume the light to have a wavelength of 0.589 micron and compute the distance along the screen from the center of the interference pattern to the first, second, and third bright fringes on either side.

2. White light is used to illuminate the slits of Prob. 1 and its extreme wavelengths will be taken as 0.38 micron for violet and 0.76 micron for red. Violet fringes appear on the screen at places where there is both reinforcement for violet light and annulment for red light. Determine the distance measured along the screen from the center of the interference pattern to the first and second violet fringes.

3. A thin piece of glass 0.02 mm thick is placed over one of the slits of Prob. 1 and this action results in shifting the center of the interference pattern 8.7 mm. What is the refractive index of the glass?

4. Green light of wavelength 0.5461 micron is incident upon a film of liquid having a refractive index of 1.45. What is the least thickness of film that will give reinforcement for the light waves that are reflected from its two surfaces when the incident light (a) is normal to the film surface and (b) makes an angle of 45° to the normal?

5. White light falls upon a film of oil on water and the interference colors are viewed from directly above. If the distance from the violet fringe of one color sequence to the next violet fringe is 0.5 cm, what is the difference in thickness of the film over this distance? Take the wavelength of violet light as 0.38 micron and the refractive index of oil as 1.45.

6. A plano-convex lens is made of glass having a refractive index of 1.62 and its focal length is 7.5 m. To observe Newton's rings, the lens is placed upon an optically flat surface and illuminated by sodium light of wavelength 0.589 micron. Compute the diameter of the fourth bright ring as observed by reflection.

7. The space between the lens and the flat surface of Prob. 6 is filled with water and the experiment on Newton's rings is repeated. Find again the diameter of the fourth bright ring.

8. It is desired to coat a glass plate that has a refractive index of 1.81 for sodium light, with a nonreflecting film to increase light transmission through it. What should be the refractive index and thickness of the surface film?

9. A Michelson interferometer illuminated by green light from mercury (wavelength = 0.5461 micron) was used to measure the width of an object. Observations showed that 635 interference fringes swept past a reference point in the field of the telescope while it moved from one side of the object to the other. Compute the width of the object.

10. The wavelengths of the blue and yellow lines of the helium spectrum were measured with a Michelson interferometer by counting the passage of

1000 fringes across the field of its telescope. For the blue line the mirror was moved 0.2357 mm and for the yellow line 0.2938 mm. What results were obtained?

11. A type of interferometer useful for measuring changes in density of gases within a test section is arranged as shown. Two glass plates, *a* and *d*, are lightly silvered to allow half the incident light to be transmitted; the other two, *b* and *c*, serve as mirrors. Assume that the incident light at *A* is parallel, that all the plates are parallel to each other, and that the light paths 1 and 2 are equal, and explain whether the emergent beams at *B* will reinforce or annul each other when the test section is absent.

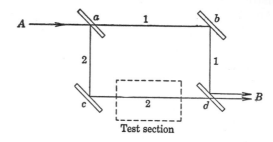

Problem 11

12. In gases the refractive index differs but slightly from unity, and it is found that the ratio $(\mu - 1)$ to the density of the gas is practically constant. The interferometer of Prob. 11 with a test section of length L is used for measuring changes of air density based on this relationship. Show that if light having a wavelength λ in vacuum undergoes n successive interferences while the density in the test section is changed from d_1 to d_2, the change of air density is given by

$$d_2 - d_1 = \frac{d_1}{\mu_1 - 1} \cdot \frac{n\lambda}{L}$$

where μ_1 is the initial refractive index of the air.

13. Yellow-green light for which the eye is most sensitive (wavelength = 0.555 micron) passes normally through a slit 1 mm wide and falls upon a screen 80 cm distant from the slit. Compute the width of the central bright band in the diffraction pattern on the screen.

14. The parallel-sided slit of Prob. 13 is replaced by a circular hole 1 mm in diameter but the other conditions of the problem remain unchanged. Compute the diameter of the central disk of the diffraction pattern upon the screen and also the diameter of the first bright ring surrounding it.

15. A telescope having a lens 10 cm in diameter is directed toward a star and focused to give a clear image. (*a*) What angle does this image subtend at the lens? (*b*) What is the least angular distance between two stars that this telescope can resolve? Take the wavelength to be 0.55 micron.

16. A camera has a lens of 6-in. focal length and is focused on a distant point source of light. If the lens is stopped to $f/8$, what is the diameter of the disk image? Take 0.6 micron as an average value for the wavelength of light.

17. Close examination of the photographs in a newspaper shows that they consist of an array of dots of various sizes regularly spaced 64 to the

inch. Consider these dots to be points, and assume the limit of the resolving power of the eye as 1 minute of arc. Beyond what distance from the eyes will such photographs blend into a uniform picture?

18. The television picture is formed by 525 scanning lines of light that are modulated by the video signals. These lines are horizontal and extend over a vertical height of 13.5 in. on the screen of the usual 21-in. receiver. Assume the lines are thin compared with the distance between them and determine the distance from the screen at which the pictures should be viewed so that the scanning lines will just merge.

19. A narrow beam of light from mercury vapor having a wavelength of 0.5461 micron is passed perpendicularly through a diffraction grating having 6000 lines per cm. Spectral lines are produced upon a screen 75 cm from the grating and parallel to it. Determine the distance along the screen from the center of the pattern to the mercury line (a) in the first-order spectrum and (b) in the second-order spectrum.

20. The grating of Prob. 19 is used with sodium light at the same screen distance. How far apart are the two yellow D lines in the second order spectrum?

21. Show that when a parallel beam of light is incident upon a grating at an angle i to the normal, its equation becomes

$$n\lambda = s(\sin \theta \pm \sin i)$$

where n is the order of the spectrum and the other symbols have the same significance as in Eq. 299.

22. The face of a crystal of sodium chloride is made up of Na^+ and Cl^- ions oriented as shown, and the square indicates the side of a unit cell. Diffractometer measurements with x-rays having a wavelength of 0.0711 millimicron show a first order reflection at the glancing angle indicated. Calculate the spacing d between crystal planes.

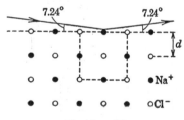

Problem 22

23. Determine the spacing of the crystal planes in sodium chloride from the facts that its molecular weight is 58.45 and its density is 2.163 gm/cm^3.

24. Tests with a beam of helium atoms incident upon a crystal of lithium fluoride showed diffraction effects similar to that produced by light, the smallest glancing angle for reinforcement being 8.65°. The distance between a lithium and a fluorine atom in the cubic cell is 2.013×10^{-8} cm. Determine the wavelength that corresponds to the helium atoms (§ 443).

39

POLARIZED LIGHT

430. Polarization of Light. The wave character of light is demonstrated by the phenomena of interference and diffraction; the transverse nature of light waves is disclosed by *polarization*. This latter phenomenon can be illustrated by a simple test using two thin plates of a mineral called *tourmaline*, the plates having been cut from the crystal in a particular manner. A beam of light is passed through one of these plates and projected upon a screen; except for a slight tinting due to the color of tourmaline and a reduction of intensity, the beam seems unchanged. However, it has been profoundly altered, as a test with the second plate placed in the light path will

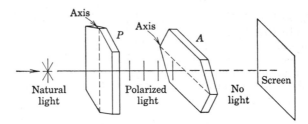

FIG. 431. Polarizing action of tourmaline

show. When the plates are held parallel the light passes through both, but when one is turned the amount of light transmitted becomes less, and when they are at right angles the light is almost entirely quenched.

A somewhat similar effect can be pictured for a mechanical wave by supposing tranverse vibrations in all planes to be set up in a rope stretched horizontally. When the rope is unobstructed the waves travel freely along its entire length, but if the test is repeated with the rope passed through a vertical slit, the horizontal components of the vibrations are blocked, and only the vertical components can travel beyond the slit. The introduction of a second slit produces no further change if it is vertical also, but if turned to the horizontal all vibrations beyond are quenched.

The significance of the test with the tourmaline plates will be considered with the aid of Fig. 431. Light is regarded as a wave in which the vibrations are transverse; that is, in planes at right angles to the line of propagation. When the vibrations constituting natural (nonpolarized) light are resolved into components, these are found equal in all directions, and a few of them

are shown on the incident ray in the figure.   Tourmaline transmits only
vibrations or their components that are parallel to the crystal axis.   Thus, in
the light transmitted by the first plate, *P*, the vibrations are restricted to a
single plane, as represented by the short vertical lines in the figure.   This
light is said to be *plane-polarized*.   The second plate, *A*, when crossed with
the first as shown, extinguishes the light, because the vibrations incident
upon it have no components along the direction in which it is capable of
transmitting.   Plate *P* is used to polarize the light and is called the *polarizer*,
and plate *A* is used to analyze the polarization and is called the *analyzer*.

It is known that light waves, like the radio waves described in Chap. 28,
are due to magnetic and electric fields which continually build up and collapse, and which are at right angles to each other.   In specifying the plane
of vibration of a light wave in this book, the plane of the electric field is
meant.

The term "polarization" implies a lack of symmetry around the axis of
propagation.   The fact that a light wave can be polarized is taken as evidence
that the wave is transverse, as a longitudinal wave appears to be inherently
symmetrical with respect to its direction of travel.

431. Polarization by Reflection.   The French engineer Etienne Malus
(1775–1812) discovered that light reflected from the surface of a transparent

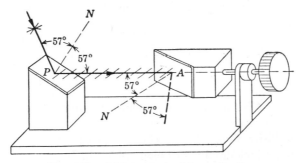

FIG. 432.   Light polarized by reflection

substance is partly polarized.   This action is indicated at *P* in Fig. 432,
which shows a beam of natural light incident upon an unsilvered glass plate.
The extent to which the reflected rays are polarized depends upon the direction of the incident light.   The angle of incidence for which the polarization becomes a maximum is called the *polarizing angle*, and is shown in the
figure between the incident ray and the normal *N*.   The value of this polarizing angle depends upon the index of refraction; for ordinary glass it is
about 57°.   Even at this angle, the amount of polarized light produced by a
single plate is relatively small, and often a pile of six to eight plates is used to
increase the intensity by combining the reflected rays from all the surfaces.

If the polarized beam from the transparent plate *P* is directed upon a
similar plate *A* that can be turned conveniently, it will be found that, when

the reflecting surfaces are parallel, reflection takes place from A as with natural light. If, however, the second plate is rotated 90° about ray PA as an axis to the position shown, there is no reflection. Thus, a transparent plate can be used to test the polarization of light by holding it in the beam at the polarizing angle and observing the relative intensities of the reflected beam as the plate is turned.

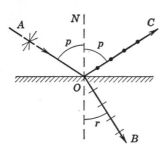

FIG. 433. Polarization of reflected and refracted rays

Fig. 433 shows a ray AO of natural light incident at the polarizing angle p upon the surface of a transparent medium. The reflected ray OC makes an equal angle with the normal N and is partly polarized, its vibrations being parallel to the surface, as represented by the dots in the figure. Most of the light is transmitted into the medium along the direction OB, the angle of refraction being r. The transmitted light is partly polarized, being deficient in those vibrations found in the beam OC.

The Scottish physicist Sir David Brewster (1781–1868) discovered that, when light impinges at the polarizing angle p upon a medium of refractive index μ, these quantities are related by the simple expression

$$\mu = \tan p \tag{301}$$

known as Brewster's Law. From this and Snell's Law of refraction, it follows that $\dfrac{\sin p}{\cos p} = \mu = \dfrac{\sin p}{\sin r}$, whence $\sin r = \cos p$. This means that $r + p =$ 90° and the angle COB is 90°; consequently for maximum polarization the reflected and refracted rays are at right angles.

432. Double Refraction. Many crystals possess the property of *double refraction*, a single incident beam being split into two beams within such a crystal. Calcite (Iceland spar, $CaCO_3$), quartz (SiO_2), and mica are doubly refracting substances.

The calcite crystal has six faces forming a rhombohedron, and the three face angles that meet at two opposite corners are 102°. A line through one of these blunt corners which makes equal angles with the three faces meeting there, or any line parallel to it, is called the *optic axis* of the crystal. A plane containing the optic axis and the normal to any face is called a *principal section*. Fig. 434 is a principal section of a calcite crystal and lines A represent the optic axis. A beam of natural light from X is shown incident normally upon an end face and two parallel beams are shown emerging from the other end face. Ray O passes through without deviation and is called the *ordinary* ray because it obeys the law of refraction. Ray E is deviated despite perpendicular incidence and is called the *extraordinary* ray. Both rays are polarized.

The direction of the rays within the crystal depends upon the direction of the incident beam. The ordinary ray travels with the same velocity regardless of its direction, the refractive index of calcite for this ray having a constant value of 1.658, as measured for the D spectral line. The extraordinary ray travels with different speeds, depending upon its direction. It if happens to advance along the optic axis, its velocity is the same as that of the ordinary ray and the two rays coincide. It if travels in any other direction, its

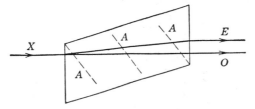

FIG. 434. Separation of rays in calcite

velocity is greater, having a maximum value along a direction at right angles to the optic axis. The refractive index of calcite for the extraordinary ray, as measured for the D spectral line, varies from 1.658 along the optic axis to 1.486 at right angles to that direction.

The wave fronts within the crystal can be located by using secondary wavelets, following Huygens' construction in Fig. 320. For the ordinary beam the wavelets have the familiar spherical shape. For the extraordinary beam they are ellipsoidal, the minor axis of the ellipsoid lying along the

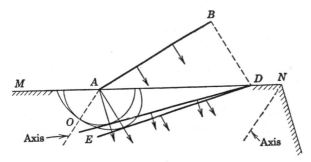

FIG. 435. Character of wave fronts in calcite

optic axis, in which direction the wavelets for the two beams coincide. These conditions are represented in Fig. 435, in which a plane wave *AB* is shown incident upon the crystal surface *MN*. The wave fronts for the ordinary and extraordinary beams are constructed as shown at *DO* and *DE*, tangent respectively to the spherical and ellipsoidal wavelets, and the corresponding rays are directed from *A* to the points of tangency. It is interesting to observe that, for the extraordinary wave, the rays are not perpendicular to the wave front.

The crystals that exhibit double refraction belong to the hexagonal and tetragonal systems. For some of these, such a quartz, the velocity of the extraordinary ray, except along the optic axis, is less than that of the ordinary ray. For these crystals, the ellipse representing the extraordinary wave front has its major axis coincident with the radius of the circular wave front of the ordinary beam, and the extraordinary ray makes a larger angle with the optic axis than the ordinary ray. Some crystals have two optic axes with characteristic angles between them; they are called biaxial crystals.

433. Polarization by Double Refraction. The polarization produced by a doubly refracting crystal is indicated in Fig. 436, which shows a principal

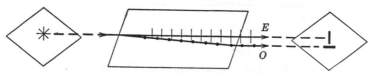

FIG. 436.   Polarization produced by calcite

section of a calcite crystal and includes views of both end faces. The vibrations of the incident natural light are resolved into components in the plane of the principal section and at right angles to this plane, and these components are transmitted by the extraordinary and the ordinary rays respectively. Thus, the emergent beams E and O are polarized at right angles to each other.

The Nicol prism, named for its inventor and used as a means of polarizing natural light, is a calcite crystal of the shape shown in Fig. 437. It is prepared by resurfacing the end faces of the crystal at an angle of 68°, sawing the crystal in two diagonally at right angles to these end planes, and cementing the two parts together with Canada balsam. The refractive index of the

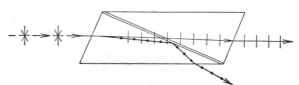

FIG. 437.   Principal section of Nicol prism

balsam, 1.53 as measured for the D spectral line, is intermediate between the refractive indices of calcite for the ordinary and extraordinary rays. The incident ray of natural light is separated as usual into ordinary and extraordinary rays. The ordinary ray is totally reflected at the balsam layer and passes to one side where it is absorbed in suitable covering materials. The extraordinary ray is transmitted as plane polarized light, its vibrations being in the plane of the principal section.

Some doubly refracting materials absorb one transmitted ray more than the other, and if the thickness is sufficient, one ray is almost completely absorbed. Such a material is called a *dichroic* substance; the best-known example is tourmaline, which transmits only the extraordinary ray and absorbs the other. The new polarizing materials utilize sulfate of iodo-quinine and even very thin layers absorb one light component effectively. In the synthetic material called *polaroid* the dichroic crystals are distributed densely in a cellulose film mounted between glass plates or bonded between transparent flexible plastic sheets. The individual crystals are needle-shaped and have girth diameters less than a wavelength of light. The average intensity of the transmitted beam is 37% of the incident light over the visible range.

434. Some Applications of Polarized Light. The introduction of polarizing substances that are relatively inexpensive, like polaroid, has made possible a number of interesting applications, two of which will be considered briefly.

The light that is reflected from matt surfaces over a range of angles contains considerable glare-light which exhibits polarization, the direction of vibration being parallel to the surface (like that of ray *PA* in Fig. 432). The glare of sunlight reflected from sidewalks and pavements can be reduced by the use of polaroid glasses arranged to transmit only vibrations in the vertical plane. The glare from paper observed in reading under desk lamps can be reduced by placing at the lamp opening a sheet of polaroid that is oriented to eliminate the horizontal vibrations.

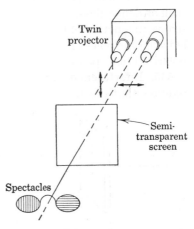

FIG. 438. Scheme for stereoscopic projection of pictures

Polarized light has also been used to give "depth" to motion pictures, making use of the stereoscopic effect described in § 419. Fig. 438 shows schematically how this may be accomplished, utilizing a twin projector equipped with polarizing screens set at right angles to each other for forming images on a ground-glass surface, and providing each observer with polaroid spectacles so oriented as to give each eye the image intended for it. Such stereoscopic projection is also possible by reflection using surfaces of fine texture preferably coated with aluminum.

435. Optical Rotation. Certain materials, notably quartz and solutions of sugar, have the property of *rotating the plane of polarization* in transmitting polarized light. This effect can be observed with a *polarimeter*, consisting of a polarizer and an analyzer, together with means for supporting the optically active substance in the light path between them.

Optical rotation is used in determining the percentage of sugar in solutions of unknown concentration. Polarimeters especially designed for testing sugar are known as *saccharimeters,* and are arranged to pass the polarized light through a tube filled with the solution under test. With the polarizer and analyzer initially crossed to give a dark field, the introduction of the sugar solution rotates the plane of polarization and hence the analyzer must be turned to a new position to restore darkness. The difference between these positions is the angle through which the plane of polarization has been rotated, or else differs from it by 180°. The rotation is found to be proportional to the length of the liquid column and to the strength of the solution, and depends also upon the wavelength of light used. With sodium light, an aqueous solution of cane sugar in a tube 10 cm long produces an optical rotation of 6.65° for a concentration of 0.1 gm of sugar per cm^3 of solution. With the same light, quartz causes a rotation of 21.72° per mm of thickness.

Faraday discovered in 1845 that some materials of high refractive index, such as dense glass, rotate the plane of polarization of light when located in a strong magnetic field. This effect can be observed by placing the specimen between the poles of an electromagnet, the pole pieces being bored so that the polarized light passes in the same direction as the magnetic field.

436. Interference Effects. To annul plane-polarized light by interference requires that the interfering waves originate from a common point of the

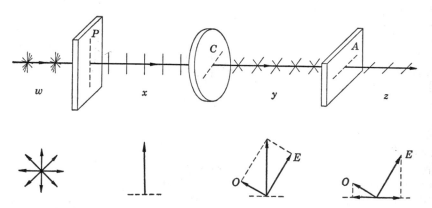

Fig. 439. Producing interference colors with crystals in polarized light. Optical axes of polarizer, crystal, and analyzer are indicated by dotted lines

source and be in phase opposition, as with natural light, and also requires that *their vibrations be in the same plane.* Interference is usually demonstrated by placing a doubly refracting substance between a polarizer and an analyzer.

The polarizer and analyzer may be either parallel or crossed; in Fig. 439 they are represented as crossed plates *P* and *A,* and the doubly refracting crystal *C* is shown between them with its optic axis inclined to the plate axes. White natural light (having transverse vibrations in all directions) entering at *w* is polarized by plate *P,* giving only vertical vibrations at *x.* These are resolved by crystal *C* into two components shown at *y,* the extraordinary ray E having its vibrations in the plane of its optic axis and the ordinary ray O having its vibrations at right angles to this plane. These rays are unequally retarded in traversing the crystal, principally because of difference in refractive index; the relative retardation can be an odd number of half wavelengths for some color in the incident light, but no interference results, because the two rays are polarized at right angles to each other. The analyzer A passes only the horizontal components of these vibrations, and in the region z beyond it the two rays can interfere and the colors resulting from the interference can be observed. The successive resolutions of the vibrations along the light path from w to z are represented in the lower part of the figure. The emergent waves overlap almost completely, although the two rays are shown separated in the figure for clearness. Thus a colorless crystal when viewed by polarized light shows colors as a result of interference, and the colors observed depend upon the thickness and refractive index of the specimen.

The arrangement described is useful in the examination of crystals and in the study of thin rock sections. When viewed with a microscope equipped with polarizer and analyzer, such sections usually appear colored irregularly and disclose details and structural differences not readily observed by other means. Such examinations enable the microscopist to determine whether a crystal is uniaxial (like quartz) or biaxial (like mica), whether it is optically active, the amount of clockwise or counterclockwise rotation of its plane of polarization, and the numerical values of its refractive indices. Such information permits him to specify to which crystal system a sample belongs and to effect its identification.

A plate of singly refracting material when substituted for the doubly refracting crystal between polarizer and analyzer produces no interference effects, since the incident ray is not split into two rays. However, many singly refracting materials, such as glass or celluloid, become doubly refracting when mechanically strained. Consequently, such substances can be tested with polarized light, either white or monochromatic. The presence of strains, not apparent when viewed in natural light, are evidenced by the appearance of interference fringes.

It was discovered by the Scottish physicist John Kerr (1824–1907) that a transparent insulator such as glass or turpentine becomes doubly refracting when located in a strong electric field. A specimen of proper thickness placed in a beam of plane-polarized light between a polarizer and an analyzer results in interference of the emergent rays from the analyzer when the field is established. With a rapidly alternating field the arrangement acts as a quick operating shutter, and this action has been used in measuring the speed of light and for a number of other purposes.

437. Elliptical and Circular Polarization. The polarized light considered thus far is plane-polarized; attention will next be directed to other kinds. It can be shown that two harmonic vibrations of equal frequency, taking place in perpendicular planes, can be combined to give elliptical motion. The shape of the ellipse depends upon the amplitudes and phases of the component vibrations. It becomes circular when the components are equal and differ in phase by one-quarter cycle.

When plane-polarized light is passed through a thin doubly refracting plate, as at *C* in Fig. 439, the components traverse the plate with different velocities and, in general, emerge displaced from each other in phase. The issuing light is said to be *elliptically polarized;* it becomes *circularly polarized* if the two components have equal amplitude and if the relative retardation is one-quarter wavelength. A doubly refracting plate designed to produce circular polarization is called a *quarter-wave* plate; its thickness and refractive indices are appropriate for the wavelength of light with which it is used. With circularly polarized light, the field remains equally bright for all positions of the analyzer.

The Dutch physicist Pieter Zeeman (1865–1943) discovered that, if a source of light is placed in an intense magnetic field, the lines of its spectra are broken into two or more components. When a line is viewed along the direction of the field, two lines appear; the two beams are circularly polarized in opposite directions. When viewed at right angles to the field, three lines appear; the outside beams are plane-polarized parallel to the field and the central one is plane-polarized at right angles to the field. Some spectral lines are resolved into four or six components. Such tests have led to important deductions concerning the structure of matter. They have also allowed the ratio of the electronic charge and mass to be evaluated, the results showing close agreement with those obtained by purely electrical methods, § 258.

438. Photo-Elasticity. The distribution of internal stresses in structural or machine parts can be observed by passing polarized light through models

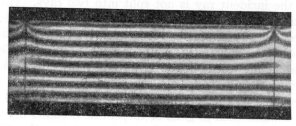

Fig. 440.   Stresses in beam shown by polarized light through model

made to scale from sheet celluloid or Bakelite, which are subjected to external forces simulating those in the actual structures. The method will be illustrated by a Bakelite model of a loaded beam. A picture of the central portion of the beam taken by circularly polarized light is shown in Fig. 440. The beam was subjected to two equal loads applied to the upper edge at the vertical lines shown and supported at two points beyond the picture and equidistant from the loads.

Throughout the region between the loads the "fibers" of the beam are stressed in tension and compression only. Under these conditions the relative retardation of the transmitted ordinary and extraordinary rays is directly proportional to the fiber stress. The dark band in the picture at midheight is the zero-order fringe at the *neutral axis*. The third fringes above and below the neutral axis are the third-order fringes and correspond to a computed stress of 1287 lb/in.² in the model. Hence each fringe represents a change in stress amounting to 1287 ÷ 3 = 429 lb/in.² Where a fringe

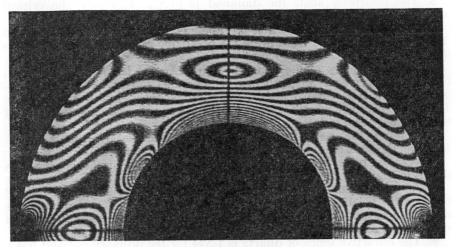

Fig. 441. Stresses in a Bakelite ring rendered visible by polarized light. (*Photograph by Professor Robert C. Veit*)

meets the edge of a loaded model made from the same sheet of Bakelite the stress at the edge is 429 times the fringe order.

Fig. 441 shows the upper half of a circular ring to which forces are applied at the left and right sides. The model was made from the same sheet of Bakelite as the beam of Fig. 440, and therefore the same stress values apply to the interference fringes. The zero order fringe or neutral point is the black dot on the vertical centerline of the ring. It is seen in counting upward from the neutral point that the fifth order fringe coincides with the top edge of the ring; hence the stress at this edge is 5 × 429 = 2145 lb/in². Below the neutral point the fringes are more numerous and more closely spaced, showing that the stresses there are higher and the stress gradient steeper. The corresponding stresses in the actual ring are determined by taking account of the relative sizes of ring and model and the relative forces applied. At the sides where the forces are applied the fringes are of high order and so closely spaced as to merge into a dark area, indicating a high stress concentration. In this case the concentrated stress is not considered objectionable since it is due to contact pressure.

PROBLEMS

1. When natural light falls upon a glass surface at an incident angle of 56.6°, the reflected beam shows maximum polarization. Find (a) the refractive index of the glass and (b) the angle of refraction within it. (c) Make a diagram showing the incident, reflected, and refracted rays in the appropriate directions.

2. A beam of light is incident upon a smooth surface of water. For what angle of incidence does the greatest amount of polarization occur in the reflected beam?

3. The polarizing angle for diamond is 67.5°. Calculate the critical angle of total reflection for this crystal.

4. A certain flint-glass prism of 60° angle produces a minimum deviation of 51° for yellow light. Determine the polarizing angle of the glass for this light.

5. If the intensity of the beam of light reflected from the analyzer in Fig. 432 is taken as I_o when surface A is parallel to surface P, then its intensity when A is rotated about PA through an angle θ is found to be $I_o \cos^2 \theta$. Through what angle has A been turned when the intensity of the reflected beam is $\frac{3}{4}$ of its maximum value?

6. Compute the speed of yellow light (D spectral line) in a calcite crystal (a) along the optic axis and (b) at right angles to the optic axis.

7. What purpose is served by the upper-right half of the Nicol prism shown in Fig. 437?

8. An aqueous solution of cane sugar that fills a tube 20 cm long is placed between the polarizer and analyzer of a saccharimeter; its presence rotates the plane of polarization through 15°. Determine the concentration of sugar in the solution.

9. The refractive index of quartz is 1.544 for the ordinary ray and has a maximum value of 1.553 for the extraordinary ray, both with respect to the D spectral line. What is the minimum thickness of a quartz plate in which these rays would annul each other?

10. Use the data of the preceding problem and determine the thickness of a quartz slab to serve as a quarter-wave plate for the D spectral line.

11. Determine the stress in the model of Fig. 441 along the outer edge of the ring (a) at a point 1 in. from the vertical centerline and (b) at a point $\frac{3}{4}$ in. above the horizontal centerline.

40

RADIATION AND ATOMIC STRUCTURE

439. Modern Physics. The branch of Physics that deals with tiny particles of matter and the wave characteristics associated with them is popularly called *Modern Physics*. A number of topics in this field have been considered in earlier chapters where they fitted well with the principles taken up; for example, the basic laws of radiation in § 186, the quantum theory in § 189, the ratio of electronic charge to mass in § 258, the cyclotron in § 259, thermionics and electronics in Chap. 27, photoelectric emission in § 315, solid-state electronics in Chap. 29, spectral series in § 390, and diffraction of x-rays in § 429.

The literature on Modern Physics is highly specialized and a study of the subject is undertaken with textbooks in particular branches. By way of introduction to these, this concluding chapter touches upon additional phases of Physics considered to be representative. The material deals with the quantum aspects of radiation, x-ray spectra, corpuscular and wave relations, relativity, radioactivity, and the nuclear structure of the atom.

440. Quantum Relations in Radiation. An understanding of radiation is made clearer by applying the quantum theory to the planetary conception of the atom, § 390. This also provides a theoretical verification of the equations for spectral series. The form of such an equation for hydrogen, due to the Swedish scientist Johannes R. Rydberg (1854–1919), was given as Eq. 276 in the section referred to and expresses the wave numbers of the hydrogen spectrum as

$$\nu = 109{,}737 \left(\frac{1}{k_2{}^2} - \frac{1}{k_1{}^2} \right)$$

where k_1 and k_2 are simple integers representing atomic energy levels, and the number is known as the *Rydberg constant*.

The single electron of a hydrogen atom will be assumed to revolve about the nucleus in a circular path of radius r at a velocity v. With a charge $-e$ on the electron and a charge $+e$ on the nucleus, both in electrostatic units, the force of attraction between them in dynes is given in § 195 as $\dfrac{e \times e}{r^2}$, where e is in statcoulombs and r in centimeters. This constitutes the centripetal force acting upon the electron of mass m gm, and amounts to mv^2/r according to Eq. 33. The linear velocity v in centimeters per second can be replaced by $r\omega$, where ω is the angular velocity, § 49, in radians per second. Under the action of this centripetal force the electron revolves in a definite orbit of radius r such that

$$\frac{e^2}{r^2} = mr\omega^2 \tag{302}$$

The energy of the revolving electron is partly potential and partly kinetic. Its potential energy is the product of the charge $-e$ and the potential V as in § 198, and hence for the electron becomes $-eV = -e\left(\dfrac{e}{r}\right)$; its kinetic energy is given by Eq. 54 as $\frac{1}{2}mv^2$. Therefore the total energy = $-\dfrac{e^2}{r} + \dfrac{1}{2}m(r\omega)^2$. This can be modified by applying Eq. 302 to give the energy in dyne·cm or ergs as

$$E = -\frac{e^2}{2r} \tag{303}$$

The two foregoing equations could be satisfied by any value of the radius r and, if no other limitation were imposed, the electron could have any conceivable energy value. Under this supposition, the spectrum of hydrogen would comprise all frequencies in accordance with Eq. 277, which states that the energy difference between a higher and lower level is $E_h - E_l = hf$; but this conclusion is contrary to fact. In order to secure agreement with the well-known hydrogen spectrum, Bohr introduced the idea of energy levels described in § 390 and assumed that the *angular momentum* of the electron in its orbit would have to be an exact multiple of $h/2\pi$, where h is Planck's constant.

The angular momentum is given in § 58 as $I\omega$, where the moment of inertia I of the single electron at a distance r from the axis of rotation is mr^2. It follows that the electron can have only particular orbits such that the angular momentum satisfies the equation

$$mr^2\omega = k\frac{h}{2\pi} \tag{304}$$

where the integer k is called the *quantum number*. This equation expresses the all-important *quantizing condition*. When the value of ω herefrom is substituted in Eq. 302, the quantizing condition indicates that the electronic orbit in hydrogen has definite radii given by

$$r = \frac{k^2 h^2}{4\pi^2 m e^2} \tag{305}$$

The energy of the electron rotating in the orbit of radius r, as given by this equation, is found by substitution in Eq. 303 to be

$$E = -\frac{2\pi^2 m e^4}{k^2 h^2}$$

and is spoken of as the energy of the atom in the kth stationary state. The energy radiated by the atom in passing from the k_1th to the k_2th stationary state is therefore

$$E_h - E_l = \frac{2\pi^2 m e^4}{h^2} \left[\frac{1}{k_2{}^2} - \frac{1}{k_1{}^2} \right]$$

When this result is merged with Eq. 277, and the frequency in that equation is replaced by the wave number ν times the speed of light c, the wave number of the spectral line emitted in the energy transfer becomes

$$\nu = \frac{2\pi^2 m e^4}{h^3 c} \left[\frac{1}{k_2{}^2} - \frac{1}{k_1{}^2} \right] \tag{306}$$

From the numerical values: $m = 9.11 \times 10^{-28}$ gm, $e = 4.80 \times 10^{-10}$ statcoulombs, $h = 6.62 \times 10^{-27}$ erg·sec, and $c = 3.00 \times 10^{10}$ cm/sec, it will be found that the coefficient of the bracketed expression agrees with the Rydberg constant for hydrogen.

The correlation of atomic energy levels and the placement of the spectral lines that has been shown to exist for hydrogen extend also to elements having many electrons and producing complicated spectra. The value of the Rydberg constant varies slightly for atoms of different mass numbers.

441. X-ray Spectra. The diffraction of x-rays by reflection from the various atomic planes of crystals, § 429, affords an accurate knowledge of the character of x-rays emitted by the elements, and this knowledge has been of great aid in determining the structure of their atoms. The radiation from the target of an x-ray tube, when investigated by reflection at all angles from a crystal, is found to consist of a continuous spectrum and a superposed bright-line spectrum extending over a range of wavelengths from about 10^{-6} to 10^{-9} cm. The continuous spectrum does not depend on the target material but the bright-line spectrum does.

The *continuous x-ray spectrum* differs in intensity over its range, increasing from very low values at the longer wavelengths to a maximum value and then falling sharply to zero at a particular shorter wavelength. This short-wave limit depends upon the potential difference across the electrodes of the x-ray tube and is independent of the target material. These facts indicate that the continuous spectrum is caused by the rapid retardation and consequent loss of kinetic energy of the electrons from the cathode of the tube as they strike the atoms of the target, or, more correctly, as they are deflected by the strong electric fields surrounding the nuclei of the target atoms.

An electron deflected from an atom usually suffers a decrease of energy, and the quantum of energy lost is emitted as radiation and is called a *photon*. The most the electron can lose is the total kinetic energy it had upon arrival at the target, but it may lose less than this amount. Consequently, the highest frequency of the x-rays (i.e., shortest wavelength) is the frequency of a photon that is emitted when the electron is stopped completely. The maximum kinetic energy of an electron on approach is Ve ergs, where V is the peak value of the potential difference across the tube and e is the charge of the electron, § 204. This is the energy of the quantum that corresponds to the highest photon frequency f_m; it is given in § 308 as

$$Ve = hf_m$$

in which Planck's constant $h = 6.62 \times 10^{-27}$ erg·sec, and the electronic charge $e = 4.80 \times 10^{-10}$ statcoulomb. Since 1 statvolt = 300 volts, and the velocity of propagation is $c = 3.00 \times 10^{10}$ cm/sec, it follows that the minimum wavelength is

$$\lambda_{min} = \frac{c}{f_m} = \frac{3.00 \times 10^{10} \times 6.62 \times 10^{-27} \times 300}{4.80 \times 10^{-10} V} = \frac{12.41}{V} 10^{-5}$$

The wavelength is in centimeters when the pd between anode and cathode of the x-ray tube is in volts. The wavelength corresponding to the maximum intensity is about $\frac{3}{2}\lambda_{min}$.

The *bright-line x-ray spectra* are characteristic of the target materials, and the spectrum for any one element consists of several well-defined groups of lines. These groups are conventionally called the K, L, M, N $\cdots$ series in the order of increasing wavelength, or decreasing energy. The wavelengths of the lines are independent of the pds across the tube terminals, but these pds do determine the intensity of the lines and whether they appear or not. The lighter elements give lines only in the first-mentioned series. The characteristic spectra of all the elements are found to be similar, but the corresponding lines of any series occur at different wavelengths for the different elements. The English physicist Henry G. J. Moseley (1887–1915) found that the wavelength for a particular line depends upon the atomic number of the element and not upon its atomic weight. The relation between wavelength λ, wave number ν, and atomic number Z is given by

$$\frac{1}{\lambda} = \nu = C(Z - \sigma)^2 \qquad (307)$$

where C and σ are constants. In this relation, known as Moseley's Law, the value of C depends on the particular line of the series while that of σ is the same for all lines of a series. The higher the atomic number of an element, the shorter is the wavelength for the particular line under consideration. Fig. 442 shows the K-series lines for four metals of atomic

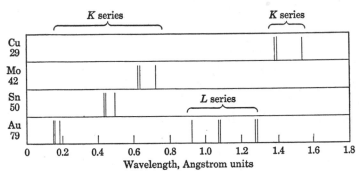

FIG. 442. X-ray spectra of copper, molybdenum, tin, and gold

numbers 29, 42, 50, and 79, and the L-series lines for the last metal only, because the others fall to the right of the chart.

Both analysis and experiment indicate that the emission of characteristic x-rays is due to the inner electrons of the target atoms. In the planetary picture of the atom, the lines of the K series are emitted when electrons from outer shells fall into the innermost one to fill vacancies there, those of the L series are emitted when electrons fall similarly to the second shell, and so on. These shells are appropriately referred to as the K and L shells. Thus, when an impinging electron collides with an atom of the target and ejects one of its electrons of the K shell, the vacancy is filled by an electron from the L shell, or one from the M shell, and so on. As a result, a line of the K series is emitted, the energy value depending on the source of the electron. If it comes from the L shell the line is called the $K\alpha$ line, if from the M shell the $K\beta$ line, and so on. The $K\beta$ line is of higher frequency than the $K\alpha$ line, because the energy difference between the M and K shells is greater than that between the L and K shells. A vacancy in the L shell is made up similarly and spectral lines of $L\alpha$, $L\beta$, $\cdots$ result.

The fact that x-ray spectra of the elements are similar except as to their wavelength scales indicates that the inner electronic structure of all but the lighter atoms is the same. In contrast, optical spectra have different characteristics from element to element and show that the outer structure of atoms differs; their lines are produced by electrons falling from a number of outer normally unoccupied levels to inner ones. Studied together with the chemical properties of atoms, both types of spectra reveal how many electrons can occupy the several shells; thus, the K shell can have 2 electrons, the L shell 8, and so on.

Energy level diagrams like that of Fig. 381 can be constructed to show the origin of x-ray spectral lines of the elements, and Eq. 276 can be extended to include their wave numbers. The modified expression for the number of waves per centimeter is

$$\nu = R(Z - \sigma)^2 \left[\frac{1}{k_2{}^2} - \frac{1}{k_1{}^2} \right] \qquad (308)$$

In this equation R is the Rydberg constant, Z is the atomic number, k_1 and k_2 are the quantum numbers for the initial and final energy levels, and σ is a constant. For hydrogen $Z = 1$ and $\sigma = 0$, and the expression reduces to Eq. 276 for the wave numbers in the infrared, visible and ultraviolet regions. It will be observed that Eqs. 307 and 308 agree in form; the value of C in the former can be evaluated readily.

Illustrative Problem

For the K series the constant σ is 0.5 and for molybdenum the atomic number is 42. Find the wavelength of the $K\alpha$ line in the x-ray spectrum of this element.

This line is produced by an electron falling from shell L of quantum number $k_1 = 2$ to shell K of quantum number $k_2 = 1$. Consequently the wave number is $\nu = 14.1 \times 10^7$ waves/cm, and the wavelength is $1/(14.1 \times 10^7) = 7.1 \times 10^{-9}$ cm, or 7.1×10^{-5} micron. This is equivalent to 0.71 Angstrom unit, § 384, and is written as 0.71 A.

Attention has also been directed to x-ray emission spectra involving the outer parts of the atoms of solids. These studies, together with those on absorption of x-rays, indicate that electrons, once removed from the inner parts of atoms, appear to belong to the solid as a whole instead of to its individual atoms, and that the energies of the electron transitions cover bands rather than specific values. This broadening of the emission lines is ascribed to the interactions of the closely packed atoms of solids, and the falling of the outer or valence electrons into vacancies produced in the inner shells of the atoms by electronic bombardment. It is expected that such studies will provide an insight to the structure of solids.

442. Corpuscular Nature of Radiation. The effects of interference, diffraction, and polarization, described in the two foregoing chapters, give ample evidence of the *wave character* of light. The same is true for radiation beyond the visible spectrum. However, the wave theory cannot explain the photoelectric effect, § 315, which supports the theory that radiation is *corpuscular* in character. The quantum theory does explain it and, moreover, gives a satisfying account of the absorption and emission of radiation in the production of atomic spectra.

In describing the photoelectric effect it was stated that: (1) when radiation is incident upon certain substances electrons are emitted, and these are often called photoelectrons to indicate their origin; (2) the velocity of their emission is not influenced by the intensity of the radiation; (3) the velocity of the photoelectrons increases with the frequency of the incident radiation; (4) the frequency must reach a certain critical value depending on the substance before emission occurs at all; (5) the number of photoelectrons emitted per unit time varies with the intensity of radiation. It has also been shown that there is no appreciable time lag between the beginning of illumination and the emission of electrons.

Since the photoelectron receives energy from the incident radiation in order to leave the substance, it is difficult to explain on the wave theory why the energy (and therefore the velocity) imparted to the photoelectron does not diminish when the radiation intensity is reduced, say by moving the source farther from the substance. The difficulty is removed by assuming that the energy is distributed discontinuously over the radiation wave front in little packets called quanta which maintain their identity in traveling from the source.

The quanta or photons have different energy values depending upon the radiation frequency, the values being given by Eq. 132, $E = hf$. The maximum energy of the expelled electrons is given by Einstein's equation as

$$\tfrac{1}{2} mv_m{}^2 = hf - w$$

where m is the mass of the photoelectron, 9.11×10^{-28} gm, v_m is its velocity in centimeters per second, h is Planck's constant in erg·seconds, f is the frequency in vibrations per second, and w is the work function in ergs. The energy values in this equation may be expressed in electron·volts, by using the conversion factor 1.602×10^{-12} ergs $= 1$ electron·volt.

The work function represents the energy required to remove one of the least firmly bound electrons, and its value differs with different substances. Its presence in the equation explains why the radiation frequency must have a sufficiently high value before emission can occur, for the minimum frequency is w/h and the corresponding maximum wavelength is hc/w, where c is the velocity of light.

Illustrative Problem

In order to have photoelectric emission from potassium, it is found that the wavelength of the incident radiation must not exceed about 0.00007 cm; how much energy is needed to remove an electron from potassium?

The work function of this element is $w = hc/\lambda = 6.62 \times 10^{-27} \times 3.00 \times 10^{10} \div 7 \times 10^{-5} = 2.84 \times 10^{-12}$ ergs, or $2.84 \times 10^{-12} \div 1.60 \times 10^{-12}$

= 1.77 electron·volts. Thus, the energy necessary to remove an electron from potassium is equal to the work done on an electron in falling through a pd of 1.77 volts.

The corpuscular theory of radiation receives further support by an effect discovered by Professor Arthur H. Compton, and now known by his name. He found that when a beam of monochromatic x-rays of high energy impinges upon one of the lighter elements like carbon, and is scattered by the element, a part of the scattered radiation exhibits an *increase in wavelength*, and this corresponds to a decrease in energy.

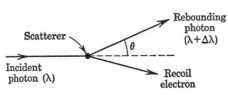

FIG. 443. Scattering of x-rays

This effect is explained on the quantum theory by stating that some x-ray photons "collide" with electrons and in doing so give up some of their energy to the electrons to set them in motion. As a result the photons rebound with diminished energy. Each direction of a rebounding photon is correlated with a certain direction of recoil of the electron, the occurrence of recoil particles in the various directions being governed by laws of probability. The condition is pictured in Fig. 443.

The change of wavelength of the scattered radiation is given by

$$\Delta\lambda = \frac{h}{mc}(1 - \cos\theta) \tag{309}$$

where θ is the angle at which the scattered radiation is observed and m is the mass of the electron. The validity of this explanation confirms the belief that all radiation behaves as particles, at least under certain conditions; for example, in its interactions with free or lightly bound electrons. Thus, light and other radiation is regarded as a swarm of photons, following each other with the speed c and differing in energy content hf in accordance with the frequency or wavelength.

443. Wave Nature of Particles. A new concept of matter was introduced in 1924 by the French physicist Louis V. de Broglie to the effect that particles of small mass, such as electrons, have a wave character like photons of radiation. By analogy with Eq. 309, these so-called "matter waves" would have a wavelength of

$$\lambda = \frac{h}{mv} \tag{310}$$

where h is Planck's constant, and m and v are the mass and velocity of the particle respectively. Experiments were being conducted at the time by Clinton J. Davisson and Lester H. Germer, physicists of the Bell Telephone Laboratories, on the reflection of electrons from the surfaces of metals, and in 1927 they produced diffraction patterns by projecting electrons upon a nickel crystal, thereby demonstrating their wave character.

Measurements of electron diffraction patterns show that the Bragg formula holds when the wavelength satisfies Eq. 310. Thus, while tests with the cloud chamber, § 446, show that electrons are undoubtedly particles, their diffraction shows that they act as light waves. In the same way atoms and molecules have been found to possess a wave character.

Fig. 444 shows a diffraction pattern of high resolution produced with a normally incident beam of electrons passing through a very thin film of cesium iodide (CsI) which is formed upon a suitable supporting foil. The molecules of such inorganic compounds, deposited by evaporation under a high vacuum, are able to move about on the foil surface and agglomerate into crystals; for the pattern shown the mean crystal dimensions were estimated at 0.02 micron or 200 A.

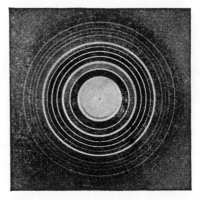

It would seem, therefore, that all particles of matter have wave characteristics and, according to the de Broglie equation, the larger their masses at a given speed, the shorter are the wavelengths. The extension of Mechanics which takes this behavior into account in dealing with particles of electronic and atomic magnitudes is called Wave Mechanics.

Fig. 444. Electron diffraction pattern. (*Courtesy of Lester H. Germer*)

The de Broglie equation is consistent with the quantum condition introduced by Professor Bohr to fix the energy levels of the normal hydrogen atom, § 440, namely, that the angular momentum of the electron moving in its circular orbit of radius r must be an integral multiple of $h/2\pi$. For the electron to exhibit a wave character, the length of its path in any stable orbit should contain an integral number of wavelengths, just as is the case with vibrating strings, § 342. Consequently, the wavelength λ should be some integer times $2\pi r$. If the integer is taken as unity

$$\lambda = 2\pi r$$

a result which may be combined with the equation for the angular momentum of the electron, namely,

$$mr^2\omega = mrv = \frac{h}{2\pi}$$

to yield Eq. 310 directly.

Illustrative Problem

Find the wavelength associated with electrons that have a kinetic energy of 100 electron·volts.

The rest mass of an electron is 9.11×10^{-28} gm, and the stated energy value is equal to $100 \times 1.602 \times 10^{-12}$ erg; hence the speed of the electrons is

$$v = \sqrt{\frac{2}{m} \, 1.60 \times 10^{-10}} = \sqrt{\frac{3.20 \times 10^{-10}}{9.11 \times 10^{-28}}} = 5.93 \times 10^8 \text{ cm/sec}$$

The de Broglie wavelength of such electron waves is, therefore,

$$\lambda = \frac{6.62 \times 10^{-27}}{9.11 \times 10^{-28} \times 5.93 \times 10^8} = 1.23 \times 10^{-8} \text{ cm} = 1.23 \text{ A}$$

444. Relativity. The fact that all motion is relative has been recognized for a long time. A person on a river steamer who looks out and sees only the water near the ship because of fog, cannot tell by observing the water moving past him whether the ship is under way or the tide is passing the ship at anchor, provided he is not assisted in this observation by other effects, such as ship vibration caused by its engine. Our own motion in walking along the street is reckoned with respect to the earth as fixed, no consideration being given to the facts that the earth rotates on its axis and travels around the sun. These and other illustrations, § 20, show that motion in space is ambiguous; it has definite meaning only when expressed relative to something that may be regarded as fixed. Einstein extended this fundamental idea of relative motion and formulated what is known as the *theory of relativity*. Much experimental evidence has been accumulated in its support, and the consequences of the theory are of great theoretical importance.

The theory postulates that (1) relative motion is the only motion that has definite meaning and (2) the velocity of light in free space is independent of the motion of the light source and observer. The first leads to the generalization that the laws of physical phenomena (for example, the laws of Mechanics) are unaffected by uniform rectilinear motion of the system of coordinates to which the physical quantities are referred. The second postulate is a statement resulting from experiment, specifically the failure to detect with an interferometer a difference of the speed of light in the direction of the earth's motion and in a direction at right angles thereto.

A surprising result of the theory of relativity is that it implies an *increase of inertia* (that is, of *mass*) *with velocity*. This variation in mass is insignificant except when the body has velocities approaching that of light. If the mass of a body at rest is represented by m_o, its mass at velocity v is

$$m = \frac{m_o}{\sqrt{1 - \dfrac{v^2}{c^2}}} \tag{311}$$

where c is the velocity of light. Thus, an electron having a mass of 9.11 $\times 10^{-28}$ gm at rest has a mass when moving with a velocity 0.9 that of light amounting to 20.9×10^{-28} gm.

The theory also indicates the equivalence of mass and energy. This equivalence can be obtained by computing the work done on a body, of rest mass m_o, in accelerating it to a velocity v, taking account of the fact that the mass increases to a value m in the transition. The result as obtained by integration shows that the kinetic energy of the body is then

$$E_k = m_o c^2 \left(\frac{1}{\sqrt{1 - v^2/c^2}} - 1 \right) \tag{312}$$

Illustrative Problem

Find the speed of electrons that have energies of 1 million electron·volts. The energy of each of these electrons is $10^6 \times 1.602 \times 10^{-12} = 1.602 \times 10^{-6}$ erg, and the rest mass of each is 9.11×10^{-28} gm. Hence, $m_o c^2 = 9.11 \times 10^{-28}$ gm $\times \left(3 \times 10^{10} \frac{cm}{sec} \right)^2 = 0.820 \times 10^{-6}$ erg, and, from Eq. 312,

$$\sqrt{1 - \frac{v^2}{c^2}} = \frac{1}{(1.602/0.820) + 1} = 0.339$$

Herefrom $v^2/c^2 = 0.885$, and consequently $v = c\sqrt{0.885} = 3 \times 10^{10} \times 0.941 = 2.82 \times 10^{10}$ cm/sec.

The combination of Eqs. 311 and 312 gives a result of great importance, namely, that the kinetic energy is c^2 times the change in mass, or

$$E_k = (m - m_o)c^2 \tag{313}$$

If $m_o c^2$ be thought of as the internal energy of the body at rest, then the total energy equivalent of the body of mass m when moving is $m_o c^2 + E_k$, or

$$E = mc^2 \tag{314}$$

The equation indicates that if a mass m were annihilated in some way, the amount of energy liberated would be mc^2. This relationship implies that the laws of the Conservation of Mass and of the Conservation of Energy are two aspects of a single law of nature.

445. Radioactivity. Shortly after the discovery of x-rays, the French scientist Antoine H. Becquerel (1852–1908) found that uranium in various states of chemical combination emitted spontaneously an invisible radiation that was capable of affecting a photographic plate and producing ionization of the air. This property possessed by uranium was later found to be shared by a number of the heavy elements, and the name *radioactivity* was applied to it. Remarkable discoveries in this field were made by the French physicist Pierre Curie (1859–1906) and his wife, Marie Curie

(1867–1934); among them may be mentioned the isolation of the elements polonium and radium from pitchblende.

It was soon found that radioactive substances emit three kinds of rays called α, β, and γ rays that are widely different in character. They can be differentiated by their power of penetrating matter and of producing ionization.

Alpha rays are particles that carry positive charges, and have been identified as the nuclei of helium atoms, each being a stable combination of two protons (i.e., hydrogen nuclei) and two neutrons. Each has a mass 4 times that of the hydrogen atom and a charge equal to that of 2 electrons. Alpha particles have velocities of the order of 2×10^9 cm/sec. As these particles move through air they produce ionization by knocking electrons out of the atoms of its constituent gases, and naturally their speed is reduced by the successive collisions. In traveling distances of, say, 10 cm in air at atmospheric pressure the α particles are slowed down to such an extent that they no longer can produce ionization. Their range is greatly reduced when they are passed through metal foil; for example, a thickness of 0.001 mm of silver is equivalent to over 2 cm of air.

Beta rays are particles that carry negative charges, and are in reality high-speed electrons. They are ejected from radioactive substances with velocities varying from 0.3 to 0.99 that of light. They are much more penetrating than α particles, but measurement of their ranges in air is difficult because of their irregular paths. The mass of the β particle is much less than that of the α particle and consequently, in colliding with electrons, the β particle is deviated from its path with each collision. In contrast, the α particle knocks the electrons out of its way and continues along a fairly straight line. The ratio e/m for β rays is not constant as it is for slow-speed electrons, because the mass of the β ray is higher at speeds comparable with the velocity of light, as explained in the preceding section.

Gamma rays are electromagnetic radiations of the same character as x-rays but have much shorter wavelengths. Crystal diffraction tests, § 429, and measurements of velocities of ejected photoelectrons show that γ rays have wavelengths ranging from about 0.005 to 1 A. The frequencies of gamma radiations are correspondingly high and therefore γ-ray photons have large energy values. The rays can pass through thicknesses of many centimeters of lead.

There is evidence to show that a γ-ray photon can be converted into matter when it impinges upon the nucleus of an atom, producing by this action an electron and a short-lived particle of equal rest mass called a *positron*. As a result the energy of the photon reappears largely as $m_o c^2$ in each particle of the electron-positron pair and the rest in the kinetic energy of the particles.

Illustrative Problem

Determine the minimum frequency of radiation required for the production of an electron-positron pair and the corresponding wavelength.

The rest mass of electron and positron together is $2 \times 9.11 \times 10^{-28}$ gm and therefore the minimum energy required for the conversion is $18.22 \times 10^{-28} \times (3 \times 10^{10})^2 = 1.64 \times 10^{-6}$ ergs. This is equivalent to 1,025,000 electron·volts or 1.025 Mev. The associated radiation frequency is given by Eq. 132 as $f = \dfrac{E}{h} = \dfrac{1.64 \times 10^{-6}}{6.62 \times 10^{-27}} = 2.48 \times 10^{20}$ per sec. The corresponding wavelength is $3 \times 10^{10} \div 2.48 \times 10^{20} = 1.21 \times 10^{-10}$ cm = 0.0121 Å.

446. Ray Tracks and Ray Counters. The investigation of radioactive rays and charged particles is carried on experimentally by observing the tracks made by them and by counting the number received per unit time. The instruments used for these purposes are all-important in experimental work in Modern Physics.

The *cloud chamber*, devised by the British physicist Charles T. R. Wilson, uses the fact that when a region saturated with water vapor is expanded suddenly, the cooling effect causes the formation of a cloud of tiny drops. These drops form upon dust or other particles and persist long enough, before they evaporate again, to allow a visual or photographic examination. In using the chamber for observing charged particles, the air is first rendered dust-free, the particles are then admitted, and immediately thereafter the air is expanded. The charged particle creates a large number of ions along its path, and a track of tiny water droplets appears as a white vapor trail against a dark background.

Tracks in a cloud chamber can be produced by α particles (helium nuclei), β particles (electrons), protons (hydrogen nuclei), and by other charged

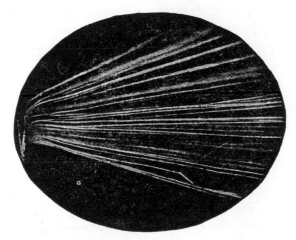

FIG. 445.   Tracks of alpha rays.   (*Courtesy of Professor W. D. Harkins*)

particles. Since electrons are much lighter and usually faster than α particles, a β ray produces fewer ions per unit length of path and its path is easily altered, consequently, the drops forming a β ray track are more widely separated than those forming an α ray track and frequently they do not lie on a straight line.

Fig. 445 illustrates the tracks made by α particles in nitrogen. The forked track shows the rare occurrence when a nitrogen nucleus captured the alpha particle that struck it and emitted a proton (upper branch); the remaining part (lower branch) constitutes the oxygen isotope of atomic mass 17.

The *bubble chamber* is a recently developed device similar to the cloud chamber, but a liquid is used instead of a gas. Actually it contains a liquefied gas such as hydrogen in a superheated condition. When a particle enters, it triggers a boiling process in the liquid and the particle leaves behind it a trail of tiny bubbles. Heavy particles produce wider tracks than light ones. The device has the advantage over the cloud chamber in that the liquid supplies more target atoms, the trail is developed faster, and the whole sequence of atomic interaction and decay occurs in a short space.

The use of magnets with cloud and bubble chambers for bending the paths of particles helps to identify their charges and their energies.

The *ray counter*, devised by the German physicist Hans Geiger, consists of a closed cylindrical chamber of thin metal or of glass with an internal metal coating, and within it a fine wire stretched along its axis, as shown in Fig. 446. The cylinder contains a gas, often air or argon, at reduced pressure. A difference of potential is maintained between the wire as anode and the cylinder as cathode, and its value is adjusted so that the

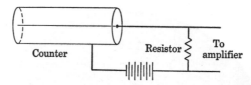

FIG. 446. Geiger counter

counter is on the verge of discharging. When a charged particle enters, it produces a number of ions and the resulting discharge can be made audible with the aid of an amplifier and a loudspeaker. The passage of particles can be counted automatically with suitable electronic equipment and counting mechanisms.

447. Radioactive Transformations. Experimental study of the disintegration of the radioactive elements by the emission of α and β rays has resulted in a definite knowledge of their successive transformations, atomic numbers, atomic masses, and stability. These elements form three groups: the uranium-radium series, the thorium series, and the uranium-actinium series.

The transformations in the first two series are illustrated graphically in Fig. 447 and the successive products are listed in the table on page 687. In the figure each inclined line downward to the left signifies the emission of an α particle; such a change causes the atom to be transformed into another having an atomic mass lower by 4 and an atomic number lower by 2, than the values for the parent atom. Each horizontal line toward the right represents the emission of a β particle; such a change is equivalent to increasing the net positive charge on the nucleus, that is, raising the atomic number by 1, without changing the mass number. The end product in both series is lead of atomic number 82, that from the uranium series having an atomic mass of 206 and that from the thorium series of 208. Another isotope of lead having an atomic mass of 207 comes from the uranium-actinium series (see Prob. 12). Elements that have the same atomic number are isotopes; thus thorium is an isotope of uranium X_1, and thorium X is an isotope of radium.

It is customary to express the stability of a radioactive element by its *half-life*, that is, the time for half of its atoms to be transformed into something else. The half-lives of the substances in the uranium-radium series and in the thorium series are listed in the table.

The number of atoms that disintegrate per unit time is proportional to the number present, hence the equation of decay can be expressed as

$$M = M_o \epsilon^{-\delta t} \tag{315}$$

where M_o is the initial mass, M is the mass at time t, ϵ the base of natural logarithms, and δ the decay constant. The half-life is found herefrom by taking $M = M_o/2$ and solving for t. It is determined experimentally with a ray counter by counting the number of particles emitted per unit time at suitable times.

448. Nuclear Structure. Before natural radioactivity became known, investigations of the atom were concerned with its outer structure, especially with the electrons in the outer shells. Changes in the arrangement of these electrons served to explain the chemical behavior of most substances, and the atomic nucleus was left out of consideration. The spontaneous liberation of particles from the radioactive elements directed attention to the nucleus and led to the realization that vast amounts of energy could be released in changing its makeup. Research on the atomic nucleus has revealed much information about its composition, has resulted in the artificial transmutation of one element into another, and has shown that nuclear reactions can be controlled and utilized.

It has been pointed out that the nuclei of atoms are composed of protons and neutrons, the two particles being nearly of the same mass. The proton has a positive electric charge that is equal in magnitude to the charge on the electron but opposite in sign; the neutron has no charge at all. For any electrically neutral atom, the number of electrons outside

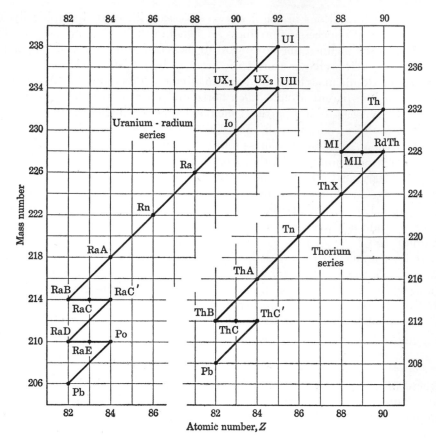

Fig. 447. Radioactive transformations of the substances in the uranium-radium and thorium series

of the nucleus equals that of protons in the nucleus. The nucleus of the lightest element, hydrogen, consists of a single proton; that of the next element, helium, has two protons and two neutrons; the nuclei of many elements that follow these sequentially have equal numbers of protons and neutrons; those of the heavier elements have more neutrons than protons.

The principal characteristic of the nucleus of an atom is its electrical charge, that is, the number of protons which it contains; this is the atomic number (Z). Another characteristic of the nucleus is its mass number (A), that is, the number of nucleons (protons plus neutrons) which it contains. If N is the number of neutrons in the nucleus, then the mass number is

$$A = Z + N$$

The mass number is the same as the relative mass in atomic mass units when rounded off to the nearest integer.

RADIOACTIVE DISINTEGRATION PRODUCTS

Uranium-Radium Series		Thorium Series	
Substance	Half-life	Substance	Half-life
Uranium I........	4.5×10^9 yr	Thorium..........	1.39×10^{10} yr
" X_1......	24.5 days	Mesothorium I....	6.7 yr
" X_2......	68 sec	" II...	6.13 hr
" II.......	2.5×10^5 yr	Radiothorium Rd	
Ionium...........	8.0×10^4 yr	Th.............	1.90 yr
Radium..........	1590 yr	Thorium X.......	3.64 days
" Emana-		" Emana-	
tion (Radon) Rn	3.82 days	tion (Thoron) Tn	54.5 sec
Radium A........	3.05 min	Thorium A........	0.16 sec
" B........	26.8 min	" B........	10.16 hr
" C........	19.7 min	" C........	60.5 min
" C'.......	1.5×10^{-4} sec	" C'.......	3×10^{-7} sec
" D........	22 yr	Lead.............	
" E........	5.0 days		
Polonium........	140 days		
Lead.............			

Every element has isotopes; their nuclei have the same number of protons and therefore the same charge, but they have different numbers of neutrons and therefore have different mass numbers. The chemical properties of the isotopes of an element are of the same kind but there are differences in the rate or extent to which reactions with them take place. In a few cases isotopes have been given distinctive names; for example, the isotope of hydrogen having a mass number of 2 is called *deuterium*, and its nucleus, composed of one proton and one neutron, is called a *deuteron*. The usual method of designating an isotope of an element R is to

MASS OF BASIC PARTICLES

Particle	Relative mass with respect to oxygen as 16 (atomic mass units)	Mass in grams (at rest)
Electron..................	0.000548	9.11×10^{-28}
Proton....................	1.00758	1.673×10^{-24}
Neutron...................	1.00893	1.675×10^{-24}
Deuteron..................	2.01418	3.343×10^{-24}
Alpha particle............	4.00276	6.644×10^{-24}

use the mass number as a superscript following the symbol of the element, and sometimes to use in addition the atomic number as a subscript in front; thus

$$R^4 \quad \text{or} \quad {}_Z R^4$$

The nucleus of ordinary hydrogen is written H^1 or ${}_1H^1$, and that of deuterium H^2 or ${}_1H^2$. In this notation the neutron is expressed as ${}_0n^1$ because its charge is zero and its mass number is one. The masses of the atomic particles, the deuteron, and the α particle are given on the preceding page.

The nucleus of oxygen, which serves as the basis of relative mass in the table ahead, is written ${}_8O^{16}$; this representation means that there are 8 protons out of a total of 16 nucleons; oxygen has the stable isotopes ${}_8O^{17}$ and ${}_8O^{18}$, but together they have an abundance of only $\frac{1}{5}$ of 1% that of ${}_8O^{16}$. If the relative abundance of the isotopes of an element is known it is possible to estimate the atomic weight from the mass numbers. For example, with boron, the abundance of ${}_5B^{11}$ is 81.6% and of ${}_5B^{10}$ is 18.4%; consequently the atomic weight of this element is $11 \times 0.816 + 10 \times 0.184 = 10.82$.

A periodic table of the elements is given in the Appendix, and includes their symbols, atomic numbers, and atomic weights. The elements listed in any one column show similar chemical behavior, while those in any row exhibit properties changing from strongly alkaline at the left to strongly acid at the right.

449. The Mass Spectrograph. The masses of atoms can be measured by passing positively charged ions of the element through electric and magnetic fields to deflect them, very much as in the determination of the charge-mass ratio of electrons, § 258. A number of instruments for such measurements have been devised; they are called *mass spectrographs*.

Fig. 448 shows a diagram of the mass spectrograph developed by Francis W. Aston of Cambridge University. Positive ions (called positive rays) enter from a discharge tube through slits S_1 and S_2 and pass through an

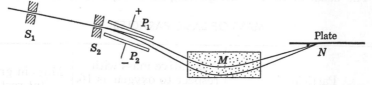

Fig. 448.   Arrangement of the Aston spectrograph

electric field between plates P_1 and P_2 and through a magnetic field M at right angles to the page. The electric field deflects the rays downward and the magnetic field deflects them upward, in both fields the ions of higher speed being deflected less than the slower ones. The field intensities are adjusted so that, whatever speeds the ions have, the rays converge to a common focus N on the photographic plate. Ions having different masses or charges are, of course, deflected differently, and only those having the same ratio of charge to mass arrive at a given point on the plate. When the ions have various masses, several lines are formed, and from their locations on the plate the atomic masses of the isotopes of an element can be determined accurately.

450. Particle Accelerators. Machines for increasing the energy of charged atomic particles to millions of electron·volts are called particle accelerators, and are used for studying the structure of the atomic nucleus and the forces that hold it together. A change in particle speed can be produced in one step as in the Van de Graaff generator, § 202, or in a number of smaller steps as in the cyclotron, § 259. Also, the change in speed can be accomplished along a straight path in the so-called linear accelerator (for example, the 1000-Mev machine at Stanford University), or along a curved path in machines variously named (for example, the 6300-Mev bevatron at the University of California). Increasing the energy of the particles is done at first by increasing their speeds and later, as the speeds approach that of light, by increasing their mass, § 444. Quite a few particle accelerators are now in operation with proton energies ranging to several billion electron·volts; one of these will be described briefly.

The proton synchrotron at the Brookhaven National Laboratory located on Long Island, New York, is illustrated in the frontispiece. It consists

Fig. 449.   Injection equipment of the Brookhaven proton synchrotron

of a giant iron ring 75 ft in diameter having an octagonal section measuring 8 ft across. Embedded near the outer rim of the ring is a flat-sided steel vacuum chamber 32 in. wide through which the protons travel. Fig. 449 shows the equipment for injecting protons from the Van de Graaff generator at the left with energies of 3 Mev into the synchrotron chamber at the right, where they circulate at higher and higher energies until they attain values in excess of 2000 Mev, and are then brought to a target in order to pierce the nuclei of its atoms. When the machine is in operation the personnel is excluded and adjustments are made by remote control.

During a 1-sec period of operation the injected protons make some 3 million trips around the vacuum chamber, and during each one they are accelerated by an electric field which gives them about 800 electron-volts of energy in a manner somewhat as in a cyclotron. This electric field is controlled by a radio-frequency oscillator, and its frequency is changed automatically to keep the orbit of the particles near the center of the vacuum chamber. The magnetic field increases continuously during the acceleration period and the final energy of the particles is determined by the maximum attainable field intensity—14,000 gausses in this synchrotron.

A still larger synchrotron is now under construction at the Brookhaven laboratory to serve both as atom-smasher and atom-maker, and to create particles now observed only infrequently in the cosmic rays from interstellar space. It will be known as an alternating-gradient synchrotron and is designed to develop proton energies up to 25,000 Mev. Such a machine is made possible by a new method of strong magnetic focusing to keep the nuclear particles in a narrow beam while traveling in a tube of relatively small cross-section.

Another procedure for exploring nuclear forces is made possible by a heavy ion linear accelerator (abbreviated Hilac) that was put in operation at the University of California in 1957. In contrast with the machines mentioned ahead for accelerating protons, deuterons, and α particles, this machine was designed to accelerate nuclei of atoms having atomic weights up to 40 in order to study the artificial elements beyond uranium and to create additional ones.

451. Binding Energy. Careful measurements show that the composite mass of a nucleus is less than the sum of the masses of the protons and neutrons of which it is composed. The difference between the mass of a nucleus and its components is a measure of the energy of cohesion of that nucleus, and indicates the energy required to break up the nucleus into those components. This difference for a given nucleus is called its *binding energy*. When divided by the number of particles in the nucleus it serves as a measure of the stability of the nucleus.

The nucleus of helium, consisting of two protons and two neutrons, would represent on a relative basis an aggregate of $2 \times 1.00758 + 2 \times 1.00895 = 4.03306$ for its components, § 448, while the nucleus itself has a total mass of 4.00276; hence the binding energy is $4.00276 - 4.03306 = - 0.03020$ in atomic mass units. In grams, the components of the helium nucleus have a mass of $2 \times 1.673 \times 10^{-24} + 2 \times 1.675 \times 10^{-24} = 6.696 \times 10^{-24}$, and the nucleus itself has a mass of 6.644×10^{-24}; hence the loss of mass is 0.052×10^{-24}. The application of Eq. 314 shows that this loss is equivalent to an energy of $E = 0.052 \times 10^{-24} \times (3.00 \times 10^{10})^2 = 46.8 \times 10^{-6}$ ergs, or $46.8 \times 10^{-6} \div 1.60 \times 10^{-12} = 29$ Mev. This illustration shows that relatively large amounts of energy are needed to separate a nucleus into its components.

The fact that a nucleus exists at all is evidence that its component particles attract one another, despite the large repulsive forces that must exist between its protons at the very small distances within a nucleus, distances of the order of 10^{-12} cm. Probably the strongest force is the attraction between protons and neutrons, as yet not fully understood. In forming a nucleus of particles that have an aggregate mass M when far apart, and a lesser mass M' when together, the total energy of the particles is changed by the amount $(M' - M)c^2$, which is the binding energy. If the binding energy per particle is plotted against the atomic masses of all atomic nuclei it is found that the elements around $A = 65$ have lower values than either the heavier or lighter elements and therefore are more stable. This would indicate that in natural radioactivity the total energy of a nucleus tends toward a minimum.

One of the present theories of the nucleus attributes the large attractive force between the proton and neutron in close proximity to another particle discovered first in the study of cosmic rays, namely the *meson*. It has a mass from 30 to 300 or more times that of an electron, and its charge may be negative or positive, or zero. Just as an electron holds two protons together in the hydrogen molecule ion, so the meson is believed to hold the proton and neutron together in the atomic nucleus.

452. Nuclear Reactions. The natural disintegration of the radioactive elements considered in § 447 is in fact the transmutation of one element into another. Such transmutation can be effected by artificial means, and the process, termed *artificial radioactivity*, is brought about by bombarding the nuclei of atoms with charged particles or neutrons. The bombardment may cause neutrons, protons, deuterons, or alpha particles to be split from the nucleus, or cause the emission of γ rays, or cause the nucleus to be split in two. Artificial radioactivity was first observed in 1934 by the French physicists Frédéric Joliot and his wife, Irene Joliot-Curie (1897–1956), daughter of the Curies who discovered radium.

The forked α-ray track shown in Fig. 445 indicates the transmutation of a nitrogen atom into an oxygen isotope. This nuclear change may be expressed in a manner similar to balanced chemical equations by writing

$$_7N^{14} + _2He^4 = _8O^{17} + _1H^1$$

or by abbreviating it to the form

$$N^{14}(\alpha, \, p)O^{17}$$

where $_7N^{14}$ is the bombarded nucleus, α or $_2He^4$ is the bullet, $_8O^{17}$ is the resulting nucleus, and p or $_1H^1$ is the emitted particle.

The parenthesis in the foregoing abbreviation is used to indicate the type of nuclear reaction; in this case it is an α particle-proton reaction. Other types of reaction are $(n, \, p)$, $(n, \, \alpha)$, $(p, \, n)$, $(p, \, d)$, $(p, \, \alpha)$, $(d, \, n)$, $(d, \, p)$, $(d, \, \alpha)$, $(\alpha, \, n)$, where n represents a neutron, p a proton, and d a deuteron. When a bombarding particle is captured by a nucleus with no particle expulsion, the reaction may be represented by $(n, \, \gamma)$ and $(p, \, \gamma)$, where γ represents the emission of a gamma-ray photon to remove the excess energy.

Energy balance must also be considered in expressing nuclear reactions. For example, in a commonly used method for producing neutrons, a beam of deuterons $(_1H^2)$ from a cyclotron, § 259, impinges upon beryllium $_4Be^9$ and changes it to boron $_5B^{10}$, emitting neutrons in the process. The complete equation for this transmutation of beryllium into boron is

$$_4Be^9 + {_1H^2} = {_5B^{10}} + {_0n^1} + Q$$

where Q, if positive, is the energy emitted and, if negative, is the energy absorbed in the process. The relative mass units of a beryllium nucleus, a deuteron, a boron nucleus, and a neutron are respectively 9.01283, 2.01416, 10.01344 and 1.00895. If these values are substituted in the foregoing transmutation equation, the energy value Q is found to be $+ 0.00460$ mass units, and this is equivalent to 4.3×10^6 electron·volts. Thus, with an incident deuteron beam of 10 Mev, the energy of the neutrons in the forward direction will be 14.3 Mev.

The nuclear reaction in which the nucleus captures the bombarding particle and causes the emission of a photon can be expressed by an equation of the type

$$_0n^1 + {_ZR^A} = {_ZR^{A+1}} + \gamma$$

wherein an element R of atomic number Z and atomic mass A captures a neutron. The resulting nucleus is an isotope having an atomic mass one unit greater than the target nucleus and is frequently radioactive; the photon emitted is a γ ray. An example of such a reaction is $Ag^{107}(n, \, \gamma)Ag^{108}$; the radioactive silver isotope subsequently emits an electron and is transmuted to a stable isotope of cadmium. Such reactions occur only for definite neutron energies, because the frequency of the photon is determined by the transition from one atomic energy level to another.

453. Nuclear Breakdown. The bombardment of heavy nuclei by neutrons renders them unstable and often causes a nucleus which captures a neutron to break apart into two fragments of comparable size instead of emitting a small particle. Such fracture is called *nuclear fission*. This effect was first observed in 1938 by Professors Otto Hahn and Fritz Strassmann of Berlin through the production of barium and krypton from the neutron bombardment of uranium, and the release of energy of the order of 200 Mev per disintegration.

It was later found that the fission of uranium 238, proactinium 231, and thorium 232 requires fast neutrons having energies between 1 and 1.5 Mev, and that only the isotope of uranium of atomic mass 235 undergoes fission with slow neutrons. Fission has also been accomplished in elements of lesser atomic numbers than ninety.

Recently the bombardment of elements near the middle of the periodic table with α particles having energies around 400 Mev resulted in the emis-

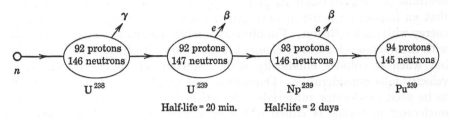

FIG. 450.   Transmutation of uranium into plutonium

sion of many nucleons. This process, called *spallation*, leaves behind a variety of nuclei of lower atomic number and mass number.

The creation of several elements that do not exist in nature has been accomplished by nuclear bombardment of uranium. The process of making neptunium and plutonium is portrayed graphically in Fig. 450. The capture of a slow neutron by $_{92}U^{238}$ forms $_{92}U^{239}$ with the emission of a γ ray; this is followed by β emission to form $_{93}Np^{239}$ and similarly to form $_{94}Pu^{239}$. In recent years the bombardment of nuclei has yielded elements 95-americium (Am), 96-curium (Cm), 97-berkelium (Bk), 98-californium (Cf), 99-einsteinium (E), 100-fermium (Fm), and 101-mendelevium (Mv).

454. Chain Reaction and the Pile. The bombardment of the nucleus of a heavy element by a neutron results not only in the fission of that nucleus but also in the production of several other neutrons. These in turn may split apart other nuclei with similar results, and the process may maintain itself as a *chain reaction*. Should all neutrons be effective in this process, fission would occur at an ever-increasing rate and all of the fissionable material would be disintegrated in a short time; the accompanying release of energy would produce an explosion of catastrophic power. The disintegration in this way of a uranium isotope was utilized in the so-called atomic bomb. A leader in this development was the Italian physicist Enrico Fermi (1901–1954) who came to America and conducted research first at Columbia University and later at the University of Chicago.

The chain reaction process was developed through a governmental project during the war, and a number of complications had to be overcome in a short time. Briefly, these complications were (1) the neutrons given off through fission were fast neutrons in that they had kinetic energies of several million electron·volts, (2) such fast neutrons are not readily caught by uranium nuclei and many of them escape from the material, (3) the uranium 238 nuclei often absorbed such neutrons without producing fission, (4) the uranium isotope 235 which is easily fissionable by slow neutrons forms only $\frac{1}{140}$ part of natural uranium, and (5) it was necessary to develop *moderators* on a large scale for reducing the energy of fast neutrons until they were immune from capture by the uranium 238 nuclei.

The material of the moderator should itself absorb relatively few of the neutrons passing through it, and it should have a low atomic weight so that an impacting neutron may give up a good proportion of its kinetic energy with each collision. For obviously, when a neutron collides elastically with the nucleus of a heavy element it rebounds with little velocity change, but when it collides elastically with a nucleus of comparable mass its velocity falls considerably. Deuterium and graphite (carbon) were found to be good moderator materials. A lattice arrangement of fissionable and moderator materials is called a *pile* or a *nuclear reactor*. Controls were provided by passageways through the pile in which rods, of material (like cadmium) that absorb neutrons strongly, can be inserted or withdrawn by remote control.

Thus, a uranium pile is a controllable machine for fundamental research on nuclei, while an atomic bomb is made of essentially pure uranium 235 and so constructed as to release energy at a colossal rate. The artificially produced element plutonium is another fissionable material which can be used for bombs, and the production of this material was the main purpose of the piles used in the government project. The pile now finds its place as a tool in the production of radioactive isotopes for medical therapy and for tracers in biological investigations, for the study of the chemical and physical aspects of atomic energy, and for the development of sources of power.

455. Thermonuclear Power. Soon after the development of the atomic bomb, experiments were devised to reverse the processes of atomic fission and spallation of heavy elements and to bring the nuclei of light elements together by *atomic fusion*. Such a process is known to release huge quantities of nuclear energy, but it requires enormous temperatures. This is believed to be the process that takes place in the interior of the sun to account for its seemingly inexhaustible supply of radiant energy. There, at temperatures of the order of 20 million ° C, the nuclei of hydrogen undoubtedly undergo fusion and form helium, four of H to each He, and the difference in mass is converted into energy.

The thermonuclear experiments led to the production of the hydrogen bomb. In this development the isotopes of hydrogen (deuterium of atomic

weight 2 and tritium of atomic weight 3) are fused at even higher temperatures, the action being triggered by the explosion of an atomic bomb containing uranium 235 or plutonium 239. Such a nuclear reaction is indicated
by the equation

$$_1H^2 + {}_1H^3 = {}_2He^4 + {}_0n^1 + 17.6 \text{ Mev}$$

and signifies the liberation of 17.6 Mev of energy. Attention is now being
directed toward harnessing the vast energy released by a hydrogen bomb
with the thought of ultimately achieving a controllable source of industrial
power from thermonuclear reactions.

PROBLEMS

1. What is the least radius of the electronic orbit in hydrogen? *Hint.*
Use Coulomb's Law to replace the statcoulomb by equivalent units.
2. Determine the wavelength of the $K\beta$ and $L\beta$ lines of the x-ray spectrum
of gold. The atomic number of this element is 79; the value of the constant
σ is 0.5 for the K series and 6.0 for the L series.
3. Light from calcium having a wavelength of 3934 A is incident upon a
sodium surface having a work function of 2.10 electron·volts. Find the
maximum velocity with which electrons leave this surface when so illuminated.
4. A beam of x-rays having a wavelength of 1.54×10^{-8} cm is scattered
by the free electrons in a graphite block. Assume that one of the x-ray
photons is scattered through an angle of 180° and find how much energy
the scattering electron receives.
5. Determine the change in wavelength of the scattered radiation of
x-rays by electrons when observed at angles of 45°, 90°, and 135° from the
incident beam.
6. What is the energy and de Broglie wavelength of helium atoms having
a velocity of 2×10^5 cm/sec? Refer to § 448 for the mass values.
7. What would be the mass of an electron relative to its rest mass if it
were projected with a speed 98% that of light?
8. Determine the percentage decrease in mass of an α particle from radium
that has its velocity decreased from 4.8×10^9 cm/sec to zero.
9. How much energy is needed to bring an electron from rest to a speed
one-third that of light in free space? Express the result in both ergs and
electron·volts.
10. The average daily energy supplied by the Consolidated Edison
Company in New York City during the year 1956 was 41.0 million kilo-
watt·hours. If all this energy could be obtained by the conversion of matter,
how much mass would have to be converted?
11. Calculate the decay constant for ionium that has the half-life listed
in the table on page 687.
12. The substances of the uranium-actinium radioactive series are believed to have the following atomic masses and atomic numbers in the order
in which the disintegration occurs: Actinouranium 235, 92; Uranium Y 231,
90; Proactinium 231, 91; Actinium (Ac) 227, 89; Radioactinium (RdAc)
227, 90; Actinium X 223, 88; Actinium Emanation (Actinon, An) 219, 86;
Actinium A 215, 84; Actinium B 211, 82; Actinium C 211, 83; Actinium C'
211, 84; Lead 207, 82. Make a chart of these transformations as in Fig.

447, and indicate which changes involve the emission of α rays and which of β rays.

13. One milligram of pure actinium contains 2.66×10^{18} atoms and would emit 4.34×10^9 α particles per second. From these facts its decay constant is found to be $4.34 \times 10^9 \div 2.66 \times 10^{18} = 1.63 \times 10^{-9}$ per sec. Determine the half-life of actinium in years.

14. The relative abundance of the isotopes of magnesium are $_{12}Mg^{24}$ 78.6%, $_{12}Mg^{25}$ 10.1%, and $_{12}Mg^{26}$ 11.3%. Estimate the atomic weight of magnesium as found in nature.

15. The isotopes of neon have the relative abundance Ne^{20} 90.5%, Ne^{21} 0.3%, and Ne^{22} 9.2% in nature. Estimate the atomic weight of neon.

16. How much energy in electron·volts would have to be supplied to a helium atom in order to disintegrate it into two hydrogen atoms and two neutrons? Assume the atomic masses of helium, hydrogen, and a neutron to be 4.00386, 1.00813, and 1.00895 atomic mass units respectively.

17. The nuclear reaction B^{10} (n, α) Li^7 indicates the transmutation of boron into lithium, and represents a loss of 0.0034 atomic mass unit. Write the full equation for this reaction in million electron·volts on the basis that 1 mass unit is equivalent to 931 Mev.

18. Fission in uranium 238 is produced by neutrons that have an energy value of 1.5 electron·volts. What is the speed of such neutrons?

19. Estimate the mass of a tritium nucleus from the data tabulated in § 448 and the fusion equation given in § 455. Express the result in atomic mass units.

APPENDIX

TABLE I. CONVERSION FACTORS

Angles

1 radian = 57.30 degrees (°)

Length

1 mile (mi) = 1760 yards (yd)
= 5280 feet (ft)
= 1.609 kilometers (km)
1 foot = 12.00 inches (in.)
= 30.48 centimeters (cm)
1 inch = 2.540 cm
1 kilometer = 1000 meters (m)
1 meter = 100 cm
= 1000 millimeters (mm)
1 millimeter = 1000 microns (μ)
1 Angstrom unit = 10^{-8} cm
= 10^{-4} μ

Area

1 square mile = 640 acres
1 acre = 43,560 ft^2
1 square foot = 144.0 in.^{2}
= 929.0 cm^2
1 square inch = 6.452 cm^2
1 square meter = 10^4 cm^2

Volume

1 cubic foot = 1728 in.^{3}
= 0.0283 m^3
1 cubic inch = 16.39 cm^3
1 liter = 1000 cm^3
= 61.0 in.^{3}
1 gallon = 231 in.^{3}
= 3.785 liters

Mass

1 slug = 32.17 pounds (lb)
1 pound = 16.00 ounces (oz)
= 453.6 grams (gm)
1 kilogram (kg) = 1000 gm
= 2.205 lb

Force

1 pound (lb) = 445,000 dynes
= 32 poundals
1 newton = 10^5 dynes

Energy

1 foot·pound = 1.356 joules
1 joule = 1 newton·meter
= 10^7 ergs
= 0.738 ft·lb
1 erg = 1 dyne·cm
1 calorie (cal) = 4.186 joules
1 British thermal unit (Btu)
= 252.0 cal
= 778 ft·lb
1 electron·volt = 1.602×10^{-19} joule
1 kilowatt·hr (kw·hr) = 3.60×10^6 joules

Power

1 horsepower (hp)
= 33,000 ft·lb/min
= 550 ft·lb/sec
= 746 watts
1 kilowatt (kw) = 1000 watts
= 1.341 hp
1 watt = 1 volt·ampere

TABLE II. USEFUL FACTS

Pressure of standard atmosphere = 76.00 cm Hg
$$= 14.70 \text{ lb/in.}^2$$
$$= 1.013 \times 10^6 \text{ dynes/cm}^2$$

Density of water = 62.4 lb/ft^3
$$= 0.0361 \text{ lb/in.}^3$$
$$= 1.000 \text{ gm/cm}^3$$

Data about the earth: Mass = 6.596×10^{21} tons
$$= 5.983 \times 10^{24} \text{ kg}$$
Radius = 3959 mi
$$= 6371 \text{ km}$$
Distance from sun (average) = 9.29×10^7 mi
$$= 1.495 \times 10^8 \text{ km}$$
Distance from moon (average) = 2.39×10^5 mi
$$= 3.84 \times 10^5 \text{ km}$$
Gravitational acceleration at surface
$$= 980.665 \text{ cm/sec}^2$$
$$= 32.173 \text{ ft/sec}^2$$

TABLE III. PHYSICAL CONSTANTS

(to four significant figures)

Charge of electron = 1.602×10^{-19} coulomb
$$= 4.802 \times 10^{-10} \text{ statcoulomb}$$
Mass of electron (at rest) = 9.107×10^{-28} gm = 9.107×10^{-31} kg
Mass of proton (at rest) = 1.672×10^{-24} gm = 1.672×10^{-27} kg
Mass of hydrogen atom = 1.673×10^{-24} gm = 1.673×10^{-27} kg
Avogadro's Number = 6.024×10^{23}
Planck's Constant = 6.624×10^{-34} joule·sec
Speed of light (in vacuum) = 2.998×10^5 km/sec
Universal gas constant per mole = 8.314 joules/°K

TABLE IV. MATHEMATICAL FACTS

$$\pi = 3.1416 \qquad \frac{1}{\pi} = 0.3183 \qquad \pi^2 = 9.870$$

Quadratic equation $ax^2 + bx + c = 0$; solution $x = \dfrac{-b \pm \sqrt{b^2 - 4ac}}{2a}$

$\sin^2 x + \cos^2 x = 1$

$\cos^2 x - \sin^2 x = \cos 2x$

$c^2 = a^2 + b^2 - 2ab \cos C$

$\dfrac{a}{\sin A} = \dfrac{b}{\sin B} = \dfrac{c}{\sin C}$

$d(C) = 0$

$d(x) = dx$

$d(x)^n = nx^{n-1}\, dx$

$d(\sin x) = \cos x\, dx$

$d(\cos x) = -\sin x\, dx$

$\sin 2x = 2 \sin x \cos x$

$2 \cos^2 x = 1 + \cos 2x$

$\displaystyle \int dx = x + C$

$\displaystyle \int x^n\, dx = \frac{x^{n+1}}{n+1} + C \text{ (except for } n = -1)$

$\displaystyle \int \frac{dx}{x} = \log_\epsilon x = 2.303 \log_{10} x$

$\displaystyle \int \sin x\, dx = -\cos x + C$

$\displaystyle \int \sin^2 x\, dx = \frac{x}{2} - \frac{1}{4} \sin 2x + C$

TABLE V. GREEK ALPHABET

A	α	Alpha	N	ν	Nu
B	β	Beta	Ξ	ξ	Xi
Γ	γ	Gamma	O	o	Omicron
Δ	δ	Delta	Π	π	Pi
E	ϵ	Epsilon	P	ρ	Rho
Z	ζ	Zeta	Σ	σ	Sigma
H	η	Eta	T	τ	Tau
Θ	θ	Theta	Υ	υ	Upsilon
I	ι	Iota	Φ	ϕ	Phi
K	κ	Kappa	X	χ	Chi
Λ	λ	Lambda	Ψ	ψ	Psi
M	μ	Mu	Ω	ω	Omega

TABLE VI. NATURAL TRIGONOMETRIC FUNCTIONS

Fifth-degree Intervals				Half-degree Intervals				Whole Degree Intervals			
Angle	Sine	Cosine	Tangent	Angle	Sine	Cosine	Tangent	Angle	Sine	Cosine	Tangent
0.0 °	.0000	1.000	.0000	12.0	.208	.978	.213	41	.656	.755	.869
.2	.0035	1.000	.0035	.5	.216	.976	.222	42	.669	.743	.900
.4	.0070	1.000	.0070	13.0	.225	.974	.231	43	.682	.731	.933
.6	.0105	1.000	.0105	.5	.233	.972	.240	44	.695	.719	.966
.8	.0140	1.000	.0140	14.0	.242	.970	.249	45	.707	.707	1.000
1.0	.0175	1.000	.0175	.5	.250	.968	.259	46	.719	.695	1.036
.2	.0209	1.000	.0209	15.0	.259	.966	.268	47	.731	.682	1.072
.4	.0244	1.000	.0244	.5	.267	.964	.277	48.	.743	.669	1.111
.6	.0279	1.000	.0279	16.0	.276	.961	.287	49	.755	.656	1.150
.8	.0314	1.000	.0314	.5	.284	.959	.296	50	.766	.643	1.192
2.0	.0349	.999	.0349	17.0	.292	.956	.306	51	.777	.629	1.235
.2	.0384	.999	.0384	.5	.301	.954	.315	52	.788	.616	1.280
.4	.0419	.999	.0419	18.0	.309	.951	.325	53	.799	.602	1.327
.6	.0454	.999	.0454	.5	.317	.948	.335	54	.809	.588	1.376
.8	.0489	.999	.0489	19.0	.326	.946	.344	55	.819	.574	1.428
3.0	.0523	.999	.0524	.5	.334	.943	.354	56	.829	.559	1.483
.2	.0558	.998	.0559	20.0	.342	.940	.364	57	.839	.545	1.540
.4	.0593	.998	.0594	.5	.350	.937	.374	58	.848	.530	1.600
.6	.0628	.998	.0629	21.0	.358	.934	.384	59	.857	.515	1.664
.8	.0663	.998	.0664	.5	.367	.930	.394	60	.866	.500	1.732
4.0	.0698	.998	.0699	22.0	.375	.927	.404	61	.875	.485	1.804
.2	.0732	.997	.0734	.5	.383	.924	.414	62	.883	.469	1.881
.4	.0767	.997	.0770	23.0	.391	.921	.424	63	.891	.454	1.963
.6	.0802	.997	.0805	.5	.399	.917	.435	64	.899	.438	2.050
.8	.0837	.996	.0840	24.0	.407	.914	.445	65	.906	.423	2.145
5.0	.0872	.996	.0875	.5	.415	.910	.456	66	.914	.407	2.246
.2	.0906	.996	.0910	25.0	.423	.906	.466	67	.921	.391	2.356
.4	.0941	.996	.0945	.5	.431	.903	.477	68	.927	.375	2.475
.6	.0976	.995	.0981	26.0	.438	.899	.488	69	.934	.358	2.605
.8	.1011	.995	.1016	.5	.446	.895	.499	70	.940	.342	2.748
6.0	.1045	.995	.1051	27.0	.454	.891	.510	71	.946	.326	2.90
.2	.1080	.994	.1086	.5	.462	.887	.521	72	.951	.309	3.08
.4	.1115	.994	.1122	28.0	.469	.883	.532	73	.956	.292	3.27
.6	.1149	.993	.1157	.5	.477	.879	.543	74	.961	.276	3.49
.8	.1184	.993	.1192	29.0	.485	.875	.554	75	.966	.259	3.73
7.0	.1219	.993	.1228	.5	.492	.870	.566	76	.970	.2419	4.01
.2	.1253	.992	.1263	30.0	.500	.866	.577	77	.974	.2250	4.33
.4	.1288	.992	.1299	.5	.508	.862	.589	78	.978	.2079	4.70
.6	.1323	.991	.1334	31.0	.515	.857	.601	79	.982	.1908	5.14
.8	.1357	.991	.1370	.5	.523	.853	.613	80	.985	.1737	5.67
8.0	.1392	.990	.1405	32.0	.530	.848	.625	81	.988	.1564	6.31
.2	.1426	.990	.1441	.5	.537	.843	.637	82	.990	.1392	7.12
.4	.1461	.989	.1477	33.0	.545	.839	.649	83	.993	.1219	8.14
.6	.1495	.989	.1512	.5	.552	.834	.662	84	.995	.1045	9.51
.8	.1530	.988	.1548	34.0	.559	.829	.675	85	.996	.0872	11.43
9.0	.1564	.988	.1584	.5	.566	.824	.687	86	.998	.0698	14.30
.2	.1599	.987	.1620	35.0	.574	.819	.700	87	.999	.0523	19.08
.4	.1633	.987	.1656	.5	.581	.814	.713	88	.999	.0349	28.64
.6	.1668	.986	.1691	36.0	.588	.809	.727	89	1.000	.0175	57.3
.8	.1702	.985	.1727	.5	.595	.804	.740	90	1.000	.0000	∞
10.0	.1737	.985	.1763	37.0	.602	.799	.754				
.2	.1771	.984	.1799	.5	.609	.793	.767				
.4	.1805	.984	.1835	38.0	.616	.788	.781				
.6	.1840	.983	.1871	.5	.623	.783	.795				
.8	.1874	.982	.1908	39.0	.629	.777	.810				
11.0	.1908	.982	.1944	.5	.636	.772	.824				
.2	.1942	.981	.1980	40.0	.643	.766	.839				
.4	.1977	.980	.2016	.5	.649	.760	.854				
.6	.2011	.980	.2053								
.8	.2045	.979	.2089								

Functions of Larger Angles

$$\sin (90 + \theta) = \cos \theta$$
$$\cos (90 + \theta) = - \sin \theta$$
$$\tan (90 + \theta) = - \cot \theta$$
$$\sin (180 + \theta) = - \sin \theta$$
$$\cos (180 + \theta) = - \cos \theta$$
$$\tan (180 + \theta) = \tan \theta$$
$$\sin (270 + \theta) = - \cos \theta$$
$$\cos (270 + \theta) = \sin \theta$$
$$\tan (270 + \theta) = - \cot \theta$$

For closer intervals in cosines and tangents from here on use co-functions of the complementary angles.

TABLE VII.   LOGARITHMS TO BASE 10

N	0	2	4	6	8	N	0	2	4	6	8
1.0	.0000	.0086	.0170	.0253	.0334	6.0	.778	.780	.781	.782	.784
1.1	.0414	.0492	.0569	.0645	.0719	6.1	.785	.787	.788	.790	.791
1.2	.0792	.0864	.0934	.1004	.1072	6.2	.792	.794	.795	.797	.798
1.3	.1139	.1206	.1271	.1335	.1399	6.3	.799	.801	.802	.803	.805
1.4	.1461	.1523	.1584	.1644	.1703	6.4	.806	.808	.809	.810	.812
1.5	.1761	.1818	.1875	.1931	.1987	6.5	.813	.814	.816	.817	.818
1.6	.2041	.2095	.2148	.2201	.2253	6.6	.820	.821	.822	.823	.825
1.7	.2304	.2355	.2406	.2455	.2504	6.7	.826	.827	.829	.830	.831
1.8	.2553	.2601	.2648	.2695	.2742	6.8	.833	.834	.835	.836	.838
1.9	.2788	.2833	.2878	.2923	.2967	6.9	.839	.840	.841	.843	.844
2.0	.301	.305	.310	.314	.318	7.0	.845	.846	.848	.849	.850
2.1	.322	.326	.330	.334	.338	7.1	.851	.852	.854	.855	.856
2.2	.342	.346	.350	.354	.358	7.2	.857	.859	.860	.861	.862
2.3	.362	.365	.369	.373	.377	7.3	.863	.865	.866	.867	.868
2.4	.380	.384	.387	.391	.394	7.4	.869	.870	.872	.873	.874
2.5	.398	.401	.405	.408	.412	7.5	.875	.876	.877	.879	.880
2.6	.415	.418	.422	.425	.428	7.6	.881	.882	.883	.884	.885
2.7	.431	.435	.438	.441	.444	7.7	.886	.888	.889	.890	.891
2.8	.447	.450	.453	.456	.459	7.8	.892	.893	.894	.895	.897
2.9	.462	.465	.468	.471	.474	7.9	.898	.899	.900	.901	.902
3.0	.477	.480	.483	.486	.489	8.0	.903	.904	.905	.906	.907
3.1	.491	.494	.497	.500	.502	8.1	.908	.910	.911	.912	.913
3.2	.505	.508	.511	.513	.516	8.2	.914	.915	.916	.917	.918
3.3	.519	.521	.524	.526	.529	8.3	.919	.920	.921	.922	.923
3.4	.531	.534	.537	.539	.542	8.4	.924	.925	.926	.927	.928
3.5	.544	.547	.549	.551	.554	8.5	.929	.930	.931	.932	.933
3.6	.556	.559	.561	.563	.566	8.6	.935	.936	.937	.938	.939
3.7	.568	.571	.573	.575	.577	8.7	.940	.941	.942	.943	.943
3.8	.580	.582	.584	.587	.589	8.8	.944	.945	.946	.947	.948
3.9	.591	.593	.596	.598	.600	8.9	.949	.950	.951	.952	.953
4.0	.602	.604	.606	.609	.611	9.0	.954	.955	.956	.957	.958
4.1	.613	.615	.617	.619	.621	9.1	.959	.960	.961	.962	.963
4.2	.623	.625	.627	.629	.631	9.2	.964	.965	.966	.967	.968
4.3	.633	.635	.637	.639	.641	9.3	.968	.969	.970	.971	.972
4.4	.643	.645	.647	.649	.651	9.4	.973	.974	.975	.976	.977
4.5	.653	.655	.657	.659	.661	9.5	.978	.979	.980	.980	.981
4.6	.663	.665	.667	.668	.670	9.6	.982	.983	.984	.985	.986
4.7	.672	.674	.676	.678	.679	9.7	.987	.988	.989	.989	.990
4.8	.681	.683	.685	.687	.688	9.8	.991	.992	.993	.994	.995
4.9	.690	.692	.694	.695	.697	9.9	.996	.997	.997	.998	.999
5.0	.699	.701	.702	.704	.706						
5.1	.708	.709	.711	.713	.714						
5.2	.716	.718	.719	.721	.723						
5.3	.724	.726	.728	.729	.731						
5.4	.732	.734	.736	.737	.739						
5.5	.740	.742	.744	.745	.747						
5.6	.748	.750	.751	.753	.754						
5.7	.756	.757	.759	.760	.762						
5.8	.763	.765	.766	.768	.769						
5.9	.771	.772	.774	.775	.777						

Notes on Logarithms

$\log 403 = 2.605$

$\log 40.3 = 1.605$

$\log 4.03 = 0.605$

$\log 0.403 = 9.605 - 10$

$\log 0.0403 = 8.605 - 10$

$\epsilon = 2.7183; \log_\epsilon 10 = 2.303$

$\log_\epsilon N = 2.303 \log_{10} N$

$\log(N^x) = x \log N$

TABLE VIII. RELATION BETWEEN MKS AND CGS UNITS

Entity	Symbol	Mks Rationalized or Unrationalized (Rationalized)	Mks Rationalized or Unrationalized (Unrationalized)	Practical	Cgs Electrostatic	Cgs Electromagnetic	Conversion Factors
Length	l	meter		......	cm		1 meter = 100 cm
Mass	m	kg		......	gm		1 kg = 1000 gm
Time	t	sec		......	sec		
Force	F	newton		......	dyne		1 newton = 10^5 dynes
Work, energy	W, E	joule		joule	erg		1 joule = 10^7 ergs
Power	P	watt		watt	$\dfrac{erg}{sec}$		1 watt = $10^7 \dfrac{ergs}{sec}$
Charge	Q	coulomb		coulomb	statcoulomb	abcoulomb	1 coulomb = 3×10^9 statcoulomb = 0.1 abcoulomb
Current	I	ampere		ampere	statamp	abampere	1 ampere = 3×10^9 statamp = 0.1 abamp
Emf, potential, potential difference	E, V	volt		volt	statvolt	abvolt	1 volt = $\dfrac{1}{300}$ statvolt = 10^8 abvolts
Resistance	R	ohm		ohm	statohm	abohm	1 ohm = $\dfrac{1}{9 \times 10^{11}}$ statohm = 10^9 abohms
Capacitance	C	farad		farad	statfarad	abfarad	1 farad = 9×10^{11} statfarad = $\dfrac{1}{10^9}$ abfarad
Inductance	L	henry		henry	stathenry	abhenry	1 henry = $\dfrac{1}{9 \times 10^{11}}$ stathenry = 10^9 abhenrys
Electric field intensity	$\mathcal{E}$	$\dfrac{volt}{meter}$ or $\dfrac{newton}{coulomb}$		......	$\dfrac{dyne}{statcoulomb}$	....	1 $\dfrac{volt}{meter}$ = $\dfrac{1}{3 \times 10^4} \dfrac{dyne}{statcoulomb}$
Magnetic flux	Φ	weber		......	....	maxwell	1 weber = 10^8 maxwells
Magnetic flux density	B	$\dfrac{weber}{meter^2}$		......	....	gauss	1 $\dfrac{weber}{meter^2}$ = 10^4 gausses
Magnetomotive force	$\mathfrak{F}$	ampere·turn	$\dfrac{1}{4\pi}$ ampere·turn	......	....	gilbert	1 rationalized mks unit = 4π unrationalized mks units = $\dfrac{4\pi}{10}$ gilberts
Reluctance	$\mathfrak{R}$	$\dfrac{ampere·turn}{weber}$	$\dfrac{1}{4\pi} \dfrac{ampere·turn}{weber}$	......	....	$\dfrac{gilbert}{maxwell}$	1 rationalized mks unit = 4π unrationalized mks units = $\dfrac{4\pi}{10^9} \dfrac{gilbert}{maxwell}$
Magnetic field intensity	H	$\dfrac{ampere·turn}{meter}$	$\dfrac{1}{4\pi} \dfrac{ampere·turn}{meter}$	......	....	oersted	1 rationalized mks unit = 4π unrationalized mks units = $\dfrac{4\pi}{1000}$ oersted

TABLE IX. PERIODIC TABLE OF THE ELEMENTS

PERIOD	GROUP 0	GROUP I	GROUP II	GROUP III	GROUP IV	GROUP V	GROUP VI	GROUP VII	GROUP VIII
I		1 HYDROGEN H 1.0080							
II	2 HELIUM He 4.003	3 LITHIUM Li 6.940	4 BERYLLIUM Be 9.013	5 BORON B 10.82	6 CARBON C 12.010	7 NITROGEN N 14.008	8 OXYGEN O 16.000	9 FLUORINE F 19.00	
III	10 NEON Ne 20.183	11 SODIUM Na 22.997	12 MAGNESIUM Mg 24.32	13 ALUMINUM Al 26.98	14 SILICON Si 28.09	15 PHOSPHORUS P 30.975	16 SULPHUR S 32.066	17 CHLORINE Cl 35.457	
IV	18 ARGON A 39.944	19 POTASSIUM K 39.100	20 CALCIUM Ca 40.08	21 SCANDIUM Sc 44.96	22 TITANIUM Ti 47.90	23 VANADIUM V 50.95	24 CHROMIUM Cr 52.01	25 MANGANESE Mn 54.93	26 IRON Fe 55.85 27 COBALT Co 58.94 28 NICKEL Ni 58.69
IV		29 COPPER Cu 63.54	30 ZINC Zn 65.38	31 GALLIUM Ga 69.72	32 GERMANIUM Ge 72.60	33 ARSENIC As 74.91	34 SELENIUM Se 78.96	35 BROMINE Br 79.916	
V	36 KRYPTON Kr 83.80	37 RUBIDIUM Rb 85.48	38 STRONTIUM Sr 87.63	39 YTTRIUM Yt 88.92	40 ZIRCONIUM Zr 91.22	41 NIOBIUM* Nb 92.91	42 MOLYBDENUM Mo 95.95	43 TECHNETIUM Tc [99]	44 RUTHENIUM Ru 101.7 45 RHODIUM Rh 102.91 46 PALLADIUM Pd 106.7
V		47 SILVER Ag 107.880	48 CADMIUM Cd 112.41	49 INDIUM In 114.76	50 TIN Sn 118.70	51 ANTIMONY Sb 121.76	52 TELLURIUM Te 127.61	53 IODINE I 126.91	
VI	54 XENON Xe 131.3	55 CESIUM Cs 132.91	56 BARIUM Ba 137.36	57–71 (LANTHANIDE RARE EARTHS)	72 HAFNIUM Hf 178.6	73 TANTALUM Ta 180.88	74 TUNGSTEN W 183.92	75 RHENIUM Re 186.31	76 OSMIUM Os 190.2 77 IRIDIUM Ir 193.1 78 PLATINUM Pt 195.23
VI		79 GOLD Au 197.2	80 MERCURY Hg 200.61	81 THALLIUM Tl 204.39	82 LEAD Pb 207.21	83 BISMUTH Bi 209.00	84 POLONIUM Po 210	85 ASTATINE At [210]	
VII	86 RADON Rn 222	87 FRANCIUM Fr [223]	88 RADIUM Ra 226.05	89 ACTINIUM Ac 227	90 THORIUM Th 232.12	91 PROTACTINIUM Pa 231	92 URANIUM U 238.07	TRANS-URANIUM ELEMENTS	

RARE EARTHS

	GROUP I	GROUP II	GROUP III	GROUP IV	GROUP V	GROUP VI	GROUP VII			
VI LANTHANIDE SERIES	LANTHANUM La 57 138.92	58 CERIUM Ce 140.13	59 PRASEODYMIUM Pr 140.92	60 NEODYMIUM Nd 144.27	61 PROMETHIUM Pm [145]	62 SAMARIUM Sa 150.43	63 EUROPIUM Eu 152.0	64 GADOLINIUM Gd 156.9		
VI		65 TERBIUM Tb 159.2	66 DYSPROSIUM Dy 162.46	67 HOLMIUM Ho 164.94	68 ERBIUM Er 167.2	69 THULIUM Tm 169.4	70 YTTERBIUM Yb 173.04	71 LUTETIUM Lu 174.99		
VII ACTINIDE SERIES	ACTINIUM Ac 89 227	90 THORIUM Th 232.12	91 PROTACTINIUM Pa 231	92 URANIUM U 238.07	93 NEPTUNIUM Np [237]	94 PLUTONIUM Pu [242]	95 AMERICIUM Am [243]	96 CURIUM Cm [243]		
VII					97 BERKELIUM Bk [245]	98 CALIFORNIUM Cf [244]				

Above the name of each element is its atomic number; below, its chemical symbol and atomic weight.
A figure within brackets indicates the mass of the most stable known isotope.
Recent additions: 99 E Einsteinium, 100 Fm Fermium, 101 Mv Mendelevium

* Also known as Columbium (41).

Courtesy of General Electric Company.

ANSWERS TO ODD-NUMBERED PROBLEMS

MECHANICS

Chapter 1—1. $_6C^{12}$; $_{29}Cu^{63}$. **3.** 145 and 333 respectively. **5.** 8848. **7.** 3960. **9.** 48.6. **11.** 4.01. **13.** 1000.027; 0.0027%. **15.** 31,300. **17.** 550 and 7830 respectively. **19.** (a) 1.567×10^{-7} cm; (b) 3.10×10^{-15} cm². **21.** 154.7.

Chapter 2—1. (a) 0.060%; (b) 1.150%. **3.** Rope a 53.1°, rope b 36.9°. **5.** 3280 ft. **7.** 13.00 mi, 22.6° north of east. **9.** 26.5 cm toward right, 40.8° down from horizontal. **11.** 3.39 mi, 36.2° south of east. **13.** (a) 2.00 ft and 3.46 ft respectively; (b) 10.00 ft and 17.32 ft respectively. **15.** 151.3 ft, 37.1° west of north. **17.** 7.07 cm.

Chapter 3—1. 17.60 and 22.0 respectively. **3.** (a) 27.8; (b) 60°. **5.** 4.11 hr. **7.** 50.0 mi/hr, 36.9° south of east. **9.** (a) 11.3° north of west; (b) 1.531 hr. **11.** (a) 45 hr 19 min; (b) 537 mi/hr; (c) 3. **13.** (a) 22.19; (b) 22.16. **15.** (a) 377 cm/sec, horizontally toward right; (b) 533 cm/sec toward right, 45° down from horizontal. **17.** (a) 35.0 mi/hr; (b) 770 ft; both in direction of motion. **19.** -1.085 m/sec². **21.** 1.433 sec and 1400 cm/sec downward respectively. **23.** (a) Upward at 60.0 ft/sec; (b) 100.0 ft/sec downward. **25.** 18.87 ft/sec toward right, 58.0° down from horizontal. **27.** (a) 0.200 cm; (b) 1.02×10^9 cm/sec, 11.3° down from horizontal. **29.** 1.161 ft. **31.** 25.0 ft.

Chapter 4—1. 40.0 cm/sec². **3.** 2.50 newtons. **5.** 600 cm/sec. **7.** 96,000 dynes. **9.** (a) 2.00×10^{-9} sec; (b) 1.098 cm. **11.** 32.5 lb. **13.** 16.05 oz. **15.** 4470 lb. **17.** 203 lb. **19.** $s = \frac{1}{2}gt^2 \sin\theta$. **21.** 1.370 sec. **23.** 46.7 cm/sec²; 46,700 dynes. **25.** 2.91 ft/sec²

Chapter 5—1. 0.977 slug·ft/sec. **3.** 60.0 cm/sec. **5.** 55,900 cm/sec. **7.** 26,100 mi/sec. **9.** (a) 16.00 ft/sec; (b) diagram; (c) 0.250. **11.** 4.15×10^6 dynes. **13.** (a) 529,000 dynes; (b) 611,000 dynes. **15.** Torque due to: W 200 lb·ft counterclockwise, R zero, f zero, P 200 lb·ft clockwise. **17.** P 400 lb, F 1520 lb, R 1680 lb. **19.** A 417 lb, B 183 lb. **21.** (a) 1016 m/sec; (b) 27.6. **23.** 34.2°. **25.** 7.25 lb.

Chapter 6—1. (a) 18,000; (b) 1200; (c) 125.7. **3.** 2.39 ft. **5.** 0.500 radian/sec. **7.** (a) 1257; (b) 267. **9.** -3.64 radians/sec² and 0.720 sec respectively. **11.** Small and large pulleys respectively -0.444 and -0.297 rev/sec²; belt -1.397 ft/sec². **13.** (a) 6.05×10^5 gm·cm²; (b) 190.0 sec. **15.** Proof. **17.** $\frac{9}{4}ML^2$. **19.** (a) 500,000 gm·cm²; (b) 57.7 cm away. **21.** 2.00 sec. **23.** $g/2$. **25.** (a) 10.64 radians/sec; (b) 5320 gm·cm²/sec; (c) 2150 dyne·cm. **27.** To A's right.

Chapter 7—1. 75,000 ft·lb. **3.** 187.5 ft·lb. **5.** Yes; 250 ft·lb. **7.** (a) 4.69 ft·lb; (b) 12.00 ft·lb; (c) 16.69 ft·lb. **9.** (a) 4.09×10^6; (b) 1.255×10^6. **11.** 328,000 ergs and 114.6 cm/sec respectively. **13.** (a) 947 ft·lb; (b) 5.03 lb. **15.** 0.340. **17.** (a) 8.94 ft/sec and 125.0 ft·lb respectively; (b) 1325 ft·lb total, work against friction 200 ft·lb, increase of E_k 125.0 ft·lb, increase of E_p 1000 ft·lb; (c) Proof. **19.** (a) 3.75 ft; (b) 3.00 in. **21.** 458 cm/sec. **23.** (a) 2140 hp; (b) 213 hp. **25.** (a) 24,000 ft·lb/sec; (b) 48,000 ft·lb/sec; (c) 60,000 ft·lb/sec.

Chapter 8—1. a 784,000 dynes, b 588,000 dynes. **3.** 76.0 lb. **5.** a 600 lb, b 800 lb. **7.** 56.5 cm. **9.** 342,000 dynes toward left, 47.0° down from horizontal; 3.46 cm from A. **11.** 0.857 lb. **13.** 3.69 in. **15.** 42.3 lb. **17.** (a) Tension 3720 lb; thrust

705

4380 lb, 31.7° up from horizontal; (b) tension 2150 lb; thrust 2230 lb, 33.3° up from horizontal. **19.** Reactions A 100.0 lb, C 60.0 lb; tension 42.4 lb. **21.** AB 5.00 lb compression, AC 3.00 lb tension, BC 4.00 lb tension, BD 3.00 lb compression.

Chapter 9—**1.** (a) 5.00 cm; (b) 0.600 sec; (c) 1.667 vib/sec; (d) 52.4 cm/sec; (e) 7.07 cm. **3.** (a) 2.00 in.; (b) 19.74 in./sec². **5.** 93.5. **7.** 0.780 vib/sec. **9.** 0.752 sec. **11.** 13.95 vib/sec. **13.** 99.3 cm and 24.8 cm respectively. **15.** 0.907 sec. **17.** 2230 gm·cm². **19.** $0.667L$.

Chapter 10—**1.** (a) Yes; (b) 0.0935 cm. **3.** (a) 113,000 lb; (b) 0.0256 in. **5.** 83,100 lb/in.² **7.** 1.494×10^{12} dynes/cm². **9.** 2.94×10^9 dynes/cm². **11.** 39.0 in.³ **13.** 5.16 vib/sec. **15.** (a) 1.000 cm/sec toward left; (b) A 7.00 cm/sec toward left, B 2.00 cm/sec toward right. **17.** 5-lb block 3.33 ft/sec and 10-lb block 2.33 ft/sec, both toward right; $e = 1.000$.

Chapter 11—**1.** 113.3. **3.** 374 lb/ft². **5.** 281 lb. **7.** (a) 312 lb/ft²; (b) 3740 lb; (c) 2340 lb. **9.** (a) 8630 lb; (b) 312 lb/ft². **11.** 159,700 lb; 852,000 lb·ft. **13.** 23,000 lb·ft. **15.** 0.908 lb. **17.** (a) 1.600 gm/cm³; (b) 0.774%. **19.** 12.00 cm³, 8.00 gm/cm³, and 8.00 respectively. **21.** 8.00 in.³, 0.0975 lb/in.³, and 2.70 respectively. **23.** (a) 0.867 cm²; (b) 7.50 cm. **25.** (a) 37.0 dynes/cm; (b) 74.0 ergs. **27.** (a) 750 dynes/cm²; (b) 18,800 dynes/cm². **29.** 51.7 dynes/cm.

Chapter 12—**1.** 901 ft·lb. **3.** 22.6 ft/sec. **5.** $v = \sqrt{2p/d}$. **7.** (a) 1400 cm³/sec; (b) 224 cm. **9.** (a) 52.3 ft/sec; (b) 27.3° up from horizontal; (c) 75.1 ft. **11.** (a) 17.28 ft/sec; (b) 248. **13.** 15.72 ft/sec; 0.318 ft. **15.** (a) 96.2 cm/sec; (b) 1210 cm³/sec. **17.** (a) 1.866; (b) 838. **19.** 51.6 ft/sec and 71.0 respectively.

Chapter 13—**1.** (a) 4.93×10^4 cm/sec; (b) 1.070. **3.** 31,800 lb. **5.** 2.02 in. **7.** 16.33 ft³. **9.** (a) 91.2; (b) 95.2; (c) 19.2. **11.** 10.20. **13.** (a) 1.200 atmospheres; (b) 0.571 gm/liter; (c) 6.00 atmospheres. **15.** (a) 2.34×10^{-23} gm; (b) 1.258 gm/liter. **17.** 544 lb. **19.** 15.15 gm. **21.** 0.00160 cm Hg.

HEAT

Chapter 14—**1.** (a) 37.0° C, 310° K; (b) −63.0° C, −81.4° F. **3.** (a) 15.30 F°; (b) 1.889 C°. **5.** 128.6. **7.** 0.234 in. **9.** 8.24 lb. **11.** 1195°F. **13.** 1.375 in.³ **15.** 12.86 gm.

Chapter 15—**1.** (a) 80,000; (b) 5620. **3.** 88.7 cal/sec. **5.** 10.19 C°. **7.** 544 cal. **9.** 58.5° C. **11.** 0.0407 cal/(gm·C°). **13.** 0.1100 cal/(gm·C°). **15.** 1800 Btu. **17.** 13.16 gm. **19.** 74.25 cm. **21.** 4130 Btu/hr. **23.** 0.265 Btu/(lb·F°). **25.** 17.68 lb of ice at 32° F unmelted. **27.** 250 lb.

Chapter 16—**1.** 25.2 lb/in.² **3.** 104.4 lb/in.² **5.** (a) 5.05%; (b) 102.0%. **7.** 34.1° C. **9.** $p_1/(T_1 d_1) = p_2/(T_2 d_2)$. **11.** Diagram. **13.** 20.0 liters, 1092° K, and 1.000 atmosphere respectively. **15.** 4.26 lb. **17.** (a) 1.640; (b) 57.0° C and 1.800×10^6 dynes/cm² respectively. **19.** (a) 13,680 and 38,270 respectively; (b) 51,950; (c) 13,680 and 27,360 respectively; (d) 41,040. **21.** (a) 75.0 lb/in.²; (b) 43.1 lb/in.² **23.** (a) 0.307 gm; (b) 0.833 atmosphere; (c) zero. **25.** (a) 49.0%; (b) 5.29 lb. **27.** 35.1%.

Chapter 17—**1.** (a) 167,400 joules; (b) 2,910,000 ft·lb. **3.** 12.84 Btu. **5.** 13.47 min. **7.** Potential energy transformed to heat; 1.171 C°. **9.** 482 ft·lb. **11.** 23.4%. **13.** (a) 61.0° F; (b) 2.63 Btu; (c) 9.90. **15.** (a) 2090 joules; (b) 375 cal; (c) 1570 joules; (d) 25.0%. **17.** 39.1 hp; 0.1 hp low. **19.** 7.35 cents. **21.** 12,000.

Chapter 18—**1.** (a) 40,100 Btu; (b) 2.81 lb. **3.** 160.0 and 1.500 respectively. **5.** 318 Btu/hr. **7.** 2190 Btu. **9.** 10,480 Btu. **11.** 5.35 m². **13.** (a) 4440 cal; (b) 3310 cal; (c) 1130 cal. **15.** 48.0 sec. **17.** (a) 5.00×10^{14} vib/sec; (b) 3.31×10^{-12} erg.

ELECTRICITY AND MAGNETISM

Chapter 19—**1.** 2, 8, 18, 32, 18, and 2; total 80. **3.** 9.49 cm. **5.** 4.61×10^{-12} newton. **7.** (a) 8.21×10^{-8} newton; (b) 9.02×10^{22} m/sec². **9.** 6.16×10^{-8} coulomb.

11. 90,000; 22,500; and 900 newtons/coulomb respectively, all directed radially away from the charge. **13.** 4.39×10^{13} m/sec^2; 4.47×10^{12} times. **15.** 36,000 newtons/coulomb toward right, 37.4° up from horizontal. **17.** Proof. **19.** 9000, 4500, and 900 volts respectively; 8.10×10^{-6} joule. **21.** (a) 1.585 m; (b) 134,400 volts. **23.** 1.027×10^7 m/sec. **25.** (a) 300,000 volts/m; (b) 0.0180 joule; (c) 0.450 newton. **27.** $v = \mathcal{E}Q/6\pi\eta r$.

Chapter 20—**1.** Explanation. **3.** 6790 dynes attraction. **5.** 1.600 oersted directed parallel to magnet and away from its north pole. **7.** 13.80 oersteds away from north pole at angle of 4.4° with line from that pole to point, veering toward south pole. **9.** 8.00 cm. **11.** (a) 4000 dyne·cm; (b) 2830 dyne·cm. **13.** 0.570 oersted; 71.4°. **15.** 0.274 oersted.

Chapter 21—**1.** (a) 5.00×10^{-7} amp; (b) 2.00×10^{-6} amp. **3.** 1.578×10^9 kw·hr. **5.** (a) 0.833 amp; (b) 360,000 joules. **7.** (a) \$15.20; (b) 3.38 cents/(kw·hr). **9.** 5.14. **11.** (a) 16.35 ohms; (b) 727 watts. **13.** (a) 3.48 amp, 0.551 ohm; (b) 344,000. **15.** 71.7 microhms; 581,000/(ohm·cm). **17.** (a) 0.1449 ohm; (b) 8.69 volts; (c) 522 watts. **19.** Upper 58.3 amp; neutral 8.33 amp; lower 50.0 amp. **21.** 100-watt lamp 144 ohms, 40-watt lamp 360 ohms; equivalent resistance 45.0 ohms. **23.** (a) 7.90 ohms; (b) 3-ohm resistor 9.70 volts and 3.23 amp, 4-ohm resistor 12.35 volts and 3.09 amp, 5-ohm resistor 38.0 volts and 7.60 amp, 6-ohm resistor 9.70 volts and 1.617 amp, 7-ohm resistor 12.35 volts and 1.763 amp, 8-ohm resistor 22.0 volts and 2.75 amp. **25.** 1-ohm resistor 1.714 amp downward, 2-ohm resistor 0.143 amp downward, 4-ohm resistor 1.571 amp to right. **27.** 2-ohm resistor 0.428 amp upward, 4-ohm resistor 1.285 amp downward, 8-ohm resistor 0.857 amp upward. **29.** I_A 511 amp; I_B 389 amp. **31.** 0.287 amp. **33.** 306 ohms.

Chapter 22—**1.** $2H_2O \rightleftharpoons H_3O^+ + OH^-$. **3.** 3.00 faradays. **5.** 12.18 kg. **7.** (a) 38.3 hr; (b) 0.1379 cent. **9.** (a) 86.0 kg; (b) 2120 ft^3; (c) 272 watt·hr. **11.** 19,450. **13.** 20.3 hr. **15.** (a) In series, 184.6 vs 58.5 amp; (b) in parallel, 480 vs 282 amp. **17.** 200. **19.** 0.644 amp upward. **21.** Battery A 1.302 amp, B 0.651 amp, and C 0.434 amp. **23.** (a) 73.7 volts; (b) explanation, 2000 ohms; (c) 1529 ohms.

Chapter 23—**1.** 29.2 oersteds, between H_1 and H_2 and 59.0° with H_1. **3.** 48.5. **5.** (a) 6.03×10^{-5} weber/m^2; (b) 6.35×10^{-5} weber/m^2, directed 71.7° from earth's component. **7.** (a) 2.25×10^{-4} weber/m^2; (b) 2.13×10^{-4} weber/m^2. **9.** (a) Zero; (b) 1.500×10^{-4} weber/m^2. **11.** (a) 10.23 amp; (b) 1.257×10^{-5} weber. **13.** 20.0 newtons downward. **15.** 0.218 microamp. **17.** Add series resistor of 27,000 ohms. **19.** 0.0526 amp. **21.** (a) 4.00×10^{-3} weber/m^2; (b) 24.0 milliamp. **23.** 3.29 webers/m^2. **25.** $F = BQv/(3 \times 10^{10})$, where B is in gausses, Q in statcoulombs, v in centimeters per sec, and F in dynes. **27.** Proof.

Chapter 24—**1.** 1690. **3.** 471 and 60.5 respectively. **5.** 340 watts. **7.** 4.00 and 19.17 respectively. **9.** (a) 0.001875 weber; (b) 0.00313 weber. **11.** (a) 880 amp·turns; (b) 1575 amp·turns/m; (c) 0.356 weber/m^2; (d) 2.30×10^{-4} weber; (e) 3.83×10^6 amp·turns/weber. **13.** 6.00 milliweber. **15.** (a) 230 volts; (b) 444 and 332 watts respectively; (c) 89.1%. **17.** (a) 20.0 amp; (b) 1.500 amp; (c) 21.5 amp; (d) 3.06 hp.

Chapter 25—**1.** 2.60 volts; 1.300 volts. **3.** 0.480 milliweber. **5.** 50.6 millihenrys. **7.** (a) 150.0 amp/sec; (b) 0.368 sec. **9.** (a) 6.33 amp; (b) 0.904 amp. **11.** 8.10 joules. **13.** (a) 300,000 volts/m; (b) 2.65×10^{-6} coulomb/m^2; (c) 5.20×10^{-7} coulomb. **15.** 6.56 μf. **17.** 0.774 ft^2. **19.** 5.30×10^{-11} coulomb/(volt·m). **21.** (a) 0.1436 m^2; (b) 0.240 joule; (c) 1.670×10^{-4} coulomb/m^2. **23.** 240 microcoulombs on each; 3-μf capacitor 80.0 volts; 6-μf capacitor 40.0 volts. **25.** 3; two in series and this pair in parallel with the third.

Chapter 26—**1.** 0.0377 volt. **3.** (a) 3600 rev/min; (b) 200 rev/min. **5.** (a) 106.0 amp; (b) 62.3 amp. **7.** 56.9 millihenrys. **9.** 7.60 ohms; 104.2 millihenrys. **11.** 4770 and 79.6 ohms respectively. **13.** (a) 87.5 volts; (b) 132.0 volts; (c) 185.6 volts. **15.** (a) 141.4 volts; (b) zero; (c) 100.0 volts; (d) 500 ohms, 0.0796 henry, 0.318 μf.

17. (*a*) 1.000 milliamp; (*b*) resistor 10.00 millivolts, each reactor 1.000 volt.
19. 0.1037 milliamp. **21.** (*a*) Capacitive branch 0.628 milliamp, inductive branch
0.846 milliamp; (*b*) 0.738 milliamp. **23.** 1688 watts. **25.** 90.0%. **27.** Primary
12.82 amp; secondary 1389 amp. **29.** 602 amp; 10,320 amp/sec. **31.** 20.9 amp.
Chapter 27—**1.** (*a*) 9.24 millivolts; (*b*) 18.72 millivolts. **3.** 970° C. **5.** 0.851. **7.** 100.
9. 1440. **11.** 2.00% low. **13.** 36.0 db.
Chapter 28—**1.** (*a*) 253 $\mu\mu$f; (*b*) 0.500 amp; (*c*) 25 ohms; (*d*) 0.31 amp. **3.** 5.00 mm;
7.04 $\times$ 10^{-24} henry·farad. **5.** (*a*) 0.333 milliamp; (*b*) 1.027 milliamp. **7.** 1.241 $\times$
10^{-4} cm. **9.** Cesium 4.41 $\times$ 10^{14} vib/sec, 2.92 $\times$ 10^{-19} joule; potassium 6.82 $\times$ 10^{14}
vib/sec, 4.51 $\times$ 10^{-19} joule. **11.** 76.0 mi/hr.
Chapter 29—**1.** (*a*) 110, 1 $\frac{1}{2}$ $\frac{1}{2}$, and $\frac{1}{2}$ $\frac{1}{2}$ 1 respectively; (*b*) (100). **3.** 2.83 $\times$ 10^{-8} cm;
1.265 $\times$ 10^{-8} cm. **5.** Proof. **7.** 5.31 $\times$ 10^{14}. **9.** 31.1/(ohm·m). **11.** 154.4 amp.

SOUND

Chapter 30—**1.** 5.50 ft. **3.** 759 ft/sec. **5.** 56.6 ft/sec and 2.83 ft respectively. **7.** 0.698
sec. **9.** 1948 ft/sec. **11.** *d* gm/cm^3, *g* cm/sec^2, λ cm, and *T* dynes/cm. **13.** (*a*) 341 m;
(*b*) 4.48 m. **15.** (*a*) 5.00 rev/min forward; (*b*) 10.00 rev/min backward. **17.** 273
mi/hr. **19.** 6.93 cm. **21.** 123,800 mi/sec. **23.** 506 vib/sec. **25.** 160,000 dynes;
sketch.
Chapter 31—**1.** 1500 vib/sec. **3.** 0.0318 erg/(sec·cm^2). **5.** 5030. **7.** (*a*) 63.0 vib/sec;
(*b*) 30.0. **9.** (*a*) 12,800 cm/sec and 50.0 cm respectively; (*b*) 33,130 cm/sec and
129.4 cm respectively. **11.** (*a*) 2783 and 8350 vib/sec; (*b*) 1392 and 4180 vib/sec.
13. 68.75, 206, and 344 vib/sec; sketch. **15.** 31.8 in. **17.** 8.34 in. **19.** (*a*) 33,250
cm/sec; (*b*) 1.41. **21.** 491 vib/sec. **23.** In vib/sec: (*a*) 417; (*b*) 385; (*c*) 390; (*d*) 400;
(*e*) 405.
Chapter 32—**1.** 40.0 db. **3.** Intensity ratio 1.778 to 1, amplitude ratio 2.67 to 1.
5. 73.3 db. **7.** 1600 ft. **9.** 0.638 mm. **11.** 0.0753 sec. **13.** 0.032 erg/(sec·cm^2).
15. (*a*) 4.82 sec; (*b*) 1.01 sec

LIGHT

Chapter 33—**1.** 20 watts; 7070 lumens. **3.** 16.9% increase. **5.** 2700 and 18.00 respectively. **7.** 55.0% greater. **9.** 91.4 candles. **11.** 65.5; 132.0 candles. **13.** (*a*) 46.3
lumens/ft^2; (*b*) 38.3. **15.** 46.5 rev/sec. **17.** (*a*) 20.6°; (*b*) 20.5″.
Chapter 34—**1.** 2.00 and 10.00 ft behind *A*; 4.00 and 8.00 ft behind *B*. **3.** Diagram.
5. Proof. **7.** 20.0, 30.0, 60.0, ∞, −20.0, −5.00, and 0 cm respectively. **9.** −5.83 cm.
11. (*a*) 0.784; (*b*) 1.275. **13.** (*a*) 32.8°; (*b*) 116,200 mi/sec; (*c*) 0.543 in. **15.** 43.6°.
17. (*a*) Sketch; (*b*) 76.9°. **19.** (*a*) Proof; (*b*) 77.1°. **21.** Rock salt; explanation.
23. 1.743 and 1.427 respectively.
Chapter 35—**1.** (*a*) Sun is a solid, liquid, or compressed gas; (*b*) calcium, hydrogen,
and oxygen present. **3.** 1.23°. **5.** (*a*) 7.6°; (*b*) 0.204°; (*c*) 7.12 mm. **7.** (*a*) 17.9°;
(*b*) 2.99°. **9.** (*a*) 5.2°; (*b*) 0.1190. **11.** 5.093 $\times$ 10^{14} and 5.088 $\times$ 10^{14} respectively,
16,980 and 16,960 per cm respectively. **13.** (*a*) White; (*b*) orange. **15.** Mercury
1.183 $\times$ 10^{15} vib/sec; 39,400 per cm. Violet limit 7.90 $\times$ 10^{14} vib/sec; 26,300 per
cm. Red limit 4.00 $\times$ 10^{14} vib/sec; 13,300 per cm.
Chapter 36—**1.** 4.22 in. **3.** 17.30 in. **5.** (*a*) 1.750; (*b*) 0.1021 cm. **7.** 15.00, 20.0,
24.0, 30.0, 60.0, ∞, −60.0, −30.0, −7.50, and 0 cm; graph. **9.** −3.90 in. **11.** (*a*)
−43.6 cm; (*b*) −13.71 cm; (*c*) diagram. **13.** Image in Prob. 1 is 7.40 times that in
Prob. 3. **15.** (*a*) 5.63 cm from object and 5.63 cm from screen; (*b*) 62.0 to 1.
17. (*a*) 24.0 cm from lens; (*b*) 9.57 cm farther from first lens. **19.** 18.75 cm behind
B; 1.50 times object size; diagram. **21.** 45.0 cm to left of lens; yes. **23.** 3.86 and

54.0 in.   **25.** Crown 2.66 in.; flint −3.92 in.   **27.** (*a*) 9.12 cm; (*b*) 21.8 cm; (*c*) 92.1 cm; diagram.

Chapter 37—**1.** −40.0 and −2.50 respectively.   **3.** (*a*) 26.7, 21.4, 15.0, and 10.9 mm respectively; (*b*) 1, 1.55, 3.17, and 6.00 respectively.   **5.** 9.74 in.   **7.** 0.00482 sec. **9.** 4.29 ft.   **11.** 3.32 × 2.27 ft.   **13.** 780; f/19.5.   **15.** Diagram; 51.5 in.   **17.** 3.00 diameters.   **19.** (*a*) 100 diameters; (*b*) 1.76 cm.   **21.** Objective 4.00 diameters; eyepiece 3.50 diameters; both together 14.0 diameters.

Chapter 38—**1.** 0.442, 0.884, and 1.326 mm respectively.   **3.** 1.580.   **5.** 1.310×10^{-5} cm.   **7.** 2.68 mm.   **9.** 0.1734 mm.   **11.** Explanation.   **13.** 0.888 mm.   **15.** (*a*) 2.77″; (*b*) 1.385″.   **17.** 4.48 ft.   **19.** (*a*) 26.0 cm; (*b*) 65.0 cm.   **21.** Proof.   **23.** 2.82×10^{-8} cm.

Chapter 39—**1.** (*a*) 1.517; (*b*) 33.4°; (*c*) diagram.   **3.** 24.5°.   **5.** 30.0°.   **7.** Explanation. **9.** 0.00327 cm.   **11.** (*a*) 1287 lb/in.^{2}; (*b*) 2574 lb/in.^{2}

ATOMIC PHYSICS

Chapter 40—**1.** 5.29×10^{-9} cm.   **3.** 6.08×10^7 cm/sec.   **5.** 0.00710 A, 0.0242 A, and 0.0413 A respectively.   **7.** 5.02 times.   **9.** 4.83×10^{-8} erg; 30,200 electron·volts. **11.** 8.66×10^{-6} per year.   **13.** 13.5.   **15.** 20.187.   **17.** $_5B^{10} + {}_0n^1 = {}_3Li^7 + {}_2He^4 +$ 3.17 Mev.   **19.** 3.01643

INDEX

Aberration, chromatic, 617; spherical of lenses, 616; of mirrors, 571
Absolute: pressure, 168; systems of units, 50; temperature scale, 214
Absorption: of light, 581, 599; of sound, 541; spectra, 587
Acceleration, angular, 88; average, 32; due to gravity, 36; force to produce, 49; in harmonic motion, 145; instantaneous, 32; linear, 31; torque to produce, 90; units of, 32
Accelerators, particle, types of, 383, 689
Accommodation of eye, 625
Achromatic lens, design of, 618
Acoustics of rooms, 542
Action and reaction, 50
Adhesion and cohesion, 178
Adiabatic process, 254
Air columns, vibration of, 524
Airfoil, lift on, 207
Airplane, forces on, 48; jet propulsion, 276
Alloys and mixtures, 2; magnetic, 392
Alpha rays, 682
Alphabet, Greek, 699
Alternating-current: circuits, 432; effective value of, 429; generators, 425, 428; measurements, 441; motors, 441; resonant circuits, 465; transformers, 438
Alternators, polyphase, 440; single-phase, 425
Ammeters, alternating-current, 441; direct-current, 376; thermo-, 450
Ampère, André M., current strength, 327; electromagnetism, 367, 371
Ampere, the, 327, 332, 373; -turns, 369, 398
Amplification by electron tube, 457; by transistor, 490
Amplifiers, electronic, 457
Amplitude: modulation of carrier, 469; of vibration, 143, 498
Analysis, spectrum, 591; wave, 520

Analyzer and polarizer, 661
Andrews, Thomas, liquefaction of gases, 255
Aneroid barometer, 200
Angle: of surface contact, 179; solid, 553; visual, 631
Ångström, Anders J., light wavelength, 587
Angstrom unit, the, 587
Angular: acceleration, 88; measurement, 13; momentum, 99; momentum of electron, 672; motion related to linear motion, 90; speed, 87; velocity, 86, 98; versus tangential velocity, 87
Anode and cathode: of cell, 350; of vacuum tube, 308
Antenna, waves from, 465
Aperture, of lens, 627; of mirror, 568
Arc lamps, 549
Archimedes, principle of buoyancy, 173, 176, 197, 205
Areas by calculation, 8
Armature of generators and motors, 399
Armstrong, Edwin H., frequency modulation, 471
Aspirator, 208
Astigmatism of eye, 627; of lens, 619
Aston, Francis W., mass spectrograph, 688
Astronomical telescopes, 629
Atmospheric electricity, 309; humidity, 259; pressure, 200; refraction, 577
Atom, structure of, 294
Atomic: bomb, 693; disintegration, 681; fission, 692; fusion, 694; mass units, 687; number, 4, 686; pile, 693; physics, 671; structure, 3, 294; weight, 4, 352, 703
Atoms and molecules, 1
Attraction, electrical, 293; gravitational, 2, 52; magnetic, 316
Atwood's machine, 60
Aurora borealis, 604